The Afro-Latin@ Reader

A John Hope Franklin Center Book

The Afro-Latin@ Reader

HISTORY AND CULTURE IN THE UNITED STATES

Edited by Miriam Jiménez Román and Juan Flores

DUKE UNIVERSITY PRESS   DURHAM AND LONDON 2010

To *afrodescendientes* everywhere

CONTENTS

VI Afro-Latinas

VII Public Images and (Mis)Representations

VIII Afro-Latin@s in the Hip Hop Zone

IX Living Afro-Latinidades

X Afro-Latin@s: Present and Future Tenses

ACKNOWLEDGMENTS

This book began as a collection of readings for the courses on Latin@s, race, and culture that we have offered at various institutions during the past twenty years. Initially the experience of Black Latin@s in the United States formed only a small part of the curriculum in those courses. But as interest in the African diaspora in the Americas as well as in the United States continued to grow, so too did the need to address the particularities of those who, like Afro-Latin@s, bridge various communities even as they constitute a community in their own right. In more recent years the emergence and expanding network of engaged scholars and activists whose work focuses on Afro-Latin@s has made possible the conceptualization and documentation of a whole new field of study and advocacy.

A compilation of this type is by necessity a collective effort and we have been fortunate in receiving unstinting cooperation from many old and new collaborators—too many, in fact, for us to mention by name. Indeed, in the process of putting this book together we have made many new friends and discovered that the network of Afro-Latin@ enthusiasts is even more extensive than we had imagined. The supportive response from all of those we approached has been extremely gratifying and has served as a vital impetus in bringing this collection to completion. We offer each of the contributors our heartfelt thanks.

We have been privileged in having access to the archives of collectors who have long appreciated the importance of Afro-Latin@ history and culture, and we gratefully acknowledge Henry Medina, José Rafael Méndez, and Mappy Torres for their contributions.

A number of photographers were especially generous in offering their work to us. We are sincerely grateful to Máximo Colón, Joe Conzo, Carlos Flores, Ted Richardson, Javier Santiago, and Cassandra Vinograd for the images of the many beautiful Afro-Latin@ faces that grace this book.

We are also very much indebted to the librarians and archivists who provided guidance and were unfailingly helpful in accessing materials. Tomaro Taylor at the University of South Florida–Tampa Library and Jennifer Cutting and Ann Hoog at the American Folklife Center of the Library of Congress deserve special mention for their efforts. We also thank Jorge Matos at the Center for Puerto Rican Studies at Hunter College for his enthusiastic cooperation over the years. At the Schomburg Center for Research in Black Culture we benefited greatly from the generous support of Diana Lachatanere, Betty Odabashian, Anthony Toussaint, and Mary Yearwood, all of whom proved yet again their professional and personal commitment to making available knowledge about the African diaspora.

At Duke University Press we offer thanks to Ken Wissoker who embraced the project from its initial conceptualization, and to the editorial staff who guided us through the intricacies of the complex editorial process. We take this opportunity to acknowledge the generous subsidy grant from the John Hope Franklin Center at Duke University. We also thank Carolyn Sattin, our graduate student assistant, for her help in the early stages of acquiring reprint permissions.

Finally, we extend our profound gratitude to all those community activists who over the decades have taken on the frequently arduous task of giving voice to the concerns of Afro-Latin@s. ¡Pa'lante!

EDITORIAL NOTE

We were not able to accommodate all of the essays in their entirety, and thus some of the longer ones have been edited for length and pertinence to our theme. In addition, in many essays the documentation has been modified for consistency or supplied where it was missing. All editorial additions and omissions are enclosed in square brackets to distinguish them from the original text. As a general rule we have chosen to capitalize the terms "Black" and "White" when they refer to social groups and to use the "@" in order to indicate gender inclusion (e.g., Latin@s).

Introduction

Afro-Latin@? What's an Afro-Latin@? Who is an Afro-Latin@? The term befuddles us because we are accustomed to thinking of "Afro" and "Latin@" as distinct from each other and mutually exclusive: one is either Black or Latin@.

The short answer is that Afro-Latin@s belong to both groups. They are people of African descent in Mexico, Central and South America, and the Spanish-speaking Caribbean, and by extension those of African descent in the United States whose origins are in Latin America and the Caribbean.

As straightforward as this definition would seem, the reality is that the term is not universally accepted and there is no consensus about what it means. The difficulties surrounding what we call ourselves reflect the complex histories of Africans and their descendants in the Americas.

And this brings us to the long answer. Broadly speaking, the word "Afro-Latin@" can be viewed as an expression of long-term transnational relations and of the world events that generated and were in turn affected by particular global social movements. Going back to the late nineteenth century and the early twentieth, Pan-Africanism signaled for the first time an explicit, organized identification with Africa and African descendants and more expansively of non-White peoples at a global level. Attendant to this process, concepts of Negritude and cultural movements like the Harlem Renaissance and Afrocubanismo gained increasing ground during the 1920s and 1930s.

The period from around mid-century and through the 1980s saw the growth of African liberation movements as part of a global decolonization process, as well as the Civil Rights and Black Power movements in the United States. In Latin America the beginnings of anti-racist organizations and the Congresos of the late 1970s introduced the first continental context for an assertive self-identification by people of African descent and a clearly articulated condemnation of anti-Black racism. Similar developments were occurring in the United States during those years, with increasing talk of "people of color" and the move from the terms "Negro" and "Colored" to Black to Afro-American or African American. With the explosive demographic increase of immigrants from Latin America and the Caribbean, the notion of a Hispanic or Latin@ pan-ethnic identity was also gaining a foothold in the same period.

As of the 1980s, spurred by the anti-apartheid struggle in South Africa, there has been a growing interest in the realities of racism on a global scale and the centrality of Africa for an understanding of this pressing political phenomenon. The concept of an African diaspora, while implicit for decades in this long historical trajectory, comes to the fore during these years and serves as the guiding paradigm in our times. Most importantly for our purposes it acknowledges the historical and continuing linkages among the estimated 180 million people of African descent in the Americas. Along with the terms "Negro," "afrodescendiente," and "afrolatinoamericano," the name Afro-Latin@ has served to identify the constituency of the many vibrant anti-racist movements and causes that have been gaining momentum throughout the hemisphere for over a generation and that attained international currency at the World Conference against Racism: Racial Discrimination, Xenophobia, and Related Intolerance, which was convened by UNESCO in Durban, South Africa, in 2001.

The term "Afro-Latin@" thus was born and reared in this transnational crucible of struggle and self-affirmation, and until recent years it has primarily been used to refer to people of African descent in Latin America and the Caribbean as a whole, even as nation- and region-specific terminology continues to hold sway. For example, depending on context a Black woman in Ecuador can identify as afrolatina, afrodescendiente, afroecuatoriana, or choteña. Since the early 1990s, however, in part as a result of the intellectual cross-fertilization between north and south, the term has gained increasing currency in the United States. Just as in Latin America, where the prefix Afro has been critical in challenging the homogenizing effects of national and regional constructs, so in the United States the term "Afro-Latin@" has surfaced as a way to signal racial, cultural, and socioeconomic contradictions within the overly vague idea of "Latin@." In addition to reinforcing those ever-active transnational ties, the Afro-Latin@ concept calls attention to the anti-Black racism within the Latin@ communities themselves. In the case of more recent immigrants these

attitudes are brought over as ideological baggage fron
tries, while for the generations-long citizens of the Uni
flect the historical location of Blackness at the bottom
archy and the Latin@ propensity to uphold *mestizaje* (r
mixture) as an exceptionalist and wishful panacea. It
challenge to the African American and English-langua;
Blackness in the U.S. context, with obvious implication:
level. Throughout the hemisphere, "afro" serves to link
clare a community of experiences and interests. Most significantly, the
prefix establishes the foundational historical and cultural connection to
Africa, an affirmation that simultaneously defies the Eurocentric ideologies that have characterized Latin America and the Caribbean.

Thus, while we recognize the primacy and historical priority of the
hemispheric usage of the term, in this volume our focus is on the strategically important but still largely understudied United States context of
Afro-Latin@ experience. What then does Afro-Latin@ mean in that context? What are and who are United States Afro-Latin@s?

Clearly the reference is to those whose numbers and historical trajectory have had the greatest significance in the United States. While
recognizing the inextricable connections to the transnational movement
or identity field ("ethno-scape") of the same name, there are conditions
and meanings that are specific to the national framework of history and
society in the United States. In some cases, transnational and domestic
experiences may even run askew of each other and show greater discontinuity than parallels. Thus, for example, despite the crucial place of Brazil—the country with a Black population second in size only to that of
Nigeria—within the Latin American context, the Brazilian presence in the
United States has been relatively small and the Afro-Brazilian negligible.
Similarly, despite the towering significance of the Haitian Revolution to
hemispheric history and the parallels that can be drawn among all immigrant peoples of African descent, in the context of the United States Haitians have consistently been distinguished—and have often distinguished
themselves—from Latin@s. Unlike the case of Afro-Latin@s, Haitians are
generally understood to be unambiguously Black.

We have identified four primary "coordinates" to a deeper and more
flexible understanding of that specific reality: group history, transnational
discourse, relations between African Americans and Latin@s, and the specific lived experience of being Afro-Latin@. The following sections consider each of these coordinates in greater depth.

First and most obviously Afro-Latin@ refers to those Latin@s of visible or self-proclaimed African descent. It is a group designation, the name for a community that historically has not tended to call itself, or to have been called, in that way; preferred terms have tended to emphasize national origin or ethnicity rather than racial identification. But Afro-Latin@s increasingly identify as such in recent years, and their group past demonstrates a sense of tradition and shared social and cultural realities. We now can speak of an Afro-Latin@ history and trace the trajectory of a collective experience through the entire span of the history of the United States.

We have taken this historical sequence as the main structuring principle of this book. Though its parts are also defined by a range of themes such as music, gender, and public representation, they proceed through the centuries and decades of Black Latin@ social and cultural experience and arrive at the present. Since the time of the European conquest and early United States colonial history, and through the nineteenth and twentieth centuries, Blacks of Spanish-language backgrounds have built up a legacy of shared and distinctive cultural values and expression that has traversed national particularities and differentiated itself from the group history of both African Americans and other Latin@s. And in the treacherous counterposition of African Americans and Latin@s that characterizes the racial discourse in this country today, Afro-Latin@s as individuals and as a group constitute a potential bridge across that ominous ethno-racial divide.

As the first readings show, the earliest manifestations of Afro-Latin@ presence actually predate the very founding of the country and even the first English settlements. As reflected in Peter Wood's title of the opening reading, the "earliest Africans in North America" were in fact Afro-Latin@s. Their role in the settlement of St. Augustine in 1565 and in the Castillo de San Marcos and the Gracia Real de Santa Teresa de Mose (Fort Mose) places them at the threshold of the nation's history. Or perhaps, given the foundational symbolism of Jamestown and Plymouth, those initial Afro-Latin@ experiences in Spanish Florida are more the antechamber of that history, the less ceremonious advance contact between European invaders and indigenous peoples. As buffers and cannon fodder, as reconnaissance scouts and militiamen, as intermediaries, and of course as attendants and slaves, Afro-Latin@s have been implicated in the forging of the North American story, complicitous with and at the same time themselves subject victims of its inhuman excesses. Afro-Latin@ culture thus not only enriches but also points to the limits and exclusions of the hegemonic Anglo-American culture and its history.

The first Afro-Latin@ historical personage, immortalized in the memorable *Relación* of Alvar Núñez Cabeza de Vaca, was the famed Estevanico el Negro. Along with the chronicler Cabeza de Vaca himself, he was one of the four survivors of the ill-starred voyage of Pánfilo de Narváez along the Florida coast in 1528. After years-long captivity among the Indian tribes of Florida, Estevanico joined Cabeza de Vaca on the long trek across the continent, traversing what is now Texas and northern Mexico. But Estevanico's unique historical role actually occurs in the years following those recounted by Cabeza de Vaca, which saw him joining the 1539 expedition of Fray Marcos de Niza to the legendary city of Cíbola (New Mexico) and providing indispensable reconnoitering and intermediary services to the campaign. And there are the unnamed Blacks whose presence marked the early history of this land long before the United States declared its own name and identity, including people like the *mulata* woman who in the 1540s was left behind in what is today Kansas, the countless frontier soldiers who served the Spanish Crown and the *casta* families who established the first settlements throughout the southwest and California. This early stage of what is now the United States clearly reveals the social constructedness of race and the negotiations necessary in societies where non-White people dominated numerically but Europeans held power. Racial mixing, the object of much current fascination and perceived by many as a new phenomenon, in fact has a long history, and as indicated by both Jack Forbes and Virginia Gould in their essays in this volume it was often the only mechanism available for improving one's circumstances within a patriarchal, racist power structure.

Though Estevanico may appear to be an isolated and idiosyncratic instance of Afro-Latin@ presence in United States history, his most distinctive cultural features (his Blackness and his Spanish language) and how those features figure in the Euro-Indian-African interaction that is to shape United States history clearly anticipate those of subsequent Afro-Latin@ generations. His dilemma of being a Black man serving as advance guard in the exploratory incursions of the White man also remains a recurrent one in the racial, political, and cultural relations of the United States through to the present.

While this prototypical positioning of the Afro-Latin@ first came into view in the sixteenth century in northern Mexico (now the American Southwest), the history of the group actually transpires in the nineteenth and twentieth centuries and in the eastern part of the country. Afro-Latin@s in the United States are preponderantly of Hispanic Caribbean origins stemming in largest numbers from Cuba, Puerto Rico, the Dominican Republic, Central America (especially Panama and Honduras), and the coastal areas of Colombia and Venezuela. The mid-nineteenth century initiates the formative period, witnessing both the centrality of African American–Latin@ historical relations in the war with Mexico—especially in the debates over the extension of slavery to Mexican territories—and the beginnings of the long-term experience of Black Cubans in southern Florida.

The burgeoning cigar industry brought thousands of Cubans, along with some Puerto Ricans and Spaniards, to the cities of Tampa, Key West, and Ybor City. The majority of the cigar workers were Afro-Cubans, while the owners and overseers were mostly White Cubans and Spaniards. After the turn of the century, and especially after the decline of the cigar industry by 1920, that population waned significantly, but between 1870 and 1940 the first sizable Afro-Latin@ community experienced the collective triumphs and hardships of prolonged group life in United States society. The Key West area was felt to be an extension of Havana, with many of the workers moving back and forth with frequency and thereby establishing the kind of cross-border cultural dynamism so characteristic of later Afro-Latin@ peoples in times closer to our own.

As recounted in the reading by Susan Greenbaum, and as later narrated in moving personal terms in the selection from Evelio Grillo's memoir *Black Cuban, Black American*, Afro-Latin@s in Florida enjoyed differential relations with other nationalities, the most complex yet most significant with White Cubans on the one hand and with African Americans on the other. Historical accounts show that while in the earlier period there existed a strong cultural and political unity among all Cubans and "Latin@s" along national and linguistic lines, their social lives were separate. The impact of post-Reconstruction and Jim Crow conditions escalated anti-Black racism and increased the need for Afro-Latin@s to establish ties with other "coloreds." Ample testimony to this unique Afro-Latin@ predicament remains available in the periodical literature and organizational documents of this historically important but largely bygone community experience.

In the course of the twentieth century the main locus of Afro-Latin@ social life shifts from Florida to New York City, and from the Cuban diaspora to that of the Puerto Ricans. Prior to the Spanish-American War and 1898 the two groups converged and united in their common struggle against Spanish colonialism, as represented in the Partido Revolucionario Cubano and its Puerto Rican section and the joint leadership of figures of the stature of José Martí, Eugenio María de Hostos, and Sotero Figueroa.

During this later-nineteenth-century period the famous Afro-Cuban General Antonio Maceo took on towering symbolic importance in Cuba and the United States, a stature that resonates in the frequent occurrence of the first name Maceo (usually pronounced máy-see-o) among African Americans. Though proclamations of racial equality were integral to the abolitionist and anticolonial rhetoric of the movement, evidence exists of the relegation and subordination of its Black members, as well as the absence and nonencouragement of any distinctive Black cultural or political agenda. Some of these Black and mulatto members of the anticolonial movement, such as Rafael Serra, Sotero Figueroa, and Pachín Marín, have their place in the course of Afro-Latin@ history in the United States.

With the United States occupation of Cuba and Puerto Rico and the ever-growing migratory presence of both populations in New York and other northeastern cities the central cultural concern of Afro-Latin@s becomes their relationship with African Americans, and more generally with an African diasporic world. This new perspective is embodied most prominently by Arturo Alfonso Schomburg, a Black Puerto Rican who took active part in the anti-Spanish liberation struggle by serving as secretary in the highly important club Las Dos Antillas under the leadership of José Martí.

Schomburg's Caribbean and Latino background has generally been eclipsed by his subsequent accomplishments as a seminal figure in the Harlem Renaissance and as one of the foremost collectors and bibliophiles of the Africana experience, which culminated in the founding of the Schomburg Center for Research in Black Culture. Given his immense educational contribution to knowledge about the Black world, which continued to include a special interest in the Caribbean, Latin America, and Spain, Schomburg may be considered the most illustrious and self-conscious of all Afro-Latin@s in the United States as well as the one whose aspirations and ambiguities seem most deeply exemplary of Afro-Latin@ social experience. For this reason we devote an entire section of the book to the life, thought, and legacy of Arturo Alfonso Schomburg.

Schomburg's life on the color line, his direct knowledge and experience of racism both in Latin America and the United States and his resultant affinity with African Americans, was also paradigmatic for Afro-Latin@s through the first half of the twentieth century. The stories of many Afro-Latin@s, both prominent and lesser known, tell of this precarious situation at the racial and cultural seams of the society. The readings in part III, and many of those that follow attest to the racial experience of Afro-Cubans such as Melba Alvarado, Graciela, Minnie Miñoso, and Mario

Bauzá, along with Afro-Puerto Ricans such as Rafael Hernández, Jesús Colón, and Piri Thomas, and the varied ways in which they navigated the color line. Ironically, for many Afro-Latin@s the overt nature of Jim Crow in the United States would actually prove to be liberatory, a refreshing change from the hypocritical rhetoric of Latin American and Caribbean racial democracy.

Since the early decades of the twentieth century the world of popular music has been a rich field of Afro-Latin@ experience, as illustrated in the selections in part IV. James Reese Europe's recruitment of the legendary Afro-Puerto Rican composer and bandleader Rafael Hernández and many other Black Boricuas into the Hellfighters Regiment Band during World War I was an event of great moment in United States Afro-Latin@ history, as was the collaboration of the Afro-Cuban innovator Mario Bauzá and Dizzy Gillespie in the forging of Afro-Cuban jazz or Cubop in the late 1940s. The special place of the pioneering work of Arsenio Rodrí-guez as analyzed in the selection by David García also warrants attention in the story of New York's Latin music as it leads up to the salsa boom of the 1970s. The complexities of the social experiences of these musical greats and their audiences, and the revolutionary changes brought to both jazz and Cuban music history, stand as a testament to Afro-Latin@ creativity and cultural resilience.

By mid-century Puerto Ricans were already outnumbering Cubans as the largest Latin@ group in New York City, and as such they were becoming the primary representatives of the Afro-Latin@ experience. The predominantly White composition of Cuban migration after the 1959 revolution contrib-uted further to this demographic change. While light-skinned Cubans re-mained the archetype, and the stereotype, of Afro-Latin@ culture in the increasingly pervasive United States mass media, it was Puerto Ricans who made up the most sizable and vocal community of Afro-Latin@s. The 1960s saw an outburst of political, literary, and cultural expression that gave voice and perspective to the particular position of young people who are both Puerto Rican and Black. To illustrate that it was not only Puerto Ricans who affirmed a militant Black nationalist position in those years we include a short reading by the Afro-Dominican Carlos Cooks. Because his activism dates back to the 1940s, Cooks is sometimes viewed as a link between the influential earlier presence of Marcus Garvey and that of Malcolm X in the 1960s. Cooks's condemnation of "hair-conking" and his exaltation of Black female beauty and pitch for Black economic self-advancement provided continuity with some of Garvey's ideas but also anticipated themes raised in Black writings of more recent years.

The ascendancy of the Young Lords Party in the late 1960s attests to the participation of Latin@s in the African American Civil Rights and Black Power movements and to the first generalized affirmation of Blackness among young Puerto Ricans born in the United States. The Young Lords leader Pablo Guzmán, generally known as "Yoruba," pointed clearly to the racism within the Latin@ community as an obstacle to the struggle for justice, and at the historical need for unity with African Americans. His present-day reflection written expressly for this collection, along with his statement as a Young Lord, mark still another landmark in United States Afro-Latin@ history. In addition to the Young Lords experience, contributions by Marta Moreno Vega and Sherezada "Chiqui" Vicioso illustrate well the transnational dimensions of this period of intense assertion of African diasporic connections, while Luis Barrios's reflection on Pentecostalism reminds us that cultural continuities can be found in unexpected spaces.

Most notable among the literary works of this transformative period is the autobiographical novel *Down These Mean Streets* (1967) by the young Black Puerto Rican–Cuban author Piri Thomas. In this work we find in sharp dramatic terms nothing short of a psychological anatomy of the Black Latin@ paradox and the tortuous struggle to affirm both identities in the presumably polarized Black-White United States racial formation. In a similar vein the so-called Nuyorican poets of the 1970s such as Pedro Pietri, Sandra María Esteves, Felipe Luciano, and Victor Hernández Cruz incorporate a strong sense of Black cultural identity in their proclamations of a United States–based Puerto Rican reality. Collaborations between these poets and such primarily African American ensembles as The Last Poets and the Third World Revelationists attest to the strong cultural bonds felt by Afro-Latin@s with their African American contemporaries. More recent poets such as Tato Laviera, Louis Reyes Rivera, Willie Perdomo, and Mariposa (María Teresa Fernández) deepen these cross-cultural insights even further; their poems ring with the contemporary significance of the Afro-Latin@ experience. We include these and other Afro-Latin@ poems in various parts of the book as illustrative of this rich cultural interaction.

The period of the 1970s was also characterized by a growing awareness of and attention to women's experiences and the centrality of issues of gender and sexuality. While we include a range of texts by and about Afro-Latinas throughout the collection, we devote part VI, "Afro-Latinas" specifically to analysis and testimony concerning heterosexual and queer experience among Afro-Latin@s. Angela Jorge's dissection of the multiple oppressions endured by Black Puerto Rican women, which dates back to the 1970s, is now a classic. Two other essays, by Marta Cruz-Janzen and

Ana Lara, are more recent and provide powerful critical reflections on the gender and sexual experience of Afro-Latinas, while Mariposa's poem on the agonies of hair straightening addresses this experience in a more direct, personal way.

The subsequent and most recent generation, which spans the period since the later 1970s, saw a waning of the 1960s level of political and cultural effervescence coupled with a demographic explosion of Latin@ populations and the ascendancy of the idea of Latinidad as a field of group identity. Both developments had the effect of pitting the nation's "fastest-growing minority" directly against the African American community in a race for numerical supremacy and resources. While the post–Civil Rights era brought a widespread reflection on race and Blackness among African Americans, especially because of the rapid rise in Black immigration from the Caribbean and Africa, Latin@ identity came to be increasingly defined as non-Black, and in some ways anti-Black.

The inadequacy of the Latin@ concept along with the need to broaden and complicate the notion of Blackness in the United States has given rise to the understanding that Latinidad and Blackness are not mutually exclusive and to a recognition of their interface in the Afro-Latin@ presence. The term "Afro-Latin@" as applied to people in the United States emerged in the early 1990s when it became clear that race matters in the Latin@ community, and that these racial realities make it a grave distortion to think of Latin@s as a monolithic group. Sociological and economic analysis as exemplified by the work of John Logan and of William Darity, Jason Dietrich, and Darrick Hamilton included in this collection, established the discrepancies within the Latin@ community according to all indicators, not to mention the racial discrimination against Black Latin@s by the wider society as well as by other Latin@s. Tanya Hernandez's discussion of legal attempts to prove discrimination at the workplace exposes some of the difficulties faced by Afro-Latin@s when race is refracted through the lens of national origin. Logan's analysis and others even suggest that by way of social experience Black Latin@s have more in common with African Americans than with the remainder of the Latin@ community.

The emerging acknowledgment of the distinctiveness of Black Latin@s within the multiracial Latin@ aggregate has not been matched by their visible presence in public and media representations of that experience. On the contrary, as is evident in the readings comprising part VII, Afro-Latin@s have faced virtually total invisibility and erasure as a possible component of either the Latin@ or the Black population: as far as the main-stream media are concerned, Latin@s are not black and Blacks are not

Latin@. And on the rare occasions when Afro-Latin@s do find their way into media or other public forms of representation (such as the Anacostia Museum's "Black Mosaic" exhibit analyzed by Ginetta Candelario in her essay), the distortions, misunderstandings, and negative stereotypes have been rampant. While this disconnect between group experience and public representation goes back generations, and certainly colored the experiences of Afro-Latin@s such as Minnie Miñoso in Major League Baseball and Juano Hernández, Eusebia Cosme, and Lucecita Benítez in the entertainment world, critical and scholarly attention to the phenomenon only came into its own in the present generation. While Carlos Flores's reflection denounces the absence of Blacks in Latino media, the essay by Ejima Baker and the one by Alan Hughes and Milca Esdaille for *Black Enterprise* suggest a greater receptivity (albeit still problematic) to Afro-Latin@s and a sensitivity to their potential role as a bridge across communities.

Finally, in more recent times the cultural tenor that has accompanied the rise of Afro-Latin@s as a group reality and designation has been set by hip hop. Since its inception, as described by Raquel Rivera and Pancho McFarland, the hip hop "zone" has been one of Afro-Latin@ cultural expression, with its main exponents and stylistic forms issuing from the collaborative creativity of African Americans and Caribbean Latin@s. Centering on the Afro-Latin@ dilemma David Lamb's novel, significantly titled *Do Plátanos Go wit' Collard Greens*, Latin@ is obviously conceived in the framework of hip-hop expressivity, and the audiences attending the theatrical version of the book are strongly Afro-Latin@ in ethnic composition. The most wildly popular musical style in the new millennium, reggaeton, which is well described in the essay by Wayne Marshall, is clearly a sequel to rap and is still within the hip hop zone. And yet with its Spanish-language lyrics and meshing of diverse Caribbean styles it appears to be even more pronouncedly Afro-Latin@ rather than African American with a Latin@/Caribbean admixture.

Transnational Discourse

While the term "Afro-Latin@s" is of recent vintage and only gains currency in our own times, the experience reaches far back in United States history and has passed through many different stages and periods in the course of generations. In addition to its deep historical foundations, an understanding of the Afro-Latin@ experience must be guided by a clear appreciation of the transnational discourse or identity field linking Black Latin Americans and Latin@s across national and regional lines. Indeed, that hemispheric link begins with the very reason for the presence of Afro-Latin@s in North America, which is the direct result of the selective migration from the countries of origin to the United States. As a general rule, migratory movements of poor and working-class people tend to have a larger proportion of African-descendant migrants, with the Puerto Rican, Dominican, and pre-revolutionary Cuban migrations providing clear evidence of this correlation.

Furthermore, no stage in Afro-Latin@ history in the United States is without some reference to home countries, whether it be personal or group memories, familial ties, or current political or social situations. This is also the case with all, or nearly so, of the readings in this collection. In some cases, such as the testimonies of Yvette Modestin, Ryan Mann-Hamilton, and Silvio Torres-Saillant, those ties are especially explicit and vital. Histories and events in Panama, the Dominican Republic, Puerto Rico, Cuba, Nicaragua, and other homelands are ever present in the lives of Afro-Latin@s in the United States, as are the ongoing effects of racial ideologies and experiences that prevail in those places of personal or family origin. As with the Latin@ concept itself, as well as the African American, it is increasingly important to resist the limitation of Afro-Latin@ to its national United States confines. That vital transnational relationship is itself an eminently Afro-Latin@ phenomenon.

Cross-Cultural Relations

Caution should be exercised when assessing the transnational dimensions of the concept of Afro-Latin@, for while it does break us out of a strictly United States–centered perspective we also run the risk of romanticized thinking about those cultural homelands or newly discovered fonts of African-based practices. One potential saving grace is that the growing and vibrant afrodescendiente movements within Latin America and the Caribbean are unmasking the inherent racism of these exoticized and folklorized versions of Black experience.

What is perhaps most particular to the United States context is that here the Afro-Latin@ problematic, or lo afrolatino, has to do with the cross-cultural relation between the Afro and the Latin@, which means most saliently the relation between Latin@s and African Americans. Thus while the concept refers first of all to the group experience of Black Latin@s themselves, the broader interaction between the two "largest minorities," including non-Afro Latin@s and non-Latin@ Blacks, bears directly on that population that is both, and conditions its social experience at every stage.

We have seen that as early as the colonial period in "Spanish Florida," the Southwest, and Louisiana, and throughout the story of Afro-Latin@s in the nineteenth century and the twentieth, Afro-Latin@s have often lived and worked alongside African Americans in a long and complex relationship characterized by both distance and embrace. For many Afro-Latin@s, such as Evelio Grillo and Arturo Alfonso Schomburg, identifying with and becoming part of the African American community turned out to be their most ready access to society in the United States, as well as their most evident recourse in the face of racist rejection by other Latin@s.

While the broader relation between Latin@s and African Americans is clearly central to an understanding of Afro-Latin@ life in the United States, it is important not to limit the concept of Afro-Latin@ to that connection and to recognize clearly the presence of a group that embodies both at once. Frequently the Afro-Latin@ idea is taken to refer to the alliance or historical symbiosis between two groups that are basically dissimilar and unrelated. A corollary and also a very common assumption is that an Afro-Latin@ is the offspring of intermarriage between a Latina or Latino and an African American. Of course, this cross-cultural experience is very widespread and may be of constitutive importance for many, as it is for María Rosario Jackson in this collection. But limiting attention to that aspect can often mean overlooking the existence of a population whose very cultural heritage is *both* African and Latin American in an organic way. Such is the case in our time of the *afromestizo* immigrants from Mexico's Pacific Coast who are creating community in California and the Carolinas, the latter of which is documented in this volume in an essay on the Winston-Salem area.

With all due caution the relative unity and solidarity between the Latin@ and African American communities is no doubt the principal field of action and interaction for the Afro-Latin@ in the United States. The building of a common agenda, and the potential mediating role of Afro-Latin@s as a living embodiment of that unity, has received growing emphasis in recent times, and it is the focal point for the political reflections of commentators like Mark Sawyer, James Jennings, and others in this volume. The gravitation of many Latin@s, including Afro-Latin@s, toward Whiteness and their attendant distance from and disdain for African American Blackness has been well documented, as is clear in the articles by Eduardo Bonilla-Silva, Ed Morales, William Darity, Jason Dietrich, and Darrick Hamilton, and others. The very presence of Latin@s of visible African descent is the most significant countervailing pressure against this divisive and self-demeaning tendency, especially as Afro-Latin@s themselves come to acknowledge and affirm their full Afro-diasporic identity. Here again the transnational dimension plays a vital role as Afro-Latin@s throughout the hemisphere reach across national borders to share experiences, grievances, tactics, and resources in a growing Black-consciousness movement. But the general recognition of the diversities within both the Latin@ and the African American communities, and the subjection of Black Latin@s to racial and cultural discrimination even among their own, is incumbent on the entire public across racial and cultural lines.

The Fact of Afro-Latinidad

Finally, Afro-Latin@ also means the distinctive and unique phenomenological experience lived at a personal level by people who are both Black and Latin@ in all aspects of their social life. Aside from and lending human concreteness to the larger historical and structural dimensions outlined above, the way that Afro-Latin@s navigate their social identities as they intersect with other Latin@s and with other Blacks is unique to them. The "fact of Afro-Latinidad" (to borrow Frantz Fanon's phrase "the fact of blackness") makes that experience distinct in basic ways from that of either non-Black Latin@s or non-Latin@ Blacks. Indeed, in a paradigmatic way this othered Blackness is common to all foreign Blacks in the United States, including Africans, Haitians, and other peoples of non-Spanish backgrounds.

These demarcations take on salient dramatic life in many of the selections included in this book, most notably perhaps in the work by Piri Thomas, in the analysis by Jairo Moreno of the relation between Dizzy Gillespie and Mario Bauzá, and in the poems of Willie Perdomo and Tato Laviera. Because of the central importance of this experiential aspect of being Afro-Latin@ we have devoted an entire section of the book, part IX, to the personal testimonies of a range of present-day United States Afro-Latin@s from different national backgrounds and walks of life.

As these life stories and countless others make clear, Afro-Latin@ is at the personal level a unique and distinctive experience and identity because of its range among and between Latin@, Black, and United States American dimensions of lived social reality. In their quest for a full and appropriate sense of social identity Afro-Latin@s are thus typically pulled in three directions at once and share a complex, multidimensional optic on contemporary society. Taking a cue from W. E. B. Du Bois, we might name this three-pronged web of affiliations "triple-consciousness." To paraphrase those unforgettable lines from *The Souls of Black Folk* (1903), in studying the historical and contemporary experience of the United States Afro-Latin@, one ever feels his three-ness, —a Latin@, a Negro, an American; three souls, three thoughts, three unreconciled strivings; three warring ideals in one dark body, whose dogged strength alone keeps it from being torn asunder. Du Bois's reference to strength and resilience bears emphasis: the multiple experiences and perspectives — including the contradictions, pain, and outrage—does not necessarily translate into pathological confusion. As many of the contributions to this volume suggest, embracing and celebrating all the dimensions of one's self has not only been possible but has also resulted in significant innovations at the personal and collective level. It is an example of how what doesn't kill you makes you strong.

To be clear, the use of the catchy term "triple-consciousness" is not intended to trump or one-up the African American particularity and struggle but rather only to point to the increased complexities of the "color line" in light of the transnational nature of present-day social experience. For when in The Souls of Black Folk Du Bois so momentously declared the problem of the twentieth century to be the color line, he was not speaking strictly of African Americans but of "the relation of the darker to the lighter races of men in Asia and Africa, in America and the islands of the sea." He recognized over a hundred years ago that these crucial social differentiations were not national but global in scope. What is new in our new century is not that transnational reach of Black experience but rather the degree to which the global and the national are intertwined with one another, and the immense political and cultural implications of this dramatic shift.

The experience of Afro-Latin@s in the United States and the emergent realities of the new century impel us, in tune with Du Bois's critical legacy, to further advance an integral global vision of race, and at the same time to articulate a keener awareness of specificities and internal complexities, both within each group and across the amplified range of groups. Here again, Du Bois's choice of language is of key interest, for in The Souls of Black Folk we have the crucial linkage of a class dimension with the heralding of cultural awakening among the oppressed nations and peoples; the word "folk," which harbors both a class and a racial reference, holds the key to comprehending the new Black and Latin@ diversity and to hailing our elusive yet persistent goal, the "dawn of freedom."

Historical Background before 1900

The Afro-Latin@ presence in the United States predates not only the nation's founding but also the first English settlements. The earliest Africans in North America were actually Afro-Latin@s. In addition to their role in the settlement of St. Augustine in 1565, Africans and their descendants were also instrumental in the exploration, conquest, and settlement of the United States Southwest. Eager to escape the caste restrictions that limited their social and economic possibilities, they were among the first to respond to the Spanish Crown's call for settlers to the sparsely populated areas of present-day Arizona, California, New Mexico, and Texas.

Members of La Unión Martí-Maceo in their Sunday best on way to an outing at Ballast Point, Ybor City, Florida, circa 1900. (Tony Pizzo Collection, Special Collections Department, Tampa Library, University of Southern Florida)

Afro-Latin@s and other non-Whites were usually the numerical majority in these early Spanish towns, a situation that encouraged—and arguably required—greater flexibility with regard to racial relations and classifications. Certainly the significance and complexity of class, race, and gender is apparent in the ways that free and enslaved men and women both complied with and defied White authority. By the mid-nineteenth century the formative period of Afro-Latinidad can be seen both in the centrality of the historical relations of African Americans and Afro-Latin@s in the war with Mexico and the Cuban-Spanish-American War and in the beginnings of the long-term experience of Black Cubans in southern Florida.

PETER H. WOOD

The Earliest Africans in North America

In the summer of 1619, a 160-ton ship from the port of Flushing in Holland sailed into Chesapeake Bay. This Dutch vessel was under the command of Captain Jope and piloted by an Englishman named Marmaduke Raynor. They were seeking to obtain provisions after a season of raiding in the West Indies. In exchange for supplies, Jope and his crew sold more than twenty Negroes to the local authorities in the struggling English colony of Virginia. These black newcomers came ashore twelve years after the founding of Jamestown and one year before the *Mayflower* arrived at Plymouth in New England. The people brought to Virginia by the Dutch man-of-war are often cited as the first persons of African ancestry to set foot on North America. But in fact, others had come before them and had traveled widely through the southern part of the continent.

The earliest Africans to reach North America arrived nearly 500 years ago as participants in the large expeditions organized by Spanish-speaking explorers. These Spaniards were the successors to Christopher Columbus, and in the generation after 1492 they fanned out across the Caribbean, competing to find a passage to the Orient and to locate gold and other riches. They exploited the local inhabitants ruthlessly as they advanced. Within several decades, constant warfare, strange diseases, and brutal enslavement had destroyed the native population of the West Indies. The Spanish colonizers immediately began searching for new supplies of labor.

One solution to the labor shortage was the transportation of additional workers from Europe, but most of these people were practicing Christians, so fellow Christians felt reluctant to exploit them. The Catholic Church in Rome and the Spanish government in Seville had less concern about exploiting non-Christian Indians, so a second option centered upon Native Americans. Expeditions were sent out from the Caribbean in various directions to the American mainland, seeking inhabitants who could be enslaved. But this strategy also presented problems. Some groups resisted fiercely, and others died rapidly from diseases the Europeans had unknowingly carried with them from across the Atlantic. The aggressive Spanish empire-builders wanted more slaves than they could get in the Americas. Thus they began to seek more distant sources of labor, and soon they focused upon a third Atlantic region: the West Coast of Africa.

By 1500, European ships had been trading along the coast of West Africa for several generations. Besides purchasing gold and ivory, they also bought slaves and transported them north for sale in Europe. Soon the Spanish began diverting some of these slave-trading vessels to the Caribbean. Many of the first African workers found themselves forced to clear land for plantations or to dig for gold and silver. But others were pressed into service as soldiers, sailors, and servants. They were present, therefore, when the Spanish conquistador Hernán Cortés marched against the Aztecs in Mexico in 1519 and when Francisco Pizarro attacked the Incas in Peru twelve years later.

Africans were also present in the early Spanish forays onto the continent of North America, as Juan Ponce de León and his successors probed Florida and the Gulf Coast in search of slaves, wealth, and a passage to the Pacific. In August 1526, for example, six Spanish ships landed on the coast of what is now South Carolina. Their commander, Lucas Vásquez de Ayllón, brought at least 500 people—men, women, and children—along with 100 horses and enough cattle, sheep, and pigs to start a settlement. They pushed south along the coast to find a suitable location, and they constructed a small village of thatched-roof huts. But within months Ayllón died, and bitter tensions arose over who should succeed him. In the midst of this struggle for control, African slaves set fire to some of the houses at night. Divided and embittered, 150 survivors straggled back to the Caribbean as winter set in. Almost all the rest—more than 350 people—died because of sickness, violence, hunger, or cold. But it was rumored that some of the Africans had escaped their bondage and remained to live among the coastal Indians.

That same winter the Spanish king approved another expedition to the Florida region, and five ships, commanded by Pánfilo de Narváez, set sail from Spain in June 1527. The following spring more than 400 soldiers and servants, including some men of African descent, landed near Tampa Bay and marched northwest. They hoped to make great conquests, but they were poorly prepared and badly led. The Indians fought fiercely to defend their own lands, and soon the invaders were separated from their supply boats and from each other. Most died in the Gulf Coast wilderness, but a few survived long enough to be taken in by local tribes. Miraculously, four such men encountered one another on the Texas coast in 1534. They evaded the tribes with whom they were living and set off across the Southwest in hopes of reaching Mexico City, the capital of the Spanish colony of New Spain.

One of these four survivors was a Spanish-speaking African named Esteban (Stephen)—the first African to emerge clearly in the pages of North American history. Another survivor was a Spanish officer named Alvar Núñez Cabeza de Vaca who wrote down their incredible story. He told how they had been enslaved by Indians and forced to haul wood and water, living on nuts, rabbits, spiders, and the juice of prickly pears. Heading west, they viewed the rolling Texas prairie with its herds of buffalo. "Over all the region," they reported, "we saw vast and beautiful plains that would make good pasture." They also marveled at the variety of languages they encountered among Southwestern Indians. Cabeza de Vaca noted that "there are a thousand dialectical differences," adding that Esteban served as their primary go-between. "He was constantly in conversation, finding out about routes, towns, and other matters we wished to know."

After eight years in America, including two years traveling together through the Southwest, the four men finally reached Mexico City in 1536—the first newcomers from Europe and Africa to cross the huge expanse of North America. When they described the massive Indian apartment dwellings they had seen (known as pueblos), gold-hungry listeners assumed they had glimpsed the legendary and wealthy Seven Cities of Cíbola. Soon Governor Antonio de Mendoza, the first Spanish viceroy of Mexico, organized a new exploration to seek out these seven mythical towns, which were supposedly surrounded by turquoise-studded walls of gold. Since the black man was a skilled translator and a seasoned guide who remained enslaved, Mendoza purchased Esteban and presented him to a Spanish friar named Marcos de Niza, who had been selected to lead the expedition. In March 1539, the friar's party, "with the Negro and other slaves, and Indians," headed northward toward what is now Arizona in search of Cíbola. According to an official report: "The Lord Viceroy having . . . news and notice of such land sent a friar and a negro, the latter having come from Florida with the others . . . as survivors of the party taken there by Pánfilo Narváez. These set out with the knowledge the negro had in order to go to a very rich country; as the latter declared, and told the friar . . .

that there are seven very populous cities with great buildings. . . . They have houses built of stone and lime, being of three stories, and with great quantities of turquoises set in doors and windows."

Esteban, familiar with the region, proceeded ahead with his two dogs and a number of Indians. As the summer heat increased, he sent wooden crosses back to the Christian friar to assure him of their progress. Finally he approached a large community—probably the pueblo of Zuni in western New Mexico. Hoping to have reached "Cíbola" at last, Esteban sent messengers ahead as usual, carrying "his great Mace made of a gourd," which "had a string of belles upon it, and two feathers one white and another red, in token that he demanded safe conduct, and that he came peaceably." But the Zunis quickly recognized the bells as Spanish. They linked this party advancing from the south with rumors of Spanish slave raiding and violence that were already circulating in the Indian markets of the region. Zuni leaders blamed the appearance of foreigners for deaths that had already occurred, and they feared a plot by which "neither man nor woman of them shall remaine unslaine."

When Esteban's messengers returned, they reported handing over the "great gourd" to the Indian magistrate. He "tooke the same in his hands, and after he had spyed the belles, in a great rage and fury hee cast it to the ground, and willed the messengers to get then packing with speed, for he knew well ynough what people they were, and that they should in no case enter the citie, for if they did hee would put them all to death." Determined in his course and confident that diplomacy could prevail, Esteban dismissed this initial rejection as "no great matter" and proceeded to approach the town. But armed men blocked his entrance to the city and confined him to an outlying building. They denied him food and water overnight, and they confiscated his trade goods. Negotiations proved unsuccessful, and when Esteban emerged the next morning, he and most of his company were attacked and killed by an angry crowd. Though "bloody and wounded in many places," several of his Indian companions managed to survive. They returned southward to inform Fray Marcos of the death of his experienced black guide.

The failure of the expeditions of Ayllón, Narváez, and Fray Marcos only increased the ambitions of other explorers. Their ventures into the American interior would also include the presence of Africans at every stage. Even before the death of Esteban at the Zuni pueblo, other black Hispanic soldiers and slaves were among those preparing to accompany Francisco Vázquez de Coronado into the Southwest and Hernando de Soto into the Southeast, and a few remain visible in the surviving accounts. Among those marching with de Soto, for example, was a man named "Gomez, a negro belonging to Vasco Gonçalez who spoke good Spanish." In 1537, de Soto had received permission to invade Florida and carve out a province for himself and his followers in the southern interior. The Spanish Crown had authorized him to raise an army, to establish three fortified towns, and to include as many as fifty enslaved Negroes in his plans. Gomez was among the black men forced to take part in this ambitious design.

When the expedition landed in Florida in May 1539, it contained 330 foot soldiers and almost as many others—artisans, carpenters, cooks, servants, and priests. They also brought herds of hogs and other livestock that would accompany their army to provide fresh meat. De Soto had taken part in Pizarro's successful campaign against the golden cities of the Incas in Peru. Now he was anxious to discover an equally wealthy kingdom of his own. But long marches through the swamps and forests of the Deep South revealed no such prize, even when he tortured local leaders for information and pushed his own company to extremes. The more de Soto's ambition was frustrated, the more ruthless his invasion became. At the Indian town of Cofitachequi near the Savannah River, he finally received gifts of pearls in the spring of 1540. But he thanked the young woman leader (or *cacica*) who had presented the pearls by making her a captive in her own region and obliging her to march with his soldiers to assure their safe passage in her domain.

De Soto's repeated cruelty toward the Native Americans assured that few would give him a kindly reception. His ruthlessness with his own army meant that many were willing to risk desertion in a strange land, especially slaves who stood to gain nothing from the entire enterprise. Several weeks after de Soto's departure from Cofitachequi, his royal Indian prisoner stepped off the path with several servants and made good her escape. Several members of de Soto's company also disappeared, including three Spanish-speaking slaves: an Indian boy from Cuba, a Berber from North Africa, and a West African—Gomez. The first two slaves eventually returned to camp and begged forgiveness, reporting that Gomez had elected to remain behind with the young Indian. Regarding the black man and the Native American woman, these informants said, "it was very certain that they held communication as husband and wife, and that both had made up their minds" to go to Cofitachequi.

So by 1540, less than fifty years after the arrival of Columbus in the Caribbean, an African ex-slave and an Indian *cacica* were living together in the southern forest. By now other European countries, jealous of Spanish wealth in the New World, were beginning to show an interest in the coast of North America. Several explorers sailing for the French king envisioned the possibility of discovering a short "Northwest Passage" from the Atlantic to the Pacific. Giovanni da Verrazzano hoped to find a route to the Orient when he examined the Outer Banks of Carolina and the mouth of New York harbor in 1524. Jacques Cartier had similar ambitions when he sailed up the broad St. Lawrence River in 1535. Even if they could not discover access to the Pacific, Spain's rivals could take advantage of the excellent fishing grounds in the North Atlantic. Or, if they dared, they could go after grander targets, attacking the Spanish galleons that sailed homeward regularly from Mexico.

The annual Spanish fleet, carrying gold and silver from the New World to Seville, followed the currents of the Gulf Stream northward along the Florida Peninsula. Foreign ships, lying in wait along that coastline, could easily attack and capture stray vessels before they headed across the Atlantic. In 1565, therefore, the Spanish established a garrison at St. Augustine on the east coast of Florida. The purpose of this small port town was to help protect the passing gold fleet from marauders and to secure Spain's claim to the Florida region against European rivals. It became the first permanent non-Indian settlement in North America, and Africans were present there from the beginning.

By 1600, roughly forty Africans had been transported to the small outpost of St. Augustine as property of the royal garrison; another sixty had arrived in the households of private individuals. These early African Americans—mostly men and mostly Spanish-speaking—were involved in erecting more than 100 Spanish-owned shops and houses and in building Fort San Marcos on the northern edge of town. They planted gardens and fished in the Matanzas River, selling their catch in the local fish market. Those who had accepted Christianity worshipped at the local Catholic church, and some drew token pay for themselves and their owners as drummers, fifers, and flag bearers in the local militia.

But living conditions were harsh, and controls at the remote outpost were limited. So some Africans escaped to live among the Indians, as Gomez and others had done several generations earlier. A Spanish document from 1605 complained that slaves had slipped away toward the south and intermarried with the Ais tribe living along the Florida coast. Those who remained in town had little reason for allegiance to their owners. The authorities feared that they would support any invader who offered them their freedom, and one official, writing in 1606, warned others to be wary of "persons of their kind, who are the worst enemies we can have." More than a century later St. Augustine would be viewed as a potential haven by a later generation of black Southerners, but that day was still far in the future.

Just as blacks, both enslaved and free, took part in the exploration and colonization of Spanish Florida, they also participated in the creation of a new colony in the Southwest. There, from the time of Esteban, Spanish raiding parties had carried Indian captives back to Mexico to work in the silver mines alongside enslaved Africans. Before the end of the sixteenth century, Mexican adventurers pushed to gain control of the populated region along the upper Rio Grande. Their reasons for immigrating to this region were many and varied: Some hoped to limit the exploitation of local Indians; some hoped to convert the Indians to Christianity; some hoped to control them and extract a profit. Government officials hoped to prevent European rivals from discovering wealth that had so far eluded the Spanish. But most of the settlers simply hoped to escape harsh conditions in old Mexico and take their chances on the rough frontier in a colony to be called *New* Mexico.

In 1595, a contract for this northern venture was awarded to Don Juan de Oñate, one of the last in a long line of ambitious and violent conquistadors stretching back to Cortés and Pizarro, de Soto and Coronado. Oñate put up the enormous wealth his father had gained from silver mining (largely with Indian and African labor) in exchange for the right to conquer, control, and exploit a vast region. His tactics proved strikingly ruthless, even in an era known for its brutality, and his grandest ambitions were never realized. In 1599 he crushed a desperate Indian revolt at the pueblo of Acoma so ferociously that he was reprimanded for his acts, and eventually he was forced to withdraw from his newly founded colony. By 1608 there was serious talk of abandoning the settlement of New Mexico altogether. Nevertheless, by 1610 a permanent mission had been established at Santa Fe, and many of those who had accompanied Oñate had demonstrated their determination to remain in New Mexico.

In 1598, the first contingent of 500 colonists heading north included persons of varied racial backgrounds and social ranks. These newcomers to the Southwest included black and mulatto (that is, mixed-race) men and women, both enslaved and free. For example, three enslaved Negro women and a variety of mulatto servants, both male and female, accompanied one wealthy Spanish settler, and other households were undoubtedly similar. Authorities in Mexico, anxious to prevent runaways from escaping to another province, ordered the death penalty for any Indian or mulatto attempting to migrate without presenting clear identification. So when several hundred reinforcements headed north in 1600, non-whites had to obtain clearance to depart. One mulatto, branded on the face as a slave, showed that his owner had given him permission to take part in the journey. Twenty-year-old Mateo Montero, another mulatto with a slave brand on his face, proved that the master who had purchased him twelve years earlier had recently granted him freedom. Isabel, a free mulatto woman traveling alone, produced an affidavit sworn by three witnesses to show that she was the legitimate daughter of a free Negro man and his Indian wife.

The century before the first Dutch slave-trading ship arrived in Virginia, therefore, had been an important and dramatic one for Africans in North America. They had experienced all of the hardships and some of the opportunities associated with transatlantic colonization. Arriving without choice, they had served where necessary and escaped where possible, proving to be every bit as opportunistic and independent as those around them. Isolated at outposts in Florida and New Mexico, they were cut off from ancestors in Africa and from most of their black compatriots on the expanding plantations of tropical America. These pioneers, few in number and spread out across the northern fringes of Spain's vast New World empire, intermarried along the way with the Africans, Europeans, and Indians whom they encountered in their amazing travels. Descendants of Gomez and Isabel and other early arrivals would live on in all the races of North America.

JACK D. FORBES

Black Pioneers

The Spanish-Speaking Afro-Americans
of the Southwest

It is not yet clear when the first African Negroes arrived in the Americas, but by the 1520s mainland North America had its first African settlers, in central Mexico and the Carolinas. Thereafter, many different kinds of Africans participated in the expansion of the Spanish Empire, including olive-skinned Muslims from North Africa and darker West Africans. In addition to these persons, there were many Spaniards of part-African ancestry, a heritage of the earlier Muslim conquest of Spain, and more recent Spanish-Negro and Indian-Negro hybrids from Haiti, Borinquen (Puerto Rico), Cuba, and Jamaica.

Africans appeared in Mexico in the earliest days of the Spanish conquest and soon were numerous enough to stage rebellions and to form rebel bands.[1] They also were recruited into most Spanish expeditions, as members of which they had penetrated into the Southwest by the 1530s. Perhaps the most famous Negro southwesterner is Estevan, a Muslim who accompanied Alvar Núñez Cabeza de Vaca from Texas to Sinaloa and then became the first non-Indian known to have entered Arizona and New Mexico in 1539. Later that same year, the Vásquez de Coronado expedition gathered together many Negroes to travel through Arizona, New Mexico, Texas, and probably Oklahoma and Kansas. As a result of this enterprise, Negroes became the first non-Indian settlers in New Mexico and, possibly, Kansas.[2]

Still other early Southwestern expeditions had Negro contingents (as did the Francisco de Ibarra party of 1565), while the Alarcón group, which explored the Colorado River in 1540, possessed at least one Muslim of unknown color. Further, the Bonilla de Leyva-Umaña Expedition left one

mulatto woman among the Indians in Kansas in the 1590s.[3] More significant, however, were the many Africans who served in Central Mexico and
became the ancestors of an extensive Afro-American progeny now estimated to compose about 10 percent of the genetic heritage of the modern-
day Mexican population.[4]

Very few Spaniards of European lineage were available to populate
newly conquered regions, and this task fell primarily to Hispanicized
natives, mixed-bloods of all kinds, and Negroes. During the seventeenth
century persons of African ancestry were present in New Mexico as colonists or soldiers, apparently, and mulattos or Eurafricans were frequently
utilized as majordomos in Spanish missions.[5] Early descriptions of the
population of Spanish towns in Durango, Chihuahua, Sinaloa, and elsewhere invariably mention mulattos, and here and there an individual is
specifically identified, as when a mulatto traveled from the Hopi villages
to southern Arizona in 1720.[6]

Many men of African ancestry were recruited into the Spanish armed
forces and, in 1744, the Marquis de Altamira wrote that many garrison
troops along the northern frontier and especially in Texas "are not Spaniards, but of other inferior qualities, and [are] ordinarily vicious. . . ." In
1760, Pedro de Labaquera asserted that most of the frontier soldiers were
mulattos of low character and without ambition.[7] These mixed-blood soldiers, however, were absolutely essential and many of their descendants
were able eventually to achieve prominence.

In 1774 a royal official asserted that the Hispano population of northern
Mexico was of Negro, Indian, and European ancestry and were so intermixed as to make it difficult for anyone to trace their ancestry.[8] Nevertheless, Spanish census records continued to enumerate race or color until
about 1800. Some interesting trends deserve comment, however.

In general, as the status of a person improved, his race changed. He
might begin life as a Negro, pure or otherwise, and end life as a mulatto or
Eurafrican, mestizo or Eurindian, or even as Español. Race, therefore, was
not definite by the late eighteenth century and many people were of such
a mixed character that they were simply de color quebrado, that is to say, "all
mixed up." Finally, ethnic designations came to be of little value in determining actual ancestry, since, for example, the child of a Spaniard and a
mestizo usually was called a Spaniard and the child of a mulatto and an
Indian was often called a mulatto. Thus many persons classified as Español in the census records were not pure-bloods and many mulattos were
actually part-Indian.[9]

Some insight into the racial characteristics of the Spanish-speaking

Southwest can be gained, however, from an examination of the situation in California. Mulattos serving in several capacities accompanied the first expeditions which occupied San Diego and Monterey in 1769. For example, Juan Antonio Coronel was a leather-jacket soldier (*soldado de cuero*) while several other Eurafricans served as muleteers. Still other part-African soldiers came with the first expeditions, or soon afterward.

It is not surprising that California was subdued by Spanish troops of mixed origin. Persons of Negro ancestry had participated in most or all of the early sea expeditions along the Pacific coast, and during the eighteenth century they formed a substantial part of Baja California's population. In 1790, for example, there were 844 non-Indians in that province, 243 of whom were classed as Españoles, 183 as mulattos, and 418 as *castas*, i.e., miscellaneous mixed-bloods. Thus, persons of recorded African ancestry constituted 21.7 percent of the population, while other mixed-bloods composed 49.4 percent and Españoles equaled 28.9 percent. Altogether, 71.1 percent of the Spanish-speaking settlers were officially of mixed origin and they formed large colonies at the mines of Santa Ana (157 mulattos, 204 castas, and 133 Españoles) and the provincial capital at Loreto (158 otras castas, 10 mulattos, and 73 Españoles).[10]

These figures are comparable to the combined statistics for both California and Baja California in 1794, which reveal that of 1,469 Spanish-speaking persons 23.2 percent were de color quebrado, i.e., part-African, and 29.3 percent were mestizos. Adding these together, 52.5 percent of the Hispanos were of officially recorded mixed origin.[11] That more than one out of every five persons in Baja California in the 1790s was of part-Negro origin may come as a surprise, but, in addition, it is probable that many persons classified as Spaniards or castas also possessed some degree of African background. In any case, many settlers from the peninsula brought their African ancestry with them to Upper California after 1769, and still other part-Negro persons were recruited in northern Sinaloa and Sonora. For example, the Juan Bautista de Anza expedition of 1775 included seven mulattos of the twenty-nine men, or approximately one out of four.[12]

More revealing, however, are census records for individual communities and districts within California. A list of the first settlers in Los Angeles in 1781 includes the following Afro-American and part-African families.

1 Antonio Mesa, negro, 36, from Los Alamos; married to Ana Gertrudes López, mulatto, 27; two children: Antonia Maria, 8; and Maria Paula, 10

2 Manuel Camero, mulatto, 30, from Chiametla; married to María Tomasa, mulatto, 24

3 José Nabarro (Navarro), mestizo, 42, from El Rosario; married to María Rufina Doretea, mulatto, 47; three children: José María, 10; José Clemente, 9; and María Josefa, 4

4 José Moreno, mulatto, 22, from Rosario; married to Guadalupe, mulatto, 19

5 Basilio Rosas, indio, 67, from Nombre de Dios, Durango; married to Maria Manuela Calistra, mulatto, 43; six children: José Maximo, 15; Carlos, 12; Antonio Rosalino, 7; Jose Marcelino, 4; Esteban, 2; and María Josefa, 8

6 Luís Quintero, negro, 65, from Guadalajara; married to Petra Rubio, mulatto, 40; five children: María Gertrudes, 16; María Concepción, 9; Tomás, 7; Rafaela, 6; and José Clemente, 3.

The total population of Los Angeles in 1781 consisted of forty-six persons, of whom twenty-six were African or part-African. Thus the Afro-American percentage was 56.5.

[. . .]

By 1790, some significant changes had occurred in Los Angeles. The total population had increased to 141, of whom 73 were classified as Españoles, 39 as mestizos, 22 as mulattos, and 7 as Indians. These figures are inaccurate, however, because many of the original settlers of 1781 had experienced a change of race in the intervening years. The table illustrates this process. The changes in racial classification were all away from Indian or mulatto and toward Español — that is, everyone acquired some fictitious Caucasian ancestry and shed Negro backgrounds — becoming, in effect, lighter as they moved up the social scale. This process had undoubtedly taken place among the individuals who were newcomers to Los Angeles in 1790, but the census data are not at hand to ascertain their earlier classifications. In any case, by correcting those inaccuracies of which we are aware, the part-African population is increased from twenty-two to thirty-two, or 22.7 percent. [. . .]

Name	Race in 1781	Race in 1790
Pablo Rodríguez	Indian	*Coyote*
		(*Coyote* refers to a mix of three-quarters Indian and one-quarter Caucasian)
Manual Camero	Mulatto	*Mestizo*
José Moreno	Mulatto	*Mestizo*

María Guadalupe Pérez	Mulatto	*Coyote*
Basilio Rosas	Indian	*Coyote*
José Vanegas	Indian	*Mestizo*
José Navarro	Mestizo	*Español*
María Rufina Navarro	Mulatto	*Mestizo* (or Indian)

During the years from 1785 to 1792, a strong tendency existed at Santa Barbara, as elsewhere, to reclassify many mixed-bloods as Español. Thus, in spite of a 25 percent increase in the total population during those years, the number of non-Spaniards remained uniform.[13]

The census for San José in 1790 includes the following Afro-Americans:

1 Antonio Romero, 40, *pardo*, from Guadalajara; married to Petra Acevez, 28, *parda*; one son (*pardo* refers to an Indian-Negro-Caucasian mixed-blood, the progeny of a mulatto and a mestizo)
2 Manuel Gonzalez, 70, Indian, from Valle de San Bartolo (Durango); married to Gertrudis Acevez, 20, parda; two sons of ages 18 and 13 (by a previous marriage, one must assume)
3 Bernardo Rosales, 46, mulatto, from Parras (Durango); married to Mónica, 28, Indian; four children
4 Manuel Amesquita, 38, mulatto, from Terrenate (Sonora); married to Graciana, 26, mulatto; four children
5 Antonio Acevez, 50, mulatto, from San Bartolomé (Durango); married to Feliciana Cortes, 50, mestiza; two children

The marriage pattern among the settlers at San Jose [shows that of] the fifteen families, only seven did not involve hybridization or hybrid lineages. Of the total number of settlers at San Jose in 1790, 24.3 percent were part-Negro and 55.5 percent were non-Español. Four years later the part-Negro proportion had been reclassified to form only 14.2 percent, while the non-Español had increased to 59.5 percent, thus indicating that some pardos and mulattos had become mestizos.[14]

Similar developments occurred at Monterey, where, in 1790, the mulattos constituted 18.5 percent of the population and the castas constituted an additional 50.2 percent. The latter group included part-Negroes as well as mestizos. The total non-Español proportion at Monterey was 74.2 percent of the population. Within one year, however, at least twenty-eight non-Españoles were reclassified as Español in the Monterey region.[15] [. . .]

Conservatively, we can estimate that at least 20 percent of the Hispano-Californians were part-Negro in 1790, while probably 25 percent of the

Hispano-Baja Californians possessed African ancestry.[16] Subsequent additions to the population of Spanish-Mexican California probably did not alter greatly the genetic heritage of the Californians, since the bulk of later immigrants were Mexicans of mixed ancestry. After about 1800, their racial character is no longer recorded but of a group of twenty-two convicts sent north in 1798, four, or 18 percent, were mulattos, six were Indians, and eight were mestizos.[17]

The physical appearance of the Spanish-speaking Californians did not, however, remain static. From the earliest intrusion of Spanish settlers in 1769, intermarriage with native Indians was encouraged both by the Spanish government and by a dearth of Spanish-speaking women.[18] Over the years, therefore, the immigrants became more Indian, genetically speaking. In addition, the Spanish-speaking people of Caucasian, Indian, and Negro ancestry steadily mixed their stocks so as to produce what amounts to a new race.

Nonetheless, the upper-class Hispano-Americans were a color-conscious people, and they were very interested in keeping track of racial ancestry. Otherwise they would not have invented so many different terms to refer to various kinds of mixtures. This race-consciousness was greatly modified in practice, however. Necessity may have forced a Spaniard to marry a mixed-blood, Negro, or Indian in cases where eligible girls were rare or absent. In addition, the Crown encouraged such mixture by allowing wealthy non-Spaniards to purchase "purity of blood" certificates; for example, a pardo could become a Spaniard in 1795 for 500 reales.[19]

Reference has already been made to persons becoming Español simply by attaining sufficient status in their own community. After about 1800 the California census records no longer enumerated persons by race, perhaps because the mixtures had become so complex and because it would be impolitic to offend so many people by reminding them of their non-Spanish origins.

All of the foregoing examples of race mixture, however, should not deceive the reader into believing that California was a racial paradise. Even when a person had achieved the official status of Español, his color, if dark, could be a handicap. The historian Charles E. Chapman noted that the *gente de razón* (Spanish-speaking citizens) "were in fact of varying shades of color. The officers and missionaries were for the most part of pure white blood, but the great majority of the rest were mestizos—part white and part Indian. In the Los Angeles district there were some mulattoes. . . . There were very marked social differences, based on rank (usually military) and blood, and very distinctly there was a Spanish Californian aristocracy."[20] Aside from his understating the extent of Negro ancestry, Chapman's statement is quite correct and is confirmed by R. H. Dana's observations in 1835:

> Those who are of pure Spanish blood, having never intermarried with aborigines, have clear brunette complexions, and sometimes, even as fair as those of English-women. There are but few of these families in California, being mostly in official stations, or who, on the expiration of their offices, have settled here upon property, which they have acquired; and others who have been banished for state offenses. These form the aristocracy, intermarrying, keeping up an exclusive system in every respect. They can be told by their complexions, dress, manner and also by their speech; for calling themselves Castilians, they are very ambitious of speaking the pure Castilian language, which is spoken in a somewhat corrupted dialect by the lower classes. . . .
>
> From this upper class [of pure Spaniards], they go down by regular shades, growing more and more dark and muddy, until you come to the pure Indian who runs about with nothing upon him but a small piece of cloth, kept up by a wide leather strap round his waist. Generally speaking, each person's caste is decided by the quality of the blood, which shows itself, too plainly to be concealed, at first sight. Yet the least drop of Spanish blood, if it be only of quadroon or octoroon, is sufficient to raise them from the rank of slaves and entitles them to a suit of clothes, boots, hats, cloak, spurs, long knife, all complete, and coarse and dirty as may be and to call themselves Españoles and to hold property, if they can get any. . . .[21]

The possession of non-Caucasian ancestry was not, of itself, enough to constitute a barrier quite as rigid as Dana would seem to indicate. An ambitious dark-skinned man might marry a light-skinned girl and produce progeny who eventually could intermarry into the "white" upper class. This latter group was not really a pure-blood caste and enough dark features appeared occasionally to allow for the acceptance of a wealthy or powerful mixed-blood.

Such indeed is the history of the Pico family, which in many ways can serve as an example of the way in which Negro genes eventually come to be dispersed widely among the "elite." The founder of the family in California, Santiago Pico, was a mestizo, while his wife was a mulatto. His sons, José Dolores, José María, Miguel, Patricio, and Francisco rose in stature by acquiring property and serving as soldiers. It was the next generation, however, which really acquired prominence; Pio Pico served

Don Pio Pico (1801–1894),
the last governor of Mexican
California, circa 1880. Born a
casta under the Spanish, Pico
became a Mexican citizen after
the war for independence, and
a U.S. citizen after the signing
of the Treaty of Guadalupe-
Hidalgo. (University of
Southern California,
Doheny Memorial Library)

as the last governor of Mexican California and Andrés Pico was a leader of the California resistance to the United States in 1846–47. This latter generation intermarried with many prominent Español families, such as the Alvarados and Carrillos, and non-Caucasian genes were widely dispersed. José Dolores Pico produced 13 children and had over 100 descendants by 1869. Miguel Pico had 228 descendants by 1860 and the other Picos usually could boast an average of 10 children per generation. Many prominent "white" Californians today are descendants of the Picos, including some who boast of the "purity" of their "Castilian" ancestry.

The change from Spanish to Mexican rule, which occurred in 1822, helped to ease the situation for mixed-bloods. Many Mexicans began to take pride in possessing vague quantities of indigenous ancestry, and several governors were dark-complexioned. Manuel Victoria (1831–1832) was described as a Negro, and José Figueroa (1833–1835) was of Aztec ancestry. Nevertheless, the upper class in California had not come to fully accept racial equality before the arrival of a contrary influence.[22]

Beginning in the 1820s, European and Anglo-American men began to settle in California and to marry Spanish-speaking women. For various reasons they tended to select mates from the more prosperous and lighter-skinned California families. This had several effects: (1) it began to lighten the color of the aristocracy still further; (2) prejudice against darker skin color was reinforced; and (3) knowledge of Indian or Negro ancestors was gradually suppressed. After the United States conquest, violently racist attitudes were introduced into the region and the Spanish-speaking Californians, quite naturally, disassociated themselves from their hybrid past. Thus commenced, incidentally, the creation of the racial mythology which is part of California's contemporary culture.

In spite of the above, African racial characteristics soon disappeared in California because the vast majority of the Spanish-speaking population intermarried freely. One of the last general references to Negroid features is found in a statement by an Anglo-American visitor in 1828 who felt that a Mexican corporal "resembled a negro, rather than a white."[23] Other pre-1848 visitors failed to note the presence of Negro characteristics and, in fact, by the 1830s, only newcomers of Afro-American ancestry were thought of as Negroes.[24] Entering the state at about the same time as the Anglo-Americans and Europeans referred to above were a number of Negroes of non-Mexican origin. The first of these was Bob, left by a Yankee ship, the Albatross, in 1816. On August 16, 1819, he was baptized at Santa Barbara as Juan Cristóbal and thereafter disappeared into the California population. A number of other Negroes arrived in 1818—among them being Fisher or Norris, who later left California, Mateo José Pascual, called a Negro or a mulatto, and a United States Negro named Francisco. In the same year, another Negro, Molina, was residing at Monterrey.[25]

Subsequently, other Afro-Americans came to California with Anglo-American groups and some became prominent in regional affairs; for example, Jim Beckworth's escapades as a mountain man, guide, and horse-thief, and Allen G. Light's service as comisario-general for Governor Alvarado in 1839. Occasional references also appear in regard to Spanish-speaking Negroes, as in 1831 when a female slave was brought to California from Peru and from 1838 to 1844 when Ignacio Miramontes, a Negro, served as corporal of the San Francisco garrison.[26] The bulk of these later Afro-American settlers would appear to have been absorbed into the Mexican-Californian population and they certainly experienced less discrimination than is evident in California today. It should be emphasized that there were almost no slaves of African ancestry in Hispano-Mexican California—only two are known for the entire period under discussion. The balance of the people whose names have been mentioned were soldiers or ex-soldiers, or civilian settlers, while a handful were servants or convicts.

California's Afro-American pioneers were fortunate in being able to live in a society where color was not an absolute barrier. In such civilian settlements as Los Angeles and San Jose especially, persons of Negro ancestry were able to rise to prominence and occupy positions of leadership. The rapid process of miscegenation allowed their children to win acceptance simply as Californios and their granddaughters frequently intermarried with incoming Anglo-Americans or Europeans. Their blood now flows in the veins of many thousands of Californians who cannot speak Spanish and who are totally unaware of their African heritage.

It is to be hoped that this survey of the importance of the Negro heritage in California and the Southwest will stimulate further research. Moreover, it is to be hoped that the story of Negroes in North America will be expanded to include those Afro-American pioneers whose descendants are not called Negroes but instead are intermixed with all of us.

Notes

1. In 1537, Spanish soldiers had to crush a revolt by Negro miners at the mines of Amtepeque. See George P. Winship, "The Coronado Expedition, 1540–1542" in *Fourteenth Annual Report of the Bureau of American Ethnology* (Washington: Smithsonian Institution, 1909), 380.

2. Ibid., 379; George P. Hammond and Agapito Rey, *Narratives of the Coronado Expedition 1540–1542* (Albuquerque: University of New Mexico Press, 1940), 262, 270, 306–7; and Gerónimo de Zárate Salmerón, "Relaciones de todas las cosas, que en el nuevo Méjico se han visto, Virreinato de Méjico," Madrid, I, 567.

3. Baltasar de Obregón, *Obregón's History*, edited and translated by George P. Hammond and Agapito Rey (Los Angeles: Metzel Publishing Company, 1928), 156, 161; Salmerón, "Relaciones de todas las cosas," 567; Herbert E. Belton, *Spanish Exploration in the Southwest* (New York: Reprint Services Corporation, 1916), 201; and Hammond and Rey, *Narratives of the Coronado Expedition*, 134–54.

4. Harold E. Driver, *Indians of North America* (Chicago: University of Chicago Press, 1961), 602.

5. When civil war broke out in New Mexico in 1640–1643, one faction was said to be composed of mestizos and mulattos. Subsequently, the same general faction was said to include "mestizos and sambahigos, sons of Indian men and Negroes, and mulattos." In 1680, Pueblo Indian rebels were aided by "confident coyotes, mestizos and mulattoes" who were able to fight on horseback and with guns as well as any Spaniard. See Patronato 244, Ramo VII, Archivo General de Indias, Sevilla, Spain; Jack D. Forbes, *Apache, Navaho and Spaniard* (Norman: University of Oklahoma Press, 1960), 127, 135, 138–39, 180; and Charles W. Hackett, *Revolt of the Pueblo Indians and Otermin's Attempted Reconquest, 1680–1682* (Albuquerque: University of New Mexico Press, 1942), ii, 322, 329, 337–39, 355.

6. How the mulatto got to the Hopi villages is a mystery. See Juan Antonio Baltasar, "De nuevos progresos . . . de la Pimería Alta" in *Apostólicos Afanes* (Mexico City: Layac, 1944), 339.

7. Marquis de Altamira al Virrey, *Biblioteca del Ministerio de Hacienda* (Madrid, 1744), 975; and Charles E. Chapman, *A History of California: The Spanish Period* (New York: Macmillan Company, 1921), 203.

8. "Reflexiones sobre el reyno de nueva españa," Virreinato de México, II, Biblioteca del Museo Navae, 568, Madrid.

9. I normally prefer to use the term "eurafrican" for a Negro-Caucasian mixed blood, but "mulatto" will be used in this paper in order to avoid implying that such mixed-bloods possessed only Negro and Caucasian ancestry. The term "mestizo" will likewise be used to refer to Indian-Spanish hybrids, although I have often used the term "eurindian" in other papers. "Eurindian" again implies a rather precise type of hybrid, while the mestizos of California were not always of Indian-Spanish ancestry alone.

10. "Censo y castas . . . 1790," C–A 50, 64, Bancroft Library, Berkeley, California. Juan Antonio Coronel was classed as a mulatto by Father Serra. See Herbert E. Bolton, editor and translator, *Palou's Historical Memoir of New California* (Berkeley: University of California Press, 1926), iii, 33.

11. "Resumen General de la Población de Ambas Californias," July 13, 1795, C–A 50, 148, Bancroft Library.

12. "Padrones y extractos . . . ," C–R 9, Carton 3, Bancroft Library.

13. "Padrón de la población de Santa Barbara," C–A 50, 6–10, and "Estado del Censo y Castas," December 31, 1792, C–A 50, 103, Bancroft Library.

14. "Padrón de Vecinos de San José," October 5, 1790, C–A 50, 61–64, and "Padrón del Pueblo San José," December 31, 1794, C–A 8, 91, Bancroft Library.

15. "Estado que manifiesta el número de Vasallos y habitantes," December 31, 1791, C–A 50, 101, Bancroft Library.

16. See the earlier summary of the Baja California population.

17. "Lista de reos para poblar la Peninsula de Californias," February 12, 1798, C–A 10, 89, Bancroft Library. The names of the mulattos were Juan José de la Luz Hernandez, José Leonicio Calzada, Casimiro Cornejo, and José Francisco Pablo.

18. Letter of Branciforte to Borica, June 4, 1797, C–A 8, 449, Bancroft Library; and Herbert Eugene Bolton, *Anza's California Expeditions* (Berkeley: University of California Press, 1930), pp. v, 104.

19. Real Cedula, February 10, 1795, C–A 8, 182–83, Bancroft Library.

20. Chapman, *History of California*, 384, 395.

21. Richard H. Dana, *Two Years Before the Mast* (New York: Harper, 1840), 72–73.

22. The color-complex was strong enough so that upper-class California women were allegedly averse to associating with the *gobernador Negro Victoria*. This tradition may, however be a later invention. See Hubert Howe Bancroft, *California Pastoral* (San Francisco: History Company, 1888), i, 284.

23. James Ohio Pattie, *Personal Narrative* (Cleveland, Ohio: Arthur H. Clark Company, 1905), 221.

24. For example, Bancroft states that there were only two Negroes in California in 1831 (*California Pastoral*, 283).

25. Hubert Howe Bancroft, *History of California* (San Francisco: History Company, 1890), 11, 230–31n, 232n, 237, 248, 277, 722.

26. Ibid., iv, 91, 741; and Bancroft, *California Pastoral*, i, 283, 617. The rank of corporal was an important one in the Hispano-Mexican armed forces.

VIRGINIA MEACHAM GOULD

Slave and Free Women of Color in the Spanish Ports of New Orleans, Mobile, and Pensacola

[. . .] Spain, France, and Britain vied throughout the eighteenth century for the region that bordered the northern Gulf of Mexico. Pensacola was founded first, by the Spanish, in 1698. The French placed a settlement a year later at Biloxi. They founded Mobile in 1702. New Orleans was settled in 1718. All three ports remained under the governance of their founders until the Treaty of Paris of 1763. Louisiana, west of the Mississippi, was ceded to the Spanish with the treaty; however, the Spanish did not gain control of the colony until 1768. Mobile and Pensacola and the regions around them were ceded to the British with the Treaty of Paris. Mobile remained under British rule from 1763 until 1780, when it was captured by the Spanish. Pensacola was captured a few months later, during 1781. The entire region remained under Spanish control until each port and the region around it was successively ceded to the United States. Louisiana was ceded first, in 1803. Mobile went next, in 1811. Neither Pensacola nor the rest of Florida was officially turned over to the Americans until 1821.

During the century that France, Spain, and England competed for control over the territory that bordered the Gulf, their colonists struggled to survive. Colonial officials encouraged their earliest settlers to establish farming communities. The settlers, however, had other ideas. In specific, colonists in Louisiana and Florida demanded that their officials import African slaves so they might establish a plantation society. There were already some slaves in the colony. A few had accompanied the early governing officials as personal servants. [. . .]

It was only after 1719 that thousands of Africans were imported into the region for the purpose of plantation agriculture. Between 1719 and 1731, twenty-two ships carrying nearly 6,000 slaves arrived in Louisiana's various ports. These ships brought slaves into the Gulf region from Juda

(Whydah), Cabinda (Angola), and Senegal. After 1731, only one other ship carrying slaves imported directly from Africa landed in French Louisiana. That was the St. Ursin, which debarked 190 slaves in 1743 from Senegal. Yet, despite the best efforts of the slaves and their masters, a suitable crop was not found. Instead, local settlers, slave and free, tried unsuccessfully to consistently produce indigo, sugarcane, tobacco, and rice. With their hopes for a profitable plantation economy dashed and with few other resources, white settlers and their African slaves struggled to survive by forming face-to-face networks based on subsistence farming and trade with the local Native Americans and one another. Subsistence farming and trade in clay, lumber, and deer hides, not plantation agriculture, defined the local economy.[1]

The failure of plantation agriculture not only redefined the economy but also had a definitive effect on the social relations of the population. Unable to establish economic and political dominance, neither planters nor merchants were able to fully subjugate their slaves. Slaves struggled with their owners for control, and in many cases managed to establish some power over their daily lives. It was more usual than not for slaves to cultivate their own plots of land and to use Sundays for worship, rest, and marketing. Nor was it unusual for slaves in the ports to live away from their owners. Slaves in colonial New Orleans, Mobile, and Pensacola often provided housing, food, and clothing for themselves and their families. Antoine LePage DuPratz wrote in 1734 that slaves in Louisiana preferred to take care of their own needs.[2]

And it was not unusual for slaves to gain their freedom during the economically and politically unstable colonial period. Some Africans and their descendants simply escaped into the swamps that surrounded the ports. Others were freed in return for faithful service and performing outstanding military feats. Still others were freed as a consequence of their ties to the free white community. The first evidence of a freed slave can be found in the sacramental records of the Cathedral of the Immaculate Conception. According to a baptismal record dated July 26, 1715, Janneton, the former slave of "Mr. Charlie," brought her son, Michel, to the church to be baptized. Janneton declared in the record that her son's father was a French soldier named La Terrier. Since Janneton was freed before she gave birth, and in Louisiana and Florida the condition of a child followed that of its mother, her son was born free. Slave women, like Janneton, often found their freedom in their relations with free men. The records do not say, but it is more than likely that La Terrier purchased Janneton's freedom from "Mr. Charlie" before the birth of their first child. Such interracial liaisons as that between Janneton and La Terrier routinely evolved in the socially fluid frontier ports, and it was not unusual for the men to purchase the freedom of the slave women with whom they cohabited. If they could not or did not free the women before they had children, they often freed them along with their children when they could. In fact, it was from just such relations as that of La Terrier and Janneton that the large and relatively influential free colored population in the Gulf region emerged.[3]

Many of the secular and religious officials viewed the interracial liaisons that were so common in the region as threatening to the social order. Father Henry La Vente, a Catholic clergyman in Mobile who wrote a memoir of his experiences in Louisiana after he returned to France in 1713, noted that the cause of the colony's spirit of irreligion was the generalized concubinage.[4] [. . .]

Father Raphael complained in a letter to Abbé Raguet in 1726 that "the number of those who maintain young Indian women or negresses to satisfy their intemperance . . . remain enough to scandalize their church and to require an effective remedy."[5] Admonitions from officials, however, appear to have been completely ignored by the region's inhabitants. The practice of white settlers taking slave women and free women of color as cohabitants continued unabated throughout the early decades of the colony. In 1766, just three years before the Spanish officially took control of the colony, Clements de Saldaño stated that it was so common for white men to keep slave women and free women of color as mistresses that no one commented on it.[6]

In order to establish a more orderly slave society, French officials in Louisiana implemented the Code noir in 1724. The Code noir, or slave law, was modeled after the 1685 Code noir that France had originally devised for its Caribbean Islands. By its intent, the Code embodied the planter philosophy of Catholicism, white supremacy, and patriarchal rule. It regulated the fundamental rights of slaves by guaranteeing them a minimum of food and providing for their baptisms and marriages. Besides regulating their fundamental rights, the code also stated that slaves could not be freed without consent of the Superior Council. After restricting slaves' access to freedom, officials placed restrictions on their ability to receive property. Freed slaves and their descendants, according to the Code, were prohibited from receiving donations *inter vivos* or *mortis causa* from whites. (Donations made between living persons were *inter vivos* and those made by a person after death were *mortis causa*.) The restrictions the French placed on freedom and the distribution of property were aimed at undermining relations between white men and slave women and free women of color. The code, it is clear, was meant to protect the race-based hierarchical nature of the social system.[7]

Despite the best efforts of the French, the Code did not prevent white settlers from cohabiting with African women and their descendants. Nor did it prevent men from freeing their cohabitants and their racially mixed offspring and providing them with property. Indeed, by the time the Spanish arrived in New Orleans in 1768, there was an already rapidly growing population of racially mixed free people of color. That is not to suggest, however, that the Spanish welcomed interracial liaisons any more than the French did. Spanish attitudes can be found scattered throughout their official correspondence. In an edict issued in 1776, Charles III of Spain emphasized that the appointed governor of Louisiana, Bernardo Galvez, establish public order and proper standards of morality. After setting forth instructions for the governance of the colony's slaves, the king pointed out that public immorality had produced a large class of "mulattos," and that a large number of "mulatto" women who were "given over to vice" lived in public concubinage with whites. If they did not marry and enter into proper employment, the king informed Galvez, he should see to their deportation.

The Spanish, in response to the king's demands, implemented specific restrictions against interracial liaisons in the Black Code of 1777. The code forbade white men from living in concubinage with free women of color or with slaves. It ordered that fines be levied against illegitimate children born of any such liaison. The fine for a child born of a free women of color and a white man was sixty piasters, which was a considerable sum. If the woman was a slave, the fine was unspecified and the child was confiscated.

It is not difficult to understand why Spanish officials, or, for that matter, officials in any of the New World slaveholding societies, believed that such liaisons threatened the social order. Since slavery in the New World was based on race, it was imperative for the white dominant class to protect its identity, or status, from contamination by those of African descent. The Spanish believed that purity of blood—*limpieza de sangre*—was necessary for the protection of the hierarchical nature of the social system, which, in turn, reinforced the distribution of property. Limpieza de sangre was originally a religious convention devised by the Spanish to distinguish and exclude Jews and Moors, whom they defined as "impure," from the Christians, whom they considered "pure." At the time that the custom of limpieza de sangre was dying out in Spain it was adapted to the colonial situation. There it was used to distinguish those of "pure" or white Caucasian European descent from those of "impure" or African descent. In his essay on New Spain, the commentator Baron Alexander Von Humboldt noted at the beginning of the nineteenth century that "in Spain it is a kind of title of nobility not to descend from Jews and Moors." It is different in America, he notes, for there it is the skin, more or less white, that "dictates the class that an individual occupies in society." Whites, Von Humboldt writes, even when riding barefoot on horseback, consider themselves members of the nobility. The distinction between black and white, slave and free, which is evident in Von Humboldt's writings, was the most important one in any society in which slavery was based in race.[8] [. . .]

The blurring of the population was later so alarming to Esteban Miró, who was appointed governor of Spanish Louisiana in 1786, that he addressed the problem in his *bando de buen gobierno*, or proclamation of good government. Newly appointed governors of the Spanish colonies, like Miró, usually addressed those issues that they found the most daunting in their inaugural addresses or bandos. It only takes a glance at Miró's bando to demonstrate that his foremost concern was the behavior and appearance of the region's free women of color. Recognizing that free women of color threatened the social stability of the region, Miró ordered them to abandon their licentious ways from which they subsisted and to go back to work with the understanding that he would be suspicious of their indecent conduct. The extravagant luxury of their dress, which was already excessive, he warned, would compel him to investigate the mores of those who persisted in such display. To ensure that their status was clearly identifiable, he ordered them to reestablish the distinction that had been manifest in their headdress. Finally, he prohibited them from wearing feathers or jewels in their hair. Instead, they were to cover their hair with head kerchiefs as was formerly the custom.[9]

Miró, like officials in Spanish America as well as Europe and other European colonies, believed that social station or status was visibly expressed through dress. In general, most of the Spanish colonial sumptuary restrictions were adapted to the colonial situation from traditional Spanish law. Spanish colonial legislation usually prohibited women of color from wearing silks, gold, silver, pearl jewelry, or mantillas. Some legislation went even further by forbidding them to wear slippers ornamented with silver bells, to own canopied beds, or to sit on rugs or cushions while attending church. Miró's sumptuary legislation directly reflected other attempts by colonial governors throughout Latin America and the Caribbean to prevent free women of color from obscuring the visible expression of status. Miró's bando that remanded the women of color in the Gulf colonies to wear the head kerchief was a completely symbolic ploy.[10]

The symbolism that Miró hoped to establish was that of women tied to slavery. After all, the slave women in the region were most closely and officially associated with work, and they were the women who traditionally wore kerchiefs to cover their heads. Thus, the intent of Miró's sumptuary law was to return the free women of color, visibly and symbolically, to the subordinate and inferior status associated with slavery. His order ignored the legal status of these women, but it also ignored their economic condition and their ties to the white community. To Miró, it was necessary for women of color who had become too light skinned or who dressed too elegantly, or who, in reality, competed too freely with white women for status and thus threatened the social order, to symbolize their ties to slavery through the simple head kerchief.[11]

There is no evidence that officials in the Gulf ports ever enforced the "tignon law," as it became known. Yet whether officials enforced the law or not, it appears that the free women of color obeyed it by adopting the habit of wearing the head kerchief. However, in acquiescing to Miró's order, free women of color thwarted it by adapting the kerchief into the stylish and flattering tignon that became a badge or mark of distinction of their race, their status, and their gender. Liliane Crété notes that the women exchanged their elegant coiffures for a tignon or a "brilliant silk kerchief, artfully knotted and perhaps enhanced with a jewel." The image seems to have attained such prominence that, in some ways, it bound very different women together in an act of defiance.[12]

Despite their rhetoric and the laws that prohibited interracial liaisons, in reality Spanish officials could do little to discourage white men from cohabiting with slave and free women of color. In fact, certain Spanish laws and traditions motivated slave women and free women of color to participate in liaisons with white men. For instance, Spanish law allowed masters to free their slaves by a simple act recorded by a notary. It also implemented the more lenient custom of *coartación*, or self-purchase. Coartación, as practiced throughout Spanish America, was an arrangement in which slaves were permitted to free themselves by agreeing with their masters on a purchase price or by arbitrating a sum through the courts. Such a policy not only allowed slaves the possibility of freedom — not only suggested to them that it was their natural right by its implications of liberty and humanity; but, in effect, loosened their master's control over them. Once freed, free people of color were allowed by Spanish law to receive *inter vivos* and *mortis causa* donations from whites. Spanish law, as implemented in New Orleans in 1769, in Mobile in 1780, and in Pensacola in 1781, encouraged a practice that had already become common. Cohabitation that had been mostly beneficial to white men during the earliest years of settlement now more directly and openly benefited their African cohabitants and their racially mixed offspring.[13]

[Extralegal liaisons were] not uncommon since the demographic imbalance in the population encouraged white men and slave women and women of color to cohabit. A sampling of census data in the colonial ports reveals this trend. For instance, the Spanish census of New Orleans for 1788 includes 5,321 inhabitants. Of those, 2,370 were described as white, 820 as free people of color, and 2,131 as slaves. The adult portion of the white population for the city had a sex ratio of 68+, which suggests that there were only 68 women for 100 men in that segment of the population. The sex ratio for the white population, however, is insignificant when compared to that of the free-colored population, which was 677+. That number meant that there were 677 free women of color for every 100 free men of color in the port in that year.[14]

A census taken in Mobile in 1805 reported that of the 1,537 inhabitants in the city in that year, 675 were white, 255 free people of color, and 607 slaves. The sex ratio for the white population, which included 383 males and 292 females, was 764+; that is, only 76 white women for every 100 white men. The 255 free people of color living in the port in 1805 had a sex ratio that, at 105+, was nearly even in that year.[15]

The 1819 census of Pensacola reported 992 inhabitants in the port. Of those, 432 were described as white, 217 as free people of color, and 343 as slaves. The white population included 234 males and 198 females, which indicates a sex ratio of 85+. The sex ratio for the free people of color was 197+, or 197 adult women for every 100 adult men. White men absent white partners would have turned to slave women and free women of color. Free women of color absent free men of color would have turned to other free men, even if they were white. Few free women of color chose to tie themselves to slave men, although there are a few examples of women who did.[16]

The demographic imbalance in the region does not, however, tell the entire story. Other evidence suggests that white men preferred cohabiting with slave women and free women of color rather than marrying white women. C. C. Robin wrote soon after Louisiana was ceded to the Union that "travelers, Creoles, residents, and everyone else in New Orleans forms alliances with these colored women and many have children of them. This license extends also to the rural regions, where the Creoles prefer to live with these women rather than to give to a white woman the title of spouse."[17] Perrin du Lac agreed with Robin's impression of the preference of white men for women of color: "As in all colonies their taste for women extends more particularly to those of color, whom they prefer to the white women."[18] The impression expressed by Robin and du Lac that some free women of color preferred to cohabit with white men rather than cohabit with or marry free men of color is verified by all the region's censuses. There are many examples of white women who were of marriageable age yet lived with their parents, and other cases in which single white women were described as heads of households.

It was also reported that some free women of color and slave women preferred liaisons with white men. John F. Watson wrote in his journal in the summer of 1805 that there were beautiful yellow women in New Orleans who had no more ambition than to become the concubine of a white gentleman. They were content, he noted, "to live at an expense of about four hundred dollars a year. Many are so maintained." He noted again, about a month later, that the women who entered in liaisons with white men were faithful. "They never desert their *maris* (de facto husband) in any case of adversity. They do not marry, because custom holds that to be odious; but that not being their fault, they are, in all respects, good as wives in general, frugal in their habits and innocent in their lives and deportment." Liaisons with white men offered slave women and free women of color opportunities they would not have found elsewhere. Again census data supports Watson's allegations that some women preferred cohabiting with white men by including multiple examples of free men of color living alone or with other free men of color. The records also demonstrate that it was also common for free men of color to cohabit with or marry slave women.[19]

It can be said without reservation that any relationship in which power was as unequal as that between white men and women of color in the early Gulf ports was exploitive. But it must also be pointed out that many of these liaisons would have been mutually beneficial to the couple and their children. As Marcus Christian, a Creole descendant of the early African and European population in New Orleans, observed over a century later, while "the female slaves were peculiarly exposed . . . to the seductions of an unprincipled master," most of the liaisons were mutually sought. White men, perhaps like Nicolas Vidal, could formulate liaisons with women outside the formal institution of marriage, and without social stigma. And women of color could acquire freedom, or property, or status and influence from their liaison with white men. There is more than a little evidence to support the argument that women of color, both slave and free, sought liaisons with white men knowing that they could exert at least a modicum of control over them. [. . .]

Yet while some slave women obviously had great difficulty in their relationships with white men, others found considerable advantage. The manumission records for New Orleans, Mobile, and Pensacola support the evidence of sex ratios derived from the analysis of the census records. Approximately three times as many women and children were freed than men, and a large number of these women found their freedom and the freedom of their children in relationships with white men. One of countless examples is that of the white Juan Robin of New Orleans who manumitted his forty-eight-year-old slave Maria and their three children: Juan Luis, eighteen; Maria Juana, twenty-seven; and Isabel, twenty. Juan Robin also freed Isabel's two daughters: Juana and Francisca.[20]

While it is impossible to calculate with certainty the frequency of interracial liaisons, a sample of the sacramental records, and in particular the baptismal records, of the St. Louis Cathedral in New Orleans suggest just how common such liaisons were. Of the 314 infants and children of slave women and free women of color baptized in the St. Louis Cathedral in 1793, 38 percent of the slave infants baptized were racially mixed while 85 percent of the children of free women of color were racially mixed. Racial mixing was consequently one of the more common features of the culture.[21]

And racial mixing frequently, but not always, led to freedom. This is particularly evident from the data from the 1793 baptismal records of the St. Louis Cathedral. That data demonstrates that 38 percent of slaves in that year were racially mixed. Confirmation records for the 64 slaves confirmed in the Plaza and at Fort Barrancas in the District of Pensacola in May 1798 demonstrate that 27, or 42 percent, of the slaves then confirmed were described as being racially mixed. Some racially mixed slaves baptized or confirmed in the ports were later freed, but many spent their lives in bondage. Some of the port's slaves were even described as extremely light-skinned or even white. Eliza Potter, a free woman of color who lived for a few months in New Orleans, witnessed a slave auction in which several women were sold. According to Potter, a great many of the women were as "white as white could be." It is not difficult to assume that all these women were racially mixed. Other documents affirm the presence of slaves who appeared to be white.[22]

Some women and their children, however, did effect their freedom and that of their children from their liaisons with white men. The census schedules demonstrate the dramatic growth of the free people of color in these ports. For example, the 1788 census of New Orleans shows that the free-colored population made up approximately 25 percent of the entire free population. By 1805, however, free people of color totaled approximately 34 percent of the free population. The population of Mobile had a similar structure. By 1805, the number of free people of color there had reached 250, or 27 percent of the entire free population. The Pensacola census of 1802 reports that free people of color made up approximately 21 percent of the free population. By 1820, however, the free people of color in the city constituted approximately 36 percent of the free population.[23]

Some slaves attained their freedom without the aid of whites. But the relationship between freedom and skin color, or racial classification, is unmistakable. For instance, of the 74 free people of color in Pensacola in 1802, 56, or 76 percent, were described by the census taker as "mulattos." Of the 145 slaves in the port in that year, 40, or 28 percent, were racially mixed. The 1787 census of Mobile offers a similar picture. There were a total of 64 free people of color in the port in that year. Of those, 49, or 77 percent, were described as racially mixed. The slave population totaled 726; of those only 86, or 12 percent, were described as racially mixed. There were 743 free people of color in New Orleans in 1791. Of those, 575, or 77 percent, were racially mixed. In the same year, there were 1,889 slaves. Of those, 285, or 15 percent, were described as racially mixed. Thus, it is clear from the available data that interracial liaisons were not only common but it was also common for white men to free their cohabitants and their children.[24]

Freedom, however, was not all that slave women and free women of color gained from their extralegal liaisons. Many women and their children also received property. Hundreds of deeds, wills, and inventories of estates contain evidence of property transferred from white men to slave and free women of color and their children. It would, therefore, be short-sighted to simply dismiss interracial liaisons as unimportant, as many have done, by pointing solely to their exploitive nature. For to focus only on the exploitive nature of the relations between white men and slave women and free women of color would be to ignore the reality of the world in which they lived. And to ignore that world would be to ignore the way in which the women participated in redefining it, despite the fears they inspired in secular and governing officials.

Notes

1. The information on the importation of the early slaves can be found in Gwendolyn Midlo Hall, *Africans in Colonial Louisiana: The Development of Afro-Creole Culture in the Eighteenth Century* (Baton Rouge: Louisiana State University Press, 1992); James Thomas

McGowan, "Creation of a Slave Society," Ph.D. diss., University of Rochester, 1976; "William S. Coker and Thomas D. Watson, *Indian Traders of the Southeastern Spanish Border-lands: Panton, Leslie and Company and John Forbes and Company, 1783–1847* (Gainesville: University Presses of Florida, 1986); and Daniel Usner, *Indians, Settlers, and Slaves in a Frontier Exchange Economy: The Lower Mississippi Valley before 1783* (Chapel Hill: University of North Carolina Press, 1992).

2. Antoine LePage DuPratz, *Histoire de la Louisiane,* 3 vols. (Paris, 1758), 1: 333–35.

3. First Book of Baptisms, entry dated July 26, 1715, Cathedral of the Immaculate Conception, New Orleans.

4. Father Henry La Vente, *Memoire de la Louisiane,* written in 1713 and 1714, Archives des Colonies, Series C, 13a, vol. 3, University of Louisiana, Lafayette.

5. Father Raphael to Abbé Raguet, May 19, 1726, Archives des Colonies, Series C, 13a, Louisiane: Correspondence generale, University of Louisiana, Lafayette.

6. Father Clements de Saldaño to Joseph Antonio de Armona, New Orleans, March 30, 1766, Biblioteca National (Madrid), Ms. Vo1.18.

7. *Le Code noir ou Edit du Roi,* Versailles, 1724; *Le Code noir, ou loi municipal,. . entreprit par Deli-dération du Cabildo en vertu des Ordres du Roi . . . consignés dans sa Lettre faite à Aranjuez le 14 de Mai 1777* (1778). Copy in the Parsons Collection, Humanities Research Center Library, University of Texas, Austin. See also Paul LaChance, "The Formation of a Three-Caste Society," *Social Science History* 18, no. 2 (summer 1994): 211–41.

8. Verena Martinez-Alier, *Marriage, Class, and Color in Nineteenth Century Cuba: A Study of the Racial Attitudes and Sexual Values in a Slave Society* (London: Cambridge University Press, 1974), 20–41. As Martinez-Alier explains for Cuba, the "metropolis laws on intermarriage, far from constituting an imposition, did no more than provide a legal framework for preexisting racial attitudes." Also see Frederick P. Bowser, "Colonial Spanish America," in *Neither Slave nor Free: The Freedmen of African Descent in the Slave Societies of the New World,* edited by David Cohen and Jack P. Greene (Baltimore: Johns Hopkins University Press, 1972); and Alexander Von Humboldt, *Ensayo Político sobre El Reino de la Nueva España,* vol. 2 (Mexico City: Porrbua, 1973), 262.

9. Esteban Miró's *bando de buen gobierno* was first proclaimed in the Cabildo, June 2, 1786. See Actas, III, Minutes for June 2, 1786, Articles 3, 6, 9, 10, New Orleans Municipal Library (microfilm). For one translation of the document, see Charles Gayarré, *History of Louisiana: The Spanish Dominion,* vol. 3 (New Orleans: James A. Greshain, 1879).

10. See Caroline Maude Burson, *The Stewardship of Don Esteban Miró, 1782–1792* (New Orleans: American Printing Company, 1940); and Frederick P. Bowser, *The African Slave in Colonial Peru, 1524–1650* (Stanford: Stanford University Press, 1974), 311–12.

11. Bowser, *The African Slave in Colonial Peru,* 311–12; François Boucher, *20,000 Years of Fashion: The History of Costume and Personal Adornment* (New York: Harry N. Abrams, 1987), 179–202; Michael and Ariane Batterberry, *Fashion: The Mirror of History* (New York: Greenwich House, 1977), 1–12; Pierre Louis Berquin-Duvallon, *Vue de la colonie Espagnole du Mississipi, ou des provinces de Louisiane et Floride occidentale* (Paris: A l'Imprimerie Expeditive, 1803), 201–47; Records of the Cabildo, June 1, 1786; *Recopilacion de Leyes de los Reynos de las Indias* (Madrid: Julián de Paredes, 1681), Libro VIII and Título V. Also, for a sampling of Spanish American sumptuary restrictions aimed at free women of color, see Richard Konetzke, *Colección de documentos para la historia de la formación social de hispano-*

america (Madrid: Consejo Superior de Investigaciones Científicas, 1962), 2: 11–12; El Prado, 22 de Noviembre de 1593, 319–22; Madrid, 29 de septiembre de 1628; John Fanning Watson, "Notitia of Incidents at New Orleans in 1804 and 1805," *American Pioneer* 11, no. 5 (May 1843): 233–36.

12. Liliane Crété, *Daily Life in Louisiana, 1815–1830*, translated by Patrick Gregory (Baton Rouge: Louisiana State University Press, 1981), 81.

13. Hans Baade, "The Law of Slavery in Spanish Louisiana," in *Louisiana's Legal Heritage*, edited by Edward F. Haas (Pensacola, Florida: Perdido Bay, 1983), 43–67.

14. Spanish Census of New Orleans, 1788, Archivo General de Indias (hereafter AGI) PC 1425.

15. Resumen General del Padrón Hecho en la Provincia de la Luisiana, Distrito de Ia Movila y Penzacola, 1788, legajo 1425.

16. Spanish Census of Pensacola, June 1, 1819, AGI legajo 1876–B.

17. C. C. Robin, *Voyages to Louisiana*, translated and edited by Stuart O. Landry Jr. (New Orleans: Pelican Publishing Co.), 250.

18. Perrin du Lac, *Travels through the Two Louisianas* (London: Richard Phillips, 1807).

19. Watson, "Notitia of Incidents at New Orleans in 1804–1805," 233–36.

20. For the best discussion of manumission in Spanish New Orleans, see Kimberly S. Hanger, "Personas de Varias Clases y Colores: Free Persons of Color in the Spanish New Orleans, 1769–1803," Ph.D. diss., University of Florida, 1991.

21. The practice of self-purchase in New Orleans is evident in the Notarial Archives of the Spanish period located in the Civil Court Building in New Orleans. Also for the debate surrounding the liberality of the Spanish practice of *coartaçion*, see Gwendolyn Midlo Hall, *Social Control in Slave Plantation Societies: A Comparison of St. Domingue and Cuba* (Baltimore: Johns Hopkins University Press, 1971), 81–135; Rebecca J. Scott, *Slave Emancipation in Cuba: The Transition to Free Labor, 1860–1899* (Princeton, N.J.: Princeton University Press, 1985), 13–14; Franklin W. Knight, *Slave Society in Cuba during the Nineteenth Century* (Madison: University of Wisconsin Press, 1970), 130–31; Elsa Goveia, "The West Indian Slave Laws in the Eighteenth Century," in *Slavery in the New World*, edited by Laura Foner and Eugene D. Genovese (Englewood Cliffs, N.J.: Prentice-Hall, 1969), 113–38; McGowan, "Creation of a Slave Society," 175–217; Baade, "The Law of Slavery in Spanish Louisiana," 67–70; and Thomas Fierhrer, "The African Presence in Colonial Louisiana," in *Louisiana's Black Heritage*, edited by Robert R. Macdonald (Baton Rouge: Louisiana State Museum, 1979), 3–31. For the nearly complete records of manumission for the Spanish colonial period in New Orleans, see the *cartas de libertad* included in the Notarial Acts, 1769–1803, housed in the Civil Court Building in New Orleans. Also, a few court cases that consider the subject of self-purchase are located in the Court Records for the Spanish period that are housed in the Louisiana State Museum in New Orleans.

22. Eliza Potter, *A Hairdresser's Experiences in High Life* (Cincinnati: By the Author, 1859), 173–74. The other documents include "Confirmations Conferred in the Piaza of Pensacola, the seventh day of May, by the Most Reverend Señor Don Luis Peñalver y Cardenas, First Worthy Bishop of this Diocese, in the present year of 1798" and "Confirmations Conferred at the Fort of Barrancas of the District of Pensacola, the twenty-first of May 1798." The confirmation lists are published in William S. Coker and G. Douglas

Inglis, *The Spanish Censuses of Pensacola, 1784–1820: A Genealogical Guide to Spanish Pensacola* (Pensacola, Florida: Perdido Bay Press, 1980).

23. The Spanish Census of New Orleans, 1797: New Orleans in 1805: A Directory and Census (New Orleans, 1936); Census de Mobile, Septiembre 12, 1805, legajo 142, Territorial Papers, Jackson, Mississippi; Padron de Panzacola, 1802, AGI PC legajo 59; Coker and Inglis, *The Spanish Censuses of Pensacola, 1784–1820.*

24. The Census of Pensacola, May 15, 1802, AGI PC legajo 59; General de la jurisdicción de la Mobila del Primero de Enero del Año 1787, AGI PC legajo 206, Mississippi Territorial Archives, Jackson, Mississippi; Census of New Orleans, November 6, 1791, Louisiana Collection, New Orleans Public Library.

SUSAN D. GREENBAUM
Afro-Cubans in Tampa

The first Cuban settlement in Florida was at Key West. A Spanish émigré cigar manufacturer named Vincente Martínez Ybor established the first new factory there in 1869. He was joined in the move by several other factory owners. Cuban cigar makers began pouring into Key West. Production there climbed from 8.5 million cigars in 1869 to 25 million in 1875. Cessation of hostilities in Cuba three years later did little to discourage the growth of this new Florida industry. By 1880, Key West's factories had increased from four to forty-four, and by 1885 there were ninety factories employing 2,811, mostly Cuban cigar makers.[1] With this growth, Key West emerged as an extremely important center of Cuban insurrectionist activities. Although a Spaniard by birth, Ybor actively supported independence for Cuba, and other factory owners shared his grievances against the colonial regime.

Cigar makers as well as manufacturers had been involved in the early stages of the independence movement, and this interest continued in exile. Worker-led revolutionary organizations had sprung up in Key West almost immediately, and the cigar makers began to vie with the more elite New York–based leadership over ideological control of Cuban independence. Conflicting interests of capitalists and aristocrats versus workers and abolitionists were no less salient in exile than they had been in Cuba. Separatist cigar manufacturers were joined in an uneasy alliance with their independence-minded workers. This somewhat unnatural state of affairs restrained labor activism but did not eliminate discontent over wages and working conditions.

The end of the Ten Years' War brought a hiatus in the patriotic partnership between workers and owners, which gave birth to a new tobacco workers union in Key West and a strike in 1879. Although workers were initially successful, the manufacturers rallied in 1881 in refusing to recognize their union. In that same year, a labor organizer was murdered in Key West, presumably at the behest of one of the factory owners.[2]

Resumption of rebel conspiracies brought Antonio Maceo and Máximo Gómez (also a general in the Cuban revolutionary army) to Key West in 1885, where the cigar manufacturers pledged strong support for the next insurrection. Unmoved by their employers' patriotic generosity, the cigar workers struck in August of that year. The strike posed a dilemma for the revolution. Manufacturers staunchly held out, and when the strike fund was depleted the strikers got offers of support from the Spanish, eager as always to capitalize on dissension among the rebel factions. Revolutionary leaders in New York intervened in the negotiations between strikers and owners, and an agreement was reached. However, the workers remained skeptical about the patrician motives of the revolutionary command, and the manufacturers took steps to preempt future labor unrest. One measure taken was a large-scale relocation of cigar factories up the west coast of Florida to the small port town of Tampa.[3]

Ybor, who had started the first factory in Key West, also pioneered in the move to Tampa. A few months after the Key West strike in 1885, Ybor and a group of Cuban and Spanish cigar manufacturers from New York made a deal with the Tampa Board of Trade. In exchange for pledges to build a cigar industry in Tampa, the local business group agreed to subsidize the purchase of land. Importantly, they also offered assurances of labor peace.[4] Although he initially planned to build only a small factory in Tampa, a massive fire in Key West destroyed Ybor's operations there in 1886, prompting him to abandon that city and concentrate all his holdings in Tampa. Other manufacturers also established factories in this new site.

Within the decade of the 1880s Tampa's population ballooned from 720 to nearly 6,000. The cigar industry was not the only factor responsible for this explosive growth, but it was a major contributor. Nearly a third of the newcomers were Cuban (1,313) and Spanish (233) cigar makers and their families. About 15 percent of the Cubans were black. There was a small influx of West Indians, some of whom were involved with cigars and the others with work on the docks. Recent arrivals also included a small group of Italians who initially had been lured into Central Florida to cut sugarcane,[5] and a small number of Romanian Jews who came to Tampa with the factories or to open businesses.[6] Not all of the new arrivals were immigrants. Tampa's booming growth of the 1880s more than tripled the size of the native-born white population, and the African American population (not counting new black immigrants) increased by 534 percent.[7] Cuban exiles in Tampa did not enter an established host community, but rather arrived in the midst of a vast economic and demographic transformation that affected all of the groups involved. [. . .]

Afro-Cuban Patriots

Both black and white Cubans took part in Tampa's transformation. Black participation is acknowledged in accounts from the period and in contemporary renditions of Tampa's role in Cuban history as well as Cuba's role in Tampa history. In these depictions Afro-Cubans play shadowy and supporting roles, and are portrayed as simple and unlettered. Many who contradicted this stereotype were either not mentioned at all or their identities as Afro-Cubans are not indicated.[8]

Tampa's best-known Afro-Cuban patriot was a woman, Paulina Pedroso. Of the many historic markers that have been erected in Ybor City, the only one that alludes to Afro-Cuban involvement in the war is a plaque that bears her likeness.[9] Locally, Pedroso is the symbol of Afro-Cuban patriotism. Her persona is plain and humble, self-sacrificing and dedicated—an embodiment of the unquestioning loyalty that Martí ascribed to Afro-Cubans in the movement. She was an undeniably important figure, and she had a particularly close relationship with Martí, but the focus on Paulina Pedroso has tended to distort the larger picture of Afro-Cuban involvement. Her gender is anomalous. Many more Afro-Cuban men than women were activists, and white Cuban women were far more numerous in the revolutionary clubs than were black Cuban women. This gendered image, which neglects the presence of men, especially men of letters and ideas, subordinates and diminishes the significance of race in this local movement. In what might appear to be a gesture of racial and gender inclusion, the stereotyped danger of black males is tamed by exclusion. The actual number of Afro-Cubans involved in these events is reduced to a handful and symbolized in a single nonthreatening figure. Paulina's husband, Ruperto, is also portrayed as a simple man with dogged loyalty to Martí and the cause.

Two other Afro-Cuban men who are recorded in early accounts, but rarely in those that are contemporary, were Bruno Roig and Cornelio Brito. Roig had a grocery store in Ybor City; the nature of Brito's establishment, which was also in Ybor City, is unknown. Brito was a director in El Club Revolucionario and was among the select welcoming party for José Martí when he first visited Tampa in 1891.[10] Roig was also centrally involved in arranging Martí's visit. As treasurer of Ignacio Agramonte, it was Roig's job to gather funds and pay the travel expenses. As José Rivero Muñiz described his role, "Bruno Roig pointed out that no one had taken notice, as if it were of secondary importance, that there would be expenses involved . . . with the trip of Martí. Everything was left in mid air until the next meeting when Roig was to present a budget covering the proposed expenses."[11]

There were many Afro-Cubans in Tampa, however, including a large group of journalists and labor activists. Several Afro-Cubans were involved with local revolutionist publications—Joaquín Granados, Emilio Planas, Julián González, Primitivo Plumas, Francisco Segura, and Teófilo Domínguez. Planas, Domínguez, and González also contributed work to well-known Cuban publications including La Fraternidad, Juan Gualberto Gómez's magazine, and Minerva, an early publication dedicated to items of interest to Afro-Cubans.[12] Domínguez's future wife, María de Jesús Viernes, was also an active supporter of Cuban independence and reportedly sewed the flag that was carried into battle when the war began in 1895.[13] In addition, there were Afro-Cubans associated with organizing revolutionary clubs, especially those that espoused labor activism and political radicalism. They included Manuel Granados, who was Joaquín's brother, and Guillermo Sorondo, who had been involved with the Reconstruction Republican Party in Key West during the early 1870s. Sorondo had also been the founder of at least two Afro-Cuban mutual aid societies in that city.[14]

Two sources that profile Afro-Cubans involved in writing and publishing—Pedro Deschamps Chapeaux's El Negro en el Periodismo Cubano en el Siglo XIX (1963) and Domínguez's Ensayos Biográficos (1899)—were written precisely because so little credit had been accorded to these individuals and their intellectual accomplishments.[15] Domínguez, author of the latter, was himself editor of a revolutionary weekly in Tampa and a close associate of Juan Gualberto Gómez.[16] He was also friends with Gustavo Urrutia, an Afro-Cuban writer who is only now gaining recognition for his role in shaping Cuban political thought.[17] Domínguez remains an undeservedly obscure figure in the history of Cuban revolutionary journalism. Between 1897 and 1899 he published a weekly literary and political magazine in Ybor City called El Sport. Listed among the founders of this publication is Generoso Campos Marquetti, an Afro-Cuban general in the liberation army who served in the Cuban legislature after independence.[18]

In addition to this magazine, only fragments of which survive, Domínguez wrote a short volume profiling some of his even lesser-known colleagues. Originally published as a series of biographical sketches in a Key West magazine in July 1898 (at the height of the final battle for Cuban independence), these pieces were reprinted by Domínguez as a book in 1899, after the war was over, along with several essays he had written about the importance of education in effecting Martí's vision for Cuba.

This publication, *Ensayos Biográficos*, includes information on Julián González, Emilio Planas, and Joaquín Granados. There are common themes in their stories — around difficult struggles to achieve an education and on early connections to independence politics and each other. Julián González, born in Havana in 1871, was a cigar maker who attended night classes sponsored by the Bella Unión Habanera. González edited a magazine named *La Pelota* (The Ball Game), which was dedicated to coverage of literature and sports and served as the official newspaper of the Cuban Baseball League of Tampa. Although not explicitly political, all proceeds from the sale of the paper were contributed to the PRC.

Emilio Planas, born in 1868, spent his early childhood in Key West where he attended classes at the San Carlos Club, the principal mutual aid organization among cigar makers in that city. Planas completed his education in Jacksonville, however, at the Goodman and Free Men Institution, a school for African Americans begun during Reconstruction. He graduated in 1888 and settled in Tampa in 1890. Planas was one of the founders of Domínguez's *El Sport* and contributed essays under the pen name Jonatas. He also started his own weekly, *El Patriota*.[19]

Joaquín Granados, the best known of this group, was born a slave in 1854. At an early age he began to write and publish political essays, and he became a protégé of Martín Morúa Delgado. Granados had collaborated with Morúa Delgado in establishing a mutual aid society in Matanzas, Cuba, in 1879.[20] Named La Armonía (Harmony), its purpose was to ease the problems that followed the end of the Ten Years' War and the gradual abolition of Cuban slavery begun in 1870.[21] Granados and his brother, Manuel, were born in Havana. Their parents were slaves, but they managed to purchase their sons' freedom at an early age. Joaquín learned cigar-making and Manuel became a barber. A self-taught scholar who won certification as a schoolteacher, Joaquín began to write poems and political essays that were published in a variety of progressive papers and magazines. He was heavily involved with Juan Gualberto Gómez and Martín Morúa Delgado, two leading Afro-Cuban intellectuals who were rivals.[22] Morúa Delgado favored complete assimilation and repudiated race consciousness. Gómez pursued a similar goal of racial equality, but based it on attacking racism and organizing collective self-help.[23] Joaquín Granados collaborated with both, serving as vice president of Gómez's Directorio Central de la Raza de Color. He worked with Morúa Delgado in Matanzas (Morúa Delgado was also founder of La Armonía) and later in exile in Key West, contributing to El Pueblo and La Revista Popular, revolutionary magazines edited by Morúa Delgado.[24]

Both Manuel and Joaquín Granados moved to Tampa in the late 1880s. Manuel had a barbershop in the Liceo Cubano where Martí got his hair cut when he was in town.[25] Both became members of the most influential revolutionary clubs—Vanguardia de Flor Crombet and Ignacio Agramonte—the former named for an Afro-Cuban general and the latter for a white Cuban patriot of the Ten Years' War. The Crombet club was later converted into La Liga Patriótica Cubana, a highly secret organization in which Manuel Granados was treasurer. Joaquín was also elected secretary of the Tampa delegation to the PRC in 1892.[26]

Guillermo Sorondo was also among the leaders of the PRC. He had been a central figure in political activities in Key West where he was associated with most of the individuals previously listed. Sociedad El Progreso, an Afro-Cuban mutual aid society he founded there, included Emilio Planas, Joaquín and Manuel Granados, Martín Morúa Delgado, and Francisco Segura.[27] Sorondo moved from Key West to Tampa in 1888, but left temporarily in 1892 to help form a Cuban colony in Ocala, a small settlement in Central Florida. This Cuban enclave was known as Martí City.[28] It collapsed in 1897, and Sorondo and his colleagues moved to Fort Tampa, a small cluster of residences in the area surrounding the port section of the town. Sorondo was head of the PRC delegation from Martí City and also was head of the Port Tampa delegation when its founders returned to Tampa.[29] Sorondo was allied with Carlos Baliño, a white anarchist who later was one of the founders of the Cuban Communist Party.[30] In Tampa, Baliño edited a paper called La Tribuna del Pueblo, to which several of the Afro-Cuban writers contributed.

Francisco Segura, another Afro-Cuban writer in Tampa during this period, had been a director with Sorondo in Sociedad El Progreso in Key West. He also relocated from Key West to Tampa in the early 1890s. Segura was an associate of Ramón Rivero, a white leader of Tampa's PRC. Segura was on the editorial staff of Rivero's magazine, La Revista de Florida.[31] Rivero also edited the official organ of the PRC, Cuba, which published writing by Segura and the other Afro-Cubans described above.[32] [. . .]

Relations with African Americans

In the same period that Afro-Cubans were being shunted to the background of white Cuban activities they were increasingly involved with African Americans. These contacts had begun earlier. Indeed, the early residence patterns of Afro-Cubans reflected more spatial integration with African Americans than was true in later years. In 1893, the Tampa city directory identified nineteen Afro-Cuban households, seven of which lived in or near the Scrub, well beyond the limits of Ybor City. One of these residents was José Valdés, who operated a restaurant at 1100 Central Avenue, squarely in the midst of African American businesses and residences. Above the store he ran a small boardinghouse, which also served as his residence. Among his tenants was Luis Garbán, the Afro-Cuban owner of a small cigar factory (a "buckeye")[33] in the back of the restaurant. Valdés's other tenants included a black cigar maker and two black laborers, all with English surnames. Any or all of them could have been West Indians, although it is equally possible that they were African Americans.

Customers in Valdés's restaurant undoubtedly included African Americans. This was the only restaurant on Central Avenue at that time. We don't know if José Valdes spoke English, but it is reasonable to assume that he did. Nor do we know what he heard and learned from his neighbors and customers, although it would have been difficult to avoid knowledge of the growing problems that they faced. This period was filled with episodes of anti-black violence and increasing pressures to exclude blacks from white spaces.

During the late 1890s, the number of black businesses on Central Avenue increased steadily as newcomers arrived and existing black business owners were forced out of the downtown area. Valdés and Garban operated inside a growing and tightening black enclave, which formed the basis of an emergent leadership structure of mostly African American business owners, pastors, journalists, and teachers. Afro-Cubans did not belong to the many clubs, lodges, and organizations that were formed in this period by African Americans, but they did join them in efforts to reverse their political misfortunes by supporting the Republican Party. José Valdés was one of twenty Afro-Cubans who registered to vote in June 1898. Others included Bruno Roig, Emilio Planas, and several individuals who later would be involved in organizing the post-independence Martí-Maceo Society. There were only about eighty African Americans who registered, but these names included several who played significant roles in the community.[34]

Baseball was another arena in which segregation promoted contact between black Americans and black Cubans. Afro-Cubans in Ybor City organized a team called the Tampa Baseball Nine. Although black and white Cubans were initially part of the same league in Tampa, by the middle of the 1890s Afro-Cuban ball players had been reassigned to the growing circuit of black teams in Florida. In May 1894, they played in Tampa against an African American team from Gainesville (about 120 miles to the north). It was a major event of the season, and four hundred black fans from Gainesville came by train to watch the game. Local African Americans also turned out in large numbers, and the "Tampa Colored Band" played music for the crowd that had assembled.[35]

More intimate relationships with African Americans were reflected in the numerous marriages between Afro-Cuban males and African American women. It is perhaps noteworthy that there were no examples of Afro-Cuban females marrying African American men. Census schedules for 1900 list sixteen Afro-Cuban–African American unions, more than 10 percent of the 156 two-parent households enumerated that year. Of these sixteen marriages fifteen included children over the age of four, indicating that the couples were already married in 1896 when *Plessy* was decided. Mixed marriages brought contact not only with American spouses but also included American in-laws and a logical connection to networks of other friends and neighbors who were black Americans.

English-speaking West Indians from Nassau and elsewhere in the Bahamas were also part of the complex linkages that drew Afro-Cubans into the larger black population of Tampa. The St. James Episcopal Church, a mostly Caribbean congregation (Jamaicans and Bahamians) that also included some Cubans, was founded in 1891 on Constant Street, just off Central Avenue. Members had come from Key West, where they previously belonged to another, earlier black Episcopal church.[36] The first pastor, Mathew McDuffie, was a prominent church and civic leader in the African American community and a strong supporter of Booker T. Washington. In 1900 fourteen Afro-Cuban men in Tampa had West Indian wives; five of these families also lived in the Scrub. Cuban members of St. James primarily consisted of these in-married spouses.

Nearly one in five Afro-Cuban families included an English-speaking wife, a factor that would have diminished the language barrier to interactions with black Americans. Kinship and neighborly relations began to develop, and school ties were also forming during this period. There were three schools in the Scrub area. The Harlem Academy, built in 1889, was a public school organized and established by members of the African

American community. St. James Episcopal began a parochial school in 1892. In 1894, St. Peter Claver Catholic Church was founded in Tampa as a mission church and school for black Catholics. The St. James's school included Cubans and Americans as well as West Indians. Some Afro-Cuban families sent their children to the Harlem Academy out of disaffection with Catholicism or an inability to pay the fees at St. Peter Claver. Several African American families, especially those who were prosperous, sent their children to St. Peter Claver, which they felt provided a superior education. [. . .]

Notes

1. Gerald Poyo, "Cuban Émigré Communities in the United States and the Independence of Their Homeland, 1852–1895," Ph.D. diss., University of Florida, 1983, 207.

2. Ibid., 221.

3. Ibid., 213.

4. Glenn Westfall, "Martí City: Cubans in Ocala," in *José Martí in the United States: The Florida Experience*, edited by L. A. Pérez (Tempe: Arizona State University Center for Latin American Studies, 1995), 10–11.

5. Gary Mormino and George Pozzetta, *The Immigrant World of Ybor City: Italians and Their Neighbors in Tampa, 1885–1985* (Urbana: University of Illinois Press, 1987).

6. Helen Jacobus Apte, *Heart of a Wife: The Diary of a Southern Jewish Woman*, edited and with essays by her grandson, Marcus D. Rosenbaum (Wilmington, Del.: SR Books, 1998); Canter Brown Jr., *Jewish Pioneers of the Tampa Bay* (Tampa, Fla.: Tampa Bay History Center, 1999).

7. Geoff Mohlman, "Bibliography of Resources Concerning the African American Presence in Tampa: 1513–1995," master's thesis, University of South Florida, 1995, 77.

8. An excellent analysis of the omission of Afro-Cuban contributions to the independence effort, a denial that is justified by reference to José Martí's admonitions against divisive discussions of race, is provided in Ada Ferrer, "The Silence of Patriots: Race and Nationalism in Martí's Cuba," in *José Martí's "Our America": From National to Hemispheric Cultural Studies*, edited by J. Belknap and R. Fernández (Durham, N.C.: Duke University Press, 1998).

9. In 1997, the Tampa/Hillsborough County Preservation Board commissioned a historic marker to be placed on the sidewalk outside of the Martí-Maceo social hall. The text, which I wrote, does include a discussion of Afro-Cubans in the War for Independence.

10. José Rivero Muñiz, *The Ybor City Story, 1885–1954*, translated by Eustasio Fernández and Henry Beltrán (Tampa, Fla.: n.p., 1976), 58.

11. Ibid., 46.

12. Carmen Montejo Arrecha, "Minerva: A Magazine for Women (and Men) of Color," in *Between Race and Empire: African Americans and Cubans before the Cuban Revolution*, edited by L. Brock and D. Fuentes (Philadelphia: Temple University Press, 1998); Teófilo Domín-

guez, *Ensayos biográficos: Figuras y figuritas* (Tampa: Imprenta: Lafayette Street, 1899), 105. [Available in the collection of the Schomburg Center for Research in Black Culture.]

13. The story about the flag was told to me by María Viernes's daughter, Fredeswinda Millet (now deceased). Her great-granddaughter, Sonia Menéndez, also had been told of the flag by María before she died. A cousin visited Cuba in the 1980s and reportedly found the flag in a small exhibit in an old municipal building in the Marianao section of Havana. Subsequent visits by others have failed to rediscover the building, but directions were vague.

14. Gerald Poyo, "Tampa Cigarworkers and the Struggle for Independence," *Tampa Bay History* 7 (1985): 227, 233.

15. Pedro Deschamps Chapeaux, *El Negro en el periodismo cubano en el siglo XIX: Ensayo bibliográfico* (Havana: Ediciones R., 1963); Domínguez, *Ensayos biográficos*, 105. [A copy of the manuscript is located in Schomburg Center for Research in Black Culture.]

16. Deschamps Chapeaux, *El Negro en el periodismo cubano en el siglo XIX*, 104.

17. Tomás Fernández Robaína, "Marcus Garvey in Cuba: Urrutía, Cubans, and Black Nationalism," in *Between Race and Empire: African Americans and Cubans before the Cuban Revolution*, edited by L. Brock and D. Fuentes (Philadelphia: Temple University Press, 1998), 123. Teófilo Domínguez's will, in the possession of his great-granddaughter Sonia Menéndez, bears the signatures of Juan Gualberto Gómez and Gustavo Urrutía as witnesses.

18. Deschamps Chapeaux, *El Negro en el periodismo cubano en el siglo XIX*, 104.

19. See also Muñiz, *The Ybor City Story*, 35.

20. Domínguez, *Ensayos biográficos*; Pedro Deschamps Chapeaux, *Contribución a la historia de la gente sin historia* (Havana: Unión de Escritores y Artistas de Cuba, 1974).

21. Phillip A. Howard, *Changing History: Afro-Cuban Cabildos and Societies of Color in the Nineteenth Century* (Baton Rouge: Louisiana State University Press, 1998), 168.

22. Pedro Serviat, "Solutions to the Black Problem," in *Afrocuba: An Anthology of Cuban Writing on Race, Politics and Culture*, edited by P. Pérez Sarduy and J. Stubbs (Melbourne, Australia: Ocean Press, 1993).

23. Aline Helg, *Our Rightful Share: The Afro-Cuban Struggle for Equality, 1886–1912* (Chapel Hill: University of North Carolina Press, 1995), 121; Ferrer, "The Silence of Patriots," 237.

24. Poyo, "Cuban Émigré Communities in the United States and the Independence of Their Homeland"; Domínguez, *Ensayos biográficos*.

25. Muñiz, *The Ybor City Story*.

26. Ibid.

27. Poyo, "Cuban Émigré Communities in the United States and the Independence of Their Homeland," 227.

28. Westfall, "Martí City."

29. Muñiz, *The Ybor City Story*.

30. Sheldon Liss, *Roots of Revolution: Radical Thought in Cuba* (Lincoln: University of Nebraska Press, 1987).

31. Poyo, "Cuban Émigré Communities in the United States and the Independence of Their Homeland," 338.

32. Ibid., 345; Domínguez, *Ensayos biográficos*.

33. ["Buckeye" was the name given to tiny cigar factories in the United States, reportedly because they made liberal use of tobacco from Ohio, the Buckeye state.]

34. *Tampa Morning Tribune*, June 1, 1898, p. 2, cols. 3–5.

35. *Tampa Times*, May 16, 1894.

36. Herman Monroe, "Centennial History of St. James Episcopal Church" (Tampa, 1991).

Excerpt from Pulling the Muse from the Drum

Rhythms arrived hidden in pageantry
of scars & piercings
Soon it was decreed
that no drummings
tóques de tambor
will be allowed
for it was a known fact
drums excited people
Masters did not want property to rebel
drum became whisper of rebellion
tongue of freedom
so feared by Spain

Yet wood & goatskin
continued their speeches
discreetly in Caribbean jungles
The language of hands hide & cedar
could not be silenced
the ancestor's mother tongue
thundering who they were
where they come from—
Oko Iyesha mo ilé mi
Iya mi ilé odo
was their muse
was their poem

We hear the sound of history
through stained walls in Little Havana
graffiti parks Lower East Side

frozen lake Wicker Park Chaaiitown
grooooved into people's struts
It is you
It is me
It is
we
unidos Latinos
A collection of feathered drums
red & white
repicando
We pulling the muse
from the drum
the muse that is we

II

Arturo Alfonso Schomburg

Arturo Alfonso Schomburg was seventeen years old when he left his native Puerto Rico to join the small exile community of anti-Spanish activists in New York City. With the exception of a brief visit in 1905 Schomburg would never return to the island; indeed, until his death in 1938 his intellectual and social life would be inextricably tied to African Americans and, more generally, to African diasporic peoples. Schomburg was one of the fore-

Arturo Alfonso Schomburg and his sister Dolores (Lola), San Juan, Puerto Rico, 1905. (Photographs and Prints Division, Schomburg Center for Research in Black Culture, the New York Public Library, Astor, Lenox and Tilden Foundations)

most collectors and bibliophiles of the Africana experience, and he was among the earliest proponents of Black studies. Given his immense educational contribution to knowledge about the Black world, which continued to include a special interest in the Caribbean, Latin America, and Spain, Schomburg may be considered the most illustrious and self-conscious of all Afro-Latin@s in the United States, as well as the one whose aspirations and ambiguities seem the most deeply exemplary of Afro-Latin@ social experience. Schomburg's life on the color line, his direct knowledge and experience of racism in the Caribbean and the United States, and his resultant affinity with other Afro-Caribbeans and African Americans were elements paradigmatic for Afro-Latin@s through the first half of the twentieth century. Almost one hundred years after Arturo Schomburg called for the study of "Negro History" he continues to serve as a symbol of diasporic unity and as an inspiration for Afro-Latin@s seeking knowledge about their African roots.

ARTHUR A. SCHOMBURG

Excerpt from "Racial Integrity: A Plea for the Establishment of a Chair of Negro History in Our Schools and Colleges. Address Delivered at the Teachers' Summer Class at the Cheney Institute, Pennsylvania, July 1913"

I am here with a sincere desire to awaken the sensibilities, to rekindle the dormant fibers in the soul, and to fire the racial patriotism by the study of Negro books. We often feel that so many things around us are warped and alienated. Let us see if we cannot agree to arrange a formula or create a basic construction, for the establishment of a substantial method of instruction for our young women and men in the material and the useful.

The object of this paper is not to revolutionize existing standards, but simply to improve them by amending them so that they will include the practical history of the Negro Race from the dawn of civilization to the present time. We are reminded that the earliest instruction was imparted orally, and that this system is still found extant in Africa and among other Oriental nations. It is useful because it trains the mind to listen and retain. The modern school with its many books, but without systematic lectures, turns out many graduates who are lacking in retentiveness and no sooner than the sound of the words has left their teachers' lips, the subject has been forgotten; and if they are called upon to explain the theme, it is reduced to an incomprehensible mass of meaningless words. The university graduate is wont to overestimate his ability, fresh from the machinery that endows him with a parchment and crowns him with knowledge, he steps into the world to meet the practical men with years of experience and mother wit. It is a contrast, the professional man with the veneer of high art, and the acquaintance with the best authors, and up to date histories demanding recognition. All these books take their proper places when applied to the white people, but when applied or measured up to the black people, they lack the substantial and inspiring. They are like meat without salt, they bear no analogy to our own; for this reason it would be a wise plan for us to lay down a course of study in Negro History and achievements, before or after men and women have left certain schools.

It is the season for us to devote our time in kindling the torches that will inspire us to racial integrity. We need a collection or list of books written by our men and women. If they lack style, let the children of tomorrow correct the omissions of their sires. Let them build upon the crude work. Let them, because of the opportunities that colleges and universities grant, crystallize the crude work and bring it out flawless. [. . .]

There have been written many histories of our people in slavery, peace and war, each serving a purpose. These books have been useful to disseminate the fragmentary knowledge to localities where the spark of learning has awakened the soul to thirst for more and better food. . . . These have been our landmarks, our rock of ages; let us place around them the inspiring love so that the scholars of today with the vast opportunities, the splendid equipment, and the great expectations of the "survival of the fittest" will be spurred to do things by which we will be remembered, and in the coming days will be heralded for racial identity, racial preservation and racial unity.

We have reached the crucial period of our educational existence. I have shown by a few examples of the past available and useful material upon which we can base our future structure. We have chairs of almost everything, and believe we lack nothing, but we sadly need a chair of Negro history. The white institutions have their chair of history; it is the history of their people, and whenever the Negro is mentioned in the text-books it dwindles down to a footnote. The white scholar's mind and heart are fired because in the temple of learning he is told how on March 5, 1770, the Americans were able to beat the English; but to find Crispus Attucks it is necessary to go deep into special books. In the orations delivered at Bunker's Hill, Daniel Webster never mentioned the Negroes having done anything, and is silent about Peter Salem. In the account of the battle of Long Island City and around New York under Major-General Nathaniel Greene, no mention is made of the eight hundred Negro soldiers who imperiled their lives in the Revolutionary War. Cases can be shown right and left of such palpable omissions. [. . .]

Where is our historian to give us our side view and our chair of Negro history, to teach our people our own history? We are at the mercy of the "flotsam and jetsam" of the white writers. The very learned Rev. Alexander Crummell, before the American Negro Academy, stated that he heard

J. C. Calhoun say that the inferiority of the Negro was so self-evident that he would not believe him human unless he could conjugate Greek verbs; and yet it must have been evident to Calhoun that in North Carolina there were many Negroes held as slaves who could read and write Arabic.[1] In those days men like Juan Latino, Amo, Capitein, Francis Williams, Rev. J. Pennington, and others could not only conjugate the Greek and Hebrew verbs, but had shown unmistakable evidences of learning, for they had received degrees from the universities of world-famed reputation. Yet in those days there were many whites unrestrained, enjoying the opportunities of education, who could not conjugate Greek roots nor verbs of the spoken language of the land. Yet this barrier was set up to persons restrained by force from the enjoyment of the most ordinary rights.

We need in the coming dawn the man who will give us the background for our future; it matters not whether he comes from the cloisters of the university or from the rank and file of the fields.

The Anglo-Saxon is effusive in his praises to the Saxon shepherds who lived on the banks of the river Elbe, to whom he pays blind allegiance. We need the historian and philosopher to give us with trenchant pen the story of our forefathers and let our soul and body, with phosphorescent light, brighten the chasm that separates us. When the fact has been put down in the scroll of time, that the Negroes of Africa smelted iron and tempered bronzes at the time Europe was wielding stone implements, that the use of letters was introduced among the savages of Europe about 1500 BC and the European carried them to America about the fifteenth century after the Christian era, that Phoenicia and Palestine will live forever in the memory of mankind since America as well as Europe has received letters from the one and religion from the other,[2] we will feel prouder of the achievements of our sires. We must research diligently the annals of time and bring back from obscurity the dormant example of agriculture, industry, and commerce, upon these the arts and sciences and make common the battle-ground of our heritage.

Notes

1. See W. B. Hodgson, *The Gospels in the Negro Patois* (New York: Cornell University Library, 1857).
2. Edward Gibbon, *Decline and Fall of the Roman Empire* (New York: Alfred A. Knopf, 1910).

JESSE HOFFNUNG-GARSKOF

The World of Arturo Alfonso Schomburg

The migrations of Arturo Alfonso Schomburg offer unique insights into the complicated question of racial identity for Afro-Latin@s in the United States. Born in Puerto Rico in 1874, to a mother of Danish West Indian origin and a father of German ancestry, Schomburg moved to New York in 1891. There he joined a community of independence activists from Cuba and Puerto Rico. He was the recording secretary for the political club Las Dos Antillas, which as part of the larger Cuban Revolutionary Party (PRC) sought to liberate the two islands from Spanish rule and establish a progressive social order in new Antillean republics. Although hardly free of racial tensions, the movement was unusual, perhaps unique, in the Americas in the 1890s for its open call for fraternity between Blacks and Whites. Party leader José Martí disavowed the reigning international scientific consensus about Black inferiority and proclaimed racial division and inequality to be a product of social prejudice. In the coming Cuban republic, Martí predicted, there would be no Blacks and Whites, "only Cubans." For Schomburg and other Puerto Rican people of color who moved to New York to join the movement, this commitment to color-blind nationalism was a great attraction.

Yet even as Schomburg participated in the multiracial coalitions of the Antillean exile community, he began to build social ties with people of African descent born in the United States and the West Indies. Many of these new friends articulated a different kind of politics that focused on international racial unity rather than on nationalism or coalitions with Whites. After the United States took possession of Cuba and Puerto Rico in 1898, the multiracial independence movement in New York dissolved. Schomburg shifted his considerable energies into Negro scholarly organizations, to use the language of the day. At the same time he helped recruit English speakers into his Spanish-speaking Masonic lodge, Sol de

Cuba. Within a decade lodge business was conducted in English and the lodge was renamed for Prince Hall, the free West Indian man who founded the Negro branch of the Masonic movement known as the Prince Hall Masons. Schomburg rose to leadership in the Prince Hall hierarchy, an important institution of the emerging African American middle class in New York.[1]

As he moved among communities of color from Puerto Rico, Cuba, the United States, and the West Indies, Schomburg dedicated himself to the collection of books and historical documents about people of African descent around the world. Negroes should emulate the Jews, he argued, by maintaining their feeling of kinship despite being scattered among nations who despise them. He held that the project of international Black unity required an international network of intellectuals and collectors who could provide firm historical footing for racial pride and unity. To that end he helped found the Negro Society for Historical Research (1911) and spent his own time and money searching out books and documents. "We need a collection or list of books written by our men and women," Schomburg wrote in 1913. "We need the historian and philosopher to give us, with trenchant pen, the story of our forefathers and let our soul and body, with phosphorescent light, brighten the chasm that separates us."[2] Documenting Negro contributions to world civilization through the science of history, he argued, would inspire the racial patriotism necessary for building an international Negro alliance across the gaps created by national boundaries and provincialism.

Schomburg's idea of history, shared with his allies in the Cuban and Puerto Rican independence movement and with his colleagues in the Negro Society for Historical Research, emerged in dialogue with dominant ideas about race and nation. White historians of the day justified colonialism and segregation by arguing that Africans and their descendants were incapable of civilization. Schomburg did not question basic assumptions about the universality of civilization, but he committed himself to the revolutionary act of disproving contemporary theories of Black inferiority. Schomburg set out to prove racist historians wrong by collecting evidence of Black poets, philosophers, composers, military heroes, novelists, and painters. Schomburg's personal collection made him an invaluable resource for the leading Black scholars of the day, including W. E. B. Du Bois, Alain Locke, and Charles S. Johnson. They published his essays and, more frequently, relied on his assistance in their own research. Then in 1926 he sold his collection to the New York Public Library. After retiring from his job as a clerk for a Wall Street firm, he took over as curator of the collection at the 135th St. Branch of the Public Library until his death in 1938. The Schomburg Center remains the premier archive for the study of Black culture and history in the United States and the world.

Although Schomburg's intellectual accomplishments were considerable, what has especially piqued public interest in him over the past decade are his migrations and his shifting racial and ethnic identities and their relationship to his intellectual projects. Schomburg was both Negro and Puerto Rican. He made a dramatic transition from nationalist politics, which saw possibilities for racial advancement through the Cuban and Puerto Rican struggle, to an explicitly racial politics on the model of an idealized Jewish diaspora. As a migrant who traveled through various societies in the aftermath of racial slavery, he engaged in a process of comparison and mutual self-recognition in conversation with the people of color he encountered. As a colonial subject, excluded from the prevailing narratives of race, nationhood, and history, he experienced a sense of dislocation and alienation that allowed him to imagine alternate forms of belonging either as an *Antillano* or as part of an international community of Black people. His story helps to show that the African diaspora was not a fixed or obvious set of relationships but rather a sense of belonging and displacement that emerged from the modern experience of Atlantic slavery, colonialism, emancipation, and migrations.

Schomburg's experience as a Puerto Rican of African descent who socialized with Black people from other parts of the world and who constructed a public identity as an American Negro runs counter to the classic accounts of how Puerto Ricans of color expressed their belonging in New York's racially segregated society and in the broader context of the Atlantic. In one of the first scholarly studies of racial prejudice in Puerto Rico, Tomás Blanco laid the foundations of this concept by describing a "natural" tendency among Puerto Ricans of African descent "to refuse, as much as possible, to be classified together with [black people from the United States,] a class of people which suffers such a high level of injustice and derision."[3] He argued that Puerto Ricans of color suffered little or no prejudice at the hands of fellow Puerto Ricans and therefore stuck together with their ethnic brethren. Few scholars still contend that Puerto Rican society is free of racism. Still, according to the prevailing view Puerto Ricans of color first naturally clung to the multiracial spaces and identities they shared with White Puerto Ricans, despite the pervasive racism practiced in those spaces. Only in response to the Black Civil Rights Movement, the thinking goes, did Puerto Ricans begin to seek an alliance with African American neighbors. In this light Schomburg seems an exceptional Puerto Rican. Indeed, recent analyses that compare Schomburg to other Puerto Rican intellectuals of color in New York in the 1920s conclude that his explicit racial politics made him a "Puerto Rican political aberration."[4]

Yet by reconstructing the world in which Schomburg lived during his early years in New York, a world that included other people of color from Puerto Rico and Cuba, we can reframe his life and its relation to a broader history of Afro-Latin@s in migration. The world of Arturo Schomburg—and of most Afro-Latin@s in New York between 1880 and 1920—was one of overlapping engagements and alliances. Men and women of color from Puerto Rico and Cuba engaged with the multiracial projects of exile nationalism while integrating into multiethnic Black neighborhoods and social institutions. Cross-racial unity of Hispanic Caribbeans in New York, while often attractive to Afro-Latin@s like Schomburg, was hardly a natural starting point from which Afro-Latin@s later diverged. These alliances emerged through the efforts of dedicated organizers in New York and always contained tensions within them. And for Latin@s with recognizable African ancestry, national or ethnic alliances as Latin@s always operated in tension with the power of local institutions to segregate by color and with the pull of social and political bonds forged around shared color.

Cuban Cigar Makers and the Prince Hall Masons

Sometime in the decade after Schomburg arrived in New York, he joined a Masonic lodge called Sol de Cuba. The founders of Sol de Cuba were cigar makers of African descent who migrated from Cuba to New York in the 1870s. They left Cuba at a moment when insurgents—White, mulatto, and Black—waged an armed struggle that sought to abolish slavery and gain independence from Spain. During this struggle, known as the Ten Years' War, underground Masonic lodges on the island served as a clandestine network of communication and conspiracy. While official Freemasonry in Cuba, under the aegis of the Gran Logia de Colón, prohibited the admission of "pardos y morenos," these irregular Masonic groups were open to men of color—a term that included men with varying degrees of African ancestry. The mixed-race lodges spread outward from the island as Cuban tobacco merchants eager to escape the insurrection and to take advantage of new U.S. tariff laws set up cigar factories in New York, Philadelphia, and South Florida. Cigar manufacturers brought with them the skilled workforce of cigar makers who, together with their bosses, made the irregular Masonic movement from the island into a form of immigrant mutual aid society with nationalist undertones. It is in this context, in June of 1880, that Manuel Coronado, Sixto Pozo, Abraham Seino, and Lafayette Marcus founded Sol de Cuba in Brooklyn. Significantly, they did not join the already existing Cuban Masonic hierarchy in New York but applied instead to affiliate with the Prince Hall Masons, an institution composed of and run by African Americans.[5]

These events are not meant to imply that the existing Masonic lodge in New York was openly segregationist. Only a few years earlier, in 1878, a Cuban physician named Ramón Ylla and a group of cigar makers in Manhattan founded the Logia Carlos Manuel de Céspedes, in honor of the founder and first symbolic leader of the Cuban insurrection. As a plantation owner Céspedes had emancipated his slaves so that they might fight in the cause of a free Cuba. He was therefore a symbol of the link between the project of independence and the project of abolition. The lodge adhered to the hierarchy of the Orden Caballeros de la Luz, which was founded some years earlier by Cuban cigar manufacturers in Philadelphia.[6] A "liturgy" published in 1879 by the Caballeros de la Luz expresses a rhetorical commitment not only to abolition but also to the project of racial and social equality. Race and class, the document instructed, were not to be taken into consideration when vetting potential brothers. The lodge Patriarch was to enforce this rule each time a new membership committee was formed, and he was to "advise" newly formed committees "that our Order recognizes equality of rights and responsibility of all men." At each meeting the lodge Patriarch raised a ritual object and told the brothers that it represented the equality of all men, White and Black, rich and poor. He then pronounced that learning, science, and morality would gradually abolish all forms of social prejudice and that "all inequality that is not based on merit is against justice."[7]

Yet if the men in the Caballeros de la Luz lodges appeared to absorb the most progressive messages of the independence movement, they did so at a moment when the movement saw itself fractured by racial and class division. In 1878 the insurrection faltered in Cuba. The White leadership surrendered to Spain, in large part because they feared the increasing power of their Black and mulatto allies. Black and mulatto leaders such as General Antonio Maceo, along with some White allies, refused to accept the truce and returned to battle in the Guerra Chiquita of 1879 and 1880. The tensions over the war and its racial politics were evident in the activities of the exile lodges. One aspirant to the lodge in Philadelphia, Manuel Suárez, renounced his candidacy in 1879 to protest the avowal of "universal fraternity" in the lodge rites. The Logia Carlos Manuel de Céspedes in New

York renamed itself Logia El Progreso, thereby distancing itself from the symbol of Cuban nationalism and abolition. For this reason the Brooklyn cigar workers who formed their own lodge in 1880 might have had good reason to expect a lukewarm welcome, if not official segregationism, in El Progreso lodge.[8]

Furthermore, a rhetorical commitment to class and racial equality did not necessarily mean that working-class men of color could actually expect to be accepted or treated equally. As Black and mulatto participants in the struggle in Cuba learned, White allies frequently held them to a higher standard on any ostensibly neutral qualities of "merit." Their supposed lack of civilization, learning, or morality could be used to exclude individuals from positions of prestige.[9] As the independence movement in Cuba split over White fears of Black insurgency, the Caballeros de la Luz membership in Philadelphia was at odds about how to deal with the tobacco workers, White and Black, who wished to join. Some brothers proposed to use lodge funds to support night classes for the instruction and intellectual uplift of poorer émigrés. This resonated with the artisan *casinos* or clubs and the anarchist popular education projects in Cuba at the time. It also paralleled institutions that Cuban intellectuals of color, notably Rafael Serra and Juan Gualberto Gómez, created in those years to uplift and incorporate the growing class of freedmen and freedwomen as Spain gradually abolished slavery. The Caballeros de la Luz, however, still led by factory owners, rejected the proposal in its preference for a more exclusive lodge and individual acts of charity toward the less fortunate. According to one member, they objected to the efforts to transform the lodge into "a *mesalina* that dedicates itself to gathering up the sons of all classes and all colors."[10] *Mesalina* here has the meaning not only of a dissolute woman but, specifically, of an upper-class woman who prostitutes herself for the benefit of lower-class clients.

With time, the prospect of belonging to the same lodges as their employers began to wear thin for many working-class Cuban exiles. Cuban cigar workers, increasingly influenced by Spanish anarchism as well as Masonic ideologies of learning, sought rather to create institutions of class solidarity and popular education.[11] By the early 1880s, the Afro-Cuban revolutionary leader Rafael Serra had brought this idea to New York. A result of this was the creation of La Liga Antillana, a night school for immigrant workers very much like the one proposed and rejected in the Caballeros de la Luz lodge in Philadelphia. Serra denounced charity, which he called "an insult," in favor of education and uplift based on full equality. La Liga Antillana was consciously multiracial and international in its membership, including "Cubans and Puerto Ricans, whites and blacks, artisans and those who are not artisans, rich and poor."[12] Serra was a believer in cross-racial unity, though, as he would later write, not in the sense of a "discriminatory and unequal unity of jockey and steed."[13] Although Serra, a man of humble origins but growing intellectual reputation, might have eventually been accepted in a lodge like El Progreso, in order to assert leadership in an organization and shape its project he chose to create his own. This may explain why the founders of Schomburg's lodge, Sol de Cuba, decided to create their own lodge rather than seek entry into Caballeros de la Luz. To express claims to full citizenship or to vindicate Black identity within the broader Masonic construct of universal "progress," these cigar makers of African descent created an independent social space that they could lead and shape to their own purposes.[14]

To do so, they sought out the institutional backing of the English-speaking African Americans in the Prince Hall Masons. While the creation of a separate Black lodge reflected a general trend toward independent organizing within Cuban society, it must also be understood in the context of a diasporic encounter particular to émigrés of color in New York. For when they left behind the cigar factories and immigrant social clubs that bound them to each other as Cubans and cigar makers, these men lived in a city divided by a color line. As a result, they had frequent and sometimes very close contact with people of color of varied backgrounds and rarely lived among Cubans identified as White. Two of Sol de Cuba's founders, Abraham Seino and Lafayette Marcus, along with at least five other lodge members married English-speaking African American women before creating the lodge. Indeed, for the men in the Sol de Cuba lodge it was far more common to marry a Black woman from the United States than a Cuban woman. None of them married White women of any nationality. Those lodge members who did not marry generally lived in rooming houses, in apartment buildings, and on blocks inhabited by Black people. Few lodge members lived in spaces mostly reserved for Whites. Even Juan Beato, the only lodge member identified by U.S. census enumerators as White, lived in an otherwise all-Black building.

In other words, whatever the state of their alliances inside the factories and clubs of the émigré community, Latin@s of color in New York parted company with White Latin@s when they returned to their homes. There they enjoyed considerable social contact with English speakers and shared experiences of the evolving color line. These men seem to have found the space for independent social organizing through an alliance with African American organizations in the United States to be a welcome alternative to the ways color constrained their membership in the Cuban community. This social and residential contact between Black Cubans and African Americans helps explain how Marcus and Coronado made their first contacts with the Prince Hall Masons. They likely had in-laws and neighbors who were in the Mt. Olive and Celestial Lodges of the Prince Hall Masons. They joined these lodges, and when their initiation was complete they applied for permission to form their own lodge. It is important to note that while Marcus and Coronado did not, or perhaps could not, affiliate with the Caballeros de la Luz, they did not simply fold into the growing Negro population among whom they lived. Neither did they abandon the project of a free and equal Cuba. Rather, they turned to a United States Negro institutional authority to form a lodge for Cuban men of color. The creation of a distinct Cuban lodge within the Prince Hall Masons may have been a gesture of separation from the broader English-speaking context in which they lived (from their brothers-in-law and fathers-in-law) as much as it was a gesture of independence as men of color within the Cuban context.[15]

Schomburg thus arrived in New York to find an already established lodge where Masonic ideologies of progress, civilization, and morality overlapped with Cuban nationalism and independent racial politics. He joined a lodge where men of color gathered to socialize in Spanish before scattering to homes in Black districts, where English, often inflected by strong southern and Caribbean accents, was the language of their wives and children. Schomburg was an example of this experience. At the age of twenty-one he married Elizabeth Hatcher, an African American woman from Virginia. The couple lived with their three sons on West 62nd St. in the Black neighborhood known as San Juan Hill. Hatcher, who died in 1900, and his two subsequent wives (also United States African Americans) brought Schomburg into close contact with North American Negro music, dance, jokes, and folklore, as well as kinship and social networks. He learned to eat new foods and apparently developed a considerable fondness for them; at one stage of his life he proposed to research and write a cookbook and social history of Negro cooking. Judging from his highly personal descriptions of "the hearty egg breads and sugar baked apples of Virginia to brains in brown butter and batter cakes with borders of crisp black embroidery in the Blue Grass, on down to rice calas and the ineffable steeped coffee, cinnamon flavored chocolate and hot toddies served in the early hours behind the sun-streaked jalousies of the Vieux Carre in New Orleans," he must have dedicated hours of loving research, in the company of family and friends, to the study of Negro culinary achieve-

Arturo Schomburg at the funeral of his mentor, John "Grit" Bruce, New York, 1924. Other mourners include Marcus Garvey (to the right of Schomburg) and members of the Prince Hall Masonic Lodge. Bruce and Schomburg cofounded the Negro Society for Historical Research in 1911. (Photographs and Prints Division, Schomburg Center for Research in Black Culture, the New York Public Library, Astor, Lenox and Tilden Foundations)

The Literary Event of the Year!

The Records of a Race in Literature History, Art and Science

GRAND OPENING

OF THE

Department of Negro History Literature and Art

IN THE

135th Street Branch of the N. Y. Public Library
103 West 135th Street

Friday, May 7th, At 8:30 P. M.

Speakers:

Dr. Hubert Harrison, staff lecturer, New York Board of Education.

Dr. Alain Locke, of Howard University.

Dr. E. H. Anderson, director of the New York Public Library and others.

SINGING OF NEGRO SPIRITUALS

Large loan collection of Negro literature by:
Mr. Arthur Schomburg   Dr. Charles Martin
Dr. Hubert Harrison and others

ALL ARE WELCOME

Auspices of Negro Literary and Historical Society and the New York Public Library

The New York Age Press

Program announcing the opening of the Department of Negro History, Literature and Art at the 135th Street Branch, New York Public Library, 1926. The new department consisted primarily of Schomburg's personal library. (Photographs and Prints Division, Schomburg Center for Research in Black Culture, the New York Public Library, Astor, Lenox and Tilden Foundations) ment.[16] Institutional ties between the Sol de Cuba lodge and the Prince Hall Masons also introduced him to a community of African American intellectuals, including John E. Bruce, who would later invite him to share in their evolving Pan-Africanist projects.

The Cuban Revolutionary Party and the Club Las Dos Antillas

When Schomburg arrived in New York in 1891 he found a community of cigar workers that, after the disillusionment of the 1880s, was again filled with excitement for the Cuban and Puerto Rican nationalist cause. During Antonio Maceo's ten years in exile in Jamaica, Central America, and New Orleans, the general had grown into an international symbol of Black resistance. By the early 1890s, Maceo shared leadership in the Cuban struggle with José Martí, a renowned journalist and poet living in New York who taught classes in Serra's Liga Antillana and attracted the loyalty of the workers who gathered there, Black as well as White. If Maceo was a symbol of heroic Black leadership, Martí was a symbol of enlightened White leadership. As most White intellectuals in the Atlantic world increasingly adopted the principles of scientific racism, Martí, like the liberal Masonic groups of the 1870s, argued that racial inequality was the result of unjust social prejudice, and that justice and morality demanded that men be judged only on their merit. In a free Cuba, he promised, there would be no Blacks or Whites, only Cubans. In a decade when nationalists in the United States and other parts of the Americas increasingly relied on race "science" to conclude that Black people were unsuited for citizenship or self-rule, Martí defended "the right of the black man to maintain and prove that his color does not deprive him of any of the abilities or rights of the human species."[17]

Martí's views of race and civilization, like those of the earlier Masonic groups, could have the effect of restricting independent Black politics. Indeed, sensitive to the Spanish accusation that a war for independence would lead to a race war, Martí opposed the formation of independent racial organizations. "The white [man] who isolates himself isolates the black [man]," he wrote. "The black [man] who isolates himself provokes the white [man] to isolate himself."[18] However, Martí's idea of a Cuba with no Blacks or Whites could also hide persistent racism and racial inequality behind a mask of race blindness. When people of color protested racial injustice, some Whites in the movement argued that the topic of race was divisive and contrary to the spirit of the Cuban cause. Martí's success at bringing elite exiles and working-class radicals together in the movement also brought a return to some of the tensions over leadership that had surfaced among the Luz de Caballeros a decade earlier. The party incorporated working-class membership, including many working-class people of color, through dozens of political clubs in New York, South Florida, and elsewhere. The artisans and self-taught intellectuals who led the revolutionary clubs engaged in a constant battle of wills to prevent elite exiles from operating independently of their influence, from expressing what one club leader called "ignorance or disdain for the will of the majority."[19]

Cubans of color in the movement, including Rafael Serra and Juan Gualberto Gómez, befriended Martí and became avid defenders of his project of racial fraternity by using the association he made between anti-racism and Cuban national identity to defend their own politics of racial advancement and citizenship. They saw support for his leadership as crucial to preserving their own role in the movement. Cubans of color participated actively in the revolutionary clubs that formed the base of the party, though few were elected to leadership positions in those clubs. A few, such as Rafael Serra, also created and sustained their own institutions. Serra presided over La Liga, a literary and educational center for Cubans and Puerto Ricans of all colors, which gave him a platform for leadership in the broader movement. Likewise, Manuel Coronado, one of the founders of Sol de Cuba, presided over the social club La Igualdad (Equality). It is not clear whether this club had a multiracial membership or was composed only of men of color, but its name suggests that Coronado, like Serra, created a social institution in which he could assert leadership and push the movement to live up to its own expressed ideals of racial and social equality.[20]

Puerto Ricans in the movement were similarly divided between elites who controlled the Puerto Rican Section of the Cuban Revolutionary Party (founded in 1895), and working-class exiles who joined the party by forming political clubs. Cuban and Puerto Ricans of color in particular were prominent in the leadership of these clubs. In 1891 the journalist Sotero Figueroa and the poet Francisco Gonzalo ("Pachín") Marín split from the Autonomista Party to join in the independence struggle. Both were men of color. In 1892, Figueroa and Marín founded the Club Borinquen, a constituent club of the Cuban Revolutionary Party, and became president and secretary, respectively. Soon thereafter Rosendo Rodríguez, a Puerto Rican cigar maker of African descent, founded Schomburg's club, Las Dos Antillas. All of the officers in Las Dos Antillas had African ancestry: Schomburg was recording secretary; and two Cubans of color, both cigar makers, became the club's treasurer and first speaker. It is not clear whether the membership of Las Dos Antillas was exclusively composed of Cubans and Puerto Ricans of color or whether this was an instance of a mixed-race club that remarkably elected only Black and mulatto officers. In either case it is clear that the social and political world Schomburg participated in was one that attracted a cohort of Puerto Ricans of color, who found space not only as members of the revolutionary clubs but also as leaders.[21]

It seems likely furthermore that their ideas about race, and commitment to racial equality, played a significant role in the decision by these Puerto Ricans to leave the Autonomistas behind and to join the Cuban movement, though they did not say so publicly.[22] Yet the party's commitment to racial and class equality was not assured. After Martí left for Cuba in 1895, the leadership of the party increasingly excluded men like Serra and Figueroa from decision making and from editorial input in Patria.[23] Figueroa and Serra joined forces to create their own newspaper, La Doctrina de Martí, in which they argued that Martí's legacy was one of unity and equality. The role of workers and of men of color in the movement was very much on the minds of the members of Borinquen and Las Dos Antillas when they met at Military Hall in October 1895, four months after Martí perished in the fighting in Cuba. A compañero named Agramonte spoke in rousing celebration of the contributions of artisans to the national cause. Then members began talking openly about race in much the same way that José Martí advocated, and in much the same way that Schomburg would for the rest of his life.

First a Colombian visitor named Haníbal Castro, on his way to join the Mambí army in Cuba, rose to speak to the crowd. Spain, he told the audience, had appealed to racist sentiments in its attempts to damage the Cuban cause. But in Colombia and Venezuela "the black race is the privileged race, which triumphed in the battles of Ayacucho and Carabobo." He continued by stating that "the black race, generous, virile, and valiant, had its cradle in Egypt, the motherland of the Negro." Black Egypt was the birthplace of civilization and progress, he told the audience. The colossal pyramids constructed by Black Egyptians had never been duplicated, even by the most intelligent of modern minds. The assembled audience began to respond heartily. "In the line of the Spanish Kings," Castro said, "there was Negro blood." "Bravo!" the crowd answered. "And today a black man is the premier Cuban." "Bravo!" they interrupted. "Maceo," Castro concluded. "¡Viva Maceo!" a voice shouted, and the crowd responded with an emphatic "¡Viva!"[24]

Castro ended by promising to risk his life to follow the Black general, and the crowd responded enthusiastically. "You could say," Schomburg wrote in his capacity as recording secretary, "that applause rained down and nearly drowned out the eloquent words of the son of Colombia."[25] The audience was comprised largely of Puerto Ricans and Cubans of color who had joined the movement chiefly because of the promise of racial advancement, as symbolized by Maceo. Beside them were working-class White allies who saw prejudices based on class and race as injustices. It is no wonder they responded enthusiastically to these words. After Castro, Sotero Figueroa spoke on the history of Puerto Rico's involvement in the struggle to abolish slavery and gain independence, which he indicated were one and the same struggle. He ended by paying homage to Juan Gualberto Gómez, the Cuban abolitionist intellectual, journalist, and independence leader and a prominent figure of the *sociedades de color* on the island. "Puerto Ricans and Cubans," Figueroa told the audience, "(there we have) this Negro, this intellect, the great Cuban Gualberto Gómez."[26]

Schomburg and the men of Las Dos Antillas cheered the idea that the Black race was a central participant in their independence movement and in that grand narrative of civilization and progress they held so dear. In so doing they articulated arguments identical to the ones that Schomburg would spend the rest of his life seeking to uphold. At the end of the meeting Schomburg looked up from taking notes and called for a final cheer for the fallen apostle José Martí. Martí, though wary of independent racial organizing, had founded a movement that accepted clubs like Las Dos Antillas, had used his influence to preserve a space for men of color to participate in the movement, and had defended the right of Black men to disprove racist theories with evidence of Black contributions to civilization. The crowd answered him with a final "¡Viva!"

Like the decision to form Sol de Cuba as a space apart from the established Cuban lodges, these meetings and conversations took place in the context of tense racial coalitions within the movement as well as in the context of a segregated city. Like the members of the Sol de Cuba lodge, the leaders of Las Dos Antillas settled among people of African descent from other parts of the Caribbean and United States. According to the 1900 federal census, for example, Rosendo Rodríguez lived in a building on Third Avenue occupied by Black families from the South. Silvestre Pivaló, the treasurer of Las Dos Antillas, lived in 1900 on a block where he and his wife Pilar were the only family enumerated as Black. But by 1910 they had moved to an all "mulatto" block where they were the only Spanish speakers. In 1900, Schomburg lived on West 62nd Street among mostly

Black neighbors. Another Las Dos Antillas officer, Francisco Araúz, lived with his wife, a Cuban woman of color, in a building on Third Avenue occupied almost entirely by African Americans. It seems that Schomburg was no more unusual in his relations with African Americans among his comrades in the Antillano independence club than among his brothers in the Sol de Cuba Masonic lodge.[27]

Indeed, when they settled in Black neighborhoods Schomburg and the other men of Las Dos Antillas were typical of most Puerto Ricans of color who lived in New York before 1920. As Jesús Colón remembered, "In those days the few Puerto Ricans around lived in the heart of the Negro neighborhood together with the Negro people in the same buildings; many times as roomers in their homes."[28] According to census data, it seems accurate to say that in those days the few Puerto Ricans of color around, about 10 percent of the total Puerto Rico–born population in the city, lived together with other people of color from the United States, Cuba, and the West Indies. Persons born in Puerto Rico and living in New York and enumerated as Black or mulatto on the United States census were more likely to marry English-speaking Black and mulatto persons than other Puerto Ricans. They frequently lodged with Blacks from the United States, Cuba, or the West Indies and almost never formed families with Puerto Ricans identified as White on the census. Practically the only exceptions to this rule were the Puerto Ricans of color who lived as servants in the homes of wealthy White Puerto Ricans.[29]

The apparent absence of any other residential contact between White and Black Puerto Ricans in New York may be explained, in part, by the problem of relying on census returns. Rather than recording the color and racial identities of these early settlers as they perceived themselves, census enumeration reflected shifting national ideas about race, codified by the color categories that Congress included in the forms: White, Black, and mulatto. The census results reflected the subjective assessment of each census taker, a judgment that was based on the physical appearance of the individual but probably also influenced by other factors such as dress, speech, family members, and neighborhood. Census takers may have been reluctant to acknowledge multiracial families and therefore may have enumerated Puerto Rican husbands and wives together in one category or the other. They may also have tended to enumerate Puerto Ricans with ambiguous features in Black neighborhoods as Black and in White neighborhoods as White. Indeed, while it is often presumed that the United States had a more rigid system of racial categories than Puerto Rico, following the "one drop rule," "White" was actually a rather fluid category in New York in the first decade of the twentieth century. Enumerators counted most of the city's foreign-born working classes as White, even though the city's elite saw them as racial inferiors. Yet it seems unlikely that context wholly trumped physical characteristics when census takers enumerated Puerto Ricans. If some Puerto Ricans had features that allowed placement in different categories according to neighborhood, some others would surely have been recognized as Black even in White neighborhoods. Furthermore, even if the census data do not identify Puerto Ricans of African descent living in White neighborhoods who may have been counted as White, they still show that of the 10 percent of Puerto Ricans in New York in this period identified as non-White, the majority formed households with people of color from other parts of the Americas (including the United States, Cuba, and the West Indies) and nearly all lived in Black-inhabited buildings and neighborhoods.

The racial politics that Schomburg and his Puerto Rican and Cuban comrades expressed in their pro-independence activism also reflected their own personal ties to the city's multiethnic Black world. Those relationships, in turn, were reflective of a broader experience of Caribbean people of color in New York before 1920. Schomburg may have been unique in his rapid rise to prominence in Negro intellectual and social circles. But he was hardly unique among his generation in his diasporic racial politics, his commitment to writing Black people into narratives of civilization and progress, or his profound social contact with African Americans from the United States.

From Sol de Cuba to Prince Hall

Schomburg's path into leadership positions in African American institutions after the breakup of the Cuban Revolutionary Party and its Puerto Rican wing set him apart from his comrades in Las Dos Antillas. Although it was common for Puerto Ricans of color of his generation to live among other Black people, none rose to such prominence in African American public life. Understanding this path requires a return to the Sol de Cuba lodge and its ties to Prince Hall Masonry.[30] According to lodge historians, after 1898 membership declined because many Cuban exiles moved back to the island. By 1911 Schomburg and other remaining lodge members decided to boost lodge membership by attracting English speakers. In essence they voted to invite their neighbors and brothers-in-law to join, and they accommodated them by switching to English in lodge meetings. Within a few years the lodge changed its name from Sol de Cuba to Prince

Hall Lodge No. 38. Schomburg translated the lodge records. The men who led the shift to English were Schomburg, a Puerto Rican with Danish West Indian heritage, and Cladius Emanuel Cyril, born in Costa Rica of Jamaican parents. The migrations of their parents within the Caribbean perhaps disposed these men to reach out to English-speaking neighbors. Still it is worth remembering that the first ties between the Sol de Cuba brothers and English-speaking neighbors had been forged in the 1870s, before Schomburg arrived in New York and before Cyril was even born.

By helping to preserve the lodge Schomburg created the conditions for his own rise to leadership within it as well as within the broader Prince Hall Masonic movement. In important ways Prince Hall No. 38 reproduced the world from which Schomburg came. In the Cuban and Puerto Rican movement, self-taught intellectuals—Black, White, and mulatto—also created their own social institutions, literary clubs, casinos, night schools, and lodges. These clubs and lodges were built around the willing adoption of norms of civilized behavior and public morals that mirrored elite institutions. Inside them cigar makers and other artisans of all colors sought to construct alternate histories of Cuba and Puerto Rico, in which they, and people like them, figured as national heroes, major literary figures, and great thinkers. In the wake of 1898, some of these comrades moved to Cuba to seek the rewards for their revolutionary sacrifices, and an outlet for their ideals, in public employment in the new republic. Greater numbers turned toward increasing labor radicalism by becoming socialists and union activists. Schomburg himself shared the humble origins of the cigar workers, but his personal and intellectual aspirations led him toward middle-class institutions and not socialism. In the Prince Hall Masons he found a community that shared his desire to disprove the theory that he was incapable of civilized behavior. Indeed, he found the space to become a leader in that community.

Schomburg's attraction to middle-class social institutions reflected his employment status. In his first years in New York Schomburg found work as a porter, but he hoped to rise to professional status by studying after work to pass the necessary exams to become a lawyer. In 1906, however, his attempts to receive a law certificate were thwarted when he could not produce evidence of sufficient schooling and the state refused to let him take the exam.[31] He instead settled in as a white-collar employee in the mailroom at Bankers Trust Company. A mailroom job would hardly be prestigious employment by today's standards, and surely it fell far short of Schomburg's ambitions. But in 1906 it was also far removed from the working-class world of the cigar factories or print shops of San Juan. While cigar workers on the islands, and in New York, faced increasing pressure from mechanization in the early decades of the century, Schomburg observed sympathetically from the relative comfort and stability of a white-collar job. While they turned from the imperfect multiracial alliances of revolutionary nationalism to the imperfect racial alliances of labor radicalism, he helped Sol de Cuba become a space for racial nationalism among middle-class Blacks of varied linguistic and ethnic backgrounds.[32]

In Prince Hall Lodge No. 38, Schomburg surrounded himself with men who shared his professional status and middle-class values. Prince Hall lodges in Brooklyn were institutions of the lower stratum of the Black middle class, a group whose class status as respectable Black men was defined by a rigid code of public behavior rather than professional achievements.[33] Like the Caballeros de la Luz, lodges selected members based on shared notions of morality, civilization, and masculinity. But while these standards allowed elites in the Caballeros de la Luz lodges to regulate the behavior of men with less education and prestige, the brothers in the Prince Hall lodges used the same ideology to glorify the image of the "self-made man."[34] Schomburg, who often suffered slights at the hands of leading Black intellectuals, pointedly expressed in his 1913 speech his Masonic attitude toward Black elites: "The university graduate is wont to overestimate his ability, fresh from the machinery that endows him with a parchment and crowns him with knowledge, he steps out into the world to meet the practical men with years of experience and mother wit."[35] It was among these men of "mother wit" that Schomburg established his class and ethnic identity in Negro New York.

Indeed, the intellectual organizations that Schomburg helped to establish with fellow Masons also helped satisfy his higher ambitions and his subversive desire to excel as a leader and an intellectual despite the racism of White society and the snobbery of the Black elite. If lodge membership secured respectability for Black men in the uncomfortable lower echelons of the middle class, becoming an officer, and then rising in the Masonic hierarchy, was an avenue for becoming a Negro notable, or a "race leader."[36] After first serving as secretary and master of the Sol de Cuba lodge, Schomburg rose quickly through the ranks of the order to become, in 1918, Grand Secretary of the Prince Hall Grand Lodge of New York State and associate editor of the *Masonic Quarterly Review*. The mentorship of John Bruce, another man of "mother wit," and Schomburg's own remarkable accomplishments as a collector, gradually increased his reputation in academic circles as well, bringing Schomburg no small satisfaction. In

1914, after Bruce helped with his election to the American Negro Academy, Schomburg wrote, "I have been elected an Academician!!! That's higher than a co-editor [Bruce had just been made co-editor emeritus of *Who's Who in Negro America*]. Thanks for your good letter of recommendation to the Academy."[37] Two years later, when he was admitted to the American Bibliographer's Society, Schomburg wrote Bruce again: "I thank you for adding more weight to my head . . . by having used your good will in electing me to membership in such an exclusive society."[38]

Conclusion

Schomburg's migrations were the product of a specific moment of overlapping diasporas in the Atlantic world, particularly the interplay in nineteenth-century New York between the multiracial world of Antillean nationalism and the multiethnic world of Black neighborhoods and organizations. When Cubans of color sought to create their own social space within the broader émigré community, they found support from the Prince Hall Masons. When Puerto Ricans and Cubans of color left the meetings of the Cuban Revolutionary Party in New York, they went home to rooming houses, apartment buildings, and even households shared with African Americans. Participating in a movement with an official rhetoric of race blindness did not mean actually being blind to racial injustice or to the bonds of solidarity that might link people of African descent across national boundaries.

Thus when the independence movement in New York broke apart in 1898, and the anti-racist alliances there vanished, Schomburg did not reach out to Black North Americans as an oppressed Puerto Rican seeking allies. He reached out to Black North Americans as a "Negro" born in Puerto Rico. He was accepted in North American Pan-Africanist circles, not because all Puerto Ricans were seen as natural allies, but because, according to the racial philosophy espoused there, foreign *Negroes* were family—related by blood. He became a respected race leader not because he immediately became an assimilated North American Negro, but because in being fluent in Spanish and competent in French Schomburg was able to serve as a correspondent and translator between North American Blacks and a network of Black intellectuals that grew within the new imperial order in the Atlantic basin. He gained prestige in the institutions of Negro New York precisely because he was something between a foreigner and a Black North American. He gained prestige among Blacks in the Caribbean by becoming a race leader at the center of the wealthiest and most powerful Black middle class in the world.

Few Cubans and even fewer Puerto Ricans lived in New York in the period when Schomburg migrated and settled in the city. Afro-Latin@s who came in later years negotiated the complications of where they belonged in contexts different from the ones that he faced, including growing Latin@ neighborhoods and evolving racial discrimination against working-class Puerto Ricans of all colors. After the Second World War racial thinking in the United States ceased to define Hebrews, Celts, and Italians as distinct "races"—White but not quite White—but preserved that status for Latin@s. While important differences remained between the reception offered to White Latin@s and Latin@s of color, that contrast was not the same as it had been in the first decades of the century.

Still, if Schomburg's life were a product of the bygone world in which he lived, it nevertheless offers key lessons for understanding the broader experience of Afro-Latin@s in the United States. Although they frequently face the presumption that one is *either* Black or Latin@, Afro-Latin@s can have experiences and social contacts that link them to *both* communities. They negotiate parallel, if differently configured, exclusions as they move between Latin American and United States societies. And like Schomburg they can find spaces to exert leadership in struggles to make Latin@ communities live up to expressed ideals of racial and class harmony, in community-wide struggles constructed around ideas of Latin@ unity, and in struggles against racism constructed around ideas of unity among people of African descent from distinct backgrounds.

Notes

1. For further biographical detail see Elinor Des Verney Sinnette, *Arthur Alfonso Schomburg, Black Bibliophile and Collector: A Biography* (New York: New York Public Library; Detroit, Mich.: Wayne State University Press, 1989); Winston James, *Holding Aloft the Banner of Ethiopia: Caribbean Radicalism in Early Twentieth-Century America* (London: Verso, 1998), 193–231; and Jesse Hoffnung-Garskof, "The Migrations of Arturo Schomburg: On Being *Antillano*, Negro, and Puerto Rican in New York, 1891–1917," *Journal of American Ethnic History* 21, no. 1 (2001): 3–49.

2. Arthur A. Schomburg, "Racial Integrity: A Plea for the Establishment of a Chair of Negro History in Our Schools and Colleges. Address Delivered at the Teachers' Summer Class at the Cheney Institute, Pennsylvania, July 1913," Negro Society for Historical Research, Occasional Papers No. 3 (Yonkers, N.Y.: August Valentine Bernier, 1913), 7, 19.

3. Tomás Blanco, *El prejuicio racial en Puerto Rico* (Río Piedras, P.R.: Ediciones Huracán, 1985 [1942]), 103. See also Lawrence Chenault, *The Puerto Rican Migrant in New York City*

(New York: Columbia University Press, 1938); and W. A. Domingo, "Gift of the Black Tropics," in *The New Negro: An Interpretation*, edited by Alain Locke (New York: Albert and Charles Boni, 1925), 342.

4. James, *Holding Aloft the Banner of Ethiopia*, 198.

5. Petition for a warrant for a new lodge to be named "Sol de Cuba," submitted to "the M.W. Grand Master of the H.F. of F.A.M. for the State of New York," in New York, June 26, 1880, Harry A. Williamson Papers, Schomburg Center for Research in Black Culture (hereafter Williamson, SCRBC). See Eduardo Torres-Cuevas, "Los cuerpos masónicos cubanos durante el siglo XIX," and Manuel Hernández González, "La Orden Cubana de los Caballeros de la Luz en el exilio norteamericano," both in *Masonería Española y Américana* (Zaragoza, Spain: Centro de Estudios Históricos de la Masonería Española, 1993). "The History of Prince Hall Lodge No. 38." Published by the Prince Hall Lodge No. 38 F. & A. M., P. H., included in a "Souvenir Program—75th Anniversary," New York, November 4, 1956, Williamson, SCRBC.

6. "Libro de Actas—Gran Logia Luz de Caballero," April 11, 1878. Logia Luz de Caballero, Manuscript Collection, Pennsylvania Historical Society, Philadelphia (hereafter Logia Luz, PHA).

7. "Liturgia Orden Caballeros de la Luz," 1879, Logia Luz, PHA.

8. "Libro de Actas," February 9, 1879, March 7, 1879, Logia Luz, PHA. See also Ada Ferrer, *Insurgent Cuba: Race, Nation, and Revolution* (Chapel Hill: University of North Carolina Press, 1999), 70–89.

9. Ferrer, *Insurgent Cuba*, esp. 170–94.

10. "Libro de Actas," March 21, 1879, Logia Luz, PHA. On the deterioration of class relations in the immigration, see Gerald Poyo, *With All and for the Good of All: The Emergence of Popular Nationalism in the Cuban Communities of the United States, 1848–1898* (Durham, N.C.: Duke University Press, 1989), 65–73.

11. "Libro de Actas," Logia Luz, PHA. See also Manuel Hernández González, "La Orden Cubana de los Caballeros de la Luz en el exilio norteamericano," in *Masonería Española y Américana* (Zaragoza, Spain, 1993).

12. For Serra's discussion of charity and La Liga, see his speech at the April 17, 1892, meeting of the PRC at Harman Hall, which was published in *Patria*, Suplemento 7, April 23, 1892.

13. Rafael Serra's "Nuestra Labor" was first published in *La Doctrina de Martí*; later it was reprinted in *Ensayos Políticos* (New York: Imprenta de P. J. Díaz, 1896), 133–34.

14. In Sol de Cuba the membership as well as the leadership seems to have been composed entirely of men of color. In this it may have been akin to the Sociedades de Color, which appeared on the island in the 1880s with the project of racial uplift and advancement. See Aline Helg, *Our Rightful Share: The Afro-Cuban Struggle for Equality, 1886–1912* (Chapel Hill: University of North Carolina Press, 1995), esp. 30–41.

15. The information in these paragraphs comes from a comparison of Sol de Cuba lodge membership lists with U.S. federal census returns for 1880 and 1900. The lodge lists are from Williamson, SCRBC.

16. See Schomburg's undated prospectus for a cookbook and social history of Negro cooking in Schomburg Papers, SCRBC.

17. Martí, "Mi Raza," *Patria*, 1893.

18. Ibid.

19. Figueroa launched this criticism of the lawyer Enrique José Varona, who led an effort by White professional exiles to draft laws for the future Cuban republic without consulting the base of the party. See *Doctrina de Martí*, January 30, 1897, cited in Josefina Toledo, *Sotero Figueroa, Editor de Patria: Apuntes para una biografía* (Havana: Editorial Letras Cubanas, 1985), 89.

20. A list of political and social clubs and the leadership was included in each issue of *Patria*. The evidence in this paragraph comes from a comparison of those leaders with the U.S. federal census returns for 1880 and 1900.

21. The evidence in this paragraph comes from a comparison between Club Borinquen and Las Dos Antillas membership lists and the U.S. federal census for 1880 and 1900. Membership information comes from early issues of *Patria*, *Antillas*, SCRBC. Another member of the Borinquen leadership, Rafael Delgado, was also a man of color. He founded and led an independent club as well, called "La Equidad." This club seemingly resembles La Igualdad and may well have been a Sociedad de Color.

22. The explanation that Figueroa and Marín published for why they left the Autonomista Party for the Cuban Revolutionary Party did not discuss the question of racial equality directly. "Del Club Borinquen al Pueblo Puertorriqueño," *Patría*, March 19, 1892.

23. Toledo *Sotero Figueroa*, 80.

24. *Antillas*, SCRBC. For the events and speeches at the Special General Assembly in "Military Hall," see Minutes from October 6, 1895.

25. Ibid.

26. Ibid.

27. These data come from a comparison of club membership with U.S. federal census returns for 1900 and 1910, consulted on Ancestry.com.

28. Jesús Colón, *A Puerto Rican in New York and Other Sketches* (New York: Mainstream Publishers, 1961), 44.

29. This data for persons born in Puerto Rico and living in New York was compiled through Ancestry.com indexes of the 1900 and 1910 federal census returns.

30. Report of the Sol de Cuba Lodge No. 38, Williamson, SCRBC.

31. Des Verney Sinnette, *Arthur Alfonso Schomburg*, 35.

32. Schomburg told Ira de A. Reid that "the Cuban Negro, who laid the foundation of the great tobacco industries in the United States . . . [has] been made useless and forced out, being substituted in a large measure by the whites and modern machinery" (Schomburg to Ira de A. Reid, July 18, 1935, Schomburg Papers, SCRBC).

33. Martin Summers, *Manliness and Its Discontents: The Black Middle Class and the Transformation of Masculinity, 1900–1930* (Chapel Hill: University of North Carolina Press, 2004), 25–65; William A. Muraskin, *Middle-Class Blacks in a White Society: Prince Hall Freemasonry in America* (Berkeley, Calif.: University of California Press, 1975), 25–42.

34. See Des Verney Sinnette, *Arthur Alfonso Schomburg*, 41, 190; and Summers, *Manliness and Its Discontents*.

35. Schomburg, "Racial Integrity," 5–6.

36. For an analysis of the importance of social clubs, dances, and elected offices in

determining the status of African Americans in the 1920s and 1930s see the sociological work by St. Claire Drake and Horace Cayton in *Black Metropolis* (Chicago: University of Chicago Press, 1940), 669–70, 688–715.

37. Schomburg to Bruce, May, 1914, Bruce Papers, SCRBC.

38. Schomburg to Bruce, September 5, 1916, Bruce Papers, SCRBC. Schomburg was also an active member and sometime officer of the Urban League, the YMCA, the Negro Society for Historical Research, the Association of Trade and Commerce, the Business and Professional Men's Forum, the Harlem Citizens League for Fair Play, the NAACP, and several fraternal organizations including Kappa Alpha Psi. See Victoria Ortiz, "Arthur A. Schomburg: A Biographical Essay," in *The Legacy of Arthur A. Schomburg: A Celebration of the Past, A Vision for the Future* (New York: New York Public Library, 1986), 63.

EVELYNE LAURENT-PERRAULT

Invoking Arturo Schomburg's Legacy in Philadelphia

I am a Venezuelan of Haitian and Venezuelan background and therefore I am an Afro-Latina. My identity as an Afro-Latina is one that I have come to embrace most strongly as a result of the twelve years that I have lived in the United States.

In January 1996 I had the honor to be appointed as the director of the Julia de Burgos Bookstore at Taller Puertorriqueño, Inc. Taller is a nonprofit arts, culture, and education organization located in North Philadelphia. For over thirty years Taller has served primarily Latin@ and, to a lesser extent, African American communities. In addition to the bookstore, Taller Puertorriqueño has an art gallery and a second building that functions as the education and theater space where after-school programs, summer camps, and a range of cultural activities take place year-round.

This was the second job I had since settling in Philadelphia. Before my move I lived for two years in Cameroon where I worked as a field biologist managing a research station. While in West Africa many of my other personal and intellectual interests began to gain strength, and I decided to put my biology career on hold for what I thought at the time was going to be a short while.

Working at Taller's bookstore gave me the opportunity to interact with many people on a daily basis, especially but not limited to the Latin@ community. By the second week on the job I began to meet other Black Latin@s who, like me, had stories to share. Many of their stories were painful, as they concerned experiences of rejection, prejudice, and discrimination within the Latin@ community. I knew what they meant, for I had experienced similar situations both in the United States and in Venezuela. After a few weeks I realized that I was not alone and that my impression that the Latin@ community harbored racist values was not unique.

Nearly all Afro-Latin@s whom I met at Taller told me how happy they felt that Taller had hired an Afro-Latina to be the face of the bookstore, which was one of Taller's most public programs. These who did not consider themselves as being of African descent had a plethora of responses to me being at Taller. Some of these Latin@s couldn't believe that I was a Latina who could speak Spanish, and many did not believe that I could be the bookstore director. When I would explain that I was Latina they would try to guess my country of origin, often citing Panama or Cuba but never Venezuela. I can't blame them because the Venezuelan community in Philadelphia is very small and most of the information that the Latin@ population receives comes from the media. These media reports often focus only on beauty pageants, which of course rarely include women of African descent.

I also had conversations with the African American visitors to Taller, who were surprised to learn that there are Black people in Venezuela. Those who had only been exposed to mainstream TV networks had a hard time imagining Latin America's diversity and the large presence of people of African descent.

Such conversations continued over the first year that I worked at the bookstore. Among Afro-Latin@s there was a common sense that prejudice and discrimination within the Latin@ community came from the tremendous lack of information and silence about our African heritage. This erasure can be traced to our colonial experience, which continues to shape the Latin American discourse on race. Specifically, in most Latin American nations the ideas of mestizaje and blanqueamiento (miscegenation and whitening) continue to be upheld as formulas for upward mobility and identity.

As my informal exchanges continued with Taller's bookstore customers, Afro-Latin@s expressed their wish to see some sort of event that could address the ignorance within the Latin@ communities about the contributions of Africa and its people to our histories and cultures. They wanted a space that could unmask the lie that Latin@ communities were free of prejudice and discrimination. I began to sense that these conversations needed to happen in a different context and with a wider audience so that many could speak and many more could hear and learn.

I proposed to Johnny Irizarry, the executive director of Taller Puertorriqueño, the idea of having a cultural space to explore the African presence in Latin@ histories and to challenge discrimination and prejudice within the Latin@ community. He was immediately enthusiastic about the idea, and together Johnny and I planned out what has been for the past twelve years the annual Arturo Schomburg Symposium. Johnny proposed the name of the venue to honor the famous Afro–Puerto Rican Arturo Alfonso Schomburg, a bibliophile and scholar who dedicated his life to collecting and writing about the achievements of Africans and the diasporas.

The first symposium featured the Afro-Puerto Rican Hector Bonilla, who at that time was admissions officer at Rutgers University, and the African American Thomas Morton, a former Peace Corps Volunteer in Latin America and a doctoral candidate at the University of Pennsylvania. Johnny proposed inviting a third guest speaker, the Afro-Puerto Rican activist and independent scholar Miriam Jiménez Román who had a long history of research on Afro-Latin@ subjects and who was then a curator at the Schomburg Center. Our three speakers volunteered their services because Taller did not have the funds to provide honoraria. The program was scheduled for February 22, 1997, during Black History Month in order to highlight the fact that Latin@s are also part of Black history.

We were enthusiastic but uncertain about whether the public would welcome and support this initiative. We were fortunate that Kevin Carter, a reporter of Afro-Cuban ancestry at the *Philadelphia Inquirer*, wrote an excellent promotional article about the symposium that appeared on the cover of the newspaper's magazine a few days before the event.

The first Arturo Schomburg Symposium was a major success. We literally ran out of space. The program was scheduled to begin at 4:00 PM but by 3:30 the place was filled with people. Miriam Jiménez Román opened the conference with a presentation about Arturo Schomburg's life and work. Hector Bonilla spoke on the social, economic, and historical contributions of Afro-Latin@s, after engaging the audience in what he calls the "Dinga or Mandiga Test." Thomas Morton shared some of his findings and insights about the Palenque San Basilio, a maroon community in northern Colombia that not only survived colonial threats and hardships but continues to the present day. Iris Brown spoke about the African presence in Puerto Rican food and, with Grupo Motivos, provided an exquisite dinner. After dinner a panel dialogue explored paths to establishing better bridges of communication and collaboration between Latin@s and African Americans. The enthusiastic crowd was so involved in the discussions that when the event was over we had to ask them to leave.

As a relatively recent arrival in Philadelphia, I don't know if any similar initiative had taken place before the first Schomburg Symposium. What I do know is that the folks who swarmed Taller looking for knowledge about Afro-Latin@s kept saying that it was about time to have this dialogue. Indeed, Philadelphia was eager to learn. People of all backgrounds had been waiting for a space of this nature to learn about how African we Latin@s really are. The annual Schomburg symposium was born, and Taller Puertorriqueño committed itself to continue with the event every February during Black History Month.

The symposium generated a positive energy and in my opinion formally introduced the notion of "Afro-Latinoness" in the region. Some attendees left the first symposium feeling that they could not wait for an entire year to continue the dialogue. People kept calling—from as far as Vancouver, Canada—to ask about the outcome of the symposium.

As a result, a group of us gathered on a Saturday afternoon in May at Taller Puertorriqueño. We were students, scholars, activists, artists, educators, and media professionals, among others, from Puerto Rico, Brazil, Haiti, Colombia, and the United States, and we were Latin@s and African Americans coming together in search of paths to growth. We talked for over eight hours, sharing the pain accumulated through years of discriminatory treatment, racist jokes, and rejection from our own community. It was a healing process for many of us, and the beginning of a project of creating more spaces and occasions for learning. We realized that by sharing our experiences we were all learning from each other as well. After several meetings we established a group named ENCUENTRO, Inc. The stated objectives of the symposium are mirrored in those of the organization, which also seeks to develop and strengthen connections between and throughout the African diaspora.

As a group ENCUENTRO, Inc. cosponsored with Mercer Community College a regional conference in New Jersey, and with the Greenfield Intercultural Center at the University of Pennsylvania a series of presentations and dialogues. In addition, ENCUENTRO, Inc. participated in several Afro-Latin@ international dialogues that took place between Afro-Latin American organizations prior to the United Nations Conference Against Racism that was held in Durban, South Africa, in 2001. Since its beginnings ENCUENTRO, Inc. has attempted to strengthen a network of Afro-diaspora activists, scholars, and artists. Currently, ENCUENTRO, Inc. maintains an electronic mailing list with information reaching about one hundred members across the nation, and the group continues to serve as a collaborator with the annual Schomburg Symposium.

Meanwhile, at Taller Puertorriqueño the symposium has continued as an annual event that each year explores a different theme or aspect of Africa and its diaspora and its connection to the Latin@ heritage. This exploration of our commonalities with the African American community and of the history behind the silence that has prevented Latin American and Latin@ cultures at large from knowing and embracing their African heritage has become an important part of the work of Taller. Over the years, themes have included spirituality and musicality; the African presence in our Latin@ and Latin American literature; common roots in dance and movement in African and Latin@ traditions; the African influence on Latin@ foods; women in the African diaspora; the African presence in Latin American and Caribbean contemporary visual arts; and the African roots of hip-hop in the Latin@ diaspora. By collaborating with other institutions, most notably Temple University and the University of Pennsylvania, Taller has been able to tap into important intellectual and organizational resources and expand its constituency.

It is impossible to narrate in detail the breadth and quality of information and expertise that has been presented at and generated through the past twelve gatherings of the Arturo Schomburg Symposium. At the symposium scholars, artists, poets, novelists, dancers, musicians, performers, filmmakers, visual artists, activists, journalists, spiritual leaders, women, men, and youth from such places as Brazil, Venezuela, Peru, Colombia, Puerto Rico, Cuba, Mexico, Jamaica, and Trinidad have come to share their expertise through talks and dialogues as well as dance performances, music and dance workshops, poetry slams, film screenings, music performances and more. And we feel that this is just the beginning.

Afro-Latin@s on the Color Line

The stories of many Afro-Latin@s, both prominent and lesser known, tell of their precarious situation at the racial and cultural seams of society in the United States. "Spanish-speaking Negroes" were viewed as outsiders even as they suffered the indignities of Jim Crow racism alongside African Americans and other Blacks. Afro-Cubans such as Evelio Grillo, Melba Alvarado, Graciela, Minnie Miñoso, and Mario Bauzá, and Afro–Puerto Ricans such as Jesús Colón and the Haslip-Viera family navigated the color line in a variety of ways, contributing their energies and talents—and

Two women at a meeting of the American Labor Party, circa 1950. (Photograph by Rómulo Lachatañeré; Photographs and Prints Division, Schomburg Center for Research in Black Culture, the New York Public Library, Astor, Lenox and Tilden Foundations; courtesy of Diana Lachatanere)

making a place for themselves—in multiple spaces. Although new immigrants to the United States encountered a variant of the same racism they had experienced in Cuba and Puerto Rico, they found opportunities which had been largely unavailable to them in their countries of origin. Ironically, for many Afro-Latin@s the overt nature of segregation would actually prove to be a refreshing change from the hypocritical rhetoric of Latin American and Caribbean "racial democracy." For those like Evelio Grillo who were born and raised in the segregated South, access to United States society came unequivocally through incorporation into the African American community. Despite a long career in which Grillo often served as a bridge between communities, when he was asked by an interviewer about his identification with African Americans, the nonagenarian immediately responded: "I *am* African American." Clearly, the color line posed a range of different options for Afro-Latin@s and depended on factors such as generation, time of arrival, phenotype, and location.

EVELIO GRILLO

Black Cuban, Black American

Black Cubans and White Cubans

While maintaining its identity as a distinctly Latin community, Ybor City, my birthplace, lies completely within the city of Tampa, Florida, which governs it. Culturally, socially, and economically a small city within a city, its residents were a mixture of white Cubans, Italians, black Cubans, black Americans, Spaniards, and a not very visible number of white Americans of European extraction. During the years between roughly 1880 and 1930, Tampa flourished at the center of the worldwide cigar-making industry. A great portion of the industry was in Ybor City, giving Tampa the identity of "Cigar-Making Capital of the World."

Ybor City (pronounced EE-bor) took its name from Vicente Martínez Ybor, one of the earliest manufacturers to build a cigar factory in Tampa.

My parents were part of the large migration of Cubans who settled in Ybor City seeking jobs in the fledgling industry. My father, Antonio, worked as a "finisher" — a very prestigious job involving the final sculpture of the cigars into identical shapes. My mother, Amparo, worked as a *bonchera*, a "buncher." She gathered the inner leaves of the cigars into the long, rounded shapes to which the finishers applied the final, prime, wrapping leaf.

While the preferred tobacco for cigars still grew in Cuba, the making of a very large proportion of the finished product, the actual cigars, took place in the United States. This strategy yielded enormous economic benefits. The machinery and materials needed to make and package the cigars abounded in the United States, and tariffs on the finished product presented no costs if they were manufactured in the United States.

Moreover, the United States provided the primary market for cigars. Enough trade moved back and forth between Tampa and Havana to support two roundtrips a week by the shipping line which served the ports.

Black Cubans and white Cubans migrated by the thousands from Cuba. Legal separation of the two races did not prevail in Cuba as it did in the United States, but discrimination along racial lines and separation along social and economic lines existed. In Cuba, affluent black Cubans moved within the society of the affluent. "Es Negro, pero es Negro blanco" (He is a black man, but he is a white black man) was an expression I heard often.

Separation of the races by residence was not practiced, although separation by economic class made for de facto segregation by race since discrimination kept black Cubans in a second-class position economically. Blacks generally did not live in luxurious houses.

However, commercial and governmental facilities were accessible to all in Cuba. Blacks attended, taught, and served as administrators in the schools. Blacks used the hospitals and clinics without limitation, and they served as staff members in most capacities. Blacks also served in the military without restrictions. The general who had led the Cuban revolution against Spain was a dark mulatto, Antonio Maceo. As Cubans entered Ybor City, however, they were sorted out. Black Cubans went to a neighborhood, immediately east of Nebraska Avenue, inhabited by black Americans and a scattering of poor whites. White Cubans had a much wider range of choices, though most of them chose to remain in Ybor City. A scattering went to live in West Tampa, across the river, in a sparsely developed section of the larger city.

Nebraska Avenue formed the western boundary of Ybor City. Twenty-second Street formed, roughly, the eastern boundary. The avenues ran east and west, with Sixteenth Avenue forming a northern limit and Sixth Avenue a southern one. From Sixteenth Avenue to roughly Twenty-second Avenue were scattered more affluent white Cubans and Italians and Spaniards, some living a semi-rural life with a cow or two, goats, and chickens.

Black Cubans worked in the factories alongside white Cubans. While my mother formed interracial friendships at work, few if any such friendships extended to visits in the homes. Nor did whites and blacks attend church together. Black Cubans had their own mutual benefit society and social center, La Unión Martí-Maceo.

Black Cubans and white Cubans worked side by side in the cigar-making industry. But I know of only one black Cuban who won a status above that of worker; that person was Facundo Acción, who achieved the highly honored position of lector, the reader.

Black Cubans and white Cubans interacted in the streets and in public places such as grocery stores, produce stands, meat markets, and in the corner saloon, where men who were not at work gathered in the afternoon to watch the throwing of the *bolita* bag and the selection of the day's number, which paid lucky ticket holders five dollars for every penny wagered.

Bolita was Tampa's version of the numbers game. A hundred small balls, each numbered, were placed in a cloth bag. A small crowd of men gathered to watch the proceedings. At the appointed hour, the bag, carefully sewn tight under the watchful eyes of the onlookers, was thrown randomly across the room to an onlooker. He, in turn, would gather one ball carefully into his hand, through the cloth of the bag, and let the other ninety-nine dangle below. One person tied a string around the lucky numbered ball and cut that section of the cloth away.

Finally, the person holding the lucky ball showed it and announced the number. Within minutes, the word rushed throughout the town, so the lucky ones could celebrate their good fortune and the unlucky ones could bemoan their fate. That is why the populace described the process as "throwing the number." That this racket enjoyed "protection" from the authorities appeared obvious. No attempt was made to hide the ceremony, held daily at the same time and in the same place.

Blacks and whites visited back and forth at wakes and funerals. A white Cuban or two might show up at the spiritualist séances to which my mother dragged me weekly. Blacks and whites belonged to the same grocery cooperative and to the same pre-pay health clinic.

My mother also took me to one meeting of a labor union, which held its meetings and celebrations in a modern labor temple. As a child, I attended a meeting held in connection with a strike or the threat of one.

Then there was baseball, to which the entire town paid homage under the leadership of Al López, legendary catcher of the Brooklyn Dodgers and a native of Ybor City. He spent much of his winters in Tampa basking in the glory of his fame.

During the World Series the local Spanish-language daily newspaper provided an elaborate mechanical display which represented the action from wherever the games were being played. Shiny metal balls represented the players, and the game could be followed as the balls moved around a magnetic board representing the playing field.

It seemed that the entirety of Ybor City gathered in front of the mesmerizing display, cheering or booing depending upon the course of the game. This was one activity I could enjoy without special permission from Mother. Many elder male friends of the family would keep watchful eyes on me. That kept her from worrying.

That was the extent of the limited association between black Cubans and white Cubans. I don't remember playing with a single white Cuban child. I remember the faces of only three white Cuban men who came to the house, two as music teachers and one as a stout, jolly Sunday boarder whom we called "Tío Pío."

With the exception of the local corner bar, which they could patronize, black Cubans did not share recreational activities with white Cubans. They were not hired as clerks, or even as menial help in the restaurants. There were no black Cuban entrepreneurs except for a tailor, a barber, and a very successful dry-cleaning establishment.

In the main, black Cubans and white Cubans lived apart from one another in Ybor City.

Black Cubans and Black Americans

In the ghetto within the ghetto located in the southwest corner of Ybor City, formed by Nebraska Avenue and Sixth Avenue, black Cubans and black Americans lived together. Black Cubans formed the larger group in this neighborhood, but neither group held local political power. A very few men developed limited power by extracting favors from the ruling groups of white Americans and, later, of Italian Americans.

Most black Americans lived west of Nebraska Avenue. No black Cubans lived there. This large section of the city above Nebraska housed solidly black American neighborhoods. They could be distinguished along social and economic lines. The closer to Ybor City, the poorer they were. The farther west one walked, toward the main shopping and commercial streets of Tampa, the more substantial the homes became and the more elaborate became the landscaping.

Public elementary schools functioned in this section, as did large black churches and funeral parlors. The Central Life Insurance Company, an important enterprise in the black American community, had its operations there also.

Central Avenue provided the bustling commercial center. Along its seven or eight block stretch were found the offices of the local dentist and the local doctor; a large drugstore (complete with modern fountain); the storefront "colored" branch of the public library; a shoemaker; two barber shops; several restaurants; real estate offices; the town's largest saloon, Moon's; the "colored" movie house, the Central Theater; and various other small businesses.

No single broad statement can encompass the relationship between black Cubans and their American counterparts. At the time of my birth, my mother's family had lived in the United States twenty-five or more years. Mother had attended elementary school in Jacksonville, Florida. This still made us rank newcomers, for black Americans traced their ancestry back for more than three centuries in the United States.

Our parents all came from Cuba and spoke little or no English. Differences in language and culture became formidable impediments to the full integration of black Cubans within the black American community.

While black Cuban children became fluent in English, our parents could not navigate the difficult waters of language and culture. Within our homes and in the Cuban community we spoke Spanish. These factors lent an edgy quality to the interactions between black Cubans and black Americans. [. . .]

A common racial identity as blacks did not bridge the gulf that existed between the two groups. Black Americans spoke English and followed Protestant religions. Black Cubans spoke Spanish and practiced Catholicism.

But other realities—such as play, school, work, friendships, love, sex, and marriage—bonded young black Cubans to black Americans. It was from black Americans that we learned about black colleges, for example. We learned that we could attend them. I don't know any black Cuban college graduate of my generation and of all the generations preceding desegregation who is not a graduate of a historically black college.

The relatively small number of black Cubans who entered college achieved nearly full integration, socially, into black American life: the language was the same, their accents the same, their dress the same. Their dating involved almost exclusively eligible black American counterparts.

Those who did not attend college went to live circumscribed lives in the Latin ghettoes of New York City, to which my generation largely migrated along with their parents. Contact with American blacks was minimal in the early days of the migration to New York City.

During the Great Depression of the early thirties they traveled to New York City in large numbers—packed ten into an eight-passenger limousine at five dollars per person, I was told. This exodus led to a vastly intensified movement of the young black Cubans, who remained in Tampa, toward black Americans. Those who stayed in Tampa enjoyed larger and larger places in black American life, as teachers, as social workers, and some as leaders in the black American community. They chose black American spouses almost exclusively. Many of them attended college, with the largest number at Florida A & M, the public university for blacks.

Our choices became clear: to swim in black American society or drown in the Latin ghettoes of New York City, never to be an integral part of American life.

This is why the experience of black Cubans who joined with black Americans is so different from that of black Cubans who remained loosely tethered to the white Cuban society. Integration presented us with simple options: join the black American society, with its rich roots deep in this country, or have no American roots at all.

We had no problems with those we knew as neighbors or schoolmates, mostly teasing and name-calling. We developed close friendships flowing from our school relationships. We did not, however, visit one another's homes very often.

The age of the automobile had just begun to flower. I know of only two black Cuban families who owned automobiles. We traveled by trolley or we walked. That meant that we had to walk through the black American neighborhoods above Nebraska Avenue if we wanted to go to the Central Theater. That sometimes became a cause for fear. The black Americans who lived in the blocks immediately above Nebraska Avenue did not always accept us, particularly those of us whom they did not know because we did not attend the public schools.

The feelings were reciprocated. Our parents' fears of black Americans were transmitted to us in the home, where they lived in isolation both from the white Cuban and black American worlds. So we young people traveled in groups, walking those dreaded blocks from Nebraska Avenue to Central Avenue and back to attend the "colored" theater to see the movie heroes of the day—Tom Mix, Rin Tin Tin—and the thrilling serials.

Some of our fears had a basis in reality, though nothing as serious as we envisioned. I remember being run home from Central Avenue during one summer when I had the duty of taking a warm lunch to my sister, Sylvia, who worked as a receptionist and assistant for the local black American dentist, Dr. Ervin.

I rode the trolley to take lunch to her, thereby assuring that the food would be warm. On the way back home, however, I walked so as to save the five cents in trolley fare. As I walked the five and one-half blocks from the trolley stop to the dentist's office, I was approached by Jason, a tall, lanky, black American classmate—a good-looking, confident boy. He had a mildly menacing look on his face. I thought I knew what he was after when he asked, "What are you doing in this part of town, Grillo?" I had had no previous direct conversation with Jason.

"Taking lunch to my sister."

"She works around here?"

"Yes, for Dr. Ervin, down the street."

"How long are you going to be up there?"

"About an hour, perhaps."

"Well, we'll be waiting for you when you come out, okay?"

"Okay!" I was intimidated, for I knew that he had no friendly business to transact with me. My tormentors, I assumed, intended to lie in wait for me to beat me up and to do other horrible things to me. I now believe that their intent was more to scare than to harm, for I was never touched during my two years at Booker T. Washington High. They could have had it in for me, for I had captured the attention of Pauline, an absolutely ravishing black American beauty whom they thought belonged to them. I had had the temerity to meet Pauline at the movies twice and to walk her home the long way, where the dark streets and trees provided wonderful settings for kissing and light petting.

So the fear was real and I took no chances. I came downstairs from the dentist's office and waited in the entryway of the building until certain that none of the feared group remained within a block of the building.

Dashing to an alley across the street in the middle of the block, I lost myself quickly within it. Then I threaded my way carefully from alley to alley, until I reached safety on the other side of Nebraska Avenue, in my own neighborhood.

This was the simple life of caste and class as it is lived out in all generations and in all places. Black Cuban cigar makers were an elite. They were highly skilled and they worked in a very intellectual environment. In Cuba they lived in the cities, and they participated in the intellectual and political life of the nation. Their rural brothers and sisters worked in the cane and tobacco fields. They did not enjoy the same level of education and social sophistication.

Some among the black Cuban cigar makers became poets, writers, artists, and musicians. They moved comfortably in the society of small tradesmen. They found their place, marginally between the upper-lower and lower-middle classes.

In Tampa they had substantial roles in the politics of Cuba; they helped to finance the Cuban war of independence against Spain and harbored the leaders of the insurrection. Moreover, they had a Spanish daily newspaper to read.

Between Nebraska and Central Avenues, on the other hand, lived many unskilled and illiterate black Americans, living what black Cuban adults considered a rough life. Though a large number of them were middle class in income, outlook, and way of life, very large numbers of them were clearly in the lowest economic and social classes. Interactions between our two groups increased only slowly, though steadily, until today the two are comfortably integrated as part of a larger black group.

In earlier days, however, a definite guardedness characterized the relationship between those who were not yet good friends. Our parents, who had limited contact with black Americans, sometimes spoke disparagingly of them, criticizing their behavior and attributing the violence that occurred within the lowest economic class to the entire black community.

As children we had intensive interaction with black Americans in school. We became good friends. We studied with them, we played with them, we fell in love with them and, as we grew older, we married them. Our feelings toward them were very positive and we were sensitive to remarks critical of them.

Reciprocally, they considered us part of the black community for that was the way we were perceived by the larger American society. Our fears of being attacked, while real, were not borne out by what actually happened. Not once were we molested. I remember only one altercation between a group of black Americans and one of black Cuban adolescents. It took place near the border between the two ghettoes. In a half-hearted rock-throwing fight that did not last very long, no one was injured, not even slightly.

We had a full calendar of community events at La Unión Martí-Maceo, our own black Cuban community center. Frequent Latin dances, traveling vaudeville shows from Cuba, and an occasional play in Spanish that we staged ourselves rounded out a busy schedule for our community.

Some of the young adult black Cubans, mostly males, attended dances held by black American organizations at our center where a large dance hall was a favored venue. In the early 1930s a "colored" movie theater, constructed in Ybor City, drew nightly a thoroughly mixed crowd of black Americans and black Cubans. The theater served also as a stopping place for road shows. Our community fluttered for days in anticipation of the appearance of Cab Calloway, then at the height of his career. Generally, however, we did not attend plays, concerts, recitals, and lectures presented in English. These were held in the large Protestant churches in the black American ghetto, where we seldom ventured other than to attend school.

There was one week during the year, however, during which the entire black American and black Cuban communities became one. Gasparilla

Day and the South Florida Fair, held in conjunction with each other and during the same week, helped greatly to cement our identities as part of one large black community.

Both communities took to the streets as one large mass, walking toward downtown Tampa to view the elaborate and exciting Gasparilla parade. Gasparilla was a pirate who, history or legend held, had roamed the waters outside of Tampa during the eighteenth century.

Tampa businessmen, dressed as pirates, rode gaily decorated floats in a long, colorful parade. We lined up for blocks to see the thrilling spectacle and to scramble for the trinkets that these pirates scattered along the route. The tradition continues to this day, and it is now integrated. We have our own black pirates, now!

The South Florida Fair held two Children's Days. On the first, called simply Children's Day, all white children entered free of charge. They included some very light mulatto (mixed black and white) children whose families were "passing" (counting themselves as white) and were allowed to do so by the white Cubans and the white American and Italian community, which had now begun to develop power in the governance of Tampa.

On Colored Children's Day, the succeeding day, black children could enter free of charge, and the two black ghettoes would empty of children early in the morning. Eager with anticipation of our funfest, for which we had been saving coins for weeks, we swarmed by the thousands to the fair. We waited impatiently for an hour or so until the gates opened.

During the wait, a babble of voices would be talking and yelling to friends:

"I'm going to head for the flying planes."

"For me it will be the electric bumping cars."

"I'll take the giant merry-go-round."

"Food, food, food, that's what I want first, a jumbo hot dog and a Coke."

"I'm not going to see the exhibits until I've done my first round of rides."

Perhaps, I hoped secretly, I would have one ride with Verdell, the unrequited love of my childhood. I followed her discreetly for twenty yards or so, but she was obviously ignoring me. So, in defeat, I withdrew from the chase. I now realize that Verdell was a child of mixed Cuban and American parentage. Her father, a Cuban, and her mother, an American, divorced when Verdell was very young. Though Verdell lived in the Cuban ghetto, she had none of her activities within it. Assuming her mother's identity, she attended a Protestant church and had her social life within the black American ghetto. She was comfortable and very popular as a black American beauty, the rage among black American boys older than I was. I believe that she considered me childish and immature. She was right.

So I spent my time at the fair in the company of young boys. We roamed the fairgrounds like adolescent bull elephants, waiting for the maturity and the strength to compete for females. We had fun, but not as much as the boys who had dates. When not so engaged I became the millstone around my sister Sylvia's neck, impeding her flirtations and fun with boys. That suited Mother just fine. She listened to Sylvia's complaints about me with little or no sympathy.

Social class, different languages, and different cultures divided the two communities. Black Cubans still built dependent relationships with black Americans, especially our black American teachers with whom we formed deep, affectionate bonds. But we lived clearly on the margins of black American society while we worked out our daily existence in the black Cuban ghetto in Ybor City. Yet our identity as black Americans developed strongly. I remember but one black Cuban hero, Antonio Maceo, the general who had led the fight for Cuba's independence from Spain. There were no photographs in my home of historically significant Cuban blacks.

My heart and mind belonged to Nat Turner, Frederick Douglass, Harriet Tubman, Sojourner Truth, Paul Laurence Dunbar, John Brown, Paul Robeson, Langston Hughes, W. E. B. Du Bois, Allison Davis, Alain Locke, and the brothers James Weldon and James Rosamond Johnson, who wrote the song very dear to my heart, "Lift Every Voice and Sing."

[*Editorial note*: The Depression that followed the stock market crash of 1929 had a profound impact on the Grillo family. Unable to find employment, his mother returned to Cuba and the rest of the family dispersed. Evelio's African American mentor encouraged him to go north to further his education and in 1934 fifteen-year-old Evelio went to live with his brother, Henry, in Washington, D.C., where he enrolled at Dunbar High School.]

At that time, three high schools were provided for blacks in Washington. Whatever their history, the schools clearly reflected a separation of students by social classes. Armstrong High, right across the street from Dunbar [High School], offered vocational education. Cardozo High School, about ten blocks away, served those who were preparing for work in the business world, largely as secretaries and bookkeepers. Dunbar served an educational elite. It dedicated itself entirely to the preparation of students

The student council of Dunbar High School, Washington, D.C., 1936. Evelio Grillo, president, sits at the center of the front row. Founded in 1870, Dunbar High was the first public high school for African Americans in the United States. (Arte Público Press, University of Houston)

for college. Students came to the schools from the black community as a whole.

Named for the celebrated black poet Paul Laurence Dunbar, the school drew its students from the large Washington black upper, middle, and upper-lower economic classes. Children of employees of the federal government, I believe, constituted a large segment of the student body. The parents of many held government jobs as elevator operators, janitors, messengers, clerical personnel, and, perhaps, some administrative personnel. Nonetheless, they earned high salaries compared to Washington's black population as a whole. Moreover, their jobs remained relatively secure during the Great Depression. They were then, as they are now, the basis of Washington's relatively large black middle class. The children of persons employed in service capacities constituted another substantial group of students. Their parents worked in the retail business establishments. Others worked in the homes of affluent families. Children of faculty members of Howard University, Miner Teachers College, of teachers in the public schools, children of professionals, small business owners, lawyers, doctors, dentists, accountants, ministers, nurses, and the like all set the tone of the school. [. . .]

Into this rarified atmosphere I was dropped. Clearly a bumpkin from the South, I was looked down upon because of my dress and my awkward, anxious demeanor. Besides, I spoke Spanish, and that, too, made me a strange one. I differed from the other students with foreign backgrounds, such as the children of diplomats from the Caribbean families. I felt more at home in the black American milieu than they did. My acculturation by the black American community of Tampa had taken. I *thought* black American. I *felt* black American. So, generally, my classmates took me in as just another black boy. There was still an uneasiness about me, but I attribute that to the differences in economic status between my classmates and me, and my blunders in verbal expressions foreign to them.

I think, too, that I tensed up in groups of boys. My mother's rigid prohibition of any play in boys' groups must have led to a certain social incompetence on my part. I believe that compensated for my insecurity by competitive, even conceited, academic functioning.

Some of my classmates became warm friends, something like my experience in Tampa. I was invited by two classmates to visit in their homes, even though I could not reciprocate because my brother and I lived in a single room in a rooming house without kitchen privileges. We ate our evening meal at a boarding house about three blocks from our home, and we scrounged for breakfast and lunch.

Only one classmate kept me off balance by drawing attention to gross language miscues and inappropriate behavior on my part. In retrospect, I believe he was threatened by my challenge to his position as one of the top students in the class.

One incident was dramatic—and traumatic for me. Jim and I met in a small group chatting in the hall. I don't remember what we were talking about, but in the midst of much laughter, I blurted out "You Negroes" in a mock-deprecating manner. Coming from anyone else in the group this would have been understood as the charade, played out almost daily by black people, of imitating white people exclaiming in exasperation about black behavior. It is very common in-group humor among blacks.

After the group dissolved, each member going to his particular class, Jim must have organized the lynching party, drawing attention to my words as an indication that I really did not consider myself black. Mrs. Brown, our homeroom teacher, apparently became aware that something was amiss. As I learned later, she spoke to one of the boys who told her what had happened. She quickly convened the members of the group who witnessed my faux pas. Having had no idea of anything unusual going on, the meeting caught me by surprise and unprepared.

Mrs. Brown introduced the subject, stating that she had become aware of a serious situation that she believed needed airing. To my complete surprise, Jim began recounting the incident and raising the question regarding my identity as a black. His face distorted with contempt for me, he had his nose tilted upward as though he were smelling something awful. No one else made any remarks. I believe that the other boys sympathized with my plight as Jim's victim.

Outraged, I attempted a few words of protest and defense, but I succeeded only in fuming. Finally, I began to sob quietly and disconsolately, feeling utterly defeated. My reaction must have sobered the group, for no one spoke for a full minute or two.

Then Mrs. Brown spoke softly. "I could not believe that what I heard actually happened. I hope that the matter has been cleared up. I know that you won't permit yourselves to be so unkind again." Actually, the boys were not very contrite, for they really had not participated fully in the travesty. They simply were following Jim, one of the two or three top students in the class, and certainly one of the most powerful.

The son of a very prominent Baptist minister, he came from a prestigious family. I believe that he fancied himself the social arbiter of the group, protecting the purity of the in-group of children of professionals. The others were more like bystanders as Jim carried out the mischievous and successful effort to put me in my place.

I was an easy target, for I had the permanent status of newcomer and outsider. I had entered Dunbar in the eleventh grade, whereas the class had established its social pecking order one year previously, in the tenth grade, and perhaps even earlier in the junior high schools. Besides, my behavior did not endear me to my classmates. I talked much more than I listened, and, in the manner of the very insecure, I had strong opinions on matters about which I knew very little. Besides, I had no pedigree. Clearly, I was near the bottom of the pecking order in "A" section. In Tampa, I had been a black boy fairly well integrated into the group. This was not the case in school in Washington. I had to earn my spurs all over again.

Jim feigned regret, condescendingly, and said words implying that, now he understood, he would permit me to remain in the circle of bona fide blacks. The other boys quickly reassured me, convinced now of my legitimacy.

I left the room confused, angry, and crestfallen. I walked home from school that afternoon in a daze. I did not tell anyone what had happened, not even Henry. I do not know why I remained silent. Perhaps I could not talk about the incident without breaking up. That provided sufficient motive for silence. Moreover, I carried a certain guilt, for I believed I must have done something wrong, since I drew this much attention. I have resented Jim all of my life. Not even his death several years ago has softened the feeling.

An unmistakable color line operated at Dunbar. Brown-skinned and light-skinned students predominated in every aspect of school life except athletics. Few very black students stood out in the school population. Those who did were academically brilliant or very talented. Their academic achievement did not always provide enhanced social status.

There was and there remains great resentment of the differential treatment accorded the dark students, especially the very dark students. To this day, some classmates refuse to participate in alumni activities, still harboring the resentment they experienced as adolescents in a color-based value system wherein they were the least prized as members.

I was brown-skinned. I passed the brown paper bag test.

"If you're light, you're all right; if you're brown, stick around; if you're black, stay back" is one ditty that the very black persons heard resentfully.

I believe I carried less baggage with respect to color. In Tampa, very [dark] students had not been as differentiated with respect to popularity and leadership roles as they were in Washington. Moreover, I was a black Cuban, a member of a definite language and cultural minority. In Tampa I had become accustomed to accepting black Americans, including a large number of very dark ones, as role models for my behavior. Generally, I escaped the resentment of my Dunbar fellow students with respect to the color issue. I navigated the Dunbar waters with relative success during my eighteen months there. My teachers were generous and kind to me. I believe that they had a special warmth for me as an underdog, having no mother or father, and living socially and economically on the other side of the tracks.

JESÚS COLÓN

A Puerto Rican in New York and Other Sketches

Little Things Are Big

It was very late at night on the eve of Memorial Day. She came into the subway at the 34th Street Pennsylvania Station. I am still trying to remember how she managed to push herself in with a baby on her right arm, a valise in her left hand, and two children, a boy and girl about three and five years old, trailing after her. She was a nice looking white lady in her early twenties.

At Nevins Street, Brooklyn, we saw her preparing to get off at the next station—Atlantic Avenue—which happened to be the place where I too had to get off. Just as it was a problem for her to get on, it was going to be a problem for her to get off the subway with two small children to be taken care of, a baby on her right arm, and a medium-sized valise in her left hand. And there I was, also preparing to get off at Atlantic Avenue, with no bundles to take care of—not even the customary book under my arm without which I feel that I am not completely dressed.

As the train was entering the Atlantic Avenue station, some white man stood up from his seat and helped her out, placing the children on the long, deserted platform. There were only two adult persons on the long platform some time after midnight on the eve of that Memorial Day.

I could perceive the steep, long concrete stairs going down to the Long Island Railroad or into the street. Should I offer my help as the American white man did at the subway door placing the two children outside the subway car? Should I take care of the girl and the boy, take them by their hands until they reached the end of the steep long concrete stairs of the Atlantic Avenue station?

Courtesy is a characteristic of the Puerto Rican. And here I was—a Puerto Rican—hours past midnight, a valise, two white children and a white lady with a baby on her arm palpably needing somebody to help her at least until she descended the long concrete stairs.

But how could I, a Negro and a Puerto Rican, approach this white lady—who very likely might have preconceived prejudices against Negroes and everybody with foreign accents—in a deserted subway station very late at night?

What would she say? What would be the first reaction of this white American woman, perhaps coming from a small town, with a valise, two children, and a baby on her right arm? Would she say: Yes, of course, you may help me. Or would she think that I was just trying to get too familiar? Or would she think worse than that perhaps? What would I do if she let out a scream as I went toward her to offer my help?

Was I misjudging her? So many slanders are written every day in the daily press against the Negroes and Puerto Ricans. I hesitated for a long, long minute. The ancestral manners that the most illiterate Puerto Rican passes on from father to son were struggling inside me. Here was I, way past midnight, face to face with a situation that could very well explode into an outburst of prejudices and chauvinistic conditioning of the "divide and rule" policy of present-day society.

It was a long minute. I passed on by her as if I saw nothing. As if I was insensitive to her need. Like a rude animal walking on two legs, I just moved on half running by the long subway platform, leaving the children and the valise and her with the baby on her arm. I took the steps of the long concrete stairs in twos until I reached the street above and the cold air slapped my warm face.

This is what racism and prejudice and chauvinism and official artificial divisions can do to people and to a nation!

Perhaps the lady was not prejudiced after all. Or not prejudiced enough to scream at the coming of a Negro toward her in a solitary subway station a few hours past midnight.

If you were not that prejudiced, I failed you, dear lady. I know that there is a chance in a million that you will read these lines. I am willing to take that millionth chance. If you were not that prejudiced, I failed you, lady. I failed you, children. I failed myself to myself.

I buried my courtesy early on Memorial Day morning. But here is a promise that I make to myself here and now; if I am ever faced with an occasion like that again, I am going to offer my help regardless of how the offer is going to be received.

Then I will have my courtesy with me again.

Greetings from Washington

John and his wife Mary went to Washington on his vacation to see the cherry blossoms, and to see Washington. John and I are good friends though we think very differently. John thinks it is too bad that "a man like you" should have such "crazy ideas!" John has one very good quality. He has a sense of humor. John also likes to tease.

So while in Washington he sent me a postcard, with a picture of the Lincoln Memorial on it. In the writing space of the card he wrote: "Greetings from Washington! City of democracy, equality, and freedom! Having a wonderful time—John and Mary." I would not doubt that perhaps John and Mary were having a wonderful time. They are white. And they had vacation money systematically put aside every week of the year for just such an occasion.

So anything can happen in Washington, D.C., capital of the United States of America. If you are white and have a little money to spend. You might even be happy if you are the kind of a person who doesn't look too closely and ask too many questions; if you are more or less insensitive to what happens to others and how the other half lives. You might even be happy in Washington, D.C.

When I said that anything can happen in Washington, I am not referring to what is taking place inside the Pentagon or in the White House, important as those things are for all of us. I am referring to everyday happenings in the lives of ordinary citizens, especially those not of the white race who go out to the United States capital.

In Washington I have seen a man break the glass in which he has served an orange refreshment to a Negro, in front of him right after the Negro had finished drinking from the glass. I have seen in Washington. . . . But what is the use? There are so many instances of race discrimination in Washington against colored diplomats, artists, scientists, and ordinary laymen that just to enumerate them will take hundreds of pages, from Marian Anderson to the end of the alphabet.

One time I went to Washington. I don't remember on what delegation or committee. It would take us at least two days to finish our business in the capital. So I took every precaution to see that I had a place to sleep at least for a night. A friend gave me a letter to a Negro family in Washington. They would have space for me to sleep for one night. The delegation went to the various offices we had to go to. After a good day's legwork from building to building we went into one of the government cafeterias—one of the few places where Negroes and whites can eat together unmolested in downtown Washington—and had our supper. We agreed on a place in which we were to meet the next morning and everybody left for the house in which a nice soft bed was waiting for him. Or so I thought.

I went to the Negro family's address to whom our mutual friend in New York had given me a very nice letter of introduction. I knocked on the door and waited. After a while, I knocked again. Then again and more persistently and strongly. A neighbor in the next apartment opened the door. "Are you looking for Mr. and Mrs. —" "Yes." "They went to New York for a few days to visit their folks in Jamaica, Long Island."

"What shall I do now?" I thought to myself. It was already around eight thirty or nine in the evening. I had a little over twenty dollars in my wallet. I went to the railroad station and returned my little overnight valise to one of the boxes in which, for twenty-five cents, you could lock anything from a briefcase to a suitcase. I wanted to be free to walk and move around without any extra weight bothering me. Then I started to look for a place to sleep.

I visited half a dozen hotels, large and medium size. They all said the same thing: No colored people allowed. When I went to three or four rather dilapidated and suspicious-looking rooming houses offering any price they asked for a cot somewhere in which to pass the night, I met with the same answer: "No colored allowed."

Suddenly I remembered that a Jewish friend had given me the telephone of a girl friend of his who worked for the government in Washington. I had it written on the margin of my *New York Times* that I had in the valise and that I had no time to read during the day. I went back to the railroad station to get the valise and the address.

By now it was eleven o'clock at night. I called the number and gave my friend's name in New York as an introduction. Then I explained my situation. Everything. She told me to come but not to take the elevator. She explained that she lived in an apartment building for whites only. If anybody knew that she was inviting a Negro to sleep at her place, she would be sure to lose her apartment. So she gave me her apartment number and detailed instructions on how to avoid being seen coming in by anybody. I will remember that night all my life. I went into that apartment building as if I were actually going to commit a crime. Avoiding everybody, walking on tiptoes as silently and stealthily as possible! And to think that I was going to do what millions of people were doing in over half the world at that very hour: Going to sleep! But in Washington, the "capital of the world's greatest democracy," I had to act like a thief just to get a place where I could go to bed and fall asleep!

The young lady shared the apartment with another office worker friend of hers. I slept on a sofa in the parlor. It was agreed that I would get up very early so that I could leave as unseen as I came in the night before. This I did. All this happened a few years ago. If you placed the two young ladies — they must be older now — right in front of me today, I confess that I would not recognize them. All I know is that both of them were waiting for my knock, dressed in their housecoats, when I came into their apartment. Wherever you are ladies, from these pages of reminiscences, thank you again. [. . .]

I remember the time that Ava Miranda and some of her friends went from Brooklyn to visit her uncle in Washington. Some of the girls were white and some were Negroes. The uncle, a Puerto Rican veteran of the First World War, had lived in Washington for many years. He was supposed to be a "small" big shot in Washington: a Puerto Rican who felt himself to be 200 percent American, who on Armistice Day was the first to be in line with his 1917 uniform, ribbons, and medals, ready to parade down Pennsylvania Avenue and show the world the equality, freedom, and liberty you could find in Washington, capital of the U.S.A. He was the kind who believed in everything that the books said — and then more. He was a Puerto Rican who had gradually and unconsciously converted himself into a flag waving, pledge taking, bigger and better 200 percent American.

As soon as the girls left the New York train, uncle took them to the first restaurant in sight. The restaurant owner insisted he would serve the white girls but not the Negro girls. Uncle was very much incensed. He felt it was his obligation to prove to the young ladies that there was equality and democracy in Washington. "I am a veteran of the First World War. Remember THAT!" he used to shout when somebody dared to doubt that he would be able to do anything about it. When they were not served at the restaurant, uncle went to the Police Department. He went to the higher authorities. There he was courteously laughed at. He made dozens of telephone calls and kept writing dozens of letters long after the young ladies returned to New York. Yes, sir, he wanted to prove to the girls that there was such a thing as equality and democracy in Washington. I heard uncle died without even being able to win an apology from the restaurant owners.

As we wrote at the beginning, there are thousands of cases to prove that even with all the late attempts to reform the reactionary racists, the government servants, and the general owning class in Washington, it will be years before a particle of racial equality and democratic treatment for any non-white coming to Washington from any part of the world would be put into practice.

Take the case of the Puerto Rican schoolteachers invited to Washington at the end of the school year in Puerto Rico. When the Puerto Rican teachers got to Washington, they were divided according to their color. The whites were housed in downtown hotels, the Negroes or those appearing to be Negroes were sent to dormitories in Howard University or in the neighborhood of that famous Negro institution of learning.

Or take the case of Rosa and Maria, her daughter. When a Puerto Rican family in Harlem told me how Rosa, an old friend of mine, visited Maria, her only daughter, working in Washington, every other weekend, I was not amazed as much as the Harlem Puerto Rican family I was visiting. I told them that those "happenings" were common in Washington, the "great democratic capital of the United States," to use John's phrase on his Lincoln Memorial greeting card.

This is the story as the family told it to me. Maria answered a federal application for a Spanish-English stenographer in Washington. We all knew that Maria was a very bright kid. A very good office worker and secretary. Maria was living with a white family in Washington. All her friends were white Americans. She was actually "passing" as white. Rosa, her mother, would not pass for anything but a Negro. Rosa's husband, Maria's father, who died when Maria was still a child, was white. This is a very familiar man-woman—or vice versa—marriage relationship in Puerto Rico.

So when Rosa went to "visit" her daughter every other weekend, Maria waited for her at the Washington train station. They walked on the streets and avenues near the train station. Maria usually had some homemade sandwiches. They ate them at some public park. Maria would not risk the possibility of going into one of the government cafeterias and finding one of her acquaintances. After the sandwiches, they walked and talked some more until the six o'clock train was about to leave for New York. Maria gave a formal train kiss to her mother and they said goodbye until two Saturdays hence.

I suppose that some Saturday, Rosa and Maria felt adventurous enough to get away from the railroad station surroundings and walk as far as the Lincoln Memorial. I imagine them there admiring the great statue of Abraham Lincoln, sitting in his imposing marble armchair high up here upon its marble pedestal in the very central point of interest in the imposing structure. I imagine Rosa and Maria being held spellbound by that modest

Flyer for a Columbus Day dance, New York City, 1932. Note the words "*Para raza blanca*" in small print at the lower right. (Jesús Colón Papers, El Centro de Estudios Puertorriqueños, Hunter College, City University of New York)

and humble figure of Lincoln and by all the humane things he stood for. And as Rosa and Maria were preparing to leave the Lincoln Memorial they would pause a minute to listen to a child holding his father's hand and reading haltingly from the south wall of the Memorial:

> FOUR SCORE AND SEVEN YEARS AGO
> OUR FATHERS BROUGHT FORTH ON THIS CONTINENT
> A NEW NATION, CONCEIVED IN LIBERTY
> AND DEDICATED TO THE PROPOSITION THAT
> ALL MEN ARE CREATED EQUAL.

I could imagine, after listening to that phrase for the ages, mother and daughter walking back in silence to the railroad station. And the daughter saying, as the train eased its way out, "I'll see you in two weeks." And the mother answering meditatively, "Yes."

Greetings from Washington!

NANCY RAQUEL MIRABAL

Melba Alvarado, El Club Cubano Inter-Americano, and the Creation of Afro-Cubanidades in New York City

Melba Alvarado was born on August 15, 1919, in Oriente, Cuba. She left for New York City at the age of fifteen and has lived there ever since. She has known and worked with some of the most important Afro-Cuban musicians, writers, and activists in New York. She frequented the Apollo Theater where she saw all the greats, including her favorites Louis Armstrong and Cab Calloway. She was a friend of the great musician Mario Bauzá and the performer Eusebia Cosme. In my discussions with Melba after I met her in the mid-1990s she spoke at length about Bauzá and his collaborations with Dizzy Gillespie and Chano Pozo. Melba described Bauzá as "un negro herido" (a wounded Black man) who was loved and respected by "el pueblo negro" (the Black public), and yet "con los blancos nunca llegó" (never made it with the Whites). Bauzá frequently performed at El Club Cubano Inter-Americano and was popular among the members. He played, Melba said, everywhere and all of the time. Only recently has Bauzá finally gained the recognition that Melba felt he deserved all along. She also knew the boxer Kid Gavilán and the baseball player Orestes (Minnie) Miñoso, and she was a fan of the Cuban All Stars baseball team. Passionate about music and musicians, she organized events in honor of Celia Cruz, Arsenio Rodríguez, Benny Moré, Olga Guillot, and Miguelito Valdés, and for over fifty years she has been one of the main organizers of El Festival Mamoncillo, a highly popular annual salsa music festival in the city.

Club life defined Melba, and she devoted most of her free time to club activity and establishing community among the different Afro-diasporic immigrants in New York. Melba was always conscious of the ephemeral and at times fleeting nature of historical memory and production, of how

Afro-Latin@s have been rendered invisible and silent because they simply do not fit larger historical narratives of immigration, race, gender, culture, and location in the United States. As Melba would say, "We are Black, but we are also Cuban, and I have always been very Cuban." For Melba being "very Cuban" did not mean that she was not Black or unwilling to be part of a larger Afro-diasporic and African American community. On the contrary, it meant that to be Cuban also meant to *be* Black. She was keenly aware that in the United States being Cuban signaled whiteness and privilege, a view that left Afro-Cubans on the margins of *cubanidad*. Afro-Cubans, as Melba explained, were only visible when they were musicians, popular artists, or sports figures. There appeared to be no space for a racially mixed working-class Cuban community that was not defined by the politics of the Cuban revolution of 1959, even though, as Melba recounted, "We were everywhere."

Melba emphasized how important it was that El Club Cubano Inter-Americano welcomed all of those who wanted to be members. No one was turned away. When asked why the club was so inclusive, Melba was quick to say that it was in direct response to the exclusion practiced in other clubs—an exclusion that was never direct nor publicly acknowledged as racial. As Melba recollected, you would get to the door of a club and they would turn you away, telling you "We reserve the right to admission." At the same time, White Cubans who she knew were not members would be admitted without question. Exclusion was also practiced through misinformation and deliberate silences. It was common for her and the other members of El Club Cubano Inter-Americano to find out after the fact, and by word of mouth, that a Cuban event, dance, or function had taken place without their knowledge. They simply had not been invited. According to Melba this happened "a lot." But perhaps what bothered her the most was when she learned that club members were often referred to by White Cubans as "los negritos del Bronx": "They [White Cubans] would call this club, 'the little Blacks of the Bronx.' That was very painful."

Melba was so proud that El Club Cubano Inter-Americano was open to all that she would make it a point to list the different nationalities of the club members. Besides Cubans, the club welcomed Puerto Ricans, African Americans, Dominicans, Jamaicans, and Haitians. The founding members were so committed to the idea of creating a safe space for "la gente negra" that one of the major stipulations was that members could not engage in any political or religious discussions while in the club. This policy allowed members from many countries to feel part of a larger Afro-diasporic community without feeling pressured to believe in the same politics or religion. Yet la cubanidad was, of course, always present. Despite the club's commitment to include everyone as members, the president had to be Cuban. After all it was, as Melba pointed out, "un club cubano."

Para acá: Migration and Community in New York, 1936–1945

On May 19, 1936, Melba Alvarado left Cuba for New York City. She was only fifteen when she left Mayarí, Oriente. The economic depression of the 1930s and the onset of World War II were not easy times for Afro-Cuban migrants in New York. As soon as Melba arrived from Cuba she worked in her father's dry cleaning business where she learned to "hacer los pasos de los abrigos y a poner los botones" (make buttonholes and sew on the buttons). At the same time that she worked she was going to school, where she learned English and earned her high school diploma.

The skills that Melba learned in her father's dry cleaning business would serve her well in the garment industry. But even though she worked in the industry for many years she rarely spoke of her jobs or work life. Melba seemed to view jobs as providing her with the income to do what she really loved to do: go to movies, dances, nightclubs, and theaters. Her favorite was the Apollo Theater in Harlem. Having no regrets whatsoever that she spent most of her life at dances and in clubs, she remarked that "Today I am satisfied. I think I saw the best Black artists here in New York at the Apollo."

Growing up in East Harlem and later the Bronx, Melba remembered the early community made up of mostly Puerto Ricans and "quite a few Cuban Blacks." African Americans lived in Harlem, while the White Cuban community resided in lower Manhattan. According to Melba, during this period the Cuban community did not interact much. It was actually more common for Afro-Cubans to associate with African Americans than with White Cubans. When asked why, Melba responded by saying: "When you were of color it didn't matter what nationality you were, you were colored. As a result many of the people that I knew who were Cubans of color would associate with Blacks [African Americans] because truly given their nationality they could not be with the Whites [Cubans] so they were with the Blacks who were the same as them."[1]

While racial divisions clearly existed among Cubans, they were never publicly acknowledged. A form of racial knowledge was practiced among Cuban immigrants where the uses and meanings of race were known but never fully articulated. You "knew" where you could work and the neighborhoods where you could live. You "knew" which clubs wanted you as a

Social event at El Club Cubano Inter-Americano, Bronx, New York, 1957. Club president Melba Alvarado is seated at the table, to the right of the flowers. (Photographs and Prints Division, Schomburg Center for Research in Black Culture, the New York Public Library, Astor, Lenox and Tilden Foundations)

member and which ones did not. You understood the "limits" of friendships and the types of conversations that were acceptable. In short, you "knew" your place.

Such practices seemed to contradict the ever-present sense that to be Cuban was enough to sustain a shared immigrant experience and identity. Yet, as the interviews show, the uses of race were critical to how Cubans would build an immigrant community. Curious to learn more, I pushed Melba to explain the multiple uses of exclusion and silence, and more importantly why Afro-Cubans accepted such practices when they were all immigrants and, as such, subject to a shared racialization. Melba's response was deceptively simple, but powerful: "Whites have always been White." Melba's answer to this question demonstrates the power of White privilege among immigrants and how such privilege can and does mitigate "foreignness." It also reveals that Afro-Cuban migrants were aware of such practices and understood their value in relation to a burgeoning politics of Afro-Cubanidad taking shape in New York. It was this more than anything else that explains why on September 17, 1945, the founding members of El Club Cubano Inter-Americano established "a club for people of color" in the Bronx, and why in the records of El Club Cubano

Inter-Americano the early members publicly stated that there was a "need for a club like this one."

Echando Pleito, Making Trouble: Power, Gender, and the Politics of El Club Cubano Inter-Americano

Melba Alvarado never married. When asked why, she states, "I liked my freedom. I liked being among artists and to learn about art, to see people in the theater." To be unmarried in the 1950s was no small feat. But for Melba such freedom was priceless. It was because she was not married that she devoted so much of her life to her activism, social life, and projects. It was probably because she was not married that she decided to run for president of El Club Cubano Inter-Americano in 1957. This was by no means easy. She experienced resistance and even hostility from some of the male members who could not fathom having a woman in control. Melba gained power and influence within the organization by serving as president of the club's subcommittees, including the Comité de Damas (Ladies' Committee), the public relations committee, and the social and club activities committee. According to Melba, women did all the *real* work of the club and for a long time they were the ones responsible for holding it together. Yet it was the men who were in control. It was when Melba pushed for change and demanded that women have a voice and a vote that the tables turned, or as she put it, "se viró la tortilla." She decided to run for president to end what had been long-standing patriarchal policy where "the women in the club were always second." She declared that "the women's club made the dinners; they did everything. And I said to myself, but we don't have a vote or a voice in the running of the club. And that's when I started making trouble."[2]

Yet women had always been instrumental to the club's founding and success. On September 7, 1945, a group of Afro-Cubans met at the home of la señora Cardenal, a Puerto Rican activist, to organize a centennial celebration in honor of Antonio Maceo, the famous nineteenth-century Afro-Cuban revolutionary leader. In the process, the members decided to form a club. There were no clubs for Afro-Cubans, and the Cuban clubs that existed at the time, El Club Cubano and the Latino Club, restricted their membership by "reserving the right to admission." During the first meeting the members decided on the most significant feature of the club: the prohibition of political and religious discussions. For Melba, the restrictions made sense. She explained. "You can have your politics at home, but in the club there are no politics. You can have the religion that you like,

like being a member of la Caridad, but here you do not discuss the oddun. And the president had to be Cuban."[3]

By banning politics and religion not only did the members believe that they were avoiding controversies and disruptions but they also hoped to eliminate any racist stereotypes associated with an Afro-Cuban club, including the history and politics of *cabildos*,[4] which were often invoked by White Cuban members to discredit Afro-Cuban clubs. Often seen as "Africanized" spaces by their White peers, it was important for the members that El Club Cubano Inter-Americano be considered "respectable" and accepted as equals by the members of the White Cuban clubs. Melba never fully explained why it was so important to maintain ties with the other Cuban clubs and their members when there were clear divisions and tensions. It was as though being Cuban was enough to sustain community even during the most difficult of times. As she would say often to me, "It's that I am Cuban and they are Cuban. I don't know what else I can say to you."

The club held its first official meeting on May 20, 1946. The first president was Generoso Pedroso and the vice president was Josefina Valdéz. Along with Valdéz, there was also a vice secretary, Arminda González, and a vice treasurer, Francisca Cardenal. Club records show that women held positions of power and organized community projects such as giving sewing lessons and teaching English to recent immigrants. As early as 1949 women members offered sewing and English classes. These classes were not incidental but rather were critical to the economic survival of the many Afro-Cuban women migrating to New York. During the 1940s and early 1950s the migration of women increased dramatically as the garment industry in the city became more lucrative. The managers in the garment industry tended to hire women over men, and Afro-Cuban, Afro-Puerto Rican, and African American women over White women, because they could pay them less. This led to an increase in the number of Cuban women employed in the garment industry.

In 1957 Melba ran for president of the club. She described the process as "a historic election and a momentous occasion." The event resulted in the losing candidate leaving and forming another club with other disgruntled male members who could not accept a woman as president. "It's that he didn't know how to lose," Melba would tell me when I asked her why she thought he took it so hard. Melba would be elected president of the club once again in 1972, and in the meantime she served in a number of different capacities, including secretary.

Notes

This piece is dedicated to Melba Alvarado. Her generosity and spirit is an inspiration and a reminder of all the histories yet to be recorded. I am deeply thankful to Miriam Jiménez Román and Diana Lachatanere who introduced me to Melba Alvarado in 1995 and encouraged me to do an oral history of her life. I would like also to thank Juan Flores and Antonio López for their suggestions and critiques. Mil gracias. All of the quotations by Melba in this piece are from my interviews with her in 1995.

1. The original quote is as follows: "Cuando tu eras de color no importa de que raza tu era, tu eras de color. Entonces muchas personas que yo conocí que eran cubanos de color se envolvían mucho con los negros [African Americans] porque verdaderamente dado su patria no podian estar con los blancos [White Cubans] pues estaban con los negros igual que ellos.

2. The original quote is as follows: "Los clubes de damas hacían las comidas, hacían todas las cosas y decía yo, pero entonces no tenemos ni voto, ni voz en la directiva. Y ese fue el pleito que yo eché."

3. The original quote is as follows: "Tu puedes tener la política que te parezca en tu casa pero dentro del club no hay política. Puedes ser de la religión que tu seas, como miembro de la Caridad, pero tu aquí ni discutes el oddun. Y tenía que ser el presidente cubano."

4. Cabildos are Afro-Cuban clubs or societies that originated in Africa and were transferred to Cuba during the eighteenth and nineteenth centuries, in particular during the period that slavery was practiced in Cuba. Some were secret while others operated as mutual aid societies. The cabildos were open only to men and were seen by outsiders as dangerous spaces where Afro-Cuban men practiced Santeria, Palo, and other religions. They were also a space where Afro-Cubans organized communities, disseminated information, and established political positions and practices. Because they were seen as sites where Afro-Cubans exhibited power, they were feared, raided, and later outlawed. Cabildos signaled a historic form of Africanization of the island and of Cubans.

ADRIAN BURGOS JR.

An Uneven Playing Field

Afro-Latinos in Major League Baseball

Anniversary celebrations of Major League Baseball's racial integration have featured widening efforts to tell the Jackie Robinson story as the story of baseball integration, and to celebrate baseball as an exemplar of integration in United States society—that is, as an economic institution that decided to address its racial misdoing (segregation) without governmental interference. Journalists inside and outside the sporting world who reflect on Robinson's legacy each year on April 15 typically focus on the place of Blacks in baseball as a barometer for race relations and social progress. Unfortunately, many commentators, either implicitly or explicitly, restrict their definition of Blackness to include only African Americans. In so doing, they minimize the international impact of baseball's integration story then and now.

The erasure of the unique standing of Afro-Latinos within the story of race and America's game captures a shift in racial understandings within the United States generally and particularly in baseball circles that has transpired during a period when Latinos have established themselves as baseball's largest minority group. The narrowing definition of Blackness effectively strips Afro-Latinos of their racial identity and marks them as ethnic (Latino) in the retelling of baseball's Jim Crow account and the redemptive story of integration. This was on prominent display in 1997 when the Major Leagues commemorated the fiftieth anniversary of integration.

As the April 15th commemoration approached, journalists and fans lamented that the Dodgers had retreated from the organization's trailblazing role of fifty years earlier. Critics pointed out that the team's roster included only one African American. The criticism heaped on the Dodgers disregarded the international ramifications of the challenge to baseball's racial divide. The 1997 Dodgers included three dark-skinned Dominicans: Raúl Móndesi, Wilton Guerrero, and Ramón Martínez. They and the hundreds of Latinos who have performed in the Major Leagues since the start of integration are all beneficiaries of Robinson's pioneering achievement that reverberated throughout the Spanish-speaking Americas. The Dominican great Felipe Alou, who debuted in 1958 and was part of the first wave of Dominicans in the Majors, named as a source of inspiration the 1948 spring training visit to the Dominican Republic by Robinson as a member of the Dodgers. Robinson's presence fascinated the twelve-year-old Alou, thereby enabling him to dream about one day also becoming a major leaguer.[1] The Cuban broadcaster Rafael "Felo" Ramírez, who witnessed Robinson's participation in the Dodgers 1947 spring training in Havana, offered a similar assessment of Robinson's importance: "He opened the door for all of them, all of the races. . . . All Latins have Jackie Robinson to thank."[2]

The Dominican trio on the 1997 Dodgers roster represented a demographic shift within baseball. That season Latinos surpassed African Americans as baseball's most numerous minority. The gap between their numbers has since widened. In 2004 foreign-born Latinos surged to over a quarter (26 percent) of all big leaguers, according to the sportswriter Travis Sawchik's calculations. Conversely, African American participation dwindled to just over 8 percent in 2007, which has produced much consternation within African American circles and for some Major League officials.[3]

Inserting Afro-Latinos back into the story of baseball integration reveals a more complex history about baseball's color line and unveils integration as a process that involved a wider series of actors than is commonly acknowledged. The controversy over the declining number of African American players in the Major Leagues, the comments of the African American player Gary Sheffield that appeared in GQ in 2007 that team officials today prefer Latinos because they are "easier to control," and the continued lack of recognition of Latino involvement in baseball integration demonstrate the stakes involved in how we define integration.[4]

A close look at baseball's segregated era reveals Latinos positioned at different locations along baseball's color line. Afro-Latinos originally were positioned as "Negro" or "colored" while their lighter-skinned compatriots entered the Major Leagues as non-White others. Importantly, their collective participation unveils baseball's color line as not merely a point of demarcation but rather a spectrum that ranged from White and inclusion to Black and outright exclusion, with other racialized locations in between. The familiar narrative of baseball integration also includes a subplot that celebrates American capitalism as a moral, self-correcting system. This subplot along with the wider narrative neglects the broader context in which the fight against Jim Crow took place within professional baseball. Specifically, it minimizes the role of Afro-Latinos and of the Latin American leagues in the campaign to overturn the segregation of baseball.

My aim in this essay, therefore, is not to invent a history that did not exist but to recast the understanding of baseball integration by reinserting Afro-Latinos. "Minnie" Miñoso and Alejandro "Alex" Pompez, among other Afro-Latinos, were not tangential to integration but instead were central actors in the events that transformed professional baseball in the United States. A focus on their contributions complicates simplistic storylines and compels a richer, more nuanced narrative. Simply put, Afro-Latinos did not enter into organized baseball as an afterthought once integration began. On the contrary, Afro-Latinos bridge the sport's segregated and integrated eras by participating in the Negro Leagues while organized baseball's color line stood in place and then by entering organized baseball as part of the generation of integration pioneers.

Striking Out Afro-Latinos

For the most part, historians have focused on the Black-White poles of baseball's color line as the main way to understand how race operated in baseball. In doing so they overlook the dynamic wherein officials of organized baseball sought to place racially ambiguous Latino players in the in-between locations along the color line by manipulating racial understandings. This process allowed lighter-skinned "White" Latinos entry into the Major Leagues as early as the 1910s. Similarly, during the player shortages in the Major Leagues during World War II, officials expanded access to medium-toned Latinos such as Roberto Estalella and Tommy (Tomás) de la Cruz—players who in the racial lexicon of Caribbean Latinos were *trigueño* (wheat colored), *jabao* (light-skinned with African features), or *café con leche*—that is, racial descriptors that indicated non-White status. Only a privileged minority of lighter-skinned Latinos gained access into the Major Leagues before Jackie Robinson and even they endured reminders that they were not necessarily viewed as fellow Whites. After performing during the 1911 and 1912 seasons with the Cincinnati Reds, the Cubans Armando Marsans and Rafael Almeida demanded salaries commensurate with their Major League peers. In the ensuing contract dispute the Reds management made clear that race figured into their position when they informed journalists that "we will not pay any Honus Wagner price for a pair of dark-skinned islanders."[5] Latinos who followed Marsans and Almeida were continually made aware that claims to a shared Whiteness were tenuous at best. White pitchers threw at them; teammates refused to room with them; and they were often not allowed to dine in the same facilities as their White American teammates.[6] This was particularly the case when a racially ambiguous Latino like Roberto Estalella entered the big leagues. The *Washington Post* columnist Shirley Povich declared that "there are many 200 per cent Americans in the big leagues" who "resent the presence of the Cuban ball players, particularly the swarthy ones like Estalella." One of Estalella's Washington Senators teammates put it bluntly by stating that most of the Senators' White players shared the perception that Estalella and other Cuban Senators were "Black—and they were treated as such."[7] These Latinos nevertheless enjoyed a degree of racial privilege. In a circuit where race and Blackness mattered, lighter-skinned Latinos and—in the late 1930s—more racially ambiguous Latinos gained access while Afro-Latinos were denied entry altogether.

Until recently most historical accounts by Latino writers scarcely dealt with the decades that Latinos performed in the Black baseball circuit in the United States (1900s–1940s). Instead they focused first on these players' limited entry into the segregated Major Leagues before engaging in a thorough analysis of Latino participation since integration. This transpired even though Latino Negro Leaguers outnumbered Latino Major Leaguers by over a four-to-one ratio during baseball's Jim Crow era. This portrayal of Latinos' baseball past made their Negro League participation seem much like a family secret, one better off hidden lest it expose that the richer legacy of Latino baseball was within the ranks of the excluded and not among the privileged Whites.[8]

The recovery of Negro League history has educated baseball aficionados about Black baseball and the challenges of operating in a segregated context. An initial recovery effort in the 1970s highlighted by Robert Peterson's *Only the Ball Was White* familiarized many with Black baseball's greats. The official recovery effort took form in 1971 when the National Baseball Hall of Fame organized a blue-ribbon committee to elect Negro League greats for enshrinement. Nine players were elected before the committee disbanded in 1978, including the Afro-Cuban Martín Dihigo, the lone Latino Negro Leaguer in the Hall of Fame until the 2006 special election. Interest declined for much of the 1980s, and another revival would not occur until Ken Burns's eighteen-hour documentary *Baseball* was shown on PBS in 1994. During this revival the Negro League historians have further illuminated the ways that Negro League players and team owners negotiated Jim Crow practices and baseball's importance within Black urban communities. However, with the notable exception of Donn Rogosin's *Invisible Men*, most works on the Negro Leagues lacked a substantive analysis of the ways that Latin America was an escape from the segregated North.

Further research into Black baseball history—which is evident in a plethora of published books and documentary films—maintained a sustained interest in the Negro Leagues into the early twenty-first century. In 2006, the completion of a landmark five-year study on Black baseball motivated the Baseball Hall of Fame to call a special election on Negro League and pre-Negro League candidates. The special election produced the Hall's largest cohort ever to be enshrined, with seventeen Negro League players and executives including three Latinos and the first woman.

The media coverage of the 2006 Hall of Fame election focused as much on who was left out as it did on who was elected. Many lamented the absence of Buck O'Neil from the list of inductees. Showcased in Ken Burns's *Baseball* series, O'Neil's endearing personality, homespun storytelling style, and lack of bitterness made him the face and voice of the Negro Leagues for many Americans. A much more muted reaction to the election's omission of the Afro-Latino Minnie Miñoso accompanied the outcry about O'Neil's "snubbing." The different reaction presents an opportunity to critically examine the ways that popular understandings about Black baseball history marginalize the place of Afro-Latinos within the story of race in "America's game."

Minimizing Miñoso

The African American Buck O'Neil and the Afro-Cuban Minnie Miñoso have come to represent different strands within the revisionist history of baseball's Jim Crow era. O'Neil embodies the southern-born African American who overcame the hurdles presented by Jim Crow. It is through his refusal to become embittered that he emerges as the iconic representative of the Negro Leagues. Conversely, many perceive the Cuban-born Miñoso as having traveled a less precarious path due primarily to his ethnicity, thereby designating him a peripheral figure within this history. A peculiar form of United States chauvinism thus minimizes what Miñoso and other Afro-Latinos endured in the struggle against Jim Crow and as members of baseball's pioneering generation. In Miñoso's case it diminishes the span of his professional career: his three seasons (1946–48) starring in the Negro Leagues; his status as the first Black Latino in the Major Leagues (1949); and his role in the integration of the Chicago White Sox (1951).

Starting in April 1951 Miñoso pioneered the integration of the Chicago White Sox, which was only the third American League club to integrate. The circumstances surrounding his pioneering season (and beyond) distinguish Miñoso from Jackie Robinson and other African American players who preceded Miñoso in the Major Leagues. Pioneering Afro-Latinos did not receive the same type of unwavering support from the Black community in big league towns as that accorded African Americans. At times, even their African American teammates questioned their standing as Black men due to their different approach to racial situations, which created ambivalent and at times bitter relations between these groups of pioneers.

Despite starting his professional career in the United States in the Negro Leagues, Miñoso nonetheless faced accusations that he was not "Black" and lacked an understanding of racial discrimination. His Cleveland teammate Harry Simpson strongly disagreed with how Miñoso dealt with United States laws and social customs that affected Blacks, and he openly castigated the Cuban. Miñoso acknowledged that he approached racial situations differently: "When I first came here, if it was against the law for a person of color to go to a certain place, I would say, 'That's the law and I will respect it.' Something like that wasn't going to hurt me."[9] That African Americans interpreted this approach as an inability to understand race and discrimination due to his Cuban background left Miñoso "surprised and a bit amused." The lack of awareness among African Americans about Cuba's racial situation startled Miñoso. Cuba was no racial paradise, he informed them. "Just as in the United States, there were many sections of Cuba, and many neighborhoods, where you only saw White people." Equally significant, he had experienced the sting of racial and cultural bias from his days playing in the Negro Leagues and as part of the Major Leagues' pioneering generation. As he reminded others, "here in this country [the United States], the signs in restaurants and buses prohibiting Blacks applied as much to me as it did them."[10]

The notion that foreign birth mitigated one's Blackness continues to detract from Miñoso's standing in baseball history. This perception hampered his chances in the Hall of Fame's 2006 special election, where the case for Miñoso hinged on his having been an integration pioneer. The Cuban native had long been caught in a peculiar situation when it came to Hall of Fame consideration since his career bridged the end of baseball's segregated era and the start of racial integration. The Hall of Fame only permits consideration for an individual candidate in one category: as a Negro Leaguer or as a Major Leaguer, but not a combination of both. Thus, the established criteria were detrimental to players like Miñoso who started their professional careers in the mid-1940s: though they were talented enough to be among the first wave of Black players acquired from the Negro Leagues, they were denied full playing opportunities in the Major Leagues due to the slow pace of integration throughout organized baseball.

The appropriateness of calling Miñoso an integration pioneer was hotly debated in the 2006 deliberations. White and African American members of the voting committee questioned how much racial antagonism Miñoso faced as a Black Latino.[11] The questioning of Miñoso as a racial pathbreaker reflects the popular belief among North Americans that growing up in a Spanish-speaking society somehow diminished the significance of one's Black skin and African ancestry after they entered United States society. This belief rationalizes efforts to separate Black Latinos into two different realms of experience: Black versus Latino. It also fuels the perception that cultural heritage somehow shielded Black Latinos from the full brunt of Jim Crow racism in spite of the historical record.

Such questions belie the reality of integration as a historical process in which Miñoso and other Afro-Latinos participated as central actors. Miñoso traversed uncharted territory as the first Black Latino in the Major Leagues. Prior to his 1949 debut, no other Latino player in the Majors had to deal openly with the challenge of being publicly received as twice different: Black and Latino. This distinguished him and the Afro-Latinos who followed from their lighter-skinned compatriots who had gained access into the segregated Major Leagues before the racial barrier was dismantled. From 1900 to 1947 fifty-four Latinos born either in the United States or elsewhere had performed in the segregated Majors. Until the Major League initiated its project of racial integration in 1947, the overwhelming majority of Latinos (over 230) participated in the Black baseball circuit since they were classified as racially ineligible for "White" organized baseball.[12]

Black Latinos dealt with overlapping processes of cultural adjustment and adaptation to United States racial practices—which varied according to region and even in local enforcement. In contrast to African Americans who found escape in local Black communities, big league towns typically lacked a thriving Latino community, with New York City and Chicago being the notable exceptions. Cultural difference exacerbated isolation. The language barrier was ever present and the English-language press seemed all too ready to poke fun at the Black Latinos due to their accents or appearance, which added another layer to their being "twice different." The Hall of Famer Orlando Cepeda stressed the trying circumstances that Miñoso and this pioneering generation encountered in dealing with the promise and limits of integration: "This is not meant to be a complaint, but the language barrier back then was so difficult. . . . Players today who come from Venezuela, Panama, and other Spanish-speaking countries . . . have no idea. That is too bad, because it diminishes a part of what Minnie has meant to so many of us."[13]

The "hot-blooded Latin" stereotype complicated the task of pioneering integration for Afro-Latinos. This stereotype cultivated the expectation that any Latino was liable to lash out, verbally or physically, at anyone: teammates, opponents, management, fans, or the press. Afro-Latinos had to demonstrate restraint on two levels when challenged on and off the field: as Latinos and as Black men. In Miñoso's case, he exhibited restraint when opposing pitchers threw brushback pitches. The Cuban led the American League in getting hit by pitches for his first four full seasons (1951–1954), and he would do so ten times in his twelve full seasons. Yet he did not charge the pitcher's mound to physically accost opposing pitchers. His cool-headed response contradicted the image of the hot-blooded Latin as well as that of the angry Black man who lacked the professional temperament to withstand adversity. In his reaction he smoothed the path for those who followed, thereby making it possible for Roberto Clemente, Felipe Alou, and Orlando Cepeda, among others, to speak more freely about maltreatment as men who were fiercely proud of being Black and Latino.

A Shared Past Diverges in the Present

The narrow definition of Blackness increasingly embraced by North American journalists and baseball historians further diminishes the contributions of Afro-Latinos like Minnie Miñoso. Cal Fussman's *After Jackie*, published to coincide with the sixtieth anniversary of baseball integration, chronicles the challenges Black players faced while pioneering integration throughout organized baseball.[14] Fussman subscribes to the narrow definition of Black that is inclusive of only African Americans. He celebrates Ernie Banks as Chicago's first Black big league star, even though Miñoso had appeared in three All-Star games by the time Banks made his 1954 debut. Equally significant, Fussman focuses on Banks despite the contemporary coverage in the mainstream newspapers *Chicago Tribune* and *Chicago Daily News* and in the nationally circulated Black weekly *Chicago Defender* that hailed Miñoso as Chicago's pioneering Black star. Fussman's narrative reminds us that this narrow definition of Black is of recent vintage, and as such it counters the integration account produced by those who witnessed integration firsthand.

A look at the all-star rosters from the 1950s through the 1970s reveals Latino stars such as Cepeda, Clemente, Miñoso, Juan Marichal, Vic Power, and Luis Tiant, among other Afro-Latinos, listed along with the African American stalwarts Hank Aaron, Banks, Bob Gibson, Willie Mays, Willie McCovey, Don Newcombe, and Frank Robinson. Together they transformed America's game. Yet it is the Afro-Latinos who have been the unwitting victims of the selective memory of the current chroniclers who chose to minimize the place of Latinos in their narratives of baseball integration and thereby make them peripheral to the story of race in baseball.

The selective, ahistorical recasting of baseball's racial past was evident in the formation of the "Black Aces," which purposefully excluded Afro-Latinos. Originally conceived by the retired African American pitcher Jim "Mud Cat" Grant, the Black Aces consisted of Black pitchers who won twenty or more games in a single Major League season, and the group promotes this select group of pitchers by organizing public appearances. The decision to exclude Afro-Latinos from the Black Aces infuriated the Black Cuban Luis Tiant. As a four-time twenty-game winner in the Majors and the son of a Negro League great, Tiant claimed he was excluded because he was not African American. The Black Aces' inclusion of Ferguson Jenkins, a Black Canadian, unveils the arbitrary decision making that upset Tiant: "I haven't been treated like a white person here. In the minor leagues, I wasn't white. I was black. We couldn't eat in the hotel. We couldn't eat in the restaurants. And now I'm not black?" Tiant asked rhetorically.[15] Even Mud Cat Grant admitted that Tiant and fellow Cuban Mike Cuellar, another four-time twenty-game winner, "had to live like we did . . . They couldn't stay in hotels, couldn't drink from the [White] water fountains."[16]

The Tiant family was intimately familiar with the challenges Black players faced in United States society and in professional baseball throughout the twentieth century. Lefty Tiant drew on his own Negro League experience in the 1930s and 1940s to discourage his son from pursuing a professional baseball career in the United States. "My father said no," Luis Tiant remarked, "because he felt there was no place in baseball for a black man. But my mother finally got him to let me try." [17] The elder Tiant confirmed this account during his lone post-retirement trip to the United States to watch his son pitch in the 1975 World Series. His words revealed the emotional scars that Jim Crow had left: "I didn't want him to come to America. I didn't want him to be persecuted and spit on and treated like garbage like I was." [18]

Integration Matters

Few Negro League owners were as well positioned to deal with the re-vamped baseball world as was Alex Pompez. Born to Cuban émigré parents and raised both in Florida and Havana, Pompez possessed an un-matched combination of professional experience and interpersonal skills as a bilingual and transnational Afro-Latino. The New York Giants organization, fully aware of Pompez's abilities as a talent evaluator, hired him in 1950 to scout Latin Americans and African Americans in the United States. Over the next twenty-two years his position would evolve into the organization's director of international scouting—the first Latino to hold such a position within the Majors.

The hiring of Alex Pompez by the Giants constituted a different approach to integration than that of the organization's Major League counterparts. Rather than strictly focusing on securing on-field talent, the Giants incorporated a vital off-field figure from the Negro Leagues. In so doing, the organization harnessed the expertise and network of contacts that Pompez had developed over his three decades in Black baseball. The lessons that Pompez had learned as a Negro League owner were central to his new work as the principal figure responsible for the flow of previously excluded talent into the Giants organization. Under his direction, the Giants procured the all-star players Willie McCovey, Orlando Cepeda, Juan Marichal, and the Alou brothers, as well as dozens of other talented African American and Latino ballplayers. Just as significant, the hiring by the Giants of Pompez illuminates the importance of including Afro-Latinos within baseball integration narratives to gain a fuller picture of the process of integration and its pivotal actors.

Pompez's behind-the-scenes efforts demonstrate that there was more to the work of integration than merely locating talent to sign. Entrusted with the organization's scouting of Black and Latino prospects, Pompez waged a lonely battle against the impatience—or worse, the racism—of colleagues not yet fully committed to the project of racial integration. During spring tryouts Pompez was the lone unwavering advocate of African

American and Latino prospects at the daily meetings where scouting directors, minor league instructors, and development personnel assessed the players, decided whom to sign, the amount of a signing bonus, and where to assign the prospect within the Giants' minor league system. "Pompez had to fight for us to stay, for us just to be given a chance," Orlando Cepeda stated emphatically.[19]

Mentoring the young African American and Afro-Latino players was an important aspect of Pompez's behind-the-scene work. He introduced them to the racial rules of social engagement. His efforts to alleviate the culture shock that the foreign-born Latinos encountered upon arrival included supervision of their living quarters, making roommate assignments (initially he assigned Dominicans with other Dominicans, Cubans with Cubans, etc.), and imparting cultural lessons that prepared them for their encounters with the media and the public. "When they first come here they don't like it," Pompez explained to the journalist Robert Boyle in a 1960 interview. "Some boys cry and want to go home. But after they stay and make the big money, they accept things as they are. . . . My main thing is to help them. They can't change the laws."[20] Felipe Alou, for one, counted himself among those who benefited greatly from Pompez's efforts to teach his young charges. "He had a car and he used to take the Latin guys to an ice cream parlor. Racism was very strong at that time in Melbourne. He wouldn't let us walk," Alou recounted. "He used to explain to us the rules of the game and also the rules for blacks. It was very important to have a man like him who knew the society so well to explain to us the limitations we had. You know, to protect us from falling into a problem of some sort."[21]

But a sense of shared struggle was not automatic for African Americans and Afro-Latinos who entered as part of organized baseball's pioneering generation. Pressed into the role of integration pioneers, tensions occasionally arose as African American and Afro-Latino players confronted the reality of reconciling the meaning of Blackness as individuals of the African diaspora from different locations within the Americas. African Americans, vastly more familiar with the idiosyncrasies of racial practice in the United States than their foreign-born Latino teammates, were annoyed when darker-skinned Latinos failed to turn to them for guidance about how to deal with segregation, or worse yet when they seemingly shunned them inside or outside the clubhouse. "I don't think I'm any better than they are," stated one African American big leaguer, "but I'm not any worse either. They think they're better than the colored guy."[22] A few African Americans accused Afro-Latino players of denying their *colored* identity, of

Roberto Clemente and Elston Howard at Yankee Stadium, n.d. In 1973 Clemente was the first Latino inducted into the Baseball Hall of Fame. (Photograph by C. Nesfield; Photographs and Prints Division, Schomburg Center for Research in Black Culture, the New York Public Library, Astor, Lenox and Tilden Foundations)

not being Black. When in an interview in 1960 one African American player was informed that some "Latin Negroes" cry when faced with segregation for the first time, he responded: "I don't cry . . . We don't cry, and we have it a hell of a lot worse than they do . . . but we're conditioned, I guess."[23]

Roberto Clemente offered a different perspective on how Black Latinos felt about their travels in the North American playing fields. In an interview with the renowned author Roger Kahn, Clemente spoke bluntly: "Me, I'm a double nigger because I'm black and a nigger because I'm Puerto Rican."[24] Relations with the English-language press undoubtedly had an impact on Clemente's view. "Anytime a fellow comes from Puerto Rico, they want to create an image. They say, 'Hey, he talks funny!' But they go to Puerto Rico and they don't talk to us. I don't have a master's degree, but I'm not a dumb-head and I don't want no bullshit from anyone."[25] Clemente's words point to how Black Latinos faced a cultural as well as a racial set of challenges. A few White teammates sympathized with Clemente's plight. "They [the press] tried to make him look like an ass by getting him to say controversial things and they wrote how the 'Puerto Rican hot dog' was 'popping off' again," Pittsburgh teammate Bill Mazeroski observed. "[Clemente] was learning how to handle the language, and writers who couldn't speak Spanish tried to make him look silly."[26]

What Jackie Robinson Day Should Look Like

The reinsertion of Afro-Latinos into baseball integration narratives moves us beyond integration as a moment where the bold action of a well-intentioned, moral-crusading (White) team executive redeemed the United States national pastime. A focus on Afro-Latinos, most specifically figures like Orestes Miñoso and Alex Pompez, integrates what has been left out of revisionist accounts of baseball integration. It underscores both the culturally specific challenges that Afro-Latinos encountered in the United States playing field and the contributions that Afro-Latinos made to the pace and shape of integration. Such a focal shift better enables us to envision integration as a process that involved a set of pioneering actors and a series of localized struggles. The point here is not to minimize the Dodgers' general manager Branch Rickey's courage in breaking with the gentleman's agreement that sustained organized baseball's color line. Neither does this focal shift diminish what Jackie Robinson encountered as the Major Leagues' first integration pioneer. Rather, the goal is to recapture the international ramifications of baseball integration and thereby acknowledge the contributions of and unique challenges faced by Afro-Latinos in the transformation of America's game.

The shift I call for enables us to rethink what Jackie Robinson Day should look like each April 15. Rather than just a solemn occasion to recall the first integration pioneer, the annual commemoration ought to honor the entire generation of pathbreakers. Such a recast commemoration would showcase the numerous actors involved at the Major League level and throughout organized baseball—that integration was simultaneously a local, national, and international story featuring well-known stars like Robinson, Larry Doby, and Minnie Miñoso, and lesser-known figures like Pumpsie Green and Ozzie Virgil. The work of integration would receive its proper acknowledgment, and the ways that the baseball diamond served as a social laboratory for all to observe would be center stage.

Honoring the generation of integration pioneers would cast new light on the contributions of Afro-Latinos by illuminating their presence in Black baseball and how integration opened new possibilities. Such a commemoration would highlight examples such as that of the Afro-Latino Orestes Miñoso who performed important social work as an integration pioneer and brought the prospect of racial healing to Chicago in the midst of racial turmoil in 1951—a year when racial protests and a race riot erupted over residential integration in several Chicago neighborhoods. In so doing, the American public can learn that contemporary Latino stars like Alex Rodríguez, Albert Pujols, Carlos Delgado, and Johan Santana, among others, are direct beneficiaries of the legacy created by baseball integration—a process in which their Afro-Latino forebears such as Miñoso were crucial participants. This is a history that merits attention at a time when African Americans and Latinos are pitted against one another and remain largely uninformed about their shared struggles inside and outside America's game.

Notes

1. Felipe Alou, interview by Larry Hogan, Tucson, Arizona, March 3, 2004.

2. Carlos Frias, "Memories of Jackie Robinson," *Palm Beach Post*, April 15, 2007, http:// www.palmbeachpost.com (site visited on April 16, 2007).

3. Sawchik, "Fair Baseball Globalization," HispanicBusiness.com, April 19, 2004, http:// www. hispanicbusiness.com (site visited on May 22, 2004). (It is unclear whether Sawchik included U.S.-born Latinos in his calculations). Mike Dodd, "Is Jackie Robinson's Legacy Fading after Six Decades?" *USA Today*, April 12, 2007, http://www.usatoday.com. See "Sheffield Criticizes Baseball for Not Recruiting More Black Players"; for details and interview with Sheffield, see www.sports.espn, posted June 6, 2007.

4. See "Sheffield Criticizes Baseball for Not Recruiting More Black Players"; for details and interview with Sheffield, see www.sports.espn, posted June 6, 2007.

5. *Havana Post*, June 25, 1913, July 7, 1913; Bretón, *Away Games: The Life and Times of a Latin Ball Player* (New York: Simon and Schuster, 1999), 98. Wagner was a Hall of Fame shortstop who played from 1897 to 1917, primarily with the National League's Pittsburgh Pirates.

6. Eddie Gant, *Chicago Defender*, July 25, 1942, quoted in Larry Lester, *Black Baseball's National Showcase: The East-West All-Star Game, 1933–1953* (Lincoln: University of Nebraska Press, Bison Books, 2002), 185.

7. Newspaper clipping, Shirley Povich, "Bob Estalella, Cuban, Is Back Again," March 14, 1938, *Washington Post*, Estalella Player File, National Baseball Library and Archive (hereafter referred to as NBLA); Bretón, *Away Games*, 100.

8. In my case I first learned about the participation of Latinos in the Negro Leagues while doing research for my senior thesis in college, although since my childhood I could recite the names of the first Major League players from every Latin American country. This, as I later found out, occurred despite direct family connections to the story of Latinos in the Negro Leagues: my paternal grandmother named one of my uncles after the Puerto Rican shortstop José Antonio Burgos who played several seasons in the Negro Leagues.

9. Marcos Breton, "Giants Lost Latin Stars," *Sacramento Bee*, August 29–30, 1993, 8.

10. Lisa Brock and Bijan Bayne, "Not Just Black: African-Americans, Cubans, and Baseball," in *Between Race and Empire: African-Americans and Cubans before the Cuban Revolution*, edited by Lisa Brock and Digna Castenada Fuertes (Philadelphia: Temple University Press, 1998), 168.

11. I had the distinct honor of serving on both the screening and voting committees for this special election. The purpose of relaying these observations about the validity of labeling Miñoso an integration pioneer is to note the pervasiveness of such thinking and not to suggest that my colleagues were ruled by racial prejudice.

12. These numbers are drawn from research I conducted for *Playing America's Game* (Berkeley: University of California Press, 2007).

13. Orlando Cepeda, foreword to *Just Call Me Minnie: My Six Decades in Baseball*, by Minnie Miñoso with Herb Fagen (Champaign, Ill.: Sagamore Publishing, 1994), xi.

14. Cal Fussman, *After Jackie: Pride, Prejudice, and Baseball's Forgotten Heroes: An Oral History* (New York: ESPN Books, 2007).

15. Mike Berardino, "Ace Issue Not Black and White," *Ft. Lauderdale Sun-Sentinel*, September 21, 2005, 1C.

16. Ibid.

17. Bill Liston, "The Man: Tiant," *1975 Boston Scorebook* (Boston: Fenway Park, 1975), 8–9; Luis Tiant Player File, NBLA.

18. Newspaper clipping, Maury Allen, "Of Destiny Man," *New York Post*, October 14, 1975, Tiant Player File, NBLA.

19. Orlando Cepeda, interview with the author, Cooperstown, New York, July 26, 2006. Willie McCovey offered a similar assessment about his early years in the Giants organization, specifically mentioning and thanking Pompez during his Hall of Fame acceptance speech in 1984.

20. Boyle, "The Private World of the Negro Ballplayer," *Sports Illustrated*, March 21, 1960, 18.

21. Alou, interview by Larry Hogan, Tucson, Arizona, March 3, 2004.

22. Boyle, "The Private World," 19.

23. Ibid.

24. Quoted in Philip Hoose, *Necessities* (New York: Random House, 1987), 102.

25. Samuel Regalado, *Viva Baseball!: Latin Major Leaguers and Their Special Hunger* (Urbana: University of Illinois Press, 1998), 123.

26. Ibid., 122–23.

GABRIEL HASLIP-VIERA

Changing Identities

An Afro-Latin@ Family Portrait

Haslip-Peña and Viera-Santiago are the names of my parents' extended families whose shifting ethno-racial identities demonstrate the arbitrariness and utter confusion of racial classification in the United States and the Spanish-speaking Caribbean. The names also illustrate how families and individuals from these areas can ignore, obfuscate, or repress an African American or Afro-Latin@ background or origin, and how different cultural and social environments can influence the adoption or construction of an ethno-racial identity by individuals or entire families in a forced or self-serving manner. In addition to the role of social privilege and prejudices, much of this confusion also reflects how census enumerators and other bureaucrats in Puerto Rico and the United States made frequent mistakes, cut corners, and often failed to apply the "one drop rule" of hypodescent to persons of African or part African background when classifying individuals by race prior to 1960, when changes in policy permitted a degree of self-identification in official and unofficial documents.[1]

The Haslip-Peña Family and Official Documents, 1909–1955

Nicholas Gabriel Haslip, my paternal grandfather, was born on the island of Curaçao in the Netherlands West Indies in 1883. He was the offspring of a European Dutch father and a woman named Regina, who was possibly of Jamaican or part Jamaican origin. Raised solely by his mother and apparently educated in the elementary and secondary schools of Curaçao, he joined the merchant marine as a young man and traveled throughout the Caribbean before establishing residence and a small dry goods store in the port of San Juan, Puerto Rico. He married Mérida Peña Torres, my paternal grandmother, who was originally from Guayama, in 1909.[2]

Jaime Haslip-Peña (age eight) and his father, Nicholas Gabriel Haslip, New York, 1923. (Courtesy of Gabriel Haslip-Viera)

Nicholas Gabriel was a man who would be described as a *jabao* or *grifo* in the Spanish-speaking Caribbean, or even as a White person, which was certainly the case when he lost most of his hair in the middle years of his life.[3] His wife Mérida was clearly someone who would be categorized as a *mulata* in the Spanish-speaking Caribbean and as Negro or Colored in the United States, which were the terms in use when she lived in New York between 1915 and 1945. At the time of his marriage in 1909, my paternal grandfather was classified as *pardo* or brown, a term traditionally used in Puerto Rico and Latin America to define persons of mixed African and European background, along with *mulato*.[4] However, in the 1910 U.S. census for Puerto Rico, he and Mérida, along with his brother-in-law, José Peña Centeño, were listed as "N" for *negro*.[5]

In the years that followed, Nicholas Gabriel's racial classification and that of his family as recorded by bureaucrats and census enumerators changed unpredictably and erratically. For example, after coming to New York and establishing residence in Brooklyn in 1915, he was listed as "black" in skin color on his February 1918 "Alien Seaman's Identification Card." However, seven months later his "race" was listed as "White" on his draft card for the U.S. military during World War I. Afterward, Nicholas Gabriel was recorded as being "White" in the 1920 census, as "White" with "dark" complexion on his 1921 "Certificate of Naturalization" (U.S. citizenship), as "yellow" in complexion on his 1923 passport application, as Negro ("NEG") in the 1930 census, and again as "White" with "dark" complexion on his military draft card for World War II.

Members of Nicholas Gabriel's immediate family and other relatives who lived in his household also experienced shifts in their racial categorization during these years, with the changes usually reflecting how he was classified. Despite the expected application of the "one drop rule," and as a result of inconsistent record keeping, Mérida, my mulata-looking paternal grandmother, was listed as "White" in the 1920 census, "Negro" in the 1930 census, and "Spanish" on her 1945 death certificate. All of my grandfather's children, including my father James (Jaime), and my uncle Julius (Julio), who had tightly curled hair and light to medium brown skin color, were listed as "White" in the 1920 census, and Negro ("NEG") in the 1930 census.[6]

This erratic pattern is also seen in my father's official records around the time of his marriage in 1937. In January of that year he was listed as having a "brown" complexion on his Merchant Marine "Protection Certificate." However, six months later he was recorded as having a "dark" complexion on his Merchant Marine "Certificate of Identification." In World War II he was also listed on his military draft card as having a "dark" complexion, but in this case the term was part of a hierarchical list of categories that ranged from "sallow" to "light, "ruddy," "dark," "freckled," "light brown," "dark brown," and finally "Black." Later, my father was also listed as "Negro" on my own 1941 birth certificate, and again as a "Negro" when he was profiled with several African American and Afro-West Indian employees of the United States Customs Service in an article published by Ebony magazine in October 1950.[7]

My father's classification as "Negro" or as a person of color probably continued in the years that followed, but other labels were also used with increasing frequency, especially after 1960 when the change in government policy allowed people to self-identify on census forms and other documents, to some degree. More often than not, my father came to be classified as a racially undifferentiated Puerto Rican, or Puerto Rican/Hispanic, but he was also listed as "White" on my younger brother's birth certificate as early as December 1951—only about a year after the publication of the article in Ebony magazine. This change in classification may have resulted from an arbitrary decision made by a hospital bureaucrat, but there was also the possibility of pressure from my father, who at this stage in his life was able to exhibit an assertive, authoritarian demeanor as a relatively tall, stocky, well-dressed official of the U.S. Customs Service. Ten years earlier, in 1941, he had also tried to change the listings for race on my own birth certificate, but with only partial success. According to the story, there was an argument with the hospital bureaucrat that resulted in a typed birth certificate which listed my mother as "White," my father as "Negro," and yours truly as "Negro," but with the word "Negro" crossed out and replaced in handwritten ink with "Puerto Rican." Thus, I may have become one of the earliest members of the "Puerto Rican" race on the U.S. mainland—a label that became commonplace for Puerto Ricans by the 1950s, along with "White," "Negro," and "Other."

The Viera-Santiago Family and Official Documents, 1910–1950

Changing racial classifications are also seen on my mother's side of my family. However, in this case there is a decided overall shift from "mixed race" categories to Whiteness in the period from 1910 to 1930, thereby providing some support for recent research and speculation on how race was classified in Puerto Rico by locally recruited agents of the U.S. Census Bureau.[8] Isidra Mercado de Santiago, my maternal great-grandmother, was classified as "*mulata*" in the 1910 census for Caimito, Río Piedras, as were her mother, Demetria Jorge de Mercado, her son, Ángel Santiago, and her daughter, María Santiago, my maternal grandmother. Isidra's son, Ángel, was also classified as "*mulato*" in the 1920 census, soon after he married and established his own household, but two years earlier he had been classified as "*negro*" on his 1918 military draft card—reflecting in this case the apparent application of the "one drop rule" of hypodescent for persons of African or part African background.

It was during the 1920 census that the move toward Whiteness clearly manifested itself in the Viera-Santiago family as a result of subtle changes in the instructions for enumerators along with other factors that may have influenced the classification of persons by race. In these records, and in contrast to the 1910 census, my great-grandmother, Isidra, now living in Santurce, was categorized as "B" for *blanca* or "White," along with my grandparents, María and Juan Viera, and their children. All of these individuals varied in appearance to some degree. Juan Viera, my maternal grandfather, was described as "looking like a typical Spaniard." My grandmother María was apparently darker but no picture of her has survived. Their children, including my mother Virginia, ranged in color from very light to medium brown, but all had very straight hair which was considered, and continues to be considered, an important factor when it comes to racial classification and the determination of status in the Spanish-speaking Caribbean. Juancho, the oldest, my mother Virginia, and two other siblings born in the 1920s, Irma and Roberto, came out looking "Spanish." In contrast, my uncles Luis, Raúl, and Ramón came out looking somewhat *trigueño* or Indian, with two other siblings, Ernesto and Francisco, falling somewhere in between. Other family members were also recorded as living in this large household in the period from 1920 to 1930. These included two younger sisters of my grandmother: Nemencia, who died soon after, and Simona Santiago Cruz, who as I remember could surely have been classified as *mulata*, along with her two daughters and her darker African-looking son, Carlos. However, in the 1930 census they too were listed as "White."

Changing Identities and Afro-Latin@ Identities

How my maternal and paternal grandparents viewed race, and how they identified racially, is unknown to me. Both my maternal grandparents died in Puerto Rico in the early 1930s. Mérida, my paternal grandmother, died suddenly and unexpectedly in her Brooklyn home in 1945, and Nicholas Gabriel died several years later in 1951 when I was ten years old. Based on what I remember and what I have learned since then, it appears that he might have tried to minimize or ignore the race issue as much as possible. He married a woman who was much darker in complexion than he was, and he had children whose color ranged from "almost White" to medium brown—all with very wavy or tightly curled hair. His friends and his work and business associates varied by race and nationality. As the head of a Curazaleño community organization in the 1930s who also spoke fluent Spanish, he worked with and was a friend of Joaquín and Jesús Colón, two dark-skinned Puerto Rican brothers who were important leaders of Brooklyn's Puerto Rican and Latino community from the late 1920s to the late 1940s. Like the Colón brothers, he may have tried to emphasize the ideals of a colorblind North American, Puerto Rican, and internationalist identity, which in part was the view asserted in the late 1960s by my uncle Robert (or Norberto) Haslip, his oldest son.[9] I remember when Robert interrupted a conversation on the race issue that I was having with my cousins by declaring that "all of this talk about race is silly" because "we are all Americans and that's the way it should be."

The ethno-racial environment that I first witnessed as a child growing up in New York's East Harlem in the late 1940s was quite complex yet seemingly harmonious. We lived in the East River Houses, an ethnically mixed "municipal housing project" that included families of mostly Italian and Irish background, some African Americans, and only four Puerto Rican families, including ours. The family discourse, especially that of my father, focused on individuals and nationality groups, except for the "colored people" (i.e., African Americans), but we were not "colored people," and it didn't matter anyway as long as they were "good people."

In 1955, we moved to the Pelham Parkway Houses, another municipal housing project in the Williambridge section of the northeast Bronx which also had a complex ethnic mix that nevertheless included very few African Americans and Puerto Ricans or other Latin@s. Proper individual and family behavior and the ideals of a colorblind society also continued to be the main tenor of the family rhetoric during this period, but the public discourse on civil rights and the politics of desegregration in the South had also begun to intervene. As it turned out, there had also been complications or trouble in the alleged racial paradise of the Haslip-Peña family all along. As I reached my teenage years, I began to hear subtle and not so subtle references to family members who had entered into marriages or relationships that were considered correct or incorrect based on the idea of "mejorar la raza"—a concept historically prevalent in Latin America and the Spanish-speaking Caribbean that encourages non-White persons to make every effort to "improve" the family racial stock by marrying White or as White as possible. What resulted in the Haslip-Peña family were racial trajectories that went in different directions depending on the relationships or the marriage decisions that were made and the neighborhoods where family members lived.

In contrast to the Haslip-Peñas, the racial trajectory of the Viera-Santiago branch followed a different path during this period because of their surnames, their time of arrival in New York, and the changes in how race was defined. My mother and her older brother were quickly defined as "White" when they came to New York in 1930–1931. When Puerto Ricans were recognized as an ethnic group and subsequently defined as an undifferentiated racial group in the years between the early 1930s and the early 1950s, they became "Puerto Rican." This was also the experience of my maternal grandmother's younger sister, Simona Santiago Cruz, who came to New York with her children in the mid-1930s. Despite their hair texture and skin color (which ranged from light to medium dark brown), they too became undifferentiated Puerto Ricans by the late 1940s.[10] They became Puerto Rican in the 1940s, and then Puerto Rican/Hispanic by the late 1960s. In recent years, some of the younger light-complexioned members of this extended family have drifted into Whiteness through intermarriage, professional status, and other factors. Others have continued to identify, or have reinforced their identity, as Puerto Ricans or Hispanics regardless of class status. In addition, some of the light and most of the darker complexioned individuals have remained working class and continue to live in East Harlem or the South Bronx. All of these trajectories illustrate how individuals and entire families from the Spanish-speaking Caribbean can successfully ignore, obfuscate, or repress an Afro-Latin@ background through intermarriage, the attainment of economic and professional status, or the acceptance or adoption of a racially undifferentiated Puerto Rican, Hispanic, or Latin@ identity.

Notes

1. Information on race was obtained primarily by enumerator observation through 1950, by a combination of direct interview and self-identification in 1960 and 1970, and by self-identification in 1980 and 1990. Information on Hispanic origin was obtained using various criteria in 1970, including self-identification (as discussed later), and was obtained using only self-identification in 1980 and 1990.

2. The records of the U.S. Census Bureau, military draft cards, and documents pertaining to the application for U.S. citizenship were obtained from databases on the Web site Ancestry.com. Other family documents such as marriage documents, seaman's papers, etc. are in the author's possession.

3. Among Puerto Ricans and other Caribbean Latin@s, a *grifo* or *jabao* is usually described as a person having a white European appearance but with tightly curled hair suggesting a degree of African ancestry. See Thomas M. Stephens, *Dictionary of Latin American Racial and Ethnic Terminology*, 2nd ed. (Gainesville: University Press of Florida, 1999), 227–28, 275–76.

4. On the word *pardo* and its origins, see Manuel Álvarez Nazario, *El elemento afronegroide en el español de Puerto Rico: Contribución al estudio del negro en América* (San Juan: Instituto de Cultura Puertorriqueña, 1974), 347, 352–53; and Stephens, *Dictionary of Latin American Racial and Ethnic Terminology*, 414, 415–18.

5. The use of this label was perhaps based on rules that were applied by the U.S. Census Bureau with regard to classification by race in 1910. See Mara Loveman and Jeronimo O. Muñiz, "How Puerto Rico Became White: Boundary Dynamics and Intercensus Racial Classification," *American Sociological Review* 72, no. 10 (December 2007): 922.

6. In the 1920 census Mérida's younger brother, José Peña Centeno, was also listed as "white" despite his dark complexion. In the 1930 census, all the other persons in the Haslip-Peña household were listed as "*negro*," including two daughters born in the 1920s, my grandmother's Amerindian-looking nephew, Tomás Peña, and four boarders who sublet rooms in the two attached apartments that my grandfather rented at 43 Sackett Street in South Brooklyn (now Cobble Hill).

7. After graduating from high school and briefly attending classes at Brooklyn College, my father became a merchant seaman (1933–1941). He worked in hotels and in the Veterans Administration Hospital in the Bronx, and he was employed by the U.S. Office of Strategic Services (OSS), where he read mail written in Spanish during World War II.

In 1943, he entered the U.S. Customs Service, where he rose from port patrol officer, to customs inspector (1947), and finally to assistant area director for the Port of New York (1972) in charge of enforcement.

8. Loveman and Muñiz, "How Puerto Rico Became White," 922.

9. On the apparent colorblind internationalist identity of the Colón brothers, see Winston James, *Holding Aloft the Banner of Ethiopia: Caribbean Radicalism in Early Twentieth-Century America* (New York: Verso, 1998), chapter 7; and Joaquín Colón López, *Pioneros puertorriqueños en Nueva York, 1917–1947* (Houston, Tex.: Arte Público Press, 2002), 25–29, 294–95.

10. Justina Santiago, another sister of my maternal grandmother, had also come to New York in the 1920s to work for a wealthy Cuban family. She eventually married an Ecuadorian, Rafael Andrade, the family chauffeur, and they had two daughters. In the 1930 census, the Andrades were listed as "Indians" (Native Americans).

¡Eso era tremendo!

An Afro-Cuban Musician Remembers

When I arrived in New York in 1943 I went to live with Mario [Bauzá] at St. Nicholas and 111th Street. I had to sleep on the sofa. So they started looking for a larger apartment so that I could have my own room and that's how we ended up on Columbus Avenue and 106th Street—where they didn't rent to Blacks because that area belonged to the Irish. Mario had a friend, a Cuban mulatto who was married to a White woman, who told him that there was an apartment available in the building across the street from his, "But they don't want Blacks. I'll tell my wife to speak to them as though the apartment is for her." And that's how we got the apartment at 944 Columbus Avenue, a two bedroom with a big living room and an enormous kitchen where everybody gathered and we had our feasts.

But God punished those Irish because their daughters started going out with the Puerto Ricans, and they weren't White Puerto Ricans! *Los irlandeses lo pagaron!* (The Irish got theirs!) Because all those girls, since they went to the same schools, those Puerto Ricans became their boyfriends, and they married and that was that. *Eso era tremendo!* New York was something else in those days.

I loved living on 106th Street and Columbus because that's where most of my friends lived. I've always gotten along well with Puerto Ricans and I have a lot of Puerto Rican godchildren. I still feel connected to El Barrio even though I have been living here [on West 73rd] for the last thirty years. But this place is for Whites. I am not White; I am Black. Not even *mulata*. *Negra*.

Back then Puerto Ricans were the majority; there were few Cubans or Dominicans and the Cubans who were here were very tiresome. We have no reason to be grateful to the Cubans. They didn't come to our performances and they had White Cuban social clubs where people of color could not

Graciela shortly after arriving in
New York City, circa 1943. (Courtesy
of the Mappy Torres Collection)

enter. They had one on Broadway and 110th like that. And there was a dance
hall on Broadway and 145th Street—the Monte Casino—where the Cuban
owner didn't allow Blacks. One time, friends of ours—a *negrita*, a Puerto
Rican, and a Spaniard—went up to the ticket booth and the Spanish girl
asked for three tickets. The man in the booth said, "Two only." "What do
you mean, 'two only'? There are three of us." He pointed to the Black girl
and said, "Because she can't come in." "What?! If she can't go in, neither
can we." And the three of them left.

But, in fact, there were many places like that, and restaurants too, where
Blacks, people of my color, couldn't enter. You had to be very light skinned.
Our orchestra was a success because of the Puerto Ricans and [African]
Americans. We played at big dancehalls, at the Audubon—where they
killed Malcolm X—and at the Hunts Point Palace, and at smaller places
like the Odd Fellows. We also played at the Palladium, the Park Plaza,
Royal Roost, and Bop City.

When Mario started playing at the Park Plaza people would say "those
Blacks can't go downtown." But first the orchestra was contracted to play
at the Royal Roost and Bop City, on Broadway and 50th Street. Since the
[African] Americans were Mario's *compañeros*—because Mario was with
Chick Webb, Cab Calloway, and all those groups—they opened the way.
Dizzy Gillespie was playing there and Mario took a tune and changed a few

things, made it Cuban, and asked Quincy Jones what he thought. "Sí Mario" he said, and that's how Mario got the idea for Afro-Cuban jazz, for what later was called Cubop. So the Blacks did go downtown and there we met many good musicians, including Harry Belafonte, with whom I recorded.

At the Royal Roost and Bop City we worked with Nat King Cole's Trio and Ella Fitzgerald, whom Mario was the first to discover. All the best singers worked with us. At the Apollo we were with Sarah [Vaughn], Dinah [Washington], Billie [Holiday], and Ella. One time at the Apollo I opened for Sarah and sang "Sí, sí, no, no"—a song that became one of my signature pieces because I added words and gestures that the audiences loved, so that I became known as "Graciela, la pintoresca." That night I received a huge ovation from the audience. I was already in the wings but Sarah laughed, pushed me out, and said, "Go on, mother fucker, go take a bow." We all got along very well, from the beginning.

In fact, when I arrived in this country in 1943, my first positive experience was with [African] Americans. I flew into Miami from Havana and then had to take the train to New York. There I was alone with my suitcase, waiting for the train. I had to use the toilet and so I looked around and saw these signs that said "White" and "colored" but I didn't know what they meant. I went into the door marked "White" and this blanca comes up to me, screaming "Get out of here! Get out of here!" And I answered in Spanish, "vete pa'l . . . [go to . . .]," and I do my business. Then back I go to wait for the train. But it's getting later and I am getting hungry and I see a little restaurant. I walk over and start to enter and this blanco yells "Get out of here! Get out of here!" and I think "Oh, my God." Just then a White woman approaches and says something I don't understand either, but she motions for me to follow her and she takes me around to the backyard where there is a kitchen and a Black man who is cooking and she shows me a chair and they gave me some food. So you see there are always a few decent White people.

Finally the train arrives and I see these baseball players that I recognized from Cuba. When I see them, I say "Oh, Campanella!" And he [Roy Campanella] says, "Oh, you Cuban?" "Sí, yo soy cubana," and I started naming Cuban ballplayers like Silvio García and Martín Dihigo, and Campanella calls out, "Come on. Come on." Then they took me to the bar because we couldn't go into the dining car and we were there having drinks until late. I got ready to go to sleep and I see a man carrying pillows and shouting "peelo, peelo," but I didn't know what he was saying. I fell asleep and when I woke up I found myself with a pillow under my head; the ballplayers had put it there.

I loved baseball and whenever we had a free Monday, Mario and I would go see a game. Especially when Jackie Robinson entered the Majors, we would go wherever he was playing, even as far as Philadelphia.

We traveled a lot, here in the United States and in Latin America and Europe and Japan—everybody loved our orchestra. We stayed at some of the best hotels and some not so good ones. In Miami, for example, for a long time Black performers had no good hotel to stay at; even Lena Horne and Sugar Ray [Robinson] and people of that category couldn't stay at the good hotels until finally they built a hotel for people of color. When our orchestra arrived in Miami in the early 1950s, we split up. Mario, the bongo player, and I, because we were *los más prietos*, went to the hotel for Blacks, *en el barrio de los negros* (in the Black neighborhood). I was very comfortable there and would even go out in my robe to sit in the patio. Machito, Johnny, and a few others who weren't as dark stayed at the White hotel. Johnny was [African] American so Machito and the other Cubans taught him some words in Spanish, like "Corre, Johnny, que nos vamos" (Hurry, Johnny, we're leaving). Things like that. But one day one of those racist White women went to the owner and asked him why he was letting Negroes stay at the hotel and he told her: "Number one, they are musicians; and number two, they are Cubans." Can you believe that? Cuban Blacks aren't Black! Boy, did I laugh. As you can see, I'm still laughing.

But things like that happened in South America too. In Bogotá, for example, Chocolate, our first trumpet, and Julián, our *conguero*, were stopped at the airport and weren't allowed to board the plane to our next gig in Lima, Peru; they were the darkest among us. The rest of us stayed at a hotel in Lima that the American millionaire Rockefeller had built. It had a restaurant and I looked in and I recognized the man from the airport who had stopped Chocolate and Julián. So I walked into the restaurant to see what would happen. There was a very large television at the bar and they were announcing that Machito and his orchestra would be playing the next day. That man, in a loud voice, said, "Not all of them because I stopped *esos dos negros* from coming in." That was in the 1960s.

But none of that surprised me because as bad as things were in the United States, they were worse in Cuba. I grew up in the barrio Jesús María, where the ships carrying Congos [Africans], and Spaniards, and all the foreigners—including the Jews—used to enter. My father started out selling root vegetables from a little cart and eventually became a wholesaler for Armor and Swift. He was a good man and out of kindness would donate food to the nuns who ran a school around the corner from our house. One day they asked him if he had any daughters and when he said that he did, they told him to bring one to the school, and he picked me. From the moment I walked in, the other little girls started up: "*Negrita*, what are you doing here?" and I shouted back my own insults. One of them called me a *negra sucia* (dirty Black) and I grabbed her and punched her. Then I went to one of the nuns and told her what had happened but she didn't believe me. So I left and refused to go back to that place. My father had to send me back to my public school.

And that wasn't the only thing. When my parents first rented the house in that neighborhood a White woman came over to my mother and verbally abused her. Black women in Cuba suffered a lot. My mother—who was a beautiful Black woman from Matanzas, the daughter of an *africana* and a Spaniard—was left an orphan at a very young age and she was given over to a Spanish woman who treated her like a slave; she had to do everything in that house. My father would see her as she ran her errands and he fell in love with her and rescued her from that place.

My mother was a very smart woman even though she had no formal education. But in Cuba even an educated woman had few opportunities. In all the years that I was in school, for example, I never saw a Black teacher. A mulata could enter a club only if she was escorted by a White man; otherwise, nothing doing. Racism in Cuba was worse than here. Eso era tremendo!

I've had a good life and few regrets. I've been everywhere and done everything. I haven't had to be running away, or covering up, or hiding from anyone. I'm proud to be a Black woman with a strong sense of my own worth. No man has ever ruled over me. That's why I never married. How was I going to support a man with my earnings? I had a love in every port. Because I was very lucky: men were always falling in love with me. You have no idea what I lost—good men—because I was in the orchestra. But I saw what happened to other women—Libertad Lamarque and Sarah Vaughn, among others—who lost it all because of their husbands.

For me the most important thing is to be proud of being Black. Because if you allow others to intimidate you, then you won't get ahead. The worst thing about being Black is to feel shame about being Black. You have to feel your strength; you are Black and . . . *pa'lante!*

Note

Interview conducted on October 27, 2007, in New York City; translated and edited by Miriam Jimenéz Román.

IV

Roots of Salsa

Afro-Latin@ Popular Music

Since the early decades of the twentieth century the world of popular music has been a rich field of Afro-Latin@ experience that provides a window on the cultural relations between Caribbean Afro-Latin@s and African Americans. James Reese Europe's recruitment of the legendary Afro-Puerto Rican composer and bandleader Rafael Hernández and other Black Bori-

Dancing to the music of Frank "Machito" Grillo and his Afro-Cuban Jazz Orchestra at the Savoy Ballroom, New York, circa 1950. (Photograph by Brown Brothers; Photographs and Prints Division, Schomburg Center for Research in Black Culture, the New York Public Library, Astor, Lenox and Tilden Foundations)

cuas into the Hellfighters Regiment Band during World War I was a great moment in Afro-Latin@ history in the United States, as was the collaboration of the Afro-Cuban innovator Mario Bauzá and the jazz great Dizzy Gillespie in the forging of Afro-Cuban jazz or Cubop in the late 1940s. The special place of the pioneering work of Arsenio Rodríguez, as analyzed in the selection by David García, also warrants attention in the story of New York's Latin music as it leads up to the salsa boom of the 1970s. The Latin boogaloo craze of the mid-1960s attests to the integral interaction of young United States-born Puerto Ricans with their African American counterparts in developing a fusion between the cha-cha and soul sounds of the time. The complexities of the social experiences of these musical greats and their audiences, and the revolutionary changes brought to both jazz and Cuban music history, stand as a testament to Afro-Latin@ creativity and cultural resilience. Poems by the Afro-Latino writers Louis Reyes Rivera and Tato Laviera, among others, evoke the power of music and dance in the cultural life of Black Latin@ communities.

RUTH GLASSER

From "Indianola" to "Ño Colá"

The Strange Career of the Afro-Puerto Rican Musician

"Jazz won the War!" declared the genre's most ardent fans at the end of 1918.[1] Beneath this rallying cry's apparent flippancy were layers of potent meaning. For the Allied victory of World War I owed a great deal to the efforts of nearly four hundred thousand African American soldiers, among whose ranks were numerous bands and singing groups that had charmed their way through France. Christened with regiment nicknames, the "Hell-fighters" of the 369th, the 350th Field Artillery Band, the "Buffaloes" of the 367th, and the "Black Devils" of the 370th put ragtime, vaudeville tunes, spirituals, and southern melodies on France's musical map.[2] Their musical conquests both symbolized the importance of American blacks in the Great War and presaged significant cultural innovations for the United States and Europe in the decades to come.

But the layers of meaning went still deeper. Within the ranks of these black soldiers was still another subculture, Puerto Rican brass and reed players who contributed their considerable talents and lung power to this musical and military effort. These men, recruited directly from Puerto Rico, were among the pioneers who introduced jazz to France. They were also among the first Puerto Rican musicians to sojourn in the mainland United States, exchanging musical ideas with their erstwhile companions and bringing new sounds back to the island.

Within the context of World War I began a process of migration and cultural exchange between two groups, African Americans and Puerto Ricans, that would last for many years. In the shadows of a later world war encounters between Cuban and black American musicians would influence bebop and produce Latin jazz and the mambo. But decades before that, Puerto Ricans and other Latinos played trumpets and tubas and composed and arranged for some of the best-known black and white jazz orchestras in the United States. In turn, they brought jazz orchestrations and harmonies back to Latino ensembles. In many respects World War I was the kickoff point for a creative intermingling that was often invisible to outsiders.

Battling Boricuas

That Puerto Ricans formed part of African American military bands was the result of the confluence of two significant historical events: Congress's passage of the Jones Act, which made Puerto Ricans citizens of the United States, in March 1917;[3] and, just one month later, Congress's declaration of war with Germany and the U.S. entry into World War I. In the flurry of registration that followed, over 236,000 Puerto Rican men were declared eligible for the draft. Nearly 18,000 of these were mustered into the U.S. armed forces. Some 4,000 soldiers were sent to guard the Panama Canal, and the rest trained in Puerto Rico. [. . .]

No Puerto Rican soldier, however, had an experience as acutely bittersweet as that of those members of the African American regimental bands who played and fought overseas. In artistic terms, to be a Negro meant to be in the vanguard of popular music; however, in social terms, it counted for innumerable abuses in the lives of these soldiers. Within just a few months these new recruits felt the sting of racism in northern and southern training camps, as well as the adulation and apparent colorblindness of the French. They were abruptly thrust into the cultures of Harlem and southern-born African Americans. A white world that saw all people of color as essentially alike expected these Puerto Ricans to identify themselves with this new ethnic group both socially and musically. [. . .]

Historic Encounters

The musicians brought to the mainland from San Juan were actually among only a handful of Puerto Ricans who fought the war in France and were part of explicitly "American" regiments. Although relatively few in number, these Puerto Ricans formed a particularly prominent part of the United States Army's most famous musical ensemble, the 369th Infantry "Hellfighters" Band, led by Lieutenant James Reese Europe. Europe himself recruited some eighteen musicians from San Juan's bands and orchestras and probably from advertisements placed in Puerto Rican newspapers.

Victoria Hernández still remembers the *"americano de color"* who arrived in Puerto Rico looking for army musicians. It was May of 1917. Her brother Rafael had left Aguadilla and toured the island with a Japanese circus, and then, like many of his peers, he had gone to San Juan in search of more musical opportunities. Now he was playing violin in the Orquesta Sinfónica of San Juan and trombone in Manuel Tizol's municipal band. He had also organized his own orchestra of a dozen musicians, which played at dances and baseball games and accompanied the silent movies in the Cine Tres Banderas.[4]

For a North American bandleader who had stepped off the boat in San Juan and was conducting a hurried search for instrumentalists, Hernández and his colleagues must have seemed a godsend. With centuries of connections to the colonial military, public bands like Tizol's were decidedly martial in instruments and orchestration. The musicians within both the band and the orchestra were adept at reading sheet music, and most could play several instruments. Europe grabbed Rafael Hernández, his brother Jesús, and sixteen more musicians and took the next boat back to New York.[5]

To date it is still a mystery how James Reese Europe found out that Puerto Rico could supply good musicians for his band. It is possible that he knew about the musicians because they had already been "discovered" by North Americans, a little over a year before. At the beginning of 1917 agents for the Victor Talking Machine Company had stopped off in San Juan as part of a recording tour of South America and the Caribbean. Several numbers by both Tizol's band and an orchestra led by Rafael Hernández ended up on their acetates.[6] Jim Europe had himself been recording for Victor since 1914 and would have had good connections with company personnel. [. . .]

Along with the different social experiences and musical repertoires of these African American and Puerto Rican musicians, there were some similarities and crossovers that promoted exchanges between the two groups during the war and later. Both African American and Puerto Rican music were based largely on the interactions between the members of a forced African diaspora and a European colonizer. Ongoing infusions of African, Latin American, Caribbean, and European migrants added to the musical melange, as did internal migrations within each country. The resemblance between the musical development of New Orleans, the birthplace of much of the most innovative African American music, and that of the islands of the French and Spanish Caribbean was particularly striking.[7]

Musically speaking, therefore, James Reese Europe and Rafael Hernández perhaps had more in common than at first met the eye. As composers and performers, they had worked within somewhat analogous musical forms. Hernández, who had begun to write songs when he was fourteen, had already composed several *danzónes*, a Cuban form with more than a passing similarity to ragtime. Both were syncopated descendants of various strains of rather march-like nineteenth-century European dance music. They were instrumental, multi-sectioned musics, featuring a series of self-enclosed musical themes that often incorporated motifs from other popular, folk, and classical songs. And what was most significant socially, both were the products of leading musicians of color who aspired to make both their music and themselves middle-class and respectable.[8]

There were musical crossovers as well as affinities between the musicians' two groups. The *danzón* and ragtime had influenced each other as a result of close commercial ties between the ports of Havana and New Orleans. James Reese Europe was himself involved in the spread throughout the United States of the tango, already popular in Puerto Rico. Europe's collaboration with dance trendsetters Vernon and Irene Castle brought the tango as well as African American–based dances such as the fox-trot before a national audience for the first time. While the people of Harlem went "tango mad" in 1914, Puerto Ricans were beginning to hear fox-trots as accompaniments to silent films and to dance to them in *casinos*.[9]

In many ways, then, the World War I interaction between African American and Puerto Rican musicians made sense. it is not surprising that it continued after the war. In New York, such collaborations were reinforced by demographic and social factors that often grouped North American blacks and Puerto Ricans together. The parallel oppressions and musical developments of the past combined with close quarters in the present to promote ongoing musical exchanges.

Music Stand Musicians

After the armistice in November 1918, the members of the 369th U.S. Infantry went home heroes both for their bravery in prolonged combat and for their music, to which "France had sung and danced and cried."[10] The entire 369th was awarded the croix de guerre. On February 17, 1919, the regiment finally had its triumphal parade up Fifth Avenue in New York City. Warmly greeted by a spectrum of the city's population, they were even more fervently cheered when they reached Harlem.

James Europe's 369th U.S. Infantry Band went on a postwar tour of the United States and began recording for the Pathé label. The Hernández brothers, Rafael Duchesne, and the other Puerto Rican band mem-

James Reese Europe and the 369th Infantry "Hellfighters" Band on shipboard, 1919. Reese recruited almost half of the band's members in Puerto Rico. (Henry Medina Archives and Services)

bers were almost certainly involved in Europe's recording of early ragtime, jazz, and blues classics, including "Indianola," "Clarinet Marmalade," and "Memphis Blues." They might have continued in a successful mainstream recording career if not for a bizarre and tragic incident. In May 1919 James Reese Europe was fatally stabbed in a quarrel with his drummer, and the band abruptly dissolved.

The honeymoon was over in more ways than one. The public's enthusiastic reception of the regimental bands and the many African American veterans with impeccable war records had led numerous black leaders to believe that racial barriers were being erased through both patriotism and good music. But the war's end heightened white racial anxieties that had been exacerbated by significant demographic changes.

During the war, xenophobic fears of "hyphenated Americans" had led government leaders to accept, albeit reluctantly, the recruitment of black and Puerto Rican troops. In the context of the anti-German hysteria these people of color were thought to be more loyal than many white immigrants and their scions. In turn, thousands of African Americans and Puerto Ricans welcomed the opportunity to prove their loyalty to the United States. By showing that they were good Americans, many blacks hoped to achieve basic social and economic rights within the United States. Similarly, leaders in Puerto Rico felt that this demonstration of loyalty would win them more economic and political autonomy for their island.

But during and after the war, as Congress sharply curtailed migration from Europe and Asia, a tremendous exodus of African Americans from the South began to change the racial contours of northern cities. In New York, this situation was compounded by the in-migration of thousands of Puerto Ricans whose economic situation on the island was deteriorating rather than improving. Once again, there were parallels between the Puerto Rican and the African American experience: members of both groups left behind the constant struggles of farming under increasingly difficult conditions or the disappearing crafts that had sustained them in urban areas to look for factory jobs in the North. Although the particularities of their cultural and economic backgrounds were quite different, Puerto Ricans and African Americans were both swept up in the tensions surrounding this adjustment between blacks and whites in the urban North. In the period during and immediately after the war there were race riots, and a revived Ku Klux Klan spread throughout many states. In New York City the two groups faced increasing segregation in housing and discrimination in jobs and unions. Within both their daily lives and their artistic careers, Puerto Rican musicians within a rigidly biracial North American society were caught up in "Negro" problems. Thus, their musical development in New York City must be understood within the context of opportunities for black artists.

Typically, the world of African American popular music not only reflected these social tensions but had its own dynamic. The postwar period demonstrates the ever-shifting fortunes of black musicians in New York City, dependent on a fickle, white-dominated music industry and audience that placed them in and out of fashion. The fate of black performers often depended both on the achievements of individual African American personalities and on a variable American racial climate rather than on a systematic and progressive acceptance by white America. Moreover, the perennial stereotypes plaguing black musicians before and during the war continued to haunt them afterward.

While the goodwill spread by the Hellfighters and other wartime bands did not eradicate existing or growing social tensions, it did create some new opportunities for black musicians. On the heels of their success during World War I, black bands became almost fixtures on Broadway during the 1920s. Indeed, James Reese Europe's work before, during, and after the war had left behind an enduring legacy: "hundreds of Clef Club and 369th Infantry Regiment musicians were now the leavening of any musical effort."[11] The efforts of black musicians before and during the war combined with a surge of Prohibition era entertainment activity to produce a new black theater. While this entertainment was generally backed and produced by whites, who received most of the financial benefits, it gave black performers an opportunity to do significant work both in Harlem cabarets and on Broadway.

The pioneers in this renaissance of black theater were Eubie Blake and Noble Sissle, alumni of the Clef Club and Hellfighters and in a sense Jim Europe's heirs. Their musical extravaganza *Shuffle Along* opened in May of 1911 at the Sixty-third Street Theater and became an instant hit. Legions of other black writers, as well as ambitious white producers, continued the trend, creating new opportunities for black actors and musicians.

Not surprisingly, some of the Puerto Rican musicians who had triumphantly marched with Jim Europe's band down Fifth Avenue in 1919 became a part of these new musical ventures, as did other recently arrived *boricuas*. Because of the lack of written records and living sources and the apparent penchant for some of those musicians to Anglicize their names under xenophobic pressure, we will probably never know just how many Puerto Rican musicians joined U.S. orchestras in the period prior to World War II. We do know, however, that a number of musicians who became well-known jazz players, particularly on brass and woodwind instruments, came from Cuba and Puerto Rico, as well as Panama, Mexico, and other parts of Latin America. Ray Coen, whose stepfather, Augusto, was a trumpeter who benefited from the receptive climate toward Puerto Rican musicians within this world, explains why they were welcomed: "The musicians who went there were what are called music stand musicians. They know how to read music, they know how to play different types of music. They were zarzuela musicians. So when [Augusto Coen] went to New York the American orchestras, the black American orchestras, were very good musicians, but they didn't have the training that the Puerto Rican musicians had. At that time there were shows. . . . Noble Sissle, they had the *Blackbirds* of 1921, 1922 on Broadway. The black American orchestras used Puerto Ricans a lot to read the parts of the Broadway shows. So there were Moncho Usera, Ismael Morales, [Rafael] Escudero, who played bass."[12]

Scant historical records confirm this participation, suggesting that many more Puerto Rican and Latino musicians formed part of these pit bands and jazz orchestras.[13] A salary list for the 1922 *Shuffle Along* company indicates that such shows could provide a good, if ephemeral, living for Puerto Rican performers. One Francisco Tizol, undoubtedly from the famous San Juan municipal bandleader's family, was listed as a musician making seventy dollars per week, more than twice as much as the show's not yet famous chorus girl Josephine Baker.[14] Other sources show Ralph [Rafael] Escudero, from Manatí, in the orchestra of the *Chocolate Dandies* in 1928. Another Puerto Rican, Ramón "Moncho" Usera, played in Lew Leslie's *Blackbirds* orchestra in the same time period. The Cuban flutist Alberto Socarrás also performed in many of these shows.[15]

The surge of white exposure to black theater, combined with a 1910s dance explosion, brought about a new general popularity for black cabaret and ballroom ensembles as well. With the advent of Prohibition, white and black entrepreneurs and organized-crime figures developed Harlem into a paradise of forbidden nocturnal pleasures for whites on slumming expeditions. In turn, the black bandleaders hired for these nightspots incorporated Puerto Rican and other Latino musicians into their groups with relative frequency. Latinos' work with black bandleaders continued even after the black shows that were a staple of Broadway during the heyday of the Harlem Renaissance had gone out of style for the second time in the still-young twentieth century. Noble Sissle must have been well pleased with the performances he saw during World War I and the black theater renaissance, because his orchestra became a veritable incubator of such musicians. Moncho Usera spent years as an important clarinetist and arranger for the group, going to France with them and starting his own jazz orchestra in Europe.[16] Oscar Madera, a violinist from a famous Puerto Rican municipal band family, recorded with Sissle from at least 1934. In turn, such musicians formed a network that helped other Latinos to get jobs. Within a few years after arriving in New York in 1930, Cuban clarinetist and trumpeter Mario Bauzá had integrated himself into this scene: "I joined Sissle after they broke up with *Shuffle Along*. Sissle opened with his orchestra in the Park Central Hotel. And they got two Puerto Rican people there, the one that got me into there—Ramón Usera, Moncho—and the other was Duchesne, Raf[ael]."[17]

Puerto Rican involvement in this postwar African American entertainment scene did not come about so automatically, but within the complexities of a multiethnic world in which they formed an ambiguous part. In the postwar period Puerto Ricans were still a nearly invisible minority among New York's ethnic populations. While an estimated 35,000 Puerto Ricans lived in New York by the war's end, the African American population there had reached about 150,000.[18] Black American musical groups received the support of both their own sizable communities and the white audiences with whom they were currently popular. Meanwhile, the tango craze had cooled, and other types of "Latin" music had not yet reached the ears of white America. There were few Latino ensembles in New York City during the 1920s, and Puerto Ricans of color were barred from participation in white orchestras. Thus Puerto Rican and Latino participation in African American ensembles was conditioned in part by their prior experiences and in part by the range of options they saw around them. At the same time, Puerto Rican instrumentalists usually did not operate exclusively within a black field. Like other musicians, they took the opportunities they could and carved some out for themselves.

When Jim Europe's band broke up, for example, ex-sergeant Rafael Hernández took off for Cuba, where he spent five years as the director of a cinema orchestra in Havana. Returning to New York in 1925, he formed his own ensemble of Puerto Rican musicians, which had a triumphant debut in the prestigious Palace theater. Hernández spent several months touring the United States with the band of Charles Luckeyth "Luckey" Roberts, one of the finest black stride pianists of his time, and soon after formed his own trío. Hernández, and undoubtedly other Puerto Ricans as well, sandwiched musical jobs with African American groups between performances in Latino musical ensembles.[19]

Puerto Rican experiences in African American orchestras were also conditioned by the needs and desires of black musicians, who were constantly battling pernicious stereotypes. Jim Europe's polished society bands before World War I and Sissle and Blake's Broadway performances afterward sought to bring dignity to African American music and theater. In Shuffle Along Sissle and Blake set out to create the first black show to feature "honest, unburlesqued, romantic love."[20] It was one of the first to eliminate the standard black and blackface minstrelsy—burnt cork, old overalls, thick dialect—and to allow black people to express universal human emotions.

Dignity was important to these musicians, who had spent years performing in impeccable dress before New York's elite, top U.S. military brass, and respectful European audiences. But the stereotype of African Americans as instinctive musicians continued to plague them and to determine their performance strategies. Pianist Eubie Blake vividly describes constraints upon black pit musicians. The band of Shuffle Along and the bands of ensuing productions had to commit entire scores to memory. "'We did that because it was expected of us,' remembers Eubie. 'People didn't believe that black people could read music—they wanted to think that our ability was natural talent.'"[21]

Puerto Rican musicians had to adapt to both white racist expectations and African American strategies to subvert stereotypes. Just as the white world believed that blacks were natural musicians, it tended to categorize all their music as "hot" or "jazz." In fact, jazz historians have often distinguished the New York African American jazz and popular music scene of the early twentieth century from its counterparts in New Orleans and other areas by the formal and elaborate arrangements and sophisticated musicianship demanded by its audiences and practiced by its performers.[22] New York–based musicians such as Ellington, Fletcher Henderson, and Don Redman were careful orchestrators and arrangers who resented being categorized as "hot" jazz musicians. Their enthusiasm for Puerto Rican musicians probably represented their desire to combat prevalent stereotypes by producing a smooth, refined sound. In an atmosphere where training often counted more than improvisational ability, Puerto Ricans and other Latinos from a municipal band background were prized figures. In addition to their reading abilities, other attributes of these musicians made them desirable for black show and cabaret bands. Duke Ellington describes being taken with a group he saw in Washington, D.C., in 1920: "Around this time I met Juan Tizol, the trombonist who came to the Howard Theater with a band from Puerto Rico led by Marie Lucas. This group impressed us very much, because all the musicians doubled on different instruments, something that was extraordinary in those days."[23]

Ellington was so impressed that several years later he invited Tizol, the nephew of San Juan's municipal bandleader, to join his orchestra in New York, starting a musical association that would last many years. In the meantime, Ellington had a chance to see another Puerto Rican performer up close when he and Ralph Escudero came up to New York together in 1922 in clarinetist Wilbur Sweatman's band. Puerto Rican musicians were thus incorporated into the defensive planning of African American musical leaders.

Other indignities and problems were chronic for black musical groups and, in turn, for their Puerto Rican members. Tuba player Ralph Escudero and Ponce trombonist Fernando Arbello both played with Fletcher Henderson, the most popular black orchestra leader in New York for much of the 1920s, for several years. When Henderson was contracted in 1924 to play in the Roseland Ballroom opposite a white band, the white musicians objected. A few months later they quit in protest.[24] Underpayment, lack of union protection, and tremendous difficulties in making sleeping and eating arrangements when on tour (usually in segregated theaters) were standard in the lives of black musicians of the period. While black shows were popular on Broadway during the 1920s, they operated on shoestring budgets, which all but evaporated during the Depression era. Only a small number of black performers made it to the big-time vaudeville theaters, and they were taboo in most of the elegant downtown hotels and night-spots. And the Harlem nightclubs where they could perform were often barred to black patrons. John Hammond, a record producer who did much to promote black musicians from the 1930s onward, was partly inspired by witnessing their struggles in this period: "The fact that the best jazz players barely made a living, were barred from all well-paying jobs in radio and in most nightclubs, enraged me."[25] Hammond remembers a rampant segregation, persisting well into the 1930s, in which mixed bands were banned in public and black and white musicians rarely knew each other. Even recording studio work with mixed personnel was risky for an ambitious white artist until near the close of the decade. In any case, white musicians and their contractors virtually monopolized studio work, just as they reaped most of the fame and money in the swing band era. The conspicuousness of a few black bands only helped to mask these conditions. As Hammond wrote in 1936, "The spectacular colored bands such as Ellington, Calloway, Lunceford, with their gleaming tympani and flashy uniforms, have given the impression that Negro musicians are on the top of the economic ladder. Little does the public know of the tremendous odds even the greatest of colored musicians must constantly battle: racketeering managers, Jim Crow unions, outright discrimination."[26] Indeed, even among the most famous black performers salaries varied greatly. Jack Schiffman, the son of the Apollo Theater owner, noted that "there wasn't any rhyme or reason to band salaries in the thirties." While Duke Ellington and Cab Calloway's bands earned several thousand dollars a week in 1932, Fletcher Henderson and his musicians got only $950. Other performers, such as comedian Pigmeat Markham, received less than a hundred dollars weekly.[27]

Community Context

The Puerto Rican musicians who participated in African American bands were caught up in their struggles to earn a living under decent conditions with as much dignity as possible. When they were performing or on tour, they had to play the same music and face the same humiliations and dangers as American blacks. When they returned home, however, their identities might undergo a change.

Puerto Rican musicians generally lived among their nonmusical *compatriotas* in working-class neighborhoods. While the demographic accident that had brought Puerto Ricans and African Americans to New York City at the same time resulted in a proximity that meant opportunities for cultural and occupational mingling for those who were musicians, it created competition for most members of both groups, who fought for jobs and housing in an era of increasing occupational and residential restrictions for people of color. Within New York, newly arrived as well as established African Americans and Puerto Ricans and other "West Indians" jostled each other for the few jobs that would accept them and apartments in the few neighborhoods not off-limits to them.

The day-to-day tensions between African Americans and Puerto Ricans were undoubtedly exacerbated by the struggles of nonwhite boricuas to come to terms with the monolithic "Negro" identity imposed upon them from the outside by a racist North American society. In case they forgot, the signs on many New York City apartment buildings that read "No Dogs, No Negroes, and No Spanish" reminded Puerto Ricans and other Latinos that many whites put them in the same inferior category as they did black Americans.[28] [. . .]

Puerto Rican artists' struggle to earn a living in New York almost inevitably involved some measure of crossover to the North American mainstream popular music scene. But that scene presented very different choices to musicians of darker and lighter complexions. The bluntly bipolar racial situation, manifested so strongly in music as well as in daily life, did a great deal to bifurcate the career paths of Puerto Rican musicians. Unlike the relatively isolated North American black and white musicians, a spectrum of Puerto Ricans might know each other intimately through Puerto Rican and New York community ties, shared professional experience on the island or mainland, or *compadrazgo* (godparenthood) or even family connections. One extreme example, given by Mario Bauzá, was of Rafael Duchesne, a relative of the World War I Hellfighters clarinetist of the same name, and his brother Miguel: "There were two [Duchesnes], Miguel and Raf. . . . When the Radio City opened, Miguel was in the pit orchestra with the Figueroa brothers [members of another famous Puerto Rican family of primarily classical musicians], and Raf Duchesne was a jazz player with the Noble Sissle orchestra. You know what happened with the two brothers? They had nothing in common. The one at Radio City used to cut his hair with a machine so they didn't see it, and tried to pass for something like half Jew. The other one had better hair, but [was] a little darker."[29]

The emotional costs of passing versus not passing must have been especially great within families such as the Duchesnes, who had such a longstanding and proud tradition of music making on the island. We can only speculate about the heavy costs dark Puerto Rican musicians faced in adjusting to the identity of the African American in the years following World War I.

Bauzá's own history gives us some idea of one black Latino's voluntary construction of an African American musical and social identity and the tensions among New York's Latinos that it both reflected and caused. Raised by white godparents in Cuba, Mario Bauzá was forced early on to confront issues of racial identity in a country that he claims was more racist than the United States. And yet musically speaking, this prodigy had training and experience paralleling that of many Puerto Rican musicians of the same era. Schooled by private teachers and in public bands, while still a boy Bauzá was playing operas, ballets, zarzuelas, and other classical works in the Havana Symphonic Orchestra. Nevertheless, Bauzá's first glimpse of Harlem in 1929, while he was recording in Victor's New York office studios with a Cuban group, fascinated him: "Here a big black race, they had everything, they had shows, they had good orchestras, good artists." Upon his return to Cuba, when his *padrino* (godfather) inquired about his future plans, he replied, "I only got one plan. I want to be with the people like me, [to] know what it is to be a black man in a black country. My roots have got to be there." Despite linguistic and cultural differences, not to mention the potentially greater prestige of playing in a symphonic orchestra in his native country, Bauzá chose to throw in his lot with African Americans playing popular music. He spent the next ten years with the orchestras of Noble Sissle, Don Redman, Cab Calloway, Chick Webb, and others. Feeling betrayed by the racism of lighter-skinned Latinos, he lived in a black section of Harlem. According to Bauzá, this horrified many Latino acquaintances, who, if they could not live downtown, were going to maintain themselves as a group apart from the unenviable North American black population: "All these Puerto Rican families wanted me to move to their house. I was a single man. 'Mario, why don't you live with us?' 'No, no, I'm working with these people and you know, I want to be with them . . . I'm making my living with them.' 'Well, all right, but you know these black people . . .' 'But I'm black too. What are you talking about?'"[30]

Not every case was as dramatic as the Duchesnes' or Bauzá's, but it was clear that white or light-skinned Latinos with talent and ambition found success, if they were lucky, in ways that were not open to even the finest Afro-Latin musicians. Such divergent career models for people so intimately connected must have caused great community tensions. Within the jazz world, for example, Louis "King" García, a trumpeter who moved to the United States in the early 1920s after working in the San Juan Municipal Band, was cited by Bauzá as "looking like a German."[31] A good player, his complexion gave him access to the Dorsey Brothers' and Benny Goodman's bands. Miguel Angel Duchesne, a cousin of the brothers cited above, spent years as orchestra leader Paul Whiteman's "hot Spanish trumpet."[32]

Since the segregation was to a certain extent one-way, however, light-skinned musicians might have multiracial career options. Juan Tizol, who was white, spent years shuttling between the orchestras of Duke Ellington and Harry James. Moncho Usera played with Xavier Cugat and arranged for him and a number of white bands as well as for Noble Sissle and black Latin ensembles.

Latin Bands

With the onset of the Depression and the scarcity of jobs, white swing bands crowded most black ensembles out of the musical scene. The band business during these years became increasingly expensive, elaborate, and centralized, and blacks were often shut out of the national tour circuits and network radio, which had become necessary for an ensemble's commercial success. Not surprisingly, the racism affecting the development of the North American popular bands in which Puerto Ricans played also had its effects on the Latin music scene coming into prominence in the late 1920s and 1930s. The difficulties experienced by most African American bands undoubtedly led to severe unemployment and underemployment for the Latino members. It is likely that the circumstances pushed many Puerto Rican and Latino musicians who had dreamed for years of creating Latin orchestras to strike out on their own.

But when Puerto Rican and other Latinos decided for commercial or personal reasons to "go back" to Latin music, the choices for darker- and lighter-skinned musicians were again geographically and racially separated. The downtown Latin "relief" bands, which alternated with featured orchestras in elegant hotels and clubs, were usually made up of whites only. While the rules may have been made by the ballrooms and hotels, the bandleaders rarely challenged them. Mario Bauzá remembers a number of them: "Well, there was a few big bands. Enrique Madriguera was one, Eddie LeBaron, the band in the Martinique, there was a band in the Stork Club, there was one in the Morocco, all the swanky places."[33] Puerto Rican

Juanito Sanabria was playing at the Havana-Madrid, and Cuban Anselmo Sacassas at La Conga. Although Xavier Cugat employed a number of Puerto Ricans in his stint at the Waldorf Astoria, he never hired those with dark skins. Singer Bobby Capó remembered that even in the 1940s, when restrictions were looser, Cugat regretfully refused his services saying, "What a pity you are so dark" because he feared a violent response in his southern tours to Capó's slightly more than olive hue. Capó also recalled that Aguadillan pianist and bandleader Noro Morales, who spent years playing at the Stork Club, had a similar policy.[34]

As in their jazz band careers, interpersonal connections among the artists made such situations ironic as well as unfair. Rafael and Victoria Hernández's family had compadrazgo ties with the Morales family. But whereas Noro and his brother Ismael, who played flute with Cugat's orchestra, had successful downtown careers performing for North American audiences, Rafael had played with the great but mostly unrecognized and unrewarded Luckey Roberts. Pedro Ortíz Dávila, known as "Davilita," became an important vocalist with uptown Latin bands and small groups, but unlike his compatriot and fellow singer Johnny Rodríguez, he never made it to the wealthy white cabaret audiences.

To a certain extent the irony worked both ways, at least for the really successful musicians. Hernández may have been restricted to uptown live-performance sites in New York, but he became internationally famous partly as a result of racism. Seeking countries where he could be a respected orchestra leader, composer, and radio personality, Hernández and his compositions traveled to Cuba, Mexico, and finally back to Puerto Rico. Conversely, the light-complexioned Latin relief bands that were fixtures in downtown ballrooms during the 1930s had a high social status in a society that equated white skin and plush surroundings with success. At the same time, their very categorization as relief bands was a ruse that allowed club owners to pay them less than union wages for work under grueling conditions. Bauzá, however, who willingly lived and worked among African Americans, got his most lucrative jobs in their musical circles. "In Harlem I was a big shot. I was one of the best-dressed musicians in Harlem. They [the other Latino musicians] were making thirty, forty dollars a week and I was making four, five hundred recording. All the black musicians, they look for me for jobs." Bauzá was making much more money in the African American ensembles than his ostensibly higher-status compatriots were making in the relief bands. He also claims that the musicianship in his groups was far superior. According to Bauzá, light-skinned Latin relief bandleaders' pandering to the racism of white club owners not only hurt them musically but socially and economically divided the Latino artistic community. Much of the tension between Afro-Latin artists and members of this light-skinned relief band workforce came out in a meeting that turned into a confrontation between Bauzá and such musicians in the late 1930s: "One day, I just arrived from the road with Chick Webb [paraphrases from letter he received]: 'Dear Brother Mario Bauzá, we want to get together such and such a day in the Toreador Night Club because we feel discriminated [against] here because the Latin bands is being classified as a relief band.' Naturally they're a relief band because they go there and play [sings] 'Oyeme Cachita, ticky ticky ticky' and the other band was a white band play show and everything else. So they didn't want that title no more, they grow up already. So I went to the reunion. I wonder what the 'brothers' got to say."[35]

Bauzá, who was the only black person in the gathering, felt that he was being used because of his prestige and connections gathered from his experience with famous African American bands. He quickly got up and made a few criticisms which he claims ended the whole meeting: "I'm working American bands, I don't work with them. They don't use nobody like me in those nightclubs, Rainbow Room, Morocco. And I say, the reason why you people been classified like that [is] the musical standard you people don't have. You people know where I am. But all the people in New York that look like me, they don't have no chance because you don't use them, so how the hell you going to call me to go and demand something to the local 802?"[36]

Accommodating the racism of the society they found themselves in, the bandleaders had failed to organize themselves along cultural lines. The net result, according to Bauzá, was a weakening of both their musical and their economic bargaining positions. Among Latino musicians in New York there was no equivalent to Jim Europe's Clef Club to bind them together as an entity or to provide an alternative to racist or inadequate performers' institutions such as the American Federation of Musicians' local.

In the meantime musicians such as Bauzá and legions of other dark-skinned Latinos were channeling their apparent liability toward the formation of an exciting uptown Latin music scene. This scene was largely made up of veterans of the African American popular orchestras. To a certain extent these artists were going back to their musical roots, thus belying the stereotyped picture of ethnics on a slow and steady road toward assimilation into "American" culture. At the same time, they were following a particular musical path shaped by their racial circumstances. Moreover, the whole concept of going back was tempered by the inevitable influence of their years in one particular kind of North American ensemble. These musicians returned to El Barrio to play Latin music before Hispanic audiences; the music itself was greatly influenced by African American jazz.

Notes

1. Emmett J. Scott, *Scott's Official History of the American Negro in the World War* (New York: Arno Press, 1969 [1919]), 306.

2. Some of the Puerto Ricans who fought and played in the 369th and other regiments were Rafael Hernández, Jesús "Pocholo" Hernández, Rafael Duchesne, Ceferino Hernández, Eligio Rijos, Gregorio Félix Delgado, Antonio González Cancel, Froilán Jiménez, Eleuterio J. Meléndez, Nicolás Vásquez, José Rosa, Genaro Torres, Leonardo Cruz, Páblo Fuentes Más, Arturo Ayala, Sixto Benítez, Angel Carrión, and Francisco Meléndez (courtesy of Donald Thompson, Río Piedras, Puerto Rico, and the National Personnel Records Center, Division of Military Records, St. Louis, Missouri).

3. Though Puerto Ricans were citizens under the law and therefore draftable, they could not vote in presidential elections and could not create binding legislation without the approval of the U.S. Congress.

4. There is some debate over whether the orchestra was known as Los Jolly Boys (Victoria Hernández, interview by the author, New York, March 27, 1989; Rafael Aponte Ledée, "Una fotografía y . . . unos chuscos," *El Nuevo Día*, January 7, 1987) or as the Sombras de La Noche (Night Shadows) (Jorge Javariz, "Trayectoria artística y discográfica de Rafael Hernández, in *El disco en Puerto Rico 1892–1965* [Ponce, Puerto Rico: Museo del Arte, 1992], 27). Aponte Ledée claims that Los Jolly Boys was formed by Hernández to compete with the Sombra de la Noche [sic], an orchestra directed by Carmelo Díaz Soler.

5. Noble Sissle, "Happy in Hell: Memoirs of Lieutenant James 'Jim' Europe" [October 1942], Manuscript Division, Arthur A. Schomburg Center for Research in Black Culture, New York, New York, 18.

6. Recording ledger, Victor Talking Machine Company, 1917, Radio Corporation of America Archives, New York.

7. See, e.g., Leonardo Acosta, *Música y descolonización* (Havana: Editorial Arte y Literatura, 1982), 183.

8. John Santos, notes for *The Cuban Danzón: Its Ancestors and Descendants*, Ethnic Folkways FE 4066; Edward A. Berlin, *Reflections and Research on Ragtime* (Brooklyn: Institute for Studies in American Music, Conservatory of Music, Brooklyn College of the City University of New York, 1987); William J. Schafer and Johannes Riedel, *The Art of Ragtime* (New York: Da Capo, 1977 [1973]).

9. Berlin, *Reflections and Research on Ragtime*, 77.

10. Little, *From Harlem to the Rhine*, 350.

11. David Levering Lewis, *When Harlem Was in Vogue* (New York: Alfred A. Knopf, 1981), 171.

12. Ray Coen, interview by the author, Río Piedras, Puerto Rico, January 1989.

13. For example, an account of a Puerto Rican musician's death, "La muerte de Yeyo," *El Nuevo Mundo*, December 29, 1928, mentions flowers being sent to the funeral home by the Blackbirds Orchestra and the McKinney's Cotton Pickers, thus indicating Yeyo's probable firsthand acquaintance with these black North American groups. Since only the most famous Puerto Rican–born players are found in jazz dictionaries, and only those who actually recorded with jazz and popular groups are found in discographies, there were probably lesser-known musicians involved in this scene who are invisible to us.

14. Robert Kimball and William Bolcom, *Reminiscing with Sissle and Blake* (New York: Viking, 1973), 127.

15. Brian Rust, *Jazz Records, 1897–1942* (Chigwell, U.K.: Storyville, 1981); Leo Walker, *The Big Band Almanac* (Pasadena: Ward Ritchie, 1989); Leonard Feather, *The Encyclopedia of Jazz* (New York: Horizon, 1960); Barry Kernfeld, ed., *The New Grove Dictionary of Jazz* (London: Macmillan, 1988).

16. Usera was an extremely important Puerto Rican musician and arranger who deserves detailed study. He worked with many groups and was for a long time the arranger for the musically nonliterate Pedro Flores.

17. Mario Bauzá, interview by the author, New York, June 2, 1989.

18. Bernardo Vega, *Memoirs of Bernardo Vega*, ed. César Andreu Iglesias, trans. Juan Flores (New York: Monthly Review, 1984), 107; American Social History Project, *Who Built America? Working People and the Nation's Economy, Politics, Culture, and Society*, vol. 2 (New York: Pantheon, 1992), 240.

19. Javariz, "Trayectoria artística y discográfica de Rafael Hernández," 28.

20. Kimball and Bolcom, *Reminiscing with Sissle and Blake*, 93.

21. Ibid., 116

22. See the account in Thomas Hennessey, "From Jazz to Swing: Black Jazz Musicians and Their Music, 1917–1935," Ph.D. dissertation, Northwestern University, 1973. While there were many highly trained African American and Creole musicians in New Orleans, many musicians in the post-ragtime jazz world were not reading musicians.

23. Duke Ellington, *Music Is My Mistress* (Garden City, N.Y.: Doubleday, 1973), 34.

24. Samuel B. Charters and Leonard Kunstadt, *Jazz: A History of the New York Scene* (Garden City, N.Y.: Doubleday, 1962), 153.

25. John Hammond with Irving Townsend, *John Hammond on Record: An Autobiography* (New York: Summit, 1977), 68.

26. John Hammond [Henry Johnson], "The Negro in the Jazz Band," *The New Masses*, November 17, 1936, 15.

27. Jack Schiffman, *Uptown: The Story of Harlem's Apollo Theater* (New York: Cowles, 1971), 151–53.

28. Esperanza Delgado, interview by the author, New York, October 21, 1988.

29. Mario Bauzá, interview by the author, New York, June 2, 1989. Ironically, Bauzá uses the racist term "better hair." Classifying people of color according to "good" and "bad" hair seems to have been as prevalent in the Spanish-speaking Caribbean as it was in the United States.

30. Mario Bauzá, interview by the author, New York, May 8, 1989.

31. Ibid.

32. Angélica Duchesne, interview by the author, Caparra Heights, Puerto Rico, January 5, 1993.

33. Mario Bauzá, interview by the author, New York, May 8, 1989.

34. Bobby Capó, interview by the author, New York, April 12, 1988.

35. Ibid.

36. Ibid.

LOUIS REYES RIVERA

Excerpt from cu/bop

they came
& they met
in the harrows of big apple slightslice
on the corners of lenox & third
down inside brooklyn harlem after hour grind spot
with their trumpets & axes
bongos & timbales
maracas & congas
chops & drums
bass & piano
bleeding needing emerging
mambo kings & bebop monarchs
mondongo fare & chittlin roast
like   yuca
          yuca
          yuca tenango
yuca yuca yuca tenango
peas & rice
greens & grits
hocks & rinds

JAIRO MORENO

Bauzá–Gillespie–Latin/Jazz

Difference, Modernity, and the Black Caribbean

"Deehee no peek pani, me no peek Angli, bo peek African."
—Luciano "Chano" Pozo, as told by Dizzy Gillespie

In his autobiography *To Be, or Not . . . to Bop*, John Birks "Dizzy" Gillespie (1917–1993) reckons that "very early, the tunes I wrote, like Pickin' the Cabbage [1940] sounded Latin oriented or expressed a Latin feeling, like putting West Indian hot sauce in some black-eye peas or hot Cuban peppers in a dish of macaroni."[1] Immediately, Gillespie turns to the figures who shaped his affinity with Latin music, noting that "this in part shows the influence of Mario Bauzá (1911–1993) and Alberto Socarrás (1908–1989). . . . But instinctively," he continues, making an intensely subjective swerve, "I've always had that Latin feeling. You'd probably have to put me in psychoanalysis to find out where it came from, but I've always felt polyrhythmic from a long way back. Maybe I'm one of those 'African survivals' that hung on after slavery among Negroes in South Carolina." Gillespie's vivid metaphorical displacements (from palate to ear, from stove to music stand), the individual agency of his musical mentors, his allusion to a deeply buried archive of cultural memory, and the specificity of his North American South Atlantic locality all form a set of mutually dependent elements in which he inscribes a known historical fact: the strong presence of what he calls "Latin" music in his practice as a jazz musician.

The historical embedding within jazz of musical forms and styles with roots in the Spanish Caribbean is the subject of much speculation.[2] Cultural and economic ties between the Caribbean and New Orleans going back to the late eighteenth century placed music into the flow of exchanges among an assortment of Black, Creole, Spanish, French, and White North American musicians. The renewed force with which Latin musics emerge in jazz beginning in the late 1910s owes to a rapid migration of musicians from postcolonial Cuba, Puerto Rico, the Dominican Republic, and Panama to New York City.[3] From the 1940s on, the focus of Gillespie's reckonings, Latin music cannot be framed as a "tinge" (after "Jelly Roll" Morton's widely circulated quip) but rather as an explicit part of musico-aesthetic experimentation by Black Cubans and Black North Americans.

The personal stories I relate come from that period. My commentaries look at these stories critically, with an eye to outlining the conditions of possibility for the emergence of Latin jazz as a distinct musical presence in New York. At the core of these stories is the encounter between Bauzá and Gillespie as a series of mutual readings and interested misreadings of cultural and identitarian ideologemes. The "Black Caribbean," as I call the cultural and historical space within which these developments take place (borrowing Paul Gilroy's influential insight in *The Black Atlantic: Modernity and Double Consciousness*), is seen as *constitutive of* and *constituted by* a conception of identity inscribed in the particular temporal and spatial dislocations of a North American modernity. It should be clear at the onset that, without detracting from its musical accomplishment, I consider the emergence of Latin jazz not so much as a celebrated contribution balanced between related expressive cultures (Gillespie), and certainly not as a "marriage" of musical styles (Bauzá), but as a tense and dynamic syncopation of sonic and social histories and temporalities. In my account, "Latin," "Cuban," or "Afro-Cuban" are integrated in the jazz tradition, but only marginally, within a decidedly modernist cognitive and psychic ambivalence that Black North American musicians experienced as they contemplated a Black Other.

Bauzá's Romance

"Welcome home, welcome to New York," said the Latina journalist greeting Bauzá at the airport on his return from a tour in 1983. "Mario," she continued, "you are one of the pioneers of Latin American musicians coming to this country." "Fifty-three years," he confirmed. "What is the difference between now and fifty-three or thirty years ago and today and a Latin American artist coming here?" she asked. "Transportation, for one thing," Bauzá replied. "It took me three and one-half days in a boat to come from Havana here, and I just come from another country in inside of five hours." Prompted to talk about the attraction that New York exerts over musicians, Bauzá framed the matter in a mixture of familial and religious metaphors: "Not only Latin American musicians, but from all over

Mario Bauzá—musician, arranger, composer, music director, bandleader, and founding father of Latin Jazz—in New York City, 1942. (Henry Medina Archives and Services)

the world come into New York, the Mecca of the music. That's all they have in their mind: New York. To me, the greatest jazz artists that this country has developed through the years and years and years [came to New York], and they want to be part of that family."[4]

Every musical culture in the West has its sacred sites, and by the early 1920s New York, along with Chicago, had been consecrated as that place for jazz. New York was an obligatory destination of sorts for musical pilgrims and also for those interested in incorporating themselves into a rapidly emerging international market centered in and around United States mass culture. Bauzá first came to New York from Havana in 1927 as a member of Antonio María Romeu's charanga orchestra. He made the boat trip of "three and one-half days" to record for RCA, whose executives were trying to market an alternative Latin fashion to the then raging tango fever. The New York City that Bauzá encountered resonated loudly in his musical imagination. Mesmerized by Gershwin's use of jazz idioms in the context of a concert piece for a large orchestra, he heard four daily performances of "Rhapsody in Blue" with the Paul Whiteman Orchestra. Uptown, Bauzá witnessed firsthand the vibrant Black cultural life of the Harlem Renaissance, noting particularly the privileges that audiences granted Black bandleaders and musicians at places such as the Lafayette and Lincoln theaters, the Smalls Paradise, and many other "shrunken spots" where people would "hang around all night," as he would later reminisce.

It was to participate in this scene that Bauzá returned in 1930 to New York, where he was determined to stay and become a "jazz musician." With the misplaced romanticism of someone having an affair in a foreign land, Bauzá did not expect, once the affair turned into a permanent relationship, having to negotiate the vicissitudes of daily life, particularly in a society intensely defined by racial and ethnic difference. It was one thing to drop in on a thriving Harlem as a visitor, and yet quite another to live and work while navigating the well-mapped territories of uptown New York City, and within those territories the ever-narrower circumscriptions of one ethnic group or another. As Bauzá notes: "So I came back by myself. It was very hard [to find] anyone to speak Spanish all day; you gotta come all the way to 116th Street to the East Side, from Lenox into Fifth, but no more than Lexington because Italians don't let Latinos walk after hours from Fifth Avenue to the East Side. That was kind of rough, but I keep myself in Harlem, what I came here for." Just how rough was it? The sign "No Dogs. No Negroes, No Spanish" found in apartment buildings in Manhattan viciously put dark-skinned Spanish speakers under a kind of double (racial and ethnocultural) jeopardy. This atmosphere of open and unbridled racism stood in contrast to the cosmopolitan 1920s in Havana, where, however heavily influenced by United States economic policies and their attendant "whitening" of the sociopolitical sphere and however marred by social and economical inequalities largely drawn around racial difference, Bauzá had had a more integrated socioeconomic space in which to navigate. He had, furthermore, enjoyed the advantages of a privileged economic upbringing with his godparents—wealthy Spaniards who, by his own account, provided him with a first-rate education and inculcated in him a spirit of cultural tolerance. And although in his early teens he had given up a scholarship to study music in Italy because of fears of racial discrimination there, race had not impeded a spectacular musical career for him at home. At age twelve, he had begun substituting for his clarinet teacher in the Havana Symphonic Orchestra (Cuba's most prestigious classical ensemble), and at sixteen the clarinet chair was his. Soon, he was also in increasing demand by the best dance orchestras. But back in Harlem, he recalled, the bleak racial landscape of a divided society accentuated the sense of cultural alienation: "Now and then, I wanna meet some people and there was no practical [way]; [there were] very, very few

Puerto Ricans." This view was held by Bauzá in spite of the fact that by the early 1920s there were approximately 35,000 Puerto Ricans in New York.

It is against this personal backdrop that Bauzá's otherwise unequivocal success as a jazz musician in New York emerges. By any standards, Bauzá accomplished his stated professional goals by entering the inner sanctum of the elite swing bands on the strength of his musical skills and personal discipline. Throughout the 1930s, he performed (on saxophone and trumpet) with the orchestras of Noble Sissle, Don Redman, Cab Calloway, and Chick Webb, among others, and in the city's most prestigious uptown club circuit that included the Savoy Ballroom and the Cotton Club. Webb, for one, designated Bauzá as bandleader, in which capacity he delegated parts, selected numbers, chose arrangers, and created set lists. Clearly, Bauzá thrived in the musical meritocracy that subtended the elite family of the New York City–based Black North American swing orchestras. This professional "family" would have overlooked his ethnic background as it did with other musicians from the Spanish-speaking Caribbean, many of whom were much sought after because of their ability to read music— a skill gained either in municipal bands or else, as was Bauzá's case, through a classical music education at conservatories in the musicians' home countries.[5]

In spite of the feelings of cultural isolation that Bauzá expressed, the empathy with Black North American culture he experienced during his first trip to Harlem did not wane. Nonetheless, it would be misguided to assume that the shared racial background erased all differences between him and his Black North American peers. Cab Calloway, for one, called Bauzá "Indian," short for West Indian. Although this marker no doubt was intended as a harmless nickname among peers, it introduced an immediately recognizable vector of distance and difference between Bauzá and other musicians in the band. That the nickname was given by the bandleader, thereby likely sanctioning its use by other band members, only accentuated the subtle asymmetry at play in the relation of a Black Cuban minority within the minority of the larger "native" Black community. In fact, such naming was institutionalized through widespread use; with the sole exception of Puerto Ricans, Black North Americans in New York identified all other immigrants from the Caribbean as "West Indians." [. . .]

The internal divisions and tensions within the Latin music scene that Bauzá diagnosed bear directly on the emergence of a musical style where Cuban dance music encounters the sound of the Black North American swing orchestra. Besides relief bands, other far more commercially successful Latin bandleaders held fast to racial segregation. This was certainly the case for Xavier Cugat, the Catalan-born Cuban musician whose orchestra became the mainstream representative of Cuban and Latin music in New York in the wake of the rumba craze that began in the early 1930s; Cugat, who like Bauzá was a child prodigy in Cuba, held forth at the Waldorf-Astoria from 1932 to 1947. Bauzá again observed the lack of representation of Black Latin musicians in music he considered unthinkable without their contribution. "Every time I seen it," he observed in *Música*, "the Latin bands was lily-white or something similar to that. Musicians of my color, they had no opportunity in those bands." The urgent desire for representation and the struggle for musico-expressive recognition and self-regulated economic options began with an analysis that no longer viewed the existing asymmetries in the binary terms of U.S. racism: "I said, 'but these people . . . they ain't with Black and they ain't with the other one, where are they? Nowhere.' So I said, 'I gotta organize a band.' That's how I organized the Machito band."

For Bauzá, Machito and his Afro-Cubans gave form to musico-cultural self-identifications that are no doubt forged by the exclusionary politics and economics of racism in New York in the late 1930s. These factors alone, however, do not fully explain why Bauzá organized an orchestra to present a new kind of music mixing Afro-Cuban and jazz elements. His response to the impersonal market networks in New York takes on a more complex and personal form, cast in deeply affective terms. "When I got [on] the boat on my own," he also said, and I believe crucially, "my homeland missed [out], and that's how I organize the Machito and his Afro-Cubans." [. . .]

Marriage and Syncopation

While Gillespie, the Black North American, speaks of combining unlikely ingredients in a dish, Bauzá, the Black Cuban immigrant, speaks of something more intimate, personal, and familial: marriage. This is a marriage in which, furthermore, his agency is complexly articulated as being both a participant and the matchmaker. Bauzá, for one, had precise plans for the musical direction that Machito and his Afro-Cubans ought to take. Determined to provide an alternative to the watered-down versions of Latin dance music performed by Cugat's big band, to give an extreme case, he accentuated the percussive elements, rhythmic sensibilities, and metric orientations of Cuban dance music and foregrounded its proclivities toward vocal and instrumental improvisation, as well as other Afro-Cuban musico-cultural markers such as call-and-response. Equally important, he put to good use the vast knowledge and accent-free command of jazz idioms that he gained in the elite swing circles. The next step, he said, was "to get the marriage of the two musics, the jazz and the Afro-Cuban music."

Bauzá defined for himself a distinctive agency in the marriage by deciding who gets married, when, and most importantly, under what conditions. His was the transculturist's approach, strategically using selected features of the (relatively) dominant musical culture (for example, orchestration and harmony, which he calls "sound") and incorporating them alongside defining features of the subaltern group's musical culture (such as rhythm). This approach redefined the overall sonic imprint of the subaltern group's music. Marked elements of the subaltern group held, in this new sound, a place of prominence in the musical surface: Spanish was the language of choice for the lyrics and dense percussion layers dominated and helped structure the compositional texture. Instrumental numbers could exhibit some of the harmonic intricacies characteristic of bebop, or could equally feature unchanging single chord vamps or *montunos*, as they are called by Cuban musicians. [. . .]

The admission of difference between two Black musical cultures introduced two distinct issues into the discourse tying rhythm to Blackness.[6] First, it signaled the existence of a rhythmic practice perhaps more fundamentally "Black" than that of Black North Americans. Second, it imposed on Black musicians a two-tiered classification of musical competency, for the readily acknowledged rhythmic complexity of the Afro-Cuban musical tradition put Black North American swing and bebop musicians at a disadvantage. Indeed, when first playing with Cuban musicians the difficulties experienced by acknowledged jazz giants such as Max Roach are legendary. These issues elicited intense feelings of loss among key Black North American musicians involved with Afro-Cuban music and raised for them what Gilroy (after LeRoi Jones) calls the "challenge of a changing same," that is, the question of "variation between Black cultures."[7] Black North American musicians responded to this challenge with their own interpretive scheme to give thematic form to the two shades of Black that were party to Bauzá's marriage. In it, Bauzá's homeland is recast (and effectively neutralized) as a screen on which the image of the true bride has been projected. Enter Dizzy Gillespie to re-solemnize the marriage between jazz and "Mother Africa."

In reference to the late-nineteenth-century accounts of drumming bans imposed on slaves in the United States, Gillespie notes that "after the drums had been outlawed and taken away our ancestors had to devise other means of expressing themselves, their emotions . . . the rhythm was in them, but they just didn't have any means, instrumentally, to put it together so that the sound could travel very far. . . . Our ancestors had the impulse to make polyrhythms, but basically they developed a monorhythm from that time on. . . . We became monorhythmic, but the Afro-Cubans, the South Americans, and the West Indians remained polyrhythmic . . . our rhythm became so basic, though, that other Blacks in the hemisphere could easily hear it" (318). Cast in a plot of tragedy, the melancholy air of this account reflects Gillespie's feelings of irreparable loss on seeing that this most treasured token of musico-cultural identity, rhythm, had been taken from him.

The kernel of Gillespie's gesture of reclamation is his statement that he had "always felt polyrhythmic from a long way back," which encapsulates his living sense of a kinship with a particular way of experiencing rhythm ("I always had that Latin feeling"). Whether or not this was a psychological projection, and whether or not it constituted a crude presentism, is both unknowable and beside the point. Still, it is possible to speculate about how Gillespie addressed the issue musically and how he went about the business of reclaiming polyrhythms for his brand of Black North American music in the mid to late 1940s. By the early 1940s, Machito and his Afro-Cubans had established itself as the preeminent Latin ensemble in New York City, and by the mid-1940s the group was holding forth at the Palladium, on 54th Street, with jazz musicians from the neighboring 52nd Street coming over to see them all the time. A veritable who's who of the jazz world, including Charlie Parker, Dexter Gordon, and Doc Cheatham, among others, played or recorded with the Machito orchestra under the musical direction of Bauzá. Bauzá's gambit had paid off. Meanwhile, Gillespie had assembled a big band for which he sought, in 1947, a conga player (an idea he remembers mentioning to Bauzá as early as 1938).

Just as he did with the marriage of Afro-Cuban music and jazz, Bauzá took the role of matchmaker. "Well, I was the cause of it, that marriage, that integration," explained Bauzá for having introduced Luciano "Chano" Pozo (1915–1948) to Gillespie. The scene of their first encounter is particularly telling of Gillespie's and Pozo's respective ideas of Blackness. "When I first heard him down there [111th Street], we talked; I mean, we didn't talk, we just looked at one another and laughed. . . . Since he couldn't speak any English, people always asked, 'Well, how do you communicate?' 'Deehee no peek pani, me no peek Angli, bo peek African,' Chano would answer" (317–18). However obvious, these power dynamics warrant mention. The linguistic barrier between the two men made Pozo a subject of Gillespie's ventriloquism. That he supplied the words in grotesquely broken and accented English speaks patently of Gillespie's structural control of their relationship and of Pozo's subordination. The dynamics surrounding their distinct fields of musical expertise were more subtle, as can be seen in the manner in which Gillespie characterized Pozo's abilities. With a distinctive mixture of paternalism and unbridled admiration, Gillespie would note that "Chano was the first conga player to play with a jazz band, and he was very unusual about playing with an understanding. There were certain things about our music that he didn't understand" (319).

In his last comment above, Gillespie is referring to the radical difference between the Afro-Cuban conception of rhythmic organization around the clave (a two-bar pattern of three and two unequal-length beats) and the jazz practice that favored single bars subdivided into three or four beats. Pozo, who could not read music, soon was taught the proper rhythmic subdivision of a jazz feel by his new boss, who would sing in Pozo's ear whenever the Cuban "got on that wrong beat. . . . He'd change immediately, it was fantastic," said Gillespie admiringly. In the give and take of his musical relationship to Pozo, Gillespie's recognition of difference remained firmly in place, and was, further, framed within specific cultural terms. "Chano had such limited knowledge of our music. He was really African, you know. He probably played when he was two and a half years old or something like that. All the Ñanigo, the Santo, the Arrara, all these different sects, the African things in Cuba, he knew, and he was well versed" (319). Deployed as an all-purpose trope, Africa, more than Cuba, was indeed the source for Gillespie's profound respect for Pozo's musicianship and expressive power, complete with a fascination with and desire for the deeply buried and authentic kind of knowledge of rhythm he felt Pozo possessed. Here, for example, the motif of a supplementarity or the dialectic tradeoff between having and not having reappears, slightly transformed: "Chano wasn't a writer, but stone African. He knew rhythm—rhythm from Africa" (320).

Notes

1. John Birks (Dizzy) Gillespie with Al Fraser, *To Be, or Not . . . to Bop* (Garden City, N.Y.: Doubleday, 1979), 171. (Additional references to this work appear as parenthetical citations in the text.)

2. The standard account of this relation, plotted as a linear narrative, appears in John Storm Roberts's *The Latin Tinge: The Impact of Latin American Music on the United States* and

Latin Jazz: The First of the Fusions, 1880s to Today (New York: Schirmer Books, 1999). A more sensitive reading of the transformations and differences of the jazz/Latin music relation, albeit one that emphasizes continuities, appears in Chris Washburne's "The Clave of Jazz: A Caribbean Contribution to the Rhythmic Foundation of an African-American Music," Black Music Research Journal 17, no. 1 (1997): 59–80. Geoffrey Jacques's "CuBop! Afro-Cuban Music and Mid-Twentieth Century American Culture," in Between Race and Empire: African-Americans and Cubans before the Cuban Revolution, edited by Lisa Brock and Digna Castañeda Fuertes (Philadelphia: Temple University Press, 1998), argues for an increasingly organic coherence in African American and Afro-Cuban musical mixtures throughout the 1940s and 1950s.

3. The work of these musicians is chronicled in Roberts, Latin Jazz. Puerto Rican musicians are closely studied in Ruth Glasser, My Music Is My Flag: Puerto Rican Musicians and Their New York Communities, 1917–1940 (Berkeley: University of California Press, 1995).

4. My transcriptions from the documentary film Música, directed by John D. Wise (produced by Gustavo Paredes Jr., NEP Productions, 1984), maintain Bauzá's original grammar, with editorial additions in brackets added only when absolutely necessary.

5. Glasser in My Music Is My Flag (68) reports that Latin musicians were often called "stand musicians" because of their music reading abilities.

6. For more on the topic, see Ronald Radano, "Hot Fantasies: American Modernism and the Idea of Black Rhythm," in Music and the Racial Imagination, edited by Ronald Radano and Philip V. Bohlman (Chicago: University of Chicago Press, 2000), 459–80.

7. Paul Gilroy, "Sounds Authentic: Black Music, Ethnicity, and the Challenge of a Changing Same," Black Music Research Journal 1, no. 2 (1991): 111.

DAVID F. GARCÍA

Contesting that Damned Mambo

Arsenio Rodríguez and the People of
El Barrio and the Bronx in the 1950s

From 1948 to 1966 the Palladium Ballroom, at Broadway and 53rd Street in Manhattan, was known among Latin@ and non-Latin@ audiences as the mecca of Latin dance music in New York City. In the early 1950s the Palladium became specifically recognized in the American mainstream media as "the home of the mambo," which featured fiery amateur and professional mambo dancers as well as the mambo big bands of the "big three": Frank "Machito" Grillo, Ernest "Tito" Puente, and Pablo "Tito" Rodríguez. Its importance to the popularization of Latin dance music in the United States is undeniable; indeed, the Palladium and the music of its top artists have constituted a dominant place in both the Latin imaginary of American popular culture and the historical canon of Latin@ popular music and culture in the United States.

A result of this dominant narrative has been that the full landscape of Latin@ music, dance, and culture in New York City during the 1950s has been largely ignored or overlooked. For example, various dancehalls, cabarets, and social clubs that were located in East Harlem or "El Barrio" and the Bronx were the sites of a vibrant music culture whose importance to resident Cuban and Puerto Rican musicians and dancers equaled, or even surpassed, that of the Palladium. The Black Cuban composer and bandleader Arsenio Rodríguez (1911–1970) was especially important to this milieu for his Cuban music repertory and unique *son montuno* style. He and his music were particularly influential among the first generation of salsa musicians, many of whom spent their formative years in El Barrio and the Bronx performing with Arsenio's *conjunto* or group and listening to its recordings.[1] As Willie Colón noted, "I always listened to [Arsenio's] records and he was our principal teacher. From him we took the feeling of Cuban music, of the orthodox *son*, for the lack of a better word."[2] The fact that Arsenio was blind (the result of a childhood accident) added to his beloved status among Cubans, Puerto Ricans, and other Latin@s in El Barrio and the Bronx.

Arsenio formed his first conjunto ensemble and popularized his son montuno style by performing primarily for the Black working class in Havana, Cuba, in the early 1940s. He expanded the old *septeto* combo—which included a lead singer (doubling on clave), two second voices (doubling on maracas and guitar), one trumpet, *tres* (a traditional Cuban guitar consisting of three double-coursed strings), double bass, and *bongó*—by adding a piano, trumpet section, and one *tumbadora* (or conga drum).[3] Although his conjuntos in Havana and New York City performed various types of Cuban dance music, including son, son montuno, guaracha, and guaguancó, the term "son montuno" refers specifically to the style of Arsenio's conjunto. Several fundamental aspects distinguished his son montuno style from those of his contemporaries in Havana and New York City: the use of *contratiempo* or highly syncopated rhythmic and melodic patterns, especially for the bass; call-and-response at different architectonic levels, including between the bass, bongó, and tumbadora; the intricate interweaving of rhythmic and melodic patterns; and, most importantly, the correlation of accented attacks in the music with important steps and bodily movements in the dance style of Cuban son. These aspects are most readily apparent in the climactic finale of his arrangements in which the parts of the conjunto come together to create simple yet syncopated, interwoven, and exciting rhythmic patterns in two-bar or, less frequently, four-bar repeating cycles.

Arsenio, his conjunto, and son montuno style were tremendously important to many residents of El Barrio and the Bronx, many of whom preferred Arsenio's music to the styles of mambo that were popular at the Palladium and that were being disseminated internationally by the popular entertainment industry. Indeed, throughout his career Arsenio maintained that the final section of his arrangements and, in general, his son montuno style, constituted the "original" and "authentic" mambo style. In an interview in the Cuban magazine *Bohemia* in 1952 Arsenio articulated such views with respect to Dámaso Pérez Prado's style of mambo: "What Pérez Prado did was to mix the mambo with American music, copied from Stan Kenton. And he did us irreparable harm with it. I'll never forgive him for that or myself for creating that damned mambo."[4]

Such claims of "inauthenticity" and "dilution," however, speak not to any empirical distinctions between an "inauthentic" and "authentic" mambo style. Instead, they reveal a resistance against and ambivalence toward the mass popularized mambo styles of Dámaso Pérez Prado, Tito Puente, and others. The Cuban Melba Alvarado, a long-time member of the social club Club Cubano Inter-Americano in the South Bronx where Arsenio was a mainstay, expressed such ambivalence: "We always danced a lot of bolero, danzón, and son. These are three típicas [traditional Cuban genres]. We didn't care too much for mambo. Mambo was played a lot, orchestras played mambo, but it wasn't something that we did with much gratification."[5] For the Puerto Rican Sara Martínez Baro, dancing to Arsenio's music evoked nostalgic feelings of "home," a sentiment that, according to Alvarado, was not associated with the mambo: "I felt good because . . . it's a beautiful style, a graceful style, a style that invariably takes a person back home, as do plena, danza, danzón, bomba, and bolero."[6]

The Music Culture of El Barrio and the Bronx

In late 1949 and early 1950 Arsenio's brother Raúl Rodríguez, who had returned to New York City before Arsenio after their 1947 visit, recruited various musicians, most of whom were Puerto Rican, to form his brother's new conjunto. After Arsenio arrived, the group, which was named Arsenio Rodríguez y Su Conjunto de Estrellas, first performed at the Teatro Triboro in El Barrio and at the St. Nicholas Ballroom in 1950. On Christmas day of that year the conjunto performed at the Palladium for the first time, along with Tito Puente's big band and several other groups.[7] For the next two years his Conjunto de Estrellas continued to perform at popular venues in Manhattan that featured mambo music and dancing, including the St. Nicholas Ballroom, the Manhattan Center, and, the most popular, the Palladium Ballroom. Some of the groups that performed with the conjunto included the big bands of Noro Morales, Marcelino Guerra, Miguelito Valdés, Tito Puente, Tito Rodríguez, and Machito.[8]

Despite the conjunto's initial success, Arsenio's relaxed son montuno style eventually proved to be incompatible with the aesthetic tastes of mambo dancers who preferred the feverish and jazz-oriented or "modern" styles of Tito Puente, Tito Rodríguez, and others. By 1957 the decline in popularity of the mambo and cha-cha accounted for the Palladium's diminishing audiences, thereby creating stiff competition among big bands for fewer jobs at the Palladium and other dancehalls in Manhattan.[9] As a result, Arsenio's conjunto had become almost entirely reliant on peripheral locales, particularly the Park Palace and Park Plaza dancehall in El

Arsenio Rodríguez (wearing dark glasses) with Rafael Cortijo and his band, New York, circa 1955. (Henry Medina Archives and Services)

Barrio and the Tropicana Club and Club Cubano Inter-Americano in the Bronx, where his conjunto had been performing regularly since its formation in 1950.[10] Unlike the majority of mambo dancers, many in the Cuban and Puerto Rican communities of El Barrio and the Bronx enthusiastically embraced Arsenio's comfortably-paced son montuno style and his típico or traditional Cuban-based repertory. In short, Arsenio's conjunto and other groups that were not active participants of the mambo scene in Manhattan fulfilled the unique musical needs of many Latin@s living in El Barrio and the Bronx, the cultural settings of which constituted a vibrant alternative to the mambo-dominated and commercially driven milieu of Manhattan's dancehalls and elite nightclubs.

El Elemento del Barrio y el Bronx

In the mid-twentieth century Puerto Ricans accounted for the overwhelming majority of Latin@s living in New York City, growing from an estimated 45 percent of Latin@s in 1940 to 80 percent in 1960.[11] The Puerto Rican population itself grew from an estimated 61,500 in 1940 to 612,574 in 1960, an increase of almost 900 percent. Neighborhoods with an established Puerto Rican population in particular, such as El Barrio as well as the South Bronx, Hunts Point, and Morrisania sections of the Bronx, grew and expanded. The Cuban population of New York City also grew, but in significantly smaller proportions relative to the Puerto Rican population. From 1940 to 1960 the Cuban population increased by 84 percent, from an estimated 23,124 to 42,694. Cubans in New York City did not form any identifiable core of settlement. Instead, they resided primarily in Puerto Rican sections, although class and race often dictated in which neighborhood Cubans settled.

Throughout the 1950s Arsenio lived in El Barrio with his wife Emma Lucía Martínez, who was born in Puerto Rico. He also regularly stayed in the Bronx with his brother Israel "Kike" Rodríguez and his family. Raúl Rodríguez also lived in the Bronx, and between 1956 and 1958 he owned the El Dorado restaurant. The South Bronx and Hunts Point areas were known for their numerous resident Cuban and Puerto Rican musicians, who in addition to Arsenio included Marcelino Guerra, René Hernández, Fernando "Caney" Storch, Alfredo Valdés, José "Joe Loco" Estévez Jr., and Pablo "Tito" Rodríguez. Other Latin@ musicians, who beginning in 1960 would spearhead the popularization of the pachanga, boogaloo, and salsa, also lived here, including Charlie and Eddie Palmieri, Manny Oquendo, Ray Barretto, Alfredito Valdés Jr., Héctor Rivera, and many more who learned from observing Arsenio's conjunto and listening to its records.[12]

Arsenio saluted the music culture of El Barrio and the Bronx in the lyrics of two of his songs—"Como se goza en El Barrio" (El Barrio Is a Lot of Fun) and "El elemento del Bronx" (The People of the Bronx)—which his conjunto recorded with Tico in 1951 and which were later released on the ten-inch LP *Arsenio Rodríguez y Su Orquesta: Authentic Cuban Mambos* in 1955. The lyrics to "Como se goza en El Barrio" describe a lively street scene stretching along Lexington Avenue from 98th to 125th streets. The song concludes with the following lines: "Si quiere bailar lo bueno, camina y venganse al Barrio. Los que viven en downtown vienen a gozar al Barrio" (If you want to dance to good music, walk to El Barrio. Those who live downtown come to have fun in El Barrio). In these lines Arsenio more than saluted El Barrio's music culture. He was urging the dancers from "downtown" (or the Palladium) to come to El Barrio and dance to "good" (or "authentic") music.

In the 1940s and 1950s, the Park Palace/Plaza, located on the corner of East 110th Street and Fifth Avenue, was the most popular dancehall in El Barrio. In its initial days of operation in the 1930s the Park Palace/Plaza catered to upwardly mobile patrons of diverse ethnic backgrounds.[13] By the early 1950s, however, it had become known for its more Cuban- and Puerto Rican-oriented dance music as well as its predominantly local working-class Cuban and Puerto Rican dancing public. The Puerto Rican Luís "Máquina" Flores, who is considered to be one of the greatest dancers of the Palladium era, vividly described the social and musical differences between the Palladium and the Park Palace/Plaza as follows:

> The Palladium always got the fascination of people because it was situated on 53rd Street and Broadway. . . . The Plaza never got in the limelight because it was smack in the middle of the ghettos. . . . But I'll tell you one thing. Machito, Arsenio, all of these bands—you never heard these people swing like they swung when they were playing at the Plaza. Because the music belonged to the ghettos. And the people that spent the money and went to the dances in droves were the people from the ghettos. . . . So all these musicians knew that they could not pull the wool over these people's eyes. . . . The Plaza had the distinction that everybody knew everybody . . . [It] had a soul of its own, it had the heart of the barrio itself, it had the essence of the poor people. . . . You could not have the same feeling in the Palladium. When you went to the Palladium you were more starchy, you know, a little more phony.[14]

While some have praised the Palladium for its egalitarian milieu,[15] Flores's observations, like Arsenio's lyrics in "Como se goza en El Barrio," suggest that from the perspective of many Latin@s in El Barrio, the music and dancing of the Park Palace/Plaza differed from that of the Palladium in terms of social class as well as musical integrity.

Similar sentiments prevailed among Cuban and Puerto Rican residents of the Bronx. In his "El elemento del Bronx" Arsenio describes a community that knows how to dance contemporary popular styles (mambo and swing) as well as Cuban styles (danzón, guaguancó, and rumba): "El elemento del Bronx, igual bailan swing que guaguancó. Igual bailan mambo que danzón. Igual bailan rumba que danzón" (The people of the Bronx, they dance swing as well as guaguancó. They dance mambo as well as danzón. They dance rumba as well as danzón). Here, he recognized both the popularity of mambo and swing and the maintenance of Cuban dance styles among "the people" (i.e., Cubans and Puerto Ricans) of the Bronx.

Such was also the case among members of the Club Cubano Inter-Americano, which from 1946 to 1960 was located on the border of the South Bronx and Hunts Point. Although the majority of its members were Cubans and Puerto Ricans of color, the social club welcomed, as Arsenio's brother Raúl emphasized, "whites, blacks, everyone!"[16] This was in contrast to other social clubs, such as the Ateneo Cubano and the Club Caborrojeño, both of which were located in Manhattan and known to discriminate against Latin@s of color through the 1950s.[17] In addition, although the Club Cubano's cultural leaning was Cuban, the Puerto Ricans who regularly attended its functions and who were not already members still felt accepted as "family." For example, as Sara Martínez Baro, Arsenio's sister-in-law and the wife of his Cuban bassist Evaristo "Cuajarón" Baro, remarked, "It was a delightful environment, one that felt as if we were all family. Everyone knew each other."[18]

The majority of the Club Cubano's members were skilled workers, including barbers and accountants, from middle-class and working-class backgrounds. The purpose of the club was to provide members and their families and friends with social and recreational activities, mostly involving the celebration of Cuban patriotic holidays. Such annual celebrations and formal dances included "La Cena Martiana" (January), which commemorated José Martí's birthday; Antonio Maceo's birthday (July) and death (December); Cuban Independence Day (20 May); carnival (February); "El baile de blanco y negro," which required black tuxedos for men and white gowns for women; and "Homenaje al excursionista" (August), which was a dance whose guests of honor were invited from Cuba. The club also hosted birthday parties for members and their families and Three King's Day and Easter celebrations for their children. In addition, members organized a dance troupe that specialized in Cuban son and danzón dancing. Most of these events were held at the club, whose size could only accommodate about one hundred persons total. As a result, club officials were unable to hire big bands because of the club's limited capacity, the proceeds from which would have been needed to pay for such bands. The club did, however, present solo piano and poetry recitals and, on occasion, small musical groups.

In January 1957, for example, the club celebrated José Martí's birthday. The political situation in Cuba had worsened in the prior month as a result of the second phase of Fidel Castro's offensive against the Batista dictatorship. Arsenio attended the club's celebration and, together with the Puerto Rican singers Luís "Wito" Kortwrite and Cándido Antomattei (who were members of his conjunto), debuted "Adórenla como Martí" ("Love Her as Martí Did"), one of Arsenio's most well-known political songs. In this song Arsenio implores all Cubans, especially the warring factions, to resolve their differences in peace and love, and to unite the country so that the sacrifices of the Cuban independence patriots would not have been in vain. The audience was moved emotionally, and its members enthusiastically applauded Arsenio's message of reconciliation.[19]

Arsenio regularly performed for the club for a modest fee, as he had done for the Black social clubs in Havana. He varied the size of the conjunto according to how much the club was able to pay. Sometimes he even performed for no fee at all. The club's officials recognized Arsenio's cooperation by regularly hiring his full conjunto to perform for the club's larger events. In any case, the Club Cubano's celebrations always involved Cuban music, whether it was played on a record player, by a trio, or in an informal jam session, such as one that included Machito, Wito Kortwrite, Arsenio, and others in 1959.

About one block east of the Club Cubano Inter-Americano was the Tropicana Club. Like the Club Cubano, its core audience as well as the performers consisted of local Cubans and Puerto Ricans. For example, in the late 1940s and early 1950s the Tropicana regularly presented Puerto Rican performers such as Juanito Sanabria, the Conjunto "Puerto Rico" de Toñito Ferrer, Conjunto Alfarona X, and Luís Cruz y Su Conjunto Marianaxis, as well as the Cuban groups of Arsenio Rodríguez and Gilberto Valdés.

During the 1950s these and other locales in El Barrio and the Bronx served a vital role in the constitution of a unique music culture in which, as Luís "Maquina" Flores and Sara Martínez Baro stated, everyone knew each other. Hence, community as well as musical style and repertory distinguished the music culture of El Barrio and the Bronx from the Palladium and its "spatial logic," which Robert Farris Thompson described as "an outer circle of rich visitors and celebrities seated at tables . . . an inner circle of Latin@ and Black dancing connoisseurs seated on the floor communally, and, in the sovereign center, the star dancers themselves."[20] And central to the music culture of El Barrio and the Bronx was Arsenio's conjunto, whose music resonated with the nostalgic feelings for "home" (i.e., Cuba and Puerto Rico) and national identities that were shared among many Cuban and Puerto Rican immigrants of El Barrio and the Bronx. Arsenio's music also had to do with authenticity and tradition, as musicians and others distinguished his son montuno style from the "modern" mambo big bands of the 1950s.

It must be remembered that as of the early 1940s, Arsenio fashioned his son montuno style according to the aesthetic predilections of the Black working class of Havana. Arsenio's importance to the people of El Barrio and the Bronx paralleled that of his importance to Havana's Black working class. First, his audience in El Barrio and the Bronx consisted of primarily working-class Cubans and Puerto Ricans of color.[21] Second, this audience favored music, like son montuno, that facilitated social dancing or, as Joe

Torres noted, "a nice tempo that you can dance to all night," in contrast to the frenetic mambo milieu of Manhattan's dancehalls, which tended to favor exhibition dancing. Similarly, in Havana, the Black working class favored his slower son montuno style over the faster styles of other Cuban conjuntos such as Conjunto Casino and La Sonora Matancera, which performed mostly for the White middle and upper classes. Indeed, in Havana Arsenio's style was referred to by musicians and dancers as *estilo negro* or a "Black style" (as opposed to the "White" styles of La Sonora Matancera and Conjunto Casino), a designation which carried over to the role of his music in New York City during the 1950s.[22]

Conclusion

The dominant historical narrative of the mambo largely overlooks Arsenio's music and career and the history of the Puerto Rican and Cuban music culture of El Barrio and the Bronx.[23] The limited scope of the mambo canon can be attributed primarily to its linear orientation, which was encapsulated by one writer as "conceived in Cuba, nurtured in Mexico, and brought to maturity in the United States."[24] That narrative, therefore, limits the significance of the early contributors to the mambo, especially Arsenio, as merely one of the originators of the mambo in Havana in the 1940s. Arsenio and his music are rarely talked about, however, in the context of the New York mambo scene of the early 1950s, even though his Conjunto de Estrellas recorded and performed regularly in the most popular mambo dancehalls along with all of the major mambo big bands, including Pérez Prado's.

What has come down to us in commercial recordings and in the American mainstream print media has significantly shaped the historical canon of the mambo and thereby limited our understanding of the extent and complexity of the history of Latin@ music in New York City in the 1950s. In focusing on the music and career of Arsenio Rodríguez we learn of the power relations and dominant aesthetic tastes that ultimately hindered his pursuit of commercial success in New York City and recognition in the American mass media. We also learn of the music culture of El Barrio and the Bronx whose residents valued, and in fact favored, the típico music of Arsenio and other Cuban and Puerto Rican groups over the mambo, despite or because of its musical "progressiveness." Most importantly, we learn that class, race, national identity, and immigration bore significantly on how the people of El Barrio and the Bronx organized their music culture and how they distinguished it from that of the Palladium and New York City's dominant mambo milieu in general.

The world of Arsenio Rodríguez and his main venues also represents an alternative to the image of the Palladium as an egalitarian place and as the destination of all Latin@s. While the Palladium did much to establish Latin popular music and dance in the American popular consciousness, much oral testimony suggests that that famed venue actually had a relatively peripheral role in the social lives of many working-class Latin@s, especially those living in El Barrio and the Bronx. Research on other conjuntos, particularly those such as Alfarona X, whose members were mostly Puerto Ricans of color, will surely provide further evidence of and insight into the complex role that subtle yet persistent forms of racism and class segregation had on the identity formations of Latin@s and their music cultures in the 1950s. This aspect of Latin@ music history in New York City also provides insight into the ideological and aesthetic origins of salsa, whose earliest originators drew both from these groups' music and from the cultural milieu of El Barrio and the Bronx of the 1950s in forming their own expressive movement in the 1960s and 1970s.

Postscript

Although it is unclear, the Park Palace and Park Plaza and the Tropicana probably closed in the late 1950s and early 1960s, respectively. The Club Cubano Inter-Americano continued to organize social functions featuring Cuban music and dancing into the 1970s. But beginning in the mid 1960s the Club Cubano's directors began to hire younger groups—such as those of Johnny Pacheco, Larry Harlow, Ray Barretto, and Willie Rosario, as well as Orquesta Típica Novel and Orquesta Broadway—more regularly than Arsenio's group.[25] Evidently, the club's directors, who were Arsenio's contemporaries in age and first-generation immigrants, began to hire groups who would attract second- and third-generation Cuban, Puerto Rican, and other Latin@ dancers to its dances.

By 1969 Arsenio had moved to Los Angeles to live with his brothers "Kike" and Raúl, and he continued to perform only sparingly with a conjunto. On December 28, 1970, Arsenio suffered a fatal stroke and was taken to Queen of Angeles Hospital in downtown Los Angeles. The stroke was brought on by his diabetes, which he had been suffering from since at least the early 1960s. On December 30, Arsenio stopped breathing and was pronounced dead. His body was flown to New York City and his wake took place at Manhattan North Chapels on 107th Street and Amsterdam

Avenue. Arsenio Rodríguez's body was laid to rest at Ferncliff Cemetery in Hartsdale in Westchester County, New York, on January 6, 1971.

Notes

The author would like to thank Juan Flores, John Storm Roberts, and Paul Austerlitz for their insightful comments on earlier versions of this essay.

1. I refer to Arsenio by his first name because it is used by almost everyone to distinguish him from other artists named "Rodríguez," which is a very common surname in Latin America.

2. Leonardo Padura Fuentes, *Los rosotros de la salsa* (Havana: Ediciones Unión, 1997), 53.

3. By 1954 in New York City Arsenio incorporated timbales into his conjunto format.

4. Vicente Cubillas Jr., "Habla Arsenio Rodríguez: ¡Ese Maldito Mambo!," *Bohemia* 44, (49) (1952): 24–25.

5. Melba Alvarado, interview with the author, Manhattan, New York, March 3, 2000.

6. Sara Martínez Baro, interview with the author, Manhattan, New York, February 19, 2000.

7. See *La Prensa* (New York City), February to April, 1950, and December 1950.

8. See *La Prensa* (New York City), January 1951 to March 1952.

9. See *El Diario de Nueva York* (New York City), May 21, 1957.

10. The Park Palace was the second-story hall, and the Park Plaza was the somewhat smaller hall on the first floor.

11. Gabriel Haslip-Viera, "The Evolution of the Latino Community in New York City: Early Nineteenth Century to the Present," in *Latinos in New York*, edited by Gabriel Haslip-Viera and Sheri Bauer (South Bend, Ind.: Notre Dame Press, 1993), 8–18.

12. Pedro Boulong, telephone interview with the author, Manhattan, New York, January 24, 2000; Orlando Marin, interview with the author, Queens, New York, January 20, 2000; Alfredo Valdés Jr., interview with the author, Manhattan, New York, October 18, 1997.

13. Except where indicated, the following discussion on the Park Palace and Park Plaza is taken from David Carp, "Report on Field Work for Place Matters/City Lore, South Bronx Latin Music Project," unpublished manuscript, 1999.

14. Juan Flores, *From Bomba to Hip-Hop: Puerto Rican Culture and Latino Identity* (New York: Columbia University Press, 2000).

15. For example, Max Salazar, *Mambo Kingdom: Latin Music in New York* (New York: Schirmer Trade Books, 2002), 87; and Steven Loza, *Tito Puente and the Making of Latin Music* (Urbana: University of Illinois Press, 1999), 222.

16. Raúl Rodríguez, telephone interview with the author, February 7, 2000.

17. Israel Berrios, telephone interview with the author, May 20, 2002; Carp, "Report on Field Work for Place Matters/City Lore, South Bronx Latin Music Project," 29. By 1960 the Club Caborrojeño had transformed from a social club to a dancehall, and the new owner discontinued its past discriminatory policies (David Carp, personal communication).

18. Sara Martínez Baro, interview with the author, Manhattan, New York, February 19, 2000.

19. Melba Alvarado, interview with the author, Manhattan, New York, March 3, 2000.

20. Robert Farris Thompson, "Teaching the People to Triumph over Time: Notes from the World of Mambo," in *Caribbean Dance from Abakuá to Zouk: How Movement Shapes Identity*, edited by Susanna Sloat (Gainesville: University Press of Florida, 2002), 341.

21. Ray Coén, telephone interview with the author, April 26, 2000.

22. See García, "Arsenio Rodríguez."

23. For example, Gustavo Pérez Firmat, *Life on the Hyphen: The Cuban-American Way* (Austin: University of Texas Press, 1994), 80; Loza, *Tito Puente and the Making of Latin Music* 163; and John Storm Roberts, *The Latin Tinge: The Impact of Latin American Music on the United States*, 2nd ed. (New York: Oxford University Press, 1999 [1979]), 123.

24. Gustavo Pérez Firmat, *Life on the Hyphen: The Cuban-American Way* (Austin: University of Texas Press, 1994), 81.

25. Most of these dances were not publicized in *El Diario–La Prensa*. See Club Cubano Inter-Americano, 1946–1996, *Club Cubano Inter-Americano Records*, 2 Boxes, Schomburg Center for Research in Black Culture.

JUAN FLORES

Boogaloo and Latin Soul

"Let's just try it out, Sonny. If it doesn't work, I'll buy you a double." Jimmy Sabater remembers the night he kept coaxing his bandleader, Joe Cuba, to play a new number he had in mind. It was 1966 at the Palm Gardens Ballroom in midtown Manhattan, and the house was packed. "It was a Black dance," Jimmy recalls, "*de morenos, morenos americanos de Harlem* and stuff, you know, they had Black dances one night a week there and at some of the other spots. So that night we were playing selections from our new album, *We Must Be Doing Something Right*, that had just come out, the one with 'El Pito' on it, you know, 'I'll never go back to Georgia, never go back . . .' The place was packed, but when we were playing all those mambos and cha-chas, nobody was dancing. So at the end of the first set, I went over to Joe Cuba and said, 'Look, Sonny' (that's his nickname). 'I have an idea for a tune that I think might get them up.' And Joe says, 'No, no, no, we got to keep on playing the charts from the new album.' Then toward the end of the second set, I went on begging him, and said, 'Look, if I'm wrong we'll stop and I'll buy you a double.' So finally he said 'OK,' and I went over to the piano and told Nick Jiménez, 'Play this' . . . Before I even got back to the timbal the people were out on the floor, going 'bi-bi, hah! bi-bi, hah!' I mean mobbed!" As Joe Cuba himself recalls, "Suddenly the audience began to dance side-to-side like a wave-type dance, and began to chant 'she-free, she-free,' sort of like an African tribal chant and dance"[1]

The new tune by the Joe Cuba Sextet was "Bang Bang." Within weeks it was recorded and released as a single which soon hit the national *Billboard* charts and stayed there for ten weeks, one of the few Latin recordings ever to reach that level of commercial success. It even outdid "El Pito," which the year before had also made the charts, and the album on which "Bang Bang" appeared, *Wanted: Dead or Alive*, was a huge hit as well. It was the heyday of Latin boogaloo, and Joe Cuba's band was at the height of its popularity. The year 1966 also saw the closing of the legendary Palladium Ballroom, an event marking the definitive end of the great mambo era in Latin music which had already been waning since the beginning of the decade. And, looking ahead to developments to come, it was some six years later at that very same Palm Gardens venue, by then called the Cheetah Club, that the Fania All-Stars were filmed in performance in the making of the movie *Nuestra Cosa* (Our Latin Thing), which is sometimes regarded as the inauguration of "salsa." Between the mambo and salsa, in the brief period spanning the years 1966–1968, the boogaloo was all the rage in the New York Latin community and beyond. It was both a bridge and a break, for with all the continuities and influences in terms of musical style, the boogaloo diverged from the prevailing models of Latin music in significant ways.

Jimmy Sabater's story about the making of "Bang Bang" helps explain the social function of boogaloo, while the song itself is characteristic of its style and musical qualities. As neighbors and coworkers, African Americans and Puerto Ricans in New York had been partying together for many years. For decades they had been frequenting the same clubs, with Black and Latin bands often sharing the billing. Since the musical revolution of the late 1940s, when musical giants like Mario Bauzá, Machito, and Dizzy Gillespie joined forces in the creation of "Cubop" or Latin jazz, the two traditions had come into even closer contact than ever, with the strains of Afro-Cuban *guaguancó, son,* and *guaracha* dance music interlacing and energizing the complex harmonic figures of big band and bebop experimentations. For African Americans, that same midcentury mambo and Cubop period corresponded to the years of rhythm and blues, from the jump blues of Louis Jordan to the shouters and hollerers and street corner doo-woppers of the 1950s. Scores of American popular tunes of those years bore titles, lyrics, or musical gimmicks suggestive of the mambo or cha-cha, while many young Puerto Ricans joined their African American and Italian partners in harmonizing the echo-chamber strains of doo-wop love songs and novelty numbers.[2]

With all the close sharing of musical space and tastes, however, there were differences and distances. African American audiences generally appreciated and enjoyed Latin musical styles, yet those who fully understood the intricacies of Afro-Cuban rhythms and came to master the challenging dance movements remained the exception rather than the rule. Most Black Americans, after listening admiringly to a set of mambos and boleros, longed for their familiar blues and R&B sounds and, by the mid-1960s, soul music. Popular Latin bands thus found themselves creating a musical common ground by introducing the trappings of Black American culture into their performances and thus getting the Black audiences involved and onto the dance floor. "Bang Bang" by the Joe Cuba Sextet, and Latin boogaloo music in general, was intended to constitute this meeting place between Puerto Ricans and Blacks, and by extension, between Latin music and the musical culture of the United States.

"Bang Bang" begins with a short piano vamp, which is then immediately joined by loud group handclapping, a few voices shouting excitedly but unintelligibly, and then a large crowd chanting in unison, "bi-bi, hah! bi-bi, hah!" The chant is repeated four times, increasing each time in intensity and accompanied throughout by the repeated piano lick, handclapping, and shouting, which is then supplemented by Jimmy Sabater on timbales, all the while building up to the resounding chorus "bang bang!" This refrain phrase is introduced by the solo vocal, then repeated over and over by the group chorus while the solo—by none other than the legendary Cheo Feliciano—goes off into a kind of skat *soneo* or adlib by blurting out random phrases mostly in Spanish and very much in the improvisational style of the *son montuno*. This lead vocal interacts with the choral "bang bang" and with the bongo bells (played, it turns out, by Manny Oquendo), and throughout the song resounds in indirect and playful dialogue with another solo voice line, in English, carried by Willie Torres, mostly exhorting the crowd and the band with slang phrases like "come git it," "sock it to me," "hanky panky," and the like. Somewhere in the middle of the four-minute recording is the line, "Cornbread, hog maw, and chitlins," repeated several times and then teased out with Spanish comments like "comiendo cuchifrito" and "lechón, lechón!" The last half of the song involves three or four false endings, as over and over the irresistible rowdy clamor is rekindled by the same piano vamp, with the solo vocal exchanges taking on a more and more gossipy and jocular tone.

Though some changes were obviously required for the studio recording of the tune, "Bang Bang" remains very much a party. Like many other popular songs of boogaloo, it reenacts a bawdy happening at the peak of its emotional and sexual energy, with instrumentals and vocals playing in full and wild association with the crowd. Joe Cuba recalls, thinking mainly of "Bang Bang," that "when I recorded in those days I always left a big boom mike overhanging above all the musicians to put in a little live effect." The musical texture of the song is a patchwork of noises, emotive outbursts, cries of glee, short musical phrases, and the recurring, abiding counterpoint of the crowd chorus and the leitmotiv piano lick. The lyrics, though of no consistent narrative or dramatic significance, nevertheless do have a meaning, which is the interplay of Black and Latin festivity and culture and the playful mingling of African American phrases and cultural symbols with those from Puerto Rican daily life. Musically this same message is carried across with the collage-like mixing of familiar trappings from mambo and R&B styles. The perspective is clearly that of the Latino, and Latin music is the main defining sound of the piece, but the traditional features and structuring principles of the Afro-Cuban model are consistently overridden by their conjoining with qualities from the R&B and soul traditions. The overall effect of the recording is one of collective celebration, gleeful partying where boundaries are set not so much by national and ethnic affiliation or even language or formalized dance movements, but by participation in that special moment of inclusive ceremony.

As "Bang Bang" illustrates, the defining theme and musical feature of boogaloo is precisely this intercultural togetherness, the solidarity engendered by living and loving in unison beyond obvious differences. Its emergence coincided with the historical moment of the Civil Rights movement and the coming of age of the first generation of Puerto Rican youths born and raised in New York City. The Latin music expert and producer René López calls boogaloo "the first Nuyorican music," and a consensus has gathered in concurrence with that description. It is the sound that accompanied the teenage years of the Young Lords and of the Nuyorican poets in the later 1960s; Piri Thomas's groundbreaking novel *Down These Mean Streets* was published in 1967. Like those experiences, it attests to the guiding, exemplary role of African American culture and politics for that generation of Puerto Ricans growing up in New York. "Bang Bang" is an explosion of excitement arising from that cultural conjunction, the linking of Puerto Rican backgrounds with the African American influences so prevalent in all aspects of social life, including of course their music and dance.

"The Boogaloo didn't die out. It was killed off by envious old bandleaders, a few dance promoters and a popular Latin disc jockey." By 1969, just three years after its explosive entry onto the New York music scene, Latin boogaloo was gone, and most musicians involved, young and older, agree with King Nando's explanation of its rapid demise. "We were the hottest bands and we drew the crowds. But we were never given top billing or top dollar. The Boogaloo bandleaders were forced to accept 'package deals' which had us hopping all over town . . . one hour here, one hour there . . . for small change. When word got out we were going to unite and no longer accept the package deals, our records were no longer played over the radio. The Boogaloo era was over and so were the careers of most of the Boogaloo bandleaders."[3]

Not everyone bemoaned its passing in equal measure, of course, or views it in such conspiratorial terms. The boogaloo was, after all, just another dance fad on the American pop scene and thus destined to a fleeting life span and instant oblivion. Latin boogaloo was more than that, as it also marked an important intervention in the history of Latin music and served as an expression of Puerto Rican and African American cultures in those pivotal years of their experience in New York. But in the name of boogaloo, rather than the broader Latin soul concept, the style was doomed to fade, as a new generation of young Latinos came to seek out something they, too, could call their own. The "next big thing" for Latin music in New York went by the name of salsa.

"The Boogaloo might have been killed off," notes the Latin music historian Max Salazar, "but Latin Soul lived on."[4] With a broader understanding of the musical and social experience called boogaloo, or salsa for that matter, and disengaging it from those commercially created categories, it becomes possible to see the continuity and coherence of the Latin–African American musical fusion in clearer historical perspective. Many of the musicians themselves preferred the idea of Latin soul all along, even during the peak of boogaloo's popularity, and the term may be seen to embrace musical styles both before and after the rise and fall of boogaloo, perhaps even including much of what has been called salsa. With the help of Salazar's guiding concept of "Afro-American Latinized rhythms," he is able to identify an entire lineage of musical follow-through on the impulse of boogaloo, an inventory that includes not only direct holdovers from the era like Louie Ramírez, Bobby Marín and his Latin Chords, and Chico Mendoza, but unexpected standbys like Johnny Pacheco and Mongo Santamaría and the Fania All-Stars, along with non-Caribbean Latinos like Santana and Jorge Dalto.

Dislodged from the power of Fania's formative influence, the term salsa itself can be thought of in more expansive and inclusive terms, and as is necessary a full twenty-five years after its "founding," it can also be conceived in its various stages and tendencies. Maybe, as Tito Ramos suggests, boogaloo should be considered part of what he calls "salsa clásica" (as opposed to the "salsa monga," or "lame salsa," of more recent years) and its repertoire be seen as a significant inclusion among the "oldies" of the genre. Certainly the music radio programming in Puerto Rico and other parts of Latin America present it in this way, as do some of the re-

Joe Bataan and the East Side Kids, New York, 1970. A participant in the boogaloo scene, Bataan continues to perform Latin soul music today. (Courtesy of Joe Bataan)

cent anthologies of Latin music from the 1960s and 1970s. The sounds of Pete Rodríguez, Joe Cuba, and Richie Ray are still adored in countries like Colombia and Venezuela, and no sharp distinction is made between those old favorites and what is called salsa.

In retrospect perhaps it is true, as some commentators claim, that the most important influence of Latin boogaloo was not even in the Latin music field but rather in the arena of Black American music. As such, states John Roberts, it was "one of the single most important factors in moving Black rhythm sections from a basic four-to-the-bar concept to tumbao-like bass and increasingly Latin percussive patterns."[5] This may be the case, but the impact started well before boogaloo, of course, and it should be no reason to understate the change that this eclipsed era brought to Latin music. Growing out of a time of "strong Puerto Rican identification with Black politics and culture," the cultural critic George Lipsitz has it, Latin boogaloo "led organically to a reconsideration of 'Cuban' musical styles . . . as, in fact, *Afro*-Cuban . . . and a general reawakening of the African elements within Puerto Rican culture. Condemned by traditionalists as a betrayal of the community, Latin Bugalu instead showed that the community's identity had always been formed in relation to that of other groups in the USA."[6] Whatever musical elements of boogaloo might have been left behind, the social context of which it was an expression—the historical raison d'être of Latin soul—has only deepened through the years.

A Latin boogaloo revival? Many of the musicians speak of a rekindled interest in boogaloo on the part of the present generation, and the huge success of Tito Nieves's *I Like It Like That* album from 1998, which also contains still another cover of "Bang Bang," is an obvious indication. They also point to the enthusiasm of fans in Puerto Rico, Latin America, Western Europe, and Japan. In England boogaloo is now classified, along with kindred styles, as "Latin Acid" or "Acid Jazz," and much is included under that umbrella, from rereleases of Hector Rivera and Mongo Santamaría's old material to the work of Pucho and other African American musicians in the Latin groove. *The Latin Vogue, Nu Yorica: Culture Clash in New York City,* and *Sabroso! The Afro-Latin Groove* are some of the compilations of recent years, and all of them include Latin boogaloo classics and related and more recent material. The Relic label has even issued a collection titled *Vaya!!! R&B Groups Go Latin,* which comprises twenty tunes by doo-wop and R&B groups from the 1950s who mixed in mambo and other Latin rhythms, starting with the Crows's "Gee" and the Harptones's "Mambo Boogie" in 1954.

But a renewal of the spirit of boogaloo in our time, and a recuperation of some of the musical experiments seemingly left by the wayside, will need to be forward-looking and not just nostalgic. With the emergence of hip-hop in the late 1970s and 1980s, another common space was forged for joint African American and Latino musical expression, and again it was Black and Puerto Rican youth from New York City who created and laid the first claim to that new terrain. As with boogaloo, it is again the African American dimension that appears most visible, but the Latino input can also be established.[7] Commercially successful acts like Mellow Man Ace and Cypress Hill introduced such fusions of rap and Latin sounds in the early 1990s, as have rappers in Puerto Rico and the Dominican Republic. Current salsa stars like La India and Marc Anthony were reared on rap and house and got their starts there, while salsa musicians as far-ranging as Manny Oquendo's Libre, El Gran Combo, and Tito Rojas have turned to rap techniques and collaborations to diversify their repertoire. Salsa in English, a long-standing crossover goal, is attempted with increasing frequency though until now with minimal musical success. Surely it is in the context of such experiments, as the adjacent and kindred Black and Latino cultures continue to intermingle, that the spirit of Latin boogaloo may live on in the years ahead. Jimmy Sabater, the all-time master of "cha-

cha with a back-beat," has that spirit in mind when he says, "Boogaloo? Boogaloo for me was basically an early form of rap."

Notes

1. See Max Salazar, "Latinized Afro-American Rhythms," in *Salsiology: Afro-Cuban Music and the Evolution of Salsa in New York City*, edited by Vernon Boggs (New York: Excelsior, 1992), 237–48.

2. See especially the work of Vernon Boggs, "Rhythm 'n' Blues, American Pop, and Salsa: Musical Transculturation," *Latin Beat* 2, no. 1 (February 1992): 16–19; and "Behind the Harptones and Mambo Boogie," *Latin Beat* 2, no. 10 (December-January 1993): 32–35. See also the 1995 LP release *Vaya!!! R & B Groups Go Latin*, on Verve, especially the liner notes by Donn Fileti.

3. King Nando, quoted in Salazar, "Latinized Afro-American Rhythms," 244.

4. Salazar, "Latinized Afro-American Rhythms," 247.

5. John Storm Roberts, *The Latin Tinge: The Impact of Latin American Music on the United States*, rev. ed. (London: Oxford University Press, 1998 [1979]), 169.

6. George Lipsitz, *Dangerous Crossroads: Popular Music, Postmodernism, and the Poetics of Place* (London: Verso, 1994), 80.

7. On the Puerto Rican role in early hip-hop, see my essay "Puerto Rocks: Rap, Roots, and Amnesia," in *From Bomba to Hip-Hop* (New York: Columbia University Press, 2000), 113–39.

TATO LAVIERA

Excerpt from the salsa of bethesda fountain

the internal dance of salsa
is of course plena
and permit me to say these words
in afro-spanish:
la bomba y la plena puro són
de Puerto Rico que ismael es el
rey y es el juez
meaning the same as marvin gaye
singing spiritual social songs
to black awareness

a blackness in spanish
a blackness in english
mixture-met on jam sessions in central park,
there were no differences in
the sounds emerging from inside
soul-salsa is universal
meaning a rhythm of mixtures
with world-wide bases

did you say you want it stronger?
well, okay, it is a root called africa
in all of us.

V

The Black Latin@ Sixties

The 1960s saw an outburst of political, literary, and cultural expression
that gave voice and perspective to the position of young people who are
both Caribbean Latin@s and Black. In anticipation of this period, the Afro-
Dominican Garveyite leader Carlos Cooks speaks to the importance of
Garvey and Malcolm X in the proclamation of Black pride and the rejection
of racism among Latin@s. Most notable among the literary works of this
transformative period is the autobiographical novel *Down These Mean Streets*
(1967) by the young Black Puerto Rican-Cuban author Piri Thomas. Here
we find in sharp dramatic terms nothing short of a psychological anatomy

Picketline protesting racial
discrimination in hiring, Bronx,
New York (circa 1960). The Civil
Rights movement extended
beyond the South and included
Spanish-speaking immigrants.
(Photograph by Curt Klemens;
Photographs and Prints
Division, Schomburg Center
for Research in Black Culture,
the New York Public Library,
Astor, Lenox and Tilden
Foundations)

of the Black Latin@ paradox, and the torturous struggle to affirm both identities. In a similar vein, the so-called "Nuyorican" poets of the 1970s such as Victor Hernández Cruz, Sandra María Esteves, and Felipe Luciano incorporate a strong sense of Black cultural identity in their proclamation of a New York–based Afro-Latin@ reality. The ascendancy of the Young Lords Party in the late 1960s attests to the participation of Latin@s in the Civil Rights and Black Power movements, and the first collective affirmation of Blackness among young Puerto Ricans in the diaspora. The historic essay by the Young Lords leader Pablo "Yoruba" Guzmán sets still another landmark in the history of Latin@s. The selections by Marta Moreno Vega on Santería and by Luis Barrios on Pentecostalism present other expressive dimensions of Afrolatinidad. Finally, the Afro-Dominicana writers Sherezada "Chiqui" Vicioso and Josefina Báez illustrate the presence of relatively new groups of Afro-Caribbeans in these transformative cultural and political movements of the period.

CARLOS COOKS

Hair Conking; Buy Black

Let's stand! Repeat after me, "One Cause, One Goal, One Destiny."

Fellow Nationalists and members of the race, the Negro is being used as a stooge for the Jews and other non-Blacks who are exploiting Black people. The Negro is a manufactured "wrongo." He is made to do wrong. He cannot do right. It is the devout policy of white supremacists to make Negroes out of every Black man, woman, and child. As we constantly point out, the word Negro is a weapon and scheme of whites to disassociate Black people from the human family and their homeland, Africa.

Slavery cut Black people in the western world adrift from Africa. In the Western world, Black people were oriented toward an alien culture and were forbidden to practice their African culture. The penalty meant death. They underwent the most macabre, diabolical, and consistent application of mental and physical torture the world has ever known. With physical torture being insufficient in converting the African into useful assets for the slave system, the Christian church was called upon to destroy the Black people's minds and turn them into Negroes. [. . .]

As Negroes, Black people have been converted into zombified caste creatures whose loyalty is permanently married to the white race; whose God and idolatry status is white; whose standards of beauty, sense of decency, and opinions on all matters are based on the set of concepts laid down by white people.

As Negroes, Black people are the stoutest defenders of white supremacy and the loudest defamers of Africa and everything pertaining to it.

Integration has been made the target of the Negroes' focus. The concentric pull of this fallacious doctrine has such a revolting effect on the behavior of Negroes that we find them at war with nature. They are disgusted with their color, hair, and physique to such a nauseating extent that they employ the use of harsh and potent chemicals to efface the handiwork of nature. Negroes are convinced that if they simulate the hair, color, and general mannerisms of the white race, they would be accepted by white society. [. . .]

The laws of science say that you can take something and make nothing out of it, but you cannot take nothing and make something out of it. In the case of Black people's hair, you have live, woolly, curly, human hair where harsh chemicals and heat are applied to kill the hair until it lays in ruin like the white people's hair or dogs' hair. You took something and made nothing out of it. But there is no known chemical or application of heat that can change the dead, straight hair of white people to the live, lovely curly hair of Black people. You cannot take nothing and make something out of it.

As Negroes, the Black people give up the best to ape the less. The Negro's hair has more sense than the Negro. After two or three weeks under the conk and hot comb applications, the hair says, "To hell with this. I am going back to Africa," and it goes back to its natural state. The Negro has to go through the conk and hot comb all over again.

The Negro is the greatest enemy of Black opportunities and racial solidarity in the path of the onward march of African Nationalism.

The constant drip of water on the hardest granite will ultimately make an impression. Likewise, the constant application of Orthodox African Nationalism to the cement mentality of the Negro will ultimately make an impression.

We must be rid of that word Negro as a racial classification of the African people. Negro is not an authentic, scientific classification of our racial group, but it is a caste name. We will begin referring to all Black people who answer to Negro as a caste people until we establish our true racial identity—Black people or Africans.

On our agenda is a call to a convention for the African people of the world. The major item on the agenda will be to get rid of that word Negro as a racial classification for our people, and to demand that we be addressed with the same dignity and respect extended to all other races and national groups.

The problem, as it projects itself upon the African people in the Americas, is economical and psychological, and we must approach it as such. It takes an economical antidote to solve an economic problem and a psychological antidote to solve a psychological problem.

As we have stated earlier, we are philosophically committed to the ideals of Marcus Garvey—African Nationalism and self-determination.

For an antidote to our economic problem, Marcus Garvey founded the

African Communities League to acquire the land, buildings, machines, tools, technology, and personnel to win, control, and dominate the commerce, business life, and body politic in all communities where Black people are the majority population.

The faults of the Black people, as Negroes, are that they rely on supernatural powers to bring about material salvation based on a misguided concept of world society. They display extreme gullibility and naiveté in accepting other people's ideas. Plus they disdain and scorn everything Black, African, or symbolic of racial unity. The results are misery, social leprosy, and political vassalage.

We find the solution to the above problem in the philosophy of the African Communities League, which is as follows: When and wherever we live in a community and are the majority population, we must own, control, and dominate the commerce, business life, and body politic of that community.

I have drawn up a concise, clear-cut, and positive program of action that will implement the above philosophy. This program is the "Buy Black" campaign. It demands Black consumers to adhere to this program of racial economic necessity, and it is dramatized by a reorientation of our shopping habits to the extent that we patronize those people belonging to our ethnic group.

The "Buy Black" campaign is the key. It will scientifically transfer the commerce, business life, and body politic of the alien parasite to its rightful owner, the Black communities. [. . .]

The "Buy Black" campaign is the primary, fundamental, and necessary activity that will give the Black people the logistics required to implement Marcus Garvey's ideals, African Nationalism and self-determination.

The masses of Blacks all over the world must embrace and support the "Buy Black" campaign. This is where the gains from this activity and program will go.

The "Buy Black" campaign is a program of action for, by, and of the African people of the world.

The "Buy Black" campaign will universally allow Blacks to taste real freedom after a long period of being denied this natural, sweet, and righteous status.

The "Buy Black" campaign will rid Black people of alien parasites in Black communities, and will prevent the outflow of the community's expenditures. Retained expenditures will go for budgets that will eliminate unemployment, poverty, crime, perversion, and alien exploitation in Black communities.

We believe in the principle of self-determination for all races. We submit that the people in Harlem and all other homogeneous African communities have the same moral and natural right to be as clannish in their patronage as other people have dramatized that they are. We advocate as a matter of sound racial economy the "Buy Black" campaign. Patronize your own race. Build a solvent foundation for your children. Help create employment and independence for your race.

One Cause, One Goal, One Destiny!

PEDRO R. RIVERA

Carlos A. Cooks

Dominican Garveyite in Harlem

Carlos A. Cooks was born in the Dominican Republic in 1913 and died in New York City in 1966. Although he seldom has been discussed in recent years, Cooks was a familiar figure in Harlem for more than three decades. Perched atop a stepladder, he delivered fiery lectures to street-corner passersby. In pronouncing on local, national, and international affairs from a Black Nationalist perspective he earned the respect of people and leaders across the community, the country, and the world. Whether he was declaring that "Black is Beautiful," or exhorting his audience to "Buy Black" Cooks consistently aimed at linking local concerns to the global Pan-African struggles.

His work in multiple organizations and public events — ranging from parades honoring Marcus Garvey, whom he always considered an ideological father, to campaigns for economic autonomy and contests celebrating Black female beauty — was all directed at inspiring a spiritual and physical journey to Africa.[1] Beyond the reach of his street echo, Cooks also articulated the universality of the African struggle for self-determination through other vehicles of his African Nationalist Pioneer Movement organization, including the *Street Speaker* magazine.

When he died on May 5, 1966, the *New York Times* noted a funeral ceremony "attended by thousands," the *Amsterdam News* labeled him "the nation's number one Black Nationalist," and Malcolm X's widow, Betty Shabazz, reputedly signed a family condolence card.[2]

Cooks is considered to be the missing link in the span from Marcus Garvey to Malcolm X, and as Charles "Nwokeojjii" Peaker implied in a forward-looking eulogy, Cooks's courageous journey turned him into a living icon of the Black liberation movement, thereby shaping the course of Pan-African struggles. In 2004, the Namibian president Samuel Nujoma visited Harlem, and "on behalf of the government and the people of the Republic of Namibia" he acknowledged Cooks and the African Nationalist Pioneer Movement as major financial contributors to his country's successful fight for independence.[3]

In his internationally acclaimed song "Guavaberry," the musician Juan Luis Guerra pays tribute to the vibrant and enduring community in San Pedro de Macoris, which is where Cooks was born and raised in the Dominican Republic. In the late 1910s, the multiethnic makeup of San Pedro contributed to its resilience, surviving even under constant harassment by the first United States Marine occupiers. Cooks's parents were originally from St. Martin, and his father was singled out and persecuted (along with other leaders) by the foreign authorities for his involvement in spreading doctrines of Black racial unity.[4] By 1922, his parents had settled in Harlem, leaving Carlos and his brother Lorenzo behind with relatives.

When Cooks crossed from Santo Domingo to Harlem in 1929, he brought with him experience and a passion that would serve to make him a militant disciple of the philosophies of Garvey. Guided by his father, Cooks was trained in local meetings of the Universal Negro Improvement Association (UNIA).[5] He also was reportedly initiated by his uncle into the Voodoo Sacree, a secret society whose influence would be reflected in Cooks's rejection of personal publicity. His exceptional oratorical skills and an impatient genius are said to have led him forward within—and beyond—the ranks and mission of the UNIA.

Appointed as an officer in the UNIA at the age of nineteen in 1932, Cooks became president of its advance division six years later. After Marcus Garvey's death in London in 1940 and the dissolution of the UNIA, Cooks tried to erect a monument in Garvey's honor, a building intended to also serve as the permanent headquarters of the succeeding African Nationalist Pioneer Movement.[6] Vowing to promote Black dignity, independence, and justice to the memory of Garvey, Cooks picked up the red, Black, and green banner to promote an unyielding radical brand of Garveyism.

While Garvey and the UNIA successfully called for the respectful capitalization of the word "Negro" in 1920, Cooks and the ANPM organized a convention in 1959 to completely abrogate the word "Negro" as a racial appellative, proposing "Black" and "African" in its stead.[7] His call for a "Negro to Black" conversion was an articulation of the rapidly evolving sensibilities in the Black community that would eventually explode into the Black Power movement. Cooks also removed "One God" from Garvey's famous admonition and replaced it with the phrase "One Cause." He thereby charged Black people to look to themselves as the main guarantors of security and freedom, even calling upon them to conquer the kingdom of heaven on earth.

In meeting halls and on busy street corners, Cooks would be heard advancing the biblical story of Lucifer's rebellion in heaven as a democratic movement against a white dictatorial God, and as an example of what Black civil rights agitation should be.[8] By the time the Black Panther Party for Self-Defense was founded, Cooks and his African Legion were remembered and respected as forerunning entities in Harlem. Collectively, individuals as diverse as the Nation of Islam minister Malcolm X, the congressman Adam Clayton Powell Jr., the Black Power leader Stokely Carmichael (Kwame Toure), and even the contemporary critic John Henrik Clarke, were among the many who left verifiable testimony of how this "young Dominican" surpassed established feats of activism, worked tirelessly to carry Garvey's program to its final consequences, and developed a practical blueprint for Black financial empowerment with his "Buy Black" forces.[9]

Until his death, Cooks mobilized community resources and channeled tangible assistance to African liberation movements. At the same time that he tried to pressure Congress to allow a Black emigrationist march to Africa, he promoted community nationalism "while you wait," and organized the Miss National Standard of Beauty Contest to encourage African natural hairstyles and other aesthetic concepts, many of which gained precedence during the Black Power movement. While not everybody was willing to follow him on some issues, many appreciated his commitment, which is why he became so respected. Cooks was a leader whose journey in Harlem was interpreted as an ignited fuse, thus setting the stage for a new era of Black radicalism in the 1960s.[10]

Notes

1. See Robert Harris, "Carlos A. Cooks: Ideological Son of Marcus Garvey," in *Carlos Cooks and Black Nationalism from Garvey to Malcolm*, compiled and edited by Robert Harris, Nyota Harris, and Grandassa Harris (Dover, Mass.: Majority Press, 1992), xi–xxiv.

2. For these and other details, see *New York Times*, July 3, 1966, 1, 39; Malcolm Nash, "Carlos Cooks, Black Nationalist Leader Buried on Long Island," *New York Amsterdam News*, May 14, 1966, 1–2; and Harris, "Carlos A. Cooks," xxiv.

3. Nujoma's speech was transmitted (and has been played back over the years) in *Afrikaleidoscope*, a radio broadcast hosted by Elombe Brath on WBAI, Pacifica Radio. As one of Harlem's top oral historians Brath is among those most responsible for keeping Cooks's name and historical legacy alive.

4. See Humberto García Muñiz and Jorge L. Giovannetti, "Garveyismo y racismo en el

Caribe: El caso de la población cocola en la Republica Dominicana," *Caribbean Studies*, 31, no. 1 (January–June 2003): 139–211.

5. Harris, "Carlos A. Cooks," xi–xii.

6. Peggy Caravantes, *Marcus Garvey: Black Nationalist* (Greensboro, N.C.: Morgan Reynolds, 2004), 112; and Harris, "Carlos A. Cooks," xii, xxi–xxiii.

7. In *Fidel and Malcolm X* (Melbourne, Australia: Ocean Press, 1993), 29–30, Rosemari Mealy provides a most insightful discussion on the significance and impact of this event, which has come to be known as the "1959 Convention."

8. Carlos A. Cooks, "Lucifer, God and Civil Rights" (dated April 10, 1966), in *Carlos Cooks and Black Nationalism from Garvey to Malcolm*, compiled and edited by Robert Harris, Nyota Harris, and Grandassa Harris (Dover, Mass.: Majority Press, 1992), 115–18.

9. Specific references can be found in *The Autobiography of Malcolm X, As Told to Alex Haley* (New York: Ballantine Books, 1999), 222; and John Henrik Clarke's "Portrait of a Liberation Scholar," in *Against the Odds: Scholars Who Challenged Racism in the Twentieth Century*, edited by Benjamin P. Bowser and Louis Kushnick, with Paul Grant (Amherst: University of Massachusetts Press, 2002), 33.

10. Stokely Carmichael (Kwame Toure) made this point in one of his last interviews, which was conducted by Elombe Brath in 1998 and aired on *Afrikaleidoscope*.

PIRI THOMAS

Down These Mean Streets

Hung Up between Two Sticks

Not long afterward me and Louie got a little bit of that shit ourselves. Only we didn't get no choice to cut out. We got hung up by a white clique from downtown as we were coming out of the RKO flick on 86th Street. There were about eight paddies. We tried to cut out, but they got us tight inside their circle. Louie quickly punched his way out and made it. It took me a little longer. I caught four belts for every one I could lay on them. Finally I got out and started putting down shoe leather. But the paddies were hot on doing me up real nice. One of them got so close to me I saw his face over my shoulder. I stopped short and he ran right into a slap with all my weight behind it. He went down on his ass and I told him cool-like, "Motherfucker, I punch men and slap punks." His boys were too near for me to play my grandstand to the most, so I started to make it. I heard him scream out from between his split lips: "You dirty, fucking shine! I'll get one of you black bastards." I screamed back, "Your mammy got fucked by one of us black bastards." *One of us black bastards. Was that me?* I wondered.

It really bugged me when the paddies called us Puerto Ricans the same names they called our colored aces. Yet it didn't bother Louie or the other fellas who were as white as him; it didn't bother Crip, or the others, who were as dark as me or darker. Why did it always bug me? Why couldn't I just laugh it off with that simple-ass kid rhyme:

> Sticks and stones may break my bones,
> But words will never harm me.

I had two colored cats, Crutch and Brew, for tight *amigos*. All the time I heard them talk about Jim Crow and southern paddies' way-out, screwed-up thinking. Crutch told me once that he was sitting on the curb down South where he used to live and some young white boys passed in a car and yelled out to him, "Hey, nigger, git outta that gutter and climb down the sewer where all you black niggers belong."

It really bugged me, like if they had said it to me. I asked Crutch if he knew any colored cats that had been hung. "Not person'ly," he said, "but my daddy knew some." He said it with a touch of sadness hooked together with a vague arrogance.

Crutch was smart and he talked a lot of things that made sense to any Negro. That was what bothered me — it made a lot of sense to me.

"You ain't nevah been down South, eh, Piri?" Crutch had asked me.

"Uh-uh. *Nunca*, man. Just read about it, and I dug that flick *Gone with the Wind*."

"Places like Georgia and Mississippi and Alabama. All them places that end in i's an' e's an' a whole lotta a's. A black man's so important that a drop of Negro blood can make a black man out of a pink-asshole, blue-eyed white man. Powerful stuff, that thar white skin, but it don't mean a shit hill of beans alongside a Negro's blood."

Yeah, that Crutch made sense.

The next day I looked up at the faces of the people passing by my old stoop. I tried to count their different shades and colors, but I gave it up after a while. Anyway, black and white were the most outstanding; all the rest were in between.

I felt the fuzz on my chin and lazily wondered how long it'd be before I'd have one like Poppa. *I look like Poppa*, I thought, *we really favor each other*. I wondered if it was too mean to hate your brothers a little for looking white like Momma. I felt my hair — thick, black, and wiry. Mentally I compared my hair with my brothers' hair. My face screwed up at the memory of the jillion tons of stickum hair oils splashed down in a vain attempt to make it like theirs. I felt my nose. "Shit, it ain't so flat," I said aloud. But mentally I measured it against my brothers,' whose noses were sharp, straight, and placed neat-like in the middle of their paddy fair faces.

Why did this have to happen to me? Why couldn't I be born like them? I asked myself. I felt sort of chicken-shit thinking like that. I felt shame creep into me. It wasn't right to be ashamed of what one was. It was like hating Momma for the color she was and Poppa for the color he wasn't.

The noise of the block began to break through to me. I listened for real. I heard the roar of multicolored kids, a street blend of Spanish and English with a strong tone of Negro American.

"Hey, man," a voice called, "what yuh doing thar sitting on your rump? Yuh look like you're thinking up a storm." It was Brew, one of my tightest *amigos*.

"Un *poco*, Brew," I said. "How's it goin' with you?"

"Cool breeze," he said.

I looked at Brew, who was as black as God is supposed to be white. "Man, Brew," I said, "you sure an ugly spook."

Brew smiled. "Dig this Negro calling out 'spook,'" he said.

I smiled and said, "I'm a Porty Rican."

"Ah only sees another Negro in fron' of me," said Brew.

This was the "dozens," a game of insults. The dozens is a dangerous game even among friends, and many a tooth has been lost between fine, ass-tight *amigos*. Now I wanted the game to get serious. I didn't know exactly why. Brew and me had played the dozens plenty and really gotten dirty. But I wanted something to happen. "Smile, pussy, when you come up like that," I said. "I'm a stone Porty Rican, and—"

"And . . ." Brew echoed softly.

I tried to dig myself. I figured I should get it back on a joke level. What the hell was I trying to put down? Was I trying to tell Brew that I'm better than he is 'cause he's only black and I'm a Puerto Rican dark-skin? Like his people copped trees on a white man's whim, and who ever heard of Puerto Ricans getting hung like that?

I looked down at my hands, curling and uncurling, looking for some kinda answer to Brew's cool echo. "Brew," I finally eased out.

"Yeah."

"Let's forget it, Brew."

"Ain't nothin' to forget, baby."

I lit a butt. Brew offered me a whole weed. "Thanks. Nice day out," I said.

"So-kay," he said, and added: "Look, I ain't rehashin' this shit just went down, but—"

"Forget it, Brew. I'm sorry for the sound."

"Ain't nothin' to be sorry about, Piri. Yuh ain't said nothin' that bad. Mos' people got some kinda color complex. Even me."

"Brew, I ain't said what I'm feeling. I was thinking a little while ago that if you could dig the way I feel, you'd see I was hung up between two sticks. I—"

"Look, Piri," interrupted Brew, "everybody got some kinda pain goin' on inside him. I know yuh a li'l fucked up with some kind of hate called 'white.' It's that special kind with the 'no Mr.' in front of it. Dig it, man; say it like it is, out loud—like, you hate all paddies."

"Just their fuckin' color, Brew," I said bitterly. "Just their color—their damn claim that white is the national anthem of the world. You know?"

"Yeah."

"When I was a little kid in school," I said, "I used to go to general assembly all togged out with a white shirt and red tie. Everybody there wore a white shirt and red tie; and when they played the national anthem, I would put my hand over my heart. It made me feel great to blast out:

My country, 'tis of thee,
Sweet land of liberty,
Of thee I sing . . .

And now when I hear it played I can't help feeling that it's only meant for paddies. It's their national anthem, their sweet land of liberty."

"Yeah, I knows, man," Brew said. "Like it says that all men are created equal with certain deniable rights—iffen they's not paddies. We uns thank you-all, Mistuh Lincoln, suh. Us black folks got through dat ole Civil War about fair, but we all havin' one ole helluva time still tryin' to git through the damn Reconstruction."

We both laughed. "That's pretty fuckin' funny if you can laugh," I said. "Let me try some of that creatin'. Be my straight man."

"What they evah do to yuh, Piri? Yuh ain't never been down South."

"No, man, I ain't," I said, remembering that Crutch had said the same thing.

"So yuh ain't never run into that played-out shit of

'If you white, tha's all right.
If you black, da's dat.'"

"Yeah, Brew," I said, "it must be tough on you Negroes."

"Wha' yuh mean, us Negroes? Ain't yuh includin' yourself? Hell, you ain't but a coupla shades lighter'n me, and even if yuh was even lighter'n that, you'd still be a Negro."

I felt my chest get tighter and tighter. I said, "I ain't no damn Negro and I ain't no paddy. I'm Puerto Rican."

"You think that means anything to them James Crow paddies?" Brew said coolly.

"Coño," I mumbled.

"What yuh say, man?"

"I said I'm really startin' to almost hate Negroes, too," I shot back.

Brew walked away from me stiff-legged. His fists were almost closed. Then he came back and looked at me and, like he wasn't mad, said, "Yuh fuckin' yeller-faced bastard! Yuh goddamned Negro with a white man's itch! Yuh think that bein' a Porto Rican lets you off the hook? Tha's the trouble. Too damn many you black Porto Ricans got your eyes closed. Too many goddamned Negroes all over this goddamned world feel like you does. Jus' 'cause you can rattle off some different kinda language don' change your skin one bit. Whatta yuh all think? That the only niggers in the world are in this fucked-up country? They is all over this whole damn world. Man, if there's any black people up on the moon talkin' that moon talk, they is still Negroes. Git it? Negroes!"

"Brew," I said, "I hate the paddy who's trying to keep the black man down. But I'm beginning to hate the black man, too, 'cause I can feel his pain and I don't know that it oughtta be mine. Shit, man, Puerto Ricans got social problems, too. Why the fuck we gotta take on Negroes,' too?" I dug Brew's eyes. They looked as if he was thinking that he had two kinda enemies now—paddies and black Puerto Ricans. "Brew," I said, "I'm trying to be a Negro, a colored man, a black man, 'cause that's what I am. But I gotta accept it myself, from inside. Man, do you know what it is to sit across a dinner table looking at your brothers that look exactly like paddy people? True, I ain't never been down South, but the same crap's happening up here. So they don't hang you by your neck. But they slip an invisible rope around your balls and hang you with nice smiles and 'If we need you, we'll call you.' I wanna feel like a 'Mr.' I can't feel like that just yet, and there ain't no amount of cold wine and pot can make my mind accept me being a 'Mr.' part time. So what if I can go to some paddy pool hall or fancy restaurant? So what if I lay some white chick? She still ain't nothin' but a white blur even if my skin does set off her paddy color."

"So yuh gonna put the Negro down jus' 'cause the paddy's puttin' yuh down," Brew said. "Ain't gonna bring nothin' from us exceptin' us putting you down too."

"Like you're putting me down?"

"I ain't put you down, Piri. You jus' got me warm with that 'I'm a Porty Rican' jazz. But I know where yuh at. You jus' gotta work some things out."

Brew shoved his big hand at me. I grabbed it and shook it, adding a slap of skin to bind it. I looked at our different shades of skin and thought, *He's a lot darker than me, but one thing is for sure, neither of us is white.* "Everything cool?" I said.

"Yee-ah. I ain't mad. I said I dig. Jus' got worried that you might turn out to be a colored man with a paddy heart."

Like Poppa, I thought, and my eyes followed a fast-moving behind going up the stoop across the street.

"Nice piece of ass," Brew said.

"Naw, Brew, I—"

"You sayin' that ain't a nice piece of ass?"

"That wasn't what I was gonna say, you horny bastard. I meant that what I want out of life is some of the good things the white man's got. Man, what some of them eat for weekday dinner, we eat for our Sunday dinner—"

"'Tain't only Porty Ricans."

"Yeah, American Negroes, too."

"Thar's a lotta white people got it kinda bad, too," Brew said. "Some even worse."

"What you doing now, man, defendin' the paddies?" I asked.

"Jus' sayin' like it is."

I thought for a long while and finally said, "I'm gonna have everything good they have for living even if I gotta take it. Fuck it, I care about me a whole lot. Even the poor white people you're talking about are down on the Negro—more so than the paddy that got bread, 'cause since the poor paddy ain't got nothin,' he gotta feel big some way, so the Negro's supposed to lie down and let the paddy climb up on his chest with his clodhoppers just so's he can feel three or four inches taller standing on another man's ribs."

"Yuh talking all this stuff, and yuh ain't evah been down South, Piri," Brew said disdainfully.

"Brew," I said with quiet patience, "you don't have to be from the South to know what's happenin.' There's toilet bowls wherever you go. Besides, I learn from you and Crutch and the others. I learn from what I read—and from the paddies."

"But it ain't exactly like being down South, Piri," Brew insisted solemnly.

"What's the matter, Brew?" I asked sarcastically. "A cat's gotta be hung before he knows what's happenin'?" I began to whistle, "Way Down Upon the Swanee River."

Brew went on like I hadn't said nothing, "So yuh can't appreciate and therefore you can't talk that much."

"That's what you say, Brew. But the same—"

"Yuh gonna jaw about the difference and sameness up here and down there," Brew broke in. "Man, you think these paddies up here are a bitch on wheels. Ha! They ain't shit alongside Mr. Charlie down thar. Down South, if one ain't real careful, he can grow up smilin' his ass off and showin' pearly whites till his gums catch pneumonia or workin' his behind off fo' nothin.'"

"Yeah, but—"

"Let me say it like it is, Piri. It ain't as bad now as when my daddy was a kid, but it's bad enough. Though I guess bad is bad, a little or a lot. Now those Indians sure had some kinda hard way to go, but they had heart."

"Whatcha mean, man?" I asked, wondering what the hell Indians had to do with all this.

"My daddy use to say that

'The Indian fought the white man and died
An' us black folk us' wagged ouah tails,
"Yas suhses," smiled and multiplied.'"

I cracked a smile and got up and yawned and stretched. "Brew," I said.
"Still here, man."

"Maybe it wasn't a bad idea to take it low when the weight was all on the other side. Dig it, man, the Indian fought the paddy and lost. And the Indian was on his own turf."

"We mighta won," Brew said.

"Yeah, we mighta, Brew," I said hollowly.

"Okay, man," Brew said, smiling.

"You know, Brew?" I said suddenly. "I'm going down South. Wanna come?"

"What fo,' man?"

"It might just set me straight on a lotta things. Maybe I can stop being confused and come in on a right stick."

My man's face screwed up like always when he wasn't sure of something. "Ah don't know, Piri," he said. "Down there it ain't like up here. You can do and say more, but down thar in some of them towns yuh jus' blow your cool and yuh liable to find yuhself on some chain gang or pickin' peas on some prison farm—or worse yet, gettin' them peas planted over yuh."

"That's okay, *amigo*, I still wanna make it. How 'bout it?"

"Ah dunno."

"Don't worry, Negro," I said. "I promise not to pull no Jim Crow act on you when we get there. Some of my best *amigos* are Negroes."

"It ain't that," Brew laughed. "It's jus' that bomb on your shoulder. We go down South and you start all that Porty Rican jazz and we's liable to get it from both sides."

"Brew, I'm serious," I said.

"So am I, man, so am I. How yuh figure on goin'?"

"Merchant Marine's the big kick around here now. All we gotta do is make it down to the NMU."

"What's that?"

"The National Maritime Union," I explained. "That's where we can take out some papers or something. Dickie Bishop works down there and we're tight, so no sweat."

"Okay man," Brew said, "Ah'm with yuh. But only on the condition you cool your role."

"Till somebody starts something?"

"Till somebody else starts, not you. An' if trouble does start, don't go looking for too much police protection down there. Mos' of the fuzzes down there are cops by day and walkin' bed sheets by night."

"I won't look for it, Brew," I said.

"Sometimes yuh don't hafta, Piri. Sometimes you don't hafta. When we gonna make it over to the NMU?"

"Mañana, man. First thing in the morning. You can meet me here around eight. Better yet, stay over my house tonight."

"On Long Island?"

"Yeah."

"You still go out there?"

"Once in a while," I said. "I still have my people there."

"Yeah, Ah know."

"Meet me about six o'clock," I said. "It's about two now."

"Tha's nice," Brew said. "It'll give me a couple hours with Alayce."

"Yeah, how is she?" I asked. "That's a nice woman."

"A-huh. She's awright. Gets me warm sometimes, but they don't come no motherfuckin' better, in or outta bed."

"Give her my regards."

"Sure will."

"Well, cool it, faggot," I smiled.

Brew grinned and said, "Dozens? Evah notice how your pappy walks?"

"Nope, I've been too busy diggin' how your mammy walks."

We laughed and slapped skin going away. I watched Brew make it and then walked off toward Penn Station. Some thoughts were still working in my mind. *Jesus, if I'm a Negro, I gotta feel it all over. I don't have the "for sure" feelin's yet.* I waved to one of the cats in front of El Viejo's candy store and kept on walking.

My daydreaming was splintered by my brother José kicking at the door in sheer panic. "Hey, who's in there?" he yelled.

Me, man, me," I yelled back. "Whatta ya want?"

"Let me in. I gotta take a piss so bad I can taste it."

"Taste good?" I asked softly.

"Dammit, open up!"

I laughed, and reached out a dripping hand and flipped the latch. José rushed in like his behind was on fire. His face had a pained look on it. "Chri-sus sake," he said, "you made me piss all over my pants."

"It'll dry, man, it'll dry."

"Aggh," he said as he relieved himself. "That feels good." I looked at my brother. Even his peter's white, I thought, just like James's. Only ones got black peters is Poppa and me, and Poppa acts like his is white, too.

"Poppa's home."

"Yeah. Hand me the towel, simple."

"Damn, Piri, you made me piss all over my pants," José said again. He pulled back the towel he was offering me and began to wipe his pants with it.

"Man, turkey, what you doin'?" I said. "You drying that piss and I gotta wipe my face with that towel."

"It'll dry, man, it'll dry."

I yanked the towel outta his hand and carefully wiped with what seemed to be the part he hadn't used. "You know somethin,' José?" I said.

"What? Jesus, I hope this piss don't stink when it dries."

"I'm goin' down South."

"Where?"

"Down South."

"What for?"

"Don't know all the way," I said, "except I'm tryin' to find somethin' out."

"Down South!" He said it like I was nuts.

"Sí. . . . I want to see what a *moyeto's* worth and the paddy's weight on him," I said.

"Whatta ya talking about? You sound like a *moto* who's high on that *yerba* shit. And anyway, what's the spade gotta do with you?"

"I'm a Negro."

'You ain't no nigger," José said.

"I ain't?"

"No. You're a Puerto Rican."

"I am, huh?" I looked at José and said, "Course, you gotta say that. 'Cause if I'm a Negro, then you and James is one too. And that ain't leavin' out Sis and Poppa. Only Momma's an exception. She don't care what she is."

José didn't look at me. He decided that looking at the toilet bowl was better. "So whatta you got to find out, eh?" he said. "You're crazy, stone loco. We're Puerto Ricans, and that's different from being *moyetos*." His voice came back very softly and his hand absentmindedly kept brushing the drying wet patch on his pants.

"That's what I've been wanting to believe all along, José," I said. "I've been hanging on to that idea even when I knew it wasn't so. But only pure white Puerto Ricans are white, and you wouldn't even believe that if you ever dug what the paddy said."

"I don't give a good shit what you say, Piri. We're Puerto Ricans, and that makes us different from black people."

I kept drying myself even though there was nothin' to dry. I was trying not to get mad. I said, "José, that's what the white man's been telling the Negro all along, that 'cause he's white he's different from the Negro; that he's better'n the Negro or anyone that's not white. That's what I've been telling myself and what I tried to tell Brew."

"Brew's that colored guy, ain't he?" José said.

"Yeah—an' like I'm saying, sure there's stone-white Puerto Ricans, like from pure Spanish way back—but it ain't us. Poppa's a Negro and, even if Momma's *blanca*, Poppa's blood carries more weight with Mr. Charlie," I said.

"Mr. Charlie, Mr. Charlie. Who the fuck is he?"

"That's the name Brew calls the paddies. Ask any true *corazón* white motherfucker what the score is," I said.

"I'm not black, no matter what you say, Piri."

I got out of the shower and sat on the edge of the tub. "Maybe not out-side, José," I said. "But you're sure that way inside."

"I ain't black, damn you! Look at my hair. It's almost blond. My eyes are blue, my nose is straight. My motherfuckin' lips are not like a baboon's ass. My skin is white. White, goddamit! White! Maybe Poppa's a little dark, but that's the Indian blood in him. He's got white blood in him and—"

"So what the fuck am I? Something Poppa an' Momma picked out the garbage dump?" I was jumping stink inside and I answered him like I felt it. "Look, man, better believe it, I'm one of 'you-all.' Am I your brother or ain't I?"

"Yeah, you're my brother, and James an' Sis, and we all come out of Momma an' Poppa—but we ain't Negroes. We're Puerto Ricans, an' we're white."

"Boy, you, Poppa and James sure are sold on that white kick. Poppa thinks that marrying a white woman made him white. He's wrong. It's just another nigger marrying a white woman and making her as black as him. That's the way the paddy looks at it. The Negro just stays black, Period. Dig it?"

José's face got whiter and his voice angrier at my attempt to take away his white status. He screamed out strong, "I ain't no nigger! You can be if you want to be. You can go down South and grow cotton, or pick it, or whatever the fuck they do. You can eat that cornbread or whatever shit they eat. You can bow and kiss ass and clean shit bowls. But—I—am—white! And you can go to hell!"

"And James is *blanco*, too?" I asked quietly.

"You're damn right."

"And Poppa?"

José flushed the toilet chain so hard it sounded as if somebody's neck had broken. "Poppa's the same as you," he said, avoiding my eyes, "Indian."

"What kinda Indian?" I said bitterly. "Caribe? Or maybe Borinquén? Say, José, didn't you know the Negro made the scene in Puerto Rico way back? And when the Spanish spics ran outta Indian coolies, they brought them big blacks from you know where. Poppa's got *moyeto* blood. I got it. Sis got it. James got it. And, mah deah brudder, you-all got it! Dig it! It's with us till game time. Like I said, man, that shit-ass poison I've been living with is on its way out. It's a played out lie about me us being white. There ain't nobody in this fucking house can lay any claim to bein' paddy exceptin' Momma, and she's never made it a mountain of fever like we have. You and James are like houses—painted white outside, and blacker'n a mother inside. An' I'm close to being like Poppa—trying to be white on both sides."

José eased by me and put his hand on the doorknob.

"Where you going?" I said. "I ain't finished talking yet."

José looked at me like there was no way out. "Like I said man, you can be a nigger if you want to," he said, as though he were talking with a ten-ton rock on his chest. "I don't know how you come to be my brother, but I love you like one. I've busted my ass, both me and James, trying to explain to people how come you so dark and how come your hair is so curly an'—"

I couldn't help thinking, *Oh, Crutch, you were so right. We shouldn't have moved to Long Island.* I said, "You and James hadda make excuses for me? Like for me being *un Negrito?*" I looked at the paddy in front of me. "Who to?" I said. "Paddies?"

Lights began to jump into my head and tears blurred out that this was my brother before me. The burning came up out of me and I felt the shock run up my arm as my fists went up the side of his head. I felt one fist hit his mouth. I wondered if I had broken any of his nice white teeth.

José fell away and bounced back with his white hands curled into fists. I felt the hate in them as his fists became a red light of exploding pain on my tender, flat nose. *Oh, God!* I tried to make the lights go away. I made myself creep up a long sinking shit-hole of agony and threw myself at José. The bathroom door flew open and me, naked and wet with angry sweat, and José, his mouth bleedin,' crashed out of the bathroom and rolled into the living room. I heard all kinds of screaming and chairs turning over and falling lamps. I found myself on top of José. In the blurred confusion I saw his white, blood-smeared face and I heard myself screaming, "You bastard! Dig it, you bastard. You're bleeding, and the blood is like anybody else's—red!" I saw an unknown face spitting blood at me. I hated it. I wanted to stay on top of this unknown what-was-it and beat him and beat him and beat him and beat him and *beat beat beat beat beat*—and feel skin smash under me and—and—and—

I felt an arm grab me. It wasn't fair; it wasn't a *chévere* thing to do. In a fair rumble, nobody is supposed to jump in. "God-dammit are you crazy?" a voice screamed. "Goddamn you for beating your brother like that. My God!—"

I twisted my head and saw Poppa. And somewhere, far off, I heard a voice that sounded like Momma crying, "What's it all about? What's it all about? Why do brothers do this to each other?"

I wanted to scream it out, but that man's arm was cutting my air from sound. I twisted and forced out, "Lemme go, Poppa. *Coño*, let me go!" And the arm was gone. I stayed on bended knees. My fists were tired and my knuckles hurt at this Cain and Abel scene. As the hurting began to leave me, I slowly became a part of my naked body. I felt weak with inside pain. I wondered why.

"José, José," Momma screamed, and I wondered why she didn't scream for me, too. Didn't she know I had gotten hurt the worst?

"Why in God's name?" Poppa was saying.

Fuck God! I thought.

"Why in God's name?"

I looked at Poppa. "'Cause, Poppa," I said, "him, you, and James think you're white, and I'm the only one that's found out I'm not. I tried hard not to find out. But I did, and I'm almost out from under that kick you all are still copping out to." I got up from my knees. "Poppa," I added, "what's wrong with not being white? What's so wrong with being *trigueño?* Momma must think it's great, she got married to you, eh? We gotta have pride and dignity, Poppa; we gotta walk big and bad. I'm me and I dig myself in the mirror and it's me. I shower and dig my peter and it's me. I'm black, and it don't make no difference whether I say good-bye or *adios*—it means the same."

Nobody said anything; everyone just stood there. I said, "I'm proud to be a Puerto Rican, but being Puerto Rican don't make the color." Still there was silence. "I'm going," I said.

"Where?" Poppa asked.

"I don't know . . ."

"He's going down South," said José, sitting on the floor with his head in his hands and the almost-blond hair, the good straight hair that could fall down over his forehead.

"Where?" Poppa asked.

I looked at José and felt sorry for me. I looked at the wall and said, "Down South. I joined the merchant marine and me and Brew's going, and—"

"Who? Brew? That's that colored boy, ain't it?" Poppa said.

"—and I wanna find out what's happening, and . . ." I wondered why everything I was saying didn't sound like it was so important to anybody, including me. I wondered why James wasn't there. I wondered why Sis wasn't there . . .

I walked away. Momma put her hand on me and she asked, "Why does it hurt you so to be *un Negrito?*"

I shook my head and kept walking. I wished she could see inside me. I wished she could see it didn't hurt—so much.

VICTOR HERNÁNDEZ CRUZ
African Things

o the wonder man   rides his space ship /
                              brings his power through
many moons
               carries in soft blood   african spirits
dance & sing in my mother's house. in my cousin's house.
black as night can be/   what was Puerto Rican all about.
                                  all about the
indios & you better believe it the african things
                                 black & shiny
grandmother speak to me & tell me of african things
                                how do latin
boo-ga-loo sound   like you
                      conga drums in the islands   you know
the traveling through many moons
                         dance & tell me black african things
I know you know.

SANDRA MARÍA ESTEVES

Black Notes and "You Do Something to Me"

For Gerry González and the Fort Apache Band

Jazz—jazzy jass juice,
Just so smooth,
so be-hop samba blue to sweet bump black.
So slip slide back to mama black—
to mamaland base black.
Don't matter could be bronx born basic street black.
Or white ivory piano coast negro dunes bembé black.
Mezclando manos in polyrhythm sync to fingers,
to keys, to valves, to strings, to sticks, to bells, to skins, to YEAH black.
Bringin' it home black.
The bad Fort Apache tan olive brown beat black.
Bringin' it all the way up fast black.
Flyin' across Miles 'n Sonny, across John, Rhasaan 'n Monk's '81,
across Dizzy blue conga Jerry horn,
'n básico Andy mo-jo black.
Across Nicky's campana timbaleando tumbao black.
'N Dalto's multi-octave chords with all those keys black.
Those multifarious dimensional openings
playin' loud—soft—hard—cold—slow—'n—suavecito black.
Playin' it runnin'—jumpin'—cookin'—greasin'—'n—sauvecito black.
Playin' it mellow, yeah mellow,
makin' it mean somethin' black.
Makin' it move, rockin' round black.
Walk with it, talk with it, wake the dead with it black.
Turnin' it out, touchin' the sky with it black.
Shakin' it suave, shakin' it loose,
shakin' it che-ché-que-re black.
Season it, sugar it, lingerin', lullaby black.

Livin' it, ALIVE BLACK!
Always lovin' it—Yeah!

Jazz,
How I love your sweet soul sounds.
Yeah,
how I love how you love me.
Yeah, how I love that deep black thang . . .

                       . . . "you do so well" . . .

Before People Called Me a Spic, They Called Me a Nigger

People always look for the beginnings of the Party. We started the Young Lords because we knew something had to be done. If we didn't find or create an organization that was gonna do something then everybody was gonna get shot, see, because it would have gotten to the point that people got so frustrated, they would just jump on the first cop they saw, or just snap, do something crazy.

At first the only model we had to go on in this country was the Black Panther Party. Besides that, we were all a bunch of readers, when we first came in we read Che, Fidel, Fanon, Marx, Lenin, Jefferson, the Bill of Rights, Declaration, Constitution—we read everything. Now there ain't too much time for reading.

We also felt that the potential for revolution had always been there for Puerto Rican people. If we had gone into the thing from a negative point of view, we wouldn't have made it, right. 'Cause a lot of times when things were really rough, it's been that blind faith in the people that keeps us going. The problem has been to tap that potential and to organize it into a disciplined force that's gonna really move on this government. Puerto Ricans had been psyched into believing this myth about being docile. A lot of Puerto Ricans were afraid to move, a lot of Puerto Ricans really thought that the man in blue was the baddest thing going.

Things were different in the gang days. Gang days, we owned the block, and nobody could tell us what to do with the street. Then dope came in and messed everything up, messed our minds up and just broke our backs— dope and anti-poverty. Anti-poverty wiped out a whole generation of what could have been Puerto Rican leaders in New York City.

For example, in '65, the time of the East Harlem riots, we held East Harlem for two days. We had the roof-tops, the streets, and the community—no pigs could go through. It was like back in the old days. A lot of people really tripped off that, a lot of the junkies who had been in gangs remembered that shit. To end it they shipped in anti-poverty. They brought it in full force, and they bought out a lot of the young cats who were leading the rebellions. A lot of dudes who were throwing bricks one day found themselves directors of anti-poverty programs the next, or workers on Mayor Lindsay's Urban Action Core.

So we had no leadership, and we had no people—our people were dying from dope. But we knew that it was there, man, 'cause we knew that the fire was there. Those of us who got together to start the thing, we knew we weren't freaks—we didn't feel that we were all that much different from the people. There's a tendency to say "the people" and put the people at arm's length. When we say "people," man, we're talking about ourselves. We're from these blocks, and we're from these schools, products of this whole thing. Some of us came back from college—it was like rediscovering where your parents had come from, rediscovering your childhood.

Our original viewpoint in founding the Party was a New York point of view—that's where the world started and ended. As we later found out, New York is different from most other cities that Puerto Ricans live in. But even in New York, we found that on a grass-roots level a high degree of racism existed between Puerto Ricans and Blacks, and between light-skinned and dark-skinned Puerto Ricans. We had to deal with this racism because it blocked any kind of growth for our people, any understanding of the things Black people had gone through. So rather than watching Rap Brown on TV, rather than learning from that and saying, "Well, that should affect me too," Puerto Ricans said, "Well, yeah, those Blacks got a hard time, you know, but we ain't going through the same thing." This was especially true for the light-skinned Puerto Ricans. Puerto Ricans like myself, who are darker skinned, who look like Afro-Americans, couldn't do that, 'cause to do that would be to escape into a kind of fantasy. Because before people called me a spic, they called me a nigger. So that was, like, one reason as to why we felt the Young Lords Party should exist.

At first many of us felt why have a Young Lords Party when there existed a Black Panther Party, and wouldn't it be to our advantage to try to consolidate our efforts into getting Third World people into something that already existed? It became apparent to us that that would be impractical, because we wouldn't be recognizing the national question. We felt we each had to organize where we were at—so that Chicanos were gonna have to organize Chicanos, Blacks were gonna have to organize Blacks, Puerto Ricans Puerto Ricans, etc., until we came to that level where we could deal with one umbrella organization that could speak for everybody. But until we eliminate the racism that separates everybody, that will not be possible.

What happened was in 1969 in the June 7 issue of the Black Panther newspaper there was an article about the Young Lords Organization in Chicago with Cha Cha Jiménez as their chairman. Cha Cha was talking about revolution and socialism and the liberation of Puerto Rico and the right to self-determination and all this stuff that I ain't *never* heard a spic say. I mean, I hadn't never heard no Puerto Rican talk like this—just Black people were talking this way, you know. And I said, "Damn! Check this out." That's what really got us started. That's all it was, man. [. . .]

When we talk about our role in terms of creating the American Revolution, we are not saying we are going to take Puerto Rican people and ship them back to Puerto Rico. We are saying that we have been here in this country for two generations—in some cases, maybe three generations—we've been here for so long, right, that it would be too convenient for us to move back now, and just create a revolution there. We're saying that we want payback for the years that we have suffered, the years that we have put up with cockroaches and rats. We had to put up with snow, we had to put up with English, we had to put up with racism, with the general abuse of America. And we are gonna hook up with everybody else in this country who's fighting for their liberation—and that's a whole lot of people. We know that the number-one group that's leading that struggle are Black people, 'cause Black people—if we remember the rule that says the most oppressed will take the vanguard role in the struggle—Black people, man, have gone through the most shit. Black people, along with Chicanos and native Americans, are the greatest ally we can have. So we must build the Puerto Rican–Black alliance. That is the basis of the American Revolution for us. Actually, the first group in America that we had a formal coalition with was the Black Panther Party. Also we must further the Latino ties, especially as we move west, and here in New York City we must work with Dominicans—to further eliminate the racism that has deeply divided Black people and Spanish people. [. . .]

Now the time has come for the Young Lords Party to begin organizing on the island. I mean, that's inevitable—we're not fighting just for Puerto Ricans in the States, we are fighting for all Puerto Ricans, you know, and in turn we're fighting for all oppressed people. In the fourth point of our Thirteen Point Program and Platform, we say we are revolutionary nationalists, not racists. That also means that we recognize the struggle of white people.

One thing we always say in the Young Lords, "Don't ever let any particular hatred you have prevent you from working. Always take it into you and let it move you forward. And if it's strong, change it, because it stops your work." We tell all Puerto Rican youth to listen to this. High-school-age Puerto Ricans are into a *big* thing about whitey, and we tell them, "Man, it's not white *folk*. What we are trying to destroy is not white people, but a system created by white people, a capitalistic system that has run away from them to the point that it is now killing white people, too." [. . .]

You know, when we meet somebody from the Third World, we immediately call them brother or sister, right. And then they have to prove to us through their practice that they are not our brothers or sisters—like Gene Roberts, who infiltrated the Panther Party. We view white people, when we first see them, with mistrust and suspicion, and then they have to show us by their practice that they are really our brothers and sisters—and that is the difference in the two.

It would be totally naive for us to openly embrace white people, even if they are in the Movement, simply because they're supposed to be revolutionary. We've gone through too many frustrations with white people in the Movement to have that happen. 'Cause you really want to hope that once you get into the Movement there ain't no more racism. But that's a joke. In many cases racism becomes sicker than what you see in the so-called "straight" world, because it's kind of like a psychopathic hero-worship. You know, everything the Panthers do is right simply because they're Black; the Young Lords are fantastic because they're Puerto Rican. That's ridiculous. The Young Lords make mistakes, and if we make mistakes we want our white *compañeros* and *compañeras* to criticize us. If they really love us, that's what they'll do. That's one of the weaknesses of the Movement, you know, that people do not want to criticize the Panthers because the Panthers are Black. But in doing that they do more harm to the Panthers than they do good. [. . .]

The Young Lords Party today is the fastest-moving group of people inside the Puerto Rican nation. We're moving faster than anybody else, and this means that all the contradictions that exist among our people are much more highlighted among us, that things come out much more quickly. That's why you have the Young Lords arguing about male chauvinism, female passivity, racism, Viet Nam. People on the street ain't talkin' about all those things yet, you know. We try to take that word "vanguard" and give it a new definition, because the definition that it has now is that the vanguard is some elitist group, that they're better than everybody else, and they tell all the other groups, "Go fuck yourself." Like, to us, the vanguard means that we have a great responsibility. It means that we are in front of the people and show the people the way, but at the same time we are among the people, because we are the people. We are also in back of the people, you know, because sometimes you got to lay back to check the people out. And that's where we get our strength from.

We're here because we are trying as best we can to take the power of the State and put that back in the hands of the people who for so long have been denied everything. It's a very deep, emotional thing, you know, for people who've been told for so long that they're fucked up, that they're niggers, spics, that they ain't worth shit, to be doing this.

We are showing people an alternative to living under a capitalistic society—an alternative to the tenement, to the street, to the workplace, to the *fanguito*. Each generation that comes up is taught that this is the only way things can be done; this is life, right? It's a fact of life that you're poor, that there are some people on top, and that most people are on the bottom. It's a fact of life that this is a dog-eat-dog world, and if you want to make it you got to make it by yourself. But we're gonna take them facts of life and turn them around. We're saying that it is gonna be a new fact of life, that what counts first is not so much the individual but the group, and in order for the individual to survive, the group, the nation, has to survive.

Before people called me a spic, they called me a nigger (2007)

From the beginning, we were always keenly aware inside the Young Lords that while we were trying to bring about changes in the society at large that would get the boot off the most downtrodden, we would also, at the same time, have to change ourselves. And we would have to try to change the very people we were trying to convince to join us in taking the bold step of confronting the status quo.

The biggest obstacle to overcome, I think, is fear. It is damn frightening to take on a power structure, to take that first step. It is almost comfortable to stay, even in the misery of where you might be. It is more secure, at first blush, to continue believing even wrong things. About yourself. Or the world around you. And how it got that way. Add on children, living paycheck to paycheck . . . yeah. Change is tough.

After fear, I think, for us in the barrio in 1969, when the Young Lords started out of New York, the next big obstacle was the relationship be-

The General Committee (The Original Five) of the Young Lords Party, left to right: Juan "Fi" Ortíz, Pablo "Yoruba" Guzmán, Juan González, David Pérez, and Felipe Luciano, New York City, summer 1968. (Photograph by Hiram Maristany/Maristany Photos)

Nellie Tanco (far right) and her brother Sammy (in hat) jamming with friends, including Felipe Luciano, New York, circa 1975. (Photograph by Máximo Colón/Max Colón Photo Collection)

tween women and men. And then, this whole thing of "race." This essay deals with the latter topic, though man and woman—well, you can fill libraries on that one.

The Lords was predominantly a Puerto Rican group, though not exclusively. We were also based in the Northeast—New York at first, then Philadelphia, Bridgeport, Newark, Hoboken, and various support groups and branches ranging from Boston to campuses in places as far-flung as Ann Arbor and Hawaii; we were in prisons, the military, and had two chapters in Puerto Rico. So our experience on "race," or "the national question," is very different from, say, our Chicano *compañeros*.

Puerto Ricans—similar to Dominicans, Cubans, and most Latino groups throughout Latin America and the Caribbean—are, mostly, a blend of genes from Spain, Africa, and the peoples indigenous to the region at the time Columbus showed up. The Native Americans. The so-called Indians: Tainos, Arawaks, Caribs. There's also touches of Dutch in there, French, *lo que sea*—but those are the three main groups.

Certain inbreeding among the aristocratic, colonial, upper classes, coupled with a fierce caste system over the generations, created the sense that the "higher" up one searched the society, the lighter skinned it got. And of course, just as in the racist United States of America, there existed the corollary that somehow "lighter" ("whiter") meant "better." And hell, a lot of things were better: Opportunity. Food. Homes. Education. Families remaining intact. Recreation. And if you don't think we still have a mountain to climb, check out the news on Univision and Telemundo, and see how they have screened out more Afro-Latin@s than even their "American" counterparts have screened out Blacks, Latin@s, and Asians. Or check out how "Spanish" radio rarely blends salsa regularly into the mix, considering it a "lower-class" music.

In New York, Puerto Ricans were growing up alongside African Americans in the same barrios, and only the fools among us (and at first there were many because who doesn't want to cling to a shred of *something* that says, "Hey, *you're* not really in the worst shape, *they* are") could not see that we had a heck of a lot in common. And it began, of course, with rhythm and dance.

As stereotypical as that may sound, come on: when people from two different cultures heard a *conga* played just right and found themselves staring across a room at each other moving in the same syncopation to that beat, it had an electricity that surpassed Steven Spielberg's aliens and Francois Truffaut tripping out together to those notes in *Close Encounters* (and if a man's eyes met a woman's across that space—well, there goes that whole male-female thing again!).

After the conga, the rest followed pretty quickly: "Chitlins?" "Cuchifritos." "Soul." "Salsa." At least half the Puerto Rican family had to pick up on having the same nappy hair as their African American cousins. It took a long, long while—but that "good hair versus bad hair" thing just couldn't cut it anymore. Y tu abuela, ¿dónde está? I used to tell David Dinkins, the former mayor of New York, that our roots went to the same slave ship. It just made different stops. Dinkins looks eerily like my father. And he claims he has a cousin who looks exactly like me.

Reality kept kicking racial bullshit in the ass. My maternal grandfather, an Afro-Latino (or Afro-Boricua, as we started saying in the Lords as a way of identifying dark-skinned Puerto Ricans), left Santiago de Cuba in 1920 to go to Tuskegee Institute in Alabama. Hello! My father, born in Nueva York, was raised by a light-skinned Puerto Rican woman who told him he was not "Black" but "White." And that as a Puerto Rican he was descended from the Spanish conquistadores. She barely mentioned the "Indios," and never included the Yorubas, Ibos, or Fulanis. Then my old man—an Afro-Boricua, if you will—signed up for the still-Jim Crow Navy in 1946.

Assigned to the aircraft carrier Midway, my father's best friend was a man from the South named Johnson. Movies were shown on the flight deck. The wooden folding chairs up front were for the white sailors. The rows in the back for the Blacks. "Come on, Johnson," my father said one night. "I see a couple of seats up front." "Whoa, Guhz-man," Johnson said in a long southern drawl, pulling back on my father's elbow. "That's fo' the White boys." "What are you talking about, we're all in this together?" My old man pulled away. "That's where the White boys sit, Guhz-man!" "I'm Puerto Rican! I'm sitting up front!"

A few minutes later, Johnson helped pull my father up from a pile of wooden chairs where he had been thrown after the "White boys" kicked his ass for being so stupid as to try and sit up front. "Ah TOL' you, Guhz-man!" "But I'm Puerto Rican," my father said in a low, slow voice, rubbing his bruises. "They don't care what kinda nigger you is, Guhz-man!"

My father told me that story every couple of years from the time I was about five. He would finish with: "So remember: you're a Black Puerto Rican!" This would drive my brown-skinned mother crazy, as she held on to the illusion a lot longer that we were somehow not "sullied" by "Black blood."

My father took me to see Malcolm X speak on the corner of 125th and Seventh when I was about twelve. He made sure we watched the news together when the sheriffs down South were hosing civil rights marchers and using electric cattle prods on them: on people just trying to vote; on people just saying "I am an American too." "I want you to see this," he would tell me. "Because in this country, those people are us."

He and my grandfather would tell me that to survive and get ahead in this country I would have to learn several languages as currency: "You have to speak perfect English. You're dark skinned, and you're poor. That's two strikes. So you have to let White folks know how educated you are by speaking *perfectly*. Now, at the same time, you live in the ghetto. You don't want people thinking you're putting on airs, or you'll get your ass kicked. So you have to speak like the brothers. Y tu *también* eres del barrio. So, you better get your Spanish together." That one took the longest time.

Think about how things have changed among us since the Young Lords, and other groups, in that regard: the good hair and bad hair nonsense. Marry someone White *para mejorar la raza*. Remember that? As a kid I remember an older, light-skinned Puerto Rican girl pointing to her bare arm when someone asked her to pick something up: "What do I look like?" she said. Meaning, *a slave? A nigger slave?*

Just before helping to start the Young Lords, I had intended to join the Black Panther Party. In fact, a Black friend and I summoned up the nerve to go to the Harlem office, with the intent of signing up. They scared the hell out of us.

But when we started the Lords, the Panthers were the model. That and the inspiration of Malcolm and Rap Brown. Now, though, thanks to founding members like Mickey Meléndez, David Pérez, and Iris Morales, we started teaching ourselves about Albizu Campos and the Nationalist Party of Puerto Rico. About Lolita Lebrón. About Ramón Emeterio Betances.

We did this while we danced at parties after a day of fighting the police, just to get basic rights, with the Panthers. Blasting James Brown *and* Tito Puente. ¡PA'LANTE!

FELIPE LUCIANO

Excerpt from Jíbaro, My Pretty Nigger

Jíbaro, mi negro lindo
De los bosques de caña
Caciques de luz
Tiempo es una cosa cósmica.

Jíbaro, my pretty nigger.
Father of my yearning for the soil,
The land,
The earth of my people.

Father of the sweet smells of fruit in my mother's womb,
the earth brown of my skin,
the thoughts of freedom that butterfly through my insides.

Jíbaro, my pretty nigger.
Sweating bullets of blood and bedbugs,
Swaying slowly to the softly strummed strains of a five string guitar
Remembering ancient empires
Of sun gods and black spirits and things that were once
So simple.

MARTA MORENO VEGA

The Yoruba Orisha Tradition Comes to New York City

In 1955, there were approximately twenty-five people in New York City who were believers in the Orisha tradition.[1] The founding member of the Orisha tradition in New York City was Babalawo Pancho Mora (Yoruba name, Ifa Morote), who arrived in New York in 1946 and, soon after, established the "first ile, or house of the orishas" there. Mora had been initiated as a high priest of Ifa in Cuba on January 27, 1944, by Babalawo Quintin Lecon, a renowned Cuban Ifa priest, and was the first babalawo in New York to practice Ifa divination.[2]

Mora's belief in this ancient tradition and his desire to maintain his belief system motivated him to found the first Orisha community in the city. From his pioneering work, the tradition has grown to include thousands of initiates from all walks of life and different ethnic groups. He has initiated several thousand godchildren from varied professions and international backgrounds, and he has traveled extensively in Latin America and nationally to perform rituals and spread the practice of Santería.[3]

On December 4, 1955, Francisco Aguabella and Julito Collazo attended their first Santería ritual in New York, a celebration to Changó (Santa Barbara) by the santero Willie, also known as "El Bolitero" (the numbers runner), an Afro–Puerto Rican initiated in Cuba by Pancho Mora's sister. Aguabella and Collazo found out about the ceremony, which took place at 111th Street and St. Nicolas Avenue in Harlem, at the world-famous Palladium nightclub, where many Latin musicians gathered and played.[4]

After observing for a time the ceremony at the home of Willie "El Bolitero," Collazo and Aguabella joined in the singing. They attracted much attention, since few people at the time knew the Yoruba chants to the orishas. As the son of the renowned santera Ebelia Collazo from barrio San Miguel in Cuba, Julito Collazo had grown up in the Orisha religion and learned the intricacies of this African-based tradition.[5] At the age of fifteen, he was accepted into a neighborhood batá drum group and began his professional career. Simultaneously, Julito became more involved with other Afro-Cuban religions and increased his knowledge of the philosophies and rituals of each sect. Under the guidance of the renowned traditional batá drummer Pablo Roche of Cuba and of the master traditional drummers Paul Diaz, Trinidad Torregrosa, Nicholas Angarica, and Miguel Somodeville, Julito Collazo became *omo* Añya, initiated in the secret knowledge of the Orisha Añya, owner of the drum.[6]

The Yoruba community between 1955 and 1959 included important figures in the entertainment field who helped promote the songs and music of the Santería tradition. The presence of Cuban musicians such as Frank "Machito" Grillo and Mario Bauzá, founder of the Afro-Cubans Orchestra, influenced Afro-American jazz as well as Latin music. Bauzá's introduction of the master Afro-Cuban drummer Chano Pozo to Dizzy Gillespie, and the incorporation of Chano Pozo—an initiate of Afro-Cuban religions—into Dizzy's orchestra, opened new musical horizons in African American jazz.

The continued collaboration among Chano Pozo, Mario Bauzá, and Dizzy Gillespie further served to popularize traditional Afro-Cuban music. Gillespie continued throughout his career to incorporate the music of Santería, the rhythms of Abakua rituals (*nañigos*), Kongo music, and others because of his close association with these Cuban musicians. Together, they developed "Cubop," the integration of two African-based musical styles. As Gillespie notes, "Chano taught us all multirhythm; we learned from the master. . . . He'd teach us some of those Cuban chants and things like that. . . . You have different ones, the Nañigo, the Arrara, the Santo (music to the Yoruba Orisha) and several others, and they each have their own rhythm. . . . They're all of African derivation."[7]

The percussionists Patato Valdéz, Candido, and Mongo Santamaría were also very influential, and the affinity of the Puerto Rican musicians culturally and musically with Afro-Cuban music and musicians established a strong bridge of exchange. Tito Puente, the internationally known Puerto Rican musician, left the Afro-Cubans Orchestra during this period to establish the Tito Puente Orchestra. The circle of musicians that formed part of his group included the Puerto Ricans Willie Bobo and Ray Barretto and the Cuban Vincentico Valdez. Although few of the Cuban musicians were initiated,[8] they were surrounded by Santería practice in Cuba, and so they brought the philosophy, belief system, and rituals with them to New York City. The passing on of these traditions to Puerto Ricans during the early days of Santería practice in New York City was critical to its growth. In fact, the first initiates in New York City were Puerto Ricans. The similarity of languages, histories, geographic location in the Caribbean, and racial and cultural expressions provided the basis for easy communication and exchange.

The center of Orisha activity was located on the Upper West Side, where most of the Afro-Cuban and Afro–Puerto Rican community resided. The Rendezvous Bar at Lenox Avenue between 113th and 114th Street, where stowaways from Cuba "hung out," and the beauty parlor Illuminada at 110th Street and Madison were popular meeting places for Orisha believers. The concentration of Latinos in these areas enhanced the familiarity between the two cultural groups and nurtured the growth of the Orisha belief system.[9]

In 1956, the Afro-Cuban percussionist Mongo Santamaría organized the first public performance of Orisha music and dance at the Palladium nightclub, in tribute to the Yoruba Orisha Chango. Julito Collazo performed songs and dances for the Orisha Chango and made a broad audience aware of this ancient African belief system.[10]

The music of Santería continued to receive popular exposure when Tito Puente asked Julito Collazo to participate in recordings of his orchestra. These recordings introduced Yoruba chants for the first time in contemporary commercial recordings in New York City. *Latin Percussions*, one of Tito Puente's classic albums, is considered the first commercial recording of Santería music.[11]

Another traditional leader who advanced Yoruba tradition in New York City was the Cuban-born Mercedes Nobles (Yoruba name, Oban Yoko), who traveled to New York in 1952. Yoko's mother was eight years old when her Afro-American grandparents moved to Cuba during World War I. In 1958, Yoko returned to Cuba and was initiated into the Yoruba tradition on March 9 as a priestess of Chango. Julito Collazo played for her first *cumpleaño de Santo*, her Orisha birthday celebration, on March 9, 1959.[12]

During the late 1950s, as the Orisha community expanded in New York City, believers would return to Cuba to perform initiations. In 1961, Oban Yoko, with the consent of her Orisha, performed the first initiation of Orisha ("mounting of the Orisha," or *hacer Santo*) on the head of Julia Franco, at 610 W. 136th Street in Manhattan. Yoko went on to establish a *casa de Santo* (House of Orisha) in New York City. When I interviewed her in 1981, she had initiated thirty-two people into the Orisha tradition, and as the first santera to initiate a recognized Orisha godchild in New York City, she established precedents for performing initiation ceremonies there. The reaction to this pioneering move was much criticized.[13] However, Oban Yoko's pioneering spirit gave Orisha a permanent home in New York, and the presence of Babalowos Pancho Mora and Bebo sanctioned this first step in initiating devotees in New York City. Not only did Yoko's courageous and pioneering action validate New York City initiations, but local initiation allowed people who could not afford to travel to Cuba to become recognized members of the Orisha community.

The influx of Cubans escaping the Cuban Revolution of 1959 further accelerated the belief in the Orisha tradition in New York City, as Joseph Murphy points out: "Since the Cuban Revolution of 1959, the United States has seen an infusion of Africanity into its melting pot. Thousands of *santeros* have come as exiles, bringing the orishas to America again. This has meant a second, if less brutal, transplantation and a second acculturation of Yoruba religion. This time an entirely new set of ethnohistorical factors has come into play as *santeros* acquire North American culture and Americans feel the impact of santería."[14] The growing community of Latinos, the establishment of *botánicas*, where ritual products could be sold, and the creation of Latino neighborhoods served to facilitate the practice of the religion, and as a consequence the presence of Orisha became increasingly public in the Latino community. The handful of practitioners in New York City in the early 1950s were joined by several thousand others by 1964, the year Pancho Mora held a public drum ceremony that attracted three thousand people, including the Latin music stars Julito Collazo and Machito.[15] During the 1960s, Mongo Santamaria also held public celebrations to the Orisha Chango in Latino *teatros*.

During this period, re-creations of Cuban batá and conga drums were used. The first *batá de fundamento* was brought to New York City from Cuba in 1979.[16] These drums were ritually prepared, given voice (*darle voz al tambor*) by Papo Angarica in Cuba, a babalawo, *omo* Añya, musician, son of a famous santero, *oriyate*, and historian. Sacred drums receive the same ritual birth as people: just as initiates are born from believers—thus maintaining and extending ritual family ties through the community—the drum is born from another sacred drum, thus establishing historical and traditional linkages.

Since there were no sacred drums in the United States before Ornelio Scull acquired his, it was not possible to "give birth" to sacred drums developed in New York City. Now, however, various sets of sacred batá drums exist outside Cuba. One set belongs to Orlando "Puntilla" Rios, *omo* Chango, *omo* Añya, who came to the United States during the Mariel Boatlift in 1981. He is one of the most influential ritual drummers and performers of the Afro-Cuban Yoruba tradition in New York City. Once he established himself in the Orisha community, he had a set of batá drums consecrated. Another set belongs to the Puerto Rican omo Añya and percussionist Louis Bauzo, who as a traditional musician and leader of a traditional dance company has helped promulgate the Orisha tradition.

The first African Americans to initiate into the Yoruba belief system were Oba Sergiman and Christopher Oliana in 1959. Already versed and initiated into the Haitian system of Vodun, they sought to expand their spiritual knowledge and cultural centeredness. Pursuing Black Power strategies to empower the African American community, Oba Sergiman opened the first African American temple in West Harlem devoted to the loas (divinities of Dahomey) of West Africa and Haiti and the orishas of Cuba (originally of Yorubaland West Africa).[17] He notes that his pride in the reclamation of Africa as part of the African American experience came with much struggle.

African Americans and Cuban Americans had to confront cultural barriers and racist attitudes before the orishas could encompass both communities. The participation of the African American community in Yoruba traditions increased Orisha exposure, but publicity made the Cuban traditional community uneasy, since many of its members were illegal aliens trying to maintain a low profile. The images of Catholic saints in Cuban and Puerto Rican Yoruba practice created another point of conflict between Latinos and African Americans, who wished to remove all images of Western European oppression from the tradition. These issues motivated African Americans to look increasingly toward Nigeria for their development in the Orisha traditional belief system.

African Americans actively sought to incorporate the orishas of Cuba and loas of Haiti into the Black Power Revolution as a means of confronting the division between the African American and Latino communities. The inclusive vision of the santeras Asunta Serrano, Mercedes Nobels, and Juana Manrique, along with Babalawo Pancho Mora, helped embrace African American initiates. In the Harlem community, African Americans discovered the gods of Africa at their back doors. The Cuban and Puerto Rican communities had brought and preserved the orishas and made them available to the African American community. The work of anthropologists and artists like Zora Neale Hurston, Katherine Dunham, Pearl Primus, Percival Borde, W. E. B. Du Bois, and others, had provided culturally grounded principles which guided the thinking, work, and practice of cultural activities of the late sixties and seventies. And Black Arts activists, in turn, incorporated the symbols, languages, images, rhythms, songs, and dress that connected our Diaspora experiences to root cultures. The work of the Puerto Rican visual artist Jorge Soto incorporated the symbols of Orisha Chango, the thunder god. The work of the African American artists Amiri Baraka, Larry Neal, and Barbara Ann Teer reflected the understanding of Yoruba philosophy and practice. The works of cultural nationalists connected political struggle to cultural expansion, thereby providing creative expressions directly connected to our historical legacies and continuity.

Notes

1. Julito Collazo, telephone interview with the author, February 1995.
2. Joseph M. Murphy, *Santería: An African Religion in America* (Boston: Beacon, 1988), 49–50.
3. Pancho Mora, interview with the author, New York, May 1981.
4. Conga drums were played at the ceremony in 1955 by the Afro-Cuban musician Arsenio Rodríquez, who came to New York City around 1949, and his brother Kiki, who was initiated with the Orisha Ogun in Cuba before coming to New York City (Julito Collazo, telephone interview with the author, February 1995). During this period, the sacred batá drums used in Yoruba ceremonies had not been introduced to New York City. The *toques* (drum ceremonies) were played with conga drums solely. Collazo's account differs from Robert Farris Thompson's statement that "Julito Collazo and Francisco Aguabella brought *batá* to the United States in 1955" (*Faces of the Gods: Art and Altars of Africa and the African Americas* [New York: Museum of American Art, 1993], 170). In actuality they brought their skill in playing the batá drums and their knowledge of *toques*. Omelio Scull introduced the first set of Cuban *fundamento* drums to New York City. The first set of sacred batá drums arrived in New York City in 1979 (Omelio Scull, interview with the author, Puerto Rico, March 1994). When Collazo first started playing *toques*, he played solo with conga drums and sang simple Yoruba chants, so that people could follow the call and response necessary in ceremonies that provide the energy to call the orishas to earth to manifest themselves.
5. Julito Collazo, telephone interview with the author, February 1995. Collazo's mother had been initiated in Cuba by an African named Dominga Latuan.
6. Pablo Roche was a major informant for the anthropologist Fernando Ortíz in his research documenting African traditions in Cuba.
7. Dizzy Gillespie, with Al Fraser, *To Be, or Not . . . to Bop* (Garden City, N.Y.: Doubleday, 1979), 319.
8. Julito Collazo, telephone interview with the author, February 1995.
9. In the early sixties, the courts became aware of the practice of Orisha when a santero accused of manslaughter killed a chicken in court before the judge who was to decide his sentence. In response to this act the judge became so irate that he had the santero deported to Cuba. In Cuba, however, the santero was freed since the laws of the United States did not apply to Cuba (Julito Collazo, telephone interview with the author, February 1995).

10. Robert Farris Thompson in *Faces of the Gods* says that the first time he saw Julito Collazo perform for the orishas was at the Palladium nightclub during the Chango presentation. They were formally introduced by the orchestra leader of the Afro-Cubans [orchestra], Frank "Machito" Grillo, child of the Orisha Chango.

11. Julito Collazo, telephone interview with the author, February 1995. Omelio Scull also participated in this first initiation *lavando Elegua y Obatalá* (washing the Orishas Elegua and Obatalá). This is part of the Orisha ritual of initiation and rebirth into the Yoruba belief system.

12. Julito Collazo, telephone interview with the author, February 1995.

13. Ibid.; Omelio Scull, interview with the author, Puerto Rico, March 1994.

14. Murphy, *Santería*, 115.

15. Ibid., 50.

16. According to Omelia Scull, Olu Añya de Oba De'e (a Yoruba name indicating ownership and name of the sacred batá drum set), a master traditional drummer, brought the drum to New York City.

17. In a presentation to the Caribbean Cultural Center in New York City, Oba Sergiman recognized the need to connect the Black activist movement to a culturally grounded philosophy and lifestyle. He identified a division within the Black Power movement between political activists and cultural activists. Sergiman's cultural activism led him to develop the first temple in West Harlem and later to establish Oyotungi Village, a Yoruba community in South Carolina.

LUIS BARRIOS

Reflections and Lived Experiences of Afro-Latin@ Religiosity

We regard Pentecostalism as an ideology adopted by people consciously
and strategically. It serves as a means by which marginalized groups
and individuals can empower themselves and construct themselves
as historical and social subjects so as to promote processes of change
involving an improvement in their material and psychological situation.
—Francisco Javier Ullán de la Rosa

It is not my intention in this brief essay to debate what should be the religion (or religions) of our Afro-Latin@ communities. Rather, I would like
to share some of the lived experiences I have had as an Afro–Puerto Rican
Anglican Catholic priest who was also initiated since childhood in the
Yoruba tradition and in the Pentecostal-charismatic tradition.

More precisely, I would like to set forth an idea that I will demonstrate
in the form of a critical ethnography, or auto-ethnography. My hypothesis
is as follows: In the process of Christian evangelization both the Afro-
Latin@ communities and those who come from Afro-descendant traditions have found in the Pentecostal-charismatic movement a sense of continuity with their ancestral spiritual traditions as well as the preservation
of many aspects of their cultural identities.

I want to break with the myth that would have us believe that Afro-
Latin@ communities only practice Afro-descendant religious traditions
such as Voodoo, Macumba, Candomblé, Orixas, Santería (Yoruba), or
Rastafarianism. I want to challenge the idea that affirming Latin@ Blackness necessarily involves the rejection of European religious traditions
and a return to African ones. Call it assimilation, colonialism, or something else, the reality is that these choices will not change because they are
enmeshed in other psychological, cultural, and political phenomena such

as acquiring power, winning over spaces, creating networks of solidarity, and recovering social identities.

While sharing my experience as a Christian spiritual guide I have in this context chosen to concentrate on Pentecostalism, which is not to deny that our Latin@ and particularly our Afro-Latin@ communities also observe other Christian traditions such as Methodist, Episcopal, or Baptist, as well as other religious traditions such as Judaism, Islam, and Buddhism. In religious terms, we are extremely diverse peoples. But in view of the strong presence and influence of the Pentecostal tradition among Afro-Latin@s I will focus my reflections on that aspect of religious life. In so doing I will pose a series of questions to myself and answer them in the form of a kind of auto-ethnography.

What Is Happening with the Catholic Church?

To be blunt, the Catholic Church has lost relevance and reverence in the people's struggles. There has been a desertion of Catholics in Latin America, and when they come to the United States this process continues. At the same time there has been a growing affiliation of the people with Protestant Christian movements, especially with Pentecostalism. It is not enough to attribute this desertion to the sexual abuse scandals on the part of criminal priests and the complicity of the religious hierarchy in covering up these crimes, or even more generally on the shortage of priests. While these are important factors, the issue is obviously much more complex. I am made aware of just how complex the situation is when in the process of people telling me about their experience in the Catholic Church they say things like "Those people are cold"; "Nobody knows each other or cares about each other"; "I just can't be myself among those people"; "I'm just going to take the communion, and that's it"; "They are backward on issues of sexuality"; and so forth.

It is also important to bear in mind that many Latinos and Latinas come from countries such as Chile, Argentina, Nicaragua, and El Salvador whose governments were run by military dictatorships and where the Church played a major role in legitimating and giving its blessing to disappearances, genocide, massacres, and a range of crimes against humanity, all the while turning its back on the people. Meanwhile, the Church goes on practicing and sanctioning androcentrism, racism, patriarchy, sexism, and heterosexism. On the other hand, it must be recognized that Vatican II, the emergence of liberation theology, and the tolerance of charismatic Catholicism, just to mention three developments, have played

A Pentecostal church member on Park Avenue in El Barrio, New York, circa 1950. (Photograph by Rómulo Lachatañeré; Photographs and Prints Division, Schomburg Center for Research in Black Culture, the New York Public Library, Astor, Lenox and Tilden Foundations; courtesy of Diana Lachatanere)

a very important role in keeping many Catholics in the fold of the Church. Nevertheless, in spite of these promising developments it is clear that such changes have not been enough, because what is ultimately at stake has to do with the relevance that people see and feel in the Church as a force in their lives.

What about the Growth of Other Christian Protestant Groups?

First of all it is necessary to recognize that evangelization has long been part of the strategy of Washington and the Pentagon in Latin America. The clear intention has been to convert people to Protestantism as part of the imperialist agenda of the United States and of George W. Bush's "American theocracy." Beyond that, it is also an anti-communist agenda deployed in counteracting the theology of liberation. The dominant classes have promoted this type of faith because it centers on the individual and not on the society. As the great Salvadorean poet Roque Dalton wrote in his "Two Religions": "When the social revolution begins to unfurl its flags, the heirs of those who crucified Christ / tell us that Christ is the only hope / precisely because he awaits us there in his / Kingdom, / which is not of this world. / This is the religion that Marx / called the 'opium of the people,' / because in this form it is but another drug to cloud / the minds of men / and hinders them from finding their way in the social struggle."[1]

Yet the growth of the Pentecostal movement has been so dramatic that further explanations are needed to account for its attraction among the people. Aside from their quantitative and qualitative increase, the evangelical Pentecostals have distinguished themselves in their ability to organize and mobilize marginalized communities and people's cultures, that is, all those that the neoliberal capitalist system has oppressed and excluded. This is why I am confident in referring to them as a social movement that has offered poor communities some options and a sense of hope.

I of course recognize that this is only part of the truth, because the answer that the evangelical Pentecostals offer is purely individualistic and does not point to the need to change the racist, sexist, heterocentric, and elitist institutions that produce oppression and exclusion in our societies. For the fact is that precisely because of racism and social discrimination the Afro-descendant communities, and especially the Afro-Latin@ communities both in Latin America and in the United States, continue to be second-class citizens. The racial, political, social, and economic marginalization that they suffer is glaring and horrific. Though Pentecostalism doesn't help to identify the causes or structural conditions of the problem, the correlation between being Black and being poor is where the Pentecostal movement has managed to sow a seed of hope and to become relevant in the lives of the people.

The contrast is glaring. On the one hand, the Catholic Church continues to be elitist, racist, and sexist. Indeed, more than Christian it is actually Roman, since all of the power is based in Rome. Pentecostalism, on the other hand, much like the practice of African traditions, tends to have independent movements and the power is decentralized and shared among the practitioners. A significant amount of power is invested in the lay people, both men and women, and improvisation is necessary because it is a sign of giving space to the divine.

What Do Afro-Latin@s Who Practice Afro-Descendant Traditions Find in Pentecostalism?

Christian evangelization has had a major impact on Afro-Latin@s, and in many cases it has involved their Afro-descendant religious practices, even though the Christian religions generally—and especially Pentecostalism—have demonized those African-based religions in a shameless way. It is clear that Pentecostalism offers something more than a movement that opens its doors to those who have been condemned here on earth, such as poor people, Black people, women, and so forth. This is why it is so important to consider the parallels between the Pentecostal movements and many of the traditions of African religions, particularly in view of the fact that Pentecostalism presents itself as an alternative to the practice of African-derived religions. It is indeed striking how many poor people, and especially poor Black people, have come to embrace these evangelical movements, so much so that we are led to ask whether they are not generating a new kind of religious syncretism like that evident in Santería. Again, it is in the face of this challenge that the Roman Catholic Church and other Christian denominations have chosen to recognize, accept, and allow for the charismatic movement within its organizations.

Is Pentecostalism a Home for Popular Cultures and Excluded Groups?

The Pentecostal movement has been a home to the people's cultures and to marginalized groups, and more broadly to those who reject excessive intellectualism and rationalism in the adoration and who promote a theology of experience. The movement reflects a need for direct personal contact with the divinity by means of sensual experience. This direct involvement by Afro-Latin@s became clear to me when one sister, whom I met in a *botánica* in the South Bronx, said to me, "Father, in this place people welcome me and make me feel good. They call me by my name, they embrace me, and don't make a big deal about it when I don't come, and they even visit me at home." Those were the very same words that this sister used when she accepted Pentecostalism.

How Do the Charismatic Movements Address
the Dualism between Good and Evil?

The role of mysticism has been very important in these religious changes. Pentecostal theology resembles that of African traditions in terms of the age-old dualism between good and evil and the struggle between God and the devil. This kind of dualistic explanation has been an important guide in everyday life, such that it represents the backbone of the religious experience. The explanations for problems of economics, health, housing, and so forth are not simply socio-economic in nature, but have to do with matters of the spirit. This is a very frequent line of analysis in both Pentecostal and African-based religions. As evidence, I invite you to go by any botánica for a consultation and then go to a place of Pentecostal worship and you will encounter the same explanations. As I was once told by a brother who was formerly a santero and is now a Pentecostal, "The devil is tempting me; it seems like they are trying to cast some evil on me. But I get rid of it by reading the Bible, doing my prayers, and observing my fasts and offerings. I am going to put a stop to that devil."

What Is the Relation between the Liturgy
and the Movement of the Body?

The Pentecostal liturgy and services tend to be replete with emotional expression. Indeed, the practice of using drums and *panderetas* (tambourines) with a fast rhythm is very common in both Pentecostal and African-based religious practices. Silence is not welcome and is viewed as a waste of time.

In this liturgy it is important to include the movement of the body and the idea of human mobility and conquered spaces. In other words, the body becomes a kind of multifaceted space representing many things, over which the individual is able to exert control. Interestingly, the body is supposed to be in constant movement, which gives rise to what is called the dance of the spirit, a very common notion in African and indigenous traditions as well as in Pentecostalism. It is in such a dance that there is a tendency to imitate the movements of nature, like those of the trees, the sea, the wind, and the animals.

In this process of receiving God into one's body there is also the need to purify the body. This is why there is such a strong emphasis on personal transformation and the practice of purification rituals, which have the effect of rejecting the need to transform this world by means of an ethic of collective experience. The moral doctrine of cleansing the body of sin and approaching God leads to a process of ongoing introspection.

As in African traditions, Pentecostalism practices a ritual of the body which establishes three emotional experiences that are generally viewed as being of central importance to the entire belief system: talking in tongues, having prophecies or visions, and practicing miraculous cures. These three bodily experiences, which are fundamental to African traditions, are not lost when the believer turns to Pentecostalism; on the contrary they are fostered because they are signs of the purification of the person and the place where divinity is revealed. "Whoever does not have the Holy Spirit and has not spoken in tongues is not a child of God. This is a mark of approval." Such were the words of a Pentecostal brother whom I met in the seminary.

What Is the Importance of Divine Possession?

I believe that divine possession or the trance state (*montarse*),[2] where there is a combination of emotional and bodily experience and expression, is among the strongest pillars of both Pentecostal and African-based religious practices. For it is in the use of the body as the temple through which the divine can enter that the site of revelation is formalized—that is, where God becomes visible by means of one's body and talks to the people. In other words, during this montarse or divine possession God uses the body as a way of communicating.

And for us Black people personal and physical reaffirmation is of extreme importance. This body full of joy and sadness, of acceptance and rejection, this body colored black that society rejects because of racism, is accepted by a divinity that enters into the body and reaffirms it as its son or daughter. In other words, this body rejected for its Blackness becomes a sacred space. Which is the same as to say that with our bodies we have created spaces of resistance, and perhaps the sacred dances or movements as in African observance are actually celebrations of liberation. It is for this reason that there is such a strong emphasis on individual health and rites of purification, because they themselves are able to cleanse this salvaged space that we call the body. As a result, a series of power relations become evident, such that Pentecostalism, like the African-descendant religions, dismantles the very inequality that devalues the bodily presence of Black people, who are then able to recapture not only power but also a sense of control over their own lives. It's like what I heard from a sister after she danced to the Spirit: "I feel like another person. How glad I am that God has accepted me as I am—Black, poor, old, and ugly—and made me His daughter. Praise be to God, for Him all the glory that is worthy of this unhappy sinner."

For this reason, by way of empowering Afro-descendant communities in their ongoing struggle within a racist, class-stratified society, the Pentecostal movement tends not to have much room for academics and intellectuals. The Afro-descendant religious traditions are based not so much on a rational experience as an emotional one. What it does have room for is for militants, and on that basis it calls for academic and intellectual activists.

Prophetic Practices

One can only marvel at the role of prophecies in the Pentecostal movement, especially in their combination with a whole range of divinations. Many people have recourse to the adoration cult, confident that God, and the divine power, will communicate not only what is happening (divination), but also what will happen (prophecy or reading the future). This type of practice, often called gifts of God given by the Holy Spirit, also lends an honorific distinction to the person who bears the messages. Divinization carries the intention of being able to correct something that is not right. In this way one is able to discover the reasons for what is happening in one's life. In other words, one seeks divine protection, as is conveyed in the saying, "Everything evil attaches itself to the Black man or woman." It is in this sense that a Pentecostal brother to whom I was giving a class on pastoral counseling said to me, "Walter Mercado doesn't know what he is missing. This knowledge doesn't come from the stars, it comes directly from God, who is telling us not only what is happening but what is going to happen."

What Is the Relevance and Reverence of an Urban Pastoral Theology?

One concern that is always present in my writings as a pastor is being able to find a way for the Church to respond to the needs of the people. What I have in mind is an urban pastoral practice that shows our respect toward the people. In this particular case, it is one which is also relevant and reverent in relation to an Afro-Latin@ agenda.

In our everyday lives our people are trying to survive in the face of at least two challenging realities: poverty and exclusion. When the Church does not have a pastoral practice that identifies, denounces, and changes these realities it becomes an institution that is irrelevant, because it does not speak the language of the people. It is also irreverent because with all its selective silence and compromised neutrality it serves to benefit the ruling class. In this way it goes on betraying the subversive evangelical principles of our brother and companion, Jesus. This irrelevance and this irreverence make the church into a burden on the backs of the people, and it thereby commits the cardinal sin *of giving religion to the people so that they don't think.* What happens is that in the African-based traditions, as in Pentecostalism as well as in other religions, the new society exists, but only in the beyond in an unknown place. That's why the emphasis is only on the personal, when it should be on both the personal and the collective.

Which is why I totally reject the religious parasitism that was invented by the ruling dominant class so as to conceal how political and economic systems were developed for the purpose of controlling the people. I also reject any religious movement that claims to be an alternative to the peoples' struggles and only serves to domesticate those struggles and the people. On the other hand, I also do not mean to promote those who reject the religious component within the realities of the people. In fact, I believe faithfully that that rejection will never happen, because the struggle for justice is not between being religious or not, or whether or not you believe in God. The question is how do we fight for justice?

Religion as a cathartic experience is unique in being a sociopsychological source for channeling personal or collective emotions that promote quietism, defeatism, and sociopolitical immobility. This is what Marx called an opiate. Rather, I am guided above all by what I am, which is a Black person trying to survive racism in all its manifestations.

Of utmost importance to me is the necessity of presenting the people with the option of a militant religion which can empower them and which reaffirms them in their struggle for self-determination. I am not one of those who continue to think that religion is a strictly private and personal matter. Religion is an eminently public, social, and political matter and I encounter the divinity in peoples' struggles. In this sense, the eradication of personal, interpersonal, institutional, cultural, and structural racism should be part of our relation with divinity, and it is a project to be realized here on earth. For this reason I believe that there should be a method of rereading the Bible from the perspective of one's reality of oppression—as a Black person, a woman, a homosexual, a young person, and so forth—so as in that way to find relevance and reverence in a divinity and be able to say that God is Black, or is a Black woman, and so forth. This is why I continue to believe in what we can call the liberation of Afro-descendant religious traditions and the liberation of Pentecostalism. That, for me, is what an urban pastoral theology should be about.

Notes

1. "Cuando la revolución social comienza a / desplegar sus banderas / los herederos de quienes crucificaron a Cristo / nos dicen que Cristo es la única esperanza / y precisamente porque nos espera allá en su / Reino, que no es de este mundo. / Esta es la religión que fue señalada por Marx / como "opio de los pueblos" / ya que en esa forma es una droga más para tupir / la cabeza de los hombres / e impedirles encontrar su camino en la lucha/social" (Roque Dalton, "Two Religions," in *Clandestine Poems/Poemas clandestinos* (Willimantic, Conn.: Curbstone Pres, 1995), 54, 56.
2. *Montarse* is a Spanish word used in African religious traditions (e.g., Yoruba) to describe trance states or the experience when the spirit takes possession of the body.

SHEREZADA "CHIQUI" VICIOSO

Discovering Myself

Un Testimonio

I first came to the United States in April 1967. Initially, I had wanted to be a lay nun and work in the barrios. Marriage repelled me, especially when I looked at my aunts, practically all of whom were divorced. I couldn't stand the idiocy of the whole scene: the danger of getting mixed up with someone when you were thirteen or fourteen, worrying about not having a boyfriend when you were sixteen. To me, becoming a nun was my path to freedom. I also wanted to study medicine. The one year I planned to stay eventually became seventeen.

My mother, who had left [for the States] a year earlier, said I should go to the United States in order to improve my English and to get to know the world before embarking on becoming a nun. I was very angry with her at the time, but she was right.

I come from a very special family with an intellectual background. On my father's side, my grandfather was a journalist and a writer, and my father is a poet and a well-known composer. My mother is a better poet than I am, but has never dared to write. She is the daughter of a peasant woman who worked in a tobacco factory and a Dominican oligarch who owned the factory and literally bought her when she was sixteen. My mother is a hybrid of two very distinct classes. I felt this when I went to school in Santiago.

In spite of having studied English in school, I found out on my arrival in New York that I didn't know very much. Like most Dominicans who come to the United States, I went to work in a factory: first a hat factory and then a button factory (the acetone in which we had to wash the buttons damaged my eyes so that I have had to wear glasses ever since). I went to night school for a while, and then was accepted into a city-sponsored intensive English program, where I was paid to study.

My next job was as a telephone operator, and I quickly acquired a reputation as being extremely courteous to the customers as my English still
wasn't all that good and I said "thank you" to everyone, even if they insulted me. Then Brooklyn College opened its doors to minority students.
They responded to a policy, initiated under the Johnson administration,
whereby colleges were paid federal funds to admit minorities. I was one
of eight Dominican students admitted to Brooklyn College.

Since there were only eight of us, and it was very tough to survive in
such a racist atmosphere, we joined up with other minority students,
principally Puerto Ricans, Blacks, other people from the Caribbean—we
formed a Third World Alliance.

This was a real threshold for me; I had never known the people from
Barbados or Trinidad, etc. My concept of the Caribbean, up to that time,
had been limited to the Spanish-speaking part, and I discovered my identity as a *caribeña* in New York.

I was also racially classified at Brooklyn College, which was an interesting experience for me. In Santo Domingo, the popular classes have a pretty
clear grasp of racial divisions but the middle and upper-middle classes
are very deluded on this point. People straighten their hair and marry "in
order to improve the race" and so on, and don't realize the racist connotations of their language or their attitude. In the United States, there is
no space for fine distinctions of race, and one goes from being *trigueño* or
indio to being "mulatto" or "Black" or "Hispanic." This was an excellent
experience for me. From that point on, I discovered myself as a Caribbean
mulata and adopted the Black identity as a gesture of solidarity. At that
time, I deeply admired and identified with Angela Davis, and ever since
then I have kept on identifying myself as a Black woman.

This opened another door; I learned about Frantz Fanon and other Caribbean theoreticians and that finished Europe for me. I learned about the triangular trade and how we had financed Europe's development. I realized
that capitalism was an impossible model to follow in our development. For
me, this was discovering a universe. I only became a feminist much later.

When I first became more radical I was very much put off by feminism
and people like Gloria Steinem and Betty Friedan—to me they were representatives of the white middle class in the United States who were busy
telling us how *we* were being screwed by machismo. In a first stage I rejected this and, up to a point, I also had a false sense of solidarity with our
men, who were racially oppressed as well. I felt that if we women criticized
our men we were only providing the racists with ammunition. This created
a conflict of loyalties for me.

Discovering myself as a woman came much later. First I had to discover that I was part of a certain geographical area, and then that I was Latin American. The great majority of the Latin American exiles converged on New York at that time—the Argentinians, the Uruguayans, the Chileans (Allende fell during those years)—so that, for me, New York became a kind of great doorway to this Latin American world.

Being in New York was very essential to my development. I would not be the woman I am today had I not gone to New York. I would have been the classic *fracasada* (failure) in my country because I know that I would not have found happiness in marriage and having children. I would have been frustrated, unhappy in a marriage, or divorced several times over because I would not have understood that within me was a woman who needed to express her own truths, articulate her own words. That, in Santo Domingo, would have been impossible.

Nevertheless for the first ten years that I lived in New York I was engulfed by a great silence; I could write nothing at all. The only poem I salvaged from this era was one about two young Puerto Ricans, aged sixteen and seventeen, who were shot by a bartender they had robbed of $100. I saw an article about it in the paper and it made me terribly sad. The poem ends with the line, "sadness has never come so cheaply." New York was, for me, a crushing kind of silence.

Still, all these experiences were being stored up inside of me. It's that kind of a process; things go in stages.

It was going to Africa that restored for me my essence as a *caribeña*. I went for three and a half months to work on coordinating the first meeting of ministers of education of the Portuguese-speaking African nations, and I discovered Amilcar Cabral, the outstanding African cultural and evolutionary theoretician. Up to that point, I had never understood the important role that culture plays in effecting change. This was a central experience for me. [. . .]

The New York experience, which was so crucial to my discovery of my Caribbean and racial identity, has made me a very, very critical person with respect to my own society. Things I never noticed before, I now see. Like racism, for example. Class differences. Santo Domingo is a very societally structured city. The situation of women is atrocious. I get almost rude about this because I can't stand the kind of sexist behavior that exists in my country. And for that, you pay the price of ostracism. It's really hard. By dint of having lived in the United States I am considered a "liberated woman," which means that the men feel they have a green light to harass me sexually while the women distrust me. That's the most painful part. You come back to your country with a sense of intimate relationship and find that, for the most part, the principal *machistas* are the women themselves. And that's terrible. You find yourself confronted by an immense hostility that is a product of their own frustration. At first you ask yourself, "What have you done to this woman to have her treat you like this?" And then you realize that you symbolize all the things that she has never been able to do and perhaps never will: leave the country, study what she wants to. She may find herself tied down by three or four children, a husband that bores her, physical confinement, etc.; and you come across as a woman who can come and go as she wishes, write, be creative and productive, freely elect the man she wants to be with, and you become, for her, an object of hatred. It's really dreadful. And with the men, you represent a challenge to try and get you because you're different, but the real challenge is to dominate you. For the women, you are all they cannot be and that must be destroyed for survival. And you have to understand that so that you don't self-destruct. You can laugh off the first two or three aggressions, but by the fourth time it really hurts.

As a writer I haven't yet been able to talk about my experiences in the United States. At some moment in the future I will. Remember that New York was an experience of great silence for me. I feel that a time will come when I will be able to surmount what happened to me in New York and I will be able to write about it. Remember, too, that the things I'm telling you in such a light vein today were wrenching experiences for me, especially discrimination. I still can't talk about it, but because I now have a better understanding of the creative process I have learned not to push the creative instincts so that they won't become artificial. I know I have to let things come to the surface. The time will come when I'll be able to do it. I've written some sociological essays and some journalistic pieces on New York for a Santo Domingo paper in order to let my people know what's happening there, but in terms of literature I haven't yet been able to draw out what I have inside.

JOSEFINA BÁEZ
Excerpt from Dominicanish

Aquí los discos traen un cancionero.
Discos del alma con afro. Con afro black is
beautiful. Black is a color. Black is my color.
My cat is black.
But first of all baseball has been very very
very good to me
Repeat after me repeat after you

IU a e o iu you
you in a secret you in a whisper
In a cloud of smoke I found my teachers.
In an LP jacket I found my teachers
Stitched suede bell bottoms on
Openly displaying their horoscope signs
Gemini capricorn pisces leo lio
In that cover I found my teachers
Los hermanos Tonga Isley
Los hermanos Isley
The Isley Brothers

VI
Afro-Latinas

The 1970s were characterized by a growing awareness of and attention to women's experiences and the centrality of issues of gender and sexuality. African American women were at the forefront of the new feminist movement by insisting on the importance of race in any analysis of women's oppression. Latina feminists for their part emphasized the cultural dimensions of their subordinate status. Efforts over the course of the last thirty years to develop more nuanced analyses of the intersectionality of race, gender, sexuality, and culture are reflected in the following selec-

Eulogia y las muchachas: Eulogia Rivera (age ninety-six), her daughter, Lydia Esther Guerra Rivera, and her granddaughters (left to right) Norma, Laura Ivette, and Denise Belén, Bronx, New York, circa 1990. (Photograph by Máximo Colón/Max Colón Photo Collection)

tions. Angela Jorge's dissection of the multiple oppressions endured by Black Puerto Rican women is a classic that dates back to the 1970s. Many of those early themes have been elaborated upon by subsequent writers—including Marta Cruz-Janzen and Ana Lara—and demonstrate their continuing relevance in the lives of Black Latina women. Lara provides powerful critical reflections on the gender and sexual experience of Afro-Latina lesbians, while Mariposa's poem on the agonies of hair straightening and the performance artist Nilaja Sun's letter on her own self-affirmation address this experience in more direct, personal ways. Spring Redd's essay offers a unique perspective with her questioning of male privilege in a context of both denial and assertion of traditional cultural roles. All of the contributors express the painful consequences when the racial and cultural prejudices faced by all Afro-Latinas are compounded and further complicated by sexism and homophobia. Most disturbing is that the lessons about the Afro-Latina's "undesirability" are often learned first within the ostensible safety of her family.

ANGELA JORGE

The Black Puerto Rican Woman in Contemporary American Society

In searching, in trying to capture, that which the Puerto Rican woman can and does bring to the feminist movement in the United States, this writer has been struck by the rather low profile of the black Hispanic woman in the struggle for woman's rights. Her apparent reticence to join and her low visibility in the movement are based, perhaps, on the belief that for her there is another struggle that, if not won, will cause her immolation, her genocide. Admittedly, this is a strong statement. However, my own personal and professional experiences, coupled with the many informal gatherings with other black Puerto Rican women in which we have invariably discussed not only our role within (or feelings about) the feminist movement, but also our role in general within the Puerto Rican community, give validity to the quality of the statement.

From these gatherings, personal observations, and experiences, some not too evident truths have emerged that need to be analyzed. First, there is a difference between the black Puerto Rican woman raised in Puerto Rico with its covert racism, often overshadowed by the issue of social class differences and colonial status and the woman raised in the United States, an openly racist society. In addition, since Puerto Ricans express racial differences according to gradations of color,[1] each classification representing a gradation of color among black Puerto Rican women will be accompanied by different attitudes and perceptions about color. The terms *mulata*, *jabá*, *trigueña*, *grifa*, *negra*, and *prieta* are all defined according to color gradations and traits.[2] Finally, differences also exist between the first, second, and third generations of black Puerto Rican women in contemporary American society that are the result of their ability or inability to cope with the racism that confronts them. Each of the differences cited warrants a detailed analysis that is long overdue, and is almost nonexistent in the literature found today about the Puerto Rican experience on the mainland. In the absence of such research, this writer has decided to limit her remarks to personal observations about the black Puerto Rican woman in our present-day society. Although many of these personal observations and conversations have taken place in New York, what will be recounted here is something that I suspect black Puerto Rican women in other areas of the United States can readily identify with.

For many, the title of this study will be unacceptable, since it will be perceived as divisive precisely at a time when the Puerto Rican people need to be united. However, it seems to me that nothing can be more obviously divisive than the exclusion of this topic in particular and of the question of color in general from the debate on Puerto Rican identity on the mainland. The uniqueness of the problems faced by the black Puerto Rican woman in American society must be discussed openly. Furthermore, these problems must not be ignored by the feminist movement that is seeking the emancipation and liberation of the Hispanic woman. The fact of being considered three minorities in one—black, Puerto Rican, and woman—is, in and of itself, a tremendous psychological burden that must be understood.

The black Puerto Rican woman's blackness is attacked from two fronts. First, American society constantly reaffirms through schooling, employment, housing, social interactions, and institutions the inferior status of black people in this country. Second, the continued denial of the existence of racism among Puerto Ricans because of the racial mixture of their population creates a sense of ambiguity in personal relationships with family and friends. The one overriding feeling generated by the ambiguity of the Puerto Rican community about color is that of guilt at having disgraced first the family and then the community by simply being black or darker than other members of the family. The popular dictum *adelantar la raza* (to go through a "whitening process" by marrying someone light-skinned, if not white) tends only to reinforce this feeling of guilt.

The imperative of this dictum and its accompanying societal commitment, whether conscious or unconscious, so rules our lives that the Puerto Rican people are progressively "whitening" themselves. This whitening process is aided by the myth of color blindness that is perpetuated by several American writers. For instance, according to Clarence Senior, "The 1950 U.S. Census classified the people of Puerto Rico as 79.9 percent white and 20.3 percent non-white. The proportion of non-whites has been dropping steadily since the 38.6 percent found in the first United States Census taken in the island in 1899."[3] He also says that "there are no . . . major differences in life chances associated with skin color in Puerto Rico and supposedly on the mainland, as are reflected in differential birth, death, and morbidity rates in the States."[4] Senior underscores his point by quoting a statement made before the New York City Board of Education by a representative of the Puerto Rican Forum that ". . . the Puerto Rican looks at himself as being wholly integrated racially."[5] The mutual contradiction between the concept of whitening, or adelantar la raza, and the supposed "wholly integrated racially" character of the Puerto Rican community is too obvious to warrant further comment. At least it is obvious to any black Puerto Rican woman who wishes to develop and maintain an integrated black identity devoid of guilt and at the same time, maintain her Puerto Rican identity.

If the Puerto Rican is so integrated and if miscegenation had solved all the problems associated with identity crisis, then Eduardo Seda Bonilla would not have found that the black Puerto Rican in the United States tends to adapt and progressively assimilate into society as a black. For many, the assimilation is so complete as to affect their speech in English to such an extent that they, according to Seda Bonilla, speak English with a southern accent. (This writer would venture to say that what he calls a southern accent may well be black English.)[6] Obviously, by the next generation—if not by the present one—the black Puerto Rican who has assimilated will no longer identify—or be identified—socially and emotionally with the Puerto Rican community.[7] The black Puerto Rican in this situation gives birth to non-Puerto Ricans. Because of the proximity of the black American community to our own, the racial attitudes of the Puerto Rican community on the mainland have been challenged to a degree that they have never been on the island. According to a Puerto Rican Forum document, although to the Puerto Rican ". . . his racial heritage is neither a subject of shame nor of particular pride—simply a fact," it is ". . . an important social fact that whereas the census allows a percentage of Puerto Ricans to classify themselves as White, the great majority of non-Puerto Ricans in the United States do not classify the great majority of Puerto Ricans as White."[8] Thus, as Clara Rodríguez notes, while "10 percent of Puerto Ricans are Negro, another 50–60 percent are non-White by social classification."[9] The mainland Puerto Rican community can continue to turn away from this challenge or it can choose to analyze it and use it as a catalyst to the undertaking of an in-depth study of the entire question of racism, within the already established issue of the Puerto Rican identity crisis.

Certainly more background information can be given to reinforce what has already been stated. First of all, this writer is defining as black, that Puerto Rican woman who would be described as *negra* or *prieta* by the Puerto Rican community. This delimitation is necessary because although the *trigueña*, *mulata*, *jabá*, and *grifa* are considered black by American racial definitions (and periodically they do experience the impact of the descendant rule that dictates that a Negro is anyone having one drop of Negro blood), each can opt to delude herself in ways not available to the black—definitely negroid—Puerto Rican woman. She can choose to emphasize her Indian and European heritage, rather than the black. It is the *prieta*, the *negra*, who is perceived beyond any doubt as black by both the American and Puerto Rican communities. There is no ambiguity about her. Her negritude in terms of hair texture, features, and finally color is undeniable. Therefore, the black Puerto Rican woman in contemporary society is in a unique position since her oppression is threefold: sex, cultural identity, and color. One would think that this three-sided oppression is sufficient; however, she is further oppressed by the act of omission or absence of literature addressing her needs. She is an endangered species that has attracted little attention or outcry from a concerned Puerto Rican professional community.

As the black Puerto Rican woman goes through the various stages of life—childhood, adolescence, and adulthood—the blackness of her skin and the clearly negroid physical characteristics make her experiences within each stage different from those of her lighter-skinned sister in the struggle for emancipation and liberation. The traumatization of the black Puerto Rican woman during childhood and adolescence is generally subtle, since she is somewhat insulated by her community (the *barrio*). Although she is a minority within a minority, identity as a Puerto Rican during the early stages of her life is fairly strong. Her early school years are spent in the neighborhood and with a Spanish surname she will definitely be identified as Hispanic. Furthermore, the negative feelings that are generated by non–Puerto Ricans in this social setting are directed against Puerto Ricans as a group and not specifically against the individual. Within the barrio, she will also be identified as Hispanic, because the neighborhoods tend to have strict demarcations that separate the black American from the Puerto Rican neighborhood, although both live in the same ghetto.

Generally, at this early stage the feelings of inadequacy and guilt are developed within the immediate family. The young black Puerto Rican woman begins to sense that everything about her—her short kinky hair, her thick lips, and most of all her color are things to be resented. Never has a kind word been said about her hair; consequently, the day she can comb her own hair is a day of jubilation. No longer is someone pulling on it and muttering invectives such as ¡Maldito sea este pelo! (Damn this hair!) or making the following statement in a martyred tone—¡Dios mío, este pelo! (Dear Lord, this hair!). This is a particularly painful experience, both physically and psychologically.

The black Puerto Rican woman must, furthermore, always be sure to keep her lips together so that the lower lip is never found hanging down. Whenever she forgets, a family member will dutifully tell her: ¡Cierra esa bemba! (Close your mouth!). These remarks are said emphatically, and never cease to bewilder. At first, it is difficult to understand why her hair and lips can bring forth such anger. Later on, she understands that she is living proof that the family failed to contribute meaningfully to the dictum adelantar la raza. She also becomes the living proof of the guilt the family feels, and finally, the receiver of the family's effort to transfer that guilty feeling to her.

As if growing up in this hostile environment were not enough, when the black Puerto Rican woman begins to develop peer-level relationships beyond the boundaries of her barrio, the traumatization becomes truly dramatic. When she begins to seek companionship with others who look like her (that is, black Americans), with those who will not reject her, she will hear ¡Con esa no juegues! (literally, "Don't play with that one!"). Nothing more is said. However, a strong and racist statement has been implicitly made, which is that one should not associate with certain people and that there is something inherently wrong with seeking out certain relationships. Now this young woman is made to believe that in addition to not being pretty, her color has the potential of making her unacceptable.

When she begins attempting to establish meaningful relationships with the opposite sex, her blackness presents still other unique problems for her. The Puerto Rican obsession with adelantar la raza makes it impossible for her to make a choice independent of the consideration of color. Whether the phrase has been said seriously or en forma de broma (jokingly) the family has reaffirmed the inferiority of her blackness and the need for her to change that situation by marrying someone very light, if not white. With such a marriage, the black Puerto Rican woman experiences the embrace of the loving family. Conversely, the rejection of a dark-skinned, or darker-skinned, potential suitor is explicit in the dictum. In fact, it is so explicit that the black Puerto Rican woman is forced automatically to do so. She quickly understands that any intimacy with a black American male is absolutely taboo, and that to engage in such a relationship is to be forced to assimilate socially into that group, essentially giving up her identity as a Puerto Rican.

With a widening of the social circle to include social activities, either at college or at the place of employment, the young black Puerto Rican woman begins to hear statements like "I didn't know you were Puerto Rican" or "You don't look Puerto Rican." This obviously becomes still another reaffirmation of her blackness, since essentially what the speaker is admitting is that her blackness takes precedence over every other consideration. For her, there is no middle ground. Even the simple daily experience of walking on the streets becomes a major trauma. In her neighborhood someone invariably would *echarle flores* (offer her a compliment). However, now that she has left the confines of her barrio and the protection of her neighborhood, she becomes one more black woman among many others. A black woman is not admired, or even glanced at, by most Latin men, since they too are operating under the dictum of adelantar la raza. An excellent example is given in a Brookings Institution study about a Puerto Rican automobile mechanic, residing in an upstate city in New York, who inserted an advertisement in an island paper for a wife, who, among other qualifications, had to be either white or mulatto.[10] The white man, too, will not look at the black Puerto Rican woman (unless he thinks she is a prostitute), since to establish a friendship that may lead to marriage, is to invite the wrath of the dominant society. The black man, on the other hand, will venture forward, but will fail to understand why his friendly overtures are rebuffed. For the black Puerto Rican woman knows that to accept his offer of friendship, of intimacy, is to invite the wrath of her family and, to some degree, of her community.

Since the outer society, the white-dominant American society, perceives the black Puerto Rican woman in terms of black versus white, she is under constant pressure to make choices within these limits only. Admittedly, she has the option of avoiding this conflict by staying exclusively within the confines of her barrio. Never venturing out of the barrio, however, does not help her to integrate the parts of herself—black, Puerto Rican, and woman—into a meaningful whole any more than does the larger racist American society, or even her assimilation into black American society. Without that integration, she is susceptible to all types of psychological pressures that force her to play an active role in her own genocide, eventually leading to a total disappearance of people like her from the Puerto Rican group. As I mentioned earlier, the role of the black Puerto Rican woman in the Hispanic woman's effort for emancipation and liberation cannot be isolated from her need to integrate within herself the three minorities that she represents.

These observations on the black Puerto Rican woman in contemporary American society have not offered solutions, primarily because none will be forthcoming until such time as the Puerto Rican community is able to recognize overtly its racism and deal with it within the context of the search for a meaningful Puerto Rican identity. While some individuals may achieve, through reflection and discussion, psychological and moral liberation from the consequences of racism, the Puerto Rican community as a whole still needs to address the wider social questions of injustice, inequality, and prejudice that are at the heart of racism in the society at large.

Notes

1. Eduardo Seda Bonilla, *Requiem por una cultura* (Río Piedras, P.R.: Editorial Edil, 1970).

2. The term *jabá* refers to someone who is light skinned but has features or hair texture that indicates African ancestry. *Trigueña* indicates an olive-skinned, dark-complexioned brunette. It is also an expression used to describe a non-white person when wishing not to use the words *negra* or *prieta*, which are generally considered offensive. *Grifa* is interchangeable with *jabá*, and both are used to describe someone who is light skinned and has Caucasian features but frizzled hair. *Prieta* means dark and swarthy, and it also infers the characteristics of tight, compact, and stingy.

3. Clarence Senior, *The Puerto Ricans: Strangers, then Neighbors* (Chicago: Quadrangle, 1965), 46.

4. Ibid., 45.

5. Ibid., 46–47.

6. Seda Bonilla, *Requiem por una cultura*, 93.

7. A classic example of an instance in which a black Puerto Rican who moves into the black American community is lost to the Puerto Rican community is Arturo Alfonso Schomburg. By the turn of the century he had moved into the black community to pursue his research on black history (although he continued to identify with the Puerto Rican community and was one of its most ardent defenders). Today, the Schomburg Center for Research in Black Culture is located in central Harlem, a predominantly black community. Schomburg's rightful place as an outstanding Puerto Rican has not been claimed by the Puerto Rican community and, consequently, many Puerto Ricans—particularly Puerto Rican blacks—are not even aware of his contribution.

8. Puerto Rican Forum, *The Puerto Rican Community Development Project: A Proposal for a Self-Help Project to Develop the Community by Strengthening the Family, Opening Opportunities for Youth and Making Full Use of Education* (New York: Puerto Rican Forum, 1964), 19.

9. Clara Rodríguez, "Puerto Ricans and the Melting Pot," *Journal of Ethnic Studies* 1 (winter 1974): 92–93.

10. Brookings Institution, *Porto Rico and Its Problems* (Washington: Brookings Institute, 1930), 8.

Something Latino Was Up with Us

Racism, as well as sexism, has played an important part in the confusion, denial, and self-hatred I have been subjected to throughout much of my life. To look at the maze of my life is to acknowledge that I am a product of two different ethnic groups and cultures. Both of these cultures, one Puerto Rican the other Black, are distinctly different and also very much alike. The members of both groups are subjected to blatant racism within the confines of the social system in the United States. They are also subjected to sexism, yet at the same time they have embraced sexism as a cultural norm and perpetuate it against each other.

In 1929 my grandmother fled an abusive husband and came to the United States from Puerto Rico with two of her daughters to obtain work. She contracted jobs for them all as domestics in Martinsville, Virginia. They worked as cooks, nannies, and all-around clean-up persons for a wealthy white Virginia family for almost ten years. Because my relatives were dark skinned and had practiced the Pentecostal faith in Puerto Rico, they integrated into the Black community in Virginia.

Eventually they moved to New York City and soon after to Cambridge, Massachusetts. By the time my mother was married in 1949, my grandmother had purchased a three-family house in the Cambridgeport section of Cambridge. My aunt had also gotten married and had children of her own. My grandmother seemed to be responsible for keeping us together, because we all lived in the house she had bought, with open doors to all three floors. We basically ate all of our meals with my grandmother and she had the first and last word on everything that went on within the families as well as in the house.

My people, because of their brown complexions, were expected to assimilate into the larger Afro-American culture. There weren't many Puerto Ricans in Cambridge, or in Massachusetts for that matter. Since my family was really turned on to Christianity they joined a Black Baptist church. All of my mother's and aunt's friends were Black and none of them spoke Spanish. The fact that my father was an American Black had an important effect on my total assimilation into Black culture as well.

However, this assimilation process was not randomly developed within me in my youth. It was pumped into my mind with fear and shame from both my family and my neighboring community while I was young. For example, as children we were not allowed to speak Spanish in the house and if we did we got a slap in the face from my mother or my aunt. My grandmother, who by the way was the strongest and most for-real feminist I've ever known, was the only person in our home who couldn't speak good English and she and my mother would get into fights all the time because she would speak Spanish to us. However, after many bitter battles she stopped and I soon lost my ability to speak my mother's native language. In the meantime, while my parents were filling me in on all of the negative stereotypes about Puerto Ricans, my own friends who actually knew I was part Puerto Rican would also say nasty little things about Puerto Ricans whenever we would see one.

By the time I was eleven I was devastated and ashamed of the female part of my family. Even though my mother and aunt tried to deculturate the Puerto Rican out of me, it was very evident to my friends who would sometimes drop by our house that something Latino was up with us. For example, since my family was lower working class and we didn't see much of a variety in foods, we ate more red rice and beans than the mind can imagine. Another thing that used to make me want to puke, especially when my friends would come by, were the big handmade dolls and red furniture that seemed to be in every corner of every room. I didn't even think about why we had them, but only felt bad that my friends made fun of them. I used to hate for my mother, but especially for my grandmother, to come outside and call me or to come to my school to pick me up. Today I feel so ashamed and shitty to say this, but I used to lie to my friends and tell them that she was a friend of the family or that I was a foster child.

Coupled with the fact that by the time I was thirteen I hated my mom for being Puerto Rican, I also started to see and resent the double-standard Puerto Rican sex roles she was trying to instill in me and in my brothers and male cousins. Because there were fifteen kids in our household, there was a lot of housework to be done. My mother thought a woman's place was in the home, doing her duty as a wife and mother, so she trained me and my sisters like a drill sergeant. She was very strict about our morality and our housework. We ironed baskets and baskets of clothes that were not to have a single "cat's face" (wrinkle) or else she would throw them all on the floor, step on them, and expect us to iron them again. At the same time my brothers were going to parties, not doing any housework, and having a ball for themselves. My sisters and I would have to wait on them hand and foot and if we complained, mom or auntie would say, "Respect that they are boys and you are supposed to serve them." If I complained about not being able to go out, she would tell me, "Boys and men can lay in the gutter and still get up and be men, but if a woman gets drunk or goes out she cannot get up and be the same person." These are just a few examples of the sexism that was being perpetuated in our home when I was a young girl.

My teenage years were filled with many mixed emotions that I was unable to face until many years later. In my early teens I not only hated my parents for being ashamed of being Puerto Rican, I also hated myself for hating being Puerto Rican. I was ashamed and afraid of being rejected by Black friends for knowing even one word of Spanish or any cultural things that weren't Afro-American. I was tired of the "off-colored" jokes they would tell about spics with their high-water pants and their pointy roach-killer shoes. I was also sick and tired of the way my mother treated me so unfairly. It seemed like she was ashamed of me and my sisters for being what she was—female.

I furthermore was enraged with my mother, my aunt, and my grand-mother for perpetuating their Puerto Rican sexist double standards on me, because they actually had all of the major economic power in our home. My father and my uncle seemed to be merely figureheads. These men made no decisions. Ultimately my grandmother had the first and last say about everything. By the 1950s grandma had opened up the first Black-owned rest home in the state of Massachusetts all by herself. Even though she wasn't formally educated, she always knew how to exist on very little, eat and spend sparingly, and invest her small paycheck. I was totally confused about mama, auntie, and grandma because I was getting a double message from them. They were telling me to conform to a female role model while at the same time I saw them bringing home the bacon and being the bosses.

One fight led to another and I moved to New York City alone on my eighteenth birthday. It was 1969 and I had a lot of hostility and anger to work on. I joined the Young Lords first and later the Black Panthers, hoping to find equality in the Black Power movement. Three years later, after a series of demonstrations and arrests, I realized I didn't quite fit. I never found the equality I was looking for and I was tired of sacrificing my consciousness for the so-called more valuable opinions and status of my brothers in the movement.

By 1972 I was traveling between New York and California, singing what we called "women's music." I was meeting many women who seemed to feel the same way I did about my oppression as a woman. After several years of this, I realized I still never felt quite right. I had hoped I would be able to make it in a women's community, but I was always at odds with their issues and never quite satisfied with their outlook on what women should be in American society. Then one day I acknowledged to myself that most of the women I was dealing with were white and middle class. Their lives and upbringings had been as different from mine as night and day. These women were aware of, but did not really have to address, the questions of racism and classism. They were focusing totally on sexism. They seemed to think that all I had to do was to eradicate sexism within society and I'd be all set for life. The early white feminists that I came in contact with ignored the fact that women of color had to first get out of the bind that racism had put them in before they could even halfway deal with sexism. This is what I did not look at when I first got involved with white feminism. I did not stop to think that I would still have to live in a world with not only Third World women, but with men too, and constantly have to deal with the racism that was being collectively thrown upon us. I associated with white women so much that I forgot I had a double problem to work with, which they did not have to work on unless they *felt* like it. For me, a Third World feminist, it was a necessity to start dealing with both sexism and racism within all walks and movements of my life.

Since 1977 I have been back in Cambridge working with Black and Latino youths around the issues of education and drug abuse. I have also been trying to work on my own racism, to understand the aspects of my Black Puerto Rican identity, and to get over that fearful twinge that I feel in my stomach whenever I'm with either group. Recently I have started a job at a battered women's shelter in Jamaica Plain where I'm able to confront problems of racism and sexism daily. This work is enabling me to better understand my own issues and to build a feminist perspective with the working-class Third World women of my community.

MARIPOSA (MARÍA TERESA FERNÁNDEZ)

Excerpt from Poem for My Grifa-Rican Sistah, or Broken Ends Broken Promises

(for my twin sister Melissa, who endured it with me)

Pinches y ribbons
to hold back and tie
oppressing baby naps
never to be free.

Clips and ribbons
to hold back and tie
imprisoning baby naps
never to have the dignity to be.

Chemical relaxers
broken ends / broken promises
activator and cream
mixed in with bitterness
mix well . . .

Keep away from children
Avoid contact with eyes
This product contains lye and lies
Harmful if swallowed

The ritual of combing / parting / sectioning
the greasing of the scalp / the neck
the forehead / the ears
the process / and then the burning / the burning

"It hurts to be beautiful, 'ta te quieta."
My mother tells me.

"¡Pero mami me pica!"

and then the running / the running to water
to salvation / to neutralizer / to broken ends
and broken promises.

Graduating from Carefree Curl
to Kitty curl / to Revlon / to super duper Fabulaxer
different boxes offering us broken ends and broken promises.

"We've come a long way since Dixie Peach,"
my mother tells me as I sit at the kitchen table.

Chemical relaxers to melt away the shame
until new growth reminds us
that it is time once again
for the ritual and the fear of
scalp burns and hair loss
and the welcoming
of broken ends
and broken
promises.

MARTA I. CRUZ-JANZEN

Latinegras

Desired Women—Undesirable Mothers, Daughters, Sisters, and Wives

Latinegras are Latinas of obvious Black ancestry and undeniable ties to Africa, women whose ancestral mothers were abducted from the rich lands that cradled them to become and bear slaves, endure the lust of their masters, and nurture other women's children. They are the mothers of generations stripped of their identity and rich heritage that should have been their legacy. Latinegras are women who cannot escape the many layers of racism, sexism, and inhumanity that have marked their existence. Painters, poets, singers, and writers have exalted their beauty, loyalty, and strength, but centuries of open assaults and rapes have also turned them into concubines, prostitutes, and undesirable mothers, daughters, sisters, and wives.

Latinegras are marked by a cruel, racialized history because of the shades of their skin, the colors and shapes of their eyes, and the textures and hues of their hair. They are the darkest *negras*, *morenas*, and *prietas*, the brown and golden *cholas* and *mulatas*, and the wheat-colored *trigueñas*. They are the light-skinned *jabás* with Black features and the *grifas* with White looks but whose hair defiantly announces their ancestry. They are the Spanish-looking *criollas*, and the *pardas* and *zambas* who carry indigenous blood.

Latinegras represent the mirrors that most Latinos would like to shatter because they reflect the Blackness that Latinos don't want to see in themselves.[1] I am a Latinegra, born to a world that denies my humanity as a Black person, a woman, and a Latina; born to a world where other Latinos reject me and deny my existence even though I share their heritage. As Lillian Comas-Diaz writes, the combination of race, ethnicity, and gender makes Latinegras a "minority within a minority."[2] Racism and sexism have been with me all my life. I was raised in Puerto Rico during the 1950s and 1960s, and lived on and off in the United States during the 1970s and 1980s. Today I still live in both worlds, and most of the gender and race themes I grew up with remain. This essay is my personal and historical narrative of the intersection of racism and sexism that has defined my life and that of other Latinegras.

Somos una raza pura / pura rebelde
(We Are a Pure Race / Pure Rebel)

"Aquí, el que no tiene inga, tiene mandinga. El que no tiene congo, tiene carabalí. ¿Y pa' los que no saben ná, tu abuela a'onde está?" This popular expression reveals what most Latinos throughout Latin America, and particularly in the Caribbean, know but wish to hide. It attests to the broad racial mixing that exists as well as to its denial. It states: "Here, those who don't have Inga, have Mandinga. Those who don't have Congo, have Carabali. And those who claim not to know, where is your grandmother at?" The Ingas, or Incas, were indigenous Indians. Mandingas and Congos were Africans. Carabalis were runaway slaves, both African and indigenous Indians, who were feared for their rebelliousness. The question "Where is your grandmother at?" publicly mocks the hypocrisy of White-looking persons who conceal their Blackness and deny their ancestral Black mothers.

Such expressions permeated my childhood and revealed the many contradictions of my world. Growing up biracial in Puerto Rico, I became aware of Latino racism at a very young age. As the child of a White Puerto Rican mother, whose family counted their drops of pure Spanish blood and resented our dark presence, and a very prieto (dark Black) Puerto Rican father, I became aware of the social and economic gulf that prevails within this purportedly harmonious, integrated society. My paternal grandparents were educated, considered middle class, and lived in a White neighborhood of paved streets and nice homes. Theirs was a neat wooden house with electricity, indoor plumbing, and a telephone. A large concrete balcony and front fence were decorated with ornamental wrought iron. Grandma kept a beautiful front flower garden. They were the only Blacks in the neighborhood, always conscious of their neighbors' watchful and critical eyes. We were careful never to set foot outside the house unless we were impeccably groomed. In contrast, the rest of my father's family lived in a predominantly Black slum on the outskirts of town. In that neighborhood, everyone was *puro prieto* (pure black). The dirt streets, the dilapidated houses, the numerous domestic and farm animals running loose, and the lack of electricity and sanitary facilities unequivocally punctuated the differences.

My siblings and I were raised in predominantly White neighborhoods and moved back and forth between two realities that seemed worlds apart. I do not recall a time when both sides of the family got together. Teachers and other adults in the community openly commented to me and my siblings that my mother had disgraced her family by marrying a Black man, while my father had elevated himself and his family by marrying a White woman. It was then that I learned how identity labels reveal the rancor of White Latinos toward Latinos of obviously non-White heritage. White Latinos are light-skinned Latinos who are usually the product of racial mixing, who profess White racial purity, and who are usually accepted as White ("social White"). While my father's family called me *trigueña*, signifying a "step up" from being Black, my mother's called me *negra* (Black) and *mulata*, signifying a step down from being White. On one side of the family we were *negros finos* (refined Blacks), while on the other side we were *una pena* (a disgrace, sorrow, and shame). Both sides of the family continually judged our looks; whoever had the most clearly defined White features was considered good-looking. I was constantly reminded to pinch my nose each day so it would lose its roundness and be sharper like those of my brothers and sisters. My younger sister was openly praised for her long flowing hair while I was pitied for my *greñas* (long mane of tangly hair). I felt fortunate, though, that at least it was long and not considered *ceretas* (short and knotty, like raisins).

When I was four my father took me to my first day of school. Later, when my mother came to pick me up and I jumped up happy to see her, my teacher exclaimed, "That can't be your mother. That woman is White." Sadly I realized for the first time that I was not like my mother or a lot of other people around me, including classmates and teachers. I recall holding hands with my parents, thereafter comparing skin colors, seeing that I was not like either one of them. Anxiously I realized that our different skin colors would always be an issue. I recall the cruel taunts of classmates, adults, and even teachers who called me *negativo*, meaning photo negative, because, while I resembled my mother, they joked that we were opposites. They often called me "Perlina" (pearly White), referring to a bleaching detergent with the picture of Black children dressed in White on the label. Peers teased that I was "una mosca en un vaso de leche" (a fly in a glass of milk) because I stood out among them. They also teased that my father was *retinto* (double-dyed Black) and *moyeto*, meaning Black and ugly. I was reminded repeatedly that my destiny could have been crueler. At least I was not *pura prieta*. At best I was *mejorando la raza* (improving the race). It was my duty to maintain and promote that improvement. These and other abuses made me sad not to be like my mother but quite relieved not to be like my father.

In retrospect, I realize that having a White mother was an asset. Our mother was easily accepted in the community, whereas our father was not. As the public ambassador of the family, Mami dealt with neighbors and negotiated many opportunities for us, especially at school. She always managed to place us with the advanced students. I learned that a Black mother would not have been very powerful because Latinegras have been socialized, through generations, to accept their inferiority to all men and Whites. As occupants of the lowest rungs on the social ladder they are looked down upon and expected to be docile, subservient, uneducated, and ignorant. I always sensed resentment by others toward Papi (Father), especially by White men. Latino men challenge each other's machismo constantly, even in unspoken ways, and the authority of a Black man is not accepted on equal terms. They commented to me that Papi thought himself *parao* (uppity), *presumído* (presumptuous), and *alzao* (elevated) because he married a White woman. The presence of an educated, successful, and very dark Black man was threatening and simply not welcomed. I dreaded my father's presence in public because he didn't elicit the warmest of responses and was only superficially treated with respect. Behind his back, peers, teachers, neighbors, and other adults called him "negro come coco" (coconut-eating Black man) an expression alluding to a popular cartoon that depicted a very dark monkey eating coconuts on a palm tree. It was clear to me that they were mocking my father for marrying a White woman.

When we moved to the United States mainland in the 1960s, concerned Latino friends advised me to emphasize my Latinness and to downplay my African traits to avoid being confused with African Americans. Some teachers advised that I might as well be Black because I would be treated like one by White Latinos and mainstream White Americans. They felt that I should prepare myself for what inevitably awaited me. Fearful, I deliberately spoke with a Spanish accent even though schools kept placing me in speech courses; I learned to use a fan gracefully, and wore my hair long and straight. Many Latinos overtly distanced themselves from me by calling me *morena* (Moorish Black), a derisive term reserved for dark-skinned Blacks, especially African Americans.

Time has passed, but the realities of such racism remain constant. Two years ago a Latino educator in Colorado told me that I was not one of them: "Hispanics are from Spain. You are not Hispanic. Everyone knows you're Black." At a Latino meeting where I raised concerns about the educational needs of African American children, I was addressed with contempt: "You ought to know; you're Black like them." A Latina friend explained, "Some Hispanics here don't want to see you as one of them because you represent everything they do not want to be. They see you as a Black person, and they don't want to be Black. They want you to stop saying you're like them." [. . .]

In the United States Blacks are usually identified as African American, and they are often considered the racialized group most discriminated against.[3] For Latinos, to be Black in the United States is a perceived liability.[4] Regardless of skin color and physical appearance, in the United States one drop of non-White blood makes the person 100 percent non-White, while in Latin America one drop of White blood makes the person whiter, or at least no longer Black or Indian.[5] In Latin America "racial impurity" can be "cleansed" and "expunged" in ascending stages; in the United States racial "impurity" designates the person and his or her future generations as unfit and undesirable.[6] In a society where "color supersedes ethnicity and culture,"[7] Black Latinos in the United States find themselves identified as African Americans by both Whites and Latinos.[8] The more Latinos become immersed in the racial ideology of the United States, the sharper and more unyielding the Black versus White dichotomy becomes, and the more powerful is their need and desire to free themselves of any and all vestiges of African ancestry.[9] Many Latinegros try to deny their Blackness and identify themselves as Hispanic like their European compatriots.

Two years ago at a conference in California I got on an elevator with two Latinas who, upon seeing me, switched their conversation from English to Spanish. When I asked them a question in flawless Spanish, they seemed surprised and remarked, "You don't look Latina!" They attempted to conceal their embarrassment and explained their surprise by telling me, "Nosotros tenemos personas como usted en nuestro país" (We [Latino Whites] have persons like you [Latino Blacks] in our own country). Since few Black Latinos from Latin American countries besides Puerto Rico are financially or legally able to migrate to the United States, these Latinas assumed that I was African American, which simultaneously meant that I could not be Latina like them. I found their explanation neither comforting nor flattering as it clearly asserted their differences and distance from all Latinegros and me. It reaffirmed my belief that Latinos in the United States prefer to deny my legitimate group membership. Their subtle, yet powerful, implication asserts that Latinegros are not true compatriots in their respective countries or in the United States. Within their native countries and within Latino groups in the United States, Latinegros live as "foreigners of both locations."[10] "You don't look Latina/o [or Hispanic]" is something Latinegros hear often not only from White Americans but from other Latinos as well. It is another example of how the ethnicity of Latinegros is repudiated.[11] [. . .]

Upon entering Cornell University in 1968, I tried joining several Latino student organizations. When that failed, I tried to establish a club for Puerto Ricans. It became apparent that Puerto Ricans from the island and those from the United States mainland did not view themselves in the same way. Puerto Ricans from the island did not want to be perceived as Black and rejected me, as well as mainland Puerto Ricans, quite shamelessly. In contrast, Puerto Ricans from the United States mainland saw their strength through unity with African American students. Many flaunted even the minutest African heritage with Afro hairstyles and African clothing. I severed ties with most Latinos from Latin America, including Puerto Rico, and sought out the African and African American communities. I styled my hair in an Afro and began wearing African clothes. I found myself in a constant struggle to find my identity. I felt obliged to prove my Blackness to other African Americans, even when they looked just like me. I was the victim of jokes because my hair would not stay up and thus was called "flat-top" and "lame-fro." I tried all sorts of styling chemicals; I even wore hairpieces and wigs. Finally, I cut my hair as short as possible. Repeatedly, African Americans told me that I must be ashamed of my African heritage because I tried to conceal it by claiming to be Latina and speaking Spanish. They insisted that Blacks were foremost a single people, regardless of where they found themselves or what languages they spoke. I was accused of thinking myself superior, on one hand, and mocked as inferior for being impure and carrying the "blood of the devil," on the other. I grew ashamed of my White heritage, prevented my mother from visiting me on campus, and worked hard to keep a dark tan. Eventually I stopped visiting Puerto Rico; I married an African American who planned to live in Africa, and I thought of adopting a traditional African name.

The culmination of my search for a legitimizing identity came when I visited Africa, "the homeland." Ironically, the search that took me halfway across the world brought me right back home. What began as a journey to establish my identity proved instead to be a dead end—I was not, nor could I ever be, an African: I was a Latinegra living among Africans in Africa. I further confirmed that I was not an African American. I had never felt so distant from my physical and psychological center. While in Africa, I could not celebrate the return to my roots because of a persistent fear of not knowing where I really belonged. I mourned the loss of all I had known myself to be and longed for the place that truly felt like home, and I resented the people who would not allow me to share a Latino home with them. The anger and frustration within me erupted, and I swore never again to allow others to tell me what I was or was not. I came back determined to claim and uphold a legitimate and rightful sense of self.

Today, I affirm proudly that I am a Latinegra whose African ancestors were brutally extracted from a distant place and time and experienced historical realities no African who stayed behind could have ever fathomed. I am a Latinegra, a Black Latina whose African heritage stands as an indelible stamp on my life. I am a Latinegra who will no longer accept the rejection and scorn of others, especially from those Latinos who share my origins. [. . .]

Madre Patria (Mother Country)

I wanted to be the Virgin Mary for the community Christmas celebration when I was in third grade in Puerto Rico. A teacher quickly informed me that the mother of Christ could not be Black. A girl with blond hair and blue eyes was selected for the role, and I was a shepherd. In middle school, also in Puerto Rico, for a school play I was assigned the role of a house servant. Only children of Black heritage played the slaves and servants. A White student with a painted face portrayed the only significant Black character; all the other characters were White. I learned then that non-Whites could not represent the nation's greatness but could only serve as servants and slaves to the great White leaders. The strongly gendered nature of many Latino cultures, particularly those directly derived from Spain, adds other enduring and significant contradictions to the Latinegra experience. Whereas my Spanish heritage taught me that women are weak and dependent, my African heritage taught me that women are strong and self-reliant. African women flourished in spite of the despair of their lives to emerge as enduring forces of cohesion and cultural transmission. My grandmother would often remind us that we were "negros finos y orgullosos" (refined [lightened] and proud Blacks). As proud as she was of our racial mixing she was equally insistent that we know our heritage. Regularly, she shared stories of our "accomplished" ancestors, especially those with education, economic well being, and social integration within the White world.

Mothers are important in Latino cultures and are visible proof of matri-lineal racial lines that cannot be concealed. Motherhood is also a paramount value within doctrines of nationalism, patriotism, and racialism endorsed by most Latino nations. Many countries around the world, including the United States and most in Latin America, revere motherhood and honor women's roles as creators and nurturers of the nations' past, present, and future. These national ideologies merge the powerful concepts of nationalism and patriotism with womanhood and motherhood to create an icon that defines and portrays these nations as inclusive of heritage both internally and to the outside world.

In Spanish, country of origin becomes *madre patria*, combining female and male symbolism. Literally, *madre patria* becomes mother of the fatherland and, ultimately, mother of the nation. In this context, nationalism and patriotism, without diminishing national patriarchy, legitimize women as bearers and nurturers of powerful men and nations. A complete national identity requires a mother. However, this powerful national icon cannot be the Black or African woman. The Latinegra cannot be the representative of the national icon of motherhood because of what she historically represents to the nation—slavery and misogyny.[12]

Cada Oveja con Su Pareja (Every Sheep with Its Partner)

A middle school teacher, who was also a family friend, punished a White classmate for dating a *puro prieto*. The school threatened to inform her parents whom she was going out with, and they were certain to be outraged. I recall sitting in the classroom after school with my inconsolable friend and the teacher, a so-called friend of my parents, debating the unfairness and hypocrisy of the situation. The teacher warned, "Cada oveja con su pareja," an admonition that interracial marriages are frowned upon even by the Catholic Church. We are all "ovejas de Dios" (God's sheep), she preached, but I felt this superficial social acceptance merely concealed deeply ingrained racial prejudices and rejection.

Family lines and marriage are significant in a culture that has historically included extended families as well as genealogical and cultural connections through *compadrazgo*, or the joining of families through oaths of honor, loyalty, and support. While often unspoken, it is understood that the presence of Blacks within a family drastically reduces its options in life. Options are very limited for Latinegr@s. There exists a sociocultural glass

Aurora Calderón, Elinor Rodríguez, and Cruz Losada, Oakland, California, 1939.
(WPA California Folk Music Project, Sidney Robertson Cowell Collection, American Folklife Center, Library of Congress)

ceiling for Latinegros, and particularly for Latinegras. The general cultural devaluation of females sets Latinegras additionally at risk. Because of the greater status and patriarchal authority bestowed on all males, regardless of race or social status, Latino cultures are more forgiving of Blackness in males.[13]

Educational and career opportunities for Latinegros remain limited. In many Latino countries most Latinegros do not have access to a secondary school education or college. Many Latinegros, and particularly Latinegras, see education, even a limited one, as the only way out of a cruel, predetermined path. Although most lack financial resources and reside in areas with poorly staffed and funded schools, those who can pursue an education do so in part to avoid the most humbling servile jobs. Most dark-skinned persons work in menial low-paying jobs; positions that require a "good appearance" or contact with the public such as receptionists, bank tellers, or secretaries tend to be closed to them. Lighter-skinned Latinegros have better opportunities because they are favored over the darker-skinned ones.

While one of the few options available for Latinegras seeking an education and career is teaching, Mami did not want us to be teachers because in

Panamanian Melba Carter and her daughter Thalia Rosario, Chicago, April 2000.
(Photograph by Carlos Flores; Las Caras Lindas Series, Carlos Flores Collection)

Puerto Rico, as in other Latin American countries, Black teachers tend to be assigned to rural schools as opposed to city schools.[14] Rural populations tend to be poorer and have greater racial mixing.[15] Nevertheless, Mami emphasized education and prohibited my sisters and me from doing any service-oriented work, even babysitting, outside of our immediate family and close friends. I always found it odd that as my girlfriends grew older their household responsibilities—caring for younger siblings, cooking, and laundering—increased, whereas our mother, on the contrary, did not teach my sisters and me many household skills. Today, I understand that she planned it that way. It remains the practice to keep Latinegras, especially educated ones, out of sight and out of mind as it is still believed that an educated Latinegra is, unquestionably, "buscando pa'rriba" (searching to move up) by marrying a White man. Stories of pregnant Latinegras abandoned by White men abound, and Mami did not want her daughters distant and alone in a very dangerous world.

In addition to a proper education, Latinegras must also find a proper marriage situation. I often overheard my mother's relatives asking, "¿Y como las vas a casar?" (How are you going to get them married?). Clearly, getting us "bien casadas" (properly married) was problematic. Apparently this was not as great a concern with my brothers. Within many Latino groups, it is more acceptable and less threatening to marry a Latinegro than a Latinegra. If a Latinegra is dark skinned, she is less socially acceptable and is considered more likely to bring the family down.[16] Properly married meant not only getting us legally married, but also married to an acceptable and upwardly mobile family. Parents prefer that sons and daughters marry "light."[17] I was constantly reminded of my responsibility, my duty, to continue the family "echando pa'lante" (moving ahead) by marrying someone lighter, hopefully someone White. In many Latin American countries White Europeans, including mainstream White Americans from the United States, have always been highly admired, and marriage to them is encouraged. To marry a White person, especially a Spaniard, European, or White American, is "dando pa'rriba" (moving up); to marry a darker person is "dañar la raza" (damaging to the race).

Although Black women are coveted sexually, they are rejected as acceptable wives; the darker the skin color and apparent Negroid features, the less acceptable the women.[18] Brown-skinned *mulatas* and wheat-colored *trigueñas* are feared within White social circles because of their White racial bloodlines. Although viewed as lesser wives and mothers than White women, *mulatas* are nevertheless perceived as better marriage partners than Black women. It is shameful enough to admit to a Black concubine in the family, but to actually bring a Black woman into the family through the sanctity of marriage is an unbearable public nightmare to many Whites. Latinegras thus represent a real threat to the family's purity and public *honra* (honor).

"Social" Whites also fear Latinegras because of *requintamiento*, or the appearance of apparent African traits that can manifest themselves in the fifth and subsequent generations. Literally translated, *requinto* refers to a return in the fifth generation. Whites with known or suspected Black bloodlines fear having children with other mulattos for this reason. Racial mixing, even remote, may *requintar* in their children, grandchildren, or great-grandchildren if they marry other non-White Latinos.[19] *Requinto* is a pejorative term for persons who are sometimes jeered as *mulatos blancos* (White mulattos), people whose parents look White but have passed on detectable African features to their children. Families that bear a *requinto* are ridiculed as *tapujos* (lies) and as *chayotes*, a term derived from a fruit— White inside and out, with a rough and prickly surface—that is said to resemble requintos "con los pelos paraos" (with hairs standing up). This is a cruel reminder that Whiteness inside and out can still fail to hide Blackness.

Many light-skinned Latinos attempt to conceal their non-White ancestors. For this reason, Latino cultures are deeply immersed in secrets. What is not stated is the fear that open discussions about race and racism may unveil personal and family mysteries. Another popular expression, "Hasta en el mantel más fino cae la mancha" (The stain falls even on the finest tablecloth), underlies the common fear that la mancha spares no one. A number of stories I've heard from other Latinegras confirm the extent of this fear. A twenty-six-year-old Latinegra I know confessed that White Latino men did not consider her attractive enough to date openly.[20] She reported that they would be her friend, they would have a clandestine affair; but open courtship and marriage was out of the question. Within her family, this Latinegra lived a different life from her mother, a "very white-looking" Mexican. Her mother was accepted as a Mexican American, while she was not. Latinos in her community constantly reminded her that she was not one of them: "I was looked down upon because I thought I was Mexican. They'd make fun of my hair. My skin is too dark. The boys especially, they'd let me know they didn't think I was attractive." And, she added, "The Mexican girls were really mean—evil. They would let me know verbally that I wasn't Mexican like them." Further, this Latinegra explained her willful refusal to learn Spanish because, as a Spanish speaker, she feared the Latino community's even crueler repudiation.[21]

This year I was told by a twenty-two-year-old Puerto Rican Latinegra, whose father is a White Latino and whose mother is a Black Latina, that her paternal family still refuses to accept her parents' marriage and children. The family discord reached the point that forced her parents to move to the United States. She added, visibly pained, that her lighter-skinned siblings are accepted "just a little bit more."

In addition, a twenty-six-year-old White Latina of Mexican American ancestry recently told me that her family did not approve of her engagement to an African American. Her family did not approve of her having dark-skinned children, particularly African American, and felt publicly dishonored and humiliated. In her words, her family had worked hard to "be White," or "as White [White American] as possible." To marry another Latino was acceptable but not as good as marrying a White American. Marrying a Latinegro was "stepping down." Marriage to an African American was the "worst that could be done," definitively "going beneath" herself and lowering the status of the entire family.

In contrast, when a Latinegra marries well, there is no end to the family's happiness. Two years ago I attended the wedding of a young Latinegra of Panamanian and Colombian parents to a mainstream White American.

Her parents held an elaborate, very public, and expensive wedding to proclaim their daughter and family's good marriage and fortune. They could not wait to see the *precioso* (beautiful), *blanquito* (White) grandchildren they were going to have. Last year I attended the wedding of a twenty-four-year-old White Mexican American woman to a Spaniard from Madrid. The woman's family was very proud, and her parents began to plan their first trip to Spain to see the *madre patria*. Ironically, this family had ancestors in Mexico but none they could name in Spain. Last month a Latina colleague chose to spend several months in Spain. When asked why not a visit to a Latin American country, her response was a contemptuous, "What for? I haven't lost anything there." As I walked through campus recently, I met a Latinegra who told me that her brother had gone to Africa to "find his roots," thereby upsetting the entire family. It seems some things never change.

Notes

1. Lillian Comas-Díaz, "LatiNegra: Mental Health Issues of African Latinas," in *The Multiracial Experience: Racial Borders as the New Frontier*, edited by Maria P. Root (Thousand Oaks, Calif.: Sage Publications, 1996), 167–90.

2. Ibid., 169.

3. Toni Morrison, "On the Backs of Blacks," *Time*, December 2, 1993, special issue: "The New Face of America: How Immigrants Are Shaping the World's First Multicultural Society," 57; and Roberto Santiago, "Negro Is a Spanish Word: The Issue of Racism Bedevils White and Black Hispanics," *Denver Post*, July 7, 1991, "Vista," 6–7, 20.

4. Delina D. Pryce, "Black Latina," *Hispanic*, March 1999, 56.

5. F. James Davis, *Who Is Black? One Nation's Definition* (University Park: Pennsylvania State University Press, 1998); Comas-Diaz, "LatiNegra," 171.

6. Marta I. Cruz-Janzen, "Y Tu Abuela A'Onde Esta?" *Sage Race Relations Abstracts* 26, no. 2 (2001): 7–24.

7. Comas-Díaz, "LatiNegra," 180.

8. Gabriel Escobar, "Dominicans Assimilate in Black and White," *Washington Post*, May 14, 1999, A2; and Mirta Ojito, "Best Friends, Worlds Apart," *New York Times*, June 5, 2000, A1, A16–7.

9. Roberto Santiago, "Negro Is a Spanish Word," 6.

10. Escobar, "Dominicans Assimilate in Black and White," 2.

11. Comas-Díaz, "LatiNegra," 168.

12. Ibid., 171.

13. Ibid., 173.

14. Isabelo Zeñón Cruz, *Narciso Descubre su Traser: El Negro en la Cultural Puertorriqueña* (Utuado, Puerto Rico: Editorial Furidi, 1974).

15. Marta Cruz-Janzen, "Racial Amnesia, Avoidance, and Denial: Race and Racism among Puerto Ricans," unpublished manuscript.

16. Comas-Diaz, "LatiNegra," 173.

17. Escobar, "Dominicans Assimilate in Black and White," 5.

18. Comas-Diaz, "LatiNegra," 186.

19. Cruz-Janzen, "Y Tu Abuela A'Onde Esta?" 21.

20. Marta I. Cruz-Janzen, "Curriculum and the Self-Concept of Biethnic and Bi-racial Persons," Ph.D. dissertation, University of Denver, 1997), 167.

21. Ibid., 170.

NILAJA SUN

Letter to a Friend

Dear _____,

I spent a good deal of last night after my show thinking about whether I should write something about my family, re-create in print the monologue I performed from my first one-woman show, or write something from my heart. Needless to say, I spent a good deal of that time crying.

When I think about being Afrolatina all of the above rings true indeed; but even truer in my heart is such a deep sense of rejection that I have felt from so many of my Latino brothers and sisters; especially growing up—not from my family but from neighbors and classmates and boys and friends. I knew one day I would have to confront this deep hurt but I don't know if I can give it the time it needs.

There is nothing like growing up and feeling ugly to your own people—especially in our culture that places beauty and "good" hair, and euro and indio features on such a pedestal. I do know one thing: I come from a heritage of strong NEGRAS who have never let any of that shit get them down. In fact, as you know, my abuelita was one of the first to own a bodega in Spanish Harlem called "El Guayama"—talk about una reina. I wish her security could rub off on me sometimes. And, I miss her still every day.

Now I perform this show that has gotten so much attention. And, for the first time, for the very first time in my life, young Latinos of all shades and features are coming up to me as if I am a star. And when they ask me what I am and I tell them I am half puertorriqueña and so many of them cheer, and high-five each other and ask for my autograph, I think about that little fea still left inside me with her kinky hair and her big lips, and her tears, so many tears and then abuelita whispers "no te apures, angelita" and I feel a little more healed.

Nilaja Sun and her grandmother, Dolores Vega Vasquez (Doña Lola), Lower East Side, New York, 1979. (Courtesy of Nilaja Sun)

Oye, don't get me wrong, I am proud to be Puerto Rican but *Ave María* what a mark it has left on me!

Blessings,
Nilaja

ANA M. LARA

Uncovering Mirrors

Afro-Latina Lesbian Subjects

I used to think I was the only one. For many lesbians, that is part of our experience.[1] Until I saw her, up on stage, her head shaved. Her mouth glowing in the stage lights as she sang. Someone, I don't remember who anymore, had told me to come to her concert. To witness her. She—the someone—thought I might like Xiomara Fortuna's music. But what I experienced was more than music. It was connection. Up on stage was a woman who looked like me—shaved head, cacao skin (mine a milk shade lighter), who was . . . a *lesbiana*.

"Is she out?"

"No. But everybody knows."

That same night, after the concert, they spotted me. The other ones. In the crowd. The other ones who had also come to be showered with possibility and light and really good, lovely, music. They saw me and asked me if I wanted a ride. We were in the Ciudad Colonial, in Santo Domingo. It wouldn't be safe for a young dyke like me alone. Someone was driving a pickup truck and I could sit in the back and join them. I had nothing to lose. I was twenty years old. I had a key to the apartment where I was staying. Who knew where the night could take me.

Digna sat across from me in the truck. She was older. With long curly hair and glossy lipsticked lips. She stared at me. I smiled back.

"I wish I could wear my hair like you do."

"Why don't you?"

"Oh to be young."

I shrugged my shoulders. Not just young. I could leave. Go back North. I didn't know it in so many words then, but I understood that my passport had a direct connection to my ability to wear my head shaved. To butch up and confuse people. Only one year earlier I had been stopped on my way out of the Dominican Republic for being "an independent woman." The airport officer had confiscated my passport, returning it only after he had succeeded in flustering me.

"You don't look like the woman in your passport."

"I know. My hair was longer."

"Are you sure this is you?"

"Yes."

"You look like . . . an independent woman."

"I am."

"Are you married?"

"No."

"Why not?"

Silence. I would not respond. My American citizenship meant I didn't have to respond.

"What does your father think of you traveling around with your hair like that?"

Silence. I did not have to be intimidated. Even if they arrested me, I could buy my way out. I would buy my way out.

"What? Are you feeling shy?"

At that point, I fingered the five dollar bill in my pocket. But not enough that he could figure it out. I looked around for my friends. They were already on the other side of security. He saw me looking.

"I'm looking for my friends."

"Where?"

I pointed. He saw the guy standing among them. The hapa (mixed race) guy who looked White. Without another word, he gave me my passport and shooed me on.

But that night on the pickup truck, I didn't let thoughts of police stop me from being there. I didn't care about the people who harassed me on the street in Santo Domingo or Boston or New York. Because I had seen her up on stage. Because I was in a pickup truck full of lesbianas in the land of my birth. And the wind felt good on my head. I squinted at Digna.

"Not that young."

Uncovering Mirrors

As Afro-Latina lesbians we move through multiple spaces simultaneously, carrying ourselves and the weight of our histories. We come without mirrors, for in the eyes of a world in which we do not yet exist, we have not yet been born. As we walk, we must at every turn choose our own birthing, we must choose that first breath. To birth ourselves. Again. And again. And again. And to find joy in that birthing. To come together as water does on a smooth surface, and in doing so become mirrors for each other.

Because of legacies of colonialism and the contemporary circumstances of neo-imperialism, for me to claim the identity of "Afro-Latina lesbian" is to embrace my choice to exist, which comes with the necessary act of reflecting on my own complicities with and challenges to the current economic, political, and social order. As I set out to write this essay I was optimistic, excited by what my research might reveal. After trudging through several libraries and search engines, in as many languages as I am lucky to speak, I came home disheartened. I cried as I told my partner that in 2008 I could not find scholarship on Afro-Latina lesbians, that I had trudged through several libraries and several floors of the local university libraries, searching for just one essay that would help me with this endeavor and found only traces and shadowed appearances—mere hints at what might or could be. What I found, I realized, was deeply reflective of my experience as a mixed-race person, but also more specifically of the world I have inherited as a self-identified Afro-Latina lesbian. And so I cried some more in realizing that I had not been imagining the sensation of fragmentation that has shaped so much of my adult experience, the same sensation that has made me seek out others who are also fearlessly claiming to be Afro-Latina lesbians. That in fact, the very real spaces and connections I have created with other Afro-Latina lesbians are largely undocumented, unreflected, and unknown. And, then, I awakened to the limitations of my education—the fact that as a postcolonial, neo-imperialist subject and object, I was putting more value on the written, catalogued, shelved book than on my own lived experience. That I had come to believe that paper was more real than flesh, words louder than voices. That I had bought into the notion that unless I was sanctified by an "other," I could not be holy. And so I wiped my tears and took out my pen and paper.

The nature of (neo)colonialism and (neo)imperialism is such that I as an Afro-Latina lesbian am posited as the repository of all that is uncivilized in our society: by my mere existence I break moral codes, I implicate the porous nature of borders, I create alliances where there should only be divisions, I make choices, I love.[2] Simultaneously, among the ranks of resisters, naysayers, and visionaries, I can be found running between the tunnels created by the fragmentary nature of identity politics in an era when identity is dissolving into mud, still solid but porous. These tunnels are at once terribly isolating and also teeming with possibilities. All I have had to do is see the possibilities in the light off the puddles of water. And remember I am not alone.

Once I was able to clear my head and move past the fragments, I came back to my own queerness, remembering what it was like to first claim myself as a lesbian. I remembered being sixteen and realizing that the rules no longer applied: I would not be getting married to a man and I didn't even have to keep my hair if I didn't want to. I had nothing to lose. Because I had always been taught to understand my gender and sexuality as something specifically heterosexual and predetermined by the "fact" of my Latinaness, claiming my own lesbianism allowed me to shed all expectations of what and who I was supposed to be. Ultimately it freed me to invent myself and to create myself and my own expectations for my own life—not just in terms of sexuality but also gender, race, ethnicity. and nationality. If I were to be walking without mirrors, then I would glean refractions of light from water.

It is this freedom of possibility to which my feminist elders Audre Lorde, Cherríe Moraga, Gloria Anzaldua, and Barbara Smith (among others) speak. This constant invention of the self, using art and activism as tools for pulling the real out of the imaginary, is an inherited practice. Naisaragi Dave makes reference to Foucault in her analysis of the ethics of queer activism in India: "A group of people that is subject to norms must, in order to survive, come up with new ways of existence. Wherever there are limits there is an imagination of transgressing these limits and that is the radical potential of being queer. That our entire lives are basically a series of limits and the fact of having all those limits in that kind of distance from the moral centre of the world, forces us, enables us, and allows us to imagine things constantly. That is the ethical possibility of being queer."[3] This analytic framework—defined as a series of possibilities—is fundamentally part of a legacy of the politics and practice of United States–based lesbians of color, and is what Audre Lorde has named an excavation of "a dark place within, where hidden and growing our true spirit rises."[4]

When I first approached this subject, I had hoped to have the space to discuss and explore how Afro-Latina lesbian subjects are affected by identity politics and transnationality and in fact by their mere existence render these concepts impotent. However, in the process of gathering research for this essay, I discovered such an enormous dearth of scholarship about Afro-Latina lesbians that my task evolved into a discussion about the process of entering my imaginary-imagination space as an Afro-Latina lesbian writer and reader researching and critically thinking about my own subjectivity and the spaces in which I do and do not find myself and others like me.[5]

My continual refusal to simply position myself as "just" Dominican is because of the history and possibility of erasure. In fall 2005 I was walking with a light-skinned Dominican sister, and when I spoke to her of my own Afro-Dominicanness, she responded, "But aren't we all Afro if we're Dominican?" I considered her face, which easily passes as ethnic White American, and the fact that she's married to a White American man and decided I didn't really agree. For though it seems ridiculous to claim Africanity within the framework of a nation of African-descended peoples, which both Haiti and the Dominican Republic are, the actual act of claiming shifts expectations and conversations. To claim Afro-Dominicanness and Afro-Latinidad confirms my relationship to the history of the people who had to be negotiated with in the establishment of the nation-state, and in doing so it also makes me complicit with the history of selling out Africanity for nationality. Simultaneously, my claim also confirms my relationship to the history of African-descended people across the entire island. I cannot afford to assume that my fellow Dominicans recognize each other as being of African descent. This is not just because of hegemonic rhetoric and policy but because of the erasure of a memory that clearly indicates the ways in which we benefited from Haitian rule in the nineteenth century and the ways in which we opened our politic to understand and absorb struggles for freedom in the land up north. These factors are illustrated best by the conversations between Du Bois and Dessalines, as well as by the living descendants of North American runaways and freed Philadelphia Blacks residing in Samaná in the northeast Dominican Republic. As an Afro-Latina specifically, my claims also evoke struggles against the supremacy of the nation-state in the policing of Afro-Latina female bodies that are best exemplified by the collected discussions at the Foro por una Sociedad Libre de Prejuicio Racial, which was convened in 1997 by the Casa por la Identidad de las Mujeres Afro in Santo Domingo, Dominican Republic.

The outcomes of this forum identified multiple ways in which Afro-Latinas (specifically Afro-Dominican) bodies are placed at the intersections of neocolonial and imperialist constructs. For example, the ways in which the bodies of Afro-Latinas are policed through the social norms established around appearance and economic participation, through forced sterilization and population control campaigns, through the control of language, media, and historical narratives; and through the control of identity by the nation-state. As Ochy Curiel states: "Estamos tan invisibilizadas como ciudadanas, que en las estadísticas no aparecemos como sector, porque no estamos segregadas por el component étnico, asumiéndose la inexistencia formal de nuestra raza" (We are so invisibilized as citizens that we don't even appear as a sector in statistical data, because the data is not segregated by ethnic composition, which creates the assumption of the inexistence of our race).[6]

What about Staceyann Chin? Isn't She a Black Latina Lesbian?

This question was posed to me at a table where I was sitting with a group of queer Chicanas and Chicanos celebrating Adelina Anthony's performance of La Angry Xicana. There was one other Black-identified person at the table with me, and one other Jew, but the majority of people at the table were United States-based Chicanas and Chicanos. I had just mentioned my heartbreak to Jackie Cuevas, a Chicana lesbian literary scholar, at how little I could find in researching this essay. I lamented by saying that even though I had crossed three separate floors of one library, and four separate libraries as well as online searches in English, Spanish, French, and Portuguese, I had still only managed to find eight Afro-Latina lesbian writers or artists and even fewer writings about Afro-Latina lesbian realities. In my head, I knew of Avotja's and Gina Anderson's pieces in Compañeras; an article from Conmoción written in 1995; Dulce Reyes Bonilla; Ana Sisnet; and two other women who are not out. I knew of the musicians Ochy Curiel, Xiomara Fortuna, and Las Krudas. I had searched the pages of Afrekete, Compañeras, This Bridge Called My Back, Carry the Word, Colonize This! and This Bridge We Call Home. I had read through Sisters, Sexperts and Queers, Making Faces/Haciendo Caras, Telling Tongues, Border-Line Personalities, and Homegirls. My search for "Afro-Latina lesbianas" on the Web had yielded porn sites and sites dedicated to "Black AND Latina," and so forth. And still this was all I could find. I was so desperate that the week before I had asked my partner, "Is Jewelle Gomez Latina? And what about Linda Villarosa? Wait, does Josefina Báez identify as a lesbian? And what about Loida Maritza Pérez—is she queer? Is Aurora Levins Morales Afro-Latina? What about Jacqueline Jiménez Polanco? And Daisy Hernández?"

And in the midst of detailing my search to Jackie, the queer Chicano performer and cultural activist Lorenzo Herrera y Lozano turned to me and asked,

"What about Staceyann Chin?"

And I responded, "Well that's the problem, isn't it? Does Latinidad encompass the English-speaking Caribbean? Staceyann is Jamaican. I'd like to think it would. But I don't think it does."

I walked away wondering what the implications of identifying Staceyann Chin as Latina would be. Could we claim her as such, and by that act expand Latinidad to include the English-speaking British-colonized Caribbean? Would doing so negate the specific particularities of history as experienced by people of the African diaspora in the English-speaking Caribbean? How might collapsing a linguistic and historic division shift conversations around political and social power? How would Blackness and Afro-Latinidad occupy space differently if Latinidad itself were expanded to include the West Indies? How has Latinidad been shaped as a construct within discourses of citizenship and resistance, within conversations around sexuality and language that have precluded such a union? What, in fact, was I looking for as I searched for Afro-Latina lesbians?

I was reminded of how ten years ago, in 1998, I attended the Encuentro Feminista Latinoamericano (Latin American Feminist Gathering) in the Dominican Republic. I best remember this gathering for two reasons: first, the ways in which the women of Brazil and Haiti took the stage and spoke in their native languages, thereby challenging the linguistic and cultural assumptions of the largely Spanish-speaking audiences as well as the racism against Haitian women by the organizing committee; and second, the storming of the capital of Santo Domingo by marchers, with lesbians at the forefront at the exact same time and date on which President Leonel had ordered the rounding up and deportation of Haitian (that is, Black) people from the Dominican Republic, thus putting African-descended feminist lesbian bodies in immediate jeopardy. Most of us who were Haitian or identified as Afro-Latinas stayed back at the hotel, and in staying back we talked about how a lack of analysis around race implicated the Dominican organizing committee's participation in racist state policies and implicated the Latin American feminist movement in racism. It is no coincidence that many of us who stayed behind identify as lesbian. At the gathering I knew of no women of the English-speaking Caribbean. There were no women from Belize or Surinam, or any of the other Francophone countries or territories besides Haiti. Not just that, but we had found each other not because there was a space or "track" on lesbianism, but because our politics and embodied experiences brought us together. What, then, does it say about the construction of Latinidad in a transnational context?

I came to Latinidad not just through a process of self-reflection that united me with other Latinas on the East Coast, but also because I was reading the works of the Chicana lesbian and feminist scholars and writers Gloria Anzaldua, Cherríe Moraga, Ana Castillo, Norma Alarcón, Sandra Cisneros, and Lorna Dee Cervantes, among others.[7] I was reading these writers in the context of also reading the works of Black American lesbians and feminists of color including Barbara Smith, Audre Lorde, Donna Kate Rushin, Pat Parker, Angela Y. Davis, June Jordan, and Alice Walker.[8] My understanding of myself as an Afro-Latina lesbian was shaped and informed by the theories developed and embedded in the stories that these women have published over the last forty years. To understand myself as an Afro-Latina I had to understand my grounding in the history of African peoples in the Caribbean, as well as in the history of women of color in the United States. And in developing a framework of Latinidad I have had to understand Chicanismo on my way to elaborating and interrogating Afro-Latinidad.

Anzaldúa not only grounds Chicana identity in the reality of the "border"—the political line dividing people into nation-states as well as the linguistic border of new ways of speaking—but also in the struggles of farm workers and laborers embodied by César Chávez and the political party La Raza Unida. Anzaldúa places the female body, the queer body, at the center of Chicanismo by being a voice behind the act of defining Chicanismo. However problematic such an assertion may be, the reality of Chicano and Chicana identities and politics is significant, especially as it relates to Afro-Latina bodies and even more specifically to Afro-Latina queer bodies.

I have spoken in many spaces and in other essays about a crisis of identity that I experienced when I first left the East Coast of the United States and moved to Califas.[9] It was the first time in my life where I entered Latina spaces in which my body's presence was questioned. Coming from an organizing context in which Latinidad encompassed Chicanismo and not the other way around (in which Chicanismo superseded Latinidad), I was met with the limitations of a pan-Latina identity. And as a result, I was driven to fight for my own cultural survival. I sought out other Afro-Latinas, finding them in the aisles of the markets that sold green plátanos as well as yellow ones. I found them in national gatherings and then just as quickly lost them as we were each swallowed up by work. We were cut off from each other by fierce identity politics that had turned in on themselves and made it almost impossible to claim each other. It almost seemed easier just to be . . . Black. An immigrant. A United States citizen. Against the war and for the people. An organizer. Latinidad gave way to the rigidity of identity-politic gate-keeping. As a result, I came to terms with a deeper and more personal understanding of the Middle Passage. In fact, the exclusion of my body and experiences from a Latina and Chicana embrace meant that I was confronted with the racism that I knew from other experiences in "Latinaness."

I have since moved to Tejas and returned to my earlier and now deeper appreciation and understanding of what a radical reading of Chicanismo can give to reshaping Latinidad. What I have come to understand since coming to live in Tejas is that Chicanismo offers me a grounding in a transnational politic that claims mestizaje and creolization as its primary organizing principle and practice against a larger rhetoric of Anglo domination or the imposition of the nation-state. This politic and practice when coupled with a disciplined push against essentialism creates deeply radical spaces in which brown bodies, Indigenous and First Nations as well as of African descent, can engage in questions of sovereignty and self-determination.

Latinidad, however, did not just arise out of Chicanismo but has a broader and fluid reach arising out of cultural practices with historic precedent in the struggles of the multitude of other "Latinas" claiming a place from which to understand not just oppression but the possibilities of social and political participation. As such, it is complicated by questions of race and racialization. As Tatiana de la Tierra writes, "*They told me, they told us: Go back where you came from.* I did not conceptualize my own otherness for many years; I just lived it. I was seven years old when my feet touched Miami asphalt. I did not speak English. I did not understand many aspects of U.S. culture, including the intense racial divide. This came much later. But I did know that I was Other, that I was inferior, that I was not meant to succeed."[10]

In discussing her coming to consciousness de la Tierra also cites the ways in which a binary system of racialization automatically posits the Latina as Other.[11] However, even in this experience of otherness, there is presupposition that otherness was not experienced in the country of origin, which is often not the case for Afro-Latinas or indigenous Latinas, who must often confront racism both in their countries of origin and of arrival. But whereas migration from the country of origin often creates a context in which national identity, or the identity of immigration itself, subverts ethnic or racial identity, this is perhaps less and less likely as the state creates ways to further control the definitions of race and ethnicity in an increasingly "Latina" society. This is clear, for example, in how the United States census has set out protocol for establishing multiple tiers of identity in determining how "Hispanics or Latinos [should] answer the race question."[12] This multiple-tier system not only serves to control the movement of racialized "Hispanic/Latina" bodies, but also to specifically identify and control the movement of specifically Black Latina bodies. This is how the one-drop rule is superimposed on immigrant bodies, thereby dissolving the lines into the control of not just "Latina" bodies but racialized Latina bodies. How then do we continue to retain complex interpretations of Latinidad without surrendering the frameworks which allow us to further solidify alliances? Juana Rodriguez discusses just this when she writes that "*Latinidad* serves to define a particular geopolitical experience but it also contains within it the complexities and contradictions of immigration, (post)(neo)colonialism, race, color, legal status, class, nation, language and the politics of location."[13]

Who polices the boundaries of identity, and in this specific case Latina identity? What specific sets of experiences lend themselves to defining Latinidad? How do we "queer" Latinidad and extend its boundaries while still preserving the ways in which Latinidad offers a social and political place to rest for bodies engaged in multiple struggles in multiple places? Does an African diasporic politic displace Latinidad or does it confirm it? What purposes does Latinidad serve in the larger social, political, and economic context of the United States when it is divorced from the particularities of language, immigrant, sexual, and cultural experiences?

Dime con quién andas y e diré quién eres
(Tell me who your friends are and I'll tell you who you are)

In my search for Afro-Latina lesbian scholarship, writings, and bodies,[14] the first article I came across appeared in *Conmoción* magazine, a now defunct Latina lesbian magazine that was printed and distributed out of Miami back in the days when the Internet did not mediate information or the movement of resources to the extent that it does now. The issue I found came out in 1995—one year before I ever knew about LLEGO (the also now defunct National Latin@ Lesbian, Gay, Bisexual and Transgender organization)[15] and the Encuentros where hundreds of Latina lesbian, gay, bisexual, and transgender (LGBT) Two-Spirit activists and artists would descend in one place. It was the same year that I saw Xiomara Fortuna in concert, and it was also the same year that I went to Brazil and found the Grupo Lésbico da Bahia, right at the edges of Pelourinho. But I didn't see *Conmoción* in 1995. I saw it in searching the libraries in 2008, and there I found a call for Afro-Latina lesbian solidarity. What was most powerful to me was the optimism and joy that the women who authored the article expressed with each other and the reader: "With that first meeting at Michigan the gathering of Latinas Negras Lesbianas has begun. In this intimate gathering the seed has been planted for a world-changing movement that challenges the dominant structures that maintain race, gender, sexuality, class and other forms of oppression in place. Most important, Latinas Negras Lesbianas are at the forefront of challenging the infrastructures of our own Latin@ communities by carving a space for a dialogue that is long overdue."[16] The documentation of the gathering of women who were working under an Afro-Latina lesbian politic made me wonder what else I am missing because of lack of access to printed materials, age and lack of access to elders, publications that don't get distributed outside of small groups, and stories that are not even printed at all. I had to reflect on how stories get passed on in my family—not while reading books but while doing dishes. Where, then, are Afro-Latina lesbians to be found? And whereas my reading of *Compañeras—A Latina Lesbian Anthology* revealed Afro-Latina oral histories and poetry to me, I had to consider how I might be defining lesbianism outside of a United States context.

I know from my own experiences of living in the Dominican Republic and Brazil that there is a distinct difference between the politics of claiming lesbian identity and claiming a life that is lesbian in its reality, without the naming. In the Dominican Republic specifically, the way in which the LGBTRR (Lesbianas, Gays, Bisexuales, Trans-generos, Raros y Raras) emerged was in a context of state-legislated, church-sanctioned, military-enforced homophobia.[17] Within this context, lesbian is not only an identity that connotes same-sex desire but also one that signals an interruption in moral and ethical social and political participation. It is also an identity that is afforded the middle and emigrant classes. In a country such as the Dominican Republic where Blackness (framed as Haitian-ness) and lesbianism continue to be punishable by law, the likelihood of someone claiming Afro-Latina lesbian as their identity must be mediated by socio-economic class—whether that be a class of emigration to the United States or Europe, or a class of education and access. As Makeda Silvera states, "There is more at risk for us than for white women. Through three hundred years of history we have carried memories and the scars of racism and violence with us. We are the sisters, daughters, mothers of a people enslaved by colonialists and imperialists."[18] The implications of this reach across borders through the immigrant body entering a larger African diasporic context.

It is here that we must turn to a different cosmology, born out of African diasporic experiences and worldviews, which again cannot be read as essential truths but rather as fluctuating relationships between people and their larger social, political, and economic contexts. And it is here that I must refer back to my question of the implications of expanding Latinidad into a larger Caribbean and Afro-Caribbean identity, for it seems that although we are all struggling with the long-term impacts of colonialism and the ongoing impact of United States imperialism on our bodies, as Caribbean bodies our West Indian, English-speaking Caribbean sisters have generated the beginnings of larger lesbian bodies of work that specifically consider lesbianism within an African diasporic context. It is here that I again invoke the names of Audre Lorde, Nalo Hopkinson, and Staceyann Chin as well as Cheryl Boyce Taylor and Cheryl Clarke. It is our sisters of the English- and French-speaking Caribbean who invoke, with their work, the words *madivinesse, mati, masisi, man royal, zami,* and *sibi*— words that can carry the weight of swords, or that of buoys, depending on their application and from whose lips they emerge. Unlike the Spanish *pata,* but more like *tortillera,* these words at once identify a woman as having desire for another woman, and simultaneously place her experience within an African diasporic and indigenous American context. The context that gives rise to *zamis* and *matis* is one in which women's strength and authority is mediated by how well she negotiates relationships in her family and community; it is usually a working-class context, a rural context—a context in which we would find Black bodies.

The process of crossing borders and entering the United States changes the identity and body politic. Whereas claiming an Afro-Latina identity challenges the expectations around both Latinidad and African diasporic identities, lesbianism undermines the heterosexual assumptions of race and ethnicity. To claim Afro-Latina lesbianism is to also raise questions of the body and of desire, citizenship, and production.

Enter Afro-Latina lesbian subjects and bodies—bodies which lack citizenship, bodies which participate in citizenship, bodies which complicate citizenship by laying claim to more than one place, space, or set of terms. Bodies which refuse to participate in the traditional modes of production which continue to be valued under a capitalist framework as highlighted by Makeda Silvera in her exploration of lesbianism in Jamaica: "Under slavery, production and reproduction were inextricably linked. Reproduction served not only to increase the labor force of slave owners, but also by 'domesticating' the enslaved facilitated the process of social control. . . . In this way slavery and the post-emancipated colonial order defined the structures of patriarchy and heterosexuality as necessary for social mobility and acceptance."[19]

If then we do not want or cannot lay claim to colonial, neocolonial, imperial, or neo-imperial definitions of Afro-Latina racialization, femininity, or sexuality, how is it that we begin to create a context in which to see each other? What is it that we must recognize in ourselves in order to recognize each other?

In discussing her own lesbian politics, Dulce Reyes Bonilla discloses how accepting a lesbian identity also required that she accept her negritude: "Tuve que esperar casi cinco años, hasta ese primer beso con la muchacha del Bronx, para empezar a confrontarme a mí misma y comprender que el mundo lo siente una más injusto cuando se trata de evadir y esconder, de meter la cabeza en la arena como el avestruz, como de cierta forma yo lo había hecho durante todo ese tiempo, no sólo con lo de mi sexualidad, sino también al rechazar mi negritud, mi pelo natural (el tal llamado pelo 'malo'), mis facciones amplias, mi cuerpo, durante mucho, mucho tiempo" (I had to wait almost five years, until I first kissed a girl from the Bronx, to begin to confront myself and to understand that the world feels that much more unjust if one tries to evade it and to hide, to stick one's head in the sand like an ostrich, as I had done all that time, not only with my sexuality, but also in rejecting my blackness, my natural hair (so-called "bad" hair), my broad features, my body for a long, long time).[20]

Her recognition of the specificity of being in the United States as a fundamental aspect of coming to herself is further noted when she writes: "La verdad es que no sé ni nunca sabré si, de haberme quedado allá [Santo Domingo], hoy hubiera estado aquí escribiendo estas páginas, pero sí tengo bien claro que el llegar a este que es hoy . . . mi otro país [Estados Unidos] tiene mucho que ver con el que yo esté aquí escribiendo este ensayo [sobre lesbianismo]" (The truth is that I don't know and I will never know had I stayed there [Santo Domingo] if I would be here today writing these pages, but I am very clear that my arriving at what is today my other country [the United States] has a lot to do with me being here writing this essay [about lesbianism]).[21]

Is Afro-Latina lesbian subjectivity thus in the claiming of oneself as such? What are the luxuries and privileges that afford the possibility of examining one's identity to the point of positioning oneself in relationship to history and a transnational politic? What is in fact the language that we use to identify ourselves and what are the points of reference? How in the world do we always manage to find each other?

If we are to engage Afro-Latina lesbian subjects we must be willing to engage what does not yet exist. If we are to engage Afro-Latina lesbian subjects we must be willing to create from what we remember. If we are to engage Afro-Latina lesbian subjects we must be willing to know there is no eternal truth, only a series of "unborrowed truths" waiting to shine in the brilliance of water reflecting back our various suns.[22]

Notes

1. We must not forget, however, that the lesbian experience is characterized by a high degree of invisibility, not only socially and culturally, but also on the personal level. Susan Wolfe and Julia Penelope say that "most lesbians spend portions of our lives invisible to ourselves as well as to others," their invisibility being "part of the social construction of a lesbian identity" (*Sexual Practice, Textual Theory: Lesbian Cultural Criticism* [Cambridge: Blackwell, 1993], 3).

2. For further discussion on lesbianism, morality, and the state, refer to M. Jacqui Alexander's essay "Transnationalism, Sexuality, and the State: Modernity's Traditions at the Height of Empire," in *Pedagogies of Crossing* (Durham, N.C.: Duke University Press, 2005), 181–254.

3. From a conversation led by Naisargi Dave and respondents Surabhi Kukke and Siddharth Narrain, at the Alternative Law Forum Website, http://www.altlawforum .org (site visited on January 18, 2008).

4. Audre Lorde, "Poetry Is Not a Luxury," in *Sister Outsider* (Freedom, Calif.: Crossing Press, 1984), 36.

5. In her introduction to the anthology *Lesbian Subjects: A Feminist Studies Reader* (Bloomington: Indiana University Press, 1996), Vicinus outlines the problematic nature of lesbian subject(ivity), which is at once a space that is implicated by the assumption of an essential, monolithic definition and a space of invisibility. She discusses the power of "not naming" and of what is "not said" or "not seen" as spaces in which definitions of lesbian subjectivity can be exploded and expanded.

6. Ochy Curiel, "El prejuicio racial desde los derechos humanos y en una perspectiva de género," in *Memoria del foro por una sociedad libre de prejuicio racial*, edited by Casa por la Identidad de las Mujeres Afro (Santo Domingo, D.R.: Editora Búho, 1997), 118.

7. It's important to note that "contrary to popular belief among Chicanos, Chicana feminism did not borrow from white feminists to create a movement. If any direct 'borrowing' was done, it was from Black feminists." Cherríe L. Moraga, *Loving in the War Years* (Boston: South End Press, 2000), 123.

8. For the purposes of this essay I have not listed all of the writings that have been influential, but I owe part of my theoretical formation to being exposed not just to Black and Chicana feminists, but also to indigenous and First Nations feminists such

as Paula Gunn Allen, Joy Harjo, Chrystos, and the Asian American and Asian, Pacific Islander, and South Asian feminists such as Maxine Hong Kingston, Arundhati Roy, Marilyn Chin, Mitsuye Yamada, Yuri Kochiyama, and Jessica Hagedorn, and later on, the Arab American feminists including Joanna Kadi, Naomi Shihab-Nye, Etal Adnan, and Bushra Rehman.

9. Regarding this crisis, see my essay "A Change of Manta," in *Telling Tongues: A Latin@ Anthology on Language Experience* (National City, Calif.: Calaca Press, Red Salmon Press, 2007).

10. From Tatiana de la Tierra, "Aliens and Others in Search of the Tribe in Academe," in *This Bridge We Call Home*, edited by Gloria Anzaldúa and Analouise Keating (New York: Routledge, 2002), 359.

11. Tatiana de la Tierra cites Lillian Manzor-Coats's work on Carmelita Tropicana within this discussion on the Latina as other (ibid., 359).

12. See U.S. Census Bureau, http://www.census.gov (site visited on January 10, 2008).

13. Juana Rodriguez, *Queer Latinidad: Identity Practices, Discursive Spaces* (New York: New York University Press, 2006), 9.

14. "Although it's taken several years since then to grow to accept me for what I am, a black, Nicaraguan lesbian, today I love myself. But I would like to know, are there any more out there? Am I the only one?" From Gina Anderson, "Carta a una compañera," in *Compañeras: Latina Lesbians*, edited by Juanita Ramos (New York: Latina Lesbian Herstory Project, 2004), 83.

15. It was in my first time attending the Encuentro, in Washington, D.C., in October 2006, that LLEGO explicitly added the bisexual and transgender identities to its name, thereby expanding its politics to reflect the shifts in gender and sexual identity that have since reshaped the LGBT movements, both in the United States and internationally.

16. *Conmoción* 1 (1995): 10. In this same article, "The Time Is Now! Black Latinas Unite at Michigan," Hilda Gutiérrez Baldoquin mentions the gathering of eight women at Michigan and the call for submissions to a Latina Negra Lesbiana anthology. To date I have not seen the anthology, but I still hold hope for it. Pa'lante Mujeres!

17. See Jacqueline Jiménez Polanco, "The Lesbian, Gay, Bisexual, Trans and Queer (LGBTQ) Movement in the Dominican Republic: A Sociopolitical and Cultural Approach," paper presented to the Program in American Culture, the Latino/Latina Studies Program, and the Department of Romance Languages and Literature at the University of Michigan, Ann Arbor, October 11, 2004.

18. Makeda Silvera, "Man Royals and Sodomites: Some Thoughts on the Invisibility of Afro-Caribbean Lesbians," in *Lesbian Subjects: A Feminist Studies Reader*, edited by Martha Vicinus (Bloomington: Indiana University Press, 1996), 174.

19. Ibid.

20. Dulce Reyes Bonilla, "Pero míja, y de dónde tú sacáte 'eso'?" in *Divagaciones bajo la luna / Musings under the Moon*, edited by Jacqueline Jiménez Polanco (Santo Domingo, D.R.: Editora Omnimedia, 2006), 45.

21. Ibid., 49.

22. "What kinds of conversations do we, as black women of the diaspora, need to have that will end these 'wasteful errors of recognition?' Do we know the terms of our

different migrations? Each others' work histories? Our different yearnings? To which genealogy of Pan-African feminism do we lay claim? . . . Which legacy of Pan-African lesbian feminism? These conversations may well have begun. If so, we need to continue them and meet each other eye to eye, black women born in this country, black women from different parts of the continent and from different linguistic and cultural inheritances of the Caribbean, Latin America, Asia, and the Pacific who experience and define themselves as black, for there is nothing that can replace the unborrowed truths that lie at the junction of the particularity of our experiences and our confrontation with history" (Alexander, *Pedagogies of Crossing*, 284).

MARIANELA MEDRANO

The Black Bellybutton of a Bongo

The blue-eyed grandmother
    blue-black ears
used to tell tales of boogie men
    of black boogie men
Stories of embroidered linen
    white sheets
    virginal sex
    secrets of pots and beans
    magic wand to cook good fortune
I lost my crystal slipper in the dust
And the prince did not soothe my bruises
Later it was all about cactus—no tulips—
In the time set for war, grandmother
Your stories slid down my skin
—black not trigueña, grandmother
    —woman not doll, abuela
Thunder came and lightning frayed the island
    —it was the drum—
    —cynical laughter bursting in curls
    tough curls fighting chemicals
    singing kinkily and happily in the air
Black mellow dark beautiful majesty
I stared it in the eye
    a wide and indivisible geography
Since then I am a doubt planting questions
    sharp arrow is my tongue
    my entire body

Before the rust I found my voice
        my eyelashes dusted time
I am a heroine in the jungle, grandmother
        I see the night patrol
            the palm trees
                the fire
        Yemaya with her belly made of water
            the areito
                Yocahu-vagua
a little black girl prays for water
the baquini multiplies flags
the box of many colors, did you forget it, abuela?
The hand closed to your bones
        shakes a spring of twigs
—don't be afraid, abuela—
Lemba greets you kindly.

VII

Public Images and (Mis)Representations

The emerging acknowledgment of the distinctiveness of Black Latin@s within the multiracial Latin@ aggregate has not been matched by their visible presence in public and media representations of that experience. On the contrary, they have faced virtually total invisibility as a possible component of either the Latin@ or the Black population: as far as the media are concerned, Latin@s are not Black, and Blacks are not Latin@s. This erasure is most apparent in the Spanish-language media where, as Carlos Flores argues, European phenotypic ideals prevail. The difficulties faced by those

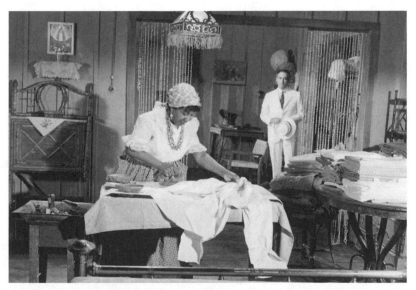

Eusebia Cosme as Mamá Dolores in the film *El Derecho de Nacer* (Mexico, 1966). (Photographs and Prints Division, Schomburg Center for Research in Black Culture, the New York Public Library, Astor, Lenox and Tilden Foundations)

few Black Latin@ entertainers who succeed in crossing the Latin@ color line can be gleaned from Yeidy Rivero's analysis of the pressures exerted on the Afro-Puerto Rican singer Lucecita Benítez to conform to racial and gender stereotypes and the negative consequences of her refusal to do so. In the Black media and other spaces of public representation, distortions, misunderstandings, and stereotypes are also common, as analyzed by Ginetta Candelario and Ejima Baker. This disconnect between group experience and public representation goes back generations and has certainly colored the experiences of Afro-Latinos like Minnie Miñoso, who played in both the Negro Leagues and Major League Baseball. But as suggested in the essay by Alan Hughes and Milca Esdaille from *Black Enterprise* magazine, there is a growing awareness of Afro-Latin@s as a potential bridge across communities.

MIRIAM JIMÉNEZ ROMÁN

Notes on Eusebia Cosme and Juano Hernández

Eusebia Cosme (1911–1976) and Juano Hernández (1896–1970) are arguably the most important Afro-Latin@ performers of the twentieth century. This is something I discovered relatively recently; although I had long been familiar with their work only now do I appreciate their significance beyond my personal experience of them.

I was first exposed to Cosme and Hernández as a kid, but in two very different contexts. Cosme was on the movie screens of the "Spanish" theaters in El Barrio where my parents would take us every few weeks to see the latest films from Mexico. Hernández, on the other hand, appeared in old black-and-white movies on the small television in our living room. In those premulticultural years, dark-brown faces were a rare sight on *either* screen, and as a child and young woman I would watch, fascinated, whenever a Black actor spoke more than a few lines. Cosme, speaking Spanish, and Hernández, with his Spanish name, each represented something I could connect to. In retrospect, I realize that they were among my earliest instructors on Black *latinidad*.

Already a well-established performer when she arrived in New York City in 1937, Eusebia Adriana Cosme y Almanza was born in Santiago de Cuba and trained in music and piano theory and declamation at Havana's Conservatorio Municipal. Her interpretive performances primarily featured Afro-Antillean poetry and literature, including the work of Nicolás Guillén, Luis Palés Matos, Andrés Eloy Blanco, and Hilda Perera Soto, and she was considered Cuba's most important *diseuse*. During the 1940s she had her own radio program, *El Show de Eusebia Cosme*, which was transmitted throughout the Spanish-speaking Americas. Cosme's first film and only English-language role was in *The Pawnbroker* (1964) in which she played a minor character as the mother of the shopkeeper's Puerto Rican assistant.

But Cosme is best known for her performances in a number of Mexican films that specifically deal with race. In *Mamá Dolores* (1971) she starred as the poor Black woman who raises the out-of-wedlock son of a wealthy White woman; the movie was a sequel to the hugely popular *El Derecho de Nacer* (1966) that broke box-office records throughout the Americas, including the United States in Spanish-language theaters. Cosme received the Premio Onix for best actress, the Mexican equivalent of Hollywood's Oscar. In *Rosas Blancas para Mi Hermana Negra* (1969) Cosme's character again takes the moral high ground by allowing her dying daughter's heart to be transplanted into the daughter of her best friend—who had earlier expressed strong anti-Black sentiments.

On one level, the casting of Cosme in these roles represented a positive development in the Mexican film industry; traditionally, Black characters were depicted by Whites or near-Whites in blackface. (For example, the "nana" in *Angelitos Negros* [1948], another classic of the post–World War II race-theme film genre, was played by the Afro-Cuban *vidette* Rita Montaner whose color was darkened artificially—and unconvincingly—by several shades.) Apparently, Cosme's color was deemed authentically Black enough. But watching Cosme on the big screen it was clear even to my unsophisticated eyes and ears (among the expressions she smilingly accepts from those who profess affection are "my little tar ball," "my little pile of soot," and "ugly negro") that her characters were disturbingly subservient and limited. In films cast almost entirely with White and near-White actors, where the other women were invariably young and shapely—or stars of the stature of the ageless Argentine Libertad Lamarque and the Mexican María Félix—Cosme was locked into the role of the middle-aged and desexualized glorified servant. Unfailingly loyal, humble, and self-sacrificing, Cosme's characters stoically endured implicit and explicit racist assaults by turning the other cheek *repeatedly* and shaming the abusers with saccharine goodness. Her few triumphs depended on the success and happiness of those she served. Frankly, I couldn't relate. I knew no Black women like that and certainly didn't want to emulate such a person. Mexican films and the *telenovelas* that followed the same basic script offered painfully conventional ideas regarding the place and role of Black and Hispanic women.

And then there was Juano.

Juano Hernández also appeared in *The Pawnbroker*—as an African American social worker. Indeed, in more than thirty films and a dozen television roles Hernández was invariably cast as an African American. He arrived in New Orleans in 1915 as an illiterate acrobat in a Brazilian traveling cir-

Juano Hernández (center) as Njogu, the Oath Giver, with Frederick O'Neal and Sidney Poitier in *Something of Value* (1957). (Courtesy of José Rafael Méndez Collection)

cus, but by 1927 he was singing in the Broadway musical *Showboat*. Other Broadway performances included *Strange Fruit* (1945) and *Set My People Free* (1948). As a radio and theater actor, he performed in all-Black productions for much of his early career. He appeared in three Oscar Micheaux films and staged his own one-man adaptation of *Othello* at New York's Belmont Theater. In 1949 he was cast in the role of Lucas Beauchamp, a man of great dignity and independence who is falsely accused of killing a White man, in the film adaptation of William Faulkner's *Intruder in the Dust*. For this role he received the Golden Globe Award for "New Star of the Year." He continued to act in Hollywood films—including *Stars in My Crown* (1950), *The Breaking Point* (1950), *Young Man with a Horn* (1950), *The Trial* (1955), *Sergeant Rutledge* (1960), and *They Call Me Mr. Tibbs* (1970)—until his death, although in increasingly smaller parts. The film historian Donald Bogle credits Hernández for "character roles of towering masculinity and surprising sensitivity," and he names him "the screen's first black separatist hero."[1] Still, Hernández was not immune from Hollywood stereotyping; as the MauMau "Oath Giver" Njogu, in *Something of Value* (1957), he plays a predictably gruesome character.

Cosme and Hernández, both immigrants to the United States, had careers that in different ways suggest the greater difficulties faced by Afro-Latin@ performers within the Latino and Latin American media. While both were critically acclaimed actors, Hernández no doubt had the more successful career. The most obvious explanation is that they operated in two distinct worlds and that opportunities were greater in Hernández's sphere. Hernández found a rich cultural community among African Americans and, as part of that Black world, was permitted a certain degree of access to the mainstream White media. The well-educated Cosme—who never lost her Spanish accent when speaking in English and by the standards of the day was "past her prime" by the time she made her acting debut—operated almost entirely within the Latin American arts community, which in the United States prior to the 1950s was relatively small, exclusive, and essentially White. At the international level, racism severely limited Cosme's options to stereotypical roles consistent with the Latin American ideology of racial democracy. Significantly, Hernández's efforts to establish a career in Puerto Rico—his birthplace and where he made his home after 1950—met with no success.

In the early 1990s I spoke with an actor who was born in Puerto Rico and raised in New York's El Barrio. During this conversation he explained to me why he had anglicized his name. He would go to casting calls for "Latinos" and be rejected because he didn't "fit the part." This was more likely to happen among Whites in the industry but he found a similar response among African Americans. And so "Pablo" became "Paul," and his surname lost its accent. But his story makes me wonder why, during a period when Black Latin@s in the film industry were practically nonexistent and when "ethnics" routinely assumed stage names, Juano Hernández kept his name. The question makes an interesting topic for speculation regarding race and ethnicity in the film industry over the course of the last sixty years. For my part I am pleased that by keeping his name Hernández became visible—and offered an alternative image of *afrolatinidad*—to those of us who sat before the screen searching for ourselves. All these years later, however, I'm still waiting for the representation of Afro-Latinas and Afro-Latinos in the field of entertainment that unequivocally acknowledges both cultural and racial identity.

Note

1. Donald Bogle, *Blacks in American Films and Television: An Encyclopedia* (New York: Garland Publishing, 1988), 401.

CARLOS FLORES

Desde el Mero Medio

Race Discrimination within the Latin@ Community

During the Operation PUSH convention, it was announced that African Americans and Latin@ leaders had signed a ten-point economic, political, and civil rights covenant. Both groups pledged to create a powerful coalition and a common national agenda.[1]

I support coalition building that works toward justice and economic and political power for African Americans and Latin@s. However, it is ironic that some Latin@ leaders and organizations seeking equal treatment and justice have ignored the issue of race within our community in terms of their treatment of Latin@s of African descent as well as indigenous people. Race discrimination is a skeleton in the closet of the Latin@ community.

The debate on race relations among Latin@s has intensified in the last decade. As a Puerto Rican of African descent, I am hopeful that the signing of this covenant will crystallize the issue. In fact, the leaders who signed the covenant should make this a priority on the coalition's agenda. The pertinent questions are: Why have Latin@s of African descent and indigenous people been excluded from gaining economic and political power? Why have their presence and their contributions been ignored?

Latin@ leaders and organizations do not want to acknowledge that racism exists among our people, so they have ignored the issue by subscribing to a national origin strategy. This strategy identifies Latin@s as a group comprising different nationalities, thereby creating the false impression that Latin@s live in a color-blind society.

It is difficult to ignore the African presence in the Americas, since 95 percent of the estimated ten million slaves brought during the slave trade were transported to Mexico, Central and South America, and the Caribbean. Yet for centuries the African presence within Latin@ society has been downplayed. The contributions of Black Latin@s to culture, music, religion, history, literature, the military, and other aspects of our society have been overlooked. Today, many Afro-Latin@s confront the same dilemma that has for decades been faced by many in the African American community—namely, not acknowledging the historical and psychological dysfunction created within their own history. I believe that the "dysfunction" is created as a result of racism and not giving proper credit to the contributions made by people of African descent. Conditioning also played a role in this dysfunction where many people of African descent adopted "whiteness" and denounced their dark skin color, i.e., the dilemma between light-skinned and dark-skinned Blacks.

In a *Chicago Tribune* commentary from 1999 titled "Minority Representation on TV" members of the newly formed African American and Latino coalition protested the lack of minority participation in the film and television industry in Hollywood.[2] Unfortunately, Latin@ leaders are not making similar demands on the Spanish-speaking media. It is rare to see Latin@s of African descent on Spanish-speaking television or in movies. It is equally rare to see them advertising products in national Latin@ magazines. For a long time, Spanish-speaking television has portrayed Latin@s of African descent and indigenous people as uneducated, lazy, sex driven, violent, sloppy, and untrustworthy.

It is even more troubling to see the Latin@ creating a perception that all Latin@s look like Ricky Martin, Julio Iglesias, and Gloria Estefan. This Eurocentric model is evident whenever you tune to Spanish-language television programming. The actors, reporters, and talk show hosts are all basically blond and blue eyed. Consider the recent coverage of the Pan American Games by Univision, a Spanish-language television network. Many of the athletes participating in the games were either Latin@s of African descent or indigenous people. In contrast, the reporters and the program anchors represented the Eurocentric model. This new coalition should question not only the exclusion of Latin@s of African descent in front of the camera but also their absence behind the cameras as producers, directors, technicians, and executives.

Juan Andrade Jr., president and founder of the United States Hispanic Leadership Institute and a member of this newly formed coalition, published a pamphlet inviting the general public to attend the institute's seventeenth annual conference in Chicago in October. The image on the cover of the pamphlet is supposed to represent Latin@ and Hispanic unity, but not one of the twenty-four individuals pictured is a Latin@ of African descent. Does this exclusion reflect an entrenched attitude, or is it an oversight on the part of our leaders?

Another concern that needs to be addressed is the myth that Latin@s of African descent are physically strong and capable of becoming great athletes, musicians, and dancers but at the same time lack intelligence. A case in point occurred in Puerto Rico in April 1998 during hearings regarding abortion and teenage pregnancy in that country. A Republican senator in the township of Fajardo indicated that his solution would be to sell white babies to Americans and keep the black babies because they are natural athletes who will build Puerto Rico's Olympic team. Although the media criticized the senator for suggesting that Puerto Rico should develop a baby factory industry, the issue of racism was swept under the rug.

At a time when the Latin@ population is expected to become this country's largest minority group, Latin@s of African descent are not considered an integral part of Latin@ society. I support the opportunity to coalesce with the African American community. However, the African American community must be aware that a racial problem does exist within the Latin@ society, and it will not disappear until the Latin@ leaders and organizations establish a serious and sincere dialogue to examine the treatment of Latin@s of African descent.

The status of the Afro-Latin@ community will be the focus of a series of events sponsored by the White House Office of Public Liaison on September 15–17, 1999. The Office of Public Liaison will provide briefings on civil rights, economic development and community empowerment, education, and other issues. On August 19–22, 1999, the Puerto Rican Commission on Civil Rights sponsored a roundtable discussion on discrimination in Puerto Rico. This commission also published a book probing the race issue among Puerto Ricans. It is entitled *Are We Racists?* The initial discussion should focus on how exclusion and negative stereotyping have affected generation after generation of Black Latin@s. It's time to send a wake-up call to many of our leaders.

Notes

1. The Operation PUSH Convention is an annual event. For the convention held in July 2000 the key theme was expressed in the title "Bridging the Gap: Moving from Margin to Mainstream." The convention's program focused on the following related social issues: the need for law enforcement to play a constructive role in society; the destructive repercussions of the criminal justice policy on disadvantaged communities; and AIDS as a growing crisis in the black community.

2. Willie T. Barrow, "Minority Representation on TV," *Chicago Tribune*, August 14, 1999, 18.

GINETTA E. B. CANDELARIO

Displaying Identity

Dominicans in the Black Mosaic of Washington, D.C.

Despite the hegemony of Indo-Hispanic ideology in the Dominican Republic, the experience of Dominican immigrants in Washington, D.C., belies the notion of a universally internalized Negrophobic and indigenist Dominican identity. The evidence lies in the life histories of Black-identified Dominican immigrants to Washington and their representation in an African American public-history museum.

Instead of conforming to national identity discourses, Dominican immigrants to Washington are more likely to identify as Black than are Dominicans anywhere else in the United States. I argue that this is so for a variety of reasons, including their regional origins in the Dominican Republic; the epoch of their migration; their age and generation; their residential and occupational patterns in Washington; and the nature of their social contact with other Latin Americans and with African Americans. They exemplify, therefore, the fact that identity is *social* rather than essential and dynamic rather than reified. Thus, in the context of a stratified, predominantly Black-identified community in Washington where Black self-identification has been imposed by the local racial order, on the one hand, and has become a means of access to economic, social, cultural, and political capital, on the other hand, Dominicans have multiple incentives to identify racially as Black.

Nonetheless, they continue also to identify ethnically as Dominican and as "Latin." Although they are demographically a national-origin minority among the new Latin@ immigrant community, which is now predominantly of Central American origins, they were also among the founding members—or, as they put it, the "old guard"—of the capital's early Latin American community. Because of this, they share similarities and differences in identity with other Latin@s and African Americans alike. At the same time, African Americans in Washington grapple with Dominicans' ethno-racial distinctiveness. This becomes evident when one examines the participation by Dominicans in Black Mosaic: Community, Race, and Ethnicity among Black Immigrants in Washington, an African American public-history project undertaken by the Anacostia Museum of the Smithsonian Institution.

When the Anacostia staff undertook the project to display Afro-Latino history and life in Washington, they were understandably perplexed and in some cases downright annoyed by the seeming unwillingness of Dominicans, Puerto Ricans, Cubans, Costa Ricans, Brazilians, and Haitians of African descent to identify simply or primarily as "Black." Internal memos and research notes for the exhibit document the ongoing dialogue among Anacostia staff, and between the staff and participants, over issues of ethno-racial and national identity.[1] Anacostia staff accustomed to the primacy of hypo-descent-based Blackness in the United States asked themselves and one another how it could be that nationality could be as salient an identity referent as race.

As Fath Ruffins has pointed out, "the use of the term diaspora to describe the experience of Black people in the Americas" by scholars of African American history and culture began in earnest in the early 1970s.[2] The African diaspora in the Americas was first made "manifest" at the Smithsonian at the 1976 Festival of American Folklife's African Diaspora Festival, organized by Bernice Johnson Reagon. As Ruffins notes, "Perhaps for the first time ever in American public history, a Black American mythos—the notion of the unity of African peoples across time and space—was presented by a preeminent cultural institution."[3] By the time the Anacostia began its discussions about Black Mosaic, in other words, the Smithsonian had had some experience presenting the African diaspora in the Americas.

However, despite the Anacostia staff's attempts to understand and present the complexity of racial identity, the ethno-racial identity of Dominicans in Washington was flattened by the structure of Black Mosaic because of its insistence on Blackness as a universal experience that predominates over ethnic or national differences. The Anacostia staff struggled with this throughout the development of the script, the recruitment of participants and community scholars, the collection of artifacts, and the preparation of the exhibit itself.

During the Trujillo era, migration out of the Dominican Republic was severely limited and controlled. Other scholars have noted that Trujillo era migrants were primarily of three types: those who Trujillo felt furthered the interests of the regime, those Trujillo felt would not undermine him, and those who were exiled.[4] Members of these groups were primarily from elite White-identified families in Santo Domingo. Dominican migration scholars have overlooked a small but interesting fourth class of migrants who arrived in the United States during this period: the domestic servants of the first two groups. Mirroring socio-racial and political conditions in the Dominican Republic at the time, these domestic-labor migrants were women who typically hailed from the traditionally English-speaking African American–descended and West Indian–heritage communities in the Dominican Republic.[5]

Ironically, it was precisely because they were poor, female, and Black that members of this group were able to leave Santo Domingo and stay in the United States, even after their employers left the country, as was often the case. Their working-class and peasant cousins, by contrast, had few opportunities to migrate and were subjected to the full force and effect of the Trujillato's ideological and repressive apparatus. Although their diplomatic-corps employers often engaged in a variety of repressive measures to retain control over their staff, including keeping their passports, many managed to remain in the United States nonetheless.

By the time Black Mosaic was being developed, some 1,779 Dominicans lived in the Center City area of Washington.[6] By 2000, the number had increased to 2,904. Center City includes the area of Washington where Dominicans tended to settle on their arrival in the capital, particularly the Adams Morgan and Adams Pleasant neighborhoods. Latin@s generally made up small percentages of the Center City population, although their presence nearly doubled from 6.82 percent in 1990 to 10.04 percent of the 2000 population. Dominicans composed a small percentage both of Hispanics (5 percent in 1990 and 2000) and a negligible percentage of the city overall (2.1 percent in 1990 and 3.5 percent in 2000). In other words, they are a small group in both absolute and relative terms.

At the same time, Dominicans were more likely than any other Latin@ group to live among African Americans and other Blacks and the group least likely to live among non-Hispanic Whites. In 2000, 45.2 percent of the city's population was Black and 39.3 percent was White. Although the dissimilarity index between Dominicans and Blacks was very high,

Dominicans tied with Puerto Ricans for the lowest index of dissimilarity between Latin@s and Blacks and with Central Americans for the highest index of dissimilarity between Latin@s and Whites. In other words, Dominicans and Puerto Ricans were the Latin@s likeliest to live among Blacks, and Dominicans and Central Americans were the Latin@s least likely to live among Whites. In addition Dominicans had the highest residential exposure levels to Blacks, average exposure levels to other Latin@s, and lowest residential exposure levels to Whites of any Latin@ subgroup. In 2000, Dominicans in Washington tended to live in neighborhoods that were 51 percent Black, 20 percent Hispanic, and 24 percent White.[7]

Black Mosaic

The participants in Black Mosaic simultaneously identified with African Americans and understood themselves to be Dominicans. In Washington they shared a sense of being racialized "Black" while being culturally distinctive as Dominican. According to the participants, their identities, high educational attainment levels, and middle-class socioeconomic standing were dynamically interrelated. In some cases, identifying as Dominican enabled them to circumvent educational and residential segregation during the 1950s. In the wake of desegregation and the successes of the Civil Rights Movement, however, identifying as Black allowed them greater access to the gains of the Civil Rights Movement and the Black Power Movement. In each of their life stories, access to education was mediated by how they identified and were identified racially. What these experiences taught them is that there were situational advantages and disadvantages to each of their ethno-racial affiliations, but that, in general, identifying as "Black" would offer them opportunities for upward mobility. Through them we gain key insights into how Dominican identity formations are responsive to local conditions and institutions.

While regular daily or weekly socializing was organized along class lines, because the Latin@ community was so limited, service staff also had fairly regular social contact with elite embassy and legation families during the 1940s and 1950s. As Ramberto Torruella, who was born and raised in Washington during the 1950s and 1960s, recalled: "The only Latinos in this town were embassy personnel, the support staff of the embassy. So we grew up with all the embassies. If the embassy of Venezuela would have a celebration to celebrate their Independence Day, all the Latinos were invited. And we'd go to the Venezuelan Embassy, eat Venezuelan food, and dance Venezuelan dances. And the same with the Mexican Embassy, the

Dominican Embassy. There was a handful; within a fifty-mile radius, there must have been one hundred Latinos. We knew every Latino in D.C. Every Latino in D.C. knew each other."[8] This working and social relationship with Latin Americans of all classes and with White Washington shielded early Dominicans somewhat from the sort of Jim Crow policies and practices that their contemporary African American neighbors and co-workers were experiencing. It also enabled the retention of a Latin American identity for the first generation and the formation of a generalized Latin@ identity for the second generation, expressed particularly through foodways, music and dance, religion, and the retention and use of Spanish.

The vast distance between African Americans and Whites in the United States had perplexed Ramberto Torruella's mother, Juana Campos, when she arrived in 1940. An astute reader of the social landscape, Doña Juana recalled more than fifty years later that "people here were separated like tuberculosis patients, Black and White apart." Neither in New York City, where her boat from the Dominican Republic had docked, nor in her hometown of Pelmar had she experienced the kind of visibly entrenched Jim Crow segregation that characterized the United States capital. Indeed, it was a new Puerto Rican friend who "instructed" the recently arrived Campos on the rules of Jim Crow. A brown-skinned woman to United States observers, Juana Campos was clearly of African descent to some degree or another and, her friend warned, likely to experience discrimination. From the first, Juana Campos was determined that neither she nor her children who were born in Washington, Ramberto and Carmen, would be constrained by Jim Crow. As Ramberto Torruella described the socioracial geography: "In those days, we were the first Latino family in the Black section. North of Columbia Road was all White. South of Columbia Road was all Black. The north side was very wealthy. The south side was the poor people. And the south side, that's where all your Black chauffeurs and nannies and cooks and housekeepers lived. So we were always on the fringe of the good area. The wealthy area. And my mom was a seamstress, and she sewed for all the rich White folks on the north side. We were raised by my mom being a seamstress sewing for the rich White folks."

For second-generation Dominicans coming of age in the 1950s and 1960s, Spanish-language use became a means of affirming a Latin@ identity, and for Afro-Latin@s it became a shield against anti-Black racism. Since appearance was not necessarily enough of a distinctive marker of foreignness for individuals who appeared Black to local segregationists, the use of languages other than English or speaking English with a foreign accent served as a salient marker of not being African American. Here

Ramberto and Carmen Torruella
in Washington, D.C., in the 1950s.
(Courtesy of Ginetta Candelario)

Ramberto's recollections of what that diplomatic exigency meant for him
and his Dominican family are instructive.

> All we spoke at home was Spanish. So we didn't know any English. All
> our friends were Spanish-speaking. And when we started learning Eng-
> lish, my mom would always say, "Never speak English in public. Always
> speak Spanish." At the People's Drug Store, Blacks couldn't eat. "No
> coloreds." Coloreds could not sit at the counters, and my mom would
> take us there, and the waitresses would look at her and look at us. We
> were actually speaking Spanish because then they'd say, "Oh, they're
> not colored; they're foreigners. You can feed them." We grew up like
> that. We grew up going everywhere because my mom knew how to
> play the game. So we grew up knowing it was important that we were
> *Dominicano*, Latino, *Dominicano*.

Doña Juana clearly understood that she and her children could be taken for
African American. She was also, it seems, aware of the foreigners' exemp-
tion. Through her use of Spanish she actively resisted the social and spatial
segregation that African American identification implied and she taught
her children to do the same. As her daughter Carmen explained, "I grew

up as White, and I fit into the White community, and it's the Black community that I've had a problem with because I don't have the baggage." The "baggage" Carmen refers to is the experience of residential and public segregation and racial violence. Growing up "as White" meant making full use of the public resources that Washington offered to Whites.

Doña Juana's refusal to be perceived as African American can be understood as a negation and a refusal of a Black identity. And, indeed, Doña Juana does not identify as Black; instead, she understands herself to be *india*, just as she did nearly sixty years ago when she left the Dominican Republic. However, soon after her arrival in Washington Doña Juana understood that her racial self-perception differed radically from the perception of both Whites and African Americans. To them, she was "Black," and that meant subordination. She understood quickly that Spanish-language use and retention would mediate anti-Black racism.

The issue for Doña Juana was not one of allegiance to one group or the other, however. Rather, it was a refusal to be relegated to second-class citizenship by either community. Doña Juana was a labor migrant who left the Dominican Republic in 1940 during the Trujillo era and shortly before the end of the decades-old U.S. Customs Receivership.[9] Her pre-migration experience of the United States, in other words, was in the context of a country deeply affected by economic, political, and military intervention by the United States. It is understandable, then, that Doña Juana did not feel herself to be caught in the horns of the United States' "American Dilemma." The issue for Doña Juana, instead, was her family's ability to negotiate both "the [United States] racial state," as Michael Omi and Howard Winant put it, and the socio-racial geography of Washington on pragmatic terms.[10]

Ironically, Doña Juana's story was at the center of Black Mosaic. The pedal-footed sewing machine with which she made her living in Washington was prominently displayed, and a picture of her alongside it at the exhibition's opening day was widely circulated in promotional materials. She derived great pleasure from her participation in Black Mosaic not because she understood herself to be a Black immigrant, but because she understood the exhibition to be a celebration of the survival of Latin American immigrants in Washington. For Doña Juana, Black Mosaic was a more permanent version of the yearly Latin American Festival she had helped establish in Washington twenty or so years earlier. Why, then, did Doña Juana participate in Black Mosaic? Simply stated, as she had done throughout her experience in Washington she ignored the racial context of the event and focused on the ethnic part of the exhibition that served her purposes. For her, Black Mosaic *was* an affirmation of her success as an immigrant and as the godmother of the Dominican community in Washington.

By contrast, for Doña Juana's children and those of their generation who came of age in Washington during the 1960s and 1970s, Black Mosaic was successful in affirming their membership in several communities: Dominican, Black, Latin@, Afro-Latin@. As was noted in Black Mosaic's section on race and ethnicity in Washington, "Afro-Latinos had to adjust to an unaccustomed social distance between the races and to U.S. classifications that sought to divide their ethnic community into two racial groups: 'Blacks' and 'Hispanics.'"[11] However, the underlying sociological and historical reasons for those affiliations were not sufficiently explored by Black Mosaic. Although it recognized and presented race and ethnicity in Latin America as distinctive from that in the United States, Black Mosaic never questioned, and therefore never explained, *why* this particular group of Latin American immigrants identified as Black.

In Washington there was and continues to be a structural incentive to Black self-identification. There, African Americans are a numerical majority, wield increasing political power, hold the vast majority of government posts and jobs, and occupy a diversity of socioeconomic statuses. (For example, just outside Washington, Maryland's Prince George's County has the highest percentage of affluent Blacks in the country).[12] In 1991, the D.C. Latino Civil Rights Task Force found that "even though Latin American residents represented between 10 and 15 percent of Washington's population, African Americans monopolized the city government as well as city services and outreach programs. None of the city council or school board members was Spanish-speaking and Latin Americans constituted only one percent of the bulging D.C. municipal workforce of forty-eight thousand."[13]

While the Dominican women arriving in Washington during the 1960s and 1970s may have come from positions of disadvantage and arrived in much more segregated communities than their New York counterparts, over the long term they have been able to experience greater upward mobility because they have been able to benefit from the political activities of African Americans. The Civil Rights Act of 1960, for example, opened up clerical jobs to African Americans, thereby prompting a shift out of domestic service and into pink-collar and white-collar labor. It was a shift that Dominican women who arrived as adults or came of age alongside

African American women in Washington experienced with them. As Maricela Medina, a Howard University alumna and former professor, put it:

> Well, in my case, I didn't have to go the Dominican route. I could go the African American route. And that was another thing that I found out, as opposed to people who think there are disadvantages to being African American. There were a lot of advantages when I went to school, because this was the time of the Civil Rights Movement. The Black Power Movement. The militancy on campus. A lot of things were changing, and there were a lot of opportunities offered to African Americans. Puerto Ricans were always included and Mexican Americans, but if you were Hispanic of any other origin, unless you qualified as African American, you weren't able to participate.

Participation for Dominican immigrants, who had made so many sacrifices to get to Washington, was, of course, of the utmost importance. In short, the combined demonstration effects of African American political activism and upward social mobility and high immigrant expectations for the second generation's success supported Black identity in the Washington context.

Choosing Ambiguity

Both Whites and African Americans expected Dominicans to declare their racial identities and, presumably, their attendant loyalties. For Whites the issue was whether one was willing to establish belongingness in the United States by rejecting Blackness and African Americans, as immigrants have been required to do historically. Maricela Medina explained it this way: "Americans period required that you make choices. . . . They put you in a separate category because you were Spanish. But they always wanted you to choose. It seemed like society was always asking you to choose between being Black and being Hispanic." African Americans, historically and contemporarily, insisted that Dominicans (and African diaspora communities generally) identify as Black. Conversely, other Latin@s insisted that ethnicity supersedes race in the structuring of Latin@ identity. As Black Mosaic explained, "Unlike other immigrants, Black immigrants must also adjust to and successfully situate themselves within two distinct environments—society at large and the African American community. Thus they must often negotiate a conflicting set of expectations."[14] Afro-Latin@s negotiated yet another "set of expectations": those imposed by the Latin@ community at large.

Julia Lara's college experience is illustrative of this issue:

> Well, it was an experience because it was for the first time when I was caught between an African American population, and a Latino population, who were not of African descent. . . . The Latino students who were not from the Caribbean did not view me as legitimately Latina because I was of African descent. These are people who, for the most part, came from South America, some from Mexico. But they were not Latinos of African descent. They were Latinos who might have been Spanish or Indian and did not recognize or value their heritage as Indian people. So being Latina and being of African descent was strange for them. And for the African American population, being of African descent yet speaking another language and having some sense of pride in where I came from and not in any way denying where I came from, was interesting to them.[15]

Lara distinguished between Latin@s from the Caribbean, who presumably are either themselves Afro-Latin@ or familiar with Latin@s of African descent, and those from South America and Mexico, who presumably are not. This group, Lara explained, did not perceive her "as legitimately Latina" because they were either unfamiliar with Afro-Latin@s or "did not recognize or value their [own] heritage as Indian people."[16] That tension over her recognition and legitimization as a Latina by other Latin@s is one that has gained increasing salience for Dominicans in Washington due to the influx and numerical predominance of Central Americans.

Until the late 1970s, the Latin American community in Washington was small and highly heterogeneous. The largest subgroups were Cubans, Dominicans, and Puerto Ricans. Although South Americans and Central Americans were present as well, the series of civil wars in Central America created a large Central American community of over 200,000 as of the 1990 census. As Terry Repak notes: "Within a single generation, Washington could claim the second largest settlement (after Los Angeles) of citizens from El Salvador to the United States and the third largest community of Central Americans overall."[17] According to the Dominicans interviewed for this project, this sea change in the ethno-racial composition and size of the Latin@ community affected African American–Latin@ race relations. Maricela Medina explained the situation as follows:

> The composition of the community now is completely different. You have mostly Central Americans . . . of Amerindian background who don't necessarily mix well with Blacks, whether Hispanic or African

American. Many of them are openly antagonistic to Blacks. They harbor many of the prejudices that Whites harbor against Blacks . . . and one of the things that bothers me is that when they talk to you—or not necessarily to me, but to a person—and they are relating something that happened to them they will always say, "El *policia negro* [The Black police officer]." My thing is: Why do you have to specify that he was Black? Because when they are talking about a policeman who is White, they don't say, "policia blanco [White police officer]." They only make the reference to race when it's a Black policeman. "El *negro* [The Black guy]." And I never thought I would learn to dislike a word like that, because I never had any problems accepting . . . I shouldn't say "never had any problems," but I don't have a problem accepting who I am or what I am. But the way that word is used carries a similar connotation to the word "nigger." I don't mean any disrespect by that, but the way it is said, it always had that kind of meaning, the expression in which they express that word. . . . And, of course, I am speaking heresy when I say this because, you know, Hispanics are not supposed to . . . We're not prejudiced, you know. It doesn't matter to us whether you're Black or White, right?

As an Afro-Latina, Medina signified her membership in the larger "Hispanic" community, which Central Americans belong to, through her use of "we" and "us." At the same time, she signaled that Blacks can be both African American and Hispanic. She took offense, therefore, at the pejorative way in which the Central Americans she had encountered use the term "Black." This anti-Black prejudice marked the tenuous nature of Dominican inclusion in the categories "Hispanic" and "Black" in Washington.

The lack of familiarity with African American history in the United States also marked Central American–African American relations in Washington. Several respondents indicated that African Americans deserved to be respected both in terms of their ancestors' status in Africa and in terms of their own survival and accomplishments in the United States. As Casilda Luna put it, "They were kings and queens in Africa, and now you want to treat them badly?" Carmen Quander expressed similar sentiments:

Something happens to the Latin American who comes here . . . to the Washington area, because everything is so divided between Black and White. And all of a sudden all of these other people become White, whereas their own. . . . They don't have Blacks in their country? Come on get out of here! And you have to remind these people, and this is why the Blacks have so much resentment toward the foreign—because they come in and they have to step on somebody. The White men have to step on somebody. So they come in and step on a Black person as lower than they are. But this is the Black man's country. They built it. They made it. They've been here much longer than the Whites. How dare you come in and condemn them in their own country?

These Dominican respondents, while sustaining a separate ethnic identity from African Americans in the United States, expressed their rejection of the Negro-phobia expressed by their Latin American peers. This is an ideology of which they are aware because they speak and understand Spanish, because they are familiar with Latin American race ideologies, and because it is part of Dominican culture.[18] While their kin and countrymen in the Dominican Republic were being encouraged to internalize an Indo-Hispanic identity based on anti-Haitianist nationalism, coming of age in the United States they witnessed and were forced to negotiate Jim Crow segregation, the Civil Rights Movement, the Black Power Movement, and Afrocentricism. Accordingly, they felt that their own histories were tied to African American history.

At the same time, as Latin@s they helped organize the first Spanish masses, the first community dances, the first Spanish-language films at the Colony Theater, the first Latin American Festival, the first bilingual education programs, and the Office on Latino Affairs.[19] They were, in other words, invested in several communities and their histories. And they had had to fight and push each to acknowledge their perspective. As Esperanza Ozuma, a hair stylist, explained:

> I consider myself Black, and I have considered myself Black since I was in my country. The difference is that when they call you Black here, it's because of problems African Americans have had with White Americans, with the differences, with what "Blacks can't be and Whites can." So that exists also in that sometimes there are Latinos and they don't know where you are from and they are talking about you and they don't know if you speak Spanish, and then after they know that you are Dominican they don't know how they're going to apologize, due to the same difference they mistake people a lot. I don't agree with that racism where you're Black and I'm lighter.

When African Americans ask her what she considers herself, she says that she responds "Black," in part because she identifies as such, but also as a gesture of solidarity. Similarly, Maricela Medina noted that "the Black Hispanics would be caught in the middle because the African Americans wanted to kick the Hispanics' butt because they were White—or, as the African Americans say, 'They think they're White.' And then the Black Hispanics would say, 'Hey man, you can't beat up my friends. How can you be a friend with that whitey?'"

Likewise, Carmen Quander, who married into a prominent African American family in Washington, recalled ongoing negotiations with Washington's African American elite: "Why do you want to take my heart and soul just because you see the color of my skin? Torruella is my last name. That's from the south of Spain. I said, 'I'm Dominican. I am a person of color. I am of the African diaspora, but you know what, you talk to me about other stuff, too, OK? We came here knowingly. I know my roots. I took my family to the grave of all of my ancestors. I am a person of color and very proud of it, but you cannot stay in that box." The "box" Quander refers to is the one that gives racial identity primacy over national or ethnic identity. It is the one based on hypo-descent that would have identified her solely as Black because she has African ancestors. As she reminded her questioner, however, she felt as connected to her European ancestors (who are from the south of Spain) as to her African ones. What is more, she felt herself to be more than the sum total of the "parts" that constitute her background. She refused to be boxed into a strictly racial identity at the exclusion of her ethnic one.

In speaking of her interactions with her co-workers at the African American beauty shop, Francia Almarante expressed a similar sentiment: "I have arrived in places where I've noticed the looks, but as soon as I speak Spanish, everything changes. Their faces change. I notice the difference immediately, from both Whites and Blacks, because Blacks here are a little discriminatory, too. They also discriminate a little bit. As soon as I speak Spanish, things change because now they know I'm not Black American. And everything changes. I did notice a bit of difference between the other Latinas who had white skin and me. They treated me better than them, friendlier. I don't know why. They identified with me more than with the other girls because I am Black." Almarante identified both with Latinas, of whatever color, and with African American women. She was, in other words, both at once. As Sofia Mora explained: "[If I am] asked where I came from, I will say I'm Dominican. But that's a nationality. It's not a race. If they want to know where I'm coming from in terms of race, then I am of African descent—recognizing that in many Latin American countries, being of African descent really means being that and some other things. But certainly I am an Afro-Latina. I am an Afro-Latina who was born in the Dominican Republic."[20] Maricela Medina was even more emphatic: "I'm still Dominican, but there is no question in my mind that I am African. Of African descent. I describe myself as a Black Hispanic woman." Almarante put it succinctly: "I am Black, but that's not all I am." For these Dominican women, physical appearance and the reception it inspired in both White and Black Washington is only part of their being in the world of Washington. The other part is formed by their social networks, which continue to consist primarily of Latin@s.

Medina, for example, attended Howard University and went on to become a member of its history faculty. She was a member of Howard, and the African American community it encompasses, for three decades. Nonetheless as she explained, "Howard changed my life, my outlook. But my social outlet was in the Hispanic community." When she left the Howard faculty to establish an insurance agency, it was Latin@s who came to be heavily represented among her clientele.

Similarly, Almarante found herself working alongside African Americans and serving many African American clients, but she continued to organize her social life primarily in the Latin@ community. She lived in Mount Pleasant, attended mass in Spanish, and went to Latin dances. Nonetheless, after several years of working with African Americans, and especially as her English language proficiency increased, she began increasingly to socialize in that community as well.

Dominican adolescent males and men who organized their social and work lives outside the home were far more exposed to anti-Black racism. Daniel Bueno, for example, arrived in the United States in 1964 at the age of sixteen. He went to work immediately. Many of his co-workers were African American men who socialized Bueno into the rule of race in Washington. As he explained:

I was an Afro-Latino teenager. The word "Afro" wasn't used. We were still divided into two races, Black and White. When we spoke Spanish in the 1960s, people would be surprised that we could speak Spanish, and we were surprised that there were so many people of color in this country because we were under the impression that they didn't exist, that here everyone was White. I experienced racism—minor, of course. I went to a restaurant in Alexandria where they didn't let me sit down in 1964. I worked for [a company that] painted cars, and they sent me to Alexandria to drop off some cars, and when it was lunchtime, you had to eat across the street. I didn't know English. I was in a group of Blacks, and when we went to the restaurant, I went in, sat down, and asked for my food. The owner came and told me that I couldn't eat there. And the guy who was with me told me, "No, ours has to be carry-out." So, in Alexandria, in the 1960s, in the early '60s and maybe in the late '60s, you still couldn't eat in certain restaurants.

Ramberto Torruella, by contrast, went through what he called his "Black phase" once he became an adolescent and went "out into the streets":

I just went Black. I went and started living in the streets. I was party-ing. I was playing basketball. I became streetwise. I was working at a shoeshine shop. I had a steady job. I was a short-order cook. I started working when I was fourteen years old, and I stayed on the streets. And then I went to the service at nineteen, as soon as I graduated from high school. I joined the military. Two weeks after I graduated I joined the service. . . . I graduated in June '63 from high school. Street Black. I was Black. And when I was in the service, it became worse, because they sent me down South. . . . They sent me to San Antonio, Texas. They sent me to Montgomery, Alabama, and they sent to me to Greenville, Mis-sissippi. This was all in 1963, before the Civil Rights Act. In Greenville, Mississippi, I got put in jail. I got into a bar fight. I went into a bar and asked for a beer, and the bartender said, "No colored here." And I said, "I'm Dominican," and they said, "You're a fucking nigger."

Again, both his work and his social life exposed Torruella to the sort of racist violence his sister Carmen was shielded from. Whether playing basketball or partying, cooking, shining shoes, or training for the Vietnam War, Torruella was reminded forcefully time and again that he was "a fuck-ing nigger," Dominican or otherwise. It is not surprising, then, that Torru-ella "went Black" for nearly two decades. He adopted an African American identity, attended a historically Black university, and refused to speak Span-ish. It was not until 1988, when he visited the Dominican Republic for the first time and "saw all these people who looked like" him, that he reclaimed a Dominican identity. Now, as he put it, "I'm all about Latin again."

Conclusion

Dominicans in Washington identify as Black nearly twice as often as Do-minicans in New York City. This is because the Dominicans in Washington form a small community, with origins in West Indian and African Ameri-can communities in the Dominican Republic, that came of age in a seg-regated southern city and in the midst of a large, economically and politi-cally diverse African American community. As Héctor Corporán put it, "I didn't have a choice." The lack of a large Dominican community, Hector explained, "creates a discontinuity from all the racial classifications that we use in Santo Domingo, which has been transplanted in New York City, but here that disappears." It is noteworthy that Washington's Dominicans have continued to sustain an identity as Dominicans—or, more universally, as Latin@s. In that regard, the story told by Black Mosaic's Dominican participants should be considered an important chapter in Dominican history.

The Dominicans who participated in Black Mosaic in Washington were world travelers in sociological and phenomenological terms. They repeatedly crossed national, racial, cultural, geographic, ideological, and social borders. The complexity of their identity narratives and displays highlights the routes they have traveled across and within those borders. If for some observers Dominican ambiguity is difficult to grasp and equivocal, for the Dominicans I interviewed in Washington it is consistent with their travel routes and destinations. The Dominicans of Black Mosaic experienced themselves as Black in Washington in ways that simultaneously linked them to and distinguished them from their African American neighbors. They could, as Maricela Medina put it, "go the African American route," but they would continue to carry their Dominican identities with them.

Notes

1. Meeting notes, Sharon Reinckens files, 1994, Black Mosaic archives, Anacostia Museum, Smithsonian Institution, Washington, D.C.
2. Fath Ruffins, "Mythos, Memory, and History: African American Preservation Efforts, 1820–1990," in *Museums and Communities: The Politics of Public Culture*, edited by Ivan Karp, Christine Mullen Kreamer, and Steven D. Lavine (Washington: Smithsonian Institution Press, 1992), 577.
3. Ibid.
4. See Franc Báez Evertsz and Frank D'Oleo Ramírez, *La immigración de dominicanos a Estados Unidos* (Santo Domingo: Fundación Friedrich Ebert, 1985); Jan Knippers Black, *The Dominican Republic: Politics and Development in an Unsovereign State* (Boston: Allen and Unwin, 1986); and Robert Crassweller, *Trujillo: The Life and Times of a Caribbean Dictator* (New York: Macmillan, 1966).
5. See Alfonso Aguilar, "Leyendas de nuestra historia: Juanita A. Campos, 54 años de vida en D.C.," *Foro*, April 28, 1994; Juana Campos, interview by Héctor Corporán in 1994 (Black Mosaic Archives, Anacostia Museum, Washington) and by the author, August 1998.
6. The Washington metropolitan area, which includes suburban counties in Maryland and Virginia, has a much larger number of Dominicans (4,760 in 1990 and 12,471 in 2000), according to the Lewis Mumford Center for Comparative Urban and Regional Research, University of Albany, http://mumfordi.dyndns.org/cen2000 (site visited

on July 25, 2005). Census data on Dominicans in Washington before 1990 were not available. Indeed, census data on Latin@s, Hispanics, and Spanish-speaking people in Washington are available only for 1940 and from 1970 onward.

7. Ibid.

8. Unless otherwise noted, this and all subsequent quotes are from interviews with Ramberto Torruella (August 1998), Frances Almarante (July 1998), Daniel Bueno (1993), Juana Campos (August 1998), Casilda Luna (1993), Maricela Medina (1993, 1998), Esperanza Ozuma (1993), and Carmen Quander (August 1998), conducted by Héctor Corporán, Olivia Cadaval, and the author.

9. The United States collected and managed Dominican customs revenues from 1905 to 1941. Since import revenues represented the principal source of currency exchange, the United States was effectively managing the Dominican economy during this period.

10. Michael Omi and Howard Winant, *Racial Formation in the United States*, 2nd ed. (New York: Routledge, 1994).

11. "Black Mosaic: Community, Race, and Ethnicity among Black Immigrants in Washington, D.C.," exhibition script (Black Mosaic Archives, Anacostia Museum, Smithsonian Institution, Washington), 86.

12. This is not to imply that African Americans in Washington are universally well off. In fact, African Americans in the capital continue to experience high poverty rates (22 percent); have median per capita incomes of $12,226, or two-thirds less than the median per capita income of $34,563 for Whites; and disproportionately fewer college and graduate degrees (see 1990 U.S. Census data, database C90S5F1A, state level statistics). That said, however, the presence of a large and visible Black middle class is sociologically relevant.

13. Terry A. Repak, *Waiting on Washington: Central American Workers in the Nation's Capital* (Philadelphia: Temple University Press, 1995), 69.

14. "Black Mosaic," exhibition script.

15. Julia Lara, "Reflections: Bridging Cultures," in "First Generation Students: Confronting Cultural Issues," special issue of *New Directions for Community Colleges* 20, no. 4 (winter 1992): 65–70.

16. There are, of course, Afro-Mexicanos and large Afro-Latin@ populations throughout Central America and South America. However, as Lara points out, these groups are generally excluded from or overlooked in their nations' imagined communities. See Edmund T. Gordon, *Disparate Diasporas: Identity and Politics in an African-Nicaraguan Community* (Austin: University of Texas Press, 1998); and Richard Graham, *The Idea of Race in Latin America, 1870–1940* (Austin: University of Texas Press, 1997).

17. Repak, *Waiting on Washington*, 1.

18. Yesilernis Peña, James Sidanius, and Mark Sawyer, "Racial Democracy in the Americas: A Latin and U.S. Comparison," *Journal of Cross-Cultural Psychology* 35 (November 2004): 749–62.

19. Olivia Cadaval, *Creating a Latino Identity in the Nation's Capital: The Latino Festival* (New York: Garland Press, 1998), 235–39.

20. "Identity," exhibition videotape (Black Mosaic archives, Anacostia Museum, Smithsonian Institution, Washington).

YEIDY M. RIVERO

Bringing the Soul

Afros, Black Empowerment, and Lucecita Benítez

I hope that the make-up they [White performers] use on their faces
cannot be taken off and that it transforms itself into tar!
—Raquel Rey, *Teve Guía*, May 13, 1973, quoting Sylvia del Villard

Puerto Ricans in the United States (and specifically Afro–Puerto Ricans)
were actively involved in African American political, social, and cultural
organizations from the early 1960s to the Black Power movement of the
mid-1960s.[1] Certainly these associations should not come as a surprise
because Puerto Ricans residing in the United States had been relegated to
racial and class locations that were similar to those of African Americans.[2]
More important, in the United States many Afro–Puerto Ricans were indeed read as African Americans. As Pablo "Yoruba" Guzmán (one of the
leaders of the 1970s Young Lords Party) recalled, "Before people called me
a spic, they called me a nigger."[3] Guzmán hints at the intertwined processes of racialization that Afro–Puerto Ricans experienced (and probably
still experience) in the states. Through the United States mainstream's
Black and White binary racial discourse, the racialization of Puerto Ricans
in general, and the rejection of Blackness that has characterized Puerto
Rico's culture, Afro–Puerto Ricans were subjected to multiple levels of
oppression. This spectrum of racial and racist practices informed the
coalitions formed in the 1960s and 1970s between African Americans,
Puerto Ricans, and Afro–Puerto Ricans and the political platform of the
Young Lords.[4]

In both Chicago and New York, the Young Lords Party (a group that was
part of the Black Panthers' Rainbow Coalition alliance) mobilized to re-
gain community control and established political ties with other minority

groups to challenge the racial and class subjugation of Puerto Rican and Latin@ communities in the United States. In addition the Young Lords included women's rights as part of its platform and criticized the machismo and homophobia ingrained in Puerto Rican and Latin@ cultures. Similar to the island's leftist movements, the Young Lords focused on Puerto Rico's independence. But as Roberto Rodríguez-Morazzani argues, for Puerto Rican radicals in New York "the legacy of Black Nationalist Malcolm X was to occupy a place equal in importance to that of Don Pedro Albizu Campos [leader of the Nationalist Party of Puerto Rico]."[5] For the radical Left based in the United States, anti-colonialism signified political freedom as well as racial consciousness. Ranging from actions such as the appropriation of names associated with Africa (for example, Yoruba), to the adoption of natural hairstyles, to the ongoing dialogues with African Americans, race and Blackness occupied important positions within the Young Lords' political and cultural platforms.

The political awareness and action of Puerto Ricans on the mainland were palpable not only in terms of grassroots community-based mobilizations but also in their use of media outlets to represent their struggles. For example, in separate studies Chon Noriega and Lillian Jiménez have demonstrated that Boricua (Puerto Rican) and Chicano activists have fought for media access, protested mainstream media stereotypes of Latin@s, and coproduced television programs on PBS addressing the Latin@ cultural heritage and issues pertinent to these communities since the late 1960s and especially during the early 1970s.[6] Furthermore, similar to Asian American, Native American, and African American filmmakers, Puerto Ricans and Chicanos have used documentary filmmaking to represent their identities and civil rights struggles.

Although the problem of racism in Puerto Rico was apparently not included in these media artifacts, all the aforementioned political, cultural, racial, mediatic, and diasporic intersections had both a direct and an indirect impact on the island. The writers from La generación de los 70 (the 1970s generation), researchers, and theater groups examined race, class, and gender within the context of colonialism and incorporated Afro-Puerto Rican and Caribbean themes in their cultural and intellectual productions.[7] Moreover, several key individuals developed sociopolitical discourses that centered on Blackness, racism, and the exaltation of Afro-Puerto Rican cultural elements.

In addition to these intellectual, literary, and theatrical cultural fronts Black identity politics were also performed in another, more visible location: Puerto Rico's commercial television. Through the appropriation of cultural elements associated with the Black Power movement in the United States, Black performers' protests against racist casting practices and the production of shows that focused on Blackness, as well as television in general (the industry, media professionals, and audiences), newspapers, and TV magazines, fostered a dialogic space that challenged the Whiteness that characterized the industry.

The 1970s televisual (and media cultures) transformations emanated from three divergent levels of political, cultural, and commercial signification: first, the Black performers' activism against racism; second, the appropriation and adaptation of television programs and concepts in the United States that addressed the topic of Blackness; and third, the United States and European fashion industry's commodification of Blackness. In other words, Puerto Rico's commercial television and media were influenced by multiple local and global political mobilizations of the 1960s and early 1970s and by the processes of desegregation that took place in media cultures in the United States.

Indeed, as numerous scholars have argued, the incorporation of Blackness in the United States media in general and commercial television in particular functioned through the ideologies of middle-class Whiteness and the depoliticization of racial struggles. However, what I foreground here are the ways in which various radical vernacular movements and commercial changes had a partial, but nonetheless crucial, impact on Puerto Rico's commercial television industry. In sum, the 1970s televisual debates directly challenged the ideology of racial equality at the heart of la gran familia puertorriqueña discourse.

The limited representation of Black bodies and the ongoing use of blackface in entertainment television programming occupied the center of the 1970s racialized struggles. Although racial categorization in Puerto Rico does not translate to racial consciousness, it should be clear that the few Black performers who were working in the industry were pivotal in televisual contestations in the 1970s. Although some artists combined their pro-independence ideology with their racial, gender, and sexual politics, Blackness and racism nonetheless served as the catalysts for their mobilization.

The 1970s televisual symbolic and actual transformations operated both individually and collectively, with some being politically motivated and others commercially driven. Nevertheless, even as these performers and media producers articulated distinct political and racial agendas, they were all fighting against the same oppressive condition: anti-Black racism. By the 1970s, the anti-Black racism in Puerto Rico's commercial television operated within three venues: blackface, cosmetic whitening, and discriminatory casting practices.

Televisual blackface began with the arrival of commercial television to Puerto Rico in 1954. For the most part, and as in radio, the *negrito* continued to be a stock buffoon-like representation in comedies and the comedy sketches included in variety shows, while the *negra* characters were depicted as submissive maids in telenovelas. In addition to the ongoing use of blackface to masquerade Whiteness, a process that I refer to as cosmetic whitening was pervasive. I identify cosmetic whitening as the practice through which features associated with a Black phenotype (such as hair or darker skin) are purposely concealed to reconstruct a mulatto body into a more White body. In other words, cosmetic whitening functioned as a camouflage that refined or disguised the flaws of racial *mestizaje*. Cosmetic whitening included tactics such as using a wig to hide Black hair or applying a light makeup foundation to whiten the *trigueña* and *trigueño* face. Obviously, mulatto bodies were primarily involved in the process of cosmetic whitening. Still, in contrast to blackface, which can be categorized as a theatrical or televisual performance, cosmetic whitening required perpetual masquerading because the televisual mulatto performer needed to maintain the illusion of Whiteness not only in front of the camera but also in public spaces.

Although both the practice of blackface and the process of cosmetic whitening drastically reduced the opportunities for Black actors and actresses in Puerto Rico's commercial television, discriminatory casting practices further limited their access. The logic used by television producers and directors (particularly in telenovelas) was simple: there were no good Black actors; thus, they had to use White performers in blackface to perform the maid characters. These media professionals never questioned their own racist equation ("Blacks" were synonymous with maids in the fictional telenovela world) or the racial constraints that informed the island's television. Consequently, in Puerto Rico's commercial television entertainment programming, Blacks occupied a particular space, one that was already fixed for them and not by them).[8] Although through various genres television constructed the nation as *mestiza* (composed of Blacks, Whites, and mulattos), racial masking and processes positioned Whiteness as the most desirable racial element within the televisual space and thus the nation.

Although Whiteness was still the norm in local television entertainment programming, the 1970s was a critical stage in the history of Puerto Rico's commercial television and media discussions of racism. The performers' militancy created an imaginary circuitry that connected Puerto Rico's Black populations to marginalized communities in the United States and to the struggles against racial oppression that informed other parts of the world.

The Racial, Gender, Sexual, and Political Ramifications of a Televisual Afro

During April 1970 Luz Esther Benítez (Lucecita), a renowned performer who was (and still is) considered one of the most talented singers in Puerto Rico and Latin America, inadvertently shocked local television audiences.[9] After years of straightening her hair and wearing wigs, Lucecita (who since the mid-1960s had been marketed as a whitened *nueva ola* [rock and roll] ballad singer) appeared with an Afro in her *El show de las 12* segment. The so-called African look stunned the press and fans, creating a controversy that not only reaffirmed the racism that is part of Puerto Rico's culture but that also rearticulated the multi-axial system of oppression related to race, gender, and sexuality. Within a period of three years Lucecita became a televisual and popular culture figure who defied Eurocentric, patriarchal, heterosexual, and right-wing political ideological discourses.

It should be clear that the African look debate that emerged in 1970 was not the first incident of racism against Lucecita. According to Javier Santiago, toward the end of the 1960s some television fans sent letters to TV magazines questioning Lucecita's Whiteness (i.e., her continual use of wigs to allegedly hide her black hair).[10] In addition, fans established an indirect racialized comparison between Lucecita and Lissette, a White Cuban immigrant who also became a youth icon in Puerto Rico during the mid-1960s. Regarding the fans' contestations, Lucecita later recalled, "There was racism. And when Lissette dyed her hair blond, the debates acquired another ingredient—the blond with the American 'look' versus the Puerto Rican *trigueña*. People said that she [Lissette] was White and that I was supposedly Black. People screamed at me all the outrageous things characteristic of an audience inflamed with a very evident racist problem."[11] While the fans' racist debates affected Lucecita's public persona at the end of the 1960s, ideologies of cultural nationalism and the emerging prejudice against the Cuban immigrant community in Puerto Rico re-inscribed Lucecita as a *mestiza*, and more important, a Puerto Rican body.

After the 1959 Cuban migration, Cubans were socially constructed as people who took jobs away from Puerto Ricans. This anti-Cuban sentiment also permeated the television industry because many Cuban media professionals (actors, actresses, directors, scriptwriters, and producers) had begun to work in Puerto Rico's commercial television, with some occupying important positions. Thus, even though Lucecita's Blackness and Lissette's Whiteness precipitated discussions among their respective fans, Lucecita's Puerto Ricanness juxtaposed to Lissette's immigrant and progressively unwelcome Cubanness temporarily disrupted some of the fans' racist contestations.

Furthermore, in 1969 Lucecita's symbolic Puerto Ricanness reached a new level of signification when she won first prize as the most talented singer at El Primer Festival de la Canción Latina del Mundo (the First Festival of Latin World Music) in Mexico City. Lucecita's international success and her still televisually constructed whitened body (her use of wigs), intertwined with Puerto Rico's cultural nationalism and delayed the racist public outburst that emerged in 1970. The Afro, however, completely destabilized her (until this point) racially, socially, culturally, and somewhat acceptably whitened triqueña and mestiza televisual body. By wearing an Afro, Lucecita disrupted the televisual containment and locations of Blackness, thus instigating a televisual racial crisis.

Television magazines played a key role in framing the debates. The media always narrated Lucecita's hairstyle as an "African look" instead of an Afro. Although the phrase (used in English) suggested a direct association with the United States, none of the magazines considered the racial, political, cultural, and social signification of the Afro within African American communities. Instead, the unexplored term "African look" seemed to associate Lucecita's hair with Africa. Still, the phrase might have contained other meanings, particularly within the context of Puerto Rico's cultural and racial ideologies and public persona. By appropriating this phrase the media were foregrounding and rejecting the supposed Africanness of Lucecita's body and thereby indirectly rearticulating official and vernacular discourses that situated Africa (and Blackness) as a present yet negligible and unwelcome element within the national body.

Initially, the media, not Lucecita, generated the public's racialized discussion. Lucecita had not intended to use her hairstyle as a symbolic reaffirmation of her Blackness. Her decision to grow an Afro was a response to an allergic reaction caused by her ongoing use of wigs. Still, regardless of Lucecita's medical condition and actual intentions, audiences and TV magazines initiated an informal campaign to censor her hairstyle and conceal her Blackness.

Following Lucecita's first television appearance with what TV magazines and newspapers categorized as an African look, audience members called Paquito Cordero (the producer of the El *show de las 12*, the creator of the late 1950s blackface character Reguerete, and one of the most powerful media professionals during the 1970s) and voiced their opposition through remarks such as, "When Lucecita appeared with that Afro, I just turned off the TV."[12] A group of Lucecita's supporters appeared with signs outside of Telemundo's building that read, "With Afro or without it, with Lucecita until the end."[13] Other fans depoliticized the Afro and Lucecita's controversy by letters supporting the hairstyle that was, according to them, the new fashion trend in New York City. However, those who were in favor of the African look apparently represented a small minority. *Vea* (a television guide magazine) initiated a survey asking readers whether they were in favor of or opposed to the African look. *Vea's* survey received 248 votes in support of the Afro and 2,823 against it.[14]

During this unexpected controversy Lucecita, who had plans to film in Spain and was required to get rid of her Afro by the film's producer, began to show signs of her politically radical transformations. In reference to her fans and the Spanish film producer's censorship of her Afro, Lucecita remarked, "This is nothing, wait until my hair keeps growing and I show up in Spain with this huge and forceful 'African look' . . . I will stop the traffic in Madrid."[15] The Afro kept growing, increasingly challenging televisual and deliberated whitening. However, alongside this racial representation of her body, Lucecita also transgressed dominant constructions of femininity by wearing "masculine" garments during her shows and public appearances.

While Lucecita began changing her style of dress at the end of the 1960s, after her appropriation of the Afro, newspapers and TV magazines began to target not only her race but also to question her femininity. For example, with her 1970 acclaimed success at the Caribe Hilton hotel's prestigious Club Caribe, one reviewer stated that "coiffed with an Afro out to here, and dressed in a rakish grey suit with tails (she is famous for not wearing skirts or dresses) Lucecita empties a cauldron of emotion onto the Caribe stage."[16] Although her talent was never doubted, her personality had now become the focus of public debate.

Lucecita, who during the beginning of her career was narrated as a shy, quiet, and humble woman, grew progressively more outspoken. Gradually, she became famous for constantly transgressing proper norms of feminine conduct by using bad words. Subsequently, she began to be categorized as difficult. Disc jockeys stopped playing her music on Puerto Rico's commercial radio stations. Finally, in March 1972, due to ongoing

Lucecita Benítez, circa 1970.
(Photograph by Javier Santiago)

pressures from the television industry, publicists, and Rambler Toyota (the sponsor of *El Show Rambler Toyota* in which Lucecita was going to participate), Lucecita straightened her hair. Soon after changing her hairstyle, she decided to stop working in television and, indeed, she let her Afro grow again.

The final dramatic changes in Lucecita's public persona occurred during 1973, when she released the album *Raza Pura* (Pure Race) with *nueva canción* (new song) Left-oriented political songs. The album openly affirmed her pro-independence political stance, symbolically represented her ideological position as a sympathizer of the Cuban Revolution, and reiterated her pride in her Blackness. These racial and political affirmations were articulated not only in the song *Soy de una raza pura* (I am from a pure race) but also on the album cover.

The song *Soy de una raza pura*, written by two men who identified with Puerto Rico's political Left movement (Tony Croatto and David Ortíz), rejects Eurocentrism, the oppressive condition of slavery, racism, and Whiteness. The lyrics detail the subjugation of Black people and the rebellious and combative "essence" of this marginalized population. *Soy de una raza pura* also positions Blackness as an integral part of the Puerto Rican nation while concomitantly ignoring the Spanish cultural and racial influences. This ideological position is clearly revealed in the stanzas, "I am borincano [from the island's Taíno name], Black, and gypsy" and "I am Taíno, I am tears, and I am also pain." Although the song in itself is an embracement of non-European cultural and racial elements, the fact that it was performed by Lucecita brought a second level of political and racial signification to its lyrics.

The album cover—designed by Antonio Martorell, a renowned Puerto Rican graphic artist and pro-independence activist—is dominated by a drawing of Lucecita. Her face and torso are painted in red and her hair is depicted as an Afro. The background for Lucecita's red figure is blue, making a connection between her Blackness and Puerto Rico's flag. Therefore, as with the song Soy de una raza pura, the album cover positions Blackness as a central element in Puerto Rico's culture, identity, and society.

With this album, Lucecita became one of the popular cultural symbols of the Puerto Rican Left and alternatively a pariah among Puerto Rico's politically conservative groups. Obviously, she became the devil incarnate for some sectors of the powerful media and right-wing anti-Castro Cuban immigrant community in both Puerto Rico and Miami. In the eyes of the Cuban immigrant community Lucecita became a cultural attaché for Fidel Castro and the Cuban Revolution; therefore, she had to be expunged from the popular culture landscape. As was expected, Lucecita was blacklisted.

Furthermore, her transgressions of femininity went beyond "male" outfits and inappropriate language. Lucecita began to use masculine adjectives when singing some of her songs and on some occasions when describing herself. Contrary to many singers who usually changed the gender-specific adjectives in song lyrics to accommodate their gender, the lyrics of Soy de una raza pura kept the masculine construction in phrases such as "Soy borincano, negro, y gitano (I am Puerto Rican, Black, and gypsy)." Moreover, when a journalist asked Lucecita about fashion and her "masculine" outfits, she, in some parts of the interview, characterized herself as a man. As Lucecita remarked, "I am a simple and humble Black male [negro] who does not know about luxurious dresses and fine jewelry. I dress as I am, as Luz Esther Benítez is. I have my own criteria as an individual, and that 'I' does not stick to fashion nor to anybody. I believe that all of us have the right to be as one feels one is, not what society imposes.[17] Later during the same interview, she reappropriated her female gender by declaring, "I am a Black woman (negra) who has struggled a lot in life." Because of her self-description as a male, together with what was considered her nonfeminine appearance and the fact that publicly she was not romantically involved with any man, rumors began to spread about her possible lesbianism.

Besides playing—in the performative and socially contravening sense—with gender, Lucecita intertwined her racial, gendered, and left-wing public performances with direct criticisms of the Catholic Church, women's oppression, and homophobia. For example, while touring in the Dominican Republic in 1973, she declared, "I am not a virgin. That is an obsolete myth . . . the Catholic Church is wrong and outdated . . . we have to accept homosexuality as an expression of love."[18] Although Lucecita never came out as a lesbian, one might say that these statements in the context of Puerto Rican and, more generally, the Spanish Caribbean's conservative and homophobic culture fueled doubts about her sexual orientation. Lucecita became a Black, pro-independence, pseudo-communist, pseudo-lesbian butch, and as such she was a direct menace to the patriarchal, White, mestizo, pro-commonwealth, pro-statehood racial, political, cultural, and gendered social order. Mainstream TV magazines and newspapers made Lucecita a media spectacle, and by 1973 she had become an outcast.

During an interview published in a left-wing magazine in 1973, Lucecita finally discussed the racism that she had experienced and the process that she endured to mask her Blackness while working in Puerto Rico's commercial television: "I am not a puppet. I never wanted to be that but they [the television industry] wanted to erase the Blackness that is part of me. They forgot that my father was Black. They wanted to refine my nose. They demanded a White Lucecita, who would fill their requirements. I felt bad but accepted. They told me that it was going to be better for me and I believed them. But the day that they took away my Afro, I cried and cried . . . I still remember and it hurts."[19]

Lucecita, the Black pro-independence woman, who sometimes constructed herself as male and at other times as female and who retained her African look, was marginalized from Puerto Rico's commercial television and mainstream culture until 1980. Within a short period of three years (1970 to 1973) Lucecita had moved from being portrayed as the beloved humble, working-class *trigueña* woman who sang love songs to one who was described as a communist and Castroite *camionera* (a word used to describe a woman as vulgar, nonfeminine, and a lesbian) and as a foulmouthed, difficult woman. Certainly, Lucecita was an active agent in her ideological and bodily transformations. Yet equally important in these narrations was the fact that Lucecita's African look and her subsequent revolutionary performances revealed the mainstream media's and some audiences' aversion to practices and discourses that challenged Puerto Rico's (and I should also say, the Spanish Caribbean's) dominant culture.

I position Lucecita as the televisual signifier of the alternative racial, political, feminist, and sexual discursive transformations that were part of some sectors of Puerto Rico's society. Lucecita's "African look" incident was the beginning of the portentous changes in her career, and it also signaled shifts in the activism of Black actors in Puerto Rico's commercial television. Indeed, no other televisual performer directly transgressed Puerto Rico's dominant multi-axial ideological discourses in the ways that Lucecita did. Moreover, her aggressive and politically up-front performances cost her many employment opportunities. Nonetheless, Lucecita's Afro was emblematic of the racial and cultural challenges that erupted in Puerto Rico's commercial television during the early 1970s.

I would like to suggest that in Puerto Rico the Afro functioned as a discursive iconography of multiple and sometimes intertwined, sometimes autonomous, counterhegemonic movements. It should be noted that, as I will further explain, just a few years after the uproar over Lucecita's hair, the Afro and soul music—by way of the locally produced and hybrid version of Soul Train—became imported and commodified cultural artifacts. Granted, many audiences may have been unaware of the hairstyle's political implications. Robin D. G. Kelley argues that in the United States the Afro became an essentialist and manufactured representation of the Black Power movement, Black community struggles, and soul music.[20] In Puerto Rico, some rebellious teenagers may have appropriated the Afro void of any political connotations. After all, in the island's vernacular culture the Afro was characterized by some as un criadero de piojos (a breeding place for lice). It follows that some young people might have used the Afro to rebel against their parents. In contrast, others might have simply appropriated the hairstyle to be defiantly fashionable. Nonetheless, I contend that the Afro acquired other meanings.

First, the hairstyle served as a reaffirmation of Puerto Rico's African heritage and as a direct affront to the island's racist ideologies and practices. Considering that in Puerto Rico's vernacular culture phrases such as mejorar la raza (improve the race) and pelo malo ("bad hair," in reference to Blacks' curly hair) represent the whitening in sexual mixing and the White-constructed normativity of the body (i.e., straightening the hair to hide the bad, Black hair), the Afro was an in-your-face resistance to hegemonic racial discourses. In other words, the Afro signified a transgression of the whitening that informs the mestizaje discourse.

Second, at least in television and in Puerto Rico's media cultures, media professionals (actors, actresses, singers, composers, etc.) who identified with Puerto Rico's independence movement appropriated the Afro. Thus, for members of this racialized, gendered, and heterogeneous group, the Afro may have been a symbol of Black empowerment, of racial struggles (in Puerto Rico, in the United States, and in other parts of the world), and of freedom from colonialism. Consequently this racial symbol galvanized a number of political movements, some racial and some that extended beyond the boundaries of race.

The multiplicity of meanings associated with the Afro are important given that some scholars in the United States have positioned the commercialization of the natural hairstyle as a negation of any political signification without considering the ways in which other transnational and Afro-diasporic communities might have *translated* and reappropriated the hairstyle. For example, Maxine Leeds Craig identifies 1970 as the year when the Afro was "drained of its meaning." She contends that "the natural, once it had become acceptable, became a mere style. As the social activism out of which the style was born fractured in array and defeat, the style referred to an increasingly distant historic period of activism."[21] In addition, Robin D. G. Kelley asserts that "by the early 1970s, on the eve of the Afro's ultimate demise, the whole 'natural' movement took another turn. . . . The Afro began to lose its specific political meaning, or at least the connection to Black nationalist politics seemed to fade into the background."[22]

The commercialization of the Afro that took place during the 1970s is undeniable. And indeed, as Kelley argues, the hairstyle's political specificity was transformed. Still, I prefer to treat the Afro as a symbol of African diasporic racial struggles, which instead of being shattered of its political meaning acquired other radical significations. In the case of Puerto Rico, I would locate the Afro as a cultural artifact that symbolically connected Puerto Ricans on the island with the African American, Puerto Rican, and Afro–Puerto Rican radical mobilizations that had taken place in the United States since the early 1960s. In other words, the Afro can be seen as a performative bodily practice that integrated the Black Power "Black is beautiful" discourse, the Young Lords, and pro-independence activism. Additionally, in the case of Puerto Rico's commercial television in general and Lucecita in particular, the Afro directly defied the practice of cosmetic whitening because, as I have previously discussed, Lucecita went through various masquerading processes to disguise her Blackness.

However, through Lucecita's televisual persona the Afro became more than a sign of Black or anticolonial empowerment. According to a member of Lucecita's fan club during the African look controversy, the imminent menace attached to Lucecita and her Afro was its racial connotation. Yet was it only her Blackness that the mainstream culture rejected? My answer is no. Although Lucecita's Afro linked Puerto Rican Blackness to the Black Power movement in the United States and the rhetoric of anti–United States imperialism that characterized alternative political discourses in Puerto Rico, Latin America, the United States, and other parts of the world, her Afro also became an emblem of gender, feminine, and even sexual transgressions. Lucecita needed to be eliminated from the island's media cultures because her Afro signified multiple and intertwined ideological contraventions. I would also argue that this is precisely why, when Lucecita staged her television comeback in 1980, she stopped performing most of her political left-wing-oriented songs, no longer constructed herself as a male, and removed all traces of an Afro or an African look. Lucecita, while still identified with the Puerto Rican Left movement, became (for the most part) a bolero singer.

Nonetheless, Lucecita's official Web site states that "the fight for her ideals is not over, her commitment is apparent, and her voice, along with a talent to make poetry and music, meld into a whole that touches our soul with a laser that cuts deep within our feelings. Lucecita is more than a light that leads the path, she beams a course with her talent and commitment to higher ideals."[23] The African look controversy is not documented on her Web site. She is now described as "the national voice of Puerto Rico." First and foremost Lucecita has embraced Puerto Rico's cultural and political nationalism's main artistic and political battle. Yet if one examines, for example, her Carnegie Hall CD from 2000, one sees that the first song is Soy de una raza pura. And, if one listens to the obviously heart-wrenching bolero Que tal te va sin mí? (How are you doing without me?), she clearly sings "Me alegro de encontrarte nuevamente. Te juro que te vez maravillosa" (I am happy to see you again. I swear that you [a female] look wonderful).[24] The racial, political, gendered, and sexual ramifications of the 1970s televisual Afro still permeate Lucecita's public persona. The difference is that today, and contrary to the African look controversy of 1970–1973, one has to pay closer attention to the subtexts of Lucecita's corporeal and verbal representations.

However, besides the African look debate of 1970–1973, the ideologies of race and Blackness in Puerto Rico's commercial television acquired a variety of complicated meanings during the early 1970s. Black actors and actresses protested the use of blackface in local television, soul music became popular, and—at the same time—a blackface female character became an iconic cultural figure in Puerto Rico.

Notes

1. See Iris Morales, "Palante, Siempre Palante: The Young Lords," in The Puerto Rican Movement: Voices from the Diaspora, edited by Andrés Torres and José A. Velázquez (Philadelphia: Temple University Press, 1998), 210–27; Roberto Rodríguez-Morazzani, "Puerto Rican Political Generations in New York: Pioneros, Young Turks, and Radicals," Centro 4, no. 1 (1992): 96–116; Basilio Serrano, "Rifle, Cañon, y Escopeta: A Chronicle of the Puerto Rican Student Union," in Torres and Velázquez, The Puerto Rican Movement, 25–43; and Komozi Woodard, A Nation within a Nation: Amiri Baraka (Leroi Jones) and Black Power Politics (Chapel Hill: University of North Carolina Press, 1999).

2. Duany, The Puerto Rican Nation on the Move: Identities on the Island and in the U.S. (Chapel Hill: University of North Carolina Press, 2002); Grosfoguel and Georas, "Latino Caribbean Diasporas in New York," in Agustín Lao-Montes and Arlene Dávila, Mambo Montage: The Latinization of New York (New York: Columbia University Press, 2001), 97–118; and Sanchez-Korrol, From Colonia to Community: The History of Puerto Ricans in New York City (Berkeley: University of California Press, 1994).

3. The Young Lords Party and Michael Abramson, Palante: Young Lords Party (New York: McGraw-Hill, 1971), 73.

4. Ibid.

5. Rodríguez-Morazzani "Puerto Rican Political Generations in New York," 106.

6. Lillian Jiménez, "From the Margin to the Center: Puerto Rican Cinema in New York," in Latin Looks: Images of Latinas and Latinos in the U.S. Media, edited by Clara Rodríguez (Boulder, Colo.: Westview Press, 1997), 188–99; and Chon Noriega, Shot in America: Television, the State, and the Rise of Chicano Cinema (Minneapolis: University of Minnesota Press, 2000).

7. Marie Ramos-Rosado, La mujer negra en la literatura puertorriqueña (Río Piedras, Puerto Rico: Editorial de la Universidad de Puerto Rico, 1999); Ana Lydia Vega, "Lafelicidad (ja, ja, ja, ja) y la universidad," El Mundo, September 23, 1990, 121; and Arlene Torres, "La gran familia puertorriqueña 'Ej Prieta De Belda' (The Great Puerto Rican Family Is Really Black)," in Blackness in Latin America and the Caribbean: Social Dynamics and Cultural Transformations, edited by Arlene Torres and Norman E. Whitten (Bloomington: Indiana University Press, 1998), 285–306.

8. I am drawing from Frantz Fanon's theories on the fixation of "Blackness" and the invisibility of the "Black" self. See Frantz Fanon, Black Skin, White Masks, trans. Charles Lam Markmann (New York: Grove Weidenfeld, 1967).

9. For information on Lucecita's career during the 1960s and a detailed and impressive documentation of la nueva ola movement in Puerto Rico, see Javier Santiago, La nueva ola portoricensis (San Juan, Puerto Rico: Editorial del Patio, 1994); and Lucecita's folders at the Fundación Nacional para la Cultura Popular, San Juan, Puerto Rico.

10. Santiago, La nueva ola portoricensis, 127.

11. Ibid.

12. Magali García Ramis, "La transformación de Lucecita," *Avance*, August 6, 1973, 21–25.

13. Santiago, "La historia detrás de un afro," *El Nuevo Día*, October 15, 2000, 129.

14. "Derrotan el 'Afro' de Lucecita," *Vea*, May 8, 1970, 46–47.

15. "Lucecita no quiere quitarse el Afro," *TeVe Guía*, June 13, 1970, 13–16.

16. "Lucecita," *San Juan Weekly*, October 3, 1970, 1.

17. María O. Olán, "No estoy en contra de nada ni de nadie . . . sino a favor de algo," *El Mundo*, September 9, 1973. See also "Lucecita explica porque estuvo retirada por un año," *Vea*, August 12, 1973, 48–49.

18. Rosendo Rosell, *Diarío las Américas*, May 24, 1973; and William Tavares, "Se define como ejemplo vivo de la liberación femenina," *El Caribe*, May 9, 1973.

19. García Ramis, "La Transformación de Lucecita," 22.

20. Robin D. G. Kelley, *Yo' Mama's Disfunktional! Fighting the Culture Wars in Urban America* (Boston: Beacon Press, 1997).

21. Maxine Leeds Craig, *Ain't I a Beauty Queen? Black Women, Beauty, and the Politics of Race* (Oxford: Oxford University Press, 2002), 107.

22. Robin D. G. Kelley, "Nap Time: Historicizing the Afro," *Fashion Theory* 1, no. 4 (1997): 347.

23. See Lucecita Benítez, official Web site, http://www.lucecita.com.

24. Lucecita Benítez, *En vivo desde Carnegie Hall* (New York: BMG Entertainment, 2000).

EJIMA BAKER

Can BET Make You Black?

Remixing and Reshaping Latin@s on
Black Entertainment Television

One lazy Wednesday morning I was lying in bed, surrounded by reading and flipping through my five hundred cable channels, desperately looking for any opportunity for further procrastination. As I came to Black Entertainment Television (BET), I was surprised to see on the screen one of my favorite Spanish-Spanglish language hosts, Julissa Bermudez, a Latina from New York City. She was reveling in her Spanglish glory, just as I had so often seen her do on Mun2 (a subsidiary of Telemundo). I began to ask myself a series of dizzying questions: Why is she on BET? Should she *not* be on BET? Who is BET trying to cater to? What does this say about how we shape so-called urban Latin@s? What does this say about the way we define "Blackness"? And most importantly, What does this say about the relationship between Latin@s and "Black" people? Are these relationships we need to rethink, or perhaps remix?

While historically a significant portion of the Latin@ community has always self-identified as White,[1] BET has nevertheless positioned itself to cater to the musical and cultural tastes of Latin@s by employing Latinas on their many programs and by running musical specials on popular Latin music, especially reggaeton. As such, BET appears to be employing the long-established White-Black racial dichotomy to court Latin@s, but at the same time it is redefining long-standing concepts of who and what is Latin@ and Black.

The truth of the matter is that this is also an exploration of my own identity and that of the ethnic and racial groups with whom I associate. I am a one-and-a-half generation immigrant woman whose family lineage includes African, Indian, Native American, and a splash of European, and I come from Trinidad—an island that was both a Spanish colony and a British one, and whose people routinely move to and from mainland Latin America. By extending a (Black) hand to their racially heterogeneous viewers, BET reminds both their Black and their Latin@ audience of their shared African diasporic identity.

At the core of my analysis of Blackness and *latinidad* is Julissa Marquez, the former VJ on Telemundo's Mun2, former co-VJ on BET's *106th & Park*, and current VJ on BET's show *The Center*.[2] Julissa was born in the Dominican Republic and raised in Queens, New York, and thus she embodies a collision of Black racial politics. The Dominican Republic has, since colonial times, had a much larger Black (by United States definitions) than White population, and today it is 90 percent Black or mulatto.[3] With a population of over nine million people, the Dominican Republic has one of the largest Black populations in the entire Caribbean.

Julissa, who looks too Black for mainstream Spanish-language television, represents what is increasingly being called the "urban Latin@" market. As a subsidiary of Telemundo, Mun2 plays the role of the (dark) intermediary between the Spanish-language stations and English- and Spanglish-language programming that caters to young Latin@s.[4] "Urban Latin@" is a euphemism for Latin@ youth who are either one-and-a-half generation or second generation (or more) and generally English or Spanglish speaking. The dichotomy between urban Latin@s and recent immigrants is emphasized by stations such as Telemundo, Galavision, and Mun2, which are creating very narrow archetypes of specific Latin@ identities. These representations of latinidad and authenticity raise the following question: Is the immigrant (who ironically generally lives in urban communities) or the urban Latin@ the real Latin@?

Julissa's move from Mun2, a station that is only carried by some cable companies, to BET, a Viacom-owned station that is part of most basic cable packages, was a major career move. The program *106th & Park* is a music video show where the studio audience actively engages with the host(s) while a countdown of the day's most popular videos plays in the background. In addition to the repartee between the hosts, the studio audience is also treated to interviews of popular musicians and actors, live performances, and on Fridays, live rap battles. Julissa shares the "look" of the majority of female hosts, guests, artists, and dancers on BET, and thus she has benefited from the nebulous distinctions between Afro-Latinas and other urban women of African descent: she has light-brown skin, long, usually straightened hair, and she dresses in a hip-hop high couture style. Julissa's ability to use English, Spanish, and Spanglish, however, also allows her to articulate the diversity of the diasporic experience in the United States.

Julissa's placement on the show 106th & Park can also be understood in the context of Harlem's history and the people who have inhabited it. By 1950 Harlem's Black population was dominated by people with roots in the United States (both northerners and southerners), Puerto Ricans, and people from the English-speaking Caribbean. Although those communities remained stable for several decades, since 1990 East Harlem has become increasingly less Puerto Rican and more Dominican, Mexican, West Indian, and West African. The neighborhood after which 106th & Park is named has experienced a constant flux of brown-skinned people, which has historically made it hard to say where Blackness begins and ends. Consequently, this neighborhood is a perfect representation of the overlap and nebulousness between so-called Black and Latin@ communities.

The music that is played on 106th & Park reflects the dominant musical lineup of BET's other shows: rap, hip-hop, R&B, occasionally reggae, and increasingly reggaeton. The rising presence of reggaeton on BET suggests that it is being accepted as Black music, albeit a different type of Black music from a different type of Black people. For example, in January 2005 BET aired a special called "Move Your Body: A Reggaeton Special." This special, which ushered in the mainstreaming of reggaeton to hip-hop audiences, chronicled the genre's roots, but it also provided insights into who BET perceives and expects its audience to be. The clip presented a narrative of reggaeton as a musical and cultural link—or hyphen—between Blacks and Latin@s, with N.O.R.E. (Noreaga of rap duo Capone-N-Noreaga) as the ideal mediator between two supposedly different worlds.

The emcee N.O.R.E., whose real name is Victor Santiago, has an Afro-American or Jamaican mother (there are conflicting narratives regarding his mother's ethnicity) and a Puerto Rican father, whose race is never discussed. It is simply assumed that his mother is Black and his Puerto Rican father is not; but how do we know that his Puerto Rican parent is not racially Black? And, to further problematize the issue, if his mother is indeed Jamaican, then why is she so often stripped of her ethnic identity and spoken of only as Black while his father's ethnicity is repeatedly emphasized? Despite the number of social commentators paraded through this television special, no one questioned the presumed racial differences between his two parents.

Performances of N.O.R.E.'s breakthrough reggaeton hit "Oye Mi Canto" are characterized by more flexible concepts of ethnic, racial, and national identities. In the music video for "Oye Mi Canto" from 2004, bikini-clad women of many shades carry flags from throughout Latin America. The concept of racial mixture is presented as gendered and the video uses women as a means of furthering that narrative. As Raquel Z. Rivera points out, Latinas are sometimes seen as a variation on Blackness, particularly since a light-skinned African American woman with "good hair" and a "mixed" racial ancestry would be hard to differentiate from the stereotypical image of a Latina.[5] As in the case of Julissa, the ethno-racial ambiguity of these attractive light-skinned women of African descent clearly accounts for much of their distinctive appeal.

The reaction of BET's audience to Julissa and reggaeton demonstrates the complexities of racial self-identification among Latin@s in a United States context. If Julissa were to simply sit silently, or was draped across the arm of the current rap star, her latinidad would not necessarily be apparent. However, Julissa is anything but silent, and she communicates her latinidad through the act of speech. Her use of Spanish marks her as distinctive, as a variation on United States–defined Blackness: a new Blackness, but Black all the same. Julissa's use of Spanish not only distinguishes her but also serves to extend a warm welcome to other Latin@s watching BET.

The welcome, however, was not as warm as the executives at BET hoped it would be, and when Julissa was chosen to be one of the interim hosts on 106th & Park, ethnic tensions between African Americans and Latin@ Blacks came into view. Heated discussions, postings, and petitions erupted on the Internet, bringing to the forefront the vexed issues surrounding the racial identities of Black people with roots only in the United States and other immigrants of African descent. One of the most popular hip-hop sites, for example, contained the following commentary: "Don't mean to be cruel but what's up with julissa being a host she's not Black do you think one of those spanish channels would hire an american Black person to host their shows i don't think so."[6]

An on-line petition with 281 signatures called for her removal from 106th & Park, employing both racial and racist commentary as well as critiques of Julissa's skill as an on-air commentator. Among those posting comments, one critic questioned BET's hiring practices: "In the whole U.S. there isn't one BLACK female qualified enough to co-host a show on BLACK Entertainment Television???." Further on, the position was dismissed as motivated by jealousy: "This petition is just Black females hating on a hot Latina. The majority of Black girls have an emotional disorder. Julissa just makes you feel inferior because you are. :-)."[7] Quite aside from the viciousness and offensive misogyny of this last comment, both posters make an explicit distinction between latinidad and Blackness. This distinction held sway even when race was considered irrelevant: "Black women are not hating on Julissa, I'm Latina and I STILL think she needs to go, please hire someone new, its not even about her race, she's just a boring host, that's all." All of which begs the question: How Black does an Afro-Latina have to be to be Black?

Despite such controversies, Julissa's position as a VJ on BET has clearly changed the relationship between BET and people of color. The BET Web site's news page has a section called "Black & Brown World," which includes news and pictorials on people of color from around the world. The channel BET Jazz, BET's sister station, also reveals a broader picture of BET's marketing strategy: almost a quarter of the programming on BET Jazz falls in their *Island Lime* framework by featuring music from throughout the Caribbean and Latin America.[8] Furthermore, the commercials on this channel include prominent foreign artists speaking either heavily accented English or Spanish.

The station BET is not simply changing how we racially define Latin@s, however, it is also challenging how we define Blackness. While the financial implications of catering to Latin@s is obvious, BET is casting a wider cultural net with its two channels and Web site than any other ethnic or race-based channel. I wonder about the implications for the future of this type of marketing. Intimate relationships between Black people, regardless of ethnicity, have already produced jazz, boogaloo, hip-hop, and now reggaeton, with each genre being intrinsically wrapped up in the politics of time and the place of interaction. Will I one day live in a world where I will (still) be flipping the channels and Telemundo will have Afro-Peruvians hosting programs and not just crying on the *Laura Show*?[9] Will I one day live in a world where BET will have a Siddi from India talking about the latest wave of Black pride spreading throughout India? Will any of these people be able to VJ a show on BET without their right to be there or their right to claim Blackness in question?

The reaction to Julissa's role as interim host on *106th & Park* and the reactions to reggaeton have shown us that there is still much work to be done before we can expect all people of color to see themselves as one multi-ethnic, multi-lingual community. At the end of the day, it seems that BET is inadvertently doing what many of us have been advocating for years: pushing the borders between Blackness and latinidad in order to accurately portray the ways in which the histories and identities of the members of these communities overlap. Julissa, reggaeton, and BET have complicated the tensions that exist between the numerous Black experiences and communities, and prompt us to seek, engage, and question new and old definitions of ourselves; we'll still be us, but just a little different, just a little new, a remix.

Notes

1. See Jorge Duany, *Puerto Rican Nation on the Move: Identities on the Island and in the United States* (Chapel Hill: University of North Carolina Press, 2001); and Silvio Torres-Saillant and Ramona Hernandez, *The Dominican Americans* (Westport, Conn.: Greenwood Press, 1998).

2. As of July 10, 2006, there were two new hosts of 106th & Park: Rocsi, a Latina, and Terrence J, a young man of African descent but unknown ethnicity. Rocsi, a native of New Orleans, is of Honduran and Chilean descent.

3. Silvio Torres-Saillant, "The Dominican Republic," in *No Longer Invisible: Afro-Latin Americans Today*, edited by the Minority Rights Group (London: Minority Rights Publications, 1995).

4. The programming on Mun2 includes shows such as 2RSLVJ (Tu eres el vj), where popular artists pick their favorite videos; *18 & Over*, an adult-themed video show; and *Reventón*, featuring the latest in Mexican and Chicano music.

5. Raquel Z. Rivera, *New York Ricans from the Hip Hop Zone* (New York: Palgrave, 2003).

6. http://www.sohh.com, no date.

7. "106 and Park Desperately Needs a New Female Co-host," http://www.petitiononline.com.

8. BET.com on TV, http://www.bet.com.

9. To be fair, in 2001 Telemundo was the first United States–based Latin@ news channel to have an Afro-Latina, Ilia Calderón, as a lead news anchor.

ALAN HUGHES AND MILCA ESDAILLE

The Afro-Latino Connection

Can this group be the bridge to a broadbased
Black-Hispanic alliance?

Cid Wilson had his first ugly run-in with racism as a teenager on a Friday afternoon. "One kid threw something at another kid," Wilson recalls. "The kid actually thought it was me." One of only eleven minorities in a senior student body of three hundred, Wilson recalls being called the "n-word" by the white teen.

"I was so infuriated with him," says the New York native. "The following Monday—it's something I'm not proud of—I looked for him and got into an actual physical altercation. That whole weekend, it was just building up inside, how angry I was."

Justifiably angry, Wilson's father was the voice of reason. James A. Wilson, a medical doctor, counseled his young son to handle racism in a more constructive way in the future: demand more of yourself and work twice as hard as your white counterparts.

Now a thirty-three-year-old Paramus, New Jersey, resident, Wilson took his father's words to heart and worked hard to excel. A former market analyst at Salomon Smith Barney, he is now a senior analyst at Whitaker Securities, a boutique investment bank, where he tracks past performance and future prospects of publicly traded stocks. Politically active, the NAACP member hopes to run for office someday. But the sting of that racial slur remains to this day.

Wilson's tale seems a familiar one to African Americans, except he's not African American. He's un puro (pure) Latino, whose parents immigrated to the United States from the Dominican Republic. Wilson, president of the Dominican American National Roundtable, is one of millions of America's Afro-Latinos who belong to both of the United States' largest minority groups. According to the U.S. Census Bureau, approximately 1.7 million of the 38.8 million Hispanics identified themselves as both Hispanic and of African descent, yet many believe this number to be much higher—closer to 3.9 million. (More than 42 percent of all Latino respondents marked a box labeled "some other race" on the census form.) Among the more famous Afro-Latinos are the Dominican baseball superstar Sammy Sosa, the retired Puerto Rican boxing champ Felix Trinidad, and the recently deceased Cuban salsa icon Celia Cruz.

And while historically attempts by Latinos and African Americans to forge economic, political, and social alliances have yielded lackluster results, it can be argued that this group—many of whom feel comfortable in both the black and Latino communities—could be the key to a much-needed business and political link between America's largest minority groups.

It's estimated that between 10 percent and 80 percent of Latinos who hail from countries like Cuba, the Dominican Republic, Colombia, Panama, Venezuela, Belize, and the United States territory of Puerto Rico have African ancestry. As the slave trade proliferated in the Americas from the 1500s through the 1800s, Europeans used Caribbean ports as a hub to transfer African slaves throughout North, Central, and South America, as part of the African Diaspora.

And some say Afro-Latinos have as much or more in common with African Americans as their lighter-skinned countrymen. Many regularly face discrimination and battle racism, both in the United States and in their native countries. Such disparaging terms as *negrito* (little black one), *pelo malo* (bad hair), or worse are commonplace for this group that often wields little political and economic power in their homelands. Poverty as well as poor educational and employment opportunities are high on the list of concerns to both African Americans and Afro-Latinos. However, the beginnings of a civil rights movement for blacks throughout Central and South America has come about fairly recently and Afro-Latinos are beginning to make some progress.

"In essence, white Latinos discriminate against black Latinos just like [white Americans] may do here," says Harry C. Alford, president and CEO of the National Black Chamber of Commerce. In order to effect change, Alford believes, "the 40 million blacks in this country need to start communicating better with the 135 million blacks in the Caribbean and South America."

The good news is that this group is beginning to come together to build a sense of pride in their African heritage by forming organizations and teaching others that Latinos come in all shades. "Blacks have already walked twice the miles we have walked," says Grace Williams, an Afro-Latino who is president of the Atlanta chapter of the National Society of Hispanic MBAS (NSHMBA). "We're starting to walk right now."

Interestingly, efforts to increase awareness regarding Afro-Latino culture and its plight can be found on the campuses of historically black colleges and universities (HBCUs). At Howard University, Nadine Bascombe heads Cimarrones, a fifty-member black student union of Caribbean, Central, and South Americans that recently expanded to include a chapter at Benedict College in South Carolina. Before Afro-Latinos can even begin to link the black-Hispanic communities, more Afro-Latinos must embrace their African heritage. "Within the population of what are considered Afro-Latinos, not all people identify with being black, so they'll join the Latino organizations because it's more of an assimilation of being white," says Bascombe, a junior. "It seems that if you relate yourself to being black it's something negative, so with that problem existing within the Afro-Latino population, not too many people run toward having an organization with that name."

Another HBCU, Spelman College, recently hosted a series of lectures, performances, and a conference looking at the African Diaspora and its impact on the Americas. A visiting group of Afro-Latinos from the Spanish-speaking nations of South America discussed their similarities based on common African heritages. "It seems [to be] apparent that Afro-Latins of various sorts see [African Americans] as role models with respect to political participation and economic success," says Sheila S. Walker, a professor of anthropology, who organized the event. "Their consciousness-raising and civil rights movements were inspired by their knowledge of ours."

There's no denying the merits of bringing these groups together from a business standpoint. "If we were to combine the African American and Hispanic community, it means a purchasing power block of one trillion dollars," says George Herrera, former president and CEO of the U.S. Hispanic Chamber of Commerce. "That kind of purchasing power and that kind of strength can basically make industry come to a standstill . . . power within our communities lays in our discretionary purchasing with corporate America, to be able to change the corporate landscape and change the dialogue of how corporate America deals with our communities." Herrera says this power can be used to affect corporate governance, procurement, and employment opportunities.

Currently, the state of black Hispanic relations in the United States is a mixed picture. Surely the media frenzy surrounding the emergence of the

Latino population as the largest minority group has lent itself to a contest-like atmosphere between the racial groups. There's also no denying that old prejudices and rivalries remain on both sides—bringing numerous challenges to overcome before any alliance can be formed.

In order for an alliance to succeed, a national agenda would have to be created that includes such issues as diversity, inclusion, and access to economic, political, and educational resources, according to Nicolas C. Vaca, a Harvard Law School graduate and the author of *The Presumed Alliance: The Unspoken Conflict between Latinos and Blacks and What It Means for America.* "Let's figure out exactly what each party needs and wants, what is important for each group, and then work out a plan for achieving it without the rose colored glasses," he recommends.

Efforts for alliances are being made on the political front. Members of the Congressional Black Caucus Foundation hosted members of the Congressional Hispanic Caucus, Congressional Black Caucus, and the Congressional Asian Pacific American Caucus in a small beach resort in Puerto Rico in October 2003. Politicians were invited for a weekend of social activities as well as political dialogue designed to foster cross-cultural understanding and facilitate the forging of common political agendas. This was the second gathering: the group met for the first time in 2002 at a New Orleans retreat.

"In order for us to work together and dialogue, we have to be able to interact, to get to know each other," says Congressman Ciro D. Rodriguez (D-TX), chair of the Congressional Hispanic Caucus. Rodriguez adds that the caucuses have worked to jointly draft a minority legislative health initiative that will be presented to senators Daschle and Kennedy.

In the meantime, hopefully, Afro-Latinos will continue on the path to becoming an economic and political force, and by doing so bring the Hispanic and black communities together. This is something Cid Wilson hopes to see. "We can honestly say we know what it's like to feel racism and discrimination—on the Latino and the African American sides," he says. "The way to build bridges is to get involved in both communities."

Whether these bridges are eventually built remains to be seen. Hailing from different countries with different cultures, the movement toward a stronger sense of Afro-Latino unity and identity must pick up speed. There is no doubt that challenges will abound, but the potential rewards are too promising to dismiss.

We spoke with several prominent Afro-Latinos to better understand the issues they face daily. Here's what they had to say.

The Cuban-American actress Gina Torres's television credits include recurring roles on the FOX drama 24 and ABC's *Alias*, as well as appearances on *Law & Order*, *The Agency*, and *Angel*. In nearly all her roles, however, she plays an African American. She hopes to take on more Latina roles in the future.

"I've gone out for several [Latina] roles," says Torres, who recently had cameo appearances in the highly successful *Matrix Reloaded* and *Matrix Revolutions* films. "It has not been my experience thus far that the people that have the power to make those [casting] decisions are ready to embrace a Latina who is dark. They like to keep it simple. You don't want complicated when you're trying to sell gum. You want to say 'that is a black person,' 'that is a Latin person,' 'that is a white person.' Everybody looks like they came from where they're supposed to come from. Let's not complicate that."

The Bronx-raised Torres admits that she gets annoyed when people assume she's not a full Latino. "That it's so out of the realm of possibility that somebody like me can be all Latina. Both my parents were born in Cuba; they came over in the mid-50s before the revolution."

Torres, who married Laurence Fishburne in 2002 after they met on the set of *Matrix Reloaded*, views her work as contributing to the struggle and making a difference. "I often say I didn't become black until I became a professional actress. It's when I realized I wasn't the Latina that America was comfortable with. I'm still not. Inside of the industry, it's changing slowly," she says. "The darkest Latina that first had name recognition was Rosie Perez, but because she sounded familiar no one made a big deal out of it. But the image the business perpetuates and is still most comfortable with is Jennifer Lopez, as was Rita Moreno in her day."

Torres says that she is comfortable with serving as a bridge between the black and Latino cultures. "As a people, we are both certainly much stronger if we align . . . we all want our children to grow up in a better place and to have better opportunities than we did," she says. "We all want the same things, we all hit a similar wall in terms of being viewed [against] standards that were set up so long ago, that we continue to bust out of and redefine. I am proof that it works."

At an early age, Maria Perez-Brown learned to live in two worlds. Born in Puerto Rico then moving to Brooklyn at the age of six, she lived in what she describes as a segregated neighborhood. "One block was all Puerto Rican and the other block was all black," she recalls. "I felt early on that my identifying quality was not only that I was Latina, but that I was a black Latina from an urban experience, with much more in common with my black friends from my neighborhood than with my Puerto Rican cousins from Puerto Rico."

In the early 1990s, Perez-Brown left the corporate world for the world of television. Now she is a successful television producer. Among her credits is creating and producing *Gullah Gullah Island*, which ran for six years and was named one of the top-ten television shows for children by TV *Guide* in 1996. She was also the creator and executive producer of *Taina*, a comedy series that aired from 2001 to 2002 on Nickelodeon about a fifteen-year-old Latina caught between two cultures: that of her traditional Latino family and the modern world of her school and friends. Perez-Brown uses her insight into both cultures to breathe life into characters that are believable and real.

"Sometimes you look at Latino shows and Latino characters in American television and you have a Jewish writer from the Upper East Side or from Los Angeles purporting to write what he thinks is a character that's Latino," she says. "What results many times is an insulting and very offensive stereotype of a character. At no point did they think it was important to find an authentic voice to write that character, or to integrate their writers, which is a pet peeve in my industry."

If African Americans and Latinos were to form lasting alliances via the Afro-Latino connection, Perez-Brown believes perception is the first thing that needs to be addressed. "The moment you start creating an image that these two groups are separate and have separate interests, you start creating a rift that allows people to divide and conquer," she says. "We can have, wield, 25 percent of the population—that is huge political power. That is a huge economic force that could make a much bigger difference than we could separately."

Embracing His Heritage

Though he's a *Black Enterprise* 100s executive, Frank Mercado-Valdes remains rooted in the Latino community. As CEO of the Heritage Networks (no. 61 on the *Black Enterprise* industrial/service 100 list, with $61.5 million in revenue) he often laments the fact that with the exception of baseball programming, Afro-Latinos are nearly nonexistent on television—even on Latino programs.

"In Latino broadcasting we're invisible because Latino broadcasting is Mexican-centric and Mexicans really don't have many blacks—they have certain pockets of Mexico where there are black populations who have been there a long time," he says, "but for the most part, you won't see black people in anything Mexican."

The son of Cuban and Puerto Rican parents, Mercado-Valdes says blacks in Latin America have an even lower standing socially than African Americans did prior to the civil rights movement. "There never was a Dr. King, a Malcolm X, or a Stokely Carmichael," says the Bronx native. "So some of them come here and shed their identity and what happens is they merge with the greater white Latino community rather than with the black community."

Mercado-Valdes's Latino heritage has influenced his business decisions. "My business niche was the African American community at first," he recalls. "I've changed the name of my company from the African Heritage Network to the Heritage Networks because I wanted to get into the perpetuation of English-language Latino programming." The syndicated network includes original properties such as *Showtime at the Apollo*, *Livin' Large*, and *Weekend* VIBE, as well as *Resurrection Boulevard*, a drama set in Los Angeles with a Latino cast.

And though he has seen prejudice firsthand in his industry, he still gets upset when he experiences it from the African American community. "I think the most frustrating thing comes from the black side of the equation—not the white. I've never had white people say 'you're not really black, are you?'" he says, "I'm always thinking 'when did I stop being black because my last name is Mercado or Valdes?'"

Mercado-Valdes says that the Afro-Latino community could be a powerful ally to both the African American and Latino communities once more civic, business, and political leaders emerge. "It's one of the things that I feel I should have been more active in that I feel like I haven't been," he confesses. "I spent so much time being black I forgot I was Latino."

VIII

Afro-Latin@s in the Hip Hop Zone

As with any new field of group identity, it is the youth and young adults who have been the first to embrace Afrolatinidad. The cultural sensibility that accompanies this new group reality and designation has been set by hip hop. Since its inception in the late 1970s and 1980s — as evident in the founding hip hop films *Wild Style* and *Style Wars* and as described in

Eli Efi and DJ Laylo performing at the Trinity International Hip-Hop Festival, Hartford, Connecticut, April 2007. (Photograph by Cassandra Vinograd; courtesy of Cassandra Vinograd)

the articles by Raquel Rivera and Pancho McFarland—the hip hop "zone" has been one of strong Afro-Latin@ cultural expression, with its main exponents and stylistic forms issuing from the collaborative creativity of African Americans and Caribbean Latin@s. Though the role of Afro-Latin@s tends to be erased or minimized, through the decades they have contributed to multiple innovations in rap, break dance, and graffiti and have been instrumental in the forging of a diasporic hip hop sensibility, one which questions, among other things, a facile notion of pan-Latin@ identity. Reggaeton, the most popular musical style in the new millennium, and well described in the essay by Wayne Marshall, is clearly a sequel to rap and still within the hip hop zone. But with its Spanish-language lyrics and meshing of diverse Caribbean styles, it appears to be even more pronouncedly Afro-Latin@ in a transnational sense, rather than African American with a Latin@-Caribbean admixture. David Lamb's novel centers on the Afro-Latin@ dilemma—from an African American perspective significantly titled *Do Plátanos Go wit' Collard Greens*—and is clearly conceived in the framework of hip hop expressivity, and the audiences attending the popular theatrical version of the book are strongly Afro-Latin@ in ethnic composition and are reared in the hip hop zone. We close the section with another sample of "hip hop literature," an episode from Sofia Quintero's novel *Divas Don't Yield*.

RAQUEL Z. RIVERA

Ghettocentricity, Blackness, and Pan-Latinidad

The people of Puerto Rico are African descendants in the same way that
the so-called slaves that they brought to [the United States of] America.
That's why we understand we are the same people and we are happy to
see our brothers representin' themselves [in hip hop].
—Dead Prez, *In the House* magazine

Journalist and poet Kevin Powell poured out a heartfelt lament in the pages
of *Vibe* magazine in which he grapples with the contradictions inherent in
what he identifies as one of the 1990s' hottest trends in U.S. popular culture in general and commercial rap music in particular: the mass marketing and glamorizing of the violence and pain of Black "ghetto" life. It dis-
tresses him that poor people's real-life tragedies are being packaged and
sold through music, television and film. But what haunts him the most is
what he perceives as a dangerous trend among young Black people: the up-
holding of a stereotypical "ghetto" mentality as a badge of honor and the
equating of that mentality with Blackness. "Suddenly, it's the move to be
from the ghetto (even if you aren't), to speak the ghettocentric language
(even when it sounds like you frontin'), and to proclaim the ghetto as the
true source of black identity—some of us call it 'representin.'"[1]

Written from the point of view of a hip hop participant, Powell's article
is an indictment of the pervasiveness within rap of a discursive and performative Blackness defined through a stereotypical "ghettocentricity."[2]
He concludes by stating that if blunt-smoking, gun-packing, forty-ounce
drinking and calling one another "niggas" and "bitches" are what the
ghetto and, by extension, Blackness are about, then "we're participating
in our own self-destruction, in true ghetto style."

Powell's article speaks to a change in rap's commercial trends. The
Afrocentric emphasis in rap of the late 1980s started shifting toward a

more ghettocentric approach in the early 1990s.[3] African Americanness did not cease to be a crucial identity marker within rap's discourse, but it became more narrowly identified as a ghetto Blackness: As Christopher Smith notes, "Rap's agenda since PE's [Public Enemy's] heyday has shifted largely from a generic concern for chronicling the black experience to one specifically about the black underclass in the ghetto. In rap's dominant market paradigm, blackness has become contingent, while the ghetto has become necessary."[4]

Focusing on West Coast "gangsta rap" during the earlier half of the 1990s, Robin D. G. Kelley ponders the confluence of class and race within the genre through artists' usage of the term "nigga":

> More common, however, is the use of "Nigga" to describe a condition rather than skin color or culture. Above all, "Nigga" speaks to a collective identity shaped by class consciousness, the character of inner-city space, police repression, poverty, and the constant threat of intra-racial violence fed by a dying economy. Part of NWA's "Niggaz4Life" on Efil4Zaggin for instance, uses "Nigga" almost as a synonym for "oppressed." In other words, "Nigga" is not merely another word for black. Products of the postindustrial ghetto, the characters in gangsta rap constantly remind listeners that they are still second-class citizens— "Niggaz"—whose collective lived experiences suggest that nothing has changed *for them* as opposed to the black middle class. In fact, "Nigga" is frequently employed to distinguish urban black working-class males from the black bourgeoisie and African Americans in positions of institutional authority.[5]

Although Kelley focuses on the commercially dominant West Coast sound of the earlier 1990s and Smith on the East Coast-based rap of the mid-to-late 1990s, both describe the same class-based narrowing of the concept of Blackness as expressed through rap.

Commercial rap's focus shifted from a Blackness primarily defined through (a narrow, nondiasporic take on) African American history and ancestry to one based more on contemporary socioeconomic conditions and lived culture (as opposed to "traditional," "inherited," or "ancestral" culture). As this shift was taking place, a slight relaxing of the ethno-racial scope of Blackness also occurred. The Blackness formerly restricted by the bounds of an ethno-racialized African Americanness began expanding to accommodate *certain* Latino groups as a population of ethnoracial Others whose experience of class and ethno-racial marginalization is in many ways virtually indistinguishable from the ghettocentric African American

Tony Tone, LA Sunshine, and Charlie Chase at Norman Thomas High School, Bronx, New York, 1980. (Photograph by Joe Conzo, Joe Conzo Photo Collection)

experience. Such Latinos could even be perceived as closer to this class-based Blackness than so-called bourgie (bourgeois) Blacks, particularly in the case of Caribbean Latinos such as Puerto Ricans, given the growing acknowledgment that they are also part of the African diaspora in the Americas.

While during the late 1980s and early 1990s hip hop frequently was described by African American participants as "a Black thing, you wouldn't understand," starting in the mid-1990s it became increasingly common to hear hip hop explained in everyday conversation, as well as in mass media and academic forums, as a "Black and Latino" phenomenon.[6] Today's near-dominant convention of describing hip hop culture—and within it, rap—as "Black and Latino," and the increased commercial visibility of Latinos/Latinas within hip hop, would not have come about had it not been for this shifting conception of Blackness that emphasizes the ghetto experience.

The short-lived MTV animated series *Station Zero*, which first was broadcast in 1999, is only one of many manifestations of this move toward the re-inclusion of Latinos as core participants in hip hop culture. The TV show featured both African American and Latino teenage characters who engaged in different facets of hip hop creativity. Journalist Joel Sosa described the character "Chino" as "definitely not afraid of his Latino

Ghettocentricity, Blackness, and Pan-Latinidad 375

heritage, he freely uses Spanish without translating for the Spanish impaired."[7] What a change from the late 1990s and even the early 1990s. What would have probably been considered back then a Latino segregationist tactic and a gesture of linguistic exclusion toward African Americans was by the late 1990s being celebrated as a sign of hip hop authenticity. New York Latinos began being acknowledged as tightly linked to hip hop's history and subsequent development. Chino was not only a "Hip Hop conscious character" struggling for artistic freedom and integrity in the face of commercial exploitation; he was also a South Bronx Latino from the very Soundview housing projects that have been central in hip hop history.

The movie *Whiteboyz*, released in 2000 and starring Danny Hoch, presents another good example of the closing hip hop legitimacy gap between Puerto Ricans and African Americans. Slick Rick, Mic Geronimo, Doug E. Fresh, Snoop Dogg, Fat Joe and Dead Prez represent the hip hop ghetto "realness" that white, rural Iowan main character Flip Dog fantasizes about. From Flip's point of view, there is no difference between Fat Joe and the rest of the rappers, even though the first is a light-skinned, green-eyed Puerto Rican and the others are dark-skinned African Americans. Flip views them all with equally adoring eyes.[8]

By the 1990s, young people of all ethno-racial affiliations, including whites, were hip hop producers and consumers. Furthermore, Blackness as signified through class-specific "nigganess" was being celebrated by many hip hop enthusiasts, regardless of their ethno-racial background. As KRS-ONE ironically commented in his popular 1995 song "MCs Act Like They Don't Know," nowadays even white youngsters call themselves "nigga." But KRS does not let his listeners forget that "White" kids' appropriation of Black language and their participation in hip hop culture takes place within a context of White supremacy, where still "the crosses burn."

By the latter part of the 1990s, rap was a central part of mainstream U.S. pop culture, a genre with multiethnic audiences all over the globe and immersed in the politics of the transnational music industry. Still, hip hop "authenticity"—based on a class-identified Blackness/nigganess—continued to be contentious ethno-racial territory, and its borders were zealously policed by its participants. The ethno-racial scope of "authenticity" expanded somewhat but only to incorporate—although not always smoothly—the "Latino" experience. This expanded ethno-racial scope was tightly woven in with contemporary socioeconomic structures.

Pee Wee Dance in DJ Tony Touch's *Tape 45* described hip hop culture as an expression of Black and Latino creativity, but warned that rap was a "white manifestation" of a longing to profit from that expression. Through his brief contribution to this 1995 mix tape, Pee Wee Dance highlights the ethno-racialized economic contentions between the Blacks and Latinos at the axis of hip hop creativity versus the "White" power structure that has taken one element of hip hop (rap), pulled it from its sociohistorical context and profited from it more than the main creators themselves.

During the second half of the 1990s, Latinos commonly were attributed a proximity to Blackness that was thought of as a product of social, political and economic circumstances, circumstances that have led to shared lived and historical experiences in the ghetto with African Americans. David Perez, a Bronx Puerto Rican who has directed videos for rap artists A Tribe Called Quest, Cypress Hill, House of Pain, Brand Nubian, Diamond D, Beastie Boys, KRS-ONE and others, explains how his growing up as a working-class Puerto Rican in New York granted him authenticity in the hip hop realm: "I look sort of white so I have to establish myself. Gotta let them know where you're coming from, what you saw when you were growing up. Then all of a sudden, they look at you, and you're light-skinned. You could be Italian Jewish, Greek. Then after you establish yourself, you become *authentic*."[9]

But Latino authenticity was not only conceived within hip hop in terms of socioeconomic structures; it was also constructed as related to Afro-diasporic ethno-racial identities, cultural history and cultural formations. The Off-Broadway production *Jam on the Groove* by GhettOriginal provides a pertinent example.[10] The cast of this hip-hop theater production consisted mostly of African Americans and Puerto Ricans, and included some of New York City's better-known Puerto Rican dancers—Crazy Legs, Ken Swift, PopMaster Fabel, Honey Rockwell, Mr. Wiggles, Rokafella, and Kwikstep. One of its pieces, entitled "Concrete Jungle," celebrated hip-hop's dance element as an expression of joy and an outlet for creativity in a context of urban blight and police brutality.

In "Concrete Jungle," a b-boy and b-girl battle is the venue where technique and inventiveness are displayed as well as a site where tensions and rivalries between African Americans and Puerto Ricans are manifested. The battle is interrupted for a moment as the offstage voice of a police officer demands that they disperse while calling them "a bunch of savages" and "nothing but shit." The dancers ignore the cop and the battle continues. The voice bursts out with another string of insults and threats, but the dancers still refuse to disperse. Gunfire rings out, as the dancers try to escape. All but one are gunned down. The sole survivor proceeds to bring everyone back to life with the beat of a drum. "Concrete Jungle" is partly an indictment of the racialization and marginalization of Latinos and African Americans as the "savages" that inhabit the New York inner-city "jungle." It also celebrates the common Afro-diasporic cultural ground of African Americans and Latinos—the drum is upheld as a symbol of tradition as well as a tool for joint present-day struggle.

But these Afro-diasporic identities shared by African Americans and Latinos involve only a sector among Latinos, namely Afro-diasporic ones. To talk about shared experiences and identities in ghettos in the United States means we must distinguish the intense similarities between African Americans and Puerto Ricans in New York from the comparatively more distinct experiences of Chicanos and African Americans in Los Angeles or Chicago and from the completely divergent experiences of African Americans and Cubans in Miami. This may seem all too obvious, yet it is another example of the specificities that are smothered under the seductive weight of the pan-Latin discourse.

The sense of a Black and Latino "us" in hip hop is intimately related to the experiences of African Americans and Caribbean Latinos—particularly Puerto Ricans—in New York City. In the words of El Barrio-raised Puerto Rican DJ and producer Frankie Cutlass: "Puerto Ricans, we grew up with Blacks. I go to the housing projects that's all you see. . . . a lot of Puerto Ricans and Blacks." [11] That is why, he says, ghetto-raised Blacks and Puerto Ricans are so similar that often they are virtually impossible to distinguish one from the other. In response to a question about the similarities in the experiences of Blacks and Latinos in the United States, Cutlass extricates his experiences from those of the Latino aggregate since he does not feel he can "speak for another culture." He feels he can talk only from his Puerto Rican vantage point.

Cuban Link, a rapper and member of the Bronx-based Terror Squad (whose most popular members are the Puerto Rican rappers Fat Joe and the late Big Punisher) answered a journalist's inquiry regarding "Latino involvement" in hip hop by discarding presumptions of pan-latinidad and narrowing down the concept to refer only to Caribbean Latinos: "It's the Caribbean Connection, baby. Puerto Ricans, Dominicans, Cubans, all. We're coming together and it's something you've got to see to believe." [12]

The explicit avowal by popular rap industry personalities and media—magazines like The Source, XXL, Blaze, Stress, and Ego Trip and rap video shows like BET's Rap City—of the historical presence and importance of New York Caribbean Latinos within hip hop has been crucial in the process of the widespread Latino legitimation as bona fide core members of the national hip hop "community" and not just *arrimaos* (interlopers) attempting to "be Black" or do a "Black thing."[13] And since latinidad often is viewed as the primary and "natural" focal point of identity for all Latinos, the fact that New York Caribbean Latinos have had the historical presence in hip hop has been automatically extended to encompass Latinos as a whole.

The acknowledgment of hip hop in both the academic and journalistic literature as an urban Black and Latino cultural expression has suffered from the perils of pan-ethnic abstraction. In the haste to rescue Latinos from historical invisibility and to acknowledge their current role within hip hop, essentialized connections—often enough based on stereotypes and exoticization—are drawn, and crucial differences among groups within the Latino pan-ethnic conglomerate are slighted.[14] The role played by New York Puerto Ricans in hip hop culture has been different from that of other Caribbean Latino groups in New York; the differences are even greater when Puerto Ricans are compared to Chicanos and other Latinos on the West Coast. But these specificities have become obscured by the growing force of *la gran familia latina* (the great Latino family) discourse within hip hop. The historical and current connections between Afro-diasporic Latinos and African Americans in New York are at times muted or even drowned out by the naturalizing call of pan-latinidad.

A 1998 feature article in *Industry Insider* magazine illustrates the case in point. Chang Weisberg, its author, laments that "Latinos in hip hop have always seemed like second class citizens in an art form they helped create," and he tries to find out why.[15] Throughout the article, Weisberg enthusiastically writes about the "sense of family" manifested among the "Latino brethren" and "Latino hermanos" who are meeting at an *Industry Insider*-sponsored summit of Latino hip hop artists. Brought together under the assumption of a family bond—Weisberg billed the summit as a "family reunion"—many of the artists themselves also celebrate in their statements the ascribed bond of latinidad.

According to Jack from the West Coast group Psycho Realm: "Since we're all Latinos, it's like we're all family." Big Punisher also alludes to a latinidad-based notion of family: "It's Latino first. That's more important than East/West. That's familia. That's La Raza." Fat Joe elaborates: "Since we're Latino, I feel that we're all spiritual in a way. It doesn't matter if you're Mexican, Puerto Rican, Cuban, Columbian [sic], or whatever. We've got something that's real different from many other cultures. No matter what's going down, we always stick together. It's about time we did this. Hopefully, we'll keep gettin' together like this and show everybody love.

It doesn't matter if you're from the West Coast or the East Coast. We're Latino. You know what I mean? We cut across all that shit."[16]

Fat Joe, Jack, Punisher and most of the other artists interviewed by Weisberg weave a family-based narrative of unity among Latinos that relies more on future projections than on lived experiences, particularly as it applies to Latinos involved in hip hop culture. Fat Joe's statement that "No matter what's going down, we always stick together" and Pun's statement that "Latinos look out for one another" express what *should be* rather than what *actually is.* The virtual lack of collaboration—particularly cross-coastal—among these artists and their vowing to work in unison *from now on* exposes this celebrated Latino unity as either still forthcoming or wishful thinking.[17] Besides, considering the article's explicit acknowledgment of "misunderstandings" and "differences" that formerly existed among some of the participating artists, the summit can be seen as more of a makeup session ("to squash beef," as Frost says) than as yet another manifestation of love and support among the Latino "familia."

Although cloaked in the benevolent, comforting and naturalizing mantle of family, the Latino unity that these artists are advocating is as much a commercial necessity and market strategy as a spiritual, familial or historical imperative. Marginalized within what Fat Joe terms a "Black business," the only option for Latinos, as expressed by most artists at the summit, is to work together and "help their own." Son Doobie, a West Coast–based Puerto Rican and a member of the group Funkdoobiest, says: "whether it's black media owned by white folks or black media owned by black folks, I know everybody wants to help their own. Basically, what we've done now is helped ourselves to the table because nobody was going to give it to us. It's time for Latinos to shine because we've been down since day one."[18]

The artists and Weisberg stress throughout the notion that Latinos have been key in hip hop since "day one." Although the Latinos who participated in hip hop's earliest history were specifically Caribbean Latinos and overwhelmingly New York Puerto Ricans, the Latino aggregate as a whole reaps the claim to hip hop historical presence and authenticity. A transcoastal, transnational Latino "us" enables this collectivization of the experience of a sector within the Latino population. The article, by not even nodding in the direction of regional and ethnic—as opposed to pan-ethnic—specificities, makes it seem as if Latino artists in different regions and of different ethnicities have faced the same obstacles and issues.

Weisberg, in his mission to celebrate Latino rap artists and hip hop culture in general, constructs a mythical pan-ethnic bond between Latino artists and portrays hip hop as a democratic, utopian space where the media is the big bad wolf: "If music is truly universal, then hip hop is its purest expression. It doesn't matter if you're Black, White, Catholic, or Gay. Hip hop has always been the cultural melting pot of free expression and open dialogue. The watering down and deterioration of hip hop's infrastructure lies in the fact that its education is left in the hands of the media."[19]

Weisberg fails to explore the tensions among Latino groups as well as those existing between African Americans and Latinos—tensions that are as much a part of hip hop history as transethnic solidarities and multiethnic cultural creation. This forced sense of harmony leads him to ignore gender power dynamics within it and even to make the ludicrous claim that homosexuality is a nonissue in hip hop.

Kevin Baxter, in a 1999 article for *The Source* suggests that the fact that "Latin culture suddenly bec[a]me so hot" in commercial terms in the late 1990s has to do with "demographics" as well as "the recent political awakening of the Latin community." Baxter mentions several movements and initiatives to illustrate "Latino" political mobilization: the Chicano Moratorium of 1970, the United Farm Workers during the 1960s and 1970s and the more recent mobilizations against California's Proposition 187.[20]

Since Baxter restricts his comments to a few West Coast–based, Chicano-dominated examples, readers unfamiliar with the topic get a myopic introduction to the history of Latino political mobilization. They may think that "Latino" political mobilization has been restricted to the West Coast, or perhaps that the movements mentioned are representative of the interests and efforts of Latinos across the nation. Baxter fails to mention, even peripherally, New York's long history of African American and Puerto Rican joint political struggles—a political history that complements an equally long history of joint cultural production of which hip hop is a part.

This type of identity-building substitutes an abstract discourse of Latino pan-ethnic solidarity in place of a more regionally based, lived-experience approach where, in the case of New York Caribbean Latinos, urban Afro-diasporic identities dominated. As the mass media visibility and momentum of a largely Hispanocentric essentialized pan-latinidad grows, so do the perceived differences between Caribbean Latinos and African Americans. Caribbean Latinos are assumed to have experiences, histories, identities and solidarities that "naturally" place them within the pan-Latino aggregate. This is not to say that there is no longer within hip hop culture a sense of an "us" between African Americans and Caribbean

Latinos in New York, or that Puerto Ricans and other Caribbean Latinos do not also resist the presumption that they share a primary, "blood"-based ancestral bond with other Latinos and only a secondary or circumstantial one with African Americans. For Puerto Ricans within hip hop, latinidad and Afro-diasporic Blackness are at times parallel, at times intersecting identity discourses; sometimes they coexist while, at other times, they may compete.

The clashing of Latino and Afro-diasporic identities is not unavoidable, for they are not mutually exclusive identities. The problem is that they are often posed as such, forcing a nonsensical choosing of sides. Ethnoracial rifts between Caribbean Latinos and African Americans within hip hop have been informed to a great extent by a larger social context in which latinidad and Blackness are often held to be nonintersecting. Hip hop, nevertheless, has been one of the contemporary social realms where Caribbean Latino Blackness has been grappled with and celebrated the most.

Whether taken up by elected officials, government bureaucrats, academics, journalists or activists, contemporary discussions of poverty, political and economic empowerment, social marginalization, crime, the prison-industrial complex and police brutality—to mention only a few issues—center around these two groups. So even in the midst of this essentializing of the pan-Latino bond, the notion of shared conditions and the need for a strategic alliance between African Americans and Latinos is not lost. Most often it is not deemed a "natural" or "primary" bond— like those among Latino groups—but one dictated by necessity. As Fat Joe states in Weisberg's article: "We can't change the world, but we want people to notice the importance of Latinos in hip hop. I want people to notice the power that we have in this industry. I want people to look at the bigger picture and realize that this isn't just about Latinos either. We need Blacks and Latinos to get together to show the strength of this hip hop game, we need to be the majority not the minority. Everybody needs to understand we're on the same fucking page."[21]

The combination of this discourse of Latino pan-ethnicity within hip hop with the sense that Blacks and Latinos are "on the same fucking page" has had the seemingly contradictory effect of extending hip hop authenticity—signified by a ghettocentric "nigganess"—to include all Latinos, but at the same time deepening the rifts between Caribbean Latinos and African Americans. Pan-latinidad has, oddly, "niggafied" certain Latino groups, such as Chicanos, through their association with New York Caribbean Latinos. Pan-latinidad also has meant, in the case of Puerto Ricans, that a group that was instrumental in hip hop's development and that had been historically associated with African Americans can now be held as nonblack under the assumptions of pan-latinidad.

These paradoxes are related to diverging assumptions about who Latinos are and what latinidad means. The union of Black and Latino under a hip hop "us" is thrown around more often than it is actually grappled with. Different assumptions can be at play when invoking that "us." Based on the Chicano model, one of these assumptions is that Latinos are "browns" who near Blackness, by virtue of sharing a parallel ghetto experience with African Americans (not necessarily sharing the same ghettos) and by virtue of their multiracial (heavily indigenous) makeup.[22] Another assumption regarding the conceptual underpinnings of latinidad is more specifically concerned with Caribbean Latinos in New York, who do share a ghetto experience with African Americans (most often the same ghettos) and an Afro-diasporic culture—thus their being even closer to Blackness.

The increasingly common reference to hip hop as a "Black and Latino" form of cultural expression cannot be understood without dwelling on the ethno-racial categories used to expand inclusiveness beyond African Americans. Puerto Ricans and other "Hispanic" Caribbeans, although Afro-diasporic peoples, are, in general, not considered and do not consider themselves "Black." Black, in its common usage in the United States as an ethno-racial category, is a synonym for African American. Exceptions are made, though, in the case of English-speaking Caribbeans. If the boundaries are stretched even more, even Francophone Caribbeans can be considered Black. But Spanish-speaking Caribbeans are a totally different story, for they are associated with the "Latino" or "Hispanic" categories rather than with Blackness or even the looser Afro-diasporic blackness. Thus, to acknowledge the historical and present role of Puerto Ricans and other Caribbean people, hip hop is explained as "Black and Latino."

Hip Hop as "Black and Latino"

Some academic commentators have restricted their discussions of Blackness, marginality, and ghettocentricity within rap to African Americans,[23] others have included Latinos as coparticipants in rap's discursive and performative constructions.[24] Most frequently, the latter are content to describe rap as a Black *and* Latino phenomenon but mention nothing about the specificities—or lack thereof—of the "Latino" experience in hip hop. Is there no mention of Latino specificities because these two groups engage—and are engaged by—Blackness in the same fashion? Or are Latinos mentioned as coparticipants due to their historical and/or contemporary importance, but the subsequent discussion of Blackness applies only to African Americans?

Christopher Holmes Smith describes rap in his article's introductory paragraph as "an expressive outlet for a marginalised and demonised urban social bloc that speaks with heavily black and Latino, predominantly masculine accents, within a staunchly white and patriarchal social order."[25] A few pages later he refers to hip hop's "African-American and Afro-Caribbean artisans." Still later he states that although rap is a contemporary expression of an "ancient African oral tradition," it is not the product of a single ethnic culture.

One of Smith's primary focuses is on exploring hip hop performance as it relates to Blackness, and he frequently refers to the African American experience. Although Smith introduces rap as an expressive form that is predominantly "black and Latino," he focuses on rap's relationship to a Blackness that is discussed solely in terms of African Americans. So where does that leave Latinos with respect to Blackness? How do they relate to and fit into it? Is this a Blackness that includes Latinos? And if that is the case, why does Smith focus only on African Americans?

It is hard to answer these questions without venturing into speculation. Smith never explains why, although he describes Latinos as coformulators, with African Americans, of rap as an "expressive artistic outlet," he never mentions them again. Is it because Latinos are included within the bounds of the Blackness being discussed or because they exist/create outside the scope of Blackness? Who are these Latinos anyway? Smith does mention another group, aside from African Americans and Latinos, as a key participant within rap when he refers to hip hop's "Afro-Caribbean artisans." Should we then assume that the "Latinos" Smith writes about are Afro-Caribbean Latinos?

Unlike Smith, other authors have made explicit their understanding of rap's internal ethno-racial dynamics when it comes to the relationship between Blackness and latinidad. Tricia Rose, for example, in her book *Black Noise* contextualizes hip hop within "Afro-diasporic cultural formations," where "Spanish-speaking Caribbean" youth are explicitly included within the African diaspora.[26] Edward Sunez Rodríguez also avoids discussing an abstract latinidad whose relationship to Blackness is unclear or unspoken, by honing in specifically on Afro-diasporic Latinos.[27]

In Smith's case, it is not at all clear if the Blackness he talks about includes Latinos (and if it does, how). Peter McLaren on the other hand, seems to imply that "blackness" and "Latinoness" are distinct but parallel ethno-racial experiences that inform rap music: "Gangsta rap is concerned with the articulation of experiences of oppression that find their essential character among disenfranchised urban *black and Latino* populations. . . . Here, blackness (or *Latino-ness*) marks out a heritage of pain and suffering."[28] But he never explains why.

Whatever reasons authors may have for not addressing how Latinos relate to rap's ghettocentric Blackness this omission leaves a lamentable gap in the literature. Is "Latino" merely the ethnic label for a group that exists within this ghettocentric Blackness? Are Latinos outside the scope of Blackness?

Notes

1. Kevin Powell, "The Ghetto," *Vibe* 3, no. 10 (December-January 1995): 49.

2. See Robin D. G. Kelley, "Kickin' Reality, Kickin' Ballistics: Gangsta Rap and Post-industrial Los Angeles," in *Droppin' Science: Critical Essays on Rap Music and Hip Hop Culture*, edited by William Eric Perkins (Philadelphia: Temple University Press, 1996), 117–58; Peter McLaren, "Gangsta Pedagogy and Ghettoethnicity: The Hip Hop Nation as Counterpublic Sphere," *Socialist Review* 25, no. 2 (1995): 9–55; and David Samuels, "The Rap on Rap: The 'Black Music' That Isn't Either," in *Rap on Rap: Straight-up Talk on Hip Hop Culture*, edited by Adam Sexton (New York: Dell Publishing, 1991), 241–52.

3. See Todd Boyd, *Am I Black Enough for You? Popular Culture from the Hood and Beyond* (Bloomington: Indiana University Press, 1997); and Christopher Holmes Smith, "Method in the Madness: Exploring the Boundaries of Identity in Hip Hop Performativity," *Social Identities* 3, no. 3 (1997): 345–74.

4. Smith, "Method in the Madness," 346.

5. Kelley, "Kickin' Reality, Kickin' Ballistics," 137.

6. See Reginald Dennis, liner notes for *Street Jams: Hip Hop from the Top, Part 2* (Los Angeles: Rhino, 1992); Roberto "Cuba" Jiménez, "Vanishing Latino Acts," *The Source*, no. 95 (August 1997): 22; Juice (TC-5) Lascaibar, "Hip Hop 101: Respect the Architects of Your History," *The Source*, no. 95 (August 1997): 47–48; McLaren, "Gangsta Pedagogy and Ghettoethnicity"; and Smith, "Method in the Madness."

7. Joel Antonio Sosa, "Station Zero: Animation for the Hip Hop Nation, *Urban Latino Magazine* 4, no. 2 (1999): 50–51.

8. However, the fact that there is only one Latino artist among Flip's rap dream team does point to the low numbers of commercial Latino rappers in a music realm overwhelmingly populated by African Americans.

9. Mandalit del Barco, "Latino Rappers and Hip Hop: Que Pasa," National Public Radio documentary, aired September 10, 1991 (emphasis added).

10. *Jam on the Groove* ran during 1995 at PS 122 in the East Village and the Minnetta Lane Theater in the West Village. The company also did an international tour. See Gabriela Bousaada, "Breaking In," *Village Voice*, August 22, 1995, 75; Jon Pareles, "Review of *Jam on the Groove* by Ghettoriginal," *New York Times*, November 18, 1995, 19.

11. Miguel Burke, "Puerto Rico . . . Ho!!! Frankie Cutlass," *The Source*, no. 90 (March 1997): 132.

12. James "Chase" Lynch, "Holdin' It Down," *Urban Latino Magazine* 3, no. 1 (1998): 34.

13. This reassessment of Latino participation did not spring up out of nowhere. Even before it became common to speak of hip hop as "Black and Latino," certain sectors held a vision of hip hop history that ran counter to the then-dominant construction of hip hop as exclusively African American.

14. For example, on the cover of the August 1999 edition of *Source* magazine, an article on the duo Beatnuts was subtitled "Dos Vatos Locos," thus assuming that West Coast Chicano self-referential terminology can be automatically made to apply to these New Yorkers of Dominican and Colombian background.

15. Chang Weisberg, "Hip Hop's Minority? Latino Artists Unite and Speak Out," *Industry Insider* 15 (1998): 50–51.

16. Ibid., 55.

17. In further illustrating that this is trumpeting of a Latino unity that has yet to materialize, Weisberg wonders, "Why haven't Latino artists worked on more projects together?" His assumption is that Latino artists *should* want to work together, and since there have been very few projects of such kind, it must be due to obstacles that should be overcome.

18. Weisberg, "Hip Hop's Minority?" 54.

19. Ibid., 51.

20. See Kevin Baxter, "Spanish Fly: Latinos Take Over," *The Source*, no. 113 (February 1999): 136–41.

21. Weisberg, "Hip Hop's Minority?" 55.

22. See Boyd, "*Am I Black Enough for You?*"; Roberto 'Cuba' Jiménez, "Vanishing Latino Acts," *The Source*, no. 95 (August 1997); William Eric Perkins, "Youth Global Village: An Epilogue," in *Droppin' Science: Critical Essays on Rap Music and Hip Hop Culture*, edited by William Eric Perkins (Philadelphia: Temple University Press, 1996), 263.

23. Nick De Genova, "Gangsta Rap and Nihilism in Black America: Same Questions of Life and Death," *Social Text* 13, no. 2 (1995); Errol Henderson, "Black Nationalism and Rap Music," *Journal of Black Studies* 26, no. 3 (January 1996): 308–39; Kelley, "Kickin' Reality, Kickin' Ballistics."

24. See Smith, "Method in the Madness"; and McLaren, "Gangsta Pedagogy and Ghettoethnicity."

25. Smith, "Method in the Madness," 345.

26. Tricia Rose, *Black Noise: Rap Music and Black Culture in Contemporary America* (Hanover, N.H.: Wesleyan University Press, 1994), 189.

27. Edward Sunez Rodríguez, "Hip Hop Culture: The Myths and Misconceptions of This Urban Counterculture" (1995 manuscript).

28. McLaren, "Gangsta Pedagogy and Ghettoethnicity," 33–34 (emphasis mine).

PANCHO MCFARLAND

Chicano Rap Roots

Afro-Mexico and Black-Brown Cultural Exchange

In 1992, the 500th year of the European presence in the Americas, Mexico officially recognized Africa as the "third root" (la tercera raíz) of its hybrid (mestizo) society and culture. Meanwhile, throughout the Mexican diaspora in the United States, Chican@s carved out a new musical culture by borrowing from and transforming a new world African culture, hip hop. By 1992, Chican@s had been rapping, break dancing, deejaying, and writing graffiti for a decade. In that year Kid Frost (later Frost), the godfather of Chicano rap, released his second compact disc, Eastside Story. One year earlier, another important rap innovator, the group Cypress Hill, released its debut album, Cypress Hill. Much like in the sixteenth century, mixed-raced Amerindians (Chican@s) and New World Africans (United States Blacks) live side by side as a result of a new economic and political order. Under Spanish colonial rule Africans and indigenous Americans remade cultures in diaspora and through mestizaje and mulataje (cultural or biological mixing involving Africans in the Americas). In the postindustrial, neo-colonial new world order, Chican@s and African Americans borrow and transform aspects of their cultures to create hip hop on the West Coast.

Chicano rap texts (music, lyrics, style, and interviews) illustrate a new millennial mestizaje/mulataje consisting of Mexican/Chican@, African (American), and European (American) elements. Analysis of the work of Kid Frost, Cypress Hill, and South Park Mexican (SPM) reveals a complex encountering of cultures that made the genre, Chicano rap, and that signals a rapidly growing trend in United States society. Hip hop culture has created a situation in which youth of Mexican and African descent in the United States can overcome obstacles to interracial communication and develop interethnic alliances that challenge the ways we think about race, culture, and politics.

New Millennial Mestizaje/Mulataje:
Diaspora, Mixture, and People of Color

Today, more than twenty million people of Mexican descent in the United States continue the process of adaptation, resistance, and hybridization that we know as mestizaje. Cultural mestizaje, our ability to adapt and survive under conditions of colonialism, became a badge of honor during the Chicano Movement of the 1960s and 1970s. We proclaimed ourselves a brown people, a mixture of Spanish and indigenous blood and American and European cultures.[1] We are a product of imperialist violence yet we survived to create something new, the Chican@s.

The Chicano Movement historian Carlos Muñoz acknowledges that Mexican mestizaje has become more complex over time, as intermarriage between Mexican Americans and people of other races increases with close proximity. He is one of few who acknowledge this more complicated notion of mestizaje. Unfortunately, Muñoz and others do not pursue the documentation of such processes. Thus, in popular and scholarly discourse, mestizaje is understood simply to refer to Spanish-indigenous mixing. Because the concept has such a long and well-accepted history, I use a new term to describe the processes of Black and Chican@ interaction that created rap and a new Chican@ identity associated with postindustrial urban living and youth culture. *Mestizaje/mulataje* suggests a further mixing of Chican@ culture and identity, one that has occurred in the late twentieth century in the urban centers of the Southwest. By adding the term *mulataje* to *mestizaje* I intend to suggest that African Diasporic cultures and peoples have been central components of syncretism and hybridization in Mexican societies, especially in postindustrial Mexico America.

Youths of color growing up in inner cities in the United States during the 1980s and 1990s had the task of maturing and developing self-conception in a period of intense denigration of their identities. This period saw what many have called a war on youth of color perpetrated by governments that, in some cases, criminalized young people's very existence. Young people who looked a certain way, listened to rap music, or had certain types of tattoos were criminalized through informal (police and private citizens singling them out and labeling them as criminal) and formal means (legislation that did not allow them to congregate or be out at certain hours). All inner-city youth of color experienced this type of racism. In the face of such denigration of their identities, young people created a subculture with a new set of values, morals, aesthetics, and identities that they imbued with positive characteristics. Today's hip hop nation consists of youth of color who identify with the music, their racial and ethnic identities, and a new mixed-race/culture worldview. Where kids of various racial and ethnic backgrounds interacted in hip hop venues (shows, concerts, clubs, street corners, youth clubs), an identity was formulated that foregrounded their common culture and marginalized their (ethnic) differences. For Chican@s, this process results from centuries of both positive and negative interactions with Africans.

From Son to Rap: Mestizaje/Mulataje in Mexico America

Beginning with Aguirre Beltran's 1946 publication of *La población negra de México* (The Black Population of Mexico), scholars have documented and shed new light on the importance of Africans to the creation of the Mexican state and culture. In 1503, the first Spanish slave ship brought Africans to the Americas; by the end of slavery in Mexico during the first half of the nineteenth century, between 250,000 and 300,000 Africans had been legally transported to Mexico (tens of thousands more were likely smuggled into Mexico), making Africans the second most populous racial group (after the indigenous group) during the colonial period.[2] With such a large presence in Mexico, Africans undoubtedly helped shape Mexican culture and Mexicanness. However, as a result of a strict racial hierarchy and later governmental initiatives to erase Blackness from Mexican national identity, the African presence in Mexico was ignored in order to focus on a Spanish-indigenous mestizaje.[3] African influence on Mexicanness is far reaching; it includes culinary, linguistic, musical, and epistemological contributions. Intermarriage and miscegenation between Africans, Amerindians, Spaniards, and Asians was also important. Key political figures such as Mexico's second president, Vicente Guerrero Saldaña, as well as José María Morelos, hero of Mexican independence from Spain, were of African descent.

Importantly for this study, Mexican musics were greatly influenced by Africans. Marco Polo Hernández Cuevas shows how "the jarocho son, the mariachi, the fandango . . . all have black African roots at the point of origin along with Amerindian, Spanish and other roots."[4] Using historical documents, Hernández Cuevas shows how rhythms, audience participation, dance, and instruments traveled from an African context to the Americas and became part of Mexican expressive culture. The Afro-Cuban son tradition serves as the foundation of two of Mexico's most important national musics, jarocho and mariachi.[5] Jarocho and mariachi music, along with African-influenced instruments such as the marimba, jarana, cajón, and tarima, have become symbols of Mexican national pride and have been identified internationally with Spanish-indigenous mestizaje.[6] Thus, the mariachi music and lyrics and dances that many non-Mexicans and Mexicans alike associate with Mexican Spanish-indigenous mestizo culture have roots in African aesthetics. The music, dance, and worldview that Mexicans brought with them in their journeys to the United States contain Africanisms that would influence Chican@ culture throughout the twentieth century and into the twenty-first.

During the twentieth century, Chican@s and United States Blacks continued the process of mestizaje/mulataje, which began during the colonial period. Here, during periods of increased interracial communication and exchange, United States denizens of African and Mexican descent shared in the creation of unique and influential youth subcultures. Gaye Johnson writes that "for as long as they have occupied common living and working spaces, African American and Chicano working-class communities have had continuous interactions around civil rights struggles, union activism, and demographic changes."[7] Matt García's research illustrates how young people have shared cultural knowledge and practices and built a common youth culture, even when residential segregation and the complex and contradictory web of racisms experienced by both groups erected barriers between them. He points out that Los Angeles dancehall promoters of the 1940s recognized that a new generation of Mexican Americans not only enjoyed Latin music styles but were also drawn to the popular swing music of the time. Swing was the music of choice for the young Mexican, Black, Filipino and White working-class practitioners of zoot culture. Dance promoters seized upon the popularity of swing and zoot culture and showcased popular swing bands at multiracial dances. In the 1950s the popularity of rock-and-roll music continued to draw a multiracial youth audience to dances. García argues further that "the racial/ethnic intermixing facilitated a blending of cultural influences . . . [and created a music that] possessed a broad-based, cross-cultural appeal, which facilitated understanding among a racially diverse audience."[8]

Such multiracial youth interaction in the middle part of the twentieth century resulted in a process of cultural exchange and borrowing that birthed low-rider culture, rock-and-roll music, and contemporary gang and street culture.[9] Both García and Johnson argue that the resultant youth subcultures challenged racial prejudices and stereotypes. García found that intercultural dancehalls along with interracial socializing at school and participation in multiracial political organizations led to improved relations between Blacks and Chican@s.[10] García's informants stated that they began to date interracially. One interviewee remembered the El Monte dancehall as "a melting pot," where interracial dating was not uncommon.

Certainly, relations between the two groups have not always been ideal. As a result of the competition for scarce resources and their uncritical acceptance of racist stereotypes imposed upon people of color by the racist, capitalist United States society, an uneasy tension and high levels of animosity have also characterized the relations between Blacks and Chican@s. Times of economic instability in the United States tend to increase racial animosity because Chican@s and Blacks are positioned among the lowest in the labor and social hierarchies, thereby increasing each group's socioeconomic difficulties and thus competition between them. Incredibly, against these odds in the middle of the 1980s, brown and Black inner-city cultural exchange led to the development of Chican@ rap and hip hop scenes throughout the Southwest. From Los Angeles, the center of Chicano rap, to small towns like Pueblo, Colorado, young Chican@s began break dancing, rapping, and deejaying. Clearly, a new mestizaje was developing.

Chicano rap and hip hop began in the early 1980s when Sugar Hill Gang's "Rapper's Delight" (1979) introduced youth of Mexican descent to the new cultural phenomenon developing in the Black and Latin@ and Chican@ barrios of New York. With this song, Chican@s and others across the Southwest were finally able to hear rap. "Rapper's Delight" and a string of early rap classics traveled quickly across the Southwest. Hip hop culture proved infectious as Chican@ and Black youth throughout the Southwest flocked to join it. By the early 1980s, following the popularity of several hip hop movies including Wildstyle, Breakin,' Breakin' II, and Beat Street, hip hop culture was firmly entrenched in many Chican@ and Black communities.

As hip hop traveled west, Ice-T and N.W.A. created a new gangsta sound. Kid Frost followed their successes with the release of Hispanic Causing Panic in 1990. With it, Frost had the first recorded Chicano rap album and the first hit, "La Raza."[11] In the same year, Lighter Shade of Brown (LSOB) dropped Brown and Proud. By 1993, the production team behind Kid Frost's and LSOB's success, G-Spot Studios, and its founder, Tony G, had a résumé that included Frost's second (East Side Drama, 1992), ALT's early albums (Another Latin Timebomb, 1992, and Stone Cold World, 1993), and LSOB's second (Hip Hop Locos, 1992). Proper Dos, a group unaffiliated with G-Spot, released Mexican Power in 1992 as well.[12] The mid-to-late 1990s saw an explosion of recorded Chican@ rap, with the music being embraced and recorded in Los Angeles to San Diego, the San Francisco Bay Area, Albuquerque, Denver, Houston, Chicago, and other locations throughout Greater Mexico.[13] Important innovators such as the Darkroom Familia, Low Profile Records, South Park Mexican, and the Cypress Hill network expanded the musical, thematic, and lyrical content of Chicano rap. In the new millennium, Chicano rap artists and entrepreneurs have continued to change the face of Chican@ hip hop culture and rap music. The Chican@ rap mestizaje now includes Brown Pride online and Digital Aztlán; the revolutionary discourse of the Divine Forces radio show and Web site; and a number of Chicano rappers and DJs from the Midwest including Los Marijuanos, DJ Payback García and Kinto Sol, and Los Nativos. An analysis of rap texts will help us more fully understand contemporary Chican@ indebtedness to Africa and African Diasporic cultures.

The Soul of Chicano Rap Music

When rap exploded across the country in the 1980s, Chican@s easily identified with the new cultural movement's social and economic conditions as well as its complex rhythmic foundations. The polyrhythmic layering at the heart of rap musical production was familiar to Chican@ youth who listened to their parents' cumbias and mambos and their older siblings' explorations of soul and funk music. Chican@s also have a long history of listening to the "oldies," the great Black soul music of the 1950s, 1960s, and 1970s often reinterpreted in rap. The strong presence of samples and interpolations of African Diasporic music in Chicano rap suggests the strong influence that Black cultures have had on Chican@ youth. Moreover, the music's heavy bass, polyrhythms, and "noise" are necessary elements to tell the stories of postindustrial urban America. "Noise" or using multilayered urban sounds as part of the musical backdrop signifies on the noisy and chaotic urban experience of youth of color.

Chicano rap music producers utilize African polyrhythmic structures as the basis for their musical production. In particular, Chicano rappers and rap producers have an affinity for using funk beats and samples in their music. This is no surprise given that the rise of recorded Chicano rap follows directly in the footsteps of the G-Funk sound of West Coast rappers and producers such as Dr. Dre. Dr. Dre pioneered the use of the funk beats and guitar riffs of James Brown's and George Clinton's groups, creating the West Coast sound.[14] Early innovators developed G-Funk so that hip hop aficionados could listen to the music in their cars. The culture of low riding found a musical companion in the slow grooves of G-Funk. Brian Cross writes that Dr. Dre always tests his music in his car to make sure it has the right mix of musical elements.[15]

While the Los Angeles Chicano rap artists such as Slow Pain, Frost, and Brownside, and others such as the San Francisco Bay Area's Funky Aztecs, borrow directly from Dr. Dre's G-Funk sound and 1970s funk, many are also fond of rapping over "laid-back" soul grooves. The sultry singing and lush instrumentation of 1970s soul provide another musical and thematic palette from which Chicanos draw. In just one album Slow Pain recognizes Marvin Gaye, Mary Wells, the O'Jays, and Smokey Robinson, funk pioneer Rick James, and new soul singers Keith Sweat and R. Kelly. Frost names some of his musical influences as Teddy Pendergrass, Earth, Wind and Fire, and Al Green. The electronic funk of the 1980s exemplified by groups like Cameo, Roger Troutman, and Zapp also provides Chicano rap with musical inspiration.

Chicano rap vocal delivery is also influenced by the vocal styles of important Black rappers. The most influential rap artist is Tupac Shakur. The flow, vocal inflections, language, and subject matter of several Chicano rappers owe their existence to Tupac's innovations. Slush the Villain, Don Ciscone (who worked with Frost on his 1999 and 2002 albums), Latino Velvet, and some Low Profile artists sound like Tupac reincarnate. Other rappers, including Frost and Brown Huero of the Brown Town Looters, publicly recognize Tupac as an important influence. On "Tha Strong Survive" from *The Ollin Project*, Brown Huero implores us to listen to Tupac's (aka Makaveli) political critique on his song "Blasphemy" from his posthumously released C D *The Don Killuminati: The Seven Day Theory*. Blunts Lla's ("step n 2 tha sun," also on *The Ollin Project*) political analysis of urban Chican@ living and his shouting of political slogans on the outro of the song draw on Tupac's style, which in turn drew upon the African American oratory tradition of Black preachers and social movement leaders.

Further, the Funky Aztecs and Tupac recorded the song "Salsa con Soul Food," which illustrates the type of inter-racial collaboration found by García and Johnson. Tupac adds a level of complication to African American and Chican@ relations in his verse as he criticizes the police for fearing positive Black-brown social relations. On "This Is LA" Delinquent Habits, a group that includes Kemo—a self-labeled "Blaxican" (biracial, Black and Mexican)—sample Tupac's "To Live and Die in L.A.," in which he acknowledges the important contributions of ethnic Mexicans to Los

Angeles by rapping that L.A. would not be the same without them. Tupac's lyric demonstrates the manner in which cultural exchange, borrowing, and transformation flow in many directions.

From the multiracial interaction apparent in much of hip hop culture, new understandings of race, politics, gender, and morality continue to develop. While these new understandings are not always liberatory or progressive (witness the extreme misogyny, homophobia, violence, and materialism of much of today's popular rap music), they have the potential to chart a new course in racial understanding between Black and brown people. The interracial cooperation at the root of Chicano rap has allowed for the destruction of debilitating racial barriers in this era when Black and brown people are forced to compete for valued resources such as jobs, housing, and education. The music of Frost, SPM, Cypress Hill, and others bears witness to the mestizaje/mulataje developing in Southwestern inner cities and to the choices of affiliation made by youth of color that challenge racial categorization.

Further, analyzing Chicano rap's new millennial mestizaje/mulataje using a lens that redefines Mexicanness or *mexicanidad* through inclusion of the Third Root of African influence allows us to see more clearly the colonial processes that have subjugated, subordinated, and destroyed people of color since 1492. The colonial experience brought people from Africa, America, and Europe together under a racial and economic caste system. Remarkably, new cultures resulted from intercultural exchange, communication, and conflict. Unfortunately, the African contribution to Mexican mestizaje/mulataje has been made invisible. Under the contemporary neocolonial new world order, Amerindians and Africans are once again mixing and melding. Out of the oppressive conditions of neglect, racism, and open hostility, Black and brown youth are creating new ways of thinking, seeing, and believing infused with the multiracial, resistant politics of the beat.

Notes

1. See Guillermo Bonfil Batalla, *Mexico Profundo: Reclaiming a Civilization* (Austin: University of Texas Press, 1996); and Carlos Muñoz, *Youth, Identity, Power* (London: Verso, 1989).

2. Hundreds, perhaps thousands, of Africans later escaped slavery in the United States by migrating to Mexico.

3. Marco Polo Hernández Cuevas, *African Mexicans and the Discourse on Modern Nation* (Lanham, Md.: University Press of America, 2004).

4. Ibid., 31–49. *Jarocho* is the term applied to the offspring of Amerindian and Black parents in Veracruz.

5. Ibid., 42–45.

6. The *tarima* is a wooden platform that is used as a drum by dancers in Mexican *ballet folklórico* who pound out rhythms with their feet. It is believed that the *tarima* was first used by Africans deprived of their drums in the Americas (ibid., 45).

7. Gaye T. M. Johnson, "A Sifting of Centuries: Afro-Chicano Interaction and Popular Musical Culture in California, 1960–2000," in *Decolonial Voices: Chicana and Chicano Cultural Studies in the Twenty-first Century*, edited by Arturo Aldama and Naomi Quiñonez (Bloomington: Indiana University Press, 2002), 316.

8. Matt García, "Memories of El Monté: Intercultural Dance Halls in Post-World War II Greater Los Angeles," in *Generations of Youth: Youth Culture and History in Twentieth Century America*, edited by Joe Austin and Michael N. Willard (New York: New York University Press, 1998), 163.

9. See García, "Memories of El Monté"; Steven Loza, *Barrio Rhythm: Mexican American Music in Los Angeles* (Urbana: University of Illinois Press, 1993); and John Yamaoka, director, *The History of Hydraulics* (video, 1998).

10. García, "Memories of El Monté," 164.

11. Kid Frost recorded the first known Chican@ rap, "Rough Cut." Reagan Kelly writes that the song was cut in 1984, but Frost states in an interview with Brian Cross that he recorded the song in 1981. See Reagan Kelly, "Hiphop Chicano: A Separate but Parallel Story," in *It's Not about a Salary: Rap, Race and Resistance in Los Angeles*, edited by Brian Cross (London: Verso, 1993).

12. Mandalit del Barco and Reagan Kelly provide thorough histories of early Chicano rappers. See Mandalit del Barco, "Rap's Latino Sabor," in *Droppin' Science: Critical Essays on Rap Music and Hip Hop Culture*, edited by William E. Perkins (Philadelphia: Temple University Press, 1996); and Kelly, "Hiphop Chicano."

13. "Greater Mexico" is a term associated with the work of Americo Paredes and has since been used by many Chican@ studies scholars. The term implies the people, territory, and culture of Mexico and the extension of Mexican-origin people, culture, and territories in the United States where ethnic Mexicans have an important presence.

14. Robin D. G. Kelley, *Race Rebels: Culture, Politics, and the Black Working Class* (New York: Free Press, 1994), 189.

15. Brian Cross, ed., *It's Not about a Salary: Rap, Race and Resistance in Los Angeles* (London: Verso, 1993), 35.

WAYNE MARSHALL

The Rise and Fall of Reggaeton

From Daddy Yankee to Tego Calderón and Beyond

That beat you've been hearing—the steady *boom-ch-boom-chick* rattling the trunks of passing cars and moving masses in the club—isn't just another fleeting hip hop trend. It's the new sound of the Americas. Make way for reggaeton, the latest Latin musical style to sweep the world and just maybe the one with the most promise of finding a permanent, prominent place not just in the United States, but in global popular culture.

Reggaeton has already accomplished something that other Latin musical forms—son, mambo, salsa, merengue, bachata—never quite attained: not only has the music ignited the imaginations of young Latinos and Latinas, but it has found unprecedented favor in mainstream United States culture. Just a few years ago the Spanish one heard on non-Latin commercial radio was limited to "Feliz Navidad" and "La Vida Loca"; now one hears fifteen to thirty minute blocks of Spanish-language pop on the same stations that promise nothing but "blazin' hip hop and R&B."

Indeed, reggaeton's inroads into hip hop's media channels may prove crucial in the genre's ability to transcend, all hype aside, the "craze" status that has marked previous spikes of interest in Latin music. In contrast to the exotic cast that has consistently marked Latin music packaged for non-Latin audiences, reggaeton enjoys a sonic profile that, for all its syncopation and sway, is heard as something more familiar, more modern, more American (in the United States–centric sense). Reggaeton artists and producers have not simply piggybacked on the success of their hip hop brethren, they have exploited and expanded hip hop's *hustle-hustle* business model, especially in such areas as shameless self-promotion, savvy cross-branding, street-team marketing, and grassroots distribution.

Reggaeton lacks much of an exotic veneer precisely because the music has not been marketed to Anglo-American audiences. At least until recently, reggaeton has been music produced by and for the pan-Latin@ community. On the main it still is, though many artists and producers now aspire to the platinum plaques that million-sellers such as Daddy Yankee and Luny Tunes have proven are within reach. Reggaeton's self-sustaining relationship to a sizeable core audience draws our attention to the most obvious underlying reason for the genre's seemingly sudden ubiquity: simple demographics.

You've heard it before: one in eight people in the United States speaks Spanish, with much higher rates in cities, while "Hispanics"—although something of a constructed category, perhaps more useful to politicians, and far from monolithic—have surpassed African Americans as the nation's largest ethnic group, with census-based projections predicting that 20 percent of the country's population will be of Hispanic origin by 2020. Latin@ migration is also increasingly circular, especially for Puerto Ricans who as United States citizens can travel within the country relatively unfettered. One effect of these seismic socio-cultural shifts is that a number of cities in the United States, especially along the coasts, have become veritable centers of the pan-Latin@ community, and the sound-scapes of New York, Miami, Boston, and other sites of migration reflect this growing presence with their cosmopolitan musical hybrids, of which reggaeton represents the latest and greatest.

So it's little surprise that the top reggaeton releases now sell in the hundreds of thousands, reggaeton performers sell out major venues across the country, and formerly ecumenical pan-Latin@ radio stations have been adopting the new, reggaeton-centric "Hurban" (Hispanic-urban) format. But perhaps even more significant is reggaeton's massive grassroots following. The music offers a set of sounds and symbols so broadly appealing that it appears to be fueling the broadest pan-Latin@ youth movement to date, which is unprecedented in its reach and appeal. From New York to Miami, Roxbury to Lowell to Springfield to Cambridge, and Cuba to Colombia to Chile, young Latinos and Latinas are using reggaeton music and style to articulate a sense of community. They are producing their own recordings, performing and marketing their music in local and regional scenes, trading mp3s and samples on the Internet, and infusing what is already a vibrant movement with exuberance, vitality, and new accents.

As a modern sound, a sound intimately related to hip hop and reggae, reggaeton gives Latin@ youth a way to participate in contemporary urban-American culture without abandoning important aspects of their heritage. This may help to explain why a Latin-Caribbean form—and not, say, a Mexican or Chicano style—has managed to captivate young Latin@s in a way that norteño never has, despite the fact that Mexican Americans constitute well over 60 percent of the Hispanic population in the United States.

Alongside the hopes and dreams of the would-be Don Omars and Ivy Queens are the hopes and dreams of record execs, media mavens, mass marketers, and other opportunists hoping to cash in on the phenomenon. With Daddy Yankee already a major commercial force on Universal, and Tego Calderón's Atlantic debut due out this year, reggaeton is poised to become a truly massive musical and cultural force.

A Brief History

Before the term "reggaeton" was coined, it went by the humbler, less marketable "Spanish Reggae" or Reggae en Español. Traveling along mass media circuits as well as diasporic networks, Jamaican popular music spread around the world in the 1960s and 1970s. Reggae arrived in places like Panama and Puerto Rico as quickly as it reached more traditional centers of migration, such as London and New York. In the case of Panama, which proudly claims reggaeton as its own, Afro-Panamanians — many of them the descendants of Jamaican migrant workers — had been performing and recording Spanish-language reggae since at least the 1970s. Tens of thousands of Jamaicans moved to Central America in search of work in the late nineteenth century and early twentieth. Having contributed to the building of the Panama Canal, many settled on Panama's Caribbean coast, maintaining connections to Jamaica even as some adopted Spanish as their native tongue. By the late 1980s and early 1990s, Afro-Panamanian artists such as El General and Nando Boom were making waves by adapting the latest dancehall reggae hits for Hispanic audiences, loosely (and sometimes closely) translating the lyrics and often singing the same, recognizable melodies over the original, Jamaican-produced riddims.

These musical translations found favor not simply in Panama but, crucially, in such pan-Latin@, pan-Caribbean centers as New York City, where Panamanians and Jamaicans mingled with Puerto Ricans, Cubans, Dominicans, and African Americans, and where such hybrid, resonant styles as Spanish-language reggae could find a receptive audience. In Puerto Rico, where rappers such as Vico C had pioneered Spanish-language hip hop, these Jamaican-inflected "translations" of popular dancehall songs had wide appeal. Dancehall reggae had already established a strong following in Puerto Rico in its own right by the early 1990s, as popular songs by Jamaican deejays such as Shabba Ranks, Cutty Ranks, and Chaka Demus

& Pliers helped to redefine the sound of contemporary club music. It was, in fact, a Shabba Ranks song, "Dem Bow," produced by Bobby Digital, which would lay the foundation for what became known as reggaeton. The underlying instrumental (i.e., *riddim*) for "Dem Bow," a minimalist production with catchy percussion, became an overwhelming favorite in Puerto Rican freestyle sessions, to the point where, for a time, Spanish-language reggae in Puerto Rico was simply called Dembow. Vocalists drew on a variety of styles, borrowing from dancehall, hip hop, and various Latin musical traditions and creating a distinctive synthesis. By the mid-1990s, a catchier tag came along, and reggaeton began to describe what was emerging as far and away the most popular music for lower-class Puerto Rican youth, at home and in the United States.

Reggaeton isn't only a snappy marketing label, it also served to distinguish a uniquely Puerto Rican style from such precursors as Latin hip hop and Reggae en Español. In this sense, the music's Panamanian roots notwithstanding, Puerto Rico does have a special claim to reggaeton. It was but a skip and a jump before it found widespread support among Hispanic youth in the United States. Circulating via channels of migration and— increasingly and importantly—on the Internet, reggaeton soon became the sound of a generation, finding footholds in a number of United States cities with significant Latin@ populations.

With a building presence in clubs and on radio in New York and Miami, a couple of breakthrough hits were all that reggaeton needed to introduce its sensuous sounds to the mainstream. With its Spanglish verses and overt pan-Latin@ pride, New York–based rapper N.O.R.E.'s "Oye Mi Canto," featuring Nina Sky and the reggaeton stalwarts Tego Calderón and Daddy Yankee, explicitly pushed and promoted reggaeton to what had become—thanks to 2003's banner year for dancehall—a reggae-friendly audience. Climbing the charts soon thereafter, Daddy Yankee's "Gasolina" became the kind of pop anthem that no one could ignore (or avoid), convincing hip hop moguls from Lil Jon to Diddy to get in on the action. In the last few years, on the heels of these hits, reggaeton has spread across the United States and the globe, but especially in Latin America, where the music's transnationalism, for all its power to animate expressions of pan-Latin@ identity, sometimes comes into conflict with national identities, as when Puerto Ricans and Panamanians debate claims over origins, or when Cuban reggaeton producers bemoan the dominance of Puerto Rican style.

Reggaeton's unmistakable *boom-ch-boom-chick* relates directly to the late-1980s and early 1990s dancehall reggae that inspired it, though it is not unreasonable for people to hear such syncopations as somehow inherently "Latin." Indeed, Jamaican reggae itself, like so many other Caribbean and American genres, bears a strong relation to Latin-Caribbean music, especially Cuban son, a genre that contributed many stylistic features to calypso and other popular music of the twentieth-century Caribbean tourist industry. One finds essentially the same rhythmic patterns, with different accents, in nearly all Caribbean pop, a product of the region's shared African, European, and indigenous cultural heritage, a high degree of inter-island migration, and more recent patterns of convergence. The same 3 + 3 + 2 subdivision that cuts compellingly across a steady 4/4 pulse can be heard and felt in Jamaican reggae and mento, Trinidadian soca and calypso, Haitian meringue and konpa, Puerto Rican bomba and plena, Dominican merengue and bachata, Cuban son and mambo, and, among others, Nuyorican salsa.

Still, for all its connections to related styles and historical precedents, reggaeton brings some new features to the table. As an utterly electronic style—usually produced on computers, drum machines, and keyboards—reggaeton embraces new possibilities for a high-tech, post–hip hop, Latin Caribbean aesthetic. This can best be heard in the unconventional approach by reggaeton producers to the snare drum. Whereas a typical recording, even in a sample-based genre such as hip hop, usually employs a single snare drum sound, reggaeton producers revel in the ability to draw from dozens of their favorite snare samples, frequently employing several in the course of a single song. By switching the snare sound every eight measures or so (and foregrounding it in the mix), they give form to what might otherwise be repetitive, subtly shifting the mood of the music in mid-verse or from verse to chorus. Reggaeton is undeniably a product of the digital age, and the genre's predilection for space-age synths, techno-indebted kick-drum crescendos, and sound effects gives the productions an unmistakable modern edge.

Reggaeton also represents a break from earlier Latin music in that it appears to have fostered a greater dialogue with non-Latin forms such as hip hop and reggae rather than the popular Spanish-language genres it has supplanted. Hip hop's emphasis on drums and reggae's taste for bass serve as cornerstones of the music. Contemporary dancehall reggae is still a vital source: reggaeton artists continue to make use of the newest riddims to emerge from Jamaica. (Ivy Queen's hit "Quiero Bailar," for instance, employs the "Liquid" riddim, produced by the Jamaican crossover guru Jeremy Harding.) And the "Dem Bow" remains a staple as it turns up in a remarkably high percentage of reggaeton tracks, sometimes quite explicitly and sometimes as a more subtle addition to the overall rhythmic texture. Indeed, reggaeton's use of the "Dem Bow" as a common building block recalls the frequent use of the "Amen" break in drum'n'bass or the "Drag Rap (Triggerman)" beat in New Orleans bounce.

If there's a prevailing sameness about the sound of reggaeton today, it's mainly a testament to the dominance of the Luny Tunes production duo. But if Luny Tunes appears content to rehash the same synth-patches, the same riffs and bass lines, and the same drum patterns, it reflects the tradition of creative reuse that takes the Jamaican example of "re-licked" riddims as a model. Just as Lenky's "Diwali" riddim, in various guises, produced a number of hit songs (Sean Paul's "Get Busy," Wayne Wonder's "No Letting Go," Lumidee's "Never Leave You"), the galloping beat for "Gasolina," especially with new layers added or prominent riffs removed, can provide a solid foundation for any number of new songs. The best reggaeton songs to date succeed not so much by offering new sounds to listeners but by using already resonant synths and samples in novel ways and leaving space for vocalists to display their creativity over familiar forms.

Nevertheless, reggaeton has become increasingly ecumenical in its approach to sample sources. Bachata, the popular Dominican genre known for its emotional ballads and plucky guitars, has been finding its way into a growing number of reggaeton productions, while salsa remixes of reggaeton hits have become common. A new song by Tego Calderón, whose *El Abayarde* (Sony International, 2003) contained interludes performed to the Afro–Puerto Rican sounds of bomba and plena, features a mix of percussive styles that point to Afro-Cuban forms as well as other Afro-Latin traditions. Given its links to hip hop and dancehall, it's not surprising that a number of recent reggaeton riddims employ the sort of "orientalist" flutes and strings that have marked so many pop songs of the last few years. And, of course, as reggaeton continues its pop ascension, reaching more and more middle-class ears, it will no doubt be shaped and styled for that audience—a penchant for overwrought singing, borrowed from pop-salsa balladry as well as *American Idol*-style shows of gospel-fried virtuosity, has already begun to take hold. In the end, the music's consistency may prove to be its greatest strength, offering an omnivorous stylistic template to producers: drop anything from a salsa break to a sitar line under that ol' *boom-ch-boom-chick* and you've got reggaeton.

Representin' (in the Doghouse)

One of the most interesting things about reggaeton's newfound success is the implication that United States audiences are finally embracing music performed in a language other than English. This may be due more to the power of the music than any sort of emerging open-mindedness, but it raises some interesting questions. Despite all the Spanish speakers living in the United States, including all the gringos who learned a little Español in high school, it seems likely that, as with Jamaican dancehall, few listeners outside of the music's core audience are able to follow all the lyrics. Those who do, especially those who find them rather scandalous, are understandably concerned with reggaeton's seemingly unabated and uncensored rise to the top. As club music first and foremost, reggaeton tends toward partying and sex as primary subjects. Descriptions of sexual acts and female bodies alternate between explicit language and innuendo, and women rarely appear as anything other than objects of the male gaze. The music's attendant dance style, *perreo* (doggy style), was seen as so salacious at one point that the Puerto Rican government attempted to ban it— a move that only affirmed reggaeton's anti-establishment character.

Reggaeton's relationship to hip hop and reggae—and the shared socio-cultural circumstances of urban poverty, high unemployment, and (co-erced) participation in the violent but profitable trans-American drug trade—go a long way toward accounting for reggaeton's focus on sex and the bleak realities of ghetto-street-thug life. But the glamorization of violence and material gain is far from being a subcultural pathology: these are the preoccupations of mainstream American culture and society, too. San Juan is no more responsible for advancing stereotypes and negative imagery than, say, Hollywood or Washington. Overlooking the inherent critique of racial injustice in reggaeton's bling-filled fantasies is to miss the boat.

Only relatively recently, with its acquisition of market power and stateside acceptance, has reggaeton reached Puerto Rico's middle and upper classes. What was previously denigrated as crude and crass now stands as a national symbol and a promising source of foreign exchange. In a place where, despite their celebrated mixedness, over 80 percent of Puerto Ricans self-identify as "White," it's no accident that a prominent reggaeton artist like Tego Calderón foregrounds his Blackness by wearing an Afro, referring to himself as "El Negro Calde," and incorporating Afro–Puerto Rican traditions. In the United States, Hispanic immigrants often find themselves living alongside, and racialized along with, African Americans and Afro-Caribbeans, so it's no surprise that reggaeton works in sympathy and solidarity with the cultural politics of hip hop and reggae.

The Future

As reggaeton increases its reach, finding a receptive audience not just in the United States and Latin America, but in Europe, Asia, and Africa, its spread will more likely resemble that of hip hop and reggae than salsa and merengue. In that sense, it will represent a break from previous transmissions of Latin music as "world music." By integrating itself into the urban music market reggaeton essentially markets itself, like hip hop and dancehall, as mainstream pop, even as underground currents and fringe movements remain vital expressions of, and contributions to, the genre's evolving sound. Top-selling artists like R. Kelly, Sean Paul, and Britney Spears are already exploring reggaeton riddims, particularly in remixes, and to that extent reggaeton is being "cleaned up" and stylized for the MTV masses. And, just as it always has, reggaeton will continue to draw from the most compelling contemporary pop, borrowing styles and samples from hip hop, versioning the latest dancehall riddims, and pushing an already tech-savvy sound further into the synthesized stratosphere.

Reggaeton will also no doubt continue its dialogue with more "traditional" Latin music: one can already hear how reggaeton's hip hop–inflected Caribbean rhythms are finding their way into other Latin genres. Salsa bands, Rock en Español groups, and Latin-tinged musicians of all stripes are now adding touches of reggaeton to their performances, often by foregrounding and accenting, if not modulating, their snare drums.

And yet, for all its power and popularity, reggaeton remains an embattled pop form: it's not reggae, it's not rap, and for some it's not Latin either. Reggaeton has been belittled by a vast array of critics, among them rockists, reggae purists, hip hop heads, upper- and middle-class Puerto Ricans, and Latin music aficionados. Purists of all sorts decry reggaeton, which makes sense for it is an inherently hybrid music. It is also, in essence, an industrial music—a high-tech product with a tendency toward, and an aesthetic based around, recycled rhythms and riffs. Although reggaeton's detractors have some valid complaints, especially with regard to the genre's most crassly commercial releases, it is clear that quite frequently they simply have not listened closely enough, or to the right things . . . or with their hips.

DAVID LAMB

Do Plátanos Go wit' Collard Greens?

While Angelita's eyes glistened brightly as she spoke to Freeman, her mother's burned with thinly veiled contempt. Like every other immigrant, she had been bombarded by negative images of African Americans blasted daily on the television, on the radio, in the newspapers and magazines. She, herself, had had a gold chain snatched by a young brotha during the chain-snatching craze of the early eighties. And that experience, coupled with the negative views and images ubiquitously dispersed throughout the media, reinforced the negative connotations associated with Blackness that she learned growing up in the Dominican Republic. In many ways, Samaná was a product of her environment. She had simply absorbed the views of the Dominican dominant classes who continue to deify the nation's Spanish and Catholic past, while simultaneously attempting to sweep under the rug the nation's African heritage. In an article in *Newsday*, the District 6 community school board member Anthony Stevens-Acevedo recalled how for decades in the Dominican Republic when Dominicans got their national ID cards if they were visibly of African descent they would be classified as "Indian." And when at sixteen he went for his ID card the clerk wrote that he was Indian, Acevedo objected and told the clerk, "I'm Black." But the clerk told him that it wasn't in his best interest to say he was Black, it would be better to say Indian. Now, as she looked at Freeman, Angelita's mom was awash in guilt, she felt that she had somehow failed her daughter. Why couldn't she be like her brother? she asked herself, wondering where she had gone wrong. Her daughter was making a terrible mistake, and she was not going to stand back and just let it happen. As soon as dinner was over she was going to tell her daughter how it was.

"You're so young, you don't understand Angelita, you have to think ahead, to improve the race."

"Think ahead; improve the race?! What kind of talk is that Mami, look at abuela."

"And that is why she married your grandfather, to improve her line."

"You know Mami, you're so blind you don't even see it. When I think of all the times you used to tell me how you would rub your milk on my head when I was a baby, so that I would have good hair. What are you saying, Mami? Yes. My hair is straight, even though it's kinda wavy, but look it's Black-Black. Would you rather it was blonde? Would you rather the full lips I got from abuela were thin like them white girls you look at in the magazines? Would you rather my skin was lighter? I bet you would. 'Stay out of the sun, you don't want to look like Haitians,' remember that Mami. Don't you see, our ancestors didn't just come from Spain, we are not conquistadors. Our ancestors came here just like the Blacks you look down on, like the Haitians you hate. In the hulls of ships, dragged off from their homelands. You know what they say, Mami, every Dominican has a little black behind the ears, you know, 'Todos los dominicanos tienen el negro detras de las orejas.' We are more like the Haitians than the Castillians. Look at what our presidente did, spending all of that money foolishly to celebrate the 500th anniversary of Columbus. And you, abuela, I mean really, using the Santos to keep me and Freeman apart."

"You don't understand Angelita, look at your sister."

"I'm not her, Mami!" Angelita yelled back, fighting back her tears. Angelita's sister, Peaches (she was so nicknamed for her fondness of the fruit of the same name as a little girl, and for those who didn't know her as a little girl for the small tattoo of peaches she had on her left ankle), had, to her mother's eternal damnation, gotten pregnant in high school. The first time Freeman saw Peaches she was the picture of subtlety. He and Angelita had just gotten back from taking Peaches's son Miguel to the movies, and Peaches had come to Angelita's to pick him up. She was dressed in a peach-colored sweater with a peach-colored leather jacket. He could see that she also had on peach-colored socks, as well as freshly painted peach-colored nails she'd just had painted at a Korean-owned nail salon. He wondered what color her underwear were. Really. Her hair had peach highlights, her earrings were peaches, and she also had two small gold chains. One said *Peaches*, and one had two small gold peaches attached to it. She was indeed the master of understatement, he thought. He'd never forget her first words, "Jo' Angelita Ah'm not votin.'" "But, why?" Her sister had asked, not really expecting a cogent answer, but wanting to hear what she had to say anyway. "'Cauz, Jo,' Dinkins ain't did nothin' for me, and 'cauz I don't trust Giuliani, he's prejudiced against Dominicans." [. . .]

When Freeman got home from dinner he was still enjoying the memory of the piononos he'd been introduced to earlier that evening, and he gave Angelita a call to let her know that he'd gotten home and to get the recipe.

"Hey, what's up, Angelita, I just wanted to call you before I went to bed. Hey, what's wrong, you sound upset? What's wrong?"

"Nothing."

"It doesn't sound like nothing, tell me, what's wrong?"

"I just got into an argument with my mother."

"About what?"

"About you?"

"About me? Why me?"

"She doesn't want me seein' any Black guys."

"Angelita, might I point out that your grandmom's, your mother's mother, is like a couple of shades darker than me."

"I know, it's like we Dominicans say, 'We all have a little black behind the ears.' Unfortunately, that's where most of us want to keep it, behind the ears."

"Damn, that's wild. Some of my older relatives tell me how when they were growin' up, if somebody called you Black, those were fightin' words. Now I can't even imagine that shit, but hey, we makin' progress. It's on us, the first generation of decolonized minds." [. . .]

After talking with Freeman, and drinking a cold bottle of Snapple lemonade to cool off, Angelita decided to make her cousin, Julia, a call. Julia had just come up in the last year from the Dominican Republic, and she worked in a beauty shop in Washington Heights. Being pretty much straight from the Dominican Republic, Julia still harbored many of her native prejudices, as Angelita was about to find out.

"Does he have good hair or bad hair?' Was Julia's first question.

"What do you mean good hair or bad hair?" An agitated Angelita asked.

"You know hair like ours, good."

"And hair like grandma's?"

"Hair like grandma's?"

"Yes, hair like grandma's."

"That's bad."

"And what makes it bad?"

"Because, you know, hair like ours is easy to manage. And girls with bad hair spend hours trying to get their hair like ours. I tell you Angelita, just the other day, I spent three hours working on this girl's hair . . ."

"Julia, grandma does not have bad hair, as a matter of fact, there's no such thing as pelo malo. How can hair be bad? Does it attack you? Is it mean? Does it enslave people? No! It's not bad, it's just different. It's only considered bad because the Spaniards put themselves on a pedestal, and made us want to look like them. Yeah, our hair is 'good' you say, but it's Black-Black, is blonde hair better? What about your complexion, is white skin better?"

As Angelita finished talking to her cousin, she heard the front door open and close, and the sounds of Fat Joe booming through a Walkman—she knew her younger brother was home. She was angry with him for missing dinner earlier, but she was glad he was home. Among all of their family, Angelita and Pablo shared a special bond. Their views and self-perception had been greatly influenced by the confluence of Afrocentricity and hip-hop, and this set them apart from the rest of their family except, maybe, the outcast Peaches, well, at least the hip-hop part, anyway.

When Freeman got off the phone with Angelita, he was still tripping about her mother's attitude. He could hear his pops typing downstairs, and he went to talk to him about it. He figured he'd have some insight since he was at the moment writing a book about Black and Latino political coalitions in New York, in addition to working on the Dinkins campaign.

"Well, Free, you've got to understand that in the Dominican Republic the Spanish quickly found themselves outnumbered by the descendants of all those Africans they'd imported, and by the revolutionary Haitians next door. And then when the Haitians took over! I mean, my goodness, the Blacks were ruling! They had to do something. When you look at the three principal leaders of the Dominican revolt against Haitian rule: Juan Pablo Duarte, Ramón Mella, and Francisco del Rosario Sánchez, they're all pretty much straight-up Spaniards. According to the historian Juan Bosch, Dominican history has been systematically slanted to create the impression that the twenty-two years of Haitian rule were marked by barbaric oppression. But according to Bosch many Dominicans supported the takeover. After all, if you were enslaved, freedom had come. And even if you weren't, under the racial order the Spanish had imposed people of African descent were at the bottom, so they also welcomed a change in the racial pecking order.

"Now, take it to America. As I was explaining, about it being in the interest of the ruling class in the Dominican Republic to sell the masses this false notion of their whiteness, or at least their Indianess (as a sort of consolation prize if they so obviously weren't 'White'), in order to ensure their support against the Haitians, so today White Americans are interested in driving a wedge between African Americans and Latinos by playing to Latino's Spanish heritage above and beyond their indigenous and African heritage. Let me put a little theoretical construct on it for you. I was just reading this paper out of the University of Chicago by Nancy Denton and Douglas Massey entitled 'Racial Segregation of Caribbean Hispanics.' These two sociologists contend that in the United States Latinos from the Caribbean are challenged by a profound confrontation between two clashing and contradictory delineations of race. In the Spanish-speaking Caribbean, they point out that race is defined along a multi-category continuum, but in the United States it's bipolar—Black or White. As a result, people from the Spanish-speaking Caribbean face pressures to identify themselves as either Black or White. Now obviously this creates a dilemma because in America, race matters—being Black means being in the downtrodden class, while being White carries advantages.

"These professors point out that another potential source of pressure could arise from the nascent formation and evolution of Latino ethnic grouping. Now before coming to the good ol' U.S. of A. most Latinos see themselves as just part of their national group, Puerto Rican, Mexican, Cuban, etcetera. In the United States, though, they begin to develop an ethnic identity based on what they have in common. They all speak Spanish, for the most part they're Catholic, and they all have roots in Latin America, accordingly then, over time, a 'Latino' ethnicity develops.

"So, if you follow this line of reasoning, then you would see that in the United States Latinos from the Caribbean are being pulled in opposite directions. On one hand, they are, as Massey and Denton say, united around their common identity as Latinos. On the other hand, they're split along racial lines as they conform to the rest of America's bipolar racial canon.

"In the last year the Atlantic Monthly has run two huge articles on the breakdown or the coming breakdown in relations between African Americans and Latinos, one specifically on New York City, dealing with Blacks and Puerto Ricans, and one on LA, dealing with Blacks and Mexicans. Now why do you think that is? When it's to White folks' advantage they talk about the particular Latino group, be it Puerto Rican, Mexican, Cuban or what have you, but when it's not in their interest to so separate them, then they'll lump them together under the rubric 'Hispanic.' Case in point: in Ed Koch's commercial endorsing Herman Badillo, at one point he refers to the candidate as the first Hispanic, and at another point as the first Puerto Rican. And even the conservative Robert Novak predicting a defection of Latinos from Dinkins, wrote of Blacks and non-Blacks, an obvious inversion of the usual white and non-white delineation of American politics. I was reading this editorial in *New York Newsday*'s New York Forum entitled 'The Coalition of Color Fades.' The White boy argues that the rift in the Black and Latino political alliance that voted Dinkins in is becoming more apparent every day. And to prove his point he cites Michael Woo's losing effort in the L.A. mayoral race. He writes that Woo lost despite winning the overwhelming percentage of Blacks' votes because he barely won the Latino vote. He ignores the low Black turnout, and the fact that Woo did indeed win the majority of Black votes and the majority of Latino votes, as well, while he lost the White vote, overwhelmingly! He also points to the Houston mayoral race where Bob Lanier, a White businessman, defeated Sylvester Turner, a Black lawyer, on the strength, according to the author, of a record turnout of Hispanic voters. What he fails to point out, however, is that in both of these cases the Hispanics he's talking about are overwhelmingly Mexican. Therefore this may or may not be relevant to the coalition between African Americans and Latinos from the Caribbean in New York City. After all, wasn't Bronx Borough president Fernando Ferrer quoted as saying that the new schools chancellor Cortines had no connection to New York's Latinos, that he didn't even speak Spanish. Yet, this article seeks to suggest that Dinkins's failure to back Cortines hurt Black and Latino relations in the city. You know what the beautiful thing about America is though, Free?"

"No."

"The beautiful thing about America is—we're all in the same boat, White folks don't care if you're one-thirty-second African or one hundred percent; for them, a nigger is a nigger. So let your girlfriend's mother protest all she wants, the forces of society dictate that the younger ones will increasingly be drawn to see their connection with us, and all of our connections with Africa."

As Freeman tossed and turned in his bed that night he remembered an earlier phone conversation he'd had with Pablo, Angelita's younger brother. He laughed when he recalled Pablo's response when he asked him what he thought of Fat Joe, whose album was at the moment blowing up. He grinned and shook his head as he repeated Pablo's response: "That nigga's dope!" "How bout that," he said to himself, "a Dominican, sounding like an African American, calling a Puerto Rican a nigga, as the word is sometimes applied in the endearment mode. Yeah, shit is funny sometimes," he said to himself, just before he lost consciousness.

SOFIA QUINTERO
Divas Don't Yield

[. . .] When I leave the building, I almost trip over a brick-colored spauld-
ing. Just as I pick it up, the little Black girl who lives on Wil's floor comes
toward me, dragging a broken broomstick. What's her name? I only know
her as Li'l Bit, which is the nickname Wil gave her.

So I say, "What's good, Li'l Bit?" I don't know much about her, but I like
her lots, and I'm not a big fan of kids (or they of mine, let me not front).
While the other girls on this block sit on the stoop fawning over their
Barbie dolls, Li'l Bit's running the streets like her little ass is on fire.

I hear this ruckus around the corner so I step off the stoop and look
up the block. The neighborhood kids are in the midst of a heated game
of stickball. I used to love that game and was pretty damned good at it,
too. I turn back to Li'l Bit, who's standing next to me now, staring down
at her ashy knees. Used to have those, too. "Why aren't you playing with
them?"

She just shrugs and holds her hand out for the ball. I give it to her and
kneel down to tighten the laces on my boots. As I do, I watch Li'l Bit throw
the ball against the building wall and swat it with her broomstick. The ball
ricochets around the plaza, and I jump up to catch it before it flies in the
street. Li'l Bit's all power, no technique, just like me before my pops gave
me a few pointers.

"So that's why they don't let you play," I say as I walk back toward
her. "You're too good for those scrubs." But L'il Bit just shakes her head,
snatches the ball from me, and fires it into the wall. "Then what? C'mon,
kid, talk to me." But I already know because as I watch her chase the ball
into the concrete flower bed, my stomach burns with the same humilia-
tion it did when I was nine years old and the neighborhood kids wouldn't
let me play with them.

Li'l Bit gets the ball and says, "They let Minerva play, and she sucks."

She tosses the ball into the air and whacks it with her broomstick with a vengeful swing. "She's the scrub, not me?"

The ball bounces off the wall right into my outstretched palm. "You need to hold the stick like this?" I say. I walk behind Li'l Bit and correct her stance. "Open your feet more. Lift your arms a little higher. Okay, now swing from your hips." Li'l Bit pulls back her arms. "No, you're swinging from your shoulders." I place my hands on her shoulders to weigh them down a bit just the way my dad had done when teaching me how to swing. Pivoting at the waist, Li'l Bit whips the stick forward and slices the air. "There you go, that's it!" I say. "Let's get out of here before we break a window."

I take her hand and lead her into the street. At the other end of the block, I see the kids playing their game. Pointing at the manhole cover, I say, "Stand over there." As I walk up the street, I pull off my sling bag and search the crowd, wondering which ones are the bullies and what nasty things they called Li'l Bit. Did they call her Brillo Pad? *Bembe* Face? Or the one I really hate . . . *cocola*. The little snots I grew up with used to call me that because they were too ignorant to realize that being Black didn't make me *not* Latina and that I understood every nasty word they were saying. And I schooled them to the fact the hard way.

Li'l Bit's African American and probably doesn't understand the Spanish insults. Not that she needs to. Regardless of what language they use, she knows they're saying some racist shit. The venom in their tones and sneers on their faces makes *bembe* just as clear as Brillo. Shit, the poor kid has it worse than I did really. If one of those little *brujas* calls her a *cocola* and Li'l Bit delivers the fat lip she has coming to her like I did, the brat can always deny that she ever said it.

I make Minerva on sight. She has to be that vanilla princess leaning against that silver Infiniti, twirling her waist-length dirty blond hair around her finger when she's supposed to be defending the box scrawled in blue chalk on the ground in front of her. The other team must be stealing third left and right. For a moment there, I want to scare a little civility into her prissy behind and send a message to all the other brats that are messing with Li'l Bit.

But I check myself because Minerva reminds me of Hazel when we were kids. Hazel was much prettier though, and probably kinder, too. For all I know, Minerva's just as innocent as Hazel had been. Hazel had no control over the vicious extremes that other kids went to to impress her, and maybe Minerva doesn't either. I seriously doubt that shit though. I'll never get the human impulse to turn cruel in the face of beauty. You'd think the opposite. Isn't beauty supposed to inspire kindness, charity, and all that? But then again, here I am thinking about going after the kid like Russell Crowe would a bellhop. I stop myself, remembering one of the immutable laws of playground politics. Li'l Bit has to show and prove. It's not going to help her for my grown-up ass to fight her battle and antagonize the most popular girl on the block. If anything, that'll make things worse for her.

Instead I drop my bag onto the ground and turn around to face Li'l Bit. "Remember what I told you," I say as I wind up and pitch the ball to her. With perfect technique, she whacks the ball, and it launches past me and into the middle of the stickball game. The boys look at each other trying to determine which one of them hit it, and I smile at Li'l Bit with loads of pride. "That's it!"

Li'l Bit jogs over to me, and I run my hand across her hair. It's soft and fluffy, and her eyes just radiate . . . She's the cutest fuckin' thing! A smile a supermodel would forgo a year of Botox for. How can anybody be mean to her? "Don't you ever let some little playahaters chase you from where you want to be, you hear me?" I say. I know that's easier said than done, so I pull the broomstick out of her hands and add, "And if they try, you grab the stick like this . . ." But then I had a better idea. "No, this is what you do. You pick out the biggest kid—the biggest boy—and you take his big head like this." I hook my arm around Li'l Bit's head into a gentle headlock.

She starts a giggling fit but waits for more instructions. Then I remember where wrestling with boys got me, and I let her go. But I don't think that Doña Myra's little fable about St. Benedict's going to work here either, so I just say, "Go tell an adult or something." That's what I'm supposed to say even though I suspect that it's probably as useless advice today as it was thirteen years ago.

"No," Li'l Bit whines. "Teach me wrestling." The kid's a pisser—I love that. She growls and throws her arms around my hips, and we both stumble as she tries to tackle me to the asphalt. I laugh as I brace myself and straighten up. Geez, Li'l Bit's already a good four six, and she's only nine. All arms and legs, too, just like me at that age. Maybe with all that height she'll grow up to be the next Naomi Campbell or Tyra Banks. God knows I sure didn't.

I throw my sling over my shoulder and give her an apologetic smile. "Can't, kid. I have to go to school."

"School? Now? Why?"

"I have to return these library books and then pick up my graduation gown." Okay, I admit I get a kick out of her disappointment. Like I said,

I'm not exactly Maria from *Sesame Street*. "Then I have to run some errands 'cause I'm going on a trip to San Francisco with my friends." After I make this trek to Fordham, I have to find myself a cheap white dress for the New York Latinas Against Domestic Violence Emergency Brides' March. No, scratch that. We're leaving on Friday morning now so that's one less thing to think about. But now that Lourdes wrecked her SUV beyond easy repair, I'll probably lose the rest of the afternoon cajoling Raul into lending me his Escalade for the road trip instead of that red sardine can he has the nerve to call a car.

"I wanna go!"

"Sure, when you graduate from college."

Li'l Bit pouts, "Who's gonna show me stuff when you're gone?"

"My boyfriend'll teach you some moves until I get back. Now go play. And remember what I said." Li'l Bit picks up her stick and barges into the stickball game as I walk hack to the Ford Tempo (technically Raul's, essentially mine). I climb into the car, place my sling bag in the passenger seat, and peek into the rearview window for one last check on Li'l Bit. She menaces the boy who caught her ball with her broomstick until he gives it back. Atta girl.

Then I catch my own reflection in the mirror. I rake my fingers through my hair, which is a dark maze encircling my face. Why would Wil want to stick his hands in that nest, let alone actually do so? I reach into my bag for the new serum, pomade, or whatever the hell it was that Hazel gave me. Still I can't bring myself to open it. I never can. And forget about all that stuff Irena says about cutting your hair to change your karma. I don't want to become one of those chicks who refuses to leave the house without her "face on" and her hair "did." I refuse to succumb to those bullshit pressures. That would make me the biggest hypocrite. You can call me a lot of things, but never a hypocrite.

So I toss the tube out my window and tear out of the parking space.

IX

Living Afro-Latinidades

What is it like to be an Afro-Latin@? As the personal stories in this section demonstrate, there is no one answer. Being Afro-Latin@ is at the individual level a unique and distinctive experience and identity, ranging as it does among Latin@, Black, and American dimensions of lived social reality. It is an experience with strong transnational elements marked by national origins, language, phenotype, and the particular context in which

René Benito Lassalle, a former carpenter and boxer, telling his story to the Afro-Puerto Rican Testimonies Project, Aguadilla, Puerto Rico, 2007. (Photograph by José Irizarry, Afro-Puerto Rican Testimonies Project)

Afro-Latin@s find themselves living. Whether their family background is traced to Panamanian, Cuban, Dominican, Puerto Rican, Nicaraguan, Honduran Garifuna, or Mexican origins, in their quest for a full and appropriate sense of social identity Afro-Latin@s are thus typically pulled in various directions at once, and they share a complex, multidimensional optic on contemporary society. Yet this simultaneous presence of multiple experiences and perspectives — including the contradictions, pain, and outrage — does not necessarily translate into pathological confusion. As many of the essays in this volume suggest, embracing and celebrating all the dimensions of one's self has not only been possible but has also resulted in significant achievements and innovations at the personal and collective level. The strength and resilience evident in these diverse life stories, and the sense of self- and social consciousness to which they attest, command admiration and respect. We close the chapter with the gripping, and humorous, dramatic poem by New York Puerto Rican Willie Perdomo, "Nigger-Reecan Blues," already a classic of Afro-Latin@ writing.

YVETTE MODESTIN

An Afro-Latina's Quest for Inclusion

To my dear father

My quest to include the voices of African descendants of Latin America in the larger dialogue of the Diaspora has had many highs and lows. One thing I am certain of is that although it is difficult to discuss race and Black pride, it is the clarity of who I am—a Black Latina woman of West Indian descent—and where I come from—a Black community that has overcome many obstacles—that gets me out of bed every morning. At the center of this quest, it is the presence of my ancestors that keeps me moving forward.

I was born and raised in Colón, Panama, and the experiences of my childhood were, I now realize, unique. Black pride flourished among the West Indian community. I lived where the nurse (my mother) was Black, the assistant branch chief of security on the Atlantic side of the Panama Canal (my father) was Black, and the firefighter, the tugboat captain, and the doctor were all Black. I did not have to look outside of my immediate surroundings to have positive images of Black people. My strong French West Indian, Bajun, and Jamaican upbringing was filled with love and pride. My grandfather, who was from Martinique, was one of the original construction workers on the Panama Canal. Growing up, I knew the French anthem because of my family's heritage; I knew the Panamanian anthem because I was born in Panama; and I knew the United States anthem because I was a "Zonian." (The territory of Panama that was owned and operated by the United States government was called the Canal Zone. Anyone born and raised in the area was considered a "Zonian.")

Segregation in the territory was very visible. The Black West Indian families lived in a separate area. They were also paid differently. The Black workers ("the Silvermen") were paid in silver while the White workers were paid in gold. There was a clear divide. Segregation, though, made people in the Black community support each other even more. They had a common history and a desire to preserve it. West Indian pride got them through these difficult times. They never thought of themselves as being less than the White man but just as good if not, at times, better. That was the way my grandfather thought. Although he was not an educated man, he radiated a sense of confidence and leadership. This camaraderie did not make things easy, but life was more livable because of it.

It's true that West Indian families did experience some privilege in this territory. They were provided with homes in the territory, as well as schools and churches. We had our own movie theaters, supermarket (or commissary as we called it), and our own swimming pool. We did not have to leave our immediate areas for anything. But we could not forget that with that privilege came a history of abuse and lack of recognition for our hard work. West Indians were brought to Panama to do a job and were paid low wages to get it done. Because of illnesses some were not paid at the end of their contract. It took many years before you began to see Black men and women in top positions. Although I did not experience the level of racism that my grandparents, parents, uncles, and aunts experienced, they did not shield us from the stories. They made it clear what they went through to get to where we were and how important it is for us to keep our heads up high and continue the legacy.

We held onto their words as the schools were integrated and the communities desegregated. We were not sure how we were going to be received but it did not matter. It was instilled in us that we deserved this and that it was time. We now had our own stories to tell. We saw it; we named it; in many ways we were able to challenge it differently than our parents and we moved through it. We responded in many ways but mainly by becoming some of the top students.

Outside of the Canal Zone area, Blacks as a whole (that is, both Afro-Caribbeans and Afro-Colonials) were treated as inferiors to the White Panamanians, especially those referred to as the *rabi blancos*, a derogatory term that literally means "white tails." They did not want to deal with us. It is a known part of Panama's history that after the construction of the Canal was completed in 1914, President Arnulfo Arias wanted all Black workers to return to their countries of birth.

In spite of our community's sense of self-worth in the face of the racism we experienced, as people of African descent we also share with others throughout Latin America an experience of general invisibility. Some countries, such as Colombia, Venezuela, Brazil, Honduras, Costa Rica, and Panama, have anti-discrimination laws and specific Black history celebrations. In others, such as Peru, Argentina, and Chile, African-descendant peoples are still fighting for full inclusion and recognition. There has been an increasing international awareness of the exclusion and poverty endured by the region's estimated 40 million indigenous people. But Blacks, mulattos or other groups with traces of African ancestry—estimated at 80 to 150 million of the total regional population of 502 million—have remained practically invisible.

This invisibility is also evident among Latinos and Latinas in the United States. I have experienced it firsthand. At a conference in North Carolina, for example, I introduced myself to another attendee. I heard her accent and asked where she was from. She responded with joy, "Honduras." When I said to her, "Somos vecinas" (We are neighbors), she replied, "Oh, I thought you were a Black woman." Fifty percent of the people from her country are of African descent.

Many of the Latinas at that conference were in deep denial about who they were around the issue of race. It took until the end of the conference for them to come up to me and have a conversation about my presentation. A few were of visible African descent, but it was clear that they did not identify themselves as such. It was very evident that a conversation on race made them uncomfortable. When they did speak to me, it was about the fact that I was fluent in Spanish. On the other hand, the African American women went from saying, "We are so different," to saying, "We have so much in common as Black women and as women." They were more receptive to me and to the conversation on the lack of inclusion of Afro-Latinas. They embraced me in my wholeness, a Black Latina woman.

In my quest for inclusion here in the United States, I have learned the negative meaning that is associated with "Blackness." I have learned that you drop a class rank because of the color of your skin; that the assumptions made of you may weigh more heavily on the negative; that the African American history I so admired and believed had moved forward, had a lot more work to do; and that African Americans are still facing a high level of injustice. I have learned that when I walk into a room full of White people, no matter what my behavior or credentials, I am immediately placed at a disadvantage because of the color of my skin. Another thing that happens is just as shocking. When people find out I'm not African American, they think better of me. Many people have told me it is because I am "a different kind of Black."

I have gone through many struggles here in the United States about my race and ethnicity, and I constantly have to explain myself. When I am in a White setting I feel that there is no point in explaining because all people see is my skin color. Some White people choose to not get stuck in that place. When I am in an African American setting I am told that I am not really Black because I am from another country and I speak another language. Some African American people choose to not get stuck in that place. When I am in a Latina setting I am seen as not "Latina enough" because of my hair and the color of my skin, even though I was born and raised in a Latin American country and my Spanish is usually at least as good as the people judging me. Some Latinas also choose to not get stuck in that place. I made the choice early on to not be minimized and to embrace, acknowledge, and celebrate that first and foremost I am a Black woman and a sister, daughter, and friend to all people of African descent.

Yet, as I now ask myself, why should people have positive images of Afro-Latinas when they don't even see a representation of us in the media? You turn on Telemundo or Univision, the Latin American TV stations, and you don't see an Afro-Latina. *Latina* magazine still has not had someone who looks like me on its cover. That magazine has been an absolute disappointment to me. After talking with a former editor of *Latina* I realized that it is all about what sells, and apparently what Latinas are saying is that Black does not sell to them. In *The Latina Bible* Sandra Guzman writes, "Many of us go around unaware that we carry baggage that prevents us from being proud of *la raza* (the people) and feeling entitled to the riches this country has to offer. Too many of us adopt a form of cultural denial . . . We are quick to claim our Spaniard *abuela* (grandmother) or deny the India or African one."[1]

The issue of hair exemplifies this. When I cut all my hair off and went natural, my Latina friends were appalled. To them I looked like "one of them"—an African American woman. I had already had the experience of having my hair long, processed, colored—all the things identified with being a Latina—and I was still questioned; I worried to some extent what this would all mean in a Latin@ setting. I had to acknowledge to myself how this all has impacted me emotionally. I felt the reactions of disgust from some people. We, both Latin@s and African Americans, have issues with natural hair. For many of us, natural means nappy and ugly. For me, it represents a sense of freedom and a confidence in one's internal and external beauty that only those who exhibit it with pride can understand. I am at my best when my hair is all out and taking its own form.

Why won't this society embrace all of who I am and what I am so proud of as a dark-skinned woman from Latin America who speaks Spanish? At an Afro-Latin@ conference in New York City I attended a few years ago, I met Christopher Rodriguez, author of *The Latino Manifesto*. After this encounter I knew that my goal would be to bring voice to the history, life, and struggles of the Afro-Latina. I wanted people to know how proud I am to be *Negra*, but I also wanted to speak about how the negativity that comes with that word has led many Latinas to deny and not embrace their *negresa*.

My experiences in the United States opened my eyes and taught me a more global perspective of my own country's history, that is, to see it not through the eyes of a child or an adolescent but as an adult who has felt what it is like to be followed around a store because she is Black. I challenge the things that are said about the Black experience or presence in Panama and remind people that the development of the country has rested on its Black presence. I challenge the status of my Black community in Colón, a forgotten province, in the larger agenda of the country. I take this one step further in including the history and experiences of other Afro-descendant communities in Latin America.

I will continue my journey in the United States, where I now reside. My quest for inclusion will continue with a strong vision of bringing peace to my future, of spreading knowledge of the African diaspora in Latin America so that I no longer have to explain myself to others. My internal and external transformations have validated for me who I am in this world and the love and pride of a community that seeks justice. At the center of this journey is the presence of my ancestors—my mother, aunts, grandparents, and uncles who continue to give me the gift of wisdom and knowledge of our past as we keep looking to our future.

Note

1. Sandra Guzman, *The Latina Bible* (New York: Three Rivers Press, 2002), 6.

RYAN MANN-HAMILTON

Retracing Migration

From Samaná to New York and Back Again

I shared very few moments with my grandfather before he passed. I remember fondly how we would sit on the front balcony, rocking back and forth, staring into each other's eyes, as he grinned his toothless smile while telling stories of days past. He was the fourth generation raised in Samaná, Dominican Republic, a descendant of the African Americans who set sail from Philadelphia, Baltimore, and New York to seek their freedom and fortune in the first Black republic of the Americas.

In the 1820s, by invitation of President Jean Pierre Boyer, African American families willing to make the journey to the new Haitian Republic were offered twenty acres of land and sustenance for four months. Most of the emigrants recruited by Boyer's emissary, Jonathan Granville, were members of the African Methodist Episcopal Church. Established by the Reverend Richard Allen and the Reverend Absolom Jones, the AME church was one of the few religious institutions that allowed Blacks to preach to their own communities.

The church was also one of the main supporters of the Underground Railroad and as such many of the immigrants were runaway slaves seeking to assert their dignity and humanity as well as pursue economic opportunities. Among them were a large number of Blacks descended from prominent family names such as the Hamiltons, Adams, and Vanderhorsts. Despite the challenges of the unfamiliar terrain, geography, and language of the new island nation, strengthened by a sincere religious belief they sought to escape the evils of slavery. The unknown was not enough to dissuade them in their quest for a better life than that available to Blacks in the United States.

The first immigrants arrived in Port au Prince on November 29th, 1824.

Subsequent voyages brought the total number of arrivals to approximately seven thousand men, women, and children. The Haitian government assigned the new immigrants to specific areas as part of their effort to populate the island with Black families that would be receptive to and supportive of the newly created nation. Upon arrival some families decided to stay in the Haitian capital, while others were assigned to settle in the communities of Puerto Plata, Samaná, Santo Domingo, and La Romana.

Most of the immigrants could read and write and spoke a British English known today as Black Vernacular English. They were called the ingleses (the English) by much of the local community, although they identified themselves as American. Many of them returned to the United States after a few months, succumbing to the pressures of their new environment. For those who remained the period of adjustment was difficult and involved reconnecting to the land that had once sustained them, as most had lived in cities and had long forgotten the toils of the land. Over the years the ingleses established a strong community that revolved around their church and their distinctive history.

In recent decades, some of the descendants of Samaná have made their way back to New York. Most of the returnees followed the same path of migration experienced by other Dominican families, but some have attempted to reclaim their particular history. My uncle was the first in our family to make his way to New York and make a home of it. He identifies as a Dominican and is heavily involved in island politics. His interest in our family history is more out of a concern for land titles and inheritance than identity. When asked about his own identity he maintains, as his birth certificate states, that he is indio. He does not view himself as Black, and he makes a distinction between himself and members of other Black communities in the United States. I recall telling my cousin our family story, explaining how once we had been slaves in the United States and the conditions under which our ancestors had migrated to the Dominican Republic. His only response was, "So we're Black?" I presumed he had entertained that notion before. I was wrong. He had never known and never shared a moment with my grandfather in the rocking chair in Samaná.

Race matters were never really discussed within my home. I understood what I was, but I had no tools to combat those who questioned me. In part this lack of affirmation led me to believe that anything in life was possible as long as I tried. It was the tired old lie of meritocracy, which I encountered directly upon arrival in the United States from Puerto Rico. Race is a subject that still cripples me from time to time. Perhaps my first memories of such a discussion were when my father announced to me that my White grandfather was really not dead, but simply had chosen never to meet us because of our Blackness. I was thirteen.

The first time I came to live in the United States I was nineteen. I imagined myself being able to hang out with the "homies" in California and insert myself into African American culture. But I had to prove myself in order to belong to any of the communities I thought I was a part of. For the Black community, I was suspicious because I spoke Spanish. For the Latino community—most of whom were Mexican and Guatemalan— I was way too dark. I had to affirm that I was both Black and Latino to both communities and slowly I was accepted, although I don't think I was ever fully trusted. I couldn't understand why I had to be one or the other and whichever I chose was the one I needed to have allegiance to. Apparently someone had forgotten to discuss the concept of diaspora.

I have encountered some of my fellow returnees to the city and talked with them about how we identified and how we're identified by others. We've spoken about the racial crossroads that we encountered upon arrival and the choices we made along the way; about being defined as one or the other but never really accepted as either; about being considered too Black to be Latino and too light skinned and culturally different to be Black—and speaking English with little or no accent. Some have chosen not to conform to the stereotypes or accept placement in that wonderful classification box that appears in the United States census. I am not "Hispanic" or a "Hispanic non-Black." I am not a "Black non Hispanic," nor just "Black." I am not an "Other." I am both, all, and much more.

The constant questioning about my history, my name, my lack of accent and my color forced me to learn more of my family's history of migration. I wasn't sure whether to respond to the questions or refute their assumptions. As this process was repeated I refined my responses and began to question the way I identified myself. Phenotypically Black, culturally Puerto Rican and Dominican, mentally liberated. Once that was clear and I acknowledged my own insecurities I understood that I, and many others, were in the same situation within the racial system of the United States.

I have made the journey back to New York perhaps aware of the return to our place in the history of this nation. But I also made my way to New York attentive to the fact that many other Afro-Latinos live in the region and I no longer have to make a choice or prove to others what or who I am. Intent on discovering more of the secrets about my forefathers and foremothers, I am convinced that my future rests in their stories. Embracing all of my identities—Puerto Rican, Dominican, American, Black—I find comfort in Afrolatinidad as the fullest expression of my multiple identities. I return to Samaná and Puerto Rico often, and I frequently discuss the details of my family history. The vision of my grandfather inspires me and has set me on my educational path. The strength of my forefathers guides me in the struggle to define an identity that I can call home, as I now do Samaná.

VIELKA CECILIA HOY

Negotiating among Invisibilities

Tales of Afro-Latinidades in the United States

When the Sandinistas stormed the National Palace in Managua, Nicaragua, in July 1979, I was already a year old and living in Crown Heights, Brooklyn. When the United States government arrested Manuel Noriega in Panama, I was about eleven years old and living in a suburb of Oakland, California. My mother is Nicaraguan, born and raised in Bluefields, Nicaragua, which is sometimes known as the Caribbean coast. My father is from Colón, Panama, or Rainbow City. And they are both Black.

That statement usually raises a few eyebrows where I live in California, where I find that most people are confused about these matters by having to negotiate among racial paradigms in the United States as a whole, and the western states in particular, where Latinidad is Mexicentric. In California, no one argues that Black people exist in Latin America—but they are Brazilians. They also do not argue that there are groups other than mestizos in Central America—but they are indigenous nations. However, the idea that African-descended peoples exist in Nicaragua (estimated as high as 13 percent of the population) and that they speak Spanish, possibly participate in ceremony, and have a continued involvement in revolutionary governments, is nearly unfathomable. Not to mention the case of Panama, where the Black population is as high as 30 percent, and not entirely West Indian, English-speaking, and Protestant. The same is true for Belize, Honduras, Guatemala, El Salvador, and Costa Rica.

Such is the background of my story, that of an Afro-Latina (Nicaraguan and Panamanian) negotiating among invisibilities.

Growing up in Panama, my father was very involved in a variety of sports, including baseball. In the Bay Area, among the various Afro-Nicaraguan communities scattered across the East Bay and the Peninsula, my father became extremely active in coaching a team and supporting the Nicaraguan softball league. The league was almost entirely composed of Afro-Nicaraguans.[1] So, when the team organized fund-raising events, soca, dancehall, and salsa music spilled from the venues. We ate fried plantains and yucca and the sounds of Creole English filled the air. On one such occasion the DJ played a banda song typical of the Pacific side of Nicaragua, where most of the mestizos live.

"What is he doing?" my cousin questioned.

"There are a bunch of pañas here.[2] They actually have the money to donate so the DJ has to make them happy," another partygoer offered.

Each year the teams from the league in the Bay Area traveled to southern California to play the Nicaraguan teams in that league. The teams had names that signified their locations in Nicaragua, and thus their identities: "Bluefields," "Atlantic Coast," "Bully's," and the all-encompassing "Nicaragua," a team of mestizos. At the tournaments, a number of games are played simultaneously while families take charge of cooking large plates of food for purchase and playing music for their patrons.

"There goes that [banda] music again. There are way more of us. We shouldn't have to listen to that crap. Besides this is a ball game. We need some uplifting music, not this stuff about someone's wife leaving him," my cousin complained.

"Whatever. I'm hungry. Which one has the best frito?"[3] I wondered aloud.

"Follow that music," my cousin answered. "Pañas don't know music but they can fry some good stuff."

I have noticed that writings about the African diaspora in Latin America recognize the various cultural forms indicative of African ancestry while at the same time pointing out the lack of racial discourse in the same locations. In Nicaragua, for example, one could listen to Bluefields music and speak Bluefields English, and therefore assert an identity apart from the national that may be equated with Blackness for those looking in. Once one is in the United States, however, that identity is completely dismissed. In 2000 the national census reported that only 2 percent of those who chose "Latino" as their ethnicity chose "Black" as their race. Half of the respondents chose "Other."

I remember when I completed the census form. I was sitting around the kitchen table with two of my cousins who were raised in Costa Rica.

" 'Ethnicity'? What are you going to check, Lucia?"[4] Mayra asked.

"Costa Rican."

"That isn't an ethnicity, it's a nationality," I responded. "Besides, you were born in Nicaragua."

"But I feel Costa Rican and what is it with these options? I'm not 'White' or 'Black.'"

"How do you figure? You look Black to me," I challenged.

"They mean Black like you, not Black from anywhere else. And there isn't any such thing in Costa Rica. Everyone is just Costa Rican."

"What makes someone Black like me?"

"Born in the United States. I don't think you can even say 'Nicaraguan.' You are African American now. So I'm putting 'Costa Rican' and checking 'Other.'"

"Me too," affirmed Mayra.

"What is your dad putting?" I asked.

"'Nicaraguan' and 'Black' probably."

"This is nuts. Here is a group of cousins and uncles. Yet, we have completely different responses on our census form!"

This was not the first time that my extended family was caught in a racial and ethnic quagmire. Most of us grew up in the Bay Area and went to the same high school, almost all at the same time. Oftentimes our peers confronted us, as our racial ambiguities became more apparent.

"Were you adopted by Mexicans?"

"You don't look African American. You look [insert any of the following: West Indian; Fijian; Samoan; Dominican; mixed with something; foreign or exotic; like you have some red in your skin]."

"You can't be Latina; there isn't a 'K' in the Spanish alphabet."

"Say something in Mexican then."

"So that is why all your cousins play soccer. Do you know how to salsa dance? I bet you can eat a bunch of peppers and it's like nothing to you."

"So that's why you all get good grades in school; you aren't really Black."

"I thought you were just Black but I could tell something was up."

"Your mom's Spanish and English sound so weird."

"Afro-Latino? Does that mean you are mixed? Who is Black, your mom or dad?"

And so on.

As far as my own self-awareness goes, I was much too fearful in high school to even walk into a "Latinos Unidos" meeting, even when they were planning to march against Proposition 187 (though illegal immigration is something my family knows quite a bit about). I was much too embarrassed to challenge my teacher in African American history when she said we would only focus our study on enslavement in the United States, although I knew 95 percent of enslaved Africans went south of the "border" and needed to at least be acknowledged. I was still too anxious as an adult when I was denied a job teaching Latin American history because "the students would rather hear that information from a Mexican colleague." And I was much too angry to speak when later, in a graduate seminar, another student informed the class that after slavery, "Black immigrants have not contributed anything to the United States as a whole, maybe just Miami and New York."

Central America suffers from the same national identity dilemmas that much of Latin America is plagued with—namely, where to place Blackness in whitening ideologies, especially when nation-building projects, post-revolutions, and United States interventions favor, and to some extent require, a unified national identity. In other words, racism, and to some extent, race, was supposedly a United States invention and therefore non-existent in Central America. Racial identities are discarded in favor of a unified national identity, despite actions to the contrary.

These national identities were critical pieces of socialist revolutionary rhetoric, especially for Nicaragua and the Sandinistas in the 1980s, in their efforts to be what the United States is not—ethnically and racially harmonious. When racial divisions become visible, they are immediately dismissed as being a figment of someone's imagination. Or, according to the dominant political discourse, the oppressed group is given complete agency in their own segregation—the people of Bluefields or the West Indians in Panama do not *want* to integrate, despite being invited. Or racism is considered something that those from the United States brought with them and began only since their arrival. Race is just one other manifestation of Central America's desire to be unlike the United States. For Central Americans these processes are complicated still further once the émigré lands in the "capitalist's backyard," and is forced to assume and grapple with a Black identity that was ignored at home. They are no longer invisible; rather they are visible, in the ways that African Americans are racialized in the United States and the West Coast in particular: non-Spanish-speaking and from the United States South. They continue to be invisible as Latin@s, because they are separate from the ways that Mexican identity is formed. And of course they continue to be invisible as Afro-Latin@s, as this identification hardly exists in the West Coast.

As a teacher and graduate student, I find myself answering questions more often than I pose them. When I am challenged or questioned about my identity, I respond by saying that Black people exist in Central America. Some are descendants of enslaved peoples; some are not. Some speak Spanish; some do not. Some are Catholic; some are Rastas; some are Garveyites. Some are immersed in hybridized identities that include native, Asian, and African nations. And when these Black people come to the United States, they continue to be Black people from Central America, negotiating among invisibilities.

Notes

1. Although my father is not from Nicaragua, like many other Blacks on the isthmus he has ancestry in Bluefields, Corn Island, and San Andres and thus shares a cultural connection with Nicaraguans.
2. *Paña* is slang for mestizo. It is a reference to España or Spain. Mestizos are those who identify as being of mixed Spanish and Native American ancestry.
3. *Frito* is a dish with fried plantains, pork, and salad, sometimes with *gallo pinto* or rice and beans, Nicaraguan style.
4. These names have been changed to respect the anonymity of the speakers.

AIDA LAMBERT

We Are Black Too

Experiences of a Honduran Garifuna

When we Black Latin@s come to this country our worlds are very differ-ent. We arrive with our own customs, our culture, our language, and it is difficult to make ourselves understood and to gain the respect of others. I myself came here over forty years ago, in 1964, when there were still very few Hondurans in New York, and even fewer Garifunas like myself. When we first got here we lived in Brooklyn, and I had to work hard so as to save and start to bring my kids over. I had six of them. Before the year was out, though, we moved to Harlem, right here on 111th Street, where we live to this day.

But those initial adjustments were hard. On my first job, at a factory in Brooklyn, I had a very mixed experience. The *puertorriqueñas* usually treated us very well and took us under their wing. But I had a supervisor who was African American, and she gave me a hard time. She seemed to be singling me out and picking on me, to the point where I had to change jobs and take work in the garment district in Manhattan. I have found that even though you are Black, the fact that you are Latina means to them that you are of another race. I know that to go up you have to climb the ladder rung by rung, but we Hondurans have moved up, step by step, even though we weren't always accepted or encouraged. I remember a time when I found some food stamps in the street and threw them away not knowing what they were. Only when I had a temporary layoff and went on unemployment did I find out that those coupons were like money. But when I tried to cash them in I again faced objections from an African American woman in the welfare office, to the point where I had to fight back and let her have it. I wound up handing her a bag of coffee grounds, so that she'd know that we are Blacks, too, as Black as they are.

Because we Garifunas are a proud people. Despite our history of resistance and affirmation, it wasn't until recently, in the 1940s, that there came any acknowledgment about our roots and historical experience. We are Africans, and Indians, and still preserve something of the original Carib language, the only people to do so. In 1948 they called all Garifuna together to unite as a people. My husband went and attended, and then brought that experience with him when we came to live here. In Honduras there are two kinds, or "levels," of Blacks: there are the "Spanish" ones who made up the slave population during the colonial period, and then there are the "ingleses"—the ones who speak English, who are mainly of West Indian roots and didn't settle in Central America until the later nineteenth century. So even in our home countries, before even coming here to the United States, we had to know how to deal with cultural differences among people. And of course with the racism of the Whites.

Again and again I have confronted the prejudice of lighter-skinned Latin@s. I always let them know, though. I remember the time I knew this Cuban man who kept saying he was White. I had to remind him that though he might think he looks White, he is the same origin as we are. I'd say to him, "You are White, but you're Black. I was born at night, and you during the day, but both from the hand of God." I had faced White discrimination back home in Honduras, so it wasn't as much of a shock when I saw anti-Black Latin@s here in New York. We feel it when we go to the bodega right here on the corner. It's owned by a Dominican, and many times he favors White customers over us. One time I was there, ready to pay for the things I had picked out, and two White guys came in. What happened was that he attended to them first, and acted like I wasn't standing there in front of him. He must think the Whites are going to find him a place in the Tower of Babel or something.

For me, though, this kind of stupidity and mistreatment has only been an incentive to advance myself, which in my opinion can only happen through education, la preparación. The Hondurans would get to know each other and socialize in the social clubs. Early on, they would mostly socialize among themselves, and many wound up getting married to people they met in this way. My own children are an example of that. I was so involved in the socializing that at one point I opened my own club, called La Lámpara (The Lamplight). Not only Hondurans but other nationalities came there, though I would specialize in having Garifuna bands so as to introduce our culture here and preserve it among our young people because we are a very small tribe here. That's what we are, a tribe. How many people knew about punta, our music? Or our language? That's why I got involved with the Desfile de la Hispanidad—the annual Hispanic Parade. It's been thirty-four years now that I have been at it, representing my country, Honduras. Even before that I belonged to the Honduran Society, *el gremio*. I've been with them so long that by now I am the only *veterana* left, which is why I was chosen to be the Honduran delegate to the Desfile. Many Latin@ groups are represented in this event, and relations are generally very good, and respectful. But it is also true that most of the delegates are White Latin@s, there are very few if any Blacks. Sometimes some of the groups are pretty racist, like the Argentines who don't invite Blacks to their dances. But they do have to invite me, because I am so actively involved. In fact, I had to push Blackness even among the Hondurans, who had never put up a Black woman for the beauty pageant. But I did, I promoted a beautiful Black *Hondureña*, and she won!

I've also seen how things change over time. Even at home, in Honduras, our Garifuna culture, and our language, is losing ground and becoming less and less familiar. And here it is even more so. My own children, as much as I try to keep the culture alive, they have their own lives and often forget whatever they learn. Not to mention my grandchildren, who were born here. I warn them about my experiences with African Americans, but they play with them, are influenced by them, and join them. They make friends with them, they identify with them, in the way they dress, and talk, and the music they listen to. And what can I do, I have to let them choose their own cultural preferences, you can't force it. The thing is, the African Americans are changing, too. With all the Latin@s around nowadays, they are having to learn how to speak Spanish, eat tortillas, and dance salsa. There are *morenos*, Black Americans, who dance salsa better than a lot of Latin@s!

The thing is, Afro-Latin@s have to come together and unite among themselves so they have more force. Unity is what gives strength. We are all *negros*, but we each have different qualities. Look at the food: the boricuas eat *mofongo*, the dominicanos eat *mangú*, and we call it *machuca*, but it is all basically the same food with different seasonings.

Note

[Interview conducted on December 26, 2007, in East Harlem, New York City; translated and edited by Juan Flores.]

MARÍA ROSARIO JACKSON
Profile of an Afro-Latina
Black, Mexican, Both

I am the United States–born daughter of an African American man and a Mexican woman. I grew up in a Black neighborhood in Los Angeles, but I spent my first eighteen summers in Mexico City where my mother's family lives. My childhood home in Los Angeles was a place where race mattered. My father was from the generation that was lashed by Jim Crow laws and then brought the civil rights movement to its peak. He was also of the generation in which many African American artists and intellectuals left the United States to find refuge in Mexico. He was proud of his heritage and passed it on to me through family stories, Black history lessons he knew I would not get in school, and the repeated reminder that despite what society would lead me to believe Black people made great contributions to civilization and I "did not come from trash."

My father loved Mexico until his death. He was fascinated by its history, culture, and people, and also, in his eyes, its non-whiteness. When he first encountered Mexico in the 1950s, coming from the United States where race was such a defining factor, he also loved the myth that in Mexico race did not matter. He was heartened by the freedoms that African Americans enjoyed in Mexico, without Jim Crow segregation. He saw art by African Americans in major cultural venues when these artists' work would not be shown in the United States. African Americans could also establish businesses and own property without dealing with racial covenants preventing this, as was the case at home. He suspected that the notion that Mexico was completely free of racism was not altogether true, and over time his suspicions were confirmed, sometimes painfully. But he continued to love the country anyway. He loved it as one loves family—warts and all.

My mother is fiercely Mexican—a small *mestiza* woman full of fire and life. At home she spoke only in Spanish to my brother and me—Spanglish was not allowed. She made sure we knew Mexican customs and could "properly" read and write in her language. Our household celebrated saints' days and 16 *de septiembre*, and our yearly summer trips to Mexico were almost sacred. My mother loved my father and his family, but she admits that, particularly early in their marriage, she did not always understand how they viewed the world—why race was so important and why everyone in his family, ranging in color from almost white (or "high yellow" in the Black vernacular) to dark brown, was called Black. When I was a small child, my mother used to claim that there was no racism in Mexico—everyone was Mexican. It was not like the United States—obsessed with race and categories. She has now lived in the United States for almost fifty years and says it has taken her decades and raising two "Black" children to better understand the racial dynamics here and to see that even in Mexico, where everyone is Mexican, there is racism too.

My view of race and racism in Mexico is influenced by my parents' experiences as well as my own. As an African American Mexican woman, over the course of my life I have felt the country's embrace and its sting. Looking at old pictures of myself as a small child among my Mexican cousins I am happy—laughing like all the rest of them—but I look somewhat different. My nose is a little flatter, my hair is much curlier, my lips are a bit fuller and I am a little darker than most of them. In Mexico City, walking through the markets with my aunts and grandmother, I was called *chata*, *chinita*, *trompudita*, and *morena*—all racial terms, though said with affection I think. I looked somewhat distinct from most people in Mexico City, but not completely unfamiliar: "*Parece costeñita*," people would say. My appearance sometimes caused people to pause briefly. They thought I was Mexican, but I was definitely not from D.F.—maybe a visitor from one of the Mexican coasts such as Veracruz or Guerrero. I was teased. People would talk to me in fake *costeño* accents and I didn't understand why. In retrospect, I can see that they were acknowledging my African features even though they may not have made the connection with Africa. They claimed me as Mexican, but they viewed me as a curiosity that belonged at the periphery of the nation.

As I grew older I became more knowledgeable about African American history and my father's interpretation of Mexican history, which included Black presidents, Morelos and Guerrero, and indigenous groups (e.g., Olmecs) with African connections. I started to identify similarities in the call and response of West African music and *son jarocho*. I traveled to Acapulco and Veracruz and saw people who looked like me, my family in the United States, and people back in my Black neighborhood in Los Angeles.

My neighborhood in Los Angeles was heavily African American. It was full of Black people of many hues who had been pioneers by integrating the predominantly White Crenshaw district, which quickly became predominantly Black upon their arrival. My neighborhood was full of school teachers and government workers, many of them with educational attainment that far exceeded their professional standing. It was the 1970s and my older brother and his contemporaries wore huge afros, to the dismay of some of the more conservative parents. It was the era of "Black Power" and time to proclaim that you were "Black and Proud." And here too, as a child I felt my community's embrace and its sting. We were "Black and Proud" just like the rest of the kids, sort of. We had been taught to be proud of our Black heritage, but often, despite all of that, we didn't feel like we were Black enough. People heard us speak Spanish. After all, most of the time my mother refused to speak to us in English. Then there was our light skin and "good" or "nice" (in the Black vernacular) not quite kinky hair. And in the summer we disappeared not to go to Texas or Louisiana like some of the other kids did, but to go south of the border to a place where my contemporaries imagined people wore sombreros, serapes, and huaraches like they did on cartoons or in the "It's a Small World" ride at Disneyland. With all that, could we still be part of the "Black and Proud" club? Did the fact that our mother was not African American eliminate us from it? Did the fact that she wasn't white make our different appearance any more palatable? We had some explaining to do. But we weren't the only ones. Some of the people in my neighborhood who were from Louisiana were Creoles and they had a whole lot of explaining to do too. They shared our physical appearance mostly. They were also Catholic and some of the elder Creoles would pepper their language with French and Creole words and phrases, which my contemporaries understood but didn't utter. Sometimes for me it was just easier to blend in with them, keep my story to myself and let them take the heat from the gatekeepers of the "Black and Proud" club.

As I got older, the Black Power movement waned. People cut their afros and I felt like there was less explaining required. Perhaps my brother, the Creole kids, and I had all finally gained entry. I'm not sure if the demands for explanations really diminished or if I just stopped hearing them, but other things captured my attention. It was the 1980s. I had to finish high school and the pressure was on because I had been taught by my father and grandfather that despite my complicated background, my light skin, and my "nice hair," I was still a little "colored" girl susceptible to all of the racism that still thrived. They drilled in me that despite whatever affirmative action programs might be available, I had "to be twice as good" as my White counterparts "to get half as far." "They can walk. You've got to run." I had heard that from them all of my life and they had the conviction and full expectation that I would be able to run just as fast as I needed to.

In college, still in Southern California, I discovered Chican@s. Growing up in an African American environment and spending summers in Mexico, I didn't have much knowledge about Chican@s. My mother didn't relate to Chicanismo when I was a child. For her that was an American concoction. She had unpleasant memories of Chican@s asking her questions about Mexico that were based on denigrating American stereotypes about Mexicans. "Are there cars in Mexico City?" Again, she was fiercely Mexican, and in the 1950s when she first came to the United States many of the people of Mexican ancestry who she encountered had been socialized to not speak Spanish and to have little regard for Mexico and Mexicans. Anyway, rather than choose to join the Black organizations or the Chican@ organizations, I tried to participate in both. But quickly I felt that I had more in common with the Black students. In dealing with the Chican@ student organizations I had flashbacks of the "Black and Proud" club from my childhood. Why didn't I have a Spanish surname? Was I really Chicana? I looked more like a Puerto Rican or Dominican. I was in the business of explaining myself again and I didn't have the energy for it, or the incentive. While I did not persist in trying to participate in the Chican@ student groups, I learned about Chican@ history and developed an appreciation for it. I shared what I learned with my mother and she began to have a different take on who Chican@s were and what their experience had been. With a better understanding, her resentment of the group turned to compassion and her grasp of race and racism in both Mexico and the United States deepened.

Even though in a United States context I affiliated and participated primarily in African American networks, I was always consciously and consistently both African American and Mexican. However, my need to be vocal about my identity has changed.

Over the years I have been in many situations where either Mexicans or African Americans didn't detect my other side and would say something negative. Sometimes I would speak up and other times I would just listen and learn. In life you go through phases, figuring out what matters, and picking your battles. In my youth and early adulthood I wanted to be clear that I was both—I felt a compulsion to identify as both African American and Mexican. As I have grown older I have felt less need to explain myself, and that has been liberating for me. If they care, let them figure it out, or not.

I am OK with the "Afro-Latina" label, which is coming into vogue. But if someone asks I say I am African American and Mexican. And in the American context I tend to say Black, or African American, first, because that has been my most significant formative experience. But it is contextual and depends sometimes on who is asking and why. For me, sometimes the two cultures are very distinct and sometimes there is confluence. I think it's important to recognize that there is integrity in both distinction and confluence. I also think it is important to remember that racial and ethnic labels are tools that can work for or against social justice.

I remember when I was in the tenth grade or so, taking my PSAT exams, and I was asked to fill out the racial box. I checked "other" because you could only pick one. Then I started realizing that some of my friends with similar or lower PSAT scores were getting college pamphlets and I wasn't getting any. I recognized that college admissions offices weren't responding to the "other" category in a way that advanced my goals. That's when I figured out that labels, a necessary evil, lead to sorting, which can have long-reaching consequences. I learned to depersonalize the categories and have become strategic when I check boxes. The boxes are no longer a source of emotional turmoil for me. The boxes are boxes. I understand them. I have learned how they are used and how to use them. I check them when I must but they don't define who I am.

ANTONIO LÓPEZ

Enrique Patterson

Black Cuban Intellectual in Cuban Miami

Miami is the capital of Cuban Whiteness. It is where, in the words of the Black Cuban exile intellectual Enrique Patterson, the long-held dream of the nineteenth-century "creole sugar-plantation ruling class (la sacarocracia criolla)" finally seemed to come true: "Cubans were White."[1]

I am talking here, of course, as much about the demographics of the old-guard Cuban exile—it was overwhelmingly White criollos who settled in Miami after 1959—as I am about its power, which naturalized Cuban Whiteness and White privilege in its everyday practice of cold war anti-revolutionary politics. Needless to say, if the exile naturalized White-ness and White privilege, it ignored, at the political level, Black Cubans and Cuban Blackness, a major omission given that every White-criollo-sanctioned Cuban nationalist movement from the nineteenth century forward has had at least to acknowledge, if not in the end fully advocate and achieve, the cause of Black Cuban justice.

Miami would "darken" over the twentieth-century course of the exile, thanks to the arriving Black and mulato and mulata protagonists of the 1980 Mariel migration and that of the 1990s balsero migration. Cuban Whiteness in the United States, meanwhile, would continue to look "off-White" in Anglo eyes, in keeping with the historic Anglo-Hispano colonial and post-colonial rivalry over the "true" claim to Whiteness and White privilege in the Americas. Yet despite these and other facts (the conflict between Miami and Washington during and after Elián González, for example, or the rela-tive "softening" of the exile's recent politics, due in part to the emerging political influence of a younger generation of Cuban-Americans born in the United States), Miami remains the capital of naturalized Cuban White-ness and White privilege. To understand latinidad in the United States, and *afro-latinidad* in particular, it is crucial to consider the history of Black *and* White Latin@ racialization in Cuban Miami.

It is in this regard that I turn to the writings of Enrique Patterson. To include Patterson in a broader discussion of United States Afro-Latin@ identity, culture, and politics is to draw the attention of both Cuban and Cuban American publics, and of the broader Latin@ communities, to the historically present yet ideologically *unseen* figure of the Cuban Black intellectual, both on the island and in the diaspora.

Since Patterson's exile to the United States in 1992, and in dozens of essays published in *El Nuevo Herald*, *Encuentro de la cultura cubana*, and elsewhere, he has pointed out the inability of the White criollo Cuban nation project to break with its racist, anti-democratic origins in Spanish colonialism. He has indicated this from a broad transhistorical perspective: the nineteenth-century uprisings against Spain, the early-twentieth-century movements to consolidate the republic, the 1959 revolution, and the Miami exile all come under his scrutiny. Patterson's critical account of *cubanidad* aligns him with other historical Black Cuban social, intellectual, and political figures in the United States, including Rafael Serra, Evelio Grillo, and Melba Alvarado. It is a disparate grouping, to be sure, each with a different attitude and method of being Black and Cuban in the United States, but it is nonetheless a coherent one in that what constitutes Black Cuban experience and knowledge for each is a resistance to both United States and Cuban White supremacist ideas and institutions. The careers of Serra, Alvarado, Grillo, and Patterson, in other words, converge on what I would term the Afro-Cuban-American difference, a concept whose meaning the documentary film *Cuban Roots/Bronx Stories* (2000) captures well. In the film a Black Cuban immigrant, reflecting on his arrival from Cuba to South Florida in the early 1960s, explains his experience of exile and Cuban racial identity thus: "As soon as we arrived in Miami, the White Cubans went one way, the Black Cubans went another."[2]

Patterson was born in 1950 in San Andrés, Oriente Province, into a middle-class Black family. A change in fortune—the family shoe factory burned down—led to a move west to Camagüey, where the young Patterson grew up. While in high school in Havana, Patterson would become disillusioned with the revolution after the Cuban state support of the Soviet invasion of Czechoslovakia. He spoke out and was expelled from the Young Communists. Beginning in 1973, he studied and taught philosophy at the University of Havana, eventually earning a degree in Hispanophone language and literature there. Expelled from the university in 1981 for further resistance to the government line, Patterson would go on to participate in the establishment of a dissident group, the Democratic Socialist Current. Eventually, after further harassment and interrogation, he sought asylum in the United States. In 1992 Patterson arrived in San Francisco, and a year later he moved to Miami. Soon thereafter, he began writing columns for El Nuevo Herald. He would go on to host two shows on Radio Martí, one of which, Café Palenque, explicitly addressed Black Cubans on the island regarding issues of racial identity and justice. His current work, as of 2007, is as a contributor to and board member of the journal Encuentro de la cultura cubana, and as a teacher at Charles R. Drew Elementary School in Liberty City, one of the historic African American neighborhoods in Miami.[3]

The main lines of Patterson's thinking are contained in two of his essays, "Cuba: La nación a la luz de las transiciones" (1997) and "Racismo, totalitarismo, y democracia" (2007). Foremost, perhaps, is the way he describes the racist ideology of Cuba's early anti-colonial intellectuals. For Patterson, "those who, in one way or another, were the originators of Cuban thought (Parreño, Saco, el Conde de Pozos Dulces, Domingo del Monte, etc.) understood Cuba, at a fundamental level, as an identity from which Blacks were excluded and whose destiny required their disappearance, sooner rather than later. In the case of [Félix] Varela, this occurred from the paternalistic view that they were beings in need of civilizing. . . . Thus the thesis of a needed 'Whitening.'"[4] Patterson translates this critique of the founding discourses of Cuban nationalism into his assessment of the Cuban revolution's failure to support Black Cuban justice—all in the broader context of his fundamental challenge to the Cuban revolution as anti-democratic. Cuban Blacks today, he writes, "live in the worst neighborhoods, hold the worst jobs, and constitute the majority of the island's penal population." He concludes that "even those who call themselves revolutionary are conservative . . . when it comes to the race problem" on the island.[5] The Cuban exile also comes under his analysis of Cuban race politics. Noticeably absent in the exile conversation on national reconciliation, Patterson argues, is "the Black issue, in spite of how fifty years of national division—historically, socially, and politically—weigh less than four hundred years of racial division. Or is racial discrimination, to them, not a national problem?"

At another level, meanwhile, Patterson comments on the crucial question of what would constitute true political freedom in contemporary Cuba. "To what degree," he asks, "can a social group assemble, freely discuss its problems, create an agenda in response, and bring it freely to the public, to the parliament, to the media, until it becomes a political program, a legal norm, an expression of power?" Such questions of democratic freedom and individual rights resonate personally and professionally with Patterson in relation to his work with Radio Martí. In reflecting on his broadcasts of *Café Palenque* with the station, he writes, "I did not allow anyone to impose a point of view on me. . . . I was totally free in the development of content." He adds that, "for the first time, we created a program produced by and directed to Afro descendents" in Cuba. Indeed, if Patterson is critical of the Cuban state's inability to respect "an expression of power" arising out of the social, he is just as critical of how state power in the United States would dictate the island's future, writing that the United States "has no right to determine when the Cuban system is democratic, nor to decide when or how democracy in Cuba has to be established."

Patterson's writing thus dislodges everyone's comfortable position on the topic of Cuba, and that is as it should be. Critics of the Cuban revolution in Miami find much to agree with in Patterson, but then they must confront his critique of how the Cuban state imagines and acts on power by wielding the historic (and, again, naturalized) power of White criollo identity, over and against the interests of Black Cubans. The Cuban government, in turn, will discredit Patterson's broadcasts over Radio Martí. "What better example is there of his compromised position," it would ask, "than that he broadcasts within the United States, the primary state sponsor of imperial violence around the world?" Yet Patterson's broadcasts do the one thing the revolution cannot, which is invite Black Cubans to imagine an island where they think and perform in civil society through their knowledge and feelings as African diasporic peoples in the Americas, where they can shape the development of the Cuban nation and its future institutions without leaving their Blackness behind.

It is difficult, in other words, to assimilate Patterson into the commonplaces of Cuban-American debate. His ideas take readers, so sure of where the question of Cuba should lead them, in multiple unexpected directions. It is perhaps fitting, then, that Patterson's work, in his own words, is "*regado*"—that is to say, "scattered"—among newspapers and academic journals both in print and online, and it includes historical analysis, literary criticism, interviews, polemics, political treatises, journalistic columns, and film reviews.[6] With his output being a kind of strategic *regadera*, or scattering, his essays have so far not been collected in book form. Patterson's intellectual *regadera* recalls how, according to the Martinican writer and intellectual Édouard Glissant, the African diasporic oral tradition of the Caribbean plantation spoke in the language of "torn-off fragments," which was a sign of the suppression of African diasporic culture by

White colonial authorities, but also of its resistance and survival.[7] Patterson's work thus resonates as a sort of post-plantation moment in Cuban Miami—the "torn-off fragments" of Black Cuban thought that the state in Cuba and, to a different degree, the exile in Miami, would prefer to banish. What is more, that Patterson writes outside of the context of his "day job" as a public school teacher in Liberty City only stresses the point, for even as he writes about Cuba he is teaching young African Americans who are the descendants of those who resisted the plantation system in its Anglo formation. This is Liberty City as a center of Cuban intellectual work—in one sense, the White Cuban sense, you can't get any less Cuban, in Miami, than that.

Patterson's essays thus narrate the history of Cuban Whiteness in the manner of the "torn-off fragment." When he reviews Rolando Díaz's film *Si me comprendieras*, a documentary on the injustices experienced by mulata and Black Cuban women working in the island entertainment industry, he writes that the film critiques the "traditional, touristic, colonizing, or White" gaze that descends from the discourses and practices of colonial plantation patriarchy and sexual violence—a gaze that would still take for granted the right to envision Cuban women of color in such misogynist terms.[8] And, in one of the most incisive readings we have of the major twentieth-century Cuban intellectual Jorge Mañach, Patterson writes that Mañach, "typically so lucid, is unaware that the White-criollo nationalist discourse is itself a 'particular' discourse, whose 'universality' results more from the mechanisms of power that impose it as 'the' discourse than because of its intellectual and ethical rigor."[9] Unveiling Whiteness as privilege and Whiteness as power, here in the cultures of Cuban gender violence against Black and mulata women and there in the intellectual tradition of theorizing national identity, is Patterson's most significant contribution to the contemporary critique of Cuba and its institutions, both on the island and in the diaspora.

Notes

1. Enrique Patterson, "Cuba: Discursos sobre la identidad," *Encuentro de la cultura cubana* 2 (1996): 66. Unless otherwise noted, all translations are mine.

2. *Cuban Roots/Bronx Stories*, directed by Pam Sporn (Los Angeles: Latino Public Broadcasting, 2000).

3. Enrique Patterson, interview with the author, December 28, 2007; Silvia Pedraza, *Political Disaffection in Cuba's Revolution and Exodus* (New York: Cambridge University Press, 2007), 231–34; and Andrea O'Reilly Herrera, ed., *ReMembering Cuba: Legacy of a Diaspora* (Austin: University of Texas Press, 2001), 34–40.

4. Enrique Patterson, "Cuba: La nación a la luz de las transiciones," *Encuentro de la cultural cubana* 6–7 (1997): 227.

5. Enrique Patterson, "Racismo, totalitarismo, y democracia," *Encuentro en la red*, November 9, 2007, http://www.cubaencuentro.com (site visited on December 24, 2007. The quotations in the three paragraphs following are also from this essay.

6. Enrique Patterson, interview with the author, December 28, 2007.

7. Édouard Glissant, *Poétique de la relation* (Paris: Gallimard, 1990), 83.

8. Enrique Patterson, "Un testimonio de negras y mulatas," *En Nuevo Herald*, March 1, 1999, 13A.

9. Patterson, "Cuba," 229.

EDUARDO BONILLA-SILVA

Reflections about Race by a *Negrito Acomplejao*

When I started talking, and later on, writing about racial matters in the mid-1980s, my father told me, "Eduardo, tú eres un negrito acomplejao" (Eduardo, you are a Black man with a complex).[1] This comment irritated me beyond belief not only because it downplayed the significance of my work on race but, more importantly, because it came from my father, whom I love dearly and who also happens to be a Black Puerto Rican. How could he, of all people, say something like this? I fought with him and reminded him of a few racial incidents in his own life. I reminded him how, when I was ten years old or so, a clerk in a shoe store treated him like dirt because he was Black (one of my first clear memories of racial discrimination). I reminded him how he had been "elevated" to "negro pero decente"[2] (Black but decent) by "White"[3] members of our family because he was a university professor. I reminded him of how he was insulted by the father of my first wife (a mulatto himself but with green eyes)[4] because he was Black. I reminded him about how few Blacks were ever hired as professors in the university and how he knew that race was a factor in this state of affairs. I reminded him of many, many things, but there was no agreement as he translated all these things as examples of individual prejudice[5] rather than of "systemic racism."[6]

This argument with my father led me to reflect on the many ways race mattered in my life as a child and as a youngster in Puerto Rico. I think of the overt ways in which race affected me, fully aware that in Puerto Rico, as in most contemporary racial orders, race also matters in ways that are not visible to those who experience discrimination (e.g., teachers not giving students equal opportunity in the classroom, employers not hiring people or denying them promotions because of racial considerations, etc.).

Very early on in my life I noticed that I received less affection from my immediate and extended family than did my siblings. Without having the tools to understand why this was the case, I struggled as a child. I pondered things no child should ponder: Why doesn't *mami* love me as much as Pedro or Karen? Why do my White family members (at the time, I did not see them as White but just as "family") seem so distant? What have I done not to deserve the same level of affection as my siblings? Although race was likely not the only reason for the lesser affection I received from my family, it was definitely a factor.[7]

As I grew up, I heard all sorts of racist statements about Blacks from some of my aunts and even from my own mother. They referred to young Blacks as *cocolos* and *cafres*,[8] and said all sorts of nasty things about the "Black side" of our family,[9] such as "You know, your aunt does not know better because she is accustomed to living in shit" or "Eduardo, *those people do not have class.*" (I struggled with these comments for a long time as I somehow felt *those people* were not just "them" but me!) And although these views were uttered in private, they must have affected social interaction as several members of the Black side of our family fought back and referred to some of the White members of my family as *blanquit@s* (whiteys).[10]

A good example of how racial perceptions affected social relations was the interaction that occurred at events such as weddings. I remember, for instance, attending weddings where these racial divisions led to what I might call a "soft" segregation: Whites and honorary Whites (such as my immediate family) sat at one set of tables while Blacks and mulatto family members sat at other tables.[11] I remember (and still observe) how social interaction among the various sides of my family varied according to their race. If the interaction was between Whites and non-Whites, the exchanges were more formal; interactions between same-race people were less formal and deeper.

As a child struggling for affection and identity, I remember how much I loved visiting members of the Black side of our family (mostly from my father's side). They always welcomed me with open arms whereas my White family members treated me in a more formal, distant manner. (I am now forty-six years old and this emotional situation has not changed at all.) As I matured and recognized (albeit incipiently) the racial roots of some of these family dynamics, I raised hell with my immediate family and created friction because my mother (a *mulata* with a Ph.D.)[12] did not like to associate with the Black side of my family. And as I gained partial racial consciousness about my own Blackness, I raised the issue vociferously every time I could. (To this day, this friction is still part of our family life and a reason why I do not travel as often as I should to my own homeland.)

Although gaining partial racial consciousness[13] gave me a tool to understand things and fight back, "seeing" how race mattered in my life was also extremely painful for me. The insults and affronts to my dignity and self-esteem experienced during my youth clearly demonstrate that race matters deeply in our Americas.

El *Negrito Acomplejao* becomes a "Blican" and Tells His Brethren What Is to Be Done

One fundamental difference between racial structurations such as that of the United States or South Africa and that of most others in the rest of the world[14] is that the former produce clear demarcations of racial groups and we versus them racial situations while "plural orders" produce malleable racial lines where racialized people are less likely to gel as groups and are thus less likely to develop a fully clear racial consciousness. Not surprisingly, it is when we—Blacks from the Americas—migrate to the United States that we develop a strong racial consciousness that then helps us revisit and rethink our personal and collective history.

I came to the United States in 1984 as a Puerto Rican with an admittedly tenuous racial consciousness. After a few years I became a "minority" and, within four years after coming to this country, I became fully racially conscious and began referring to myself as a Black Puerto Rican (I started my racial identity process before the current movement toward the usage of the term "Afro-Latin@"). As a sort of joke, I refer to myself nowadays as a "Blican" (Black Puerto Rican), thus poking fun at Tiger Woods who labeled himself "Cablinisian" (Caucasian, Black, Indian, and Asian).

And what can a Blican tell Afro-Latin@s about what they will experience in the United States and what they can do to fight back?

1. For those new to the United States racial boat, be prepared. In the "mean streets" of America you are not likely to be recognized as a "Latin@."[15] Instead, you are more likely to be viewed and treated as a *negr@* (a Black person). This will have monumental implications for your life, and you had better learn this lesson quickly.

2. Afro-Latin@s must resist the temptation to participate in the game of racial innocence that their families play. That is, we must learn our histories and not repeat the nonsense we hear in our communities, such as the idea that racism is just a United States problem and that we do not have racial problems "back home."

3. We must understand that our Latin@ communities are also internally fractured by race and that, therefore, the "enemy" for us here is not just

White gringos. Watch out for friends and families telling you about the "morenos" or the "molletos" (two terms Latin@s use to refer to African Americans). Today they talk about them, but tomorrow they will talk about you. And the lessons about plural orders and the experiences I've narrated about my life in Puerto Rico may happen to you here with Latin@s, so watch out for blanquit@s in your communities.

4. Although I believe that Afro-Latin@s must develop solidarity with African Americans, I also know that African Americans can treat us as "lesser" Blacks. Thus, we must also work hard to educate Black folks here. We must let them know that we, Blacks from the Americas, have a longer presence and history in the "New World." We must also remind them that "Blackness" is a construction and, as such, many of the folks they count as Black came from the Caribbean and Latin America. And this historical trend will continue, so it is in their best interest to be more pluralistic and understanding of us, Afro-Latin@s. Coalition politics go both ways!

5. Afro-Latin@s will notice that Whites treat some Latin@s better than them. They may also notice that some Latin@s are liked by Whites and that many Whites mingle with Latin@s of a certain look (those who look White). They will further notice how these Latin@s are more likely to experience success and occupational mobility (how many Afro-Latin@ professors do we have in colleges and universities?). And some Afro-Latin@s will wonder and ponder. I say, wonder and ponder no more. Latin@s come in all shades and the lighter Latin@s, much like light-skinned African Americans, are more likely to be liked by White folks.[16]

6. Latin@s in power in the political, social, cultural, and economic fields are likely to be the light-skinned ones. Afro-Latin@s must begin the struggle to get admitted to colleges, to be represented in TV (Univision, for example, seems to believe all Latin@s are light skinned), to assure that the few affirmative-action-inspired jobs and positions for Latin@s also go to them and not only to the usual suspects (White Latin@s). This strategy will be called "divisive" by some, but we must stand strong and firm. The demand for full representation of all Latin@s cannot be sacrificed at the altar of "unity."

7. Those who, like me, have a Latin@ "accent" will experience the double whammy of racial and ethnic discrimination.[17]

The life of Afro-Latin@s in the United States, therefore, entails a triple rather than "double consciousness."[18] We are Latin@s, but we are Afro-Latin@s. And we are people of African descent, although many African Americans see us as not of their kin. Thus, we navigate life as Blacks, as

Latin@s, and as a special segment of the American people with a special sight (now, after much pain, I see this sight as a gift).

But the racial landscape and racial practices in the United States are changing and those changes will have important implications for Afro-Latin@s. The traditional bi-racial order of the country (White versus non-White) is slowly morphing into a Latin America–like order.[19] As such, new racial spaces and racial practices are emerging before our very eyes. Most notably, I contend, an intermediate racial space for "in-betweeners" (honorary Whites) is being carved. This space will allow Latin@s who possess phenotypic and cultural capital to stake a claim to honorary—and maybe even to complete—Whiteness. Further, in the apparently more fluid emerging racial order, dark ontologies are sharing a space at the bottom with African Americans and other dark-skinned minorities (I label this space "the collective Black"). Thus, for example, although Black Cubans and White Cubans are all Cubans and many live in Miami, their life chances are totally different; Black Cubans seem to have all but joined African Americans at the bottom of the United States (racial) well.[20] Accordingly, Afro-Latin@s must work politically with others in the collective Black racial space to achieve racial justice. That justice is highly unlikely to come from Whites or, increasingly, from White Latin@s who will have the option to play out a new racial game as "honorary" or even as "real" Whites.

Final Words from the Black Man from Puerto Rico

I said almost all I wanted to say in this essay. I engaged in forbidden discussions likely to anger some but, hopefully, to serve as inspiration to many others. I outlined issues and subjects (e.g., how race fractures families in the Americas and how that is central to the reproduction of the racial order, etc.) that I hope others will work on in a systematic fashion in the future. I discussed personal matters that I have never discussed publicly in the hope that others will join me in exposing how deeply the tentacles of racism work in our America and in our own souls. I have done so hoping that people of color in the Americas wake up and begin analyzing in a serious fashion how race has affected their lives. We must expose how much discrimination we have suffered so that we can begin changing the terrain of discussion and action from the limited concept of prejudice to the more complex notion of systemic racism.

We must work hard to examine and uncover the practices and mechanisms at play that produce and maintain racial privilege at the economic, political, social, and psychological-attitudinal levels. Based on my knowledge of the almost invisible, now-you-see-it, now-you-don't way race operates in our societies, I believe it is likely that analysts will unearth a system of *racismo solapado* like that in most of Latin America and the Caribbean and akin to the one I have argued rules public racial interactions in post–civil rights America.[21]

This process ought to be connected to organizational and political efforts to force race from the background to the foreground. These processes may help Afro-Latin@s in the Americas to develop their incipient consciousness and move from a "race in itself" to a "race for itself" level of consciousness. In my case, like that of so many Afro-Latin@s, it was the "shock therapy" of navigating the in-your-face racial order of the United States that led me to wake up and accept my Blackness. Now, at forty-six, I can tell anyone who cares to listen that I am not a *negrito acomplejao* but a proud Black man from Puerto Rico!

Notes

1. This is an abbreviated version of a longer piece in progress entitled "Las historias prohibidas de pulgarcito: Reflections about Race by a 'Negrito Acomplejao.'" In the Spanish-speaking countries in the Americas with a significant African influence, words with the ending *ado* are usually shortened to *ao*. Thus, the word *acomplejado* is pronounced *acomplejao* or the word *pescado* (fish) is pronounced *pescao*. For the specific case of Puerto Rico, see Manuel Alvarez Nazario, El elemento afronegroide en el español de Puerto Rico, contribución al estudio del Negro en América (San Juan, P.R.: Instituto de Cultura Puertorriqueña, 1961).

2. Throughout the Americas, and under the myth of racial democracy, our racist culture remains intact. I grew up listening to sayings such as "Black but decent," "You are Black but have a white soul," "Blacks will screw up, either when they come in or on their way out." For the case of Puerto Rico, see Isabelo Zenón Cruz, Narciso descubre su trasero: El negro en la cultura puertorriqueña, 2 vols. (Humacao, P.R.: Ediciones Fundí, 1974, 1975). For the case of the Dominican Republic, see Ninfa Partiño Sánchez, "Relaciones interétnicas en República Dominicana: Racismo y antihatianismo," in El racismo en las Américas y el Caribe, edited by José Almeida Vinueza (Quito, Ecuador: Abya-Yala, 1999), 97–126.

3. When I refer to the White members of my family, I mean White by Puerto Rican standards. Our standards are more flexible than those of the United States, and many Puerto Rican "Whites" would not be regarded as such in the United States.

4. In the Americas, the construction of race includes more components than in the United States, where phenotype and acknowledged ancestry dictate, for the most part, racial classification. Hence, it is possible for "mixed people" (a funny notion, as we are all "mixed") who have *pelo bueno* (good hair), light eyes, European facial features, or

even nonmorphological characteristics such as education, "high" culture, or money, get "elevated" to Whiteness or at least to honorary Whiteness in our societies.

5. In the Americas, cases of discrimination are interpreted by most people as instances of "prejudice" (see Tomás Blanco, El prejuicio racial en Puerto Rico, edited by Arcadio Díaz Quiñones (Río Piedras, P.R.: Ediciones Huracán, 1985). This allows for any systemic pattern to be reframed as an individual-level problem.

6. Joe R. Feagin, Systemic Racism: A Theory of Oppression (New York: Routledge, 2006).

7. As an adult, I got confirmation from my own mother about how a nightmare she suffered as a child created an emotional block that affected how she interacted with me. The details are not essential to this story, but the fact remained that she read me through that nightmare negro. The racist component of this story, and the fact that it connects my mother's tragedy to the racial grammar of the West, is how she processed her negative experience with one Black person as symbolic of the "evil" in all Blacks. On this issue, see chapter 5, "The Fact of Blackness," in Frantz Fanon, Black Skin, White Masks (New York: Grove Press, 1967). See also Fanon's discussion of the influence of race on the affective networks within families in the Caribbean (191).

8. These two words are of African origin, and in Puerto Rico they refer to the poor, Black, and unrefined.

9. Families are always regarded in the Americas as "extended families" and most families have "Black" or "Indian" sides.

10. The word blanquit@ literally means "whitey," but it is used in Puerto Rico to refer to people with money. However, since the people who have had money throughout Puerto Rican history have been, for the most part, White people, the word has an unmistakable racial component to it.

11. Segregation in plural racial orders is usually "soft" because of the level of racial mixing. This explains in part why, for example, residential segregation is not so prominent in Latin America. Missing in most analyses is an understanding of (1) the extent of soft segregation, (2) the extent of hierarchy in social interactions, and (3) the existence of deep practices of segregation in marriages and social interaction among the White elites in these societies. Puerto Rico has a Spain-oriented Puerto Rican and Cuban elite with its own clubs (Casa Cuba, Club Naútico de San Juan, Casa de España, etc.) that help maintain racial-cultural "purity" among these folks. Thus, they may live in a "plural society," but they maintain a White habitus. See Eduardo Bonilla-Silva, Racism without Racists, 2nd ed. (Lanham, Md.: Rowman and Littlefield, 2006).

12. Explaining inter-racial relations in the Americas is, and will be, a central challenge for social analysts in the future.

13. In plural racial orders, it is very hard to gain full racial consciousness. The structure of these societies not only forbids talking about race but fosters a nationalist sense of self (We are all Puerto Ricans!).

14. Because it was in the United States that "race studies" emerged, the analysis of racial matters still follows their logic and traditions. This has produced a scholarship that tries to explain the many from the few—that is, we still try to explain most of the racial situations in the world based on concepts, ideas, and analyses based on the racial experience of the United States. I have criticized this stand in essays in my book

with Tukufu Zuberi, *White Logic, White Methods: Racism and Methodology* (Lanham, Md.: Rowman and Littlefield, 2008).

15. I borrow the term "mean streets" from Piri Thomas, *Down These Mean Streets* (New York: Knopf, 1967).

16. Edward Telles and Edward Murgia, "Phenotypic Discrimination and Income Differences among Mexican Americans," *Social Science Quarterly* 71, no. 4 (1990): 682–96.

17. Bonnie Urciuoli, *Exposing Prejudice: Puerto Rican Experiences of Language, Race, and Class* (Boulder, Colo.: Westview Press, 1996); Alberto Dávila, Alok K. Bohara, and Rogelio Sáenz, "Accent Penalties and the Earnings of Mexican Americans," *Social Science Quarterly* 74 (1993): 902–116.

18. W. E. B. Du Bois, *The Souls of Black Folk* (New York: Signet Classic, 1995).

19. Bonilla-Silva, *Racism without Racists*, 2nd ed. (Lanham, Md.: Rowman and Littlefield, 2006).

20. Correspondents of the *New York Times*, *How Race Is Lived in America* (New York: Henry Holt and Company, 2001).

21. Bonilla-Silva, *Racism without Racists*.

SILVIO TORRES-SAILLANT

Divisible Blackness

Reflections on Heterogeneity and Racial Identity

Blackness is divisible by as many contexts in which it might occur. Blackness mattered to the second-century BCE Roman playwright Publius Terentius Afer (commonly known as Terence), and to Alexander Sergeyevich Pushkin, the towering Romantic poet in Frederick the Great's Russia, differently from the ways it mattered to the Surinamese political thinker Anton de Kom in the 1930s or his contemporary in the United States, Marian Anderson, the revered operatic singer from Philadelphia. When it comes to the race question—hardly a subject suitable for scientific demonstration—personal experience can adequately compete with other forms of knowledge in the power to lay out the issue under discussion. With that in mind, I would like to start my reflections by allowing myself the indulgence of bearing witness. I shall cite a few incidents that strike me as emblematic of the complexity of racial identity. I present each as a vignette that I hope may elicit conversation about the diversity of the experiences that often place us face to face with the social and political significance of a Black person's phenotype as she or he interacts with the inhabitants of a world informed by the racial imagination.

The first vignette takes place in Moscow, where in 1984 I had the good fortune of visiting as a guest of the USSR Academy of Sciences thanks to a Russian scholar whose acquaintance I had made while pursuing graduate studies at New York University. On a particular Sunday afternoon I ventured to the circus on my own, my guide having already done enough escorting and orienting earlier in the week. I must have arrived at the circus after the show had already started, for I found no line or crowd outside. The deserted entrance area made all the more conspicuous the tall, thin figure of a Black man, dressed in a well-fitting dark-gray suit, standing near the door as if he were waiting for someone on the way in or out. Possibly only a few years older than I was at the time, he stood there straight and motionless, his gaze fixed on some distant point. Having already politicized the significance of my Blackness, I felt inclined to approach him and greet him in racial solidarity, Black brothers that we were in the midst of our vast Slavic surroundings. For a quick moment, I had the distinct impression that he might have felt the same way. I hesitated, though, for it dawned on me that I could not tell where he came from and did not know what language to address him in. Immediately, whole arrays of alien cultures, distant lands, and foreign tongues that I could not presume to speak began to parade through my mind, exponentially increasing the chance that my attempt at communication with him across language and difference might fail terribly. After a moment of uncomfortable hesitation, I desisted from concretizing my gesture of racial solidarity, choosing instead to go my way while he remained standing where I had found him.

The second vignette I have previously narrated, where I have told about a time when, while teaching at a college in the City of New York, I was approached by a colleague who was working with a group in the creation of a Black Faculty Caucus. In truth, some members of the organizing group had proposed my inclusion on account of my color, but others had second thoughts on account of my coming from a Spanish-speaking nation. Giving me the benefit of the doubt, the group agreed to let me decide whether or not I belonged in the caucus. My African American colleague put the question thus: "Do you consider yourself more Black than Hispanic, or more Hispanic than Black?" Finding the question disarming, I was unable to quantify the immaterial. I was too fearful of saying the wrong thing and merely spent sentences galore in aimless circumlocution. My indecision made me suspect in the eyes of my colleague, with the predictable result that I never heard about the Black caucus again."[1] My sharing of that story during the April 2002 conference Transnationalism, Gender, and the Changing Black World, held under the auspices of the African American Studies Department at Syracuse University, produced an expected corollary, when a prominent feminist scholar of the African diaspora who was one of the main speakers queried me about the episode. As a consummate Afrocentrist, she did not share my perplexity about the ethnoracial binary with which the Black caucus had confronted me. This became evident when, approaching me during the break, she would have me explain what she termed "the politics of the hesitation" that I had just related. Her body language and tone gave me grounds for sensing the indictment that would follow if I entered the conversation that she sought to provoke, one in which I could tell she would have a compelling prescription concerning how I should have located my ethnoracial identity in the episode narrated and the troubling implications of the fact that I didn't. Therefore, I politely evaded the question and managed to gear our exchange in the direction of less fractious terrain.

This latter incident and its corollary show the pressures that racialized beings may experience to fit prescriptive molds and regulatory narratives of racial identity. People of mixed ancestries seem to encounter the most difficulty since regimes of racial identity have often depended on the rule of homogeneity, the presumption that we have one root, not many, that, counterintuitive as it may sound, to claim more than one origin is to be less.

That the dead, no less than the living, may have to respond to the vigilant demands of ethnoracial border patrols protecting group identities from people with multiple roots stands out in the case of a racially mixed labor activist who died in 1942 at the age of ninety after a life dedicated to promoting the creed of equality and social justice. A biography co-written by Carolyn Ashbaugh, a researcher in women's labor history, calls her Lucy Parsons, privileges her Black origins, and dismisses her own self-attribution of Hispanic roots as an unfortunate denial of "her own Black ancestry."[2] Her Mexican American biographers, on the other hand, call the same labor advocate Lucía González Parsons and celebrate her as "an important early radical Chicano reformer."[3] Alfredo Mirande and Evangelina Enriquez succinctly evoke the squabble over the ethnicity of Gonzáles Parsons in their book on Mexican American women, but in the end they too end up asserting one of her ancestries over the other when they declare her to be a full-fledged Chicana.[4] Neither side seems to feel comfortable with the notion that the labor activist in question may have been both Black and Hispanic, that both sides can lay an equal claim to her legacy, and that her service to humanity was made greater precisely by her expansive vision of the struggle for justice and equality, meaning one which did not circumscribe her field of operation to the race or ethnicity of the workers whose well-being formed the core of her political cause.

The third vignette takes me back to the fall of 1998, when I served on the literature panel of the Mid-Atlantic Arts Foundation in Baltimore, Maryland. I recall bonding with the panel's two other males—one Black, the other White, and both from the United States. After completing our work, we found ourselves enjoying mirthful drinks at the bar of the hotel where we stayed. As the hours of our gleeful conversation passed, I noticed a distinct pattern in the triangular architecture of our colloquy. The volume of animated words that flowed between my two companions greatly surpassed the number of utterances either of them exchanged with me. Though we had known one another for the same length of time, a mere day and a half, partook of a common interest in literature, and shared a disposition to serve in state arts councils, I sensed that I could not succeed at steering my third of the conversation. Try as I may, I failed to assert myself as a natural speaker at the table of conviviality. I, the Hispanic, my dark-skinned hue notwithstanding, could not compete with the attention and enthusiasm that kept my Black and White associates going with reciprocal zest. I found myself resigned to playing a supporting role as a tributary to the main dialogue, intermittently expanding or wittily inflecting the core chat between my Black and White co-panelists. While never desisting from my occasional feeder remarks to confirm my still active role at the night's verbal intercourse, in my mind I mused about the long history of attraction and repulsion that mysteriously bonded my Black and White interlocutors in a way that rendered my presence tertiary. In 1998, I had lived in the United States for a good twenty-five years, and then, as now, my spoken English lacked an American inflection and listeners wishing to locate the provenance of my accent often end up befuddled. Whether the dynamic at the table would have varied radically had my Black and White acquaintances not detected in my voice the surviving trappings of the foreigner remains a matter of conjecture.

The final vignette took place in the fall of 2002 at a Peruvian restaurant in Chicago, where four light-skinned Latin@ colleagues and I went to dine following a day-long editorial meeting as we prepared to launch the journal *Latino Studies*. Three in our cohort had been born in the United States and spoke English as their native language. On the other hand, I had come to the United States at the age of eighteen from a Spanish-speaking country where I completed my education through secondary school. The nice waiter assigned to our table greeted the gathering in Spanish, explained the specials of the day, and proceeded counterclockwise to take our orders, beginning with the colleague to my right. When he finally reached me, for some reason he felt compelled to code-switch, asking for my order in English. This linguistic detail did not escape the notice of my four colleagues, and once the waiter was no longer within hearing range, we all proceeded to interpret—as scholars are wont to do. In unison we concluded that my Blackness had prevented the nice Peruvian gentleman from recognizing my Hispanicity. His failure to recognize a Black person as Hispanic ironically reverberates with the reticence of the African American colleague who in my earlier vignette regarded my unwillingness to undermine my Hispanic origins as a feature that rendered me ineligible for bona fide

Blackness. Another layer of irony emerges with the Peruvian waiter. He may have correctly identified us as Latino academics on our way from a scholarly conference, a by no means unreasonable supposition given the proximity of the restaurant to the Chicago campus of the University of Illinois. If that was the case, one would have to forgive his blunder when he took me for a non-Latino. My experience reveals that Afro-Latin@s rarely sit at the table of conversation in Latino scholarly fora. When participating in learned events in which Latin@ academics analyze the past, the present, and the future of the U.S. Hispanic population, I have often been among the very few Afro-Latin@s to address the august lecture hall. At any rate, the incident shows that the rule of homogeneity may operate with equal rigidity among people of Latin American origin and African Americans when assessing the ethnoracial identity of groups or individuals.

Taken together, the four vignettes combine to describe a picture of complexity that frames my racial experience as an African-descended Dominican, an Afro-Latino, illustrating the difficult ethnoracial location of Black Hispanics in the United States. The picture, I would propose, points to the instability of identitarian formulations, urging us to exercise caution when we deploy Blackness as a transnational category with the ambition to map the human experience of populations beyond the source of their immediate heritage. The foregoing anecdotes would seem to discourage our overemphasizing the bond of solidarity that a common skin hue or a shared sense of African ancestry will automatically trigger across the historical divides of nationality, ethnic loyalty, language, and political dogma, among other concrete factors of social identity. Certainly the commonality of their Blackness did not deter the deployment of Hutu violence against the Tutsi population during the Rwandan genocide of 1994. Neither do we need such extreme examples of horrendous mass murder in geographically remote locations to show creases within any holistic or global configuration of Blackness. New York City, which has been the recipient of so many waves of Black migrations from the Caribbean, Africa, and the southern United States, can suffice to provide an ample field for illustration. The 1973 novel *The Friends* by Rosa Guy, a native of Trinidad who arrived in Harlem at age seven in 1932, offers suggestive glimpses of the tension often created by the presence of West Indian cultural difference among the more numerous African American inhabitants of the Black capital of the United States. The novel evokes the complicated friendship between the Caribbean girl Phyllisia Cathay and the African American Edith Jackson. Classmates in Phyllisia's Harlem school mocked her West Indian accent and constantly called her names — "'monkey' was one of the nicer ones."[5] Her older sister Ruby, who attends a different school, does not face similar harassment from her peers because she has strategically decided to mitigate the trappings of her difference unlike her younger sibling. Explaining to their mother, she reports thus: "After all, Mother, you know how Phyllisia is. If she did not try to act so smart and know-it-all, she would not be opening up her mouth and continually be reminding the children where she comes from."[6] Disheartened by her travail in school, as compared with her sister's smoother ride in hers, Phyllisia receives a boost to her self-confidence when their mother, disapproving of Ruby's cultural self-annulment, encourages her to continue to act precisely as she had done even if it brought her a measure of trouble: "You are a West Indian girl going to school in New York and you are proud. What happens in this school will happen in any other. So if you must fight, you must."[7]

The Afro–Puerto Rican Arturo Alfonso Schomburg—coming to New York from the Caribbean like Rosa Guy, but unlike her having received his education in a language other than English—was seventeen when he left his island of birth in 1891, and although he played a key role in the intellectual awakening that gave rise to the Harlem Renaissance, he came to the United States at an age when he could not easily erase the thickness of his accent and the foreignness of his diction when he communicated in English. The historian Jesse Hoffnung-Garskoff notes that in New York Schomburg settled among a community of cigar makers, a labor enclave of Puerto Rican and Cuban nationalists who promoted the cause of Cuban independence from Spain, standing out as the organizer of a revolutionary club called Las Dos Antillas (The Two Antilles). With the demise of the Cuban independence movement as a result of the entrance in the war of the United States, which converted the original national liberation struggle into a war between empires, after 1898 Schomburg gravitated toward an explicitly racialized political cause as an advocate of Pan-Africanism and a promoter of knowledge on the achievements of Blacks throughout the world. That impetus led to his dedication to collect books and documentary materials dealing with the most diverse aspects of the Black experience globally, culminating in an impressive collection that he "stored and catalogued in his home in Brooklyn" until in 1926 he sold it to the New York Public Library, "laying the foundation for one of the world's richest archives for the study of Black culture."[8]

During the 1920s and 1930s Schomburg became a visible public figure in Black intellectual circles, collaborating with the likes of W. E. B. Du Bois, Alain Locke, and Charles S. Johnson and mentoring younger writers of the Harlem Renaissance such as Langston Hughes and Claude McKay. Despite his determination to establish the locus of his identity within the sphere of United States Blackness, he did not succeed at shedding the markers of his ethnic difference, thereby at times earning the mockery of his associates for the way he used the English language. While editing one of Schomburg's articles in 1937, Locke had this to say about him as a writer: "My good loyal friend Schomburg can gather facts but he cannot write. He was trained in Porto Rico on florid Spanish and his English is impossible."[9] Probably in reaction to his failure to gain full acceptance within the realm of North American Blackness, in the last portion of his productive life Schomburg "began reasserting his own Hispanic origins and tried desperately to rekindle the interest of Black North Americans in the rest of the Black world."[10]

Guy, a novelist, fictionalizes the ethnic antipathy that a West Indian girl encounters among African American classmates in a Harlem school, and Hoffnung-Garskof, a historian, teases out of Schomburg's biography the difficult migration of a Hispanophone Afro–Puerto Rican who endeavors to enter the identity space of North American Blacks, the bond presumably afforded by their common African ancestry proving at times precarious in both cases. The creases within Blackness that these instances dramatize receive insufficient attention from chroniclers seeking to map the experience of the African diaspora globally or even regionally with the result that their narratives often assume sufficient and necessary conditions of racial solidarity among peoples of African descent across countries or ethnically differentiated communities. An expectation of uniformity in the ways those populations live, feel, and speak about their race pervades the narratives in question with the occasionally deleterious result that particular groups of nations that deviate in speech or action from the operative norm may earn disqualifying portrayals. The prevailing narrative exhibits a tendency to pathologize populations that insufficiently glorify their Blackness, charging them with collective self-hatred and construing them as downright exceptional in their ill-guided reticence to identify with the Black inhabitants of the planet wherever they might live.

The overview of the state of Blackness in Latin America offered by The Miami Herald starting in the second week of June 2007 provides a case in point. The newspaper ran a series of feature articles that ostensibly sought to describe the conditions of people of African descent throughout Latin American societies. With each article written by a different columnist, the five-part series entitled "A Rising Voice: Afro-Latin Americans" undertook coverage of racial self-affirmation of Blacks in present-day Cuba and the extent to which Afro-Brazilians have through their public stances and the advocacy of their grassroots organizations increasingly challenged their country's myth of a racial democracy. One article in the series chronicles the progress made by Afro-Nicaraguans in their quest to attain full citizenship, thereby stressing the discernible momentum of Black advocacy there.[11] But incontestably the article that proved most memorable dealt with Dominicans. Entitled "Black Denial" and penned by the *Miami Herald* foreign correspondent Frances Robles, it provoked the most reaction from readers nationally.[12] Typically, the article dramatizes the reticence of Dominicans to accept their Blackness; their obsessive commitment to Whiteness as a national value; the pervasiveness of Negrophobia that even the darkest among them reflect, as illustrated by the testimony of the Purdue University professor Dawn F. Stinchcomb, an African American who reports having experienced in Santo Domingo racial antipathy of a magnitude so disconcerting that it made her memories of growing up in the South rosy by comparison; and, finally, the proverbial anti-Haitianism whereby Dominicans disqualify their island neighbors.

Published on June 13, 2007, as part 2 of the series, the article by Robles on the state of Blackness in Dominican society and among U.S. Dominicans in the United States brought in an unprecedented number of responses, including close to one hundred electronic mail messages. Most of the replies, says the author, were from Dominican women wishing to thank her for revealing the truth, but along with them came a share of "hate mail." Robles had occasion to discuss the repercussion caused by her piece during an interview she landed, thanks to the impact of her article, on Michel Martin's program *Tell Me More* on National Public Radio. She emphasized the magnitude of the response by indicating that it surpassed the interest elicited by anything she had written since she started working for the *Miami Herald*, even when her subjects dealt with hot Cuban issues, a not insignificant comment given the anti-Castro and generally conservative crusade that forms the kernel of the paper's coverage. The article contained much caricature that aimed to illustrate the ignorance of Dominicans about themselves as racial beings and the extremes to which they would go to distance themselves from Blackness, whether theirs or that of others. During the interview, Robles further enriched the colorful details with which she had embellished the print story, stating, for instance, that in the Dominican Republic a Black woman cannot go outside or use public transportation wearing her hair in its natural state without enduring verbal insult or having people physically stick combs into her hair.[13] When asked by Martin if she had met anybody during her data-gathering visit to the Dominican Republic who revealed any sanity about the matter, Robles explained that the very few people she met who showed any intellectual or cultural awareness about their race had all studied in the United States.

Given such manner of depiction, it's no wonder, indeed, that the article by Robles incited widespread condemnation of Dominican Negrophobia, thereby eliciting various letters to the editor including one by none other than the prestigious Haitian-American fiction writer Edwidge Danticat. Two pronouncements in particular demanded the resignation of the sociologist Ramona Hernández, the director of the Dominican Studies Institute at the City College of New York, for Negrophobic remarks that the article attributes to her. The wider resonance of her article relative to the others in the five-part series has little to do with the merits of Robles as a journalist. Instead it has to do primarily with the fact that, when it comes to the race question, Dominicans offer much juicier material than any other national community in the hemisphere. Strangely, this juiciness cannot be explained by any peculiarly Dominican idiosyncracy that sets this population aside from all others throughout the region in matters of race. The Dominican case does not differ radically from the overall state of Blackness in the Americas. One can think of locales as significant as Cartagena de Indias, on the Atlantic coast of Colombia, which unlike the Andean and the Pacific regions of the country has an overwhelming Black majority, and there too public displays of Negrophobia occur. The exceptionality imputed to Dominicans in this regard cannot withstand even a swift empirical observation of racial relations in the Americas. Ironically, in the diaspora we find Dominicans demonstrating a greater propensity to classify themselves as Black than any other Latino subgroup, and largely we owe to them the growth of Afro-Latin@s in the United States population census in 2000, a fact that remains overlooked by commentators insisting on the self-hatred of Afro-Dominicans.

Irrespective of what their actual racial practice or beliefs might be, however, Dominicans carry the burden of a stigma concerning their alleged racial delusion. If I can allow myself a conjecture, I would speculate that the stigma can perhaps be traced to the manner in which the knowledge of Dominican society entered the sphere of Black studies in the United States academy beginning in the 1960s when ethnic studies initiatives throughout the country emerged. Typically represented as racially benighted, Dominicans appear "backward" and "confused" on account of their inability or reticence to proclaim Blackness as their principal social identity. A statement in Leslie B. Rout Jr.'s volume *The African Experience in Spanish America*,

1502 to the Present Day (1976) encapsulates the tone and the tenor of the prevailing wisdom about Dominicans and race. Closer to being an indictment than an attempt to explain, his judgment seems final: "A mulatto nation situated in the Negroid Caribbean is undoubtedly ailing if it cannot accept its racial image. Dominicans may feel constrained to call each other white, but it is hard to say who is deceived. In view of these considerations, the glorification of Caucasian features by the mulatto majority is disturbing and, for the black minority, psychologically disjunctive."[14]

The discourse of Black studies on Dominicans has focused almost exclusively on the anti-Haitian and Negrophobic pronouncements of the cadre of intellectuals funded by the government of Generalissimo Rafael Leonidas Trujillo, the dictatorship that kept the population under rigid control for three decades, during which assassinations of suspected dissidents were the order of the day, and that perpetrated the horrendous massacre of Haitian immigrants and Dominicans of Haitian descent along the Haitian-Dominican border in 1937, adding a ghastly Dominican chapter to the annals of crimes against humanity. As a result of that emphasis, Dominicans entered the discourse of Black studies antithetically to Haitians. The white supremacist Eurocentric leanings of the Trujillo intelligentsia came to represent how Dominicans thought, whereas Haitian attitudes were evoked via the exalted heroism and racial self-respect of Toussaint L'Ouverture. Naturally, the representation of Dominicans suffered since they came into the discourse as known quantity, as hermeneutically processed entities, as explained phenomena, needing neither further understanding nor additional scrutiny. It should come as no surprise, therefore, that they should disappear from the bibliography on the Black diaspora in the Americas. The Dominican chapter of the Black experience remained absent or gravely understudied until the 1990s, when Dominican-descended scholars began to insert themselves in the United States academic industry in significant numbers. The lack of serious consideration of race among Dominicans has allowed for the longevity of the scheme of thought that posits anti-Haitian attitudes strictly as a feature of Haitian-Dominican relations rather than the global phenomenon that we might otherwise recognize it to be.

Apart from allowing unexamined doxa to pass as scholarly interpretation, much else is lost to the story of global Blackness by the omission or trivialization of its Dominican chapter: the primacy of Santo Domingo as inaugural site of the African presence in the Americas, as birthplace of the plantation—the economic institution that gave Blackness its modern significance—as locus of the first insurrections of enslaved Africans, and as cradle of the Maroon tradition during the colonial period. With the advent of the republic in 1844, Dominican Blacks and mulattos resisted the Creole independence movement, causing it to incorporate racial equality in its agenda—hence the anti-slavery decree that the nascent government produced as its very first juridical act. When the decree became law, the newly minted Dominican Republic declared itself a sanctuary for any slaves arriving on its shore by granting them automatic freedom and citizenship. Although the country achieved its independence by separating from Haitian rule, the first Dominican government made an open invitation to Haitians by offering them protection if they wished to stay in the country. During the 1830s and 1860s, Haitian and Dominican revolutionaries collaborated in their common struggle against tyrannical regimes at home and annexationist invasions coming from abroad. They have historically exchanged martyrs and freedom fighters such as the Dominican-descended Charlemagne Peralte who led the Caco rebellion against the United States invasion of Haiti in 1915, and the Haitian-born poet Jacques Viau Renaud who died in Santo Domingo fighting in the nationalist trenches against the United States invasion of 1965. One could then be forgiven for believing that when the literary stars Edwidge Danticat and Junot Diaz—the former born in Haiti, the latter in the Dominican Republic—jointly author a *New York Times* op-ed piece denouncing the deportation of Haitian immigrants by the Dominican government, they may be following the call of a memory of Haitian-Dominican collaboration that goes back many generations. Perhaps the same historical instinct informed the Haitian and Dominican students at City College of New York who throughout the 1980s shared the same office space for the headquarters of both the Haitian and Dominican Students Association, or the student leadership that initiated the tradition of an annual Haitian and Dominican gala dinner at the University of Massachusetts, Amherst, or the Syracuse University students who began the practice of holding a spring celebration called Quisqueya Night that pays tribute to the heritages of Haiti and the Dominican Republic.

A closer look at the Dominican chapter of the Black experience may also be able to clear the radar screen on which Haiti is placed when anti-Haitianism is regarded as a Dominican aberration rather than a historical, global Western harassment. We need only remember that Haiti came into being as a sovereign state in the midst of circumstances that shook the economic, political, social, and moral foundations of the world that Western colonialism had created. Haiti's birth as a republic offended the Christian West. In general the Western world, whose stability, wealth, and power by the beginning of the nineteenth century depended on the success of a plantation economy that swallowed slave labor like a boa constrictor, had nothing to celebrate when the enslaved population of Saint Domingue dismantled the source of Western well-being. Witness the grief that President George Washington expressed when he learned about the loss of the French colony, and the solidarity, the empathy, that Thomas Jefferson voiced for the plight of French planters forced to leave the island of their wealth due to the vengeful wrath of the insurgents. Resentment against Haitian revolutionaries caused the United States to refuse to recognize Haiti as an independent nation for over sixty years. Anti-Haitianism in the United States precedes the birth of the Dominican Republic. By 1844 American statesmen and publicists had already amassed a large body of anti-Haitian discourse. By the beginning of the twentieth century the defamatory portrayal of Haiti had become so firmly established that Jacques Nicolas Léger, envoy extraordinary and minister plenipotentiary of Haiti in the United States, set out to rectify the image of his country while he served in Washington, D.C., by publishing a book, written in English, called *Haiti, Her History and Her Detractors* (1907), in which he explores history to find the origin of "the persistent calumnies" endured by Haiti. Ironically, almost sixty years later, when the anthropologist Melville J. Herskovitz published his *Life in a Haitian Valley* (1964), he felt compelled to devote his opening sentences to bewail the "condescension and caricature" that had predominated, "especially in recent years," in popularized representations of Haiti, suggesting that very little had changed. In short, anti-Haitianism, a Western creation with the United States playing a leading role, belongs to the whole world that emerged from the colonial transaction. Dominicans play a rather minor role in it.

As I try to extract metadiscursive knowledge from the composite scenario that the preceding pages have offered, I come to the realization that I do not have a theory with which to sum up the whole in one large interpretive swoop, other than, perhaps, a conspiracy theory. To express it succinctly I would borrow the words of Junot Diaz, who told me once, only half tongue-in-cheek, that Dominicans exist to enable Whites to dissemble their own Negrophobia and to assist people of color in their tragic need to collude with Negrophobic regimes that they have lacked the power to dismantle. Given the important role they play, Junot would say, if Dominicans did not exist they would have to be invented. We need to look more closely at the multiple areas of contention within the sphere of Blackness, as the vignettes with which I started are intended to indicate. I volunteer two more for the sake of closing the circle that my prefatory remarks opened.

In one I am in the classroom, and after the first week of classes I quickly strike a friendly rapport with an African American student whom I had seen on campus for a couple of semesters prior to her taking my course. She too remembered that we had greeted each other in amiable gestures but had not had a conversation. When we spoke in the classroom, and she had heard my accent, she told me that she had misconstrued my identity when we passed each other on the quad; namely, she had thought I was Black. I thought of my skin hue and the bona fide African ancestry of which I am the result and said in my mind, "So did I." In the other vignette I am serving on a search committee, which is evaluating candidates for a faculty position in literature. After months of labor and deliberations—from the preliminary reading of applications, to the study of writing samples, to MLA interviews, to campus visits—a disturbing pattern became discernible to me involving the way the other Black person in the committee handled the candidacy of Black applicants. Too many coincidences made it indubitably clear: she found merit only in Black candidates who, as far as one can deduce, shared her own national origins. Blackness alone was not welcome if it came from elsewhere. Lest I violate the rule of confidentiality by which search committee members are bound, I shall refrain from further detail in this example. Suffice it to say that discovering the pattern saddened me considerably. The pattern, in my view, reflects a schism within the territory of Blackness, a schism the understanding of which would require delving into the history that was informing my colleague in the search committee. Multiplying that history by as many societies in the Americas, in Africa, and everywhere else where Blackness occurs renders it quite clear that the formulation of an unproblematic transnational configuration of Blackness needs first to attend to its hurdles, its creases, the heterogeneity that makes it exponentially divisible.

Notes

1. Silvio Torres-Saillant, "Dominican Blackness and the Modern World," in *Perspectives on Las Américas: A Reader in Culture, History, and Representation*, edited by Matthew C. Gutman, Félix V. Matos Rodríguez, Lynn Stephen, and Patricia Zavella (Malden, Mass.: Blackwell Publishing, 2003), 283–84.

2. Carolyn Ashbaugh, *Lucy Parsons: American Revolutionary* (Chicago: Illinois Labor History Society, 1976), 66, 268.

3. Matt S. Meir and Feliciano, *Dictionary of Mexican American History* (Westport, Conn.: Greenwood, Rivera, 1981), 149.

4. Alfredo Mirande and Evangelina Enriquez, *La Chicano: The Mexican American Woman* (Chicago: University of Chicago Press, 1979), 91.

5. Catherine A. Sunshine and Keith Q. Warner, eds., *Caribbean Connections: Moving North* (Washington, D.C.: Network of Educators on the Americas, 1998), 119.

6. Ibid., 122.

7. Ibid.

8. Jesse Hoffnung-Garskof, "The Migrations of Arturo Schomburg: On Being Antillano, Negro, and Puerto Rican in New York, 1891–1938," *Journal of American Ethnic History* 21, no. 1 (2001): 3.

9. Cited in ibid., 37.

10. Ibid., 38.

11. Audra Burch, "Afro-Latin Americans: A Rising Voice," *Miami Herald*, June 10, 2007.

12. Frances Robles, "Black Denial," *Miami Herald*, June 13, 2007.

13. Frances Robles, interview by Michel Martin, *Tell Me More*, National Public Radio, June 16, 2007.

14. Leslie B. Rout Jr., *The African Experience in Spanish America, 1502 to the Present Day* (Cambridge: Cambridge University Press, 1976), 288.

WILLIE PERDOMO

Nigger-Reecan Blues

—Hey, Willie. What are you, man? Boricua? Moreno? Que? Are you
    Black? Puerto Rican?
—I am.
—No, silly. You know what I mean: What are you?
—I am you. You are me. We the same. Can't you feel our veins drinking
    the same blood?

    —But who said you was a Porta-Reecan?
    —Tu no ere Puerto Riqueño, brother.
    —Maybe Indian like Ghandi-lndian?
    —I thought you was a Black man.
    —Is one of your parents white?
    —You sure you ain't a mix of something like Cuban and Chinese?
    —Looks like an Arab brother to me.
    —Naahhh, nah, nah . . .You ain't no Porty-Reecan.
    —I keep tellin' y'all: That boy is a Black man with an accent.

If you look real close you will see that your spirits are standing right
    next to our songs. Yo soy Boricua! Yo soy Africano! I ain't lyin'. Pero
    mi pelo is kinky y curly y mi skin no es negro pero it can pass . . .

    —Hey, yo. I don't care what you say. You Black.

I ain't Black! Every time I go downtown la madam blankita de Madison
    Avenue sees that I'm standing next to her and she holds her purse just
    a bit tighter. Cabdrivers are quick to turn on their *Off-Duty* signs when
    they see my hand in the air. And the newspapers say that if I'm not in
    front of a gun you can bet I'll be behind one. I wonder why . . .

—Cuz you Black, nigger!

Don't call me no nigger. I am not Black, man. I had a conversation with
my professor and it went just like this:
"So, Willie, where are you from?"
"I'm from Harlem."
"Ohhh. Are you Black, Willie?"
"No, but we all the same and—"
"Did you know our basketball team's nationally ranked?"

—Te lo estoy diciendo, brother. Ese hombre es un moreno. Miralo!

Mira, pana mio, yo no soy moreno! I just come out of Jerry's Den and
the coconut spray on my new shape-up is smelling fresh all the way
up 125th Street. I'm lookin' slim and I'm lookin' trim and when
my compai Davi saw me he said: "Coño, Papo, te parece como un
moreno, pana. Word up, kid, you look just like a light-skin moreno."

—What I told you? You Black my brother.

Damn! I ain't even Black and here I am suffering from the young Black
man's plight / the old white man's burden / and I ain't even Black,
man / a Black man I am not / Boricua I am / ain't never really was /
Black / like me . . .

—Y'all leave that boy alone. He got what they call the "nigger-reecan
blues."

I'm a spic! I'm a nigger!
Spic! Spic! Just like a nigger.

Neglected, rejected, oppressed and dispossessed
From banana boats to tenements
Street gangs to regiments
Spic, spic, spic. I ain't nooooo different than a nigger!

X

Afro-Latin@s: Present and Future Tenses

Race matters in the Latin@ community. Sociological, economic, and legal analyses as exemplified by the work of John Logan, Tanya Hernández, William Darity, and others, help to document the differences within the Latin@ community according to all indicators, not to mention the racial discrimination against Black Latin@s perpetrated by the wider society. The building of a common agenda between the Latin@ and African American communities, and the potential mediating role of Afro-Latin@s as a living embodiment of that unity, has received growing emphasis in recent times and is the focal point for the political reflections of commentators like Ed Morales, Mark Sawyer, and James Jennings. At the same

Ignacia Bermúdez, daughter of Guatemalan immigrants, Bronx, New York, 2008. (Photograph by Miriam Jiménez Román)

time, the gravitation of many Latin@s, including Afro-Latin@s, toward Whiteness, and their attendant distancing from and disdain for African American Blackness, or Blackness more generally, has serious implications for future generations of new immigrants. While the very presence of Latin@s of visible African descent is the most significant countervailing pressure against this divisive and self-demeaning tendency, increasingly Afro-Latin@s are taking more assertive measures and actively challenging traditional notions. Organized efforts to acknowledge and affirm their full African diasporic identity *and* their full membership in the Latin@ community have grown in recent years and include consciously establishing coalitions across national lines.

JOHN R. LOGAN

How Race Counts for Hispanic Americans

Hispanics are now the largest minority group in the United States. They are also quite diverse. A previous Mumford Center report analyzed differences among Hispanics by national origin.[1] This report assessed racial differences among Hispanics. Census data do not allow us to measure how people are actually perceived in the neighborhoods where they live and work and go to school, but they do enable us to count Hispanics with different racial identifications, compare them in terms of social and economic background, evaluate their residential integration with Whites, Blacks, and other Hispanics, and assess whether other characteristics of their neighborhoods are more similar to the neighborhoods where Whites, Blacks, or other Hispanics live.

Since 1970 the United States census has asked all Americans to identify their race and, separately, whether they are Hispanic. This means Hispanics can be of any race. It is widely understood that there is a small Black minority among Hispanics. Less well known is that only about half of Hispanics in Census 2000 identified themselves in standard racial categories such as White, Black, or Asian on their census form. Nearly as many people instead wrote in their own term, most often "Latino," "Hispanic," or a similar word. Many of these people might be perceived by non-Hispanics as "White"—but apparently they do not see themselves in that way. In this report they are referred to as "Hispanic Hispanics."

We find substantial differences among these Hispanic racial groups:

— Hispanic Hispanics are the fastest-growing segment, and very likely they will soon be an absolute majority of Hispanic Americans.
— There are nearly a million Black Hispanics. These people have a socioeconomic profile much more similar to non-Hispanic Blacks

than to other Hispanic groups, and their neighborhoods have nearly as many Black as Hispanic residents. Many Black Hispanic children have a non-Hispanic Black mother or father.

—A very small share of Mexicans identifies as Black. Still, there are nearly a quarter million Black Mexicans in the United States. Dominicans and Puerto Ricans are most likely to identify as Black. Cubans, in contrast, mostly identify as White.

—White Hispanics have the highest socioeconomic standing, they live in closest proximity to non-Hispanic Whites, and their neighborhoods have a more affluent class composition than those of other Hispanic groups.

—A strong predictor of racial identification of Hispanics is the racial mix of the metropolitan region where they live. Among metros with the largest Hispanic populations, Miami has the highest share of White Hispanics; New York has the highest share of Black Hispanics. In California and Texas, Hispanic Hispanics generally are the majority of Hispanics.

Technical Issues: Measuring Race among Hispanics

The Census Bureau treats race and Hispanic origin as distinct concepts, although often users of census data and the Census Bureau itself combine them to compare information about non-Hispanic Blacks and Hispanics.[2] Census 2000 switched the order of the question "Is this person Spanish/ Hispanic/Latino?" and the question on race identification, thereby asking the Hispanic origin question before the race question. This change may have affected Hispanics' response to the race question.

One source of information for this report is the set of microdata from the 1980, 1990, and 2000 censuses (Public Use Microdata Samples, or PUMS). These data files allow maximum flexibility in the creation of categories of race and Hispanic origin, and they make it possible to tabulate many social and economic characteristics of Hispanics by their self-reported race. However, they are sample data and they are most reliable at the national level.

For information on specific metropolitan regions and census tracts within them, we rely on pre-tabulated summary files from Census 2000 (SF1 and SF3). Use of these files is complicated by the fact that people were able to report multiple races in this census, but summary files available at this time report data for only a few of the possible combinations.

For the purposes of this study, we classify Hispanics into the following categories:

—*Hispanic Hispanics.* Persons who identified as "other race" (most often writing in "Hispanic" or a similar term) alone or in combination with another specific race. The census refers to these people as "some other race" Hispanics.

—*Black Hispanics.* Persons who identified as "Black" alone or in combination with another race. There is some overlap in the summary file data between this category and the Hispanic Hispanic category. About 120,000 Hispanic Hispanics also identified themselves as Black.

—*White Hispanics.* Persons who identified neither as "other race" nor as "Black." A more complete label for this group would be "White, Asian, or Native American." However, analysis of microdata shows that 96 percent in this category identified only as White.

Size and Characteristics of Hispanic Racial Subgroups

Table 1 shows the evolution of the Hispanic population of the United States by race for 1980, 1990, and 2000 (calculated from PUMS data for each year). The Hispanic population more than doubled in this period.

The category that we call "White Hispanic" is still the largest. It included nearly two-thirds of Hispanics in 1980, declining to a 54 percent share in 1990, and then just below half in 2000.

In 1970, only 700,000 Hispanics identified themselves as "some other race." Since then, however, this group that we call Hispanic Hispanics has risen to about a third in 1980, 44 percent in 1990, and 47 percent in 2000.

A small but steady share of Hispanics identified as Black in all three years, just under 3 percent. Though a small percentage, the number of Black Hispanics has grown from under 400,000 to over 900,000 in the period.

Who among Hispanics identifies as Black or Hispanic rather than White? Table 2 shows that Black Hispanics are very distinctive. They are much less likely to be immigrants compared to the average Hispanic (28 percent compared to 41 percent for all Hispanics), and much less likely to speak a language other than English at home (61 percent compared to 79 percent). They have an advantage in education (with a mean of 11.7 years, nearly a high school level, compared to 10.5 years for all Hispanics). On the other hand their actual economic performance is worse, with a lower

Table 1. Racial Composition of the Hispanic population of the United States, 1980–2000

	1980		1990	
Hispanic Hispanic	4,979,240	33.7%	9,426,634	44.2%
Black Hispanic	388,240	2.6%	633,516	2.9%
White Hispanic	9,397,240	63.7%	11,776,701	53.9%
Hispanic Total	14,764,720	100.0%	21,836,851	100.0%

Table 2. Socioeconomic characteristics of Hispanic groups and Blacks, 2000

	FOREIGN BORN	SPEAK OTHER LANGUAGE	YEARS OF EDUCATION	MEDIAN INCOME
White Hispanic	38.8%	75.7%	11.0	$39,900
Hispanic Hispanic	43.8%	82.6%	9.9	$37,500
Black Hispanic	28.2%	60.8%	11.7	$35,000
Hispanic Total	40.9%	78.6%	10.5	$38,500
Non-Hispanic Black	6.4%	6.3%	12.5	$34,000

median household income ($3,500 below the Hispanic average), higher unemployment (more than 3 percentage points above the Hispanic average), and a higher poverty rate (31.5 percent compared to 26.0 percent).

Table 2 also allows a comparison of Black Hispanics to non-Hispanic Blacks. Like Black Hispanics, non-Hispanic Blacks had a lower median income ($34,000), higher unemployment rate (11.0 percent), and higher rate of poverty (29.7 percent) than did the average Hispanic. Compared to Black Hispanics, non-Hispanic Blacks were slightly poorer but had lower rates of unemployment and poverty and higher education. The main differences between them were related to nativity. Non-Hispanic Blacks in 2000 were much less likely to be foreign born (6.4 percent). In this respect, Black Hispanics fall in between African Americans (all born in the United States) and Afro-Caribbeans, a majority of whom are foreign born.

White Hispanics have the highest incomes and lowest rates of unemployment and poverty. The table shows that Hispanics who identified themselves as "other race" in the census—those we call Hispanic Hispanics—fall squarely between White Hispanics and Black Hispanics in their income, unemployment, and poverty levels. However, they are the

		GROWTH	
2000		1980–1990	1990–2000
16,700,055	47.4%	89.3%	77.2%
939,471	2.7%	63.2%	48.3%
17,601,942	49.9%	25.3%	49.5%
35,241,468	100.0%	47.9%	61.4%

UNEMPLOYED	BELOW POVERTY
8.0%	24.1%
9.5%	27.7%
12.3%	31.5%
8.8%	26.0%
11.0%	29.7%

Hispanic group with the highest proportion of foreign-born members and they are most likely to hold onto the Spanish language.

We can also use PUMS data to classify the Hispanic racial groups by national origin, as reported by the census. Table 3 shows that Cubans are most likely to identify as White, and Dominicans are least likely. Dominicans are the most likely to identify in the other two categories.

The highest share of Black Hispanics is found among Dominicans (12.7 percent). There are about 100,000 Black Dominicans, who are especially prominent in New York City. Puerto Ricans also have a higher than average share of Black Hispanics (8.2 percent), and the highest number of Black Hispanics are Puerto Rican (more than a quarter million). Though a very small percentage of Mexicans are Black Hispanics, this group still includes nearly a quarter million persons.

More detailed analysis shows that about half of Black Hispanics are children under the age of eighteen. What is the role of racially mixed parentage in the identification of these children as Black Hispanics? This question cannot be fully answered, because the majority of Black Hispanic children do not live with both parents. However, based on those cases

Table 3. National Origins of Hispanics by race, 2000

	WHITE HISPANIC		HISPANIC HISPANIC	
Mexican	10,324,597	49.3%	10,406,214	49.7%
Puerto Rican	1,661,577	49.0%	1,450,124	42.8%
Cuban	1,071,596	85.4%	123,427	9.8%
Dominican	197,939	24.3%	514,185	63.1%
Central American	746,847	42.1%	956,540	53.9%
South American	854,785	61.1%	522,762	37.4%
All Others	2,744,601	48.6%	2,762,803	48.2%
Total	17,601,942	49.9%	16,700,055	47.4%

Table 4. Hispanic children living with both parents, by their own race and race of their parents, 2000

Total White Hispanic children	3,355,395	100.0%
Both parents White Hispanic	2,407,052	71.7%
One parent non-Hispanic White	650,477	19.4%
Other combinations	297,866	8.9%
Total Hispanic Hispanic children	3,310,500	100.0%
Both parents Hispanic Hispanic	2,798,957	84.6%
One parent White Hispanic or Black Hispanic	195,863	5.9%
Other combinations	315,680	9.5%
Total Black Hispanic children	133,500	100.0%
Both parents Black Hispanic	40,700	30.5%
One parent non-Hispanic Black	60,394	45.2%
Other combinations	32,406	24.3%

where both parents are present, the microdata allow us to tabulate the race of the child along with the race of each parent.

Table 4 presents the results for all Hispanic children under eighteen who live with both parents. A large majority of White Hispanic children have parents who are both White Hispanic (over 70 percent). An even higher share of Hispanic Hispanic children have parents who are both Hispanic Hispanic (85 percent). In contrast, it is rare that a Black Hispanic child has two Black Hispanic parents (only 31 percent). For nearly half the Black Hispanic children, one of the parents is non-Hispanic Black. In

BLACK HISPANIC		TOTAL
221,905	1.1%	20,952,716
277,765	8.2%	3,389,466
59,341	4.7%	1,254,364
103,361	12.7%	815,485
72,823	4.1%	1,776,210
21,956	1.6%	1,399,503
182,320	3.2%	5,653,724
939,471	2.7%	35,241,468

many of the remaining cases, one parent is identified as Black Hispanic, while the other parent is White Hispanic or Hispanic Hispanic.

This result suggests that intermarriage is the most important source of the Black Hispanic population, with a strong likelihood of having a non-Hispanic Black parent. Research using non-census data sources would be required to assess to what degree the same is true for older Black Hispanics.

Geographic Distribution

As would be expected—if only because of the differences by national origin—the Hispanic racial groups are unevenly distributed around the country. Table 5 lists the six metropolitan regions with more than a million Hispanics and shows their racial composition.

Miami stands out with nearly 90 percent White among its Hispanic residents. New York, reflecting in part its Puerto Rican and Dominican communities, is unusual with nearly 10 percent Black Hispanics.

There is a more general phenomenon operating here. The racial composition within the Hispanic population is closely related to the area's overall racial and ethnic mix. Metropolitan regions with large non-Hispanic White populations tend to have a larger share of White Hispanics; those with larger Hispanic populations tend to have more Hispanic Hispanics; and those with larger non-Hispanic Black populations have more Black Hispanics. This pattern is demonstrated in table 6.

—In metros that are less than 70 percent non-Hispanic White, the White share among Hispanics is only 53 percent. In those that are

Table 5. Racial composition of the Hispanic population, 2000 (metros with more than 1,000,000 Hispanic residents)

	HISPANIC TOTAL	WHITE HISPANIC	HISPANIC HISPANIC	BLACK HISPANIC
Los Angeles–Long Beach	4,242,213	44.7%	54.3%	1.1%
New York	2,339,836	41.8%	49.0%	9.2%
Chicago	1,416,584	49.3%	48.9%	1.8%
Miami	1,291,737	86.2%	10.9%	2.9%
Houston	1,248,586	53.8%	45.1%	1.2%
Riverside–San Bernadino	1,228,962	44.9%	53.9%	1.3%

Table 6. Racial composition of the Hispanic population according to the overall racial mix of the metropolitan region, 2000

METRO PERCENT WHITE	WHITE HISPANIC	HISPANIC HISPANIC	BLACK HISPANIC
Less than 70%	53.0%	42.0%	5.0%
70–85%	53.9%	41.0%	5.0%
More than 85%	59.8%	35.5%	4.6%
Total	55.6%	39.5%	4.9%
METRO PERCENT HISPANIC	WHITE HISPANIC	HISPANIC HISPANIC	BLACK HISPANIC
Less than 5%	58.3%	35.2%	6.5%
5–10%	51.7%	44.0%	4.3%
More than 10%	52.7%	45.2%	2.0%
Total	55.6%	39.5%	4.9%
METRO PERCENT BLACK	WHITE HISPANIC	HISPANIC HISPANIC	BLACK HISPANIC
Less than 5%	57.3%	39.6%	3.1%
5–10%	54.7%	40.9%	4.4%
More than 10%	54.4%	38.5%	7.0%
Total	55.6%	39.5%	4.9%

more than 85 percent White, the White share among Hispanics is 60 percent.

—Where Hispanics are less than 5 percent of the population, Hispanic Hispanics are only 35 percent of this group. Where they are above 10 percent of the population, Hispanic Hispanics have a 45 percent share.

—Where the population is less than 5 percent Black, Black Hispanics have only a 3 percent share of all Hispanics, but this rises to 7 percent in places where more than 10 percent of residents are Black.

This pattern is consistent with two kinds of processes that could influence people's racial identification. First, there is the phenomenon of intermarriage, already mentioned above. The racial mix of an area directly influences the odds that a given Hispanic person will marry another Hispanic, or a non-Hispanic White, or a Black person. This choice may affect their own racial identity and certainly will influence that of their offspring. Second, there may be a broader cultural process by which people assume an identity more consistent with the larger community where they live. This would help explain what leads White Hispanics and Hispanic Hispanics to different racial choices, despite the overall similarities in their social and economic position.

Neighborhood Characteristics of Hispanics by Race

A final comparison of Hispanics with different racial identification is in terms of the kinds of neighborhoods where they live. Specifically, how segregated are these Hispanic subgroups from Whites and Blacks who are non-Hispanic? What are their neighborhoods like with respect to class composition and nativity of residents? The relevant information is shown in tables 7–8, which are based on a weighted average of all metropolitan regions in the nation (counting regions more heavily if more members of the particular Hispanic subgroup live there). Neighborhood characteristics are based on the census tract where people live. (Recall that the categories of race and Hispanic origin from the summary file data partially overlap with one another; the sum of the categories is greater than the Hispanic total.)

The degree to which two groups live together in the same neighborhoods or in separate neighborhoods is one of the best indicators of social connections between them. In this respect there is a very clear and consistent contrast between White Hispanics and Black Hispanics.

Table 7. Residential pattern of metropolitan Hispanic groups and Blacks, 2000

	WHITE HISPANIC	HISPANIC HISPANIC	BLACK HISPANIC	NON-HISPANIC BLACK
Segregation (Index of Dissimilarity) from:				
Non-Hispanic Whites	45.5	57.3	61.8	64.6
Non-Hispanic Blacks	50.3	49.1	35.0	0.0
White Hispanics	0.0	17.3	34.1	55.0
Hispanic Hispanics	17.6	0.0	30.7	54.1
Black Hispanics	31.5	30.4	0.0	33.7
In average group member's neighborhood:				
% non-Hispanic White	39.6	34.1	34.0	33.3
% non-Hispanic Black	9.3	11.5	28.2	51.0
% Hispanic	43.8	46.7	31.1	11.4
% White Hispanic	26.2	22.5	15.2	5.5
% Hispanic Hispanic	19.1	25.9	15.9	5.8
% Black Hispanic	0.8	1.0	2.2	0.9
Total population (SF1 definitions)	18,027,799	15,324,344	972,892	30,381,389

Table 8. Neighborhood characteristics of metropolitan Hispanic groups and Blacks, 2000

	WHITE HISPANIC	HISPANIC HISPANIC	BLACK HISPANIC	NON-HISPANIC BLACK
In average group member's neighborhood:				
Median household income	$41,037	$37,806	$36,479	$36,200
% Below poverty	17.7	20.1	21.3	20.4
% Homeowners	55.4	49.5	43.5	52.8
% Foreign-born	27.4	28.7	23.7	11.6
% Speak other language at home	47.0	49.1	37.7	17.2

White Hispanics are less segregated from non-Hispanic Whites (D = 45.5) than from non-Hispanic Blacks (D = 50.3). They typically live in neighborhoods that are almost as White (39.6 percent) as they are Hispanic (43.8 percent), and where only a small share of the population is non-Hispanic Black (9.3 percent). Black Hispanics are the most segregated from Whites (D = 61.8), and their segregation from Blacks is unusually low (D = 35.0). They live in neighborhoods where there are nearly as many Black (28.2 percent) as White residents (34.0 percent).

Black Hispanics and non-Hispanic Blacks have very similar segregation from Whites. Non-Hispanic Blacks on average live in metropolitan regions where their segregation from non-Hispanic Whites is 65. The typical non-Hispanic Black person's neighborhood is 33 percent White. The difference, of course, is that Black Hispanics live in much more Hispanic environments than do Blacks.

Hispanic Hispanics are as segregated from Blacks as are White Hispanics, but at the same time they are more segregated from Whites.

Compared to other Hispanic groups, Black Hispanics' neighborhoods have the lowest median income, the highest share of poor residents, and the lowest share of homeowners. Finally—partly reflecting their own relatively low proportion of foreign born individuals—they live in neighborhoods with the lowest percentage of immigrants and neighbors who speak a language other than English in their homes.

Again a comparison with non-Hispanic Blacks is useful. Their typical neighborhood has a median income of $36,200 and a poverty rate of 20.4 percent—almost the same as Black Hispanics, and quite distinct from White Hispanics. However, their neighborhoods have higher levels of homeownership (52.8 percent) and lower shares of immigrants and non-English-language speakers.

White Hispanics live in neighborhoods with a higher class standing and also more immigrants and non-English speakers. Hispanic Hispanics have some similarities to White Hispanics: they live in places where more than a quarter of their neighbors are immigrants and nearly half speak another language. However, the income level and poverty rate of their neighborhoods is closer to Black Hispanics than to White Hispanics. And homeownership in their communities is at a middle point between the two other Hispanic groups. In these respects, as is also true with several socioeconomic characteristics shown in table 2, Hispanic Hispanics are intermediate between Black and White Hispanics.

Whether Hispanics choose to identify their race as White, Hispanic, or Black is not a matter of purely personal preference—it reflects the social position of group members.

This is most evident in the case of the smallest group, Black Hispanics. Their individual characteristics such as income and unemployment make them in many ways more similar to non-Hispanic Blacks than to other Hispanic groups. Whether Hispanics identify themselves as Black is directly responsive to the size of the Black community where they live. Nearly half of Black Hispanic children have a non-Hispanic Black mother or father. Black Hispanics have a very low level of segregation from non-Hispanic Blacks. And they live in neighborhoods with very similar class composition to non-Hispanic Blacks.

Users of census data have been reluctant to classify Black Hispanics together with non-Hispanic Blacks, perhaps because of the distinctive linguistic background and national origins of Black Hispanics. However, there is considerable diversity within the non-Hispanic Black community, and groups such as Africans and Afro-Caribbeans are quite distinctive in their socioeconomic composition and neighborhood patterns. Haitians and some African-born Blacks are not native English speakers. And in fact the typical level of segregation between African Americans and Afro-Caribbeans is greater than that between non-Hispanic Blacks and Black Hispanics.

Black Hispanics potentially provide a bridge between the Black and Hispanic communities. On the basis of social similarity, if it is necessary to combine them with another group, there are now better reasons to classify Black Hispanics as Black than as Hispanic.

Legally there is no obstacle to treating Black Hispanics as both Black and Hispanic. Federal policy is enunciated in Bulletin No. 00–02 of the Office of Management and Budget (March 9, 2000) regarding counting of residents in cases of agency monitoring and enforcement: "If the enforcement action requires assessing disparate impact or discriminatory patterns [the agency will] analyze the patterns based on alternative allocations to each of the minority groups."[3] This means that Black Hispanics may be counted as both Hispanics and as Blacks. More specifically, when evaluating complaints about civil rights violations, federal agencies are instructed to categorize data in the way that is most meaningful for that complaint (e.g., if the complaint is about Hispanic political representation, Black Hispanics would be counted as Hispanics). This study shows that the question needs to be taken seriously. Routinely treating all Hispanics as a single separate group may seriously misrepresent the social reality in a given place.

Because of their numbers—now more than sixteen million, and growing more rapidly than other Hispanic groups—it is even more important to be aware of the distinctiveness of Hispanics who identify neither as Black nor as White. These are the newest Hispanics, in terms of the share who are foreign born or speak Spanish in their homes. Hispanic Hispanics are intermediate between White and Black Hispanics on several of the measures studied here. They are unlikely to be "Black" in the sense of having a non-Hispanic Black parent. But they are clearly less advantaged in many respects than are Hispanics who identify themselves as White.

Federal policy does not require that this Hispanic group be separately identified. Indeed, for some purposes its members are routinely reclassified into another racial category. For example, the Census Bureau's post-census population estimates "impute" a race such as Black, White, or Asian to people who identify as "some other race." This practice is justified by the fact that other vital statistics on which estimates are based do not distinguish "Hispanic Hispanics." It does conform to the Office of Management and Budget's minimum requirements for race reporting (White; Black; American Indian and Alaska Native; Asian; and Native Hawaiian and Other Pacific Islander). But the distinctiveness and explosive growth of this segment of the Hispanic community in the United States make it important to understand what it represents.

Possibly White Hispanics reflect an assimilationist tendency within the Hispanic community, a tendency for those who are somewhat more advantaged and who live in metropolitan areas with smaller Hispanic populations to become more integrated with the White majority. To some extent they are also rooted in intermarriage between Hispanics and non-Hispanic Whites. Still, their socioeconomic standing is considerably lower than that of non-Hispanic Whites, they are moderately to highly segregated from non-Hispanic Whites, and they live in less advantaged neighborhoods.

The rise of Hispanic Hispanics may represent a different social tendency that is consistent with the continuing gaps between Hispanics of any race and a non-Hispanic White majority. Though Hispanics are undoubtedly aware of the Black-White color line in American society, this report offers evidence that they increasingly reject these racial categories and assert a distinct Hispanic ethnic identity. It makes sense that such a development would draw more heavily on immigrants and find more resonance in parts of the country where there is a more substantial Hispanic presence. The recent rapid growth of a Hispanic population that is not fully integrated into the mainstream economy offers conditions that support such a cultural turn and suggests that it will deepen in coming years.

Notes

The Mumford Center research assistants Hyoung-jin Shin and Jacob Stowell contributed to the analyses reported here.

1. John R. Logan, "The New Latinos: Who They Are, Where They Are," report from the Lewis Mumford Center, SUNY, Albany, September 10, 2001.

2. Background information about the Census Bureau's approach can be found at www.census.gov/population/www/socdem/compraceho.html.

3. "Guidance on Aggregation and Allocation of Data on Race," Office of Management and Budget, Bulletin No. 00–02, March 9, 2000, www.whitehouse.gov/omb (site visited on October 22, 2009).

WILLIAM A. DARITY JR., JASON DIETRICH,
AND DARRICK HAMILTON

Bleach in the Rainbow

Latino Ethnicity and Preference for Whiteness

For the North American country of Mexico and the Caribbean countries of Cuba and Puerto Rico—the major sources of Latino immigration to the United States—estimates run as high as 75 percent of their populations consisting of persons of modern African descent.[1] Conservative estimates indicate that persons of African descent constitute anywhere from 5 to 13 percent of South America's population.[2]

Specific countries in South America—Guyana, Suriname, French Guiana, Brazil, and Colombia—are reported to have African-descended population shares that amount to one-quarter or more of their citizenry.[3] For Caribbean countries like Jamaica, the Dominican Republic, Haiti, the Bahamas, Barbados, and Guadeloupe, the proportion of the population that is of African descent has been estimated at 85 to 95 percent.

Therefore, it would seem surprising that the proportion of all respondents among Latinos who self-describe themselves as Black or "Negro" in the United States censuses is very small (see tables 1 and 2). In both the 1980 and 1990 censuses, regardless of gender, less than 3 percent of all Latino respondents self-identified themselves as Black. Preliminary data from Census 2000 indicate that the proportion still remains unchanged. Data on Latinos taken collectively in United States censuses is dominated heavily by Mexican ancestry respondents. Mexican ancestry respondents constituted more than 60 percent of all Latinos in the 1980 and 1990 census (table 1) using the 5 percent Public Use Microdata Samples (PUMS). But among the smaller subset of Latinos who tend to self-identify as Black, the respondents weigh most heavily from countries other than the three major ones contributing to the Latin American presence in the United States.

Table 1. Distribution of Latinos by racial self-identification in the
1980 and 1990 censuses (5% PUMS)

	1980	1990
Males		
Non-Black Cubans	8,192	10,992
Black Cubans	219	353
Non-Black Mexicans	70,424	120,005
Black Mexicans	846	561
Non-Black Puerto Ricans	13,876	17,596
Black Puerto Ricans	471	711
Non-Black other Spanish	25,705	41,100
Black other Spanish	1,121	2,085
Females		
Non-Black Cubans	7,133	9,225
Black Cubans	223	275
Non-Black Mexicans	44,924	92,738
Black Mexicans	857	469
Non-Black Puerto Ricans	8,987	14,588
Black Puerto Ricans	309	598
Non-Black other Spanish	21,226	35,738
Black other Spanish	1,052	2,063

In tables 1 and 2 the "Other Spanish" category consists primarily of persons from Central and South America. In the 1990 census, independent of racial identification, 22 percent reported ancestry from Spain, 12 percent from El Salvador, 9 percent from Colombia, 8 percent from the Dominican Republic, and 6 percent from Guatemala. The "Other Spanish" category constituted more than 40 percent of all Latinos who self-identified as Black in the 1980 census and close to 60 percent of all Latinos who self-identified as Black in the 1990 census.

Among those persons in the "Other Spanish" category reporting themselves to be Black, the distribution by national origin is quite different from their overall representation in the category. Twenty-five percent of Dominicans, 37 percent of Panamanians, and 10 percent of Hondurans reported themselves to be Black. The only other countries of origin where the percentage exceeded 4 percent were Costa Rica and Venezuela in the "Other Spanish" category. Countries such as Colombia and Peru, despite

Table 2. Percentage of Latino national groups self-reporting race as Black in the 1980 and 1990 census (5% PUMS)

	MALES		FEMALES	
	1980	1990	1980	1990
Cubans	2.6	3.1	3.0	2.9
Mexicans	1.2	0.5	1.9	0.1
Puerto Ricans	3.3	3.9	3.3	3.9
Other Spanish	4.2	4.8	5.9	5.5

large African ancestry populations, did not have a percentage of respondents self-classifying themselves as Black that exceeded 2 percent.

What Is at the End of the Rainbow?

Clara Rodriguez has stressed the tendency of Latinos to eschew both the categories of Black and White and instead to opt for some intermediate or alternative category of racial identification—that is, a racial "Other" category.[4] This is not consistent with our findings. This is generally true for Mexican-ancestry respondents, perhaps in part due to an embrace of Native American and Aztec ancestry. In the 1990 census more than 45 percent of Mexican male and female respondents self-identified themselves in a racial category that was neither White nor Black. But less than 10 percent of Cuban, Puerto Rican, and Other Spanish respondents, regardless of gender, selected a category distinct from Black or White. In both 1980 and 1990 fewer than 8 percent of Puerto Rican respondents self-identified themselves in a racial category other than White.

Indeed, the evidence is compelling that there is a strong Latino preference for racial self-identification as White, not Black or some intermediate category between the ostensibly dichotomous color poles. The Latino aversion to self-identification as Black is pronounced in table 2 where proportions of each of the four Latino national groups that reported themselves as Black in the 1980 census are displayed. Note that among Mexican respondents, less than 1 percent of the men and women said they were Black in 1990. The rate only approaches 4 percent for Puerto Ricans.

The low frequency of self-reported Blackness is especially stark in the 1990 census for Cubans. The 1980 census, taken in 1979, would not have reflected the impact of the 1980 Mariel boatlift immigrants, phenotypically darker than the earlier immigrants, on Cuban American demography. The 1990 census, on the other hand, should have included the 1980 immigrants, but the proportion of men and women declaring themselves to be racially Black was virtually unchanged.

Customarily, it is asserted that the Latin American understanding and conceptualization of race is dramatically different from that in the United States. The conventional wisdom has it that racial classification in Latin America is gradational based on phenotype, while it is dichotomous and based on genotype in the United States.[5] Gina Sanchez has made parallel claims for Cape Verdeans.[6] This perspective has led Clara Rodriguez to declare Puerto Ricans a "rainbow people," virtually devoid of race prejudice and solely amused and entertained by their phenotypical variations.[7] [. . .]

Collective Passing

If racial classification were solely a matter of phenotype or ascriptive appearance in Latin America, then there should be a close correspondence between individuals' physical appearance and their racial self-classification on a gradational scale. That does not appear to be the case.

Angelo Falcón reports on a set of results from the 1989–1990 Latino National Political Survey (LNPS) for 561 Puerto Rican respondents drawn from forty metropolitan areas in the United States.[8] Respondents' skin color was rated as very dark, dark, medium, light, and very light by the interviewers. The respondents were asked to self-classify themselves by race in an open-ended fashion. Responses that did not fall into the categories of Black or White were clustered by the researchers conducting the study under the label "Latino referent." Hence, "Latino referent" includes racial self-characterization linked to nationality (e.g., Hispanic, Chicana, Aztec) but also racial self-characterization linked to color in categories falling between Black and White (e.g., mulatta, moreno).

In Falcón's examination of the LNPS sample, most Puerto Ricans (58 percent) described themselves as White, while 38 percent chose a racial category that placed them in the Latino referent category. Falcón interprets these results as broadly supportive of the "rainbow people" hypothesis.[9] We disagree, particularly since the aversion toward self-identification as Black is evident again. Only 4 percent of Puerto Rican respondents reported themselves to be Black.

More compelling is that the resistance to self-identification as Black remained strong among those who ascriptively would be most likely to be viewed by others as Black. Furthermore, a clear preference was demon-

Table 3. Racial self-identification by skin color and rating by interviewers of Puerto Rican, Mexican, and Cuban respondents

PUERTO RICAN RESPONDENTS SKIN-COLOR RATING BY INTERVIEWERS					
RACIAL SELF-IDENTIFICATION	VERY LIGHT	LIGHT	MEDIUM	DARK	VERY DARK
White	70.4%	70.6%	55.2%	30.6%	33.4%
Other (Latino referent)	29.6%	28.8%	41.2%	59.0%	29.2%
Black	—	0.6%	3.6%	10.4%	37.4%
Number of cases	78	175	218	71	19

MEXICAN RESPONDENTS SKIN-COLOR RATING BY INTERVIEWERS					
RACIAL SELF-IDENTIFICATION	VERY LIGHT	LIGHT	MEDIUM	DARK	VERY DARK
White	71.0%	62.9%	48.4%	37.2%	37.5%
Other (Latino referent)	29.0%	36.9%	51.6%	62.2%	59.4%
Black	—	0.2%	—	0.6%	0.1%
Number of cases	162	396	599	288	32

CUBAN RESPONDENTS SKIN-COLOR RATING BY INTERVIEWERS					
RACIAL SELF-IDENTIFICATION	VERY LIGHT	LIGHT	MEDIUM	DARK	VERY DARK
White	99.4%	97.8%	91.4%	72.7%	9.1%
Other (Latino referent)	0.6%	1.6%	7.1%	12.1%	9.1%
Black	—	0.6%	1.5%	15.2%	81.8%
Number of cases	165	321	140	33	11

strated to be classified as White rather than as an intermediate category. Thirty-three percent of the very dark respondents classified themselves as White, 31 percent of the dark respondents did the same, and 55 percent of the medium (brown) respondents—the most numerous based on the interviewers' scale—said they were White. In short, a significant proportion of the darkest-skinned Puerto Ricans were inclined to leapfrog self-identification in an intermediate "other" category altogether and place themselves in the White category. None of the very light or light respondents characterized themselves as Black.

Tyrone Forman has utilized the LNPS to replicate the Falcón study as well as present results for Mexican-origin and Cuban-origin respondents.[10] His findings are reported in table 3. Only 4 out of 1,477 (0.3 percent of the sample) Mexican-origin respondents classified themselves as Black, yielding a percentage similar to the frequency in the 1990 census.

There also is evidence of the stronger Mexican tendency to choose the intermediate category for racial self-classification, although that weakens as skin shade lightens. There still is a remarkably high percentage of darker-skinned persons opting for the White category.

There were a total of 670 Cuban respondents, a mere 18 (2.7 percent) of whom said they are Black. In this case, aside from the very dark Cubans there is a clear preference for self-identification as White with little attention given to the intermediate category. In none of these cases is there evidence of a neutral outlook about racial categories, nor much evidence of a rainbow of colors. There is evidence of a flight toward Whiteness.

Forman's results for Puerto Ricans, based on a slightly larger sample (571 observations), closely parallel Falcón's findings. One-third of the respondents classified as dark or very dark by the interviewers identified themselves as White. Half of the respondents with medium (brown) complexions self-identified as White racially.

Additional pieces of qualitative evidence are relevant. The anthropologist France Twine's ethnographic study of a northeastern Brazilian community reveals that phenotypically White individuals would display prominently photographs of their lightest-complexioned relatives but hide or suppress images of relatives whose features and skin shade provided too much evidence of an African ancestry.[11] Similarly, Marta Cruz-Janzen reports on the tendency of light-skinned Latinos to hide their Black ancestry behind a web of intrafamilial secrecy.[12] If only phenotype mattered in social classification, genealogical history would be irrelevant.

Furthermore, an issue of *Time* magazine celebrating an ostensible gravitation of the United States toward the putative Latino gradational model of racial types opens with the following anecdote: "One day when Carlos [Aguilar, son of Peruvian immigrants] was little, another child asked him: 'Did you come here riding on a donkey?' Aguilar was upset, and there was a small scuffle. The family still remembers the flap. 'People think if you have black hair you must be Mexican or illegal,' says his mother Ada, 'but my grandfather,' she proudly adds, 'was of Spanish descent.' 'Peruvians are a combination of the Incas and the Spanish, and the Spanish come from Germany, France, Italy, Arabia—it's a never-ending story.'"[13] Ada Aguilar's comments are revealing. In addition to her denigration of Mexican immigrants, she explicitly privileges her own Spanish ancestry over all others in response to the racism confronted by her son. She neglects to mention that Peruvians also are descendants of enslaved Africans who were brought into western South America as laborers. Again, Blackness is being suppressed rather than being treated as another rich color in the rainbow. Genotype matters significantly in her construction of racial identity.

Cruz-Janzen refers to this pattern of Latino denial of Black ancestry as "the most blatant manifestation of Latino racism."[14] She labels it "historical amnesia." We call it "collective passing" by Latinos.

A Black Night Is Falling?

A purely genotypical characterization of race classification in the United States (the "one drop" rule) also is misleading. The salience of phenotype can be demonstrated by the connection between skin shade and life chances in the United States. Richard Seltzer and Robert Smith's inquiry using the 1982 General Social Survey subsample of 510 Blacks, where interviewers classified Black respondents as dark, medium, and light skinned, shows that dark-skinned Blacks fare worse on all social indicators.[15] Verna Keith and Cedric Herring used the 1979–1980 National Survey of Black Americans where interviewers had coded Black respondents' skin shades and found results parallel to Seltzer's and Smith's.[16] Darker skin shade was associated with lower income, inferior employment, and less education. Mark Hill's more recent longitudinal inquiry provides similar evidence.[17]

James Johnson found that being darker complexioned lowered a Black man's odds of being employed in Los Angeles by 52 percent after controlling for age, schooling, and criminal record.[18] Two studies using the data from the 1979 National Chicano Survey found similar results among Mexican Americans.[19] In a sample where interviewers judged respondents not only on skin shade but also for the correspondence of their facial features with more European or more Native American types, Chicanos with darker skin and less European (more Native American) features had lower earnings and lower socioeconomic status, and they faced a greater degree of labor market discrimination.

Christina Gomez used 1993–1994 Boston Social Survey Data to explore the impact of skin shade on life chances for 354 Puerto Rican and Dominican men and women.[20] While she found no correlation between skin shade and wages for the women in the sample, she found that darker skin was associated with lower wages among the men. [. . .]

The critical point is that this body of evidence points to the salience of skin shade as a factor relevant to variation in intragroup economic outcomes and points to the manifest effect of phenotypical variation in the United States. Genotype alone does not completely characterize the operation of race in the United States. Gradational variations along an indicator

Table 4. Black relative wage outcomes by skin tone for women
(MCSUI: Atlanta, Boston, and Los Angeles)

SKIN SHADE	NUMBER OF OBSERVATIONS (1)	WAGES AS A PERCENTAGE OF WHITE FEMALE WAGE (2)
Dark	302	87.2
Medium	321	83.5
Light	95	89.9

Table 5. Black relative wage outcomes by skin tone for men
(MCSUI: Atlanta, Boston, and Los Angeles)

SKIN SHADE	NUMBER OF OBSERVATIONS (1)	WAGES AS A PERCENTAGE OF WHITE FEMALE WAGE (2)
Dark	176	70.5
Medium	150	78.5
Light	43	88.4

like skin tone have an impact. Genotype also matters among Latin Americans; phenotype also matters in the United States.

Conclusions

We close with five final observations:

1. African Americans are somewhat unique in embracing a Black identity. This may be due to the effect of exits by passing of those Blacks most inclined to identify as White during the century-long Jim Crow era. Latin Americans, in contrast, tend to flee identification with Blackness. Hence, color or racial commonality is unlikely to be a pole for intergroup solidarity between them.

2. Discrimination does not have a uniform impact across all members of broadly construed ethnic and racial groups. As the results reported here indicate, the economic outcomes can vary by skin shade.

3. The difference between self-classification and social classification of race is especially important to consider among Latinos. Census data

only provide information on self-classification. This is valuable in pointing toward potential anomalies and toward a Latino preference for Whiteness given the distribution of phenotypical attributes in a population that shares significantly in recent African ancestry. But census data need to be augmented with studies that simultaneously combine interviewee (self-classification) and interviewer (social classification) reports on racial identity.

4. Racial self-identification involves choice, and individual selection need not correspond to the social construction of racial categories. In Latino populations in the United States the individual selection frequently does not match social classification. But, unlike the implications of the "rainbow people" metaphor, individual racial self-identification among Latinos does not proceed in a fashion that reveals neutrality toward the racial categories. The processes governing the choice, especially the Latino preference for identification with Whiteness, is an important subject for further inquiry as to the effects of phenotype on economic outcomes. It suggests that future research on race and social outcomes will need to treat race as an endogenous variable, particularly in studies that include Latino populations. This insight will inform our own work when we extend our inquiry in this area by using the 2000 census.

5. These results suggest that popularly reported expectations that the United States will have a non-White majority by the mid-twenty-first century should be muted. If most recent immigrant populations prefer the racial status of being classified as White—and if the existing White majority accepts those who are relatively lighter as such—sufficiently flexible boundaries of Whiteness could maintain a White majority in the United States indefinitely.[21] Ironically, the same flexibility historically has not been extended openly to African Americans, regardless of their skin shade. Hence those African Americans who opted to obtain the privileges of Whiteness had to "become" White by passing. After all, if everyone could become White, then there would be no privilege associated with Whiteness. Such privilege is the reason racial boundaries persist.

Bleach in the Rainbow Revisited (November 2007)

In mid-2003, John Logan issued a report through the Lewis Mumford Center at the University of Albany documenting Latina and Latino (Logan prefers to use the term "Hispanics" throughout his report) patterns of race identification in Census 2000 for the United States. The report takes at face value, with negligible interrogation of potential anomalies and conundrums, descriptive statistics that can be extracted directly from the census. In particular, Logan does not problematize the self-reported responses to the race question. Given the prevalence of what has been called the "bleaching" phenomenon among Latinas and Latinos—the preference for Whiteness[22]—it is essential to explore the whorl of subtexts that underlie many Latina and Latino respondents' answers to the race question.

Race as a socially designed identity can be established by self-classification (own classification) or by social classification (classification by others). In both cases, an individual's phenotype and/or genotype may play a role in the process of categorization. The Latino National Political Survey (LNPS) taken in 1989–1990 asked Mexican, Puerto Rican, and Cuban ancestry respondents to answer an open-ended question about their race. Interviewers also "graded" respondents on their skin shade on a five-point Likert-type scale; an individual would be graded as "very light," "light," "medium," "dark," or "very dark" by their interviewer. More than 30 percent of the 454 dark and very dark respondents said their race was "White" as did more than half of the 957 medium-complexioned interviewees. Most surprising, among Cubans over 90 percent of the 140 persons graded as having a medium skin tone said they were "White." Overall, about 70 percent of all respondents said that their race was "White"; virtually none of the interviewees graded as light or very light claimed their race was "Black."[23]

In addition, the LNPS reveals a general reluctance on the part of Latin@s two decades ago to self-identify as Black, regardless of their skin shade. Only 4 out of 1,477 Mexican-origin respondents in the sample said they were Black. Among a total of 670 Cuban-origin respondents, only 18 persons reported their race as Black. A mere 21 Puerto Rican respondents out of a total of 561 said they were Black. In a survey where interviewees had the option of choosing a nationality or culturally based race referent, including their country of origin or "Hispanic" or "Latino," or color categories other than Black or White for their race, the predominant choice was "White." And it was a choice taken by a large proportion of the respondents with the darkest skin shades.

The aversion toward self-identification as Black persists across censuses over time. In both the 1980 and 1990 censuses less than 3 percent of all Latinas and Latinos self-identified as Black, despite coming from countries where estimates indicate that upward of 75 percent of the populations consist of persons of modern African descent.[24] In Census 2000, the proportion of Latinas and Latinos self-reporting their race as Black was largely unchanged at 2.7 percent.[25]

It is noteworthy that the proportion of Latin@s reporting their race to be White also fell in Census 2000 to marginally less than half of all respondents (49.9 percent). What has changed dramatically between the point at which the LNPS was taken and Census 2000 is the proportion of Latinas and Latinos who use either "Hispanic" or "Latino" as their race identifiers. By Census 2000 close to half of the Latina and Latino respondents (47.4 percent) said their race was "Hispanic" or "Latino," a trend that my coauthors and I had not fully grasped when we wrote the original version of "Bleach in the Rainbow."

Logan suggests that there is evidence of a growing inclination among Puerto Ricans in the United States to claim a Black racial identity.[26] By Census 2000, he observes, 8.2 percent of Puerto Ricans said they were Black. This is misleading. Census 2000 was the first in fifty years where the race question was asked in Puerto Rico itself, and close to 8 percent of the respondents there reported their race as Black while less than 2 percent of Puerto Ricans in the contiguous United States said they were Black.[27] This should not be interpreted as an indicator of greater Black consciousness on the part of Puerto Ricans on the island. After all, over 80 percent of Puerto Ricans on the island said their race is "White" while slightly less than half of the Puerto Ricans in the contiguous United States chose to self-identify racially as White. Puerto Ricans in the contiguous United States do share in the growing inclination to self-identify racially as "Hispanic" or "Latino."

Logan also incorrectly asserts that Dominicans have the highest rate of self-identification as Black among Latinas and Latinos, with a 12.7 percent rate. The rate of Black self-identification actually is greater among Panamanians.[28]

The critical reader must be alert to the fact that a Latina's and Latino's racial self-identification as White or Latino does not provide a clear indicator about their appearance or how they will be viewed by others in the communities where they live. Many "White Hispanics" in Logan's enumeration may well be perceived as Black by others. At minimum, to the extent that they are darker-complexioned, they may be subjected to pervasive colorism penalties in the United States. Evidence from the 1992–1995 Multi-City Study of Urban Inequality shows that darker- and medium-complexioned Black men in the United States suffer discriminatory wage losses three to four times as great as those faced by lighter-complexioned Black men relative to White males.[29] A study utilizing data from the 2003

New Immigrant Survey demonstrates that shorter and darker-skinned immigrant males suffer high levels of discrimination in American labor markets.[30]

Indeed, Logan seems genuinely surprised to discover that although the small percentage of Latinas and Latinos who self-report their race as Black in Census 2000 do worse than other Latinas and Latinos on a variety of economic indicators, they have a mean level of schooling that is more than a full year higher than that of other Latinas and Latinos.[31] This "discovery" is consistent with an earlier finding of much higher levels of discriminatory losses in earnings against "Black Latinas and Latinos" in comparison with those who reported a non-Black racial identity in the 1980 and 1990 censuses.[32] Indeed, because of the widespread Latina and Latino resistance to embracing a Black identity, those Latin@s who self-report their race as Black in the censuses are very likely to have phenotypical attributes that would lead them to be perceived as Black by others—and therefore subject to the economic penalties associated with Blackness in a racist society.

In a new study Golash Boza and I used both the Latino National Political Survey and the more recent National Latino Survey (2002) to examine what factors are associated with Latin@ racial choices.[33] What is critical in this context is our treatment of race *as a choice* for the respondent. We found, among other results, that the longer Latinas and Latinos live in the United States, the less likely they are to say their race is White and the more likely they are to say they are "Latino" or "Hispanic." If they are bilingual or English dominant in language skills they are more likely to choose a race classification other than White.

Using the National Latino Survey (NLS), we find some mild evidence for the vaunted "social whitening" hypothesis or the idea that as an individuals' income rises they become more likely to choose "White" as their race identifier. But there is an important qualifier here: the NLS, unlike the LNPS, was a phone survey and there are no skin shade controls available in the data. If Latinas and Latinos who are lighter earn more—which is demonstrably true in the LNPS—then we probably are not finding support for the social whitening hypothesis at all. We are only finding additional evidence of the privileges associated with lighter skin and more evidence of a material basis for many Latinas' and Latinos' preference for Whiteness, regardless of how they might actually look themselves.

Notes

William A. Darity Jr. is the sole author of the section "Bleach in the Rainbow Revisited (November 2007)" on page 493 to 496.

1. Marta Cruz-Janzen, "Latinegras: Desired Women–Undesirable Mothers, Daughters, Sisters and Wives," *Frontiers* 22, no. 3 (2001): 174.

2. Adam Halpern and France Twine, "Antiracist Activism in Ecuador: Black-Indian Community Alliances," *Race and Class* 42, no. 2 (2000): 19–20.

3. Inter-American Dialogue: Race Report, "Afro-Descendants in Latin America: How Many?" January 2, 2003, http://www.thedialogue.org (site visited on April 19, 2005).

4. Clara Rodriguez, "Race, Culture, and Latino 'Otherness' in the 1980 Census," *Social Science Quarterly* 73, no. 4 (1992): 930–37.

5. Clara Rodriguez and Hector Cordero-Guzman, "Placing Race in Context," *Ethnic and Racial Studies* 15, no. 4 (1992): 523–42; Rodriguez, "Race, Culture, and Latino 'Otherness' in the 1980 Census."

6. Gina Sanchez, "The Politics of Cape Verdean Identity," *Transforming Anthropology* 6, nos. 1–2 (1997): 54–71.

7. Clara Rodriguez, *Puerto Ricans: Born in the USA* (Boston: Unwin Hyman, 1989).

8. Angelo Falcón, "Puerto Ricans and the Politics of Racial Identity," in *Racial and Ethnic Identity: Psychological Development and Creative Expression*, edited by Herbert Harris, Howard Blue, and Ezra Griffith (New York: Routledge, 1995).

9. Ibid., 200.

10. Tyrone Forman, "Racial Self-Identification and Interviewers' Skin Color Rating among Puerto Ricans, Mexicans, and Cubans: National Latino Political Survey," unpublished manuscript, Department of Sociology, University of Michigan, n.d.

11. France Twine, *Racism in a Racial Democracy: The Maintenance of White Supremacy in Brazil* (New Brunswick, N.J.: Rutgers University Press, 1998).

12. Cruz-Janzen, "Latinegras," 180.

13. "The New Face of Race," *Time*, September 28, 2000, 38.

14. Cruz-Janzen, "Latinegras," 176.

15. Richard Seltzer and Robert C. Smith, "Color Differences in the Afro-American Community and the Differences They Make," *Journal of Black Studies* 21 (1991): 279–86.

16. Verna M. Keith and Cedric Herring, "Skin Tone and Stratification in the Black Community," *American Journal of Sociology* 97 (1991): 760–78.

17. Mark E. Hill, "Color Differences in the Socioeconomic Status of African American Men: Results of a Longitudinal Study," *Social Forces* 78, no. 4 (2000): 1437–60.

18. James H. Johnson Jr. with Elisa Bienenstock and Jennifer Stoloff, "An Empirical Test of the Cultural Capital Hypothesis," *Review of Black Political Economy* 23 (1995): 7–27.

19. Carlos H. Arce with Edward Murgania and W. Parker Frisbee, "Phenotype and Life Chances among Chicanos," *Hispanic Journal of Behavioral Studies* 9 (1987): 19–33; Edward E. Telles and Edward Marguia, "Phenotype, Discrimination, and Income Differences among Mexican Americans, *Social Science Quarterly* 71 (1990): 682–94.

20. Christina Gomez, "The Continual Significance of Skin Color: An Exploratory Study of Latinos in the Northeast," *Hispanic Journal of Behavioral Sciences*, 22, no. 1 (2000): 94–103.

21. Jonathan Warren and France Twine, "White Americans, The New Minority? Non-Black and the Ever-Expanding Boundaries of Whiteness," *Journal of Black Studies* 28, no. 2 (1997): 200–18.

22. William Darity Jr., Jason Dietrich and Darrick Hamilton, "Bleach in the Rainbow: Latin Ethnicity and Preference for Whiteness," *Transforming Anthropology* 13, no. 2 (October 2005): 103–9.

23. Ibid., 105–6.

24. Cruz-Janzen, "Latinegras," 174.

25. John R. Logan, "How Race Counts for Hispanic Americans," report from the Lewis Mumford Center, SUNY, Albany, July 14, 2003, 4.

26. Ibid.

27. Matthew Christenson, "Census 2000 in Puerto Rico: Response to the Questions on Race and Hispanic Origin," paper presented at the annual meeting of the Population Association of America, Minneapolis, Minnesota, May 1–3, 2003, 6.

28. Logan, "How Race Counts for Hispanic Americans," 4.

29. Arthur Goldsmith, Darrick Hamilton, and William Darity Jr., "Shades of Discrimination: Skin Tone and Wages," *American Economic Review* 96, no. 2 (May 2006): 242–45.

30. Joni Hersch, "Skin Color, Immigrants, and Discrimination," paper presented to the Kirwan Institute for the Study of Race and Ethnicity, Ohio State University, December 2, 2007.

31. Logan, "How Race Counts for Hispanic Americans," 3.

32. William Darity Jr., Darrick Hamilton, and Jason Dietrich, "Passing on Blackness? Latinos, Race and Earnings in the USA," *Applied Economics Letters* 9, no. 13 (October 2002): 847–54.

33. Tanya Golash Boza and William Darity Jr., "Latino Racial Choices," *Ethnic and Racial Studies* 31, no. 5 (September 2008): 899–934.

ED MORALES
Brown Like Me?

The Iowa Brown and Black Forum. There it was, superimposed on the bottom corner of the screen going to commercial break just after Al Sharpton tore into Howard Dean's affirmative-action hiring record. Hosted by MSNBC's Lester Holt, an African American, and Maria Celeste Arraras, a Puerto Rico–born anchor for Telemundo, this last debate before the Iowa caucuses helped introduce a new phrase into the American political lexicon. Black and brown. "Do you have a senior member of your cabinet that was Black or brown?" Sharpton prodded, and Dean turned red (again).

Although Sharpton and the Iowa group use this phrase to promote Black-Latino unity, the first time I remember hearing it was when, on the occasion of the quincentennial of Columbus's journey to the Americas (and the aftermath of the Rodney King riots), the *Atlantic Monthly* published "Blacks vs. Browns," by the *Los Angeles Times* reporter Jack Miles. In a significant challenge to the binary view of American racial politics, Miles uncovered the hidden truth about the riots, that there was substantial Latino involvement in what was widely portrayed as a Black and White confrontation. Yet he did not regard this as evidence of an alignment of Black and Latino interests. On the contrary, he predicted that "America's older black poor and newer brown poor are on a collision course."[1]

According to Miles, the civil rights era coalition between Blacks and Latinos was threatened by an emerging class conflict. Fearful of the "nihilistic" tendencies in Black urban culture, he claimed, White and Asian employers were increasingly passing over poor Blacks in favor of Latino immigrants, who were willing to work for lower wages. "Blacks are the most oppressed minority, but it matters enormously that whites are no longer a majority," wrote Miles. "And within the urban geography of Los Angeles, African-Americans seem to me to be competing more directly with Latin Americans than with any other group."[2]

A year earlier, Charles Kamasaki and Raul Yzaguirre of the National Council of La Raza had published a ground-breaking paper that corroborated Miles's argument. Yzaguirre and Kamasaki recounted several instances when African American leaders had failed to support Latino causes. In 1975 the NAACP opposed an extension of the Voting Rights Act that benefited Latinos, while the Leadership Conference on Civil Rights opposed a similar extension of the act in 1982. The NAACP declined to oppose employer sanctions under the Immigration Reform and Control Act; throughout the 1980s the LCCR was indifferent to increasing protection for Latinos against employment discrimination, while only nominally opposing the English-only movement. The paper concluded that "growing tension between the two communities . . . threatens the ability of Blacks and Hispanics to develop strong, sustainable coalitions."[3]

These ominous predictions are echoed in Nicolas C. Vaca's book *The Presumed Alliance: The Unspoken Conflict between Latinos and Blacks and What It Means for America.* But unlike Miles and Kamasaki and Yzaguirre, whose arguments he cites, Vaca, a lawyer and scholar based in the Bay Area, wants to posit the adversarial aspects of the relationship between Blacks and Latinos as a fact of life. In making this argument, Vaca, who fancies himself a maverick, claims he is simply facing up to realities that Latino intellectuals and activists have sidestepped because of "knee-jerk," "politically correct" assumptions about Black-Latino solidarity. He is so convinced of this that he lost an old Latino friend in a public argument over whether to write the book. "Why dig up dirt," writes Vaca, "ruffle feathers, destroy the illusion of unbroken unity between Blacks and Latinos, bleeding the colors of the Rainbow Coalition by giving the dreaded gringo the ammunition my former friend told me I was providing? The simple answer is that the ethnic landscape has changed."[4]

Vaca's argument hinges on the demographics laid out in the opening chapter "The Latino Tsunami: The Browning of America." He cites statistics that forecast exponential population growth, which will cast California and the Southwest in an increasingly "brown" hue by midcentury, and the related "hypergrowth" of Latino communities in areas like Atlanta as well as Raleigh, Greensboro, and Charlotte, North Carolina, with the influx of new, mostly Mexican, immigrants. This demographic transformation will inexorably generate increasing conflict as Latinos—who have long been underrepresented in political office, in part because immigrants can't vote, and who have long felt their concerns are not taken seriously—seek representation equal to their numbers. In cities like Los Angeles, where African Americans wield a measure of political power,

Blacks are increasingly digging in to resist a numerically superior brown rival.

In chapter 3, "Who's the Leader of the Civil Rights Band?" Vaca analyzes the landmark case *Mendez v. Westminster*, which challenged the existence of separate schools for Mexican Americans and "helped lay the groundwork for the ruling in *Brown vs. Board of Education* eight years later." By establishing a Latino claim to a history of oppression by White America, Vaca is also trying to establish that African Americans were not the only pioneers of the civil rights struggle, and that Latinos deserve a share of the movement's benefits. Unfortunately, he uses these arguments to blame another victim. The villains invariably turn out to be African Americans, who are threatened by demographic changes and shut Latinos out of political office, while refusing to acknowledge that anyone's suffering could ever be as great as theirs. In the chapter "Somewhere Over the Rainbow Coalition," Vaca curiously draws from the Stokely Carmichael and Charles Hamilton classic *Black Power* to argue that "feel-good statements" and an idealistic "squinty-eyed view" held by out-of-touch activists "does not square with what has happened in the real world." By invoking Carmichael and Hamilton's observation that different groups in a coalition will tend to act in their own interest, he is merely invoking a tautology that could be made about almost any political coalition. Vaca goes on to cite several studies showing that in Los Angeles, Blacks often block Latinos from obtaining municipal employment. This competition is "one of many examples of how zero-sum conflict trumps any idealized notion of Latino-Black cooperation."[5] But there is no discussion in this chapter of the private sector, either with respect to the hiring practices of small businesses or with respect to falling wages, which Latino immigrants are more likely to accept than African Americans.

All of which is not to say that Vaca is entirely wrong. Although he doesn't take into account that Mexican American citizens are also displaced in the job market by immigrants (including fellow Latinos), and that some established Mexican Americans do not favor pro-immigration legislation, this conflict scenario accurately represents the Latino experience in the South and Southwest. Los Angeles has seen Black-Latino political conflict (and cooperation) since the early days of the civil rights movement. Although the city's eighteenth-century founders were multiracial Mexicans of indigenous, African, Chinese, and Spanish blood, Los Angeles has not elected a Latino mayor in more than a century, and Blacks and Latinos have often voted for different candidates. The 1965 Watts riots, a predominantly African American uprising, focused attention on the plight of Black

Angelenos but not on the barrios, while the Black-Jewish liberal coalition that swept Tom Bradley into power further isolated Mexican Americans from political power. An even greater rift developed when janitorial jobs, once the preserve of African American union members, were turned over to non-unionized Mexican immigrants by union-busting janitorial firms. Despite Antonio Villaraigosa's strong candidacy in the 2001 mayoral race, he was not able to draw enough Black votes from James Hahn, a White liberal whose father was a favorite of African Americans.

Vaca shows that the conflict between Blacks and Latinos in California is historically rooted in a dynamic that is particular to that part of the country. After it was absorbed by the United States following the Mexican-American War, the Southwest's primary racial divide was between Anglos and Latinos (and to a lesser extent East Asians), with African Americans coming into the mix later on, beginning in the 1930s. In Vaca's account of phenomena like segregated Mexican American–only schools and the lynching of Mexican Americans, African Americans are portrayed as late-comers to the West's zero-sum battle for resources. That is, despite African Americans' claim to primary "minority" status, "Black suffering does not necessarily trump Latino suffering."[6]

Vaca's argument is true as far as it goes—which isn't far at all. As he points out, Mexican Americans make up about 60 percent of the total Latino population in the United States, and their experience in Los Angeles (particularly in the neighborhood of Compton) has been marked, at times, by tensions with African Americans. But the question of Black-brown relations is national in scope, and Vaca's analysis reflects a distinctly West Coast and ultimately parochial perspective. His chapters on Black-Latino political strife in Los Angeles and Houston focus almost entirely on the Mexican American version of Latino interests. In an attempt to counterbalance this, Vaca offers an analysis of Black-Latino relations in Miami (a reverse-case scenario, where the White Cuban American elite has historically refused to share public-sector power with African Americans and Afro-Caribbeans) and, in the book's least-coherent chapter, of the 2001 mayoral race in Puerto Rican–dominated New York. Miami is clearly an aberrant case, because that city's Latino immigration was dominated by lighter-skinned members of Cuba's upper and middle classes fleeing Castro's revolution, and New York's complex ethnic politics, in which Latinos and Blacks have entered into various coalitions with each other and with Whites, is apparently beyond Vaca's expertise.

Although he rarely uses the word "brown" to describe Latinos, Vaca's assertion of a sharp separation between Black and Latino is consistent with the "brown perspective" associated with a group of influential West Coast Latino writers. While it can serve as a useful color-coded signifier for being Latino, "brown" obscures the fact that Latinos come in the full spectrum of racial hues, very much including Black. West Coast brownologists like the essayist Richard Rodríguez and Gregory Rodriguez, the *Los Angeles Times* commentator and New America Foundation fellow, consistently categorize Latinos as distinctly separate from African Americans, a third, mestizo, wheel in the American race dialogue. Although Rodríguez and Rodriguez (no relation) are more diplomatic than Vaca in declaring that historic Latino suffering could never approach Black suffering, the most important subtext in both writers' output is their effort to erect explicit barriers between Blacks and Latinos.

Richard Rodríguez's concept of brown is, to be sure, semantically playful in invoking UPS's current ad campaign along with sodomy in describing this "undermining brown motif, this erotic tunnel." Brown can be read here as the messy multiethnic muddle that America is seemingly becoming through rising rates of Latino intermarriage, a Utopian space from which, as the Mexican writer José Vasconcelos once suggested in his work *La Raza Cósmica*, humanity could launch its next great leap. In his recent book of essays, *Brown*, Rodríguez describes how growing up as an "honorary White" allowed him to escape linkages with the Black culture of suffering. When a Black professor at a public forum uses the phrase "blacks-and-Latinos" as a "synonym for the disadvantaged in America," Rodríguez recoils in discomfort. His most fervent desire for the African Americans he has so much compassion for is "White freedom. The same as I wanted for myself."[7] By this he means freedom from "culture" or "race," a desire expressed in various ways by ideologues like Ward Connerly and writers like Shelby Steele.

Gregory Rodriguez in an editorial in the *Los Angeles Times* in 2003 went to great lengths to give African Americans their due as the undisputed kings of suffering. "Even as Latinos exert growing influence on American politics and culture, blacks will continue to have a more powerful claim on America's moral imagination," he wrote. "Their history of slavery and segregation ensures that African-Americans will not be displaced in their role as the preeminent 'other' in U.S. society." But apparently this moral authority is directly proportional to the ability to inspire the kind of fear that Jack Miles's *Atlantic Monthly* article evoked. "Latino immigrants generally do not instill the same fear among whites that Blacks can. The social distance between brown and white has never been as great as that between Black and white."[8]

Well, that may be true, but what if you were one of the millions of Latinos who are not brown but actually Black (a genetic condition given only passing reference by brownologists), or even stranger, strongly identify with African culture regardless of skin tone? One doesn't have to look too far in United States Latino letters to find representatives of this point of view. Witness Lisa Sanchez-Gonzalez's fascinating meditation, in *Boricua Literature*, in which she contrasts William Carlos Williams and Arturo Schomburg (both of Puerto Rican heritage) and the roles they played in defining how Latinos have manifested themselves not just as brown but as "White" and "Black" in America. Hip-hop, the most dynamic and commercially successful musical form in the world today, emerged as a joint creative effort between Blacks and Latinos, as both Juan Flores's *From Bomba to Hip-Hop* and Raquel Rivera's *New York Ricans from the Hip Hop Zone* have recently demonstrated. These texts are not merely evidence of "identification" with African Americans but a reflection of a shared, lived experience engendered by the proximity of Black and Latino neighborhoods in northeastern cities and the Caribbean islands, as well as an acknowledgment of shared African genetic heritage. *Pace* Vaca, this shared history, though no guarantee of Black-Latino solidarity, can translate into a set of overlapping political interests.

Call these writers the leading edge of the East Coast–based Caribbean alternative to the brown perspective on Black-Latino relations, if you are daring enough or have the energy to accept even more categories in the increasingly complicated debate over race in America. One might argue that these works are merely part of a "Puerto Rican exception," to borrow a phrase from the neoconservative Linda Chavez, who used it to describe intractable Puerto Rican poverty in her notorious 1992 treatise *Out of the Barrio: Toward a New Politics of Hispanic Assimilation*. But although Puerto Ricans make up less than 10 percent of United States Latinos (roughly 17 percent if you count island Puerto Ricans, all United States citizens), and other Latin American countries with Afro-Caribbean affinities (including the Dominican Republic, Venezuela, Colombia, and Cuba) only add another 5 to 7 percent, this perspective has always been crucial when examining the relations between Blacks and Latinos in the United States. And the Puerto Rican experience formed a pattern that Dominicans are following, despite the fact that they entered this country as immigrants. One of the major projects recently proposed by the Upper Manhattan Empowerment Zone is the creation of an Afro-Dominican cultural center in Washington Heights.

Vaca's take on New York's sometimes troubled Black-Latino political coalitions in his chapter "The Big Manzana" starkly reveals the limitations of West Coast brownology. Vaca concludes that mayoral candidate Freddy Ferrer foolishly believed in the potential of a Black-Latino coalition (which had elected David Dinkins in 1989), only to be betrayed by Al Sharpton, who withheld his support until the last minute, denying Ferrer his best chance. What Vaca fails to understand is that Ferrer had a history of shying away from African American issues, and in part for this reason he was never wholeheartedly embraced by the Puerto Rican community, a significant portion of which is Black. Vaca recounts that Ferrer was strongly in the running until (a) the 9/11 terror attacks, which occurred the day of the scheduled Democratic primary, drove the city into the arms of minority-unfriendly Rudolph Giuliani; and (b) the stepped-up mailings of a *New York Post* cartoon depicting Ferrer as a Sharpton puppet ruined him with White voters. While Vaca wrongly argues that Sharpton's refusal to help out a Latino is evidence that Ferrer was sabotaged by Black self-interest (Sharpton initially demanded Ferrer's support for a slate of Black candidates in exchange for his endorsement), the implication is that Ferrer's mistake was his attempt to appeal to Black voters. Freddy violated the brownologists' rule of keeping your distance.

Vaca's underlying project, it seems, is to free Latinos from any guilt they might feel about pursuing their own interests. Latinos, he argues in his conclusion, are not responsible for the plight of African Americans. And, he adds, because Latinos are not responsible, they come to the table with a clear conscience. Latinos come from "another land, living a life apart from the black-and-white vision of the world described by Black literature."[9] As Vaca points out, the Latin American idea of race was always more supple and nuanced than that of the United States. In Latin America, large communities of escaped and freed slaves were able to flourish, and with the abolition of slavery, Jim Crow laws were never adopted. While there is a grain of truth to the idea that Latin America's openness to racial mixing contrasts with the notorious "one-drop" rule in the United States, that doesn't mean its conscience is clear. Latin America was a major player in the slave trade, it has a long legacy of anti-Black attitudes, and Latinos often bring those attitudes with them when they come north. Slur words like *moyeto* that refer to people of African descent and qualifiers like *pelo malo* (bad hair) did not originate in the United States. In fact, Afro-Latinos are beginning to organize in countries like Brazil, Colombia, and Honduras to address government policies of benign neglect. Representatives Charles Rangel and John Conyers, with the support of both the Congressional Black Caucus and the Congressional Hispanic Caucus, are pushing for an "Afro-Latino Resolution" asserting that United States funding to

Latin American countries should come with a provision recognizing the difficult economic and social conditions of the approximately 80 to [150] million Afro-Latinos.

In truth, the relations between Blacks and Latinos have never been as plain as Black and White, as Tatcho Mindiola, Yolanda Flores Niemann, and Nestor Rodriguez show in their valuable work of analytic sociology, *Black-Brown Relations and Stereotypes*.[10] The book's measured discussion of Black-Latino relations in Houston, in which attitudes are revealed through extensive questionnaires, contrasts markedly with Vaca's inflammatory selection of anecdotes from a single article published in March 2001 in the *Charlotte Post*, in which Blacks were quoted as saying things about Mexican immigrants like "they're taking all of our jobs . . . they could be plotting to kill you and you would never know." But the two groups have at times successfully worked together on the West Coast, and Black-Latino relations in New York are never completely smooth. While researching a piece about Spanish Harlem last year, I encountered strains between African American and Latino politicians fighting over whether to call the region East Harlem or Spanish Harlem. The Harlem political machine that propped up Dinkins has often outmaneuvered and sometimes sabotaged Latino politicos. But whether or not you think Sharpton was posturing for influence, he did spend three months in jail over Vieques. And how do Vaca's theories hold up in Freehold, New Jersey, where a Black Baptist church is providing sanctuary for Mexican immigrant day laborers whose case is being represented by the Puerto Rican Legal Defense and Education Fund? In the end, brownologists like Vaca question the value of a brown-Black alliance in the same way many *mestizos* in Latin America distinguish themselves from Blacks.

The brownologists' excitement is fueled by an explosion of immigrants who are willing to work long, hard hours and who, unlike United States citizen Puerto Ricans, are not eligible for welfare. But as anyone who has studied inner-city youth or picked up a copy of *Urban Latino* magazine knows, after a few generations many Latinos start to look more and more like African Americans. It's in places like Chicago, with its mix of Puerto Ricans, Mexicans, and Blacks, and Spanish Harlem, whose demographics are beginning to resemble Chicago's, that much of the work of Black-Latino relations will be done. As the New York University professor Arlene Dávila says in her forthcoming book, *Barrio Dreams*, "The relationship between Mexicans and Puerto Ricans . . . echoes that of Blacks and Puerto Ricans, at least in regards to a history of cooperation and competition."[11] Aren't we always cooperating and competing with everyone we love?

Migration to the United States has allowed many darker-skinned or Afro-Latinos (primarily from the Caribbean, but increasingly from South America) to embrace an African identity that was suppressed in their native countries. The fiction of Dominican-Americans like Nelly Rosario and Junot Diaz, and of Puerto Ricans like Edgardo Vega Yunque and Piri Thomas, is part of a new understanding of Latino identity that could not have formed in the postcolonial culture of Latin America. When Richard Rodríguez, referring to the probability that most African Americans have White blood in their genetic history, declares that "the last white freedom in America will be the freedom of the African American to admit brown,"[12] I can only wonder, when will the brownologists be free to admit Black?

Of course, racial cross-identification is only a preliminary step in the difficult process of creating and maintaining political alliances between oppressed groups. Vaca's book might be helpful in clearing the ground for future cooperation between Blacks and Latinos by acknowledging points of contention. But the book is more likely to have the effect of reinforcing what generations of immigrants have been taught: that estrangement from Blackness is the key to success in America.

Notes

1. [Jack Miles, "Black vs. Brown," *Atlantic Monthly*, October 1992, 52.]
2. [Ibid.]
3. [Charles Kamasaki and Raul Yzaguirre, "Black-Hispanic Tensions: One Perspective," paper presented at the annual meeting of the American Political Science Association, Washington, 1991.]
4. [Nicolas C. Vaca, *The Presumed Alliance: The Unspoken Conflict between Latinos and Blacks and What It Means for America* (New York: HarperCollins, 2004), 15.]
5. [Ibid., 49, 61.]
6. [Ibid., 189.]
7. [Richard Rodríguez, *Brown* (New York: Viking Penguin, 2003), 142.]
8. [Gregory Rodriguez, "Morality Play Stays the Same," *Los Angeles Times*, June 22, 2003.]
9. [Vaca, *The Presumed Alliance*, 191.]
10. [Tatcho Mindiola, Yolanda Flores Niemann, and Nestor Rodriguez, *Black-Brown Relations and Stereotypes* (Austin: University of Texas Press, 2002).]
11. [Arlene Dávila, *Barrio Dreams: Puerto Ricans, Latinos, and the Neoliberal City* (Berkeley: University of California Press, 2004), 21.]
12. [Richard Rodríguez, *Brown*, 142.]

Against the Myth of Racial Harmony in Puerto Rico

We denounce the firmly entrenched myth of a homogeneous Puerto Rican race, which allegedly resulted from the harmonious fusion of the Taínos, Spaniards, and Africans. We may be connected but we are not merged.

On September 5–11, 2007, three women and two men from western Puerto Rico traveled to Montreal, Canada, to attend the twenty-seventh International Congress of the Latin American Studies Association (LASA). This association is an intercontinental organization that brings together researchers, activists, and cultural workers who are committed to studying and intervening in Latin American and Caribbean intellectual, political, and cultural production. Our group represented an ongoing collaborative research project titled Afro-Puerto Rican Testimonies: An Oral History Project in Western Puerto Rico, which began in August 2006 with the support of the Faculty of Arts and Sciences of the University of Puerto Rico and the Otros Saberes initiative of LASA. More than twenty project participants — community leaders, professors, and students from the University of Puerto Rico, Mayagüez — have collaborated since 2006 to accomplish one of our main goals: to defy the conventionally established lore that confines Blackness and Afro-Puerto Rican identity to allegedly self-contained regions of Puerto Rico, notably the municipalities of Loíza and Carolina in the east and Ponce and Guayama in the south.

We have compiled an oral history archive comprised of thirty-two testimonies by Afro-Puerto Ricans from the towns of Aguadilla and Hormigueros. This extensive collection of one hundred hours of recorded interviews and over fifteen hundred pages of transcripts is complemented by a photographic and videographic archive that documents the narrators as well as the collective process of designing and implementing the oral history project. We gathered testimonies from former residents of the Central La Eureka in Hormigueros and from residents or former residents of Aguadilla. The narrators give voice to the diversity of these western Afro-Puerto Rican communities in terms of gender, age, occupation, social class, sexual preference, migration history, family composition, religion, and so forth.

In Hormigueros we conducted a community oral history project informed by *eurekeños* (displaced residents and workers) of La Eureka, a sugar cane plantation that was geographically and socially segregated throughout most of the twentieth century and bears in the twenty-first century the traces of this marginalization. Nearly three decades have elapsed since La Eureka began to be dismantled and its residents were forced to relocate (many to the adjacent Barrio Lavadero, others to neighboring towns, and still others to New York and New Jersey). Yet to this day the former residents of La Eureka and their descendents are often stigmatized as "los negros de la Eureka," a term originally meant as an insult in the White supremacist discourse of Hormigueros and Puerto Rico in general but then reclaimed as an affirmative collective identity by many contemporary eurekeños. On the other hand, in Aguadilla we conducted a life history project informed by narrators who are not bound by a collective "community" of reference but who represent a diversity of experiences and processes of Afro-Aguadillan@s, and consequently, Afro-Puerto Rican identity formation.

We were invited to participate in LASA's 2007 International Congress as one of the six groups funded by its Otros Saberes initiative, which promotes collaborative research between academics and indigenous and Afro-Latin American peoples. After the congress we participated in a collaborative research workshop with fellow grant recipients from Colombia, Brazil, Nicaragua, Mexico, and Ecuador. As the most incipient project we were greatly enriched by this exchange, which familiarized us with the problems, experiences, challenges, and aspirations of compañeros and compañeras who struggle for the right to racial, economic, and educational equality and, in some cases, for the right to live.

The arduous but fertile path that we have trekked over the past months has defined our current course of action. We stand together to firmly repudiate the following issues: first, the objectionable and unfounded myth of racial equality in our country; second, the alleged gradual "whitening" of the Puerto Rican population, which reached the pinnacle of absurdity in 2000 when 81 percent of those polled by the United States Census Bureau self-identified as "White"; and third, the myth of racial homogeneity.

We denounce the firmly entrenched myth of a homogeneous and singular Puerto Rican "race," which allegedly resulted from the harmonious fusion of the Taínos, the Spanish, and the Africans. We might be connected but we are not merged; the "making" of the Puerto Rican nation has been a conflicted and complex process. The so-called harmonious integration of the "three races" stemmed from the imposition of Eurocentric power over the Taínos and the Africans; the "fusion" resulted from the rape and coercive sexual appropriation of subordinated indigenous and African women. The European axis of our national history was brutal and implacable and asserted its power through the decimation of Taínos and the exploitative subordination of Africans through the cruel institution of slavery.

In light of this, we urge Afro-Puerto Ricans and all Puerto Ricans to reject the myth that we are all the product of an "indissoluble fusion of three races." We are conditioned, from an early age, to give credence to the dogma that as a result of this so-called fusion, we are all "equal." Yet our life experiences and those related by our narrators demonstrate that some seem to be "more equal" than others. We fervently affirm our Afro-Puerto Rican identity as an unfettered aspect of our collective identity. Thus we reject hegemonic constructs that insidiously contribute to perpetuate marginality and injustice and to legitimate the powers that be—those who, "coincidentally," are not Afro-Puerto Ricans.

The mythical view that the Puerto Rican is the fusion of three races, compounded by the perfunctory declaration that all Puerto Ricans are African on one side or on the other ("el que no tiene dinga tiene mandinga"), has operated to silence, veil, and marginalize Afro-Puerto Ricans. The state and the political parties, the church, the academy, the public education system as well as other institutions, including the family, have all conspired in this operation. Together they have exerted an ideological and psychological control that has often precluded Afro-Puerto Ricans from speaking as one to collectively denounce and defy our discrimination and marginalization. This is why we have seldom come together, as Afro-Puerto Ricans, to define our collective agendas and fight, independently, for our common interests. We have been co-opted, "instructed" to regurgitate the dominant ideology—which is always the ideology of the dominant sectors. This is why it's so common for Black men and women to resent and slander the Black or mulatto man or woman who advocates for his or her rights and proudly affirms his or her Afro-Puerto Rican identity.

For these reasons, we have chosen to use oral history to record testimonies about the experiences and life histories of contemporary Afro-Puerto Ricans in the western part of the archipelago; document the processes of identity construction that take place at the local level; and register the individual and collective ways in which we resist the "whitening" project that has characterized Puerto Rican history.

We will no longer tolerate the racist affront of television and radio talk shows that "entertain" the masses at the expense of Afro-Puerto Ricans, who are often stereotyped and ridiculed. We will condemn the absence of Afro-Puerto Ricans in the senate and in executive and judicial bodies, where our presence is and has historically been negligible. We will repudiate the silencing, marginalization, and exoticism of contemporary Afro-Puerto Rican subjects, communities, and cultural expressions. The testimonies of our narrators propel us to keep working together, join our forces and pursue a collective agenda. In recording their memories and listening to their voices, we have become *testigos*, witnesses of their histories, which are a significant part of our history. As testigos we are committed to struggling jointly for true equality, which can only be achieved when Afro-Puerto Ricans are justly regarded, respected. and rewarded in our society.

LISA HOPPENJANS AND TED RICHARDSON
Mexican Ways, African Roots

Children fresh off school buses run through the door, clutching the dollar bills that their mothers gave them to pick up milk or bread. They use the change to buy Jolly Ranchers, Tootsie Rolls, and bubble gum out of the buckets that line the counter.

Men, their clothes dirty from construction work, stroll in and pay twenty-five cents for single cigarettes to start their afternoons.

Women with babies on their hips navigate the narrow aisles, rounding up staples for that night's dinner—chorizo or ham, tortillas or bread, black beans or baked beans. Amid the bustle at Titi's Convenience Store in the Skyline Village apartment complex, the Mexicans and blacks brush by each other in the aisles, yet exchange few words.

Though Mexican and black children in the apartment complex play together—a love of riding Hot Wheels spans cultures—the adults live side by side in different worlds. They are separated by language, suspicion, and stereotypes. But these neighbors have more in common than they realize.

Depending on the day, the radio may be playing mariachi music or hip-hop, a nod to the store owner Marina Arrellanes's son, Rey David, who works with her when he's not in school. "My son likes that music," she said. "His friends are all black."

While a Mexican woman sifts through a bin of green peppers and tomatoes, Arrellanes rings up a sale for a black man buying Ruffles and a Mountain Dew. She doesn't tell him that he is the same color as her grandfather.

Mexicans pride themselves on their mestizo culture. They are proud of the mixture of indigenous and European heritage that most Mexicans share. But there is another source of mestizo heritage that is less recognized—African slaves.

Their descendants, Afro-Mexicans, inhabit the Costa Chica, a narrow, coastal region stretching two hundred miles along the Pacific Ocean in southern Mexico. Many Mexicans don't even know they exist. Afro-Mexicans are estimated to make up less than 1 percent of Mexico's population of 105 million, but they are a majority of the 30,000 Hispanics that officials have estimated to be living in Forsyth County.

Bobby Vaughn, an assistant professor of sociology at Notre Dame de Namur University in Belmont, California, has studied the Afro-Mexicans of the Costa Chica, which includes research in Winston-Salem. Vaughn estimates that about 80 percent of Winston-Salem's Hispanic population is from the Costa Chica.

Vaughn learned of Afro-Mexicans when he spent two semesters in Mexico City studying Spanish and political science in the early 1990s. He scraped up some money for a bus ride to the coast of the Mexican state of Guerrero during his spring break. He arrived in Caujinicuilapa, known as Cuaji, the largest town in the region, on a hot day. "I saw black people, and I was dumbfounded," he said. "I saw old men who looked like my grandfather."

A Single Pioneer

Patterns of Mexican migration to specific cities in the United States often can be traced to a single pioneer. By most accounts, the story of how Afro-Mexicans arrived in Winston-Salem begins with Biterbo Calleja-García. In 1978, Calleja-García was working in Tejas Ranchos, Texas, when a coyote, a guide who helps illegal immigrants cross the border, told him that there was more money to be made in North Carolina.

"Who knows how he knew to bring me here, but he knew," Calleja-García said. "He said, 'You're gonna make a lot of money there.'"

In fact, he began earning $3.35 an hour working seventeen acres of tobacco with his two sisters off Union Cross Road. They lived in a trailer on the farm and worked from 7 AM to 10 PM May through November. They returned to Mexico during the off-season. Calleja-García spread the word to friends and relatives back home in Cuaji and to many who were already working in Santa Ana, California. In Winston-Salem, he told them, there is work.

For ten years, Calleja-García had the same boss in North Carolina. In 1988, he got his papers to work legally in the United States. He stopped his annual returns to Mexico in 1989 and took a job in roofing. Soon, he switched to a construction job, pouring cement for a company in Kernersville, earning $4 an hour, then $6. He started renting a two-bedroom house in the Waughtown section of Winston-Salem with about twelve others who came from California.

"After that, many that I didn't know began to come," he said.

Most, like Calleja-García, crossed the border illegally. Some are paid off the books; others get fake work documents or work under false names. Others come legally on a temporary work visa. And some, again like Calleja-García, attain legal working status at some point after they get here.

In Winston-Salem, the immigrants moved into jobs in construction, into factories packaging T-shirts and toiletries, and assembling window frames and drainage pipes for swimming pools. They moved into bakeries and the kitchens of restaurants. They opened their own restaurants and shops, hiring family members and friends.

Calleja-García stuck with construction. In 1992, he found a job pouring concrete for a company in Archdale. His starting pay was $9.50 an hour, and he wound up helping build megastores such as Home Depot, Lowe's, and Wal-Mart along Hanes Mall Boulevard. By the time he was laid off in 2002, he was earning $18 an hour. He found work with a construction company in Greenville, South Carolina, and returned to Winston-Salem on the weekends. The travel was worth it. In Cuaji, a day laborer might earn 120 pesos, or $10 a day, half of what he was earning per hour in North Carolina.

Understanding Heritage

In Cuaji, the name Winston-Salem is familiar.

A North Carolina license plate hangs on the blue pickup truck of a fisherman who used to work in a bakery in Winston-Salem. In a pool hall, a Carolina-blue baseball cap stands out amid a sea of cowboy hats. A man wearing a Duke T-shirt works on a ranch, roping cattle to be vaccinated.

Many residents have spent some time working in Winston-Salem, while others have friends or family members here now. Those who have returned or remained behind said they prefer the open spaces of Mexico's small towns and the absence of the rules and regulations found in the United States.

The Afro-Mexicans know that they look different from their country-men, but they have only recently begun to truly understand their heritage.

The people have their own story about how blacks came to live in the

Costa Chica region. The story, passed down by mothers and grandmothers for generations, tells of a shipload of slaves that crashed at Punta Maldonado, a rocky beach twenty miles from Cuaji. The slaves are said to have sought refuge in the surrounding hot and densely wooded region. These escaped slaves formed small, isolated communities, one of the largest being Caujinicuilapa. Over generations, the slaves mixed with native Mexicans. Some people believe that the descendants of these original slaves—thought to be no more than two hundred in number—now populate the entire Costa Chica.

Marina Román told the shipwreck story to her teenage son, Silvestre, one afternoon in the living room of their small apartment in Skyline Village. Silvestre was skeptical.

"We're from Aztec warriors," insisted Silvestre, whose classmates mistook him for an African American when he started school in the United States.

Then explain why the people in this part of Mexico are so dark, his mother responded.

"It's all because of the sun," Silvestre said.

Historians tell a different story. Many agree that the first blacks arrived to the Costa Chica in the second half of the sixteenth century in the company of a Spanish slaver, el Mariscal de Castilla.

In the Afro-Mestizo Museum in Cuaji, one of the town's most well-maintained buildings, Hector Senteno Mejía, a history student from the University of Toluca in Mexico, studied a floor-to-ceiling map depicting slave-trade routes from Africa to Central and South America.

"The majority of people in Mexico don't know about Afro-Mexicans," said Mejía, who was in Cuaji for two weeks studying the remnants of African culture that remain there.

Mejía disputed the shipwreck myth. He said that slaves came from Guinea and Congo by way of Patagonia and settled more widely and more systematically in the Costa Chica.

"Blacks were too dispersed throughout the region to have come from the same shipwreck," he said.

In recent years, there has been a new emphasis among some in Mexico, and some outside, on recognizing the African roots of those in the Costa Chica.

According to Vaughn, the political organization of Afro-Mexicans began during the 1990s. On the public level, Mexico's Federal Office of Popular Culture funded a program called Nuestra Tercera Raíz (Our Third Root) that explored the presence of blacks throughout Mexico. It also funded the Afro-Mestizo Museum, which opened in 1999. A grassroots movement led by a priest from Trinidad, Father Glyn Jemmott, simultaneously gained momentum.

Arturo Cruz Montero, who owns a casket store in Cuaji, said he thinks that about half the people in the town are interested in their African heritage. Montero attended an annual gathering to discuss Afro-Mexicans and their heritage in Cuaji in March 2002. He said that there were white and black visitors, many of them academics from the United States. He said that the meeting drew six hundred people, nearly six times the number who had attended the first such gathering in 1997.

"It's beautiful when your children know where they are from," he said.

Getting Past Barriers

The cultural differences are evident every day in Skyline Village, as are the simple ways that people try to get beyond those barriers—and sometimes succeed. One warm spring day at Titi's Convenience Store, a young black woman fanned herself with her hand, telling Arrellanes, "es caliente," using a Spanish word for "hot." But caliente means "spicy," a different type of hot. Arrellanes gently corrected her. "Es calor," she said.

At least once a day, Arrellanes is affectionately called "Miss Titi" by her black customers, who take their cue from the misspelled sign out front— "Titi's Convience Store." Arrellanes laughed as she explained the origin of the store's name. Titi was a nickname she gave her son. It's a type of small monkey.

On a Saturday in March, a black baseball coach, Arthur Green, went door to door in the apartment complex, recruiting players for Little League tryouts later that day at a nearby park. He did not speak Spanish, and the Mexicans greeted him with suspicion as he explained why he was there. Suspicion is a constant for those here illegally when an American stranger knocks on the door. None of the Mexicans sent their children to the tryouts.

One night, Tequilla Wilson, a young black woman attending Winston-Salem State University, met some of her Mexican neighbors in a desperate effort to complete her Spanish homework. She wandered around the complex, searching for anyone who could help her out. Some Mexican neighbors kindly obliged.

For the most part, the blacks and Mexicans keep to themselves. The apartment complex, once named Columbia Terrace, was built about 1950

Rosa Colón welcomes Teka Crawford and daughter Alma Tavira Colón to the Colón's Spague Street home in Winston-Salem, North Carolina, 2005. (Photograph by Ted Richardson; courtesy of Ted Richardson)

Rey David Arrellanes glances toward his mother, Marina Arrellanes, who runs the convenience store at Skyline Village in Winston-Salem, North Carolina, 2005. (Photograph by Ted Richardson; courtesy of Ted Richardson)

as the first low-income housing project in the city. For years its residents were predominantly black, but in the 1990s Hispanics began to move in. The process has accelerated in the past four years, and today the complex's 169 units are about evenly split between blacks and Mexicans, mostly from the Costa Chica.

In this and other neighborhoods around the city, Mexicans and blacks live side by side, a condition that can create tension.

The city's Human Relations Department investigates and mediates complaints of discrimination, and it studies and promotes ways to increase positive community relations. Director Wanda Allen-Abraha said that her department has heard "all kinds of misconceptions and stereotypes" about Hispanics and blacks.

Some blacks, Allen-Abraha said, complain that Hispanics get special tax breaks or are able to get business loans more easily than blacks. They say that Hispanics pack too many people into one house or apartment.

On the other hand, Allen-Abraha said, Hispanics complain that African Americans have too many children out of wedlock, are all on welfare, and resent the Hispanics for taking jobs.

Allen-Abraha said she attributes much of the tension to economic factors. "We have had a lot of downsizings and closings in our region," she said. "With the general overall downturn of the economy, I think that's making people compete even more for jobs."

She predicted that as black, Hispanic, and white children grow into adults, relationships between the city's ethnic groups will improve and there will be a greater acceptance of other cultures.

"I think you'll see a change in attitude," she said. "I don't think people will have much of a choice."

As a start, the city's Human Relations Commission and the Winston-Salem chapter of the National Association for the Advancement of Colored People are sponsoring a forum Thursday at 6 PM at El Cordero de Dios Moravian Church at Waughtown and Peachtree streets to encourage dialogue between the two groups.

In some ways, the forum is an acknowledgment that the Mexicans, who have slowly come to dominate areas of town, are here to stay.

Marina Arrellanes certainly is.

She works at her store seven days a week, 8:30 AM to 8:30 PM, except on Saturday and Sunday, when she opens at 9. She worked on Easter and on Christmas. The morning of April 7, though, Arrellanes locked the door of Titi's at 7:30 AM. She was wearing a light pink dress and clutching a big, black purse and a stack of papers.

On this day, she would become a citizen.

The room at the Charlotte sub-office of U.S. Citizenship and Immigration Services slowly filled with sixty citizens-to-be from thirty-three countries. Most had entourages of family and friends armed with disposable cameras and flowers. Arrellanes was alone. Her son was at school, her husband at work.

She tucked a small American flag into her purse as she took her oath.

Citizenship means that she can work permanently in the country where she has already lived for sixteen years. It means that she can always stay here with her three children—two of whom are citizens and one who is working on her citizenship application. Most of all, it means that she can bring her mother, whom she hasn't seen in four years, to the United States for a visit, even if, as she learned later, she must wait a year to do so.

After her swearing-in, Arrellanes returned to Winston-Salem for a short, celebratory lunch at a Mexican restaurant.

By early afternoon, she had reopened Titi's, slightly overdressed, her half-day vacation over.

TANYA KATERÍ HERNÁNDEZ
Afro-Latin@s and the Latin@ Workplace

Afro-Latin@s are an enigma for the United States courts of law. In the jurisprudence of antidiscrimination law, "Black" has long been understood to be solely a reference to African Americans, and non-Latin@ Whites are understood to primarily be the agents of discrimination. Within that context, when Afro-Latin@s assert discrimination by other Latin@s, it presents a conundrum that does not fit the traditional narrative of discrimination in the United States. The context of employment discrimination provides a useful case study of the racial dislocation of Afro-Latin@s by law.

For instance, in the 2004 case *Arrocha v.* CUNY,[1] a self-identified Afro-Panamanian tutor of Spanish sued the City University of New York (CUNY) for failure to renew his appointment as an adjunct instructor, claiming a violation of Title VII's prohibition against race and national-origin discrimination in the workplace. The plaintiff alleged that the Latin@ heads of the Spanish Department at Medgar Evers College discriminated against "*Black* Hispanics," and that there was "a disturbing culture of favoritism that favor[ed] the appointments of *White* Cubans, Spaniards and *White* Hispanics from South America."[2] Yet the court dismissed his legal claims of "race" and "national-origin" discrimination under Title VII of the Civil Rights Act of 1964 because the judge did not understand how a color hierarchy informs the ways in which Latin@s subject other Latin@s to racism and national-origin bias. Indeed, the national-origin claim was dismissed on summary judgment because five of the eight adjunct instructors who were reappointed were natives of other South or Central American countries such as Argentina, Peru, and Mexico, as well as the Dominican Republic. In dismissing the national-origin claim because the Afro-Panamanian plaintiff's employer reappointed natives from other South and Central American countries instead of him, the *Arrocha* court treated all Latin@s as interchangeable and incapable of national-origin discrimination against other Latin@s.

Yet, the interchangeability of Latin@'s perspective in *Arrocha* fails to appreciate the ways in which internal Latin@ national-origin bias is rooted in a racialized hierarchy of Latin American countries, where countries perceived as European are viewed as more advanced than those more significantly populated with people of indigenous descent or those of African descent. In the list of countries the judge thought equivalent, Latin American racial constructs would rank Argentina as a highly valued White country, followed by Peru and Mexico with their indigenous populations, followed finally by the Dominican Republic and the plaintiff's own country of origin, Panama, because they are countries populated by more people of African descent. For Latin@s influenced by Latin American racial paradigms where each country has a racial identification, a diverse workforce of Latin@s is not the immediate equivalent of a bias-free context. Nor is a color preference divorced from a racialized ideology within the Latin@ context. The Latino studies scholars Nicholas de Genova's and Ana Ramos-Zayas's observation that "intra-Latino divisions seem always to be entrenched in the hegemonic denigration of African Americans" applies equally to the denigration of Blackness in general.[3]

The presumption that the pan-ethnic identifier of Latin@ or Hispanic precludes discrimination among various Latin@s is also apparent in other Latin@ inter-ethnic employment discrimination cases. This, of course, directly contravenes the Supreme Court mandate in *Castaneda v. Partida* against presuming that intra-ethnic and intra-racial discrimination cannot exist.[4] Treating Latin@s as racially interchangeable also denies them protection against national-origin discrimination when the employer's agents are also Latin@s. The Supreme Court's own definition of national origin as referring "to the country where a person was born, or, more broadly, the country from which his or her ancestors came,"[5] conflicts with the way the judges lump all Latin@s into one undifferentiated group.[6] Certainly, where a non–Latin@ White employer is alleged to have discriminated against a Latin@, the binary non-Latin@ White versus Latin@ context may justify the simple reference to the plaintiff as a "Latin@" or "Hispanic" with standing to bring a national-origin claim.[7] However, where a Latin@ plaintiff from a particular country is alleging national-origin discrimination at the hands of a Latin@ from another country of origin, it would be nonsensical to ignore the distinctions in country of origin and the racial connotations of each country. Similarly, it would defy logic to presume that an employer's preference for one Latin@ ethnic group or race over another should insulate the employer from an inquiry about discriminatory intent as long as the employer hires Latin@s generally.

Afro-Latin@ plaintiffs don't fare much better when they bring their claims as Title VII "color" discrimination cases within Latin@ workplaces. In the case of Felix v. Marquez,[8] Carmen Felix, a Puerto Rican of what she termed "partial African ancestry," was terminated from employment as a secretary with the Office of the Commonwealth of Puerto Rico in Washington, D.C. (OCPRW) at the behest of both the Puerto Rican Administrator of the office, Jose Cabranes, and the Puerto Rican supervisor Providencia Haggerty. While the Felix v. Marquez case is noteworthy for its recognition of how "the plaintiff's skin tone and phenotype used in tandem with genealogy operated as racial markers,"[9] the court opinion still presented a confused assessment of Latin@ experiences with colorism. To prove her claim of color discrimination, Carmen Felix introduced the personnel cards of twenty-eight fellow employees to demonstrate that only two others were as dark as or darker than she, and she argued that there was thus a prevailing bias against dark-skinned employees in the office in the allocation of promotions that privileged what she termed "White" employees with higher-ranked positions. The judge purported to dispute Carmen Felix's premise of dark-skin bias by visually inspecting the photographs himself and then enumerating the employees that Felix had presumably misclassified as White when in the judge's view they were some shade of brown.

The judge then went on to say that "these observations tend to contradict the placement of a rigid line between white and non-white employees [of the OCPRW] drawn by Felix in her testimony and reflect the fact that a substantial number of Puerto Ricans have mixed ancestry."[10] And therein the judge misperceived the actualization of colorism within Latin@ communities (and workplaces such as the OCPRW), because the persons the judge viewed as brown skinned were perceived by Felix and perhaps her coworkers as "White" by virtue of their phenotype, hair texture, and socioeconomic class and not simply because of their skin shade.

There exists a vast social science literature which documents the ways in which Latin@s often manifest White-skin preferences in their mode of self-identification and choice of associations in ways that recall and mirror Latin American racial ideology.[11] What this literature demonstrates, in particular, is how Latin@ expressions of color bias are intimately connected with assessments of phenotype, hair texture, size and shape of noses and lips, and socio-economic class standing. Latin@ race labeling thus factors in considerations of bodily features other than color that are considered to be racial signifiers of denigrated African ancestry.[12] Accordingly, when a plaintiff like Carmen Felix in a predominantly Latin@ workplace enumerates the coworkers deemed to be "White," she is referring to coworkers who have achieved that racial characterization not simply because of their skin color.

For example, what the social science literature indicates is that two individuals can be of the same light skin shade but if one has African facial features and hair texture then a Latin@ would not likely categorize such an individual as White absent indicators that the person was wealthy or of high social status.[13] In turn, the non-Whiteness attributed to that light-skinned person with African features would better position another light-skinned person with less prominent African features to be perceived as White in that context. In essence, Latin@s treat racial categorization in a functional manner. In any given context there are functional Whites and Blacks regardless of their degree of pigmentation. But while this Latin@ categorization scheme is fluid and context specific, it still forms the foundation for racially exclusionary conduct.[14] In other words, the absence of precision in Latin@ racial categorization methods does not mitigate the allocation of social benefits based on the approximation to Whiteness.

The complexity of a Latin@ racial hierarchy cannot be captured by a simplistic assessment of employee skin shades. Thus, what the *Felix v. Marquez* judge failed to appreciate is how nuanced and perverse Latin@/Latin American assessments of color and status are. Instead the judge fell prey to the Latin@/Latin American romanticization of racial mixture (*mestizaje*) as being an indicator of racial ambiguity and harmony.[15] Thus the court recognizes colorism as a cognizable claim that is a particularly "appropriate claim for a Puerto Rican to present" given the mixture of races that presumably make rigid racial categories harder to apply for purposes of a racial discrimination claim, but the court uses that very recognition of racial mixture to undermine the ability to mount a successful colorism claim. The irony of the judicial failure to appropriately assess the colorism claim of the Afro-Puerto Rican plaintiff Felix is that the case was decided by District Court Judge John Helm Pratt. Judge Pratt, until his death in 1995, was known as an important defender of civil rights and discrimination law. For instance, in 1977 and 1983 he issued orders requiring the federal government to combat bias in schools against minority groups, women, and the handicapped.[16] Judge Pratt was a White man born in New Hampshire in 1910, but some of his most significant decisions made progress in the area of individual freedom and civil rights. Yet even this defender of civil rights in the United States was unable to understand the complexity of Latin@ color discrimination.

This is in part because the federal employment discrimination legislation of Title VII of the Civil Rights Act of 1964 provides separate categories of "race," "color," and "national origin" for what is viewed as impermissible discrimination. As a result, judges have fallen prey to the notion that the categories are mutually exclusive and do not relate or reinforce each other, despite the fact that the statute does not provide definitions of what race, color, and national-origin discrimination are or how they differ. This tunnel vision hampers judges from understanding intersectional claims where the various categories overlap in one person's experience of discrimination.[17] As a result, a "color" claim gets reduced to a simplistic consideration of skin color variation. The judicial inclination is to act as a spectrometer rather than examining how the full scope of colorism's racial preoccupations are deployed against Latin@s of African descent in the Latin@ workplace. There is a direct clash between the judicial focus on color as uniquely a dimension of chromatic differences and the "Latin@" conceptualization of color as a taxonomy informed by hair texture, phenotype features, class, place, and space. Consequently, the situational deployment of Latin@ colorism is overlooked by the judges. This hinders an appropriate assessment of Latin@ colorism claims.

It is also interesting to note that when African Americans or other non-Latin@ persons of African descent present colorism claims, courts have been disinclined to focus on degrees of skin color. The legal scholar Taunya Lovell Banks observes that this is because of the view that with respect to African Americans and non-Latin@ immigrants of African descent, one drop of Black blood makes one Black and that there are no degrees of Blackness in the United States cultural mindset for persons other than Latin@s.[18]

Conclusion

The current status of employment discrimination jurisprudence does not adequately serve Afro-Latin@s who experience racial discrimination by other Latin@s. This is because judges do not know how to assess allegations of discrimination when they are brought forth by Afro-Latin@s in Latin@ workplace settings with Latin@ supervisors. Latin@ discrimination against Afro-Latin@s defies the traditional legal narrative of non-Latin@ White versus African American discrimination. In order for employment discrimination jurisprudence to be properly developed, Latin@ lawyers and others who care about these issues will need to take on the work of confronting the existence of anti-Black sentiment in the Latin@ community and then tailoring their litigation strategy to better educate the judiciary about Latin@ racial diversity and Latin@ racial attitudes.

Notes

1. 2004 WL 594981 (E.D.N.Y. Feb. 9, 2004).

2. Id. at 7.

3. Nicholas de Genova and Ana Y. Ramos-Zayas, *Latino Crossings: Mexicans, Puerto Ricans, and the Politics of Race and Citizenship* (New York: Routledge, 2003), 214 (discussing the ethnographic study of Latino racial attitudes in Chicago).

4. *Castaneda v. Partida*, 430 U.S. 482, 499 (1977). ("It would be unwise to presume as a matter of law that human beings of one definable group will not discriminate against other members of their group.")

5. *Espinoza v. Farah Mfg. Co.* 414 U.S. 86, 88 (1973); see id. at 89. ("The only direct definition given the phrase 'national origin' is the following remark made on the floor of the House of Representatives by Congressman Roosevelt, Chairman of the House Subcommittee which reported the bill: 'It means the country from which you or your forebears came.'") See also *Storey v. Burns Int'l Sec. Servs.*, 390 F. 3d 760, 766 (3d Cir 2004) (Scirica, C. J., concurring) (noting that a plaintiff with a national-origin claim must "trace ancestry to a nation outside of the United States" and thus a "Confederate Southern-American" is not a valid national-origin class under Title VII). But see *Earnhardt v. Commonwealth of Puerto Rico* 744 F. 2d 1, 2–3 (1st Cir. 1984) (holding that in Puerto Rico a plaintiff born in the continental United States can assert a national-origin discrimination claim). For an in-depth critique of the current limitations of the legal definition for national origin, see Juan F. Perea, "Ethnicity and Prejudice: Reevaluating 'National Origin' Discrimination Under Titale VII," *Wm & Mary Law Review*, no. 35 (1994): 805, 857 (proposing that Congress legislate an expansive definition of "national origin" that includes discrimination based upon ethnic traits such as alienage status and language preference).

6. See Gloria Sandrino-Glasser, "Los Confundidos: De-Conflating Latinos/as' Race and Ethnicity," *Chicano–Latino Law Review*, no. 19 (1998): 69, 73 (detailing the ways Latinos are inappropriately depicted as a homogeneous group). Symbolic homogenization is not restricted to Latinos.

7. It is probably for this very purpose that while the EEOC does not define national origin, it chooses to define national-origin discrimination "broadly as including, but not limited to, the denial of equal employment opportunity because of an individual's, or his or her *ancestor's place of origin*; or because an individual has the physical, cultural or linguistic characteristics of a national origin group" (29 C.F.R sec. 1606.1 [2007] [emphasis added]). Accordingly, at least one district court has permitted Latino plaintiffs to bring national-origin discrimination allegations based upon their "Spanish-speaking characteristic" alone where a non-Latin@ White defendant may have had no actual knowledge of the plaintiff's exact place of origin but instituted policies that dis-

parately impacted and discriminated based upon the foreignness of the plaintiffs. See *Alemendares v. Palmer*, 2002 U.S. Dist. LEXIS 23258, at 31 (N.D. Ohio Dec. 2, 2002) ("Because plaintiffs have linguistic characteristics of a particular national origin group—as required in the EEOC's definition of 'national origin discrimination'—they have sufficiently pled a claim of national origin discrimination. Plaintiffs' Spanish-speaking characteristics reflect their national origin").

8. *Felix v. Marquez*, 27 Empl. Prac. Dec. P 32,241, 1981 WL 275 (D.D.C. Mar. 26 1981).

9. Taunya Lovell Banks, "Colorism: A Darker Shade of Pale," UCLA *Law Review*, no. 47 (2000): 1705–46.

10. *Felix v. Marquez*, 27 Empl. Prac. Dec. P 32,241, 1981 WL 275, at * 8 n. 6 (D.D.C. Mar. 26, 1981).

11. Nancy A. Denton and Douglas S. Massey, "Racial Identity among Caribbean Hispanics: The Effect of Double Minority Status on Residential Segregation," *American Sociological Review*, no. 54 (1989): 790–808; Laura Padilla, "Internalized Oppression and Latinos." *Texas Hispanic Journal of Law and Policy*, no. 7 (2001): 61–113; Eric Uhlmann, Nilanjana Dasgupta, Angelica Elgueta, Anthony G. Greenwald, and Jane Swanson, "Subgroup Prejudice Based on Skin Color among Hispanics in the United States and Latin America." *Soc. Cognition*, no. 20 (2002): 198–225.

12. Sonya M. Tafoya, "Shades of Belonging: Latino/as and Racial Identity," *Harvard Journal of Hispanic Policy*, no. 17 (2004/2005): 58–78.

13. Carmen Luz Valcarel, "Growing Up Black in Puerto Rico," in *Challenging Racism and Sexism: Alternatives to Genetic Explanations*, edited by E. Tobach and B. Rosoff (New York: Feminist Press, 1994), 284–94.

14. Marta I. Cruz-Janzen, "Y Tu Abuela A'onde Esta?" SAGE *Race Relations Abstracts*, no. 26 (2001): 7–24.

15. Ariel E. Dulitzky, "A Region in Denial: Racial Discrimination and Racism in Latin America," in *Neither Enemies nor Friends: Latinos, Blacks, Afro-Latinos*, edited by A. Dzidzienyo and S. Oboler (New York: Palgrave Macmillan, 2005), 39–59.

16. Pam Belluck, "John H. Pratt, 84, Federal Judge Who Helped Define Civil Rights" (obituary), *New York Times*, August 14, 1995.

17. See, e.g., Kimberle Williams Crenshaw, "Demarginalizing the Intersection of Race and Sex: A Black Feminist Critique of Antidiscrimination Doctrine, Feminist Theory, and Antiracist Politics." *University of Chicago Legal Forum*, no. 1989 (1989): 139.

18. Taunya Lovell Banks, "Colorism: A Darker Shade of Pale."

MARK SAWYER

Racial Politics in Multiethnic America

Black and Latin@ Identities and Coalitions

In Little Havana, Miami, a young Afro-Cuban woman went into a "Cuban" hair salon. She politely asked in Spanish how she might make an appointment to have her hair done. The proprietor of the salon snapped back in English, "We don't work on Black hair here—you will have to go somewhere else." The women in the salon then went back to conversing in Spanish and the Afro-Cuban woman left dejected.

The vignette is more than a story about rude treatment by a business owner. It is a case of race making in which the Afro-Cuban woman, seeking to reaffirm her "Cubanness," was being cast out of being Cuban within the United States and told to seek her fortune with African Americans. The story serves as a sign for how the unresolved issue of racism within Latin@ communities toward Latin@s of darker hues might contribute to preventing interethnic alliances with African Americans. However, this essay not only looks at this side of the equation of Black-Latin@ relations but addresses how the unwillingness of African Americans to recognize experiences of racial groups other than the United States-born Black experience also contributes to problems in coalitions.

In this essay I explore how conflicts among Blacks and Latin@s have been nurtured both by the unresolved racism within Latin@ communities that has its origins in their respective countries of origin and by the frequently parochial way in which African Americans privilege the United States-born Black experience and fail to recognize the struggles of immigrants of all colors. These narrow definitions of social, cultural, and political identity prevent interethnic alliances and foment ethnic conflict among groups that share substantial political interests and issue concerns. However, there have been notable points of cooperation among

Blacks and Latin@s. Ultimately, if we exclude ideologically conservative Cuban Americans from the analysis, it becomes easier to find meaningful patterns of both convergence and difference of interests on political issues. Further, by engaging common interests and bridging identities like Afro-Latin@s, it is possible to forge a progressive politics that includes the concerns of both groups and challenges the sharp distinctions between Black and Latin@ that many commentators currently attempt to highlight.

Electoral Politics

Historically, there has not been a consistent pattern of political interaction between United States Blacks and Latin@s. Patterns of cooperation, conflict, and ambivalence have been hallmarks of Black and Latin@ relations. However, there is a growing literature by commentators, such as Nicolas Vaca, who emphasize difference and conflict.[1] They point to a variety of cases without reference to the more mixed record.

For instance, 54 percent of Blacks in California voted for Proposition 187, compared to 46 percent of Latin@s. The bill was supported by Governor Pete Wilson and would have denied services to undocumented immigrants. However, that figure is far below the 65 percent of Whites that supported Proposition 187. While Proposition 187 was explicitly anti-Latin@, the rhetoric surrounding Proposition 209, the anti-affirmative action initiative supported by Governor Wilson, was more explicitly anti-Black.[2] Though Proposition 209 passed, a solid majority of African Americans and Latin@s in California voted against the initiative. Black and Latin@ voters seemingly learned from the rotating-target politics of the California initiative process and voted against the anti-bilingual initiative 227. However, the case that looms large for Vaca and others is the defeat of Antonio Villaraigosa's bid to become the first Latino mayor of Los Angeles. Villaraigosa lost because of lower than necessary Latin@ voter turnout and because 80 percent of Black votes were cast for James Hahn, a White candidate.[3] While Hahn had significant support among the Black leadership due to his father's legacy of representing the African American community, he ran a campaign largely aimed at garnering conservative White voters in the San Fernando Valley by using the crime issue. Hahn used racist advertisements targeting Villaraigosa that were reminiscent of the Willie Horton advertisements from the Bush-Dukakis campaign.

While Vaca points to some disappointing results, there are equally encouraging examples of coalitions between African Americans and Latin@s around the country. For example, in the California recall election, Lieu-tenant Governor Cruz Bustamante received a higher percentage of Black votes than Latin@ votes in his losing effort.[4] However, it was the defec-tion of White democrats to Schwarzenegger after attacking Bustamante on racialized issues like Indian gaming and driver's licenses for undocu-mented immigrants that cost Bustamante the governor's mansion. Still, Latin@ and Black coalitions do not always spell defeat. In Chicago, Harold Washington was elected in 1983 and 1987 from a progressive coalition that included Mexicans, Puerto Ricans, Blacks, gays and lesbians of all colors, and reform-minded Whites. Washington reformed city government and gained control of the city council in his second term only by expanding and supporting Latin@ insurgent city council candidates against ethnic Whites. He also pushed legislation that allowed undocumented immi-grants to vote in local school council elections. The Washington coalition set the conditions for the creation of the first Latin@ majority congres-sional seat now held by Luis Gutiérrez, a former Washington ally. Gains for Mexicans and Puerto Ricans in Chicago synergistically aided Black politi-cal power.[5] Similarly, in Georgia in 2003 Sam Zamarippa was elected to the Georgia House of Representatives in an overwhelmingly Black district of Atlanta that includes the Martin Luther King Jr. Center and Ebenezer Baptist Church. In Texas, Black voters supported the election of Henry Cisneros who became the first Latino mayor of San Antonio. In another case, Black and Latin@ voters came together in Denver to help elect first Federico Peña and later the African American Wellington Webb as mayors. There is also a mixed record in the area of public opinion.[6]

Public Opinion

Traditionally, public opinion research about race has focused predomi-nantly on White attitudes about Blacks. Only recently have studies begun to challenge this approach and to search for alternative paradigms to de-scribe minority attitudes as well as interminority relations.[7] While this re-search is in its infancy, it is clear that paradigms used to explain White atti-tudes about Blacks also serve to frame the attitudes of Latin@s and Blacks about each other. Yet, for the most part, Blacks and Latin@s share support for affirmative action and generally support a social democratic agenda in government and spending much more than do Whites or Asians.[8] Un-like White Americans, an overwhelming majority of Blacks and a large number of Latin@s opposed the United States invasion of Iraq in 2003.[9] Despite Vaca's argument that Whites have more in common with Blacks than with Latin@s, public opinion data show that Blacks and Latin@s are far closer on most issues than either are to Whites.[10] But what about the question of competition? While Nicolas Vaca allows for some ideological convergence in his work, he asserts that, on a microlevel, there are simply different "interests."[11]

Though Blacks see some decline in their political power as a result of growing numbers of Latin@s, they largely see these gains as "fair." Many Blacks recognize that growing Latin@ political power may result in less power for African Americans, but they also do not believe that Latin@s are sufficiently represented in local government.[12] These nuances lead to facile misinterpretations of conflict among Blacks and Latin@s. For example, in their book Black Pride, Black Prejudice, Paul Sniderman and Thomas Piazza interpret as "anti-immigrant" the fact that a majority of Blacks believe that growing numbers of immigrants in their community will necessitate more taxes and spending on public services.[13] However, since most Blacks generally support social spending it is difficult to assume that this is not merely a factual account of how rising populations will necessitate more services. In fact, in many cities where populations would have fallen without the presence of immigrants, it can be argued that immigration has preserved middle-class jobs for many Black service providers. Black social workers, teachers, bus drivers, postal workers, and the like have benefited from the expansion and maintenance of city services driven by immigration.

While there is some perception of job competition among Blacks and Latin@s, as well as anti-Black attitudes on the part of Latin@s and anti-Latin@ attitudes among Blacks, these attitudes never rise to the levels of those held by Whites who are not involved in similar neighborhood competition. In fact, for Blacks and Latin@s it appears that social contact in neighborhoods reduces rather than exacerbates tensions.[14] In other words, it appears that to the extent that African Americans express anti-immigrant sentiment, those sentiments do not correlate with racist stereotypes but are more about jobs and employment. For Whites anti-Latin@ racism drives their views about immigration. Thus, public opinion matches the mixed picture of the electoral process, with no clear conclusion to be drawn about the prospects of Black and Latin@ relations.[15]

Since the empirical picture is so mixed, it is important to inquire about what is behind the emphasis on conflict among Blacks and Latin@s. Clearly, one cannot excuse the White power structure. From this point of view, an emphasis on the competition and conflict between Blacks and Latin@ is an effort to discipline Latin@ ideology and political behavior and prevent Black and Latin@ political alliances. However, although one could describe it as a simple divide-and-conquer strategy doing so would ignore the significant role that Black and Latin@ agents play in creating and maintaining conflict. Indeed, the agents of this process are numerous. They include the White Left, which has grown weary of "identity politics" on behalf of Blacks and others; right-wing politicians who seek to isolate Blacks and incorporate Latin@s into the right; and African American political agents who, in the wake of the erosion of gains acquired during the civil rights era, want to hold onto Black status as the most important minority. Other agents are xenophobic Whites who are uncomfortable with the changing racial character of United States society, and finally, Latin@s who feel that the route to social mobility is through emphasizing their difference from Blacks who have traditionally been at the bottom of the racial hierarchy in the United States.[16]

The Limits of Black and Latino Politics

African Americans have in some ways come to attack other expressions of "difference" as a way to protect the particularity of the African American predicament and its consequences. Hence, gender, sexual orientation, and in some cases class have today fallen prey to a construction of a "universal" but narrow Black identity.[17] Much like women and gays and lesbians, Black immigrants from Africa, Latin America, or the Caribbean must choose to either be Black or assert their ethnic identity as if the two were mutually exclusive. Cathy Cohen calls this process secondary marginalization.[18] Hence, the multiplicity of Black experiences outside and within the United States has not come together to form a broader, more inclusive dialogue.[19]

The inability to see the Black experience in broader diasporic terms prevents the development of a new Black politics that incorporates issues of immigration and citizenship along with traditional Black concerns that might provide a bridge of interests between African Americans and Latin@s. In addition, the consistent place of African Americans at or near the bottom of the American racial hierarchy creates suspicion about joint struggles with other racial ethnic groups who may after some limited gains leave the African American community behind. In this case, Afro-Latin@s or Latin@s with significant levels of African ancestry do not become bridges between the communities but rather become examples of how no one wants to be Black in the United States. The Latin@ history of denying the very existence of Black heritage along with the sociocultural practice of whitening only further damages the possibility of interethnic cooperation.

Latin@s are both potentially Whites and "others." For instance, the construction of Jennifer Lopez (J-Lo) as an exotic other who, when necessary, plays the role of an Italian woman shows the schizophrenia that greets United States Latin@s. J-Lo is interesting because the media tried very hard to make her White and to emphasize Black and Latin@ differences through her. Her use of the dreaded word "nigger" in her performance with rapper Ja Rule, for example, was discussed in the media as if it had been said by a White woman instead of a Latina. In this case, J-Lo was able to traverse the difficult racial boundaries by reemphasizing her relationship with Puff Daddy (now P-Diddy) and her connection to Bronx street culture. J-Lo represents an often-suppressed history of hip hop culture that in its inception was as much Jamaican and Puerto Rican as African American.[20] However, this controversy and Hollywood's portrayals of J-Lo emphasize the attempt to portray Latin@s as "potential Whites."

Concepts of whitening within Latin@ culture have existed since the advent of Latin American nations.[21] Active attempts to create "White" and modern nations were explicitly connected with ideas that racial mixture would eliminate the negative racial influences of Blacks and indigenous peoples. As national myths grew that all were mixed and moving toward White, discussions of racism that assumed that Blacks damaged the national character disappeared, as did assertions of the unique experience of Afro-Latin@s.[22] The construction of national identities around mestizo or white somatic norms denied the existence of racism and Black populations more generally.[23]

It should be no surprise that upon arriving in the United States, Latin@s are slow to identify with Blacks. After all, not only are Blacks at the bottom of the racial hierarchy but Latin Americans and United States Latin@s have consistently denied the problems of racism and the existence of blackness in their home countries and in their communities.[24]

The identity of the Latin@ as being exclusive of Black forces Afro-Latin@s to choose either to be Black or to be Latin@. The denial of blackness can be so intense that it is both sad and comical. Dominicans have taken it so far that they have resurrected a myth of indigenous heritage in order to explain their dark skin.[25] The obviously Black baseball star of the Chicago Cubs, Sammy Sosa, for instance, becomes an *indio* (Indian) rather than a Black, since according to this national myth and tradition Dominicans "cannot be Black."[26] The same goes for figures like the pitcher Pedro Martínez of the Boston Red Sox. However, Dominicans are not the only examples of this, and many of them after years in the United States identify as Black.[27] In Central American countries such as Mexico, Honduras, and El Salvador Blackness has literally been erased from the national history and consciousness. Despite their nappy hair, full lips, and dark skin many Central Americans find it impossible to think that African heritage plays a significant role in their racial makeup. This denial extends to myths that slavery never existed in their countries and Blacks never set foot on the land.

Given these facts, it is no secret that politics in the western United States with its high concentrations of Central Americans and Mexicans frequently involve less inter-ethnic cooperation than places in the East. It is also not surprising that the Cuban American community that once enforced racial segregation while in control of Cuba has frequently been anti-Black in its political activities in the United States context.[28] Any study of Latin@ politics that does not represent the diversity of the Latin@ experience in terms of race, gender, sexual identities, and ideology erases Blackness from the Latin@ experience and ends up presenting Latin@s as "ethnics" who are closer to Whites. Yet it is through recognizing the diversity of Latin@s that the possibilities for a truly progressive politics arise. Moreover, it is the unresolved issue and invisibility of Blackness within Latino communities that prevent bridges and encourage antagonism with African Americans.

Thus, a broad and multi-spectrum "Latin@" identity that recognizes diversity is important. Public opinion evidence points to the fact that those who have such a pan–Latin@ identity or who identify as Blacks feel closer and more willing to enter into coalitions with African Americans.[29] Thus, when pan–Latin@ identity accommodates and recognizes the diversity of the Latin@ experience, it becomes a progressive alternative to identities that emphasize brownness as an alternative to Blackness or country-specific identities. Latin@s who speak English and have either been born in or lived in the United States for many years are more likely to feel closer to Blacks. Thus, we can say that negative notions about Blackness from their countries of origin play a substantial role in Latin@ attitudes about Blacks. It is also notable that many Puerto Ricans and Dominicans feel more commonality with Blacks than with Whites. A full 50 percent of Puerto Ricans feel they have a lot in common with Blacks, while 44 percent feel they have a lot in common with Whites. Further, even Salvadorans feel they have slightly more in common with Blacks than with Whites, but the numbers may fall within the margin of error.[30] These numbers speak to the necessity to research Black experiences in countries of origin and to

Program flyer for Race, Reason, Rhythms, an event in Washington, D.C., organized by Fiesta DC and Grupo Afro Descendiente, February 2008. (Courtesy of Rolando Roebuck)

interrogate anti-Black racism in Latin America. Since Mexicans are the largest group, there is a need for studies that address the problem of race in Mexican history, politics, and culture.

The Primacy of Diaspora Research and Consciousness

The Latin American myth of racial democracy alerts us to the danger of emphasizing color-blind alternatives without having first achieved racial equality. It silences those who want to articulate their experiences of exclusion based upon race and legitimizes a de facto "mainstream color" that ultimately comes to be accepted as the society's norm. In the United States this impulse is likely to erase African Americans from the political landscape, ignore Afro-Latin@s as well as Latin@s with indigenous features, and finally offer conditional acceptance into the mainstream solely to light-skinned Latin@s. In this context, what are the alternatives?

The concept of diaspora presents an interesting alternative to this political problem. It is not only analytically correct to understand that the experience of African people cannot be confined within the boundaries of the nation-state. In the case of Blacks and Latin@s, it becomes a political necessity. By examining the overlapping experiences and cultures of people of African descent both within and outside of the United States, we can create a discussion about racism in Caribbean and Latin American countries as well as reveal connections and a sense of shared struggle. Rather than creating divisions, diaspora research presents opportunities to understand the interesting alternative of how Black identities can be thought of in more flexible terms and how Black culture can be integrated into national cultures.[31] This integration and struggle better approximate the problem of race in the post–civil rights era and can be instructive for African Americans in terms of understanding barriers to political mobilization.

However, diasporic consciousness is not a panacea. It can only be an effective tool in the United States context if connected to expanding integration of African American and Latin@ interests through expanded labor organizing and an emphasis on core issues such as access to education, housing, health care, and police reform. These issues, together with cultural factors and research challenging the parochial nature of both Black and Latin@ politics, can create grassroots visionary leadership that establishes lasting bonds rather than the limited patterns of convergence, ambivalence, and conflict that have plagued Black-brown relations to date. In many ways, Afro-Latin@s become a metaphor. They are both Black and Latin@, though not quite completely accepted as either. The struggle for citizenship, the fractal patterns of racial exclusion within United States society and the Latin@ community, and the substantial ambivalence of the African American community are further complications that position Afro-Latin@s at a point on the crossroads of political identities that represents a space for greater cross-cultural understanding or the tragedy of missed opportunity.

Politics on the Ground

Culture and diasporic research do have their limits. Close attention to emergent coalitions among Blacks and Latin@s can shed light on issues related to Blacks and Latin@s and help to formulate a progressive political agenda for the twenty-first century. Such a politics must be locally and internationally grounded and cover issues that are of paramount concern to both groups, including a living wage, health care, globalization, education, human rights, and United States foreign policy.

On the issue of immigration, Blacks must recognize that they have no interest in defending nativist and racist policies driven by White conservatives that only benefit business elites. Although such a recognition is already evident, it has not been acknowledged by critics like Vaca. The response of Black leaders and groups to the Immigrant Workers Freedom Ride of 2003 was a step in the right direction. Groups like the NAACP and the Urban League, along with individuals like Jesse Jackson and Congressman John Lewis, joined with labor organizations and African American freedom riders to support the cause of human rights for immigrants.[32]

While economic issues are critical, other foreign policy concerns are also important rallying points for coalition building. While many among the African American and Latin@ communities alike may have opposed the war in Iraq, members of both disproportionately serve in the military for economic reasons. The United States policy toward the island of Vieques in Puerto Rico drew protests from Latin@s as well as prominent African Americans such as the Reverend Al Sharpton who was arrested and jailed for three months. Ongoing struggles for freedom and sovereignty throughout the region also may galvanize African Americans and Latin@s. The Bush administration's aid in overthrowing President Jean-Bertrand Aristide in Haiti in March 2004 parallels its support of regime instability in Venezuela. As more countries respond to the pain of neoliberalism, it is incumbent upon Blacks and Latin@s in the United States to encourage respect for democracy. In terms of international politics, the recent move by the Congressional Black Caucus and Congressional Hispanic Caucus, led by Congressman Charles Rangel, to recognize the situation and concerns of Afro-Latin@s in the context of major transformations in Latin American economics and politics is a powerful first step. It is both symbolically and substantively important. However, much of politics is still local, and local coalitions must form.

The mass incarceration of African American and Latin@ youth and adults is an issue that has not been given enough attention. Both communities share this burden equally and have strikingly similar interests in seeing a criminal justice system that is fair and focused on rehabilitation. Improving urban schools and increasing affordability and access to higher education are also issues that bring Latin@s and African Americans together. On these issues there is no divergence of interests. Similarly, supportive minority set-aside programs and protecting living-wage jobs are issues that bond Latin@s and African Americans and must be emphasized. These issues cut across class and ethnic lines in both communities. Latin@s and African Americans share support for affirmative action, and its defense must be cast in multiethnic terms. African Americans should not and cannot fight the battle for affirmative action alone nor can they rhetorically exclude Latin@s from the struggle.

The possibility of building Black and Latin@ political coalitions rests upon the development of mutual understanding and building bridges across political interests. A focus on the practical issues that bond Latin@s and African Americans to a common political agenda, mediated through labor organizations and other community groups, needs to be emphasized. Issues of race and culture need to be confronted by both groups. While we cannot ignore that popular perceptions are politically significant, it is also important to keep in mind, contrary to Vaca's assertions, that the argument that Latin@s take jobs from African Americans has never actually been proven in the context of social science research, and widespread African American antipathy toward Latin@s or immigrants has also never been proven. We cannot let the assumptions of these conflicts go unchecked or be discussed in simplistic terms, nor can we allow repetition of these assumptions in the media to make them true.

Afro-Latin@s must not remain invisible. Their struggle in the United States and around the Americas highlights the problem of racism toward Latin@ and within Latin@ communities. Constructively engaging with the concerns of Afro-Latin@s also challenges the ethnocentrism and xenophobia that can at times plague African American discourse. A focus on social justice, human rights, and cultural recognition and respect challenges and undercuts conflict and forms the foundation for coalition politics.

Notes

1. Nicolas Vaca, *The Presumed Alliance: The Unspoken Conflict between Latinos and Blacks and What It Means for America* (New York: Rayo, 2004).
2. Otto Santa Ana, *Brown Tide Rising: Metaphors of Latinos in Contemporary American Public Discourse* (Austin: University of Texas Press, 2002).
3. Vaca, *The Presumed Alliance*.
4. Matt A. Baretto and Ricardo Ramírez, "Minority Participation and the California Recall: Latino, Black, and Asian Voting Trends, 1990–2003," PS: *Political Science & Politics* 37, no. 1 (2004): 11–14.
5. Dianne Pinderhughes, "An Examination of Chicago Politics for Evidence of Political Incorporation and Representation," in *Racial Politics in American Cities*, edited by Rufus Browning, Dale Marshall, and David Tabb (New York: Longman, 1997).
6. Rodney F. Hero, "Latinos and Politics in Denver and Pueblo, Colorado: Differences, Explanations, and the 'Steady-State' of the Struggle for Equality," in *Racial Politics in*

American Cities, edited by Rufus Browning, Dale Marshall, and David Tabb (New York: Longman, 1997).

7. J. Eric Oliver and Janelle Wong, "Intergroup Prejudice in Multiethnic Settings," *American Journal of Political Science* 47, no. 4 (2003): 567–82; Fu Mingying, "Opposing Affirmative Action: Self-Interest, Principles, or Racism," paper presented at the annual conference of the Midwestern Political Science Association, Chicago, Illinois, April 3–6, 2003; Karen M. Kaufmann, "Cracks in the Rainbow: Group Commonality as a Basis for Latino and African-American Political Coalitions," *Political Research Quarterly* 56, no. 2 (2003): 199–210.

8. Fu, "Opposing Affirmative Action."

9. "Survey of Latino Attitudes on a Possible War with Iraq," report on poll conducted by the Pew Hispanic Center, University of Southern California, February 18, 2003.

10. Oliver and Wong, "Intergroup Prejudice in Multiethnic Settings"; Fu, "Opposing Affirmative Action."

11. Vaca, *The Presumed Alliance*.

12. Paula McClain et al., "What's New about the New South?: Race, Immigration, and Intergroup Relations in a Southern City," paper presented at the annual meeting of the American Political Science Association, Philadelphia, August 27, 2003.

13. Paul Sniderman and Thomas Piazza, *Black Pride, Black Prejudice* (Princeton, N.J.: Princeton University Press, 2003).

14. Oliver and Wong, "Intergroup Prejudice in Multiethnic Settings."

15. Wellinthon García and Georgia Duerst-Lahti, "Entering the Agenda: Framing Dominican Americans in Politics," paper presented at the annual meeting of the Western Political Science Association, Portland, Oregon, March 2004.

16. Vaca, *The Presumed Alliance*; Richard Rodríguez, *Brown* (New York: Penguin, 2003); Lydia Chavez, *The Color Bind: The Campaign to End Affirmative Action* (Berkeley: University of California, 1998).

17. Cathy Cohen, *The Boundaries of Blackness: AIDS and the Breakdown of Black Politics* (Chicago: University of Chicago Press, 1999).

18. Ibid.

19. Rogers, "Afro-Caribbean Immigrants, African Americans, and the Politics of Group Identity."

20. Juan Flores, *From Bomba to Hip-Hop* (New York: Columbia University Press, 2000).

21. N. L. Stepan, *The Hour of Eugenics: Race, Gender, and Nation in Latin America* (Ithaca, N.Y.: Cornell University Press, 1991); Melissa Nobles, *Shades of Citizenship: Race and the Census in Modern Politics* (Stanford, Calif.: Stanford University Press, 2000).

22. Mark Q. Sawyer, "Cuban Exceptionalism: Group-Based Hierarchy and the Dynamics of Patriotism in Puerto Rico, the Dominican Republic, and Cuba," *Du Bois Review* 1, no. 1 (2004): 93–113; J. Sidanius, Y. Peña, and M. Sawyer, "Inclusionary Discrimination: Pigmentocracy and Patriotism in the Dominican Republic," *Political Psychology* 22 (2001): 827–51.

23. Michael G. Hanchard, *Orpheus and Power: The Movimiento Negro of Rio de Janeiro and São Paulo, Brazil, 1945–1988* (Princeton, N.J.: Princeton University Press, 1994); Sawyer, "Cuban Exceptionalism."

24. Sawyer, "Cuban Exceptionalism"; Yesilernis Peña, James Sidanius, and Mark Sawyer, "Racial Democracy in the Americas: A Latin and United States Comparison," *Journal of Cross-Cultural Psychology* 35 (November 2004): 749–62.

25. S. Torres-Saillant, "The Dominican Republic," in *No Longer Invisible: Afro-Latin Americans Today*, edited by Minority Rights Group (London: Minority Rights Publications, 1998), 109–38.

26. It is interesting to note that following the Sammy Sosa corked-bat scandal, African American callers to sports radios in Chicago supported Sammy Sosa and charged that the attack by the league, white sports writers, and callers was "racist."

27. S. Torres-Saillant and Ramona Hernández, *The Dominican Americans* (New York: Greenwood Publishing Group, 1998).

28. S. I. Croucher, *Imagining Miami: Ethnic Politics in a Postmodern World* (Charlottesville: University Press of Virginia, 1997); Sawyer, "What We Can Learn from Cuba."

29. Kaufmann, "Cracks in the Rainbow."

30. Ibid., 203.

31. Anani Dzidzienyo, "Conclusions," in *No Longer Invisible: Afro-Latin Americans Today*, edited by Minority Rights Group (London: Minority Rights Publications, 1995), 345–58; Leslie B. Rout Jr., *The African Experience in Spanish America, 1502 to the Present Day* (New York: Cambridge University Press, 1976); Pierre-Michel Fontaine, ed., *Race, Class and Power in Brazil* (Los Angeles: University of California Press, 1982); Abdias do Nascimento and Elisa Larkin Nascimento, *Africans in Brazil: A Pan-African Perspective* (Trenton, N.J.: Africa World Press, 1992); Hanchard, *Orpheus and Power.*

32. For an account of the Immigrant Workers Freedom Ride of 2003 and a list of the many organizations that supported it, see the group's Web site at www.iwfr.org.

JAMES JENNINGS

Afro-Latinism in United States Society

A Commentary

The concept of Afro-Latinism reminds me of Langston Hughes's powerful and enduring poem "I, Too, Sing America," which starts off, "I am the darker brother. They send me to eat in the kitchen when company comes." For this discussion about Afro-Latin@s is not new. "I, Too, Sing America" was written in 1926 and it is a poem that can be related to many situations today as United States society continues to grapple with racial and ethnic demographic changes and persisting injustices. In fact, the Afro-Latin@ concept also has a rich history dating back to this period and even earlier. I think of the musings of José Celso Barbosa, for example, as the Black president of the Republican Party in Puerto Rico in the very late nineteenth century. He wondered if Black Puerto Ricans might enjoy better opportunities "con los gringos del norte" than with their own White Puerto Rican brethren. This was a most important question in that the United States invaded Puerto Rico in 1898 and the issue of race in Puerto Rico, given the weight of race in United States society, could not be easily ignored. Throughout the decades of the twentieth century, many Latin@ artists and intellectuals raised questions about what it meant to be both Black and Latin@ in the Latin@ world. The question, or discussion, regarding the concept of Afro-Latin@ reemerges very powerfully again in the 1960s and 1970s. Perhaps one of the dynamics that made the Young Lords so attractive to Latin@ and African American youth was precisely that it was part of an Afro-Latin@ political movement. Though received as controversial in some African American and Latin@ quarters, the very point of the poem "Jíbaro, My Pretty Nigger" by Felipe Luciano, one of the members of the Black nationalist–oriented Last Poets, was that an important element of the Latin@ experience is African.

This concept or idea remains powerful today for a number of reasons, the most obvious being the demographic changes that have occurred as a result of globalization and transnationalism. The growing racial and ethnic diversity in United States society has also meant an increasing diversity within these very same communities of color. Today, the Black community is composed of various ethnicities, as is the case with the Latin@ and Asian communities. Ethnic diversity means that terms like "the Latin@ community" or "the Asian community" present erroneous monolithic impressions about these groups. It also means that a term like "African American," as widely accepted as it has become, may now be a demographic misnomer. By the same token, there are many people from Haiti, Nigeria, Brazil, Colombia, Cuba, and Panama, for example, who may not call themselves African American but will say that they are Black.

This ethnic diversity is changing the social agendas that have been traditionally associated with these groups. An issue like bilingual education, for example, traditionally a "Latin@" issue in many places, is rapidly becoming a "Black" issue as a result of the growing ethnic diversity within Black urban communities. Ethnic and racial diversity within what we have understood to be the Latin@ community is also encouraging challenges to the notion that race, or racism, is absent among Latin@s. As the Latin@ population continues to grow, social and economic differences between various Latin@ groups may place in question the notion of a Pan-Latin@ consciousness.

But the focus on the concept of Afro-Latin@ involves much more than simply a demographic dynamic. This concept can emerge as a potential cultural and political tool for the expansion of social and economic democracy both in this country and throughout the Americas. I would propose that there are four main aspects of this role.

First, this concept forces a revisiting of social history and the dominant paradigm of race relations in United States society. Just as Black studies, Chican@ and Puerto Rican studies, and women's studies all challenged dominant ideas and research about race and ethnicity in this country when they emerged in the 1970s, the concept of Afro-Latin@ represents a challenge to the dominant paradigm of race relations in United States society today.

What I refer to as the "Gunnar Myrdal paradigm" is still the dominant explanation for race and race relations and class relations in United States society. Myrdal's classic work *An American Dilemma* (1944) contained two essential components as part of this dominant model for analyzing race and race relations. One is that the problem with race has more to do with

Organizers of the 2006 Haitian and Dominican Open Forum, an event held at Riverside Church in New York. From left to right: Kathleen, Alba Mota, Rosemary Almonte, Mathylde Frontous, Alix Almond, Holly Guzman, Winnie Siclait, Ruthzee Louijene, Jennifer Calvin, and Kaity Trinidad. (Photograph by Tequila Minsky, © 2006)

prejudice than with structural inequality, and the second is that we live in a Black and White society. (It is this paradigm, by the way, that provided the foundation for the Clinton Commission on Race and the subsequent race conversations in a few town halls across the nation during Clinton's administration.) Of course, the concept of Afro-Latin@ explodes this notion with history, demography, and the reality of groups of people that include both Black and White and beyond. The concept enhances the civic dialogue in this country about race and class by reminding people that race is far more complex than the White and Black bi-polar presentation in many discussions, both popular and scholarly.

Second, the concept of Afro-Latin@ also helps to expose a racial hierarchy in this country that actually protects the increasing concentration of wealth on behalf of corporate interests. By racial hierarchy I mean, simply, that Whiteness is on top. One can look at cultural dynamics, political power structures, health disparities, economics, and occupation and, regardless of the progress that people of color are making, still see gaps between people who are White in this country and those who are not White. Some Latin@s and immigrants who come to this country may decide to join a niche in this racial hierarchy. The concept of Afro-Latin@ exposes the inherent yet often overlooked racism of this arrangement. It serves as a critique of Latin@ voices that choose to ignore it, and shows how it is a system for distributing social and economic benefits to certain groups. In other words, it's very hard to argue, for example, that Latin@s as a group are making it in society because they are different from African Americans—for example, the idea that they work harder, have a greater reflection of family values, or value education. Then when one turns to the social experiences of Afro-Latin@s—who are also certainly Latin@s—the intellectual and experiential weakness of the model is exposed. There must be something else that explains social and economic mobility because Afro-Latin@ folks are Latin@s, yet they seem not be making it, as may be the case for "other" Latin@s.

A third point that highlights the power of this concept is that the Afro-Latin@ perspective encourages us to focus on coalitions between communities of color. I don't mean to ignore or play down the potential and actual conflict between communities of color. A Black and brown political and economic divide, in particular, should not be minimized. Such a divide of course discourages public policy that would expand economic democracy and challenge the continuing concentration of wealth in this society. A Black and brown coalition is key to exposing and resisting this growing inequality in the concentration of political and economic power.

While these contentions have been a reality, we must not overlook the important history of political collaboration between African American and Latin@ communities in United States society. In an essay in *Black Commentator*, Jorge Mariscal reminds us that "contact between Chicano and Black activists was often intense. In 1967, Tijerina began a close relationship with SNCC, the Black Panthers, and other militant groups. Chicanos participated in the New Politics Conferences and the Poor People's Campaign. One of Dr. King's planned stops after visiting striking sanitation workers in Memphis in April of 1968 was to have been Delano, California, and a meeting with César Chávez. The meeting never happened; the spectre of a brown/Black coalition may have been one reason why."[1] Alas, this story does not sell, for the mainstream media tends to sensationalize the conflict and invisibilize instances—indeed, *teachable moments*—of political and economic collaboration. Should this not also be a focus of our commentaries and guest columns and books?

Let me provide a few examples of how these groups have worked together. Though it may not be evident that it was the concept of Afro-Latin@ that triggered successful coalitions, the Latin@ concept is certainly some part of this story. I will focus on Boston, where I live and work. It will appear to be a somewhat unlikely offering for Boston, which has been colloquially described as the "citadel of White America." The fact is that today the majority of the city's population is Black, Latin@, and Asian. Yes, Boston is majority people of color today. Some interesting and telling coalitions between the African American, Latin@, and Asian communities have emerged, and the concept of Afro-Latin@ was part of the glue in some of these coalitional developments. The Mel King mayoral campaigns in 1979 and 1983 were very important in this regard. The redistricting campaigns in this city also involved relatively strong coalitions between communities of color—Black, Latin@, and Asian.

Nelson Merced, the first Puerto Rican state representative, was elected primarily based on a Black voting base. Latin@s also voted for Nelson Merced, of course, as did a few Whites. But it was a Black voting base that put Nelson Merced into the state legislature as the first Latin@ elected state representative. More recently a strong alliance of Black and Latin@ activists helped elect Felix Arroyo as the first Latin@ city-wide elected official in the city council. Though he was defeated in the last election as a city-wide candidate, he won twice and helped to build a strong alliance with other African American and Asian elected officials. Such an alliance can serve as a foundation for challenging corporate power in a city like Boston. Last year Sam Yoon was elected the first Asian American city-wide council member. In all of these instances, what stands out is that there was a focus on progressive politics, one that emphasized the expansion of economic democracy for all people. This is an important lesson that we don't hear too much about in our media.

Finally, Afro-Latin@s can also help to expand bridges of communication between African Americans and the growing immigrant communities. Stephen Steinberg, author of *The Ethnic Myth* and a former writer for the *New York Times*, notes that "there is a black ambivalence towards immigration."[2] There are many reasons for this ambivalence about immigration among African Americans. Some of it has to do with perceived economic threats: "They're taking our jobs!" There is also a sense that the struggles of African Americans, which resulted in the expansion of social and economic democracy, is taken for granted. It also has to do, in part, with a system that emphasizes "ethnic leap-frogging" as a way to achieve social and economic mobility versus the building of alliances based on class interests.

The dominant discourse on immigration has two faces to it. The first is that immigration is a threat to the United States as a White, Protestant Christian nation. This is suggested in Samuel P. Huntington's *The Hispanic Challenge to America* (2004). But the other face of the dominant discourse on immigration is the suggestion—even made by some advocates of immigration rights—that these new groups represent model ethnic minorities. They have strong family values, as if African Americans do not; they work hard, as if African Americans do not; they believe in the American dream, as if African Americans do not. Part of this discourse is that America is the perfect society and that immigrants are rushing to our shores because we do have it right in terms of how we are organized and how we deal with issues of wealth, class, and certainly race. This part of the discourse eliminates the need to examine and challenge structural inequalities in United States society that are manifested in persistent poverty, high unemployment and underemployment, growing income inequality, and the increasing criminalization of Black and Latin@ youth in urban areas.

The concept of Afro-Latin@ thus has the potential to serve as a bridge between communities that are presented on opposite sides in the terms of this dominant discourse on immigration. Because Afro-Latin@s are Black and Latin@ and, in many cases, immigrants, the concept of Afro-Latin@ can help to raise the historical consciousness of Black, Latin@, and immigrant youths. In the Black community, there has to be an acknowledgment of the historical impact that immigration has had in the very development and empowerment of the African American community in this country. In the Latin@ immigrant communities, there has to be a historical consciousness that touches upon or allows for an understanding of the role of race in our own home countries, but also the role of African Americans in the struggle for justice and equality.

An Afro-Latin@ perspective immediately exposes ignorance about race and culture in this society and in other places. It helps to expose opportunistic agendas on the part of certain leaders in both communities. How can African Americans see Latin@s as culturally or socially alien and not to be trusted, when the presence of Afro-Latin@s is integral to the latter group? And how can Latin@ leaders see the Black community as the "other" when the presence of Blacks in the Latin@ community becomes more and more evident and explicit? Furthermore, it is clear that advocates of immigrant rights must challenge forthrightly the racial inequality and treatment that people of color, and especially Blacks, have received in this society, as well as the racism within the Latin@ community itself.

It is for these reasons that Langston Hughes's poem "I, Too, Sing America" resonates for me in a discussion about Afro-Latin@s. Although the Afro-Latin@ concept has been "kept in the kitchen" ("Y tu abuela, dónde está?" as the well-known Puerto Rican saying has it), it too has been growing strong. It, too, like Langston's poem, can be a powerful resource for the building of a better society for all people. I therefore propose that the idea and reality of Afro-Latin@s can be used to expand communication and collaboration among a range of racial and ethnic groups. This is critical because political relationships between Blacks, Latin@s, and Asians is now a crucial ingredient for mobilizing effective coalitions to challenge the economic and corporate status quo, and thereby put issues of economic democracy on the table of public dialogue and action. Afro-Latin@s can play a decisive role in moving all communities of color out of the kitchen and to a rightful place at the table of collective dialogue and action. To paraphrase another line of that unforgettable poem, "Afro-Latin@s will be at the table when company comes."

Notes

1. Jorge Mariscal, "A Chicano Looks at the Trent Lott Affair," *Black Commentator*, no. 25, January 16, 2003, www.blackcommentator.com.
2. Stephen Steinberg, "Immigration, African Americans, and Race Discourse," *New Politics*, 10, no. 3 (summer 2005), www.newpolitics.mayfirst.org.

SOURCES AND PERMISSIONS

Part I

"The Earliest Africans in North America," from Peter H. Wood, "The Earliest Africans in North America," in *Strange New Land: Africans in Colonial America* (New York: Oxford University Press, 2002), 1–2. Reprinted with permission of Oxford University Press, Inc.

"Black Pioneers: The Spanish-Speaking Afro-Americans of the Southwest," from Jack D. Forbes, "Black Pioneers: The Spanish-Speaking Afroamericans of the Southwest," *Phylon* 7, no. 3 (1966): 233–46. Reprinted with permission of Clark Atlanta University.

"Slave and Free Women of Color in the Spanish Ports of New Orleans, Mobile, and Pensacola," from Virginia Meacham Gould, "'A Chaos of Iniquity and Discord': Slave and Free Women of Color in the Spanish Ports of New Orleans, Mobile, and Pensacola," in *The Devil's Lane: Sex and Race in the Early South*, edited by Catherine Clinton and Michele Gillespie (New York: Oxford University Press, 1997), 232–45. Reprinted with permission of Oxford University Press, Inc.

"Afro-Cubans in Tampa," from Susan D. Greenbaum, *More Than Black: Afro-Cubans in Tampa*, New World Diasporas Series (Gainesville: University Press of Florida, 2002), 58–60, 68–72, 82–84. Reprinted with permission of the University Press of Florida.

"Pulling the Muse from the Drum," from Adrián Castro, *Cantos to Blood and Honey* (St. Paul, Minn.: Coffee House Press, 1997), 40–42. Reprinted with permission of the author.

Part II

"Racial Integrity: A Plea for the Establishment of a Chair of Negro History in Our Schools and Colleges," from Arthur A. Schomburg, Negro Society for Historical Research, Occasional Paper No. 3 (Yonkers, N.Y.: August Valentine Bernier, 1913).

Part III

"Black Cuban, Black American," from Evelio Grillo, *Black Cuban, Black American* (Houston: Arte Público Press, 2000), 6–17, 62–71. Reprinted with permission of the publisher, © 2000 Arte Público Press, University of Houston.

"A Puerto Rican in New York and Other Sketches," from Jesús Colón, *A Puerto Rican in New York and Other Sketches* (New York: International Publishers, 1982), 115–17, 119–25. Reprinted with permission of the publisher.

Part IV

"From 'Indianola' to 'Ño Colá': The Strange Career of the Afro–Puerto Rican Musician," from Ruth Glasser, *My Music Is My Flag: Puerto Rican Musicians and Their New York Communities, 1917–1940* (Berkeley: University of California Press, 1995), 52–55, 64–78. © 1995. The Regents of the University of California.

Excerpt from "cu/bop," from Louis Reyes Rivera, *Scattered Scripture* (Brooklyn: Shamal Books, 1996), 41–43. Reprinted with permission of the author.

"Bauzá–Gillespie–Latin/Jazz: Difference, Modernity, and the Black Caribbean," from Jairo Moreno, "Bauzá–Gillespie–Latin/Jazz: Difference, Modernity, and the Black Caribbean," *South Atlantic Quarterly* 103, no. 1 (winter 2004): 81–99. © Duke University Press. Revised selection, with permission of the publisher.

"Boogaloo and Latin Soul," from Juan Flores, *From Bomba to Hip-Hop* (New York: Columbia University Press, 2000), 79–86. Copyright © 2000 Columbia University Press. Reprinted with permission of the publisher.

"the salsa of bethesda fountain," from Tato Laviera, *La Carreta Made a U-Turn* (Houston: Arte Público Press, 1992), 67–68. Reprinted with permission from the publisher, © 1992 Arte Público Press, University of Houston.

Part V

"Hair Conking; Buy Black," from Carlos Cooks, *Carlos Cooks and Black Nationalism from Garvey to Malcolm*, edited by Robert Harris, Nyota Harris, and Grandassa Harris (Dover, Mass.: Majority Press, 1992). Reprinted with permission of the publisher.

"Down These Mean Streets," from Piri Thomas, *Down These Mean Streets* (New York: Knopf, 1967), 95–104, 119–28. Copyright © 1967 by Piri Thomas. Copyright renewed 1995 by Piri Thomas. Reprinted with permission of Alfred A. Knopf, a division of Random House, Inc.

"African Things," from Victor Hernández Cruz, *Mainland* (New York: Random House, 1973), 64. Reprinted with permission of the author.

"Black Notes and 'You Do Something to Me,'" from Sandra María Esteves, *Bluestown Mockingbird Mambo* (Houston: Arte Público Press, 1990), 75–76. Reprinted with permission from the publisher, © 1990 Arte Público Press. University of Houston.

"Before People Called Me a Spic, They Called Me a Nigger," from Pablo "Yoruba" Guzmán, in Michael Abramson, *Palante: Young Lords Party* (New York: McGraw-Hill, 1971), 52–60. Reproduced with permission of The McGraw-Hill Companies.

"Jíbaro, My Pretty Nigger," from Felipe Luciano, in *Puerto Rican Poetry*, edited by Roberto Marquez (Amherst: University of Massachusetts Press, 2007), 410–11. Reprinted with permission of the author.

"The Yoruba Orisha Tradition Comes to New York City," from Marta Moreno Vega, *African American Review* 29, no. 2 (summer 1995), special issue on the music, 201–6. Reprinted with permission from the author.

"Discovering Myself: Un Testimonio," revised version of "An Oral History (Testimonio)," in *Daughters of the Diaspora: Afra-Hispanic Writers*, edited by Miriam DeCosta-Willis (Kingston, Jamaica: Ian Randle, 2003), 313–18. Reprinted with permission of the author.

"Dominicanish," from Josefina Báez, Dominicanish (New York: I Ombe, 2000), 26–27. Reprinted with permission of the author.

Part VI

"The Black Puerto Rican Woman in Contemporary American Society," from Angela Jorge, in *Puerto Rican Woman*, edited by Edna Acosta-Belén (Westport, Conn.: Greenwood, 1986), 134–41. Reprinted with permission of Greenwood Publishing Group Inc. Westport, Conn.

"Something Latino Was Up with Us," from Spring Redd, in *Home Girls: A Black Feminist Anthology*, edited by Barbara Smith (New Brunswick, N.J.: Rutgers University Press, 1983), 52–56, © 1983, 2000 by Barbara Smith. Reprinted with permission of Rutgers University Press.

"Poem for My Grifa-Rican Sistah, or Broken Ends Broken Promises," from Mariposa (María Teresa Fernández), *Born Bronxeña* (New York: Bronxeña Books, 2001), 13–14. Reprinted with permission of the author.

"Latinegras: Desired Women–Undesirable Mothers, Daughters, Sisters, and Wives," from Marta I. Cruz-Janzen, *Frontiers: A Journal of Women Studies* 22, no. 3 (2002): 168–74, 176–83. Reprinted with permission of the University of Nebraska Press. Copyright © 2002 by Frontiers Editorial Collective.

"The Black Bellybutton of a Bongo," from Marianela Medrano, in *Regando Esencias/The Secret of Waiting*, Collección Tertuliando No. 2 (New York: Ediciones Alcance, 1998), 13–14. Reprinted with permission of the author.

Part VII

"Desde el Mero Medio: Race Discrimination within the Latino Community," from Carlos Flores, "Desde El Mero Medio: Race Discrimination Within the Latino Community," in "Celebrating the African Heritage of the Americas," *Diálogo* no. 5 (winter/spring 2001): 30–31. Copyright Center for Latino Research at DePaul University, Chicago, Ill. Reprinted with permission of *Diálogo*.

"Displaying Identity: Dominicans in the Black Mosaic of Washington, D.C.," from Ginetta E. B. Candelario, selections from chapter 3, "I Could Go the African American Route," *Black Behind the Ears: Dominican Racial Identity from Museums to Beauty Shops* (Durham, N.C.: Duke University Press, 2007), 129–76. Copyright 2007, Duke University Press. All rights reserved. Reprinted with permission of the publisher.

"Bringing the Soul: Afros, Black Empowerment, and Lucecita," from Yeidy M. Rivero, *Tuning Out Blackness* (Durham, N.C.: Duke University Press, 2005), 68–85. Copyright 2005, Duke University Press. All rights reserved. Reprinted with permission of the publisher.

"The Afro-Latino Connection: Can This Group Be the Bridge to a Broadbased Black-Hispanic Alliance?," from Alan Hughes and Milca Esdaille, *Black Enterprise Magazine*, February 2004, 111–18. Reprinted with permission of the publisher.

Part VIII

"Ghettocentricity, Blackness, and Pan-Latinidad," from Raquel Z. Rivera, *New York Ricans from the Hip Hop Zone* (New York: Palgrave Macmillan, 2003), 97–110 (selection). Reproduced with permission of Palgrave Macmillan.

"Chicano Rap Roots: Afro-Mexico and Black-Brown Cultural Exchange," from Pancho McFarland, "Chicano Rap Roots: Black-Brown Cultural Exchange and the Making of a Genre," *Callaloo* 29, no. 3 (2006): 939–54 (selection). © Charles H. Rowell. Reprinted with permission of The Johns Hopkins University Press.

"The Rise and Fall of Reggaeton: From Daddy Yankee to Tego Calderón and Beyond," from Wayne Marshall, *Boston Phoenix*, January 19, 2006, www.thephoenix.com. Reprinted with permission of the author.

"Do Plátanos Go wit' Collard Greens?," from David Lamb, *Do Plátanos go wit' Collard Greens?* (New York: I Write What I Like, 1994). Reprinted with permission of the author.

"Divas Don't Yield" from Sofia Quintero, *Divas Don't Yield* (New York: One World/Ballantine, 2006), 11–15. Reprinted with permission of the author.

Part IX

"Nigger-Reecan Blues," from Willie Perdomo, *Where a Nickel Costs a Dime* (New York: Norton, 1996), 19–21. Copyright © 1996 by Willie Perdomo. Reprinted with permission of W. W. Norton & Company, Inc.

Part X

"How Race Counts for Hispanic Americans," from John R. Logan, "How Race Counts for Hispanic Americans," 1–12 (Albany, N.Y.: Lewis Mumford Center, SUNY Press, 2003). Reprinted with permission of the author.

"Bleach in the Rainbow: Latino Ethnicity and Preference for Whiteness," from William A. Darity Jr., Jason Dietrich, and Darrick Hamilton, "Bleach in the Rainbow: Latin Ethnicity and Preference for Whiteness," *Transforming Anthropology* 13, no. 2 (October 2005): 103–9. Reprinted with permission of Wiley-Blackwell.

"Brown Like Me?" from Ed Morales, "Brown Like Me," *The Nation*, March 8, 2004, 23–27. Reprinted with permission from *The Nation* magazine.

"Mexican Ways, African Roots," from Lisa Hoppenjans and Ted Richardson, *Winston-Salem Journal*, June 19, 2005. Reprinted with permission of the publisher.

"Racial Politics in Multiethnic America: Black and Latina and Latino Identities and Coalitions," from Mark Sawyer, in *Neither Enemies Nor Friends*, edited by Anani Dzidzienyo and Suzanne Oberler (New York: Palgrave Macmillan, 2003), 266–79 (selection revised by author). Reproduced with permission of Palgrave Macmillan.

CONTRIBUTORS

Afro-Puerto Rican Testimonies: An Oral History Project in Western Puerto Rico is a collective initiative involving scholars and students from the University of Puerto Rico, Mayagüez and community leaders from the towns of Aguadilla and Hormigueros. Their project draws from the memories of local Afro-Puerto Ricans to challenge the official discourse on national identity and to dispel the myth of racial democracy in Puerto Rico.

Josefina Báez is a writer, performer, teacher, and director who was born in La Romana, Dominican Republic, but has spent most of her life in New York. She is the founder and director, since 1986, of the Latinarte/Ay Ombe Theatre troupe collective. Her best-known work is the performance piece *Dominicanish* (2000).

Ejima Baker is an artist and academic whose work focuses on popular culture, race, and gender. She has a BA in Africana studies and music and an MA in ethnomusicology, and she is currently a student in the anthropology program at the New School.

Luis Barrios is an associate professor in psychology and ethnic studies at John Jay College of Criminal Justice, City University of New York. He is also an associate priest at St. Mary's Episcopal Church in Manhattan and a community activist. Since 1997 he has been a weekly columnist for *El Diario/La Prensa*, one of the oldest Spanish-language newspapers in the United States. His research concerns street organizations, the juvenile criminal justice system, popular religion, and immigrant rights.

Eduardo Bonilla-Silva is a professor of sociology at Duke University. His publications include *Racism without Racists* (2006) and *White Logic, White Methods: Race, Epistemology, and the Social Sciences* (2008), coauthored with Tukufu Zuberi.

Adrian Burgos Jr. is an associate professor of history at the University of Chicago, Urbana-Champaign and author of *Playing America's Game(s): Baseball, Race, and Latinos, 1868–1959* (2008).

Ginetta E. B. Candelario is an associate professor of sociology and Latin American and Latin@ studies at Smith College. Her publications include *Black Behind the Ears: Blackness in Dominican Identity, from Museums to Beauty Shops* (2007) and the coedited volume *Generizando: Los estudios de género en la República Dominicana al inicio del tercer milenio* (2005).

Adrián Castro is a poet, performer, and interdisciplinary artist whose publications include *Cantos to Blood & Honey* (1997) and *Wise Fish: Tales in 6/8 Time* (2005). Born and raised in Miami, he is a Babalawo and herbalist.

Jesús Colón (1901–1974) was born in Puerto Rico and then migrated to New York in 1917. A life-long activist and labor organizer, Colón was a regular columnist for labor and community newspapers, including the *Daily Worker*, *Mainstream*, and *Liberación*, the most important forum in New York for progressive writers from Latin America and the Caribbean. In addition to *A Puerto Rican in New York and Other Sketches* (1961), he is the author of a collection of articles, *The Way It Was* (1993).

Marta I. Cruz-Janzen is an assistant professor in the Department of Secondary Education at Metropolitan State College of Denver. She is the coauthor of *Educating Young Children in a Diverse Society* (1994).

William A. Darity Jr. is an arts and sciences professor of public policy studies and professor of African and African American studies and economics at Duke University. Most recently he coauthored *Economics, Economists, and Expectations: Microfoundations to Macroapplications* (2004) and coedited *Boundaries of Clan and Color: Transnational Comparisons of Inter-Group Disparity* (2003).

Jason Dietrich is an economist with the U.S. Office of the Comptroller in Washington. His published research includes work on labor economics.

Milca Esdaille is a freelance writer who publishes in general and business magazines, both as a ghostwriter for clients and under her own name.

Sandra María Esteves, a Puerto Rican–Dominican, was born and raised in the Bronx. She was executive producer of the African Caribbean Poetry Theater, a Bronx-based arts organization. Her poetry volumes include *Bluestown Mockingbird Mambo* (1989), *Tropical Rains: A Bilingual Downpour* (1984), and *Yerba Buena* (1981).

María Teresa Fernández (Mariposa) is a poet, playwright, educator, and human rights activist born to Puerto Rican parents. She has published widely and is the author of *Born Bronxeña: Poems on Identity, Love and Survival* (2001). She has performed in many university and community settings throughout the United States and Puerto Rico.

Carlos Flores is a longtime community activist in Chicago's Puerto Rican community and the former project coordinator for Project Kalinda, at the Center for Black Music Research at Columbia College in Chicago. A prolific photographer and documentarian, he is the founder and director of the Afro-Latino Institute in Chicago.

Juan Flores is a professor in the Department of Social and Cultural Analysis at New York University. He is the translator of *Memoirs of Bernardo Vega* (1984) and *Cortijo's Wake* by Edgardo Rodríguez Juliá (2004), and coeditor of *On Edge: The Crisis of Latin American Culture* (1992) and the *Companion to Latina/o Studies* (2007). His most recent books include *From Bomba to Hip-Hop: Puerto Rican Culture and Latino Identity* (2000) and *The Diaspora Strikes Back: Caribeño Tales of Learning and Turning* (2008).

Jack D. Forbes is a professor emeritus and former chair of Native American studies at the University of California, Davis, where he has served since 1969. He has authored numerous articles and books, including *Africans and Native Americans* (1993).

David F. García is an assistant professor in ethnomusicology at the University of North Carolina, Chapel Hill. His publications include *Arsenio Rodríguez and the Transnational Flows of Latin Popular Music* (2006).

Ruth Glasser is a lecturer and the Waterbury Program Coordinator at the University of Connecticut. She has worked on a variety of academic and community-based endeavors including books, curriculum projects, oral history projects, and exhibits. Her publications include *My Music Is My Flag: Puerto Rican Musicians and Their New York Communities, 1917–1940* (1995) and *Caribbean Connections: Dominican Republic* (2004).

Virginia Meacham Gould is a member of the faculty of history at Our Lady of the Holy Cross College in New Orleans. She is the author of *Chained to the Rock of Adversity: To Be Free, Black, and Female in the Old South* (1998) and coeditor of *No Cross, No Crown: Black Nuns in Nineteenth Century New Orleans* (2002).

Susan D. Greenbaum is a professor in the Department of Anthropology at the University of South Florida. Her book *More Than Black: Afro-Cubans in Tampa* (2002) was the recipient of a number of awards, including the 2003 Choice Award for Outstanding Academic Book.

Evelio Grillo was born and raised in Tampa, Florida, in the 1920s and 1930s. He attended Dunbar High School in Washington, D.C., and Xavier College in New Orleans, and he earned an MA in social work in 1953 from the University of California, Berkeley, after serving in World War II. During a long career in Oakland, California, he served as a social worker, community organizer, and political advisor.

Pablo "Yoruba" Guzmán was born in East Harlem to a Cuban father and Puerto Rican mother, and raised in the South Bronx. A founding member of the radical Young Lords Party in the late 1960s, he is now a senior correspondent for CBS-TV in New York.

Darrick Hamilton is an assistant professor at Milano: The New School for Management and Urban Policy. He has published articles on disparities in wealth, homeownership, and labor market outcomes.

Gabriel Haslip-Viera, a professor in the Department of Sociology at the City College of New York, specializes in the history of pre-Columbian and colonial Mexico and the history of Latino communities in New York City. His books include *Crime and Punishment in Colonial Mexico* (1999) and the edited volumes *Latinos in New York: A Community in Transition* (1996) and *Taíno Revival: Critical Perspectives on Puerto Rican Identity and Cultural Politics* (2001).

Tanya Katerí Hernández is a professor at Fordham University School of Law. She teaches courses on property, trusts and estates, critical race theory, and race and the law and has published extensively on issues of race, ethnicity, and the law.

Victor Hernández Cruz was born in Aguas Buenas, Puerto Rico, and raised in New York's Lower East Side. His many volumes of poetry include *Snaps* (1968), *Mainland* (1973), *Red Beans* (1991), and *Maraca* (2001).

Jesse Hoffnung-Garskof is an associate professor of history and American culture at the University of Michigan. He is the author of *A Tale of Two Cities: Santo Domingo and New York after 1950* (2008).

Lisa Hoppenjans was a reporter at the *Winston-Salem Journal* and is currently a law student at Duke University.

Vielka Cecilia Hoy is a doctoral student in African diaspora studies and cofounder of the Afro-Latino Working Group at the University of California, Berkeley. She is also an education consultant for the Oakland Unified School District.

Alan Hughes is the managing editor of *Black Enterprise* magazine.

María Rosario Jackson is a senior research associate and director of the Culture, Creativity and Communities Program at the Urban Institute in Washington, D.C. She earned a doctorate in urban planning from the University of California, Los Angeles.

James Jennings is a professor of urban and environmental policy and planning at Tufts University. His edited volumes include *Race, Neighborhoods, and the Misuse of Social Capital* (2007), and he is the author of *Welfare Reform and the Revitalization of Inner City Neighborhoods* (2003).

Miriam Jiménez Román is the executive director of afrolatin@ forum, a research and resource center focusing on Black Latinos in the United States. For over a decade she researched and curated exhibitions at the Schomburg Center for Research in Black Culture, where she also served as the assistant director of the Scholars-in-Residence Program. She is currently a visiting scholar in the Africana Studies Program at New York University.

Angela Jorge is an associate professor emerita in the Humanities and Languages Department at the State University of New York, Old Westbury. In addition to her work on gender and race, she is the author of "Mesa Blanca: A Puerto Rican Healing Tradition."

David Lamb was born in Queens, New York, and is a graduate of Hunter College, the Woodrow Wilson School of Public and International Affairs at Princeton University, and New York University School of Law. He has written and produced two plays, *Plátanos y Collard Greens* (based on his novel *Do Plátanos Go wit' Collard Greens?*) and *From Auction Block to Hip Hop*.

Aida Lambert was born in Honduras and has lived and worked in New York since 1964. She is a long-term activist in the Latino community.

Ana M. Lara is an Afro-Dominican writer and performance artist. She was born in the Dominican Republic and raised in East Africa and Mount Vernon, New York. Her novel *Erzulie's Skirt* was a Lambda Literary Award finalist in 2007. She is currently a graduate student at Yale University.

Evelyne Laurent-Perrault, the daughter of Haitian immigrants to Venezuela, is originally from Caracas. One of the founders of Encuentro, Inc., a Philadelphia-based Afro-Latin@ organization, she is currently pursuing a doctorate in history at New York University.

Tato Laviera is a poet, playwright, and cultural educator who was born in Puerto Rico but has spent most of his life in New York. His books of poetry include *La Carreta Made a U-Turn* (1979), *Enclave* (1981), *AmeRícan* (1985), *Mainstream Ethics* (1988), and *Mixturao* (2008).

John R. Logan is a professor of sociology and Director of the Spatial Structures in the Social Sciences Initiative at Brown University. He is coauthor of *Urban Fortunes: The Political Economy of Place* (1987), and his most recent edited book is *The New Chinese City: Globalization and Market Reform* (2001).

Antonio López is an assistant professor in the English Department at George Washington University, where he specializes in Latin@ literary and cultural studies. He is completing a book on Afro-Cuban literary and popular culture in the United States from the 1920s to the present.

Felipe Luciano was a cofounder of the Young Lords Party and an original member of The Last Poets. He is a two-time Emmy Award winner for his reporting for WNBC.

Ryan Mann-Hamilton is of Dominican background and was raised in Mayagüez, Puerto Rico. A doctoral student in cultural anthropology at the City University of New York graduate school, he is a founding member of the afrolatin@ forum, a research and advocacy organization.

Wayne Marshall is the Florence Levy Kay Fellow in Ethnomusicology at Brandeis University. Specializing in the intersections between Caribbean and American popular music, he received his doctorate from the University of Wisconsin, Madison, in 2007. He is a coeditor of the anthology *Reggaeton* (2009).

Pancho McFarland is assistant professor of sociology at Chicago State University. Originally from New Mexico, he recently published *Chicano Rap: Gender and Violence in the Postindustrial Barrio* (2008).

Marianela Medrano is a Dominican writer and psychotherapist who has lived in Connecticut since 1990. She holds a Ph.D. in psychology, and her volumes of poetry include *Oficio de vivir* (1986), *Los alegres ojos de la tristeza* (1987), *Regando esencias/The Scent of Waiting* (1998), and *Curada de espantos* (2002).

Nancy Raquel Mirabal is an associate professor of Raza/Ethnic studies at San Francisco State University. She is coeditor of *Technofuturos: Critical Interventions in Latina/o Studies* (2005) and author of "Displaced Geographies: Latina/os, Oral History, and the Politics of Gentrification in San Francisco's Mission District."

Yvette Modestin, a native of the Republic of Panama, is the founder and director of Encuentro Diaspora Afro in Boston, and regional coordinator of the Red de Mujeres Afrolatinoamericanas, Afrocaribeñas y de la Diáspora.

Ed Morales is a journalist whose work has appeared in a variety of national magazines and newspapers, including the *Village Voice* and the *Nation*. He is the author of *Living in Spanglish* (2003) and *The Latin Beat: The Rhythm and Roots of Latin Music from Bossa Nova to Salsa and Beyond* (2008).

Jairo Moreno is an associate professor of music at the University of Pennsylvania. As a bassist with Ray Barretto he earned five Grammy nominations. He is the author of *Musical Representations, Subjects, and Objects: The Construction of Musical Thought in Zarlino, Descartes, Rameau, and Weber* (2004).

Marta Moreno Vega is founder and president of the Franklin Williams Caribbean Cultural Center African Diaspora Institute and cofounder of the Global AfroLatino and Caribbean Initiative. She is the author of *The Altar of My Soul: The Living Traditions of Santería* (2000) and *When the Spirits Dance Mambo* (2004), the latter of which is also the title of her documentary film.

Willie Perdomo is the author of *Where a Nickel Costs a Dime* (1996), *Smoking Lovely* (2003), and *Visiting Langston* (2005), which won the 2004 Beyond Margins Award of the PEN American Center. A native of East Harlem, he currently teaches at Friends Seminary and the Bronx Academy of Letters.

Graciela (Pérez Gutiérrez), called "the First Lady of Latin Jazz," was born in Havana in 1915. She began her singing career in Cuba as a teenager with Grupo Anacaona, an all-female band. She settled in New York in 1943, joining her brother Frank "Machito" Grillo and her brother-in-law Mario Bauzá and their Afro-Cuban Jazz Band. Her 2004 album *Inolvidable*, with the percussionist Cándido Camero, was nominated for a Grammy award.

Sofia Quintero is a writer, activist, and educator best known by her pen name, Black Artemis. Born into a working-class Puerto Rican–Dominican family in the Bronx, where she still resides, her novels include *Explicit Content* (2004), *Picture Me Rolling* (2005), and *Divas Don't Yield* (2006).

Spring Redd was active in the women's and Third World communities in Boston.

Ted Richardson is a photojournalist at the *News and Observer* in Raleigh. He continues to cover a wide range of issues affecting Latin@s in North Carolina.

Louis Reyes Rivera is a poet and essayist whose books include *Who Pays the Cost* (1976), *This One for Me* (1977), and *Scattered Scripture* (1996). In recent years he has offered workshops and hosted poetry and jazz presentations at Sistas' Place in Brooklyn.

Pedro R. Rivera was born in the Dominican Republic. He is a doctoral student in history at Howard University, Washington, D.C.

Raquel Z. Rivera is a writer and independent researcher. She is the author of *New York Ricans from the Hip Hop Zone* (2003) and coeditor of *Reggaeton* (2009). A singer-songwriter, she is a founding member of Yaya, an all-women's musical collective dedicated to Dominican *salves* and Puerto Rican bomba.

Yeidy M. Rivero is an associate professor of communications and culture at Indiana University. In addition to *Tuning out Blackness: Race and Nation in the History of Puerto Rican Television* (2005), her publications include "Broadcasting Modernity: Cuban Commercial Television 1950–53."

Mark Sawyer is an associate professor of African American studies and political science and the Director of the Center for the Study of Race, Ethnicity and Politics at the University of California, Los Angeles. He is the author of *Racial Politics in Post Revolutionary Cuba* (2006).

Nilaja Sun is a native of the Lower East Side who has worked as a teaching artist in New York City schools for more than eight years. An actress and playwright, she was the solo performer and writer of *No Child . . .* , a critically acclaimed off-Broadway hit that received numerous awards including an Obie.

Piri Thomas was born Juan Pedro Tomás of Puerto Rican and Cuban parents in New York City's Spanish Harlem in 1928. *Down These Mean Streets* was originally published in 1967, and it has been in print ever since. His other works include *Savior, Savior, Hold My Hand* (1972) and *Seven Long Times* (1975).

Silvio Torres-Saillant is the William P. Tolley Distinguished Professor of English at Syracuse University. His publications include *The Dominican-Americans* (1998) and *An Intellectual History of the Caribbean* (2006). He was born and raised in the Dominican Republic.

Sherezada "Chiqui" Vicioso is a poet, essayist, and political advocate for women's rights in the Dominican Republic. Her books include *Viaje desde el agua* (1981), *Un extraño ulular trajo el viento* (1985), *Julia de Burgos, la nuestra* (1990), and *Internamiento* (1992).

Peter H. Wood is a professor emeritus of history at Duke University. The lead author for the United States survey textbook *Created Equal*, he is actively involved with diverse public history projects. In addition to *Strange New Land* his books include *Black Majority: Negroes in South Carolina from 1670 through the Stone Rebellion* (1996) and *A Bee in the Mouth: Anger in America Now* (2007).

INDEX

baseball, 127–42; Clemente, 138–39, 139; Cuban All Stars, 120, 152; Jackie Robinson Day, 139–40; Miñoso, 129, 131–35, 139–40, 141n11; Negro Leagues and, 129–34; Pompez, 129, 136–37; racial integration anniversary celebration, 127–29; Robinson, 127–29, 132, 153; in Tampa, 58, 101

Bataan, Joe, and the East Side Kids, 204

Bauzá, Mario, 8, 120, 150–53, 164, 168–72, 174n29, 177–85, 179, 246. *See also* Afro-Cuban jazz (Cubop)

Belafonte, Harry, 152

Benítez, Luz Esther (Lucecita), 347–56, 350

Bermúdez, Ignacia, 469

"Black Bellybutton of a Bongo" (Medrano), 314–15

Black-Brown Relations and Stereotypes (Mindiola, Niemann, and Rodriguez), 506

Black Cuban, Black American (Grillo), 6, 99–112

Black Entertainment Television, 358–63

Blackness: Afro-Latin@s and, 1–3; Latinidad and, 10–11, 14–15, 302–4, 358–63, 383, 384, 540–46; Young Lords Party and, 9, 235–43, 540

"Black Notes and 'You Do Something to Me'" (Esteves), 233–34

Blanco, Tomás, 72, 451n5

Bonilla, Dulce Reyes, 310

boogaloo, 199–206

Bruce, John, 86–87

Caballeros de la Luz (Masonic lodge), 74–77, 80, 86

Cabeza de Vaca, Alvar Núñez, 5, 21, 27

California: Afro-Latin@s pre-1900s, 17–18, 29–36; Baja California, 29, 31–32; changing demographics of, 500–501; electoral politics and, 528–29; intermarriage in, 35; Latin@ impact on electoral politics, 528–29; mixed ancestry immigrants from Mexico and,

13, 29–36, 502; Proposition 187, 381, 528; San Diego, 29

Calloway, Cab, 166, 167

Campanella, Roy, 152

Club Cubano Inter-Americano, El, 120–26, 123, 189, 192–94, 196

Census 2000, 493–96. *See also* U.S. Census Bureau

Chavez, Linda, 504

Chicago, 132, 133–35, 139, 506, 528–29, 532. *See also* Young Lords Party

Chican@s, 305–7. *See also* Mexico, Mexicans

Chinn, Staceyann, 303–4

cigar workers, 6, 51, 73–79, 85–86, 105, 458

class solidarity: Caballeros de la Luz (Masonic lodge) and, 74–77, 80, 86; La Liga Antillana, 75–76, 80

Clemente, Roberto, 138–39, 139

Club Borinquen (political club), 80–81, 90n21

coalition building, 6, 7–8, 364–70, 527–39, 543–44

Coén, Ray, 163

Colón, Jesús, 8, 113–19

Colón, Willie, 187–88

color consciousness: Alvarado, 120–26, 123; Bauzá, 120, 150–53, 164, 168–72, 174n29, 177–85, 179, 246; El Club Cubano Inter-Americano, 120–25, 189, 192–94; Colón, 8, 113–19; Cubans and, 99–112, 120–25; Graciela, 150–54, 151; Grillo, 6, 13, 99–112, 109; Haslip-Viera family, 142–49, 143; Masonic lodges and, 76–79; Alvarado, 120–26; Miñoso, 129, 131–35, 139–40, 141n11; in music clubs, 151; New Orleans and, 38, 41–43, 45, 46–47, 49n21, 363n2; Puerto Ricans and, 296–97; racial classification and, 142–49, 143; women and, 269–75; work opportunities and, 289–94; workplace discrimination and, 520–26; Ybor City, Florida, 99–112. *See also* racial identification

Juan Flores is a professor in the Department of Social and Cultural Analysis at New York University.

Miriam Jiménez Román is the executive director of afrolatin@ forum, a research and resource center focusing on Black Latin@s in the United States. She is currently a visiting scholar in the Africana Studies Program at New York University.

Library of Congress Cataloging-in-Publication Data

The Afro-Latin@ reader : history and culture in the United States /
edited by Miriam Jiménez Román and Juan Flores.
p. cm.
"A John Hope Franklin Center Book."
Includes bibliographical references and index.
ISBN 978-0-8223-4558-9 (cloth : alk. paper)—ISBN 978-0-8223-4572-5 (alk. paper)
1. African Americans. 2. Hispanic Americans. 3. African Americans—Relations with Hispanic Americans. 4. United States—Ethnic relations. I. Jiménez Román, Miriam, 1951– II. Flores, Juan, 1943– III. Title: Afro-Latino reader. IV. Title: Afro-Latina reader.
E185.615.A37 2010
305.800973—dc22   2010005176